The Best Teachers' Test Preparation for the

CSET®
Multiple Subjects
Plus Writing Skills

Michelle DenBeste, Ph.D.
Associate Professor & Chair, History
California State University, Fresno
Fresno, CA

Maire Mullins, Ph.D.
Associate Professor of English
Pepperdine University
Malibu, CA

Melissa Jordine, Ph.D.
Lecturer, History
California State University, Fresno
Fresno, CA

Ted Nickel, Ph.D.
Professor Emeritus, Psychology
Fresno Pacific University
Fresno, CA

James L. Love, M.A.T.
Instructor, Physics
Richland College
Dallas, TX

Jin H. Yan, Ph.D.
Assistant Professor, Kinesiology
California State University, East Bay
Hayward, CA

Jean O. Charney, Ph.D.
Jean Charney Editorial Services
Fort Collins, CO

Research & Education Association
Visit our website at
www.rea.com

The content specifications for the CSET: Multiple Subjects Test were created and implemented by the California Commission on Teacher Credentialing in conjunction with National Evaluation Systems, Inc., a unit of Pearson Education, Inc. For further information visit the CSET website at *http://www.cset.nesinc.com.*

For all references in this book, CSET® and California Subject Examinations for Teachers® are trademarks of the California Commission on Teacher Credentialing and Pearson Education, Inc., or its affiliate(s), which have not reviewed or endorsed this book.

Research & Education Association

61 Ethel Road West
Piscataway, New Jersey 08854
E-mail: info@rea.com

THE BEST TEACHERS' TEST PREPARATION FOR THE CSET®: MULTIPLE SUBJECTS TEST PLUS WRITING SKILLS

Printed in the United States of America

Library of Congress Control Number 2007940940

ISBN-13: 978-0-7386-0334-6
ISBN-10: 0-7386-0334-1

REA® is a registered trademark of
Research & Education Association, Inc.

About the Authors

Jean O. Charney, Ph.D., received her Ph.D. in Linguistics, her M.A. in Linguistics, and her B.A. in Anthropology from the University of Colorado. Her doctoral dissertation was "A Grammatical Sketch of the Comanche Language." From 1985 to the present, she has worked as an expert freelance editor, researcher, writer, and transcriber.

From 1977 through 1980, Dr. Charney was research assistant for a Siouan Languages Archiving Project at her alma mater. For 10 years beginning in 1987, she was production manager and editor of oral history projects for the Nebraska counties of Nye, Lincoln, Eureka, and Esmeralda.

In the 1990s, she helped create manuscripts of ethnographic studies of small communities for the AMS Press and prepared dictionary and grammatical materials for the Southern Ute Indian Tribe's language preservation program. From 1999 through 2006, she was a Composition Aide in the Poudre R-1 School District in Fort Collins, Colorado. For the past five years she has done work as an Editorial Assistant at the *Journal of Atmospheric and Oceanic Technology*, published by the American Meteorological Society.

In 1994, Dr. Charney published *A Grammar of Comanche* with the University of Nebraska Press. Along with this publication, she is a co-author of REA's test preparation book for the ACT.

Michelle DenBeste, Ph.D., is Associate Professor and Chair of the history department at California State University, Fresno. Dr. DenBeste continues to actively research, discuss and publish material in the fields of Russian history and the history of women. Her numerous publications include "Emerging Professionalism: Women Physicians in Late Imperial Russia," published in Review Journal of Philosophy and Social Science (Vol. XXVII, 2002, 275-294) and "Publish or Perish? The Scientific Publications of Women Physicians in Late Imperial Russia," in Dynamis: The International Journal of the History of Medicine, Vol. 19, 1999, 215-240. She has also been actively involved in creating and teaching the World History course at Fresno State University, and sponsoring conference panels in regard to specific aspects of teaching World History.

Melissa Jordine, Ph.D., is a Lecturer in the history department at California State University, Fresno. Dr. Jordine teaches courses on World History, Modern European History and Military History. She has presented papers at both regional and national conferences and is currently working on an article relating to the image of Erwin Rommel and the German forces who fought in North Africa during World War II. She has also been actively involved in the San Joaquin History Social Science Project. This project sponsors summer seminars and lectures designed to increase the knowledge of secondary school teachers in regard to current scholarship and resources relating to topics covered by the California Social Science Standards.

James L. Love, M.A.T., teaches part-time at Richland College, Dallas, Texas, and runs a tutoring service. He has taught Advanced Placement- and International Baccalaureate-level physics in Texas secondary schools and holds two advanced degrees from the University of Texas at Dallas. In the course of his distinguished teaching career, Mr. Love, now semi-retired, won a number of National Science Foundation and U.S. Department of Energy awards for advanced study and training at national labs, including Kitt Peak Observatory, the Fermi Laboratory, and the Thomas Jefferson Laboratory. He continues a seven-year association with International Baccalaureate as an examiner for extended essays in physics.

Maire Mullins, Ph.D., serves as Co-editor and Poetry Editor of the journal *Christianity and Literature* and teaches as a Visiting Lecturer in the Social Action and Justice Seminar at Pepperdine University. Her articles on Walt Whitman have appeared in *Tulsa Studies in Women's Literature, The Walt Whitman Quarterly Review, The Walt Whitman Encyclopedia* (Garland P, 1998), *Tohoku Journal of American Studies* (Sendai, Japan), and *The American Transcendental Quarterly*. She has also written articles on Willa Cather, Hisaye Yamamoto, Isak Dinesen, and William Butler Yeats, and published in the journal *Academic Leader*.

Ted Nickel, Ph.D., Professor Emeritus in psychology at Fresno Pacific University, received his B.A. from Tabor College and his M.A. and Ph.D. in psychology from UCLA. His desire always has been to be a teacher. Several years teaching at the elementary level, including special education, concluded in teaching at the college level for 31 years. During that period he taught in the Early Childhood Education Program at UCLA under Norma Feshbach, at the University of Tulsa, Tabor College, and for 18 years at Fresno Pacific University. His long career also included several administrative positions (Associate Dean of Arts and Sciences at University of Tulsa, Vice President at Tabor College, and Dean of the Graduate School at Fresno Pacific University). He has been an active reviewer of books and films, primarily for *Scientific American,* has presented papers at conventions, and has been published in refereed journals. Skiing and the building and flying of airplanes are his primary avocational interests.

Jin H. Yan, Ph.D., is an Assistant Professor of kinesiology at California State University, East Bay, at Hayward. He received his Ph.D. and post-doctoral training from Arizona State University, and an M.A. from San Jose State University. His area of expertise is in the field of lifespan/developmental motor control and learning. Over the last 10 years Dr. Yan has worked extensively with individuals at all ages and with various levels of motor, physical, and cognitive capabilities (including motor disorders of children with ADHD or learning disabilities, and seniors with Alzheimer's disease). He enjoys physical activities like basketball, golfing, and swimming.

About Research & Education Association

Founded in 1959, Research & Education Association (REA) is dedicated to publishing the finest and most effective educational materials—including software, study guides, and test preps—for students in middle school, high school, college, graduate school, and beyond.

REA's Test Preparation series includes study guides for all academic levels in almost all disciplines. Research & Education Association publishes test preps for students who have not yet completed high school, as well as high school students preparing to enter college. Students from countries around the world seeking to attend college in the United States will find the assistance they need in REA's publications. For college students seeking advanced degrees, REA publishes test preps for many major graduate school admission examinations in a wide variety of disciplines, including engineering, law, and medicine. Students at every level, in every field, with every ambition can find what they are looking for among REA's publications.

REA's publications and educational materials are highly regarded and continually receive an unprecedented amount of praise from professionals, instructors, librarians, parents, and students. Our authors are as diverse as the subject matter represented in the books we publish. They are well-known in their respective fields and serve on the faculties of prestigious high schools, colleges, and universities throughout the United States and Canada.

Acknowledgments

In addition to our authors, we would like to thank **Larry B. Kling,** Vice President, Editorial Services, for supervising development; **Pam Weston**, Vice President, Publishing, for setting the quality standards for production integrity and managing the publication to completion; **Jeff LoBalbo,** Senior Graphic Designer, for electronic preflight support; **Christine Saul,** Senior Graphic Designer, for cover design; **Gunnar E. Carlsson, Ph.D.,** of Stanford University, **Edward L. Condren, Ph.D.,** of the University of California, Los Angeles, **Ralph A. Smith, Ph.D.,** of the University of Illinois at Urbana-Champaign, and **Eleanor Willemsen, Ph.D.,** of Santa Clara University for technically editing the manuscript; **Ellen Gong** and **Cheryl Pedersen** for proofreading the manuscript; **Alice Leonard,** Senior Editor, and **Molly Solanki,** Associate Editor, for coordinating revisions; **Rachel DiMatteo,** Graphic Designer, and **Kathy Caratozzolo** of Caragraphics, for typesetting revisions.

CONTENTS

CHAPTER 1 PASSING THE CSET: MULTIPLE SUBJECTS   1

Know the Format 4

How to Use this Book 5

Scoring the CSET 6

Studying for the CSET 7

CSET Test-Taking Strategies 8

The Day of the Test 9

CSET Study Schedule 10

CHAPTER 2 READING, LANGUAGE, AND LITERATURE REVIEW   15

Prose 16

Poetry 29

Language and Linguistics....................................54

CHAPTER 3 HISTORY AND SOCIAL SCIENCE REVIEW   63

World History: Ancient Civilizations Through

        Early Modern Times 67

River Valley Civilizations 68

The Rise of Advanced Civilizations 74

Trade and Migration in the Ancient World 82

Rise of World Religions...84

Civilizations in the Middle Ages 89

Renaissance, Reformation, and Enlightenment................101

United States History: Pre-Colonial Times Through the

        Industrial Era 126

Beginnings of European Exploration.............................131

Beginnings of English Colonization................................139

Contents

Attempts at Stronger Control of the Colonies..................149

The Colonies and the Coming American Revolution 156

The War for Independence 159

Development of the New Nation and the Constitution.......164

The Constitution of the United States 166

Westward Expansion and Conflict 182

Expansion and Economic Growth of the U.S. 185

Slavery in the U.S. 192

Continuation of Westward Expansion 195

The Civil War and Reconstruction..................................201

California History: Pre-Columbian Development

              Through the Present Day.................209

CHAPTER 4   SCIENCE REVIEW   221

Structures and Properties of Matter 222

Principles of Motion and Energy....................................224

Life Science 232

Structure of Living Organisms and their Functions

       (Physiology and Cell Biology) 232

Living and Nonliving Components in Environments

       (Ecology)..236

Life Cycle, Reproduction and Evolution

       (Genetics and Evolution) 239

Earth and Space Science..242

The Solar System and the Universe (Astronomy).............242

The Structure and Composition of the Earth (Geology) 245

The Earth's Atmosphere (Meteorology) 249

The Earth's Water (Oceanography)................................250

Planning and Conducting Experiments............................251

CHAPTER 5   MATHEMATICS REVIEW   255

Arithmetic...255

Algebra..271

Measurement and Geometry..290

Statistics, Data Analysis, and Probability........................301

CHAPTER 6   PHYSICAL EDUCATION REVIEW   **305**

Benefits of Diet and Exercise 305

Principles of Cardiovascular Fitness..............................306

Aerobic Exercise..307

Low-Impact Aerobics...308

Anatomy and Physiology...308

Sports and Games 309

Health and Diet..312

First Aid 316

Movement Education 317

Psychological and Social Aspects of Physical Education ...320

CHAPTER 7   HUMAN DEVELOPMENT REVIEW   **323**

Student Development and Maturation............................325

Theories of Cognitive Development..............................326

Nature and Nurture 331

Learning Styles 339

Study Strategies...345

Jointly Constructed Meaning 348

Abuse and Neglect of Children:

   Factors of Risks and Treatment............................352

CHAPTER 8   VISUAL AND PERFORMING ARTS REVIEW   **355**

Aesthetic Perception and Creative Expression 356

Cultural Heritage 359

Historical Survey 360

Dance, Theater, Opera, Popular Musical Theater, and

   Ethnic/Folk Traditions...371

Critical Judgment..374

Contents

PRACTICE TEST 1   **377**

Answer Sheets 379

Subtest I: Reading, Language & Literature,
                  History & Social Science................................381

Constructed-Response Questions...................................397

Subtest II: Science, Mathematics................................399

Constructed-Response Questions...................................412

Subtest III: Physical Education, Human Development,
                  Visual and Performing Arts 417

Constructed-Response Questions...................................431

Answer Key..433

Detailed Explanations 435

PRACTICE TEST 2   **479**

Answer Sheets 481

Subtest I: Reading, Language & Literature,
                  History & Social Science................................485

Constructed-Response Questions...................................500

Subtest II: Science, Mathematics................................503

Constructed-Response Questions...................................518

Subtest III: Physical Education, Human Development,
                  Visual and Performing Arts 521

Constructed-Response Questions...................................538

Answer Key..541

Detailed Explanations 543

APPENDIX: CSET: WRITING SKILLS TEST
Review and Sample Essays   **587**

INDEX   **607**

CSET

**California Subject Examinations
for Teachers: Multiple Subjects**

Passing the CSET:
Multiple Subjects

Passing the CSET: Multiple Subjects

The California Subject Examinations for Teachers: Multiple Subjects is one of the most comprehensive educator certification exams in use today. Covering seven subject areas and requiring writing as well as analytical skills, the CSET: Multiple Subjects Test is designed to ensure that only well-rounded, competent educators are certified to teach in the state of California. The CSET: Multiple Subjects Test is a lengthy, challenging exam, and may cover material that you have not studied in several years. But by studying the information and proven strategies in our book, you will be well on your way to succeeding. REA provides you with everything you need to know to achieve a passing score. Every type of question, every subject area, and every skill needed to pass the exam is given complete coverage. The information in this book, coupled with your dedication, will get you certified. Let's start by learning a little bit about the background of the exam.

In California, a **Multiple Subject Teaching Credential** enables one to teach any subject in a self-contained classroom. While this credential is good for grades K–12, in practice it is used mostly in elementary schools. A California **Single Subject Teaching Credential** enables the holder to teach a specific subject in a departmentalized class. Again, the Single Subject Credential allows the holder to teach in grades K–12; however, its most prevalent use is for getting certified in middle and secondary schools.

The focus of this book is the CSET: Multiple Subjects Test, which is administered by National Evaluation Systems, Inc. (NES). CSET: Multiple Subjects is part of NES's series of teacher certification exams, which also includes the California Basic Educational Skills Test. For more information on the CSET series in general, or the CSET: Multiple Subjects examination in particular, contact NES as follows:

National Evaluation Systems, Inc.
P.O. Box 340813
Sacramento, CA 95834-0813
Phone: (916) 928-0244
Website: *www.cset.nesinc.com*

Know the Format

The CSET consists of three distinct subtests, each containing both multiple-choice and constructed-response items. By and large, this exam has the feel of the straightforward fill-in-the-oval kind of exam you've seen many times in your educational career. The balance of the CSET, however, features items that require you to write short, focused responses. Thus, the exam is of considerable breadth and scope. Don't be daunted: One-hundred forty-three multiple-choice and 11 constructed-response questions covering seven subject areas may sound like a lot, but let's take a look at a breakdown of the questions by subject.

	Subject	Number of Questions	Number of Constructed-Response Questions
Subtest I	Reading, Language and Literature	26	2
	History and Social Science	26	2
Subtest II	Science	26	2
	Mathematics	26	2
Subtest III	Physical Education	13	1
	Human Development	13	1
	Visual and Performing Arts	13	1

You'll notice that the test favors core subjects like math and English by a ratio of 2 to 1 over physical education and human development. While all areas of the test are important, the exam is biased toward math, science, English, and history. Knowing this will allow you to play to your strengths and tailor your study time accordingly.

Each testing session is five hours in length. You may choose to take up to three CSET: Multiple Subjects subtests per session. Subtest I consists of Reading, Language and Literature, and History and Social Science. Subtest II consists of Science and Mathematics, while Subtest III encompasses Physical Education, Human Development, and Visual and Performing Arts. Individual subtests are not timed.

How to Use this Book

When Should I Start Studying?

It's never too early to start studying for the CSET. With so many subject areas to cover, the more time you have, the better. We've included an eight-week study schedule, but the format is very flexible. If you've only got a few weeks before your test date, you'll have to make some adjustments. If you've got a few months, then extend the time allotted to each section in the study schedule. Remember, the more time you spend studying, the more confident and prepared you'll feel on test day.

About the Review Sections

The review material in this text has been compiled in accordance with explicit guidelines provided by National Evaluation Systems, Inc. California currently adheres to these standards. By using the review material in conjunction with the practice tests, you should be well prepared for the actual CSET: Multiple Subjects Test. At some point in your educational experience, you have probably studied all the material that constitutes the test. For most candidates, however, this was most likely some time ago. The reviews will serve to refresh your memory of these topics, and the practice tests will help you gauge which areas you need to work on.

Scoring the CSET

How Do I Know If I've Passed the Exam?

NES administers several versions of the CSET, and these versions vary in their level of difficulty just as the scoring weight of each question varies. For this reason, there is no single formula that you may use to convert your raw score into a scaled score. Responses to multiple-choice questions are machine scored. Test scores are based on the number of questions answered correctly. No penalty is assessed for guessing.

The Content-Response Exercises also are difficult to score. A scoring guide is included in the Content-Response Exercises practice exam, as are sample essays against which you can judge your work. You may want to have a professor or another test candidate judge your work against our sample essays. If you are honest with yourself about the quality of your work, however, there is no reason why you cannot score your responses yourself. Each response is graded on a four-point scale, 0–3.

A quick reference guide to the approximate weight value of the scoring for the complete CSET: Multiple Subjects test (Subtests I, II, and III):

Test	Number of Questions	Score weight
Multiple Choice	143	approx. 70%
Constructed-Response	11	approx. 30%

To pass the test, you will need to answer roughly 85, or 60 percent, of the multiple-choice questions correctly and score an average of about "2" on the constructed-response questions. If you don't achieve a passing score on your first practice test, don't worry. That's what diagnostic exams are for. Use what you learned about your strengths and weaknesses to focus your study.

About six weeks after you take the actual exam, you'll get your official score report from NES. Sit down, take a deep breath, and open it. The numbers on that score report will reflect your *scaled score*. Your scaled score is the total value of the questions you answered correctly based on your unique test administration.

Passing scores are as follows:

Test	Passing
Subtest I	220
Subtest II	220
Subtest III	220

Remember, each subtest is scored indiviually. Therefore, there is not an overall minimum score to obtain to pass the CSET: Multiple Subjects test. You must pass all three subtests to pass the complete exam.

Studying for the CSET

There is no one correct way to study for the CSET. You must find the method that works best for you. But there are some general guidelines to follow. Let's take a look at some of the basics:

Be Realistic

How long has it been since you were on the *other* side of that desk? Depending on your specific areas of interest, it may have been years since you were in a history class, a math class, or an art history class. In addition to the time it's going to take to actually learn (or even *re*learn) the material that's tested on the CSET, it's going to take a while to simply acclimate yourself to this kind of study again. Account for this time when planning your study, and more importantly, remember this advice when you get frustrated, because you can't simply breeze through our math or history reviews. Allow yourself to be amazed at how much you've forgotten. In two weeks, you'll be amazed at how much you've learned.

The Double-it-Plus-Two Rule

Our study schedule is a good guide to how to plan your study time, but it's painted with a fairly broad brush. When planning your study for an evening rather than a week, use the Double-it-plus-two rule. Estimate how long it will take you to read a specific chapter or subsection. Then double it, and add two. For example, if you think it will take an hour to study the Physical Education Review, set aside four hours. This will account for study breaks, interruptions, and all the other miscellaneous demands placed upon your time in an average day. By carrying out a more realistic study plan, you'll retain more, especially if you are not frustrated by the inevitable distractions to your study time.

Know Thyself

Some candidates prefer to set aside a few hours every morning to study, while others prefer to study at night before going to sleep. Only you can determine when and where your study time will be most effective, but it is helpful to be consistent. You may retain more information if you study every day at roughly the same time. Use our study schedule as a guide, but remember, no one knows what works for you better than you do.

When taking the practice tests, remember to try to duplicate the actual testing conditions as closely as possible. A quiet, well-lit room, free from such distractions as the television or radio is preferable. As you complete each practice test, take a good look at your score reports and thoroughly review the explanations. Information that is wrong for one item may be correct for another, so it will be helpful to you to absorb as much data as possible. Keep track of your scores so you can gauge your progress accurately, and develop a clear sense of where you need improvement.

CSET Test-Taking Strategies

Listed here are several must-do strategies to help you succeed on the CSET.

➤ *Read all of the possible answers.* Even if you believe you have found the correct answer, read all four options. Often answers that look right at first prove to be "magnet responses" meant to distract you from the correct choice.

➤ *Eliminate obviously incorrect answers immediately.* It's always better to guess than not answer at all. Even if you have absolutely no idea what the correct answer might be, you have a 25 percent chance of being correct. Increase those chances by eliminating the answers you know are wrong. Points are not deducted for incorrect answers, so don't leave anything blank.

➤ *Work calmly and steadily.* You have a five-hour session to complete as many subtests (up to three subtests total) as you choose to take. Individual subtests are not timed so don't feel pressured to spend a certain amount of time on any one item. Work at your own pace as you attempt to achieve a comfortable rhythm of answering questions. Timing yourself while you take the practice tests will help you learn to use your time wisely.

➤ *Be sure that the oval you are marking corresponds to the number of the question in the test booklet.* The multiple-choice section of the CSET is graded by a computer, which has no sympathy for clerical errors. One incorrectly placed response can upset your entire score.

The Day of the Test

Try to get a good night's rest, and get up early on the test day. Have a good breakfast, as a growling stomach could prove distracting to yourself and the other candidates and, moreover, your brain will function better with proper nourishment. Dress in layers. The testing center will be comfortable only for the proctor. Arrive early. Acclimate yourself to the room. Put yourself at ease by noticing any funny pictures or, say, odd cracks in the ceiling. The point is to minimize distractions once the clock starts ticking.

Before you leave for the testing center, make sure you have your valid admission ticket, as well as photo identification. The name on your ID must match the one on your registration. If the name on your identification differs from the name in which you are registered, you must provide official verification of the change (e.g., marriage certificate, court order). You will also need to bring several sharpened No. 2 pencils, as none will be provided at the test site. Basic four-function calculators will be provided for examinees taking CSET: Multiple Subjects Subtest II. Directions for the use of the calculator, however, will not be provided. Communication devices, such as cellular phones, are forbidden in the testing center. Possession or use of such devices could result in the voiding of your test score. No eating, drinking, or smoking is permitted during the test, so make sure to get those things out of the way beforehand.

Make sure you report to the test facility for each assigned test session at the time indicated on your admission ticket. If you arrive at a test session late, you may not be admitted. If you are admitted late, you will not be given any additional time beyond the scheduled end of the test session, and you will be required to sign a statement acknowledging this. When you have finished the test(s) or subtest(s) or when the test session ends, your test materials will be collected and you will be allowed to leave. After the test, go home and sleep for a day or so. You've earned it.

CSET Study Schedule

The following study course schedule should provide all the time you need to pass the CSET: Multiple Subjects examination. If you have more than eight weeks, add any extra time you have to Weeks 2 and 7. No matter which schedule works best for you, the more time you devote to studying for the CSET, the more prepared and confident you will be on the day of the actual test.

Week	Activity
1	Take the first test as a diagnostic exam. Your score will be an indication of your strengths and weaknesses. Study your score reports and review the explanations for the questions you answered incorrectly.
2 and 3	Study REA's CSET review material. Highlight key terms and information. Take notes on the important theories and key concepts since writing will aid in the retention of information.

4 and 5   Review your references and sources. Use any other supplementary material which your counselor and the California Commission on Teacher Credentialing recommend.

6   Condense your notes and findings. You should have a structured outline detailing specific facts. You may want to use index cards to aid you in memorizing important facts and concepts.

7   Test yourself using the index cards. You may want to have a friend or colleague quiz you on key facts and items. Take the second full-length practice test. Review the explanations for the questions you answered incorrectly.

8   Study any areas you consider to be your weaknesses by using your study materials, references, and notes. Retake the tests using the extra answer sheets provided in this book.

CSET

**California Subject Examinations
for Teachers: Multiple Subjects**

Review

Reading, Language, and Literature Review

"Words are some of the most powerful and important things I know . . . Language is the tool of love and the weapon of hatred. It's the bright red warning flag of danger—and stone foundation of diplomacy and peace."—Anonymous

The potency of language is evident in its utility and diverse forms. Without language, humankind would be incapable of conceptualizing ideas. Literature provides a forum to express the versatility of language. The art of literature paints language in many forms such as satire, poetry, and novels, which are discussed in the Reading, Language, and Literature section. Reading offers the opportunity to learn language and the different ways it can be expressed. The reading of this section will allow you to express your expertise on related topics to be tested on the CSET.

Prose

General Rules and Ideas

Students are sometimes confused as to what exactly prose is. Basically, prose is **not** poetry. Prose is what we write and speak most of the time in our everyday intercourse: unmetered, unrhymed language. Which is not to say that prose does not have its own rhythms—language, whether written or spoken, has cadence and balance. And certainly prose can have instances of rhyme or assonance, alliteration, or onomatopoeia. Language is, after all, **phonic.**

Furthermore, **prose** may be either **fiction** or **non-fiction**. A novel (like a short story) is fiction; an autobiography is non-fiction. While a novel (or short story) may have autobiographical elements, an autobiography is presumed to be entirely factual. Essays are usually described in other terms: expository, argumentative, persuasive, critical, narrative. Essays may have elements of either fiction or non-fiction, but are generally classed as a separate subgenre.

Satire, properly speaking, is not a genre at all, but rather a **mode**, elements of which can be found in any category of literature—from poetry and drama to novels and essays. Satire is a manifestation of authorial attitude (tone) and purpose. Our discussion of satire will be limited to its use in prose.

But we have not addressed the initial question: "Why do people write prose?" The answer depends, in part, on the writer's intent. If he wishes to tell a rather long story, filled with many characters and subplots, interlaced with motifs, symbols, and themes, with time and space to develop interrelationships and to present descriptive passages, the writer generally chooses the novel as his medium. If he believes he can present his story more compactly and less complexly, he may choose the novella or the short story.

These subgenres require from the reader a different kind of involvement than does the essay. The essay, rather than presenting a story from which the reader may discern meaning through the skillful analysis of character, plot, symbol, and language, presents a relatively straightforward account of the writer's opinion(s) on an endless array of topics. Depending upon the type of essay, the reader may become informed (expository), provoked (argumentative), persuaded, enlightened (critical), or, in the case of the narrative essay, better acquainted with the writer who wishes to illustrate a point with his story, whether it is autobiographical or fictitious.

Encountering satire in prose selections demands that the reader be sensitive to the nuances of language and form, that he detects the double-edged sword of irony, and that he correctly assesses both the writer's tone and his purpose.

Readers of prose, like readers of poetry, seek aesthetic pleasure, entertainment, and knowledge, not necessarily in that order. Fiction offers worlds—real and imagined—in which characters and ideas, events and language, interact in ways familiar and unfamiliar. As readers, we take delight in the wisdom we fancy we have acquired from a novel or short story. Non-fiction offers viewpoints which we may find comforting or horrifying, amusing or sobering, presented by the author rather than by his once-removed persona. Thus, we are tempted to believe that somehow the truths presented in non-fiction are more "real" than the truths revealed by fiction. But we must resist! Truth is not "genre-specific."

Reading Novels

Most literary handbooks will define a novel as an extended fictional prose narrative, derived from the Italian *novella*, meaning "tale, piece of news." The term "novelle," meaning short tales, was applied to works such as Boccaccio's *The Decameron*, a collection of stories which had an impact on later works such as Chaucer's *Canterbury Tales*. In most European countries, the word for **novel** is **roman**, short for **romance**, which was applied to longer verse narratives (Malory's *Morte d'Arthur*), which were later written in prose. Early romances were associated with "legendary, imaginative, and poetic material"—tales "of the long ago or the far away or the imaginatively improbable;" novels, on the other hand, were felt to be "bound by the facts of the actual world and the laws of probability" (*A Handbook to Literature*, C. Hugh Holman, p. 354).

Fast Facts

The novel has, over some 600 years, developed into many special forms which are classified by subject matter: detective novel, psychological novel, historical novel, regional novel, picaresque novel, Gothic novel, stream-of-consciousness novel, epistolary novel, and so on. These terms, of course, are not exhaustive nor

Most literary handbooks define a novel as an extended fictional prose narrative, derived from the Italian *novella*, meaning "tale, piece of news."

mutually exclusive. Furthermore, depending on the conventions of the author's time period, his style, and his outlook on life, his *mode* may be termed **realism**, **romanticism**, **impressionism**, **expressionism**, **naturalism**, or **neo-classicism** (Holman, p. 359).

Our earlier description of a novel (" . . . a rather long story, filled with many characters and subplots, interlaced with motifs, symbols, and themes, with time and space to develop interrelationships and to present descriptive passages") is satisfactory for our purposes here. The works generally included on the CSET are those which have stood the test of time in significance, literary merit, and reader popularity. New works are incorporated into the canon which is a reflection of what works are being taught in literature classes. And teachers begin to teach those works which are included frequently among the questions. So the process is circular, but the standards remain high for inclusion.

Analyzing novels is a bit like asking the journalist's six questions: what? who? why? when? where? and how? The "what" is the story, the narrative, the plot, and subplots. The most important of these questions, however, is the "why." The critic's job is to discover "why" the author of a piece of writing chose to include in it the ideas and the very words a reader sees before him or her. That Gabriel's wife Gretta, in James Joyce's *The Dead,* must have loved that seventeen-year-old boy Michael Furey who died years ago holds less interest for the critic than understanding why Joyce gave him that particular name, why Gretta is reminded of the boy through a song, why she falls asleep thinking about the boy, what he represents to her now, and why Joyce names his novella *The Dead.*

Most students are familiar with Freytag's Pyramid, originally designed to describe the structure of a five-act drama but now widely used to analyze fiction as well. The stages generally specified are **introduction** or **exposition, complication, rising action, climax, falling action,** and **denouement** or **conclusion**. As the novel's events are charted, the "change which structures the story" should emerge. There are many events in a long narrative; but generally only one set of events comprises the "real" or "significant" story.

However, subplots often parallel or serve as counterpoints to the main plot line, serving to enhance the central story. Minor characters sometimes have essentially the same conflicts and goals as the major characters, but the consequences of the outcome seem less important. Sometimes the parallels involve reversals of characters and situations, creating similar yet distinct differences in the outcomes. Nevertheless, seeing the parallels makes understanding the major plot line less difficult.

Sometimes an author divides the novel into chapters—named or unnamed, perhaps just numbered. Or he might divide the novel into "books" or "parts," with chapters as subsections. Readers should take their cue from these divisions; the author must have had some reason for them. Take note of what happens in each larger section, as well as within the smaller chapters. Whose progress is being followed? What event or occurrence is being foreshadowed or prepared for? What causal or other relationships are there between sections and events? Some writers, such as Steinbeck in *The Grapes of Wrath*, use intercalary chapters, alternating between the "real" story (the Joads) and peripheral or parallel stories (the Okies and migrants in general). Look for the pattern of such organization; try to see the interrelationships of these alternating chapters.

Of course, plots cannot happen in isolation from characters, the **who?** element of a story. Not only are there major and minor characters to consider; we need to note whether the various characters are **static** or **dynamic**. Static characters do not change in significant ways—that is, in ways which relate to the story which is structuring the novel. A character may die, i.e., change from alive to dead, and still be static, unless his death is central

> Analyzing novels *Fast* is a bit like asking *Facts* the journalist's six questions: what? who? why? when? where? and how?

to the narrative. For instance, in Golding's *Lord of the Flies*, the boy with the mulberry birthmark apparently dies in a fire early in the novel. Momentous as any person's death is, this boy's death is not what the novel is about. However, when Simon is killed, and later Piggy, the narrative is directly impacted because the reason for their deaths is central to the novel's theme regarding man's innate evil. A dynamic character may change only slightly in his attitudes, but those changes may be the very ones upon which the narrative rests. For instance, Siddhartha begins as a very pure and devout Hindu but is unfulfilled spiritually. He eventually does achieve spiritual contentment, but his change is more a matter of degree than of substance. He is not an evil man who attains salvation, nor a pious man who becomes corrupt. It is the process of his search, the stages in his pilgrimage, which structure the novel *Siddhartha*.

We describe major characters or "actors" in novels as **protagonists** or **antagonists**. Built into those two terms is the Greek word *agon,* meaning "struggle." The *prot*agonist struggles **toward** or for someone or something; the *ant(i)*agonist struggles **against** someone or something. The possible conflicts are usually cited as man against himself, man against man, man against society, or man against nature. Sometimes more than one of these conflicts appears in a story, but usually one is dominant and is the structuring device.

A character can be referred to as **stock**, meaning that he exists because the plot demands it. For instance, a Western with a gunman who robs the bank will require a number of stock characters: the banker's lovely daughter, the tough but kindhearted barmaid, the cowardly white-shirted citizen who sells out the hero to save his own skin, and the young freckle-faced lad who shoots the bad guy from a second-story hotel window.

Or a character can be a **stereotype**, without individuating characteristics. For instance, a sheriff in a small Southern town, a football player who is all brawn, a librarian clucking over her prized books, or the cruel commandant of a POW camp.

Characters often serve as **foils** for other characters, enabling us to see one or more of them better. A classic example is Tom Sawyer, the Romantic foil for Huck Finn's Realism. Or, in Lee's *To Kill a Mockingbird*, Scout serves as the naive observer of events which her brother Jem, four years older, comes to understand from the perspective of the adult world.

Sometimes characters are **allegorical**, standing for qualities or concepts rather than for actual personages. For instance, Jim Casey (initials "J. C.") in *The Grapes of Wrath* is often regarded as a Christ figure, pure and self-sacrificing in his aims for the migrant workers. Or Kamala, Siddhartha's teacher in the art of love, whose name comes from the tree whose bark is used as a purgative; she purges him of his ascetic ways on his road to selfhood and spiritual fulfillment.

Other characters are fully three-dimensional, "rounded," "mimetic" of humans in all their virtue, vice, hope, despair, strength, and weakness. This verisimilitude aids the author in creating characters who are credible and plausible, without being dully predictable and mundane.

The interplay of plot and characters determines in large part the **theme** of a work, the **why?** of the story. First of all, we must distinguish between a mere topic and a genuine theme or thesis; and then between a theme and contributing *motifs*. A **topic** is a phrase, such as "man's inhumanity to man;" or "the fickle nature of fate." A **theme**, however, turns a phrase into a statement: "Man's inhumanity to man is barely concealed by 'civilization.'" Or "Man is a helpless pawn, at the mercy of fickle fate." Many writers may deal with the same topic, such as the complex nature of true love; but their themes may vary widely, from "True love will always win out in the end," to "Not even true love can survive the cruel ironies of fate."

To illustrate the relationship between plot, character, and theme, let's examine two familiar fairy tales. In "The Ugly Duckling," the structuring story line is "Once upon a time there was an ugly duckling, who in turn became a beautiful swan." In this case, the duckling did nothing to merit either his ugliness nor his eventual transformation; but he did not curse fate. He only wept and waited, lonely and outcast. And when he became beautiful, he did not gloat; he eagerly joined the other members of his flock, who greatly admired him. The theme here essentially is: "Good things come to him who waits," or "Life is unfair—you don't get what you deserve, nor deserve what you get." What happens to the theme if the ugly duckling remains an ugly duckling: "Some guys just never get a break?"

Especially rewarding to examine for the interdependence of plot and theme is "Cinderella:" "Once upon a time, a lovely, sweet-natured young girl was forced to labor for and serve her ugly and ungrateful stepmother and two stepsisters. But thanks to her Fairy Godmother, Cinderella and the Prince marry, and live happily ever after."

We could change events (plot elements) at any point, but let's take the penultimate scene where the Prince's men come to the door with the single glass slipper. Cinderella has been shut away so that she is not present when the other women in the house try on the slipper. Suppose that the stepmother or either of the two stepsisters tries on the slipper—and it fits! Cinderella is in the back room doing the laundry, and her family waltzes out the door to the palace and she doesn't even get an invitation to the wedding. And imagine the Prince's dismay when the ugly, one-slippered lady lifts her wedding veil for the consummating kiss! Theme: "There is no justice in the world, for those of low or high station;" or "Virtue is not its own reward?"

Or let's say that during the slipper-test scene, the stepsisters, stepmother, and finally Cinderella all try on the shoe, but to no avail. And then in sashays the Fairy Godmother, who gives them all a knowing smirk, puts out her slipper-sized foot and cackles hysterically, like the mechanical witch in the penny arcade. Theme: "You can't trust anybody these days;" or, a favorite statement of theme, "Appearances can be deceiving." The link between plot and theme is very strong, indeed.

Skilled writers often employ **motifs** to help unify their works. A motif is a detail or element of the story which is repeated throughout, and which may even become symbolic. Television shows are ready examples of the use of motifs. A medical show, with many scenes alternately set in the hospital waiting room and operating room, uses elements such as the pacing, anxious parent or loved one, the gradually filling ashtray, and the large wall clock whose hands melt from one hour to another. And in the operating room, the half-masked surgeon whose brow is frequently mopped by the nurse; the gloved hand open-palmed to receive scalpel, sponge, and so on; the various oscilloscopes giving read-outs of the patient's very fragile condition; the expanding and collapsing bladder manifesting that the patient is indeed breathing; and, again, the wall clock, assuring us that this procedure is taking forever. These are all motifs, details which in concert help convince the reader that this story occurs in a hospital, and that the mood is pretty tense, that the medical team is doing all it can, and that Mom and Dad will be there when Junior or Sissy wakes up.

But motifs can become symbolic. The oscilloscope line quits blipping, levels out, and gives off the ominous hum. And the doctor's gloved hand sets down the scalpel and shuts off the oscilloscope. In the waiting room, Dad crushes the empty cigarette pack; Mom quits pacing and sinks into the sofa. The door to the waiting room swings shut silently behind the retreating doctor. All these elements signal "It's over, finished."

Fast Facts ▶ **Motifs can become symbolic.**

This example is very crude and mechanical, but motifs in the hands of a skillful writer are valuable devices. And in isolation, and often magnified, a single motif can become a controlling image with great significance. For instance, Emma Bovary's shoes signify her obsession with material things; and when her delicate slippers become soiled as she crosses the dewy grass to meet her lover, we sense the impurity of her act as well as its futility. Or when wise Piggy, in *Lord of the Flies,* is reduced to one lens in his specs, and finally to no specs at all, we see the loss of insight and wisdom on the island, and chaos follows.

Setting is the **where?** element of the story. But setting is also the **when?** element: time of day, time of year, time period or year; it is the dramatic moment, the precise intersection of time and space when this story is being told. Setting is also the atmosphere: positive or negative ambiance, calm, chaotic, Gothic, Romantic. The question for the reader to answer is whether the setting is ultimately essential to the plot/theme, or whether it is incidental; i.e., could this story/theme have been told successfully in another time and/or place? For instance, could the theme in *Lord of the Flies* be made manifest if the boys were not on an island? Could they have been isolated in some other place? Does it matter whether the "war" which they are fleeing is WWII or WWIII or some other conflict, in terms of the theme?

Hopefully, you will see that the four elements of plot, character, theme, and setting are intertwined and largely interdependent. A work must really be read as a whole, rather than dissected and analyzed in discrete segments.

The final question, **how?**, relates to an author's style. Style involves language (word choice), syntax (word order, sentence type and length), the balance between narration and dialogue, the choice of narrative voice (first person participant, third person with limited omniscience), use of descriptive passages, and other aspects of the actual words on the page which are basically irrelevant to the first four elements (plot, character, theme, and setting). Stylistic differences are fairly easy to spot among such diverse writers as Jane Austen, whose style is—to today's reader—very formal and mannered; Mark Twain, whose style is very casual and colloquial; William Faulkner, whose prose often spins on without punctuation or paragraphs far longer than the reader can hold either the thought or his breath; and Hemingway, whose dense but spare, pared-down style has earned the epithet, "Less is more."

Reading Short Stories

The modern short story differs from earlier short fiction such as the parable, fable, and tale, in its emphasis on character development through scenes rather than summary: through *showing* rather than *telling*. Gaining popularity in the nineteenth century, the short story generally was realistic, presenting detailed accounts of the lives of middle-class personages. This tendency toward realism dictates that the plot be grounded in *probability*, with causality fully in operation. Furthermore, the characters are human with recognizable human motivations, both social and psychological. Setting—time and place—is realistic rather than fantastic. And, as Poe stipulated, the elements of plot, character, setting, style, point of view, and theme all work toward a single *unified* effect.

However, some modern writers have stretched these boundaries and have mixed in elements of nonrealism—such as the supernatural and the fantastic—sometimes switching back and forth between realism and nonrealism, confusing the reader who is expecting conventional fiction. Barth's "Lost in the Funhouse" and Allen's "The Kugelmass Episode" are two stories which are not, strictly speaking, *realistic*. However, if you approach and accept this type of story on its own terms, you will be better able to understand and appreciate it fully.

Unlike the novel, which has time and space to develop characters and interrelationships, the short story must rely on flashes of insight and revelation to develop plot and characters. The "slice of life" in a short story is of necessity much narrower than that in a novel; the time span is much shorter, the focus much tighter. To attempt anything like the panoramic canvas available to the novelist would be to view fireworks through a soda straw: occasionally pretty, but ultimately not very satisfying or enlightening.

The elements of the short story are those of the novel, discussed earlier. Because the material in a short story is so concentrated, the author's choice of point of view may be especially significant. A narrator may be *objective*, presenting information without bias or comment. Hemingway frequently uses the objective *third-person* narrator, presenting scenes almost dramatically, i.e., with a great deal of dialogue and very little narrative, none of which directly reveals the thoughts or feelings of the characters. The third-person narrator may, however, be less objective in his presentation, directly revealing the thoughts and feelings, of one or more of the characters, as Chopin does in "The Story of an Hour." We say that such a narrator is fully or partially *omniscient*, depending on how complete his knowledge is of the characters' psychological and emotional makeup. The least objective narrator is the *first-person* narrator, who presents information from the perspective of a single character who is a participant in the action. Such a narrative choice allows the author to present the discrepancies between the writer's/reader's perceptions and those of the narrator.

One reason the choice of narrator, the point of view from which to tell the story, is immensely important in a short story is that the narrator reveals character and event in ways which affect our understanding of theme. For instance, in Faulkner's "A Rose for Emily," the unnamed narrator who seems to be a townsperson recounts the story out of chronological order, juxtaposing events whose causality and significance are uncertain. The narrator withholds information which would explain events being presented, letting the reader puzzle over Emily Grierson's motivations, a device common in detective fiction. In fact, the narrator presents contradictory information, making the reader alternately pity and resent the spinster. When we examine the imagery and conclude that Miss Emily and her house represent the decay and decadence of the Old South which resisted the invasion of "progress" from the North, we see the importance of setting and symbol in relation to theme.

Similarly, in Mansfield's "Bliss," the abundant description of setting creates the controlling image of the lovely pear tree. But this symbol of fecundity becomes ironic when Bertha Young belatedly feels sincere and overwhelming desire for her husband. The third-person narrator's omniscience is limited to Bertha's thoughts and feelings; otherwise we would have seen her husband's infidelity with Miss Fulton.

In O'Connor's "Good Country People," the narrator is broadly omniscient, but the reader is still taken by surprise at the cruelty of the Bible salesman who seduces Joy-Hulga. That he steals her artificial leg is perhaps poetic justice, since she (with her numerous degrees) had fully intended to seduce him ("just good country people"). The story's title, the characters' names—Hopewell, Freeman, Joy; the salesman's professed Christianity, the Bibles hollowed out to hold whiskey and condoms, add to the irony of Mrs. Freeman's final comment on the young man: "Some can't be that simple . . . I know I never could."

The *initiation story* frequently employs the first-person narrator. To demonstrate the subtle differences which can occur in stories which ostensibly have the same point of view and general theme, let's look at three: "A Christmas Memory" (Capote), "Araby" (Joyce), and "A & P" (Updike).

Early in "A Christmas Memory," Capote's narrator identifies himself:

The person to whom she is speaking is myself. I am seven; she is sixty-something. We are cousins, very distant ones, and we have lived together—well, as long as I can remember. Other people inhabit the house, relatives; and though they have power over us, and frequently make us cry, we are not, on the whole, too much aware of them. We are each other's best friend. She calls me Buddy, in memory of a boy who was formerly her best friend. The other Buddy died in the 1880's, when she was still a child. She is still a child.

Buddy and his cousin, who is called only "my friend," save their meager earnings throughout the year in order to make fruitcakes at Christmas to give mainly to "persons we've met maybe once, perhaps not at all . . . Like President Roosevelt . . . Or Abner Packer, the driver of the six o'clock bus from Mobile, who exchanges waves with us everyday. . . " Their gifts to one another each year are always handmade, often duplicates of the year before, like the kites they present on what was to be their last Christmas together.

Away at boarding school, when Buddy receives word of his friend's death, it "merely confirms a piece of news some secret vein had already received, severing from me an irreplaceable part of myself, letting it loose like a kite on a broken string. That is why, walking across a school campus on this particular December morning, I keep searching the sky. As if I expected to see, rather like hearts, a lost pair of kites hurrying toward heaven."

Buddy's characterizations of his friend are also self-revelatory. He and she are peers, equals, despite their vast age difference. They are both totally unselfish, joying in the simple activities mandated by their economic circumstances. They are both "children."

The story is told in present tense, making the memories from the first paragraphs seem as "real" and immediate as those from many years later. And Buddy's responses from the early years ("Well, I'm disappointed. Who wouldn't be? With socks, a Sunday school shirt, some handkerchiefs, a hand-me-down sweater and a year's subscription to a religious magazine for children. *The Little Shepherd*. It makes me boil. It really does.") are as true to his seven-year-old's perspective, as are those when he, much older, has left home ("I have a new home too. But it doesn't count. Home is where my friend is, and there I never go.").

The youthful narrator in "A & P" also uses present tense, but not consistently, which gives his narrative a very colloquial, even unschooled flavor. Like Buddy, Sammy identifies himself in the opening paragraph: "In walks these three girls in nothing but bathing suits. I'm in the third checkout slot, with my back to the door, so I don't see them until they're over by the bread." And later, "Stokesie's married, with two babies chalked up on his fuselage already, but as far as I can tell that's the only difference. He's twenty-two, and I was nineteen this April." The girls incur the wrath of the store manager, who scolds them for their inappropriate dress. And Sammy, in his adolescent idealism, quits on the spot; although he realizes that he does not want to "do this" to his parents, he tells us " . . . it seems to me that once you begin a gesture it's fatal not to go through with it." But his *beau geste* is ill-spent: "I look around for my girls, but they're gone, of course . . . . I could see Lengel in my place in the slot, checking the sheep through. His face was dark gray and his back stiff, as if he'd just had an injection of iron, and my stomach kind of fell as I felt how hard the world was going to be to me hereafter."

Like Buddy, Sammy tells his story from a perch not too distant from the events he recounts. Both narrators still feel the immediacy of their rites of passage very strongly. Buddy, however, reveals himself to be a more admirable character, perhaps because his story occurs mainly when he is seven—children tend not to be reckless in the way that Sammy is. Sammy was performing for an audience, doing things he knew would cause pain to himself and his family, for the sake of those three girls who never gave him the slightest encouragement and whom he would probably never even see again.

In "Araby," the unnamed narrator tells of a boyhood crush he had on the older sister of one of his chums: "I thought little of the future. I did not know whether I would ever speak to her or not or, if I spoke to her, how I could tell her of my confused adoration. But my body was like a harp and her words and gestures were like fingers running upon the wires." She asks the boy if he is going to Araby, a "splendid bazaar," and reveals that she cannot. He promises to go himself and bring her something. But his uncle's late homecoming delays the boy's excursion until the bazaar is nearly closed for the night, and he is unable to find an appropriate gift. Forlornly, "I turned away slowly and walked down the middle of the bazaar . . . . Gazing up into the darkness I saw myself as a creature driven and derided by vanity; and my eyes burned with anguish and anger." This narrator is recounting his story from much further away than either Buddy or Sammy tells his own. The narrator of "Araby" has the perspective of an adult, looking back at a very important event in his boyhood. His "voice" reflects wisdom born of experience. The incident was very painful then; but its memory, while poignant, is no longer devastating. Like Sammy, this narrator sees the dichotomy between his adolescent idealism and the mundane reality of "romance." However, the difference is in the narrator's ability to turn the light on himself; Sammy is still so close to the incident that he very likely would whip off his checker's apron again if the girls returned to the A & P. The "Araby" narrator has "mellowed," and can see the futility—and the necessity—of adolescent love.

Reading Essays

Essays fall into four rough categories: **speculative**, **argumentative**, **narrative**, and **expository**. Depending on the writer's purpose, his essay will fit more or less into one or these groupings.

The **speculative** essay is so named because, as its Latin root suggests, it *looks* at ideas; explores them rather than explains them. While the speculative essay may be said to be *meditative*, it often makes one or more points. But the thesis may not be as obvious or clear-cut as that in an expository or argumentative essay. The writer deals with ideas in an associative manner, playing with ideas in a looser structure than he would in an expository or argumentative essay. This "flow" may even produce *intercalary* paragraphs, which present alternately a narrative of sorts and thoughtful responses to the events being recounted, as in White's "The Ring of Time."

The purposes of the **argumentative** essay, on the other hand, are always clear: to present a point and provide evidence, which may be factual or anecdotal, and to support it. The structure is usually very formal, as in a debate, with counterpositions and counterarguments. Whatever the organizational pattern, the writer's intent in an argumentative essay is to persuade his reader of the validity of some claim, as Bacon does in "Of Love."

Narrative and **expository** essays have elements of both the speculative and argumentative modes. The narrative essay may recount an incident or a series of incidents and is almost always autobiographical, in order to make a point, as in Orwell's "Shooting an Elephant." The informality of the storytelling makes the narrative essay less insistent than the argumentative essay, but more directed than the speculative essay.

Students are probably most familiar with the expository essay, the primary purpose of which is to explain and clarify ideas. While the expository essay may have narrative elements, that aspect is minor and subservient to that of explanation. Furthermore, while nearly all essays have some element of persuasion, argumentation is incidental in the expository essay. In any event, the four categories—speculative, argumentative, narrative, and expository—are neither exhaustive nor mutually exclusive.

As non-fiction, essays have a different set of elements from novels and short stories: **voice**, **style**, **structure**, and **thought**.

Voice in non-fiction is similar to the narrator's tone in fiction; but the major difference is in who is "speaking." In fiction, the author is not the speaker—the **narrator** is the speaker. Students sometimes have difficulty with this distinction, but it is necessary if we are to preserve the integrity of the fictive "story." In an essay, however, the author speaks directly to the reader, even if he is presenting ideas which he may not actually espouse personally—as in a satire. This directness creates the writer's **tone**, his attitude toward his subject.

Style in non-fiction derives from the same elements as style in fiction: word choice, syntax, balance between dialogue and narration, voice, use of description—those things specifically related to words on the page. Generally speaking, an argumentative essay will be written in a more formal style than will a narrative essay, and a meditative essay will be less formal than an expository essay. But such generalizations are only descriptive, not prescriptive.

Structure and thought, the final elements of essays, are so intertwined as to be inextricable. We must be aware that to change the structure of an essay will alter its meaning. For instance, in White's "The Ring of Time," to abandon the *intercalary* paragraph organization, separating the paragraphs which narrate the scenes with the young circus rider from those which reflect on the circularity and linearity of time, would alter our understanding of the essay's thesis. Writers signal structural shifts with alterations in focus, as well as with visual clues (spacing), verbal clues (*but, therefore, however*), or shifts in the kind of information being presented (personal, scientific, etc).

Thought is perhaps the single element which most distinguishes non-fiction from fiction. The essayist chooses his form not to tell a story but to present an idea. Whether he chooses the speculative, narrative, argumentative, or expository format, the essayist has something on his mind that he wants to convey to his readers. And it is this idea which we are after when we analyze his essay.

Orwell's "Shooting an Elephant" is an often anthologized narrative essay recounting the writer's (presumably) experience in Burma as an officer of the British law that ruled the poverty-ridden people of a small town. Orwell begins with two paragraphs which explain that, as a white, European authority figure, he was subjected to taunts and abuse by the natives. Ironically, he sympathized with the Burmese and harbored fairly strong anti-British feelings, regarding the imperialists as the oppressors rather than the saviors. He tells us that he felt trapped between his position of authority which he himself resented, and the hatred of those he was required to oversee.

The body of the essay—some eleven paragraphs—relates the incident with an otherwise tame elephant gone "must" which had brought chaos and destruction to the village. Only occasionally does Orwell interrupt the narrative to reveal his reactions directly, but his descriptions of the Burmese are sympathetically drawn. The language is heavily connotative, revealing the helplessness of the villagers against both the elephant and the miserable circumstances of their lives.

Orwell recounts how, having sent for an elephant gun, he found that he was compelled to shoot the animal, even though its destruction was by now unwarranted and even ill-advised, given the value of the elephant to the village. But the people expected it, demanded it; the white man realized that he did not have dominion over these people of color after all. They were in charge, not he.

To make matters worse, Orwell bungles the "murder" of the beast, which takes half an hour to die in great agony. And in the aftermath of discussions of the rightness or wrongness of his action, Orwell wonders if anyone realizes he killed the elephant only to save face. It is the final sentence of the final paragraph which directly reveals the author's feelings, although he has made numerous indirect references to them throughout the essay. Coupled with the opening paragraphs, this conclusion presents British imperialism of the period in a very negative light: "the unable doing the unnecessary to the ungrateful."

Having discovered Orwell's main idea, we must look at the other elements (voice, style, structure) to see *how* he communicates it to the reader. The voice of the first-person narrative is fairly formal, yet remarkably candid, using connotation to color our perception of the events. Orwell's narrative has many complex sentences, with vivid descriptive phrases in series, drawing our eye along the landscape and through the crowds as he ponders his next move. Structurally, the essay first presents a premise about British imperialism, then moves to a gripping account of the officer's reluctant shooting of the elephant, and ends with an admission of his own culpability as an agent of the institution he detests. Orwell frequently signals shifts between his role as officer and his responses as a humane personage with *but*, or with dashes to set off his responses to the events he is recounting.

Poetry

Opening a book to study for an examination is perhaps the worst occasion on which to read poetry, or about poetry, because above all, poetry should be enjoyed; it is definitely "reading for pleasure." This last phrase seems to have developed recently to describe the reading we do other than for information or for study. Perhaps you personally would not choose poetry as pleasure reading because of the bad name poetry has received over the years. Some students regard the "old" poetry such as Donne's or Shelley's as effete (for "wimps" and "nerds" only, in current language), or modern poetry as too difficult or weird. It is hard to imagine that poetry was the "current language" for students growing up in the Elizabethan or Romantic eras. Whereas in our world information can be retrieved in a nanosecond, in those worlds there was plenty of time to sit down, clear the mind, and let poetry take over. Very often the meaning of a poem does not come across in a nanosecond and for the modern student this proves very frustrating. Sometimes it takes years for a poem to take on meaning—the reader simply knows that the poem sounds good and it provokes an emotional response that cannot be explained. With time, more emotional experience, more reading of similar experiences, more life, the reader comes to a meaning of that poem that satisfies for the time being. In a few more years that poem may take on a whole new meaning.

This is all very well for reading for pleasure but you are now called upon, in your present experience, to learn poetry for an important examination. Perhaps the first step in the learning process is to answer the question, "Why do people write poetry?" An easy answer is that they wish to convey an experience, an emotion, an insight, or an observation in a startling or satisfying way, one that remains in the memory for years. But why not use a straightforward sentence or paragraph? Why wrap up that valuable insight in fancy words, rhyme, paradox, meter, allusion, symbolism, and all the other seeming mumbo-jumbo that explicators of poetry use? Why not just come right out and say it like "normal people" do? An easy answer to these questions is that poetry is not a vehicle for conveying meaning alone. Gerard Manley Hopkins, one of the great innovators of rhythm in poetry, claimed that poetry should be "heard for its own sake and interest even over and above its interest or meaning." Poetry provides intellectual stimulus, of course. One of the best ways of studying a poem is to consider it a jigsaw puzzle presented to you whole, an integral work of art, which can be taken apart piece by piece (word by word), analyzed scientifically, labelled, and put back together again into a whole, and then the meaning is complete. But people write poetry to convey more than meaning.

T.S. Eliot maintained that the meaning of the poem existed purely to distract us "while the poem did its work." One interpretation of a poem's "work" is that it changes us in some way. We see the world in a new way because of the way the poet has seen it and told us about it. Maybe one of the reasons people write poetry is to encourage us to *see* things in the first place.

Fast Facts
Poets write to awaken the senses.

Simple things like daffodils take on a whole new aspect when we read the way Wordsworth saw them. Why did Wordsworth write that poem? His sister had written an excellent account of the scene in her journal. Wordsworth not only evokes nature as we have never seen it before, alive, joyous, exuberant, he shows nature's healing powers, its restorative quality as the scene flashes "upon that inward eye/Which is the bliss of solitude." Bent over your books studying, how many times has a similar memory of the quality of nature's power come to you? Maybe a summer beach scene rather than daffodils by the lake is more meaningful for you, but the poet captures a moment that we have all experienced. The poet's magic makes that moment new again.

If poets enhance our power of sight they also awaken the other senses as powerfully. We can hear Emily Dickinson's snake in the repeated "s" sound, or sibilance, of the lines:

His notice sudden is—
The Grass divides as with a Comb—
A spotted shaft is seen—

and because of the very present sense of sound, we experience the indrawn gasp of fearful breath when the snake appears. We can touch the little chimneysweep's hair "that curled like a lamb's back" in William Blake's poetry and because of that tactile sense, we are even more shocked to read that the child's hair is all shaved off so that the soot will not spoil its whiteness. We can smell the poison gas as Wilfred Owen's soldiers fumble with their gas masks; we can taste the blood gurgling in their poisoned lungs.

Poets write, then, to awaken the senses. They have crucial ideas, but the words they use are often more important than the meaning. More important still than ideas and sense awakening is the poet's appeal to the emotions. And it is precisely this area that disturbs a number of students. Our modern society tends to block out emotions—we need reviews to tell us if we enjoyed a film, a critic's praise to see if a play or novel is worth our time. We hesitate to laugh at something in case it is not the "in" thing to do. We certainly do not cry—at least in front of others. Poets write to overcome that blocking (very often it is their own blocking of emotion they seek to alleviate), but that is not to say that poetry immediately sets us laughing, crying, loving, hating. The important fact about the emotional release in poetry is that poets help us explore our own emotions, sometimes by shocking us, sometimes by drawing attention to balance and pattern, sometimes by cautioning us to move carefully in this inner world.

Poets tell us nothing really new. They tell us old truths about human emotions that we begin to restructure anew, to reread our experiences in light of theirs, to reevaluate our world view. Whereas a car manual helps us understand the workings of a particular vehicle, a poem helps us understand the inner workings of human beings. Poets frequently write to help their emotional life—the writing then becomes cathartic, purging or cleansing the inner life, feeding that part of us that separates us from the animal. Many poets might paraphrase Byron, who claimed that he had to write or go mad. Writer and reader of poetry enter into a collusion, each helping the other to find significance in the human world, to find safety in a seemingly alien world.

This last point brings any reader of poetry to ask the next question: Why read poetry? One might contend that a good drama, novel or short story might provide the same emotional experience. But a poem is much more accessible. Apart from the fact that poems are shorter than other genres, there is a unique directness to them which hinges purely on language. Poets can say in one or two lines what may take novelists and playwrights entire works to express. For example, Keats' lines—

Beauty is truth, truth beauty,—that is all
Ye know on earth, and all ye need to know—

studied, pondered, open to each reader's interpretations, linger in the memory with more emphasis than George Eliot's *Middlemarch*, or Ibsen's *The Wild Duck*, which endeavor to make the same point.

In your reading of poems remember that poetry is perhaps the oldest art and yet surrounds us without our even realizing it. Listeners thrilled to Homer's poetry; tribes chanted invocations to their gods; today we listen to pop-song lyrics and find ourselves, sometimes despite ourselves, repeating certain rhythmic lines. Advertisements we chuckle over or say we hate have a way of repeating themselves as we use the catchy phrase or snappy repetition. Both lyricists and advertisers cleverly use language, playing on the reader's/listener's/watcher's ability to pick up on a repeated sound or engaging rhythm or inner rhyme. Think of a time as a child when you thoroughly enjoyed poetry: nursery rhymes, ball-game rhythms, jump-rope patterns. Probably you had no idea of the meaning of the words ("Little Miss Muffet sat on a tuffet..." a tuffet?!) but you responded to the sound, the pattern. As adults we read poetry for that sense of sound and pattern. With more experience at reading poetry there is an added sense of pleasure as techniques are recognized: alliteration, onomatopoeia; forms of poetry become obvious—the sonnet, the rondelle. Even greater enjoyment comes from watching a poet's development, tracing themes and ideas, analyzing maturity in growth of imagery, use of rhythm.

To the novice reader of poetry, a poem can speak to the reader at a particular time and become an experience in itself. A freshman's experience after her mother's death exemplifies this. Shortly after the death, the student found Elizabeth Jenning's poem "Happy Families." Using the familiar names of the cards, Mrs. Beef and Master Bun, the poet describes how strangers try to help the family carry on their lives normally although one of the "happy family" is "missing." The card game continues although no one wants it to. At the end the players go back to their individual rooms and give way to their individual grief. The student described the relief at knowing that someone else had obviously experienced her situation where everyone in the family was putting up a front, strangers were being very kind, and a general emptiness prevailed because of that one missing family member. The poem satisfied. The student saw death through another's eyes; the experience was almost the same, yet helped the reader to reevaluate, to view a universal human response to grief as well as encourage her to deal with her own.

On reading a poem the brain works on several different levels: it responds to the sounds; it responds to the words themselves and their connotations; it responds to the emotions; it responds to the insights or learning of the world being revealed. For such a process poetry is a very good training ground—a boot camp—for learning how to read literature in general. All the other genres have elements of poetry within them. Learn to read poetry well and you will be a more accomplished reader, even of car manuals! Perhaps the best response to reading poetry comes from a poet herself, Emily Dickinson, who claimed that reading a book of poetry made her feel "as if the top of [her] head were taken off!"

Before such a process happens to you, here are some tips for reading poetry before and during the examination.

Before the Exam

1. Make a list of poets and poems you remember; analyze poems you liked, disliked, loved, hated, and were indifferent to. Find the poems. Reread them and for each one analyze your *feelings*, first of all, about the poetry itself. Have your feelings changed? Now what do you like or hate? Then paraphrase the *meaning* of each poem. Notice how the "magic" goes from the poem, i.e., "To Daffodils:" the poet sees many daffodils by the side of a lake and then thinks how the sight of them later comforts him.

2. Choose a poem at random from an anthology or one mentioned in this introduction. Read it a couple of times, preferably aloud, because the speaking voice will automatically grasp the rhythm and that will help the meaning. Do not become bogged down in individual word connotation or the meaning of the poem—let the poetry do its "work" on you; absorb the poem as a whole jigsaw puzzle.

3. Now take the puzzle apart. Look carefully at the title. Sometimes a straightforward title helps you focus. Sometimes a playful title helps you get an angle on the meaning. "Happy Families," of course, is an ironic title because the family playing the card game of that name is not happy.

4. Look carefully at the punctuation. Does the sense of a line carry from one to another? Does a particular mark of punctuation strike you as odd? Ask why that mark was used.

5. Look carefully at the words. Try to find the meaning of words with which you are not familiar within the context. Familiar words may be used differently: ask why that particular use. Having tapped into your memory bank of vocabulary, if you are still at a loss, go to a dictionary. Once you have the *denotation* of the word, start wondering about the *connotation*. Put yourself in the poet's position and think why that word was used.

6. Look carefully at all the techniques being used. You will gain these as you progress through this section and through the test preparation. As soon as you come across a new idea—"caesura" perhaps—learn the word, see how it applies to poetry, where it is used. Be on the lookout for it in other poetry. Ask yourself questions such as why the poet used alliteration here; why the rhythm changes there; why the poet uses a sonnet form and which sonnet form is in use. Forcing yourself to ask the why questions, and answering them, will train the brain to read more perceptively. Poetry is not accidental; poets are deliberate people; they do things for specific reasons. Your task under a learning situation is to discover why.

7. Look carefully at the speaker. Is the poet using another persona? Who is that persona? What is revealed about the speaker? Why use that particular voice?

8. Start putting all the pieces of the puzzle together. The rhythm helps the meaning. The word choice helps the imagery. The imagery adds to the meaning. Paraphrase the meaning. Ask yourself simple questions: What is the poet saying? How can I relate to what is being said? What does this poem mean to me? What does this poem contribute to human experience?

9. Find time to read about the great names in poetry. Locate people within time areas and analyze what those times entailed. For example, the Elizabethans saw a contest between secular love and love of God. The Romantics (Wordsworth, Coleridge, Keats, Shelley, Byron) loved nature and saw God within nature. The Victorians (Tennyson, Blake) saw nature as a threat to mankind and God, being replaced by the profit cash-nexus of the Industrial Age. The moderns (T.S. Eliot, Pound, Yeats) see God as dead and man as hollow, unwanted, and unsafe in an alien world. The Post-Moderns see life as "an accident," a comic/cosmic joke, fragmented, purposeless—often their topics will be political: apartheid, abortion, unjust imprisonment.

10. Write a poem of your own. Choose a particular style; use the sonnet form; parody a famous poem; express yourself in free verse on a crucial, personal aspect of your life. Then analyze your own poetry with the above ideas.

During the Exam

You will have established a routine for reading poetry, but now you are under pressure, must work quickly, and will have no access to a dictionary. You cannot read aloud but you can:

1. Internalize the reading—hear the reading in your head. Read through the poem two or three times following the absorbing procedure.

2. If the title and poet are supplied, analyze the title as before and determine the era of the poetry. Often this pushes you toward the meaning.

3. Look carefully at the questions which should enable you to "tap into" your learning process. Answer the ones that are immediately clear to you: form, technique, language perhaps.

4. Go back for another reading for those questions that challenge you— theme or meaning perhaps—analyze the speaker or the voice at work— paraphrase the meaning—ask the simple question "What is the poet saying?"

5. If a question asks you about a specific line, metaphor, or opening or closing lines, highlight or underline them to force your awareness of each crucial word. Internalize another reading emphasizing the highlighted area—analyze again the options you have for your answers.

6. Do not waste time on an answer that eludes you. Move on to another section and let the poetry do its "work." Very often the brain will continue working on the problem on another level of consciousness. When you go back to the difficult question, it may well become clear.

7. If you still are not sure of the answer, choose the option that you *feel* is the closest to correct.

Go home, relax, forget about the exam—read your favorite poem!

Verse and Meter

As children reading or learning poetry in school, we referred to each section of a poem as a verse. We complained we had ten verses to learn for homework. In fact the word **verse** strictly refers to a line of poetry, perhaps from the original Latin word "versus:" a row or a line, and the notion of turning, "vertere," to turn or move to a new idea. In modern use we refer to poetry often as "verse" with the connotation of rhyme, rhythm, and meter but we still recognize verse because of the positioning of lines on the page, the breaking of lines that distinguish verse from prose.

The verses we learned for homework are in fact known as **stanzas:** a grouping of lines with a metrical order and often a repeated rhyme which we know as the **rhyme scheme.** Such a scheme is shown by letters to show the repeating sounds. Byron's "Stanzas" will help you recall the word, see the use of a definite rhyme and how to mark it:

"Stanzas"

(When a man hath no freedom to fight for at home)	
When a man hath no freedom to fight for at home,	*a*
Let him combat for that of his neighbors;	*b*
Let him think of the glories of Greece and of Rome,	*a*
And get knocked on the head for his labors.	*b*

To do good to mankind is the chivalrous plan,	*c*
And is always as nobly requited;	*d*
Then battle for freedom wherever you can,	*c*
And, if not shot or hanged, you'll get knighted.	*d*

The rhyme scheme is simple: *abab* and your first question should be "Why such a simple, almost sing-song rhyme?" The simplicity reinforces the **tone** of the poem: sarcastic, cryptic, cynical. There is almost a sneer behind the words "And get knocked on his head for his labors." It is as if the poet sets out to give a lecture or at least a homily along the lines of: "Neither a lender nor a borrower be," but then undercuts the seriousness. The **irony** of the poem rests in the fact that Byron joined a freedom fighting group in Greece and died, not gloriously, but of a fever. We shall return to this poem for further discussion.

Certain types of rhyme are worth learning. The most common is the **end rhyme**, which has the rhyming word at the end of the line, bringing the line to a definite stop but setting up for a rhyming word in another line later on, as in "Stanzas": home . . . Rome, a perfect rhyme. **Internal rhyme** includes at least one rhyming word within the line, often for the purpose of speeding the rhythm or making it linger. Look at the effect of Byron's internal rhymes mixed with half-rhymes: "combat . . . for that"; "Can/And . . . hanged" slowing the rhythm, making the reader dwell on the harsh long "a" sound, prolonging the sneer which almost becomes a snarl of anger. **Slant rhyme**, sometimes referred to as half, off, near or approximate rhyme, often jolts a reader who expects a perfect rhyme; poets thus use such a rhyme to express disappointment or a deliberate let-down. **Masculine rhyme** uses one-syllable words or stresses the final syllable of polysyllabic words, giving the feeling of strength and impact. **Feminine rhyme** uses a rhyme of two or more syllables, the stress not falling upon the last syllable, giving a feeling of softness and lightness. One can see that these terms for rhyme were written in a less enlightened age! The terms themselves for the rhymes are less important than realizing or at least appreciating the effects of the rhymes.

If the lines from "Stanzas" had been unrhymed and varying in metrical pattern, the verse would have been termed **free**, or to use the French term, *"Vers libre,"* not to be confused with **blank verse**, which is also unrhymed but has a strict rhythm. The Elizabethan poets Wyatt and Surrey introduced blank verse, which Shakespeare uses to such good effect in his plays, and later, Milton in the great English epic, *Paradise Lost*. Free verse has become associated with "modern" poetry, often adding to its so-called obscurity because without rhyme and rhythm, poets often resort to complicated syntactical patterns, repeated phrases, awkward cadences, and parallelism. Robert Frost preferred not to use it because, as he put it, "Writing free verse is like playing tennis with the net down," suggesting that free verse is easier than rhymed and metrical. However, if you have ever tried writing such verse, you will know the problems. (Perhaps a good exercise after your learning about meter is to write some "free" verse.) T.S. Eliot, who uses the form most effectively in "The Journey of the Magi," claimed that no *"vers"* is *"libre"* for the poet who wanted to do a good job.

Such a claim for the artistry and hard work behind a poem introduces perhaps the most difficult of the skills for a poet to practice and a reader to learn: meter. This time the Greeks provide the meaning of the word from *"metron,"* meaning measure. **Meter** simply means the pattern or measure of stressed or accented words within a line of verse. When studying meter a student should note where stresses fall on syllables—that is why reading aloud is so important, because it catches the natural rhythm of the speaking voice—and if an absence of stressed syllables occurs there is always an explanation why. We "expect" stressed and unstressed syllables because that is what we use in everyday speech. We may stress one syllable over another for a certain effect, often using the definite article "THE well known author . . . " or the preposition "Get OUT of here!" Usually, however, we use a rising and falling rhythm, known as **iambic rhythm**. A line of poetry that alternates stressed and unstressed syllables is said to have **iambic meter**. A line of poetry with ten syllables of rising and falling stresses is known as **iambic pentameter**, best used by Shakespeare and

Milton in their blank verse. The basic measuring unit in a line of poetry is called a **foot**. An **iambic foot** has one unstressed syllable followed by a stressed marked by ∪ /. Pentameter means "five-measure." Therefore **iambic pentameter** has five groups of two syllables, or ten beats, to the line. Read aloud the second and fourth, sixth and eighth lines of "Stanzas," tapping the beat on your desk or your palm, and the ten beat becomes obvious. Read again with the stresses unstressed and stressed (or soft and loud, short or long, depending on what terminology works for you) and the iambic foot becomes clear.

Tapping out the other alternate lines in this poem you will not find ten beats but twelve. The term for this line is **hexameter**, or six feet, rather than five. Other line-length names worth learning are:

monometer	one foot	**dimeter**	two feet
trimeter	three feet	**tetrameter**	four feet
heptameter	seven feet	**octameter**	eight feet

Other foot names worth learning are:

the **anapest,** marked ∪ ∪ /, the most famous anapestic line being:

"Twas the night before Christmas, when all through the house . . . "

the **trochee,** marked / ∪, the most memorable trochaic line being:

"Double double toil and trouble . . . "

the **dactyl,** marked / ∪ ∪ / ∪ ∪, the most often quoted dactylic line being:

"Take her up tenderly . . . "

Old English poetry employs a meter known as **accentual meter**, with four stresses to the line without attention to the unstressed syllables. Contemporary poets tend not to use it, but one of the greatest innovators in rhythm and meter, Gerard Manley Hopkins, used it as the "base line" for his counterpointed "Sprung Rhythm." Living in the nineteenth century, Hopkins produced poetry that even today strikes the reader as "modern," in that the rhymes and rhythms often jar the ear, providing stressed syllables where we expect unstressed and vice versa. The rhythm was measured by feet of from one to four syllables, and any number of unstressed syllables. Underneath the rhythm we hear the "regular" rhythm we are used to in speech, and an intriguing counterpoint develops. One stanza from "The Caged Skylark" will show the method at work:

As a dare-gale skylark scanted in a dull cage
Man's mounting spirit in his bone-house, mean house, dwells—
That bird beyond the remembering his free fells;
This in drudgery, day-labouring-out life's age.

The stress on "That" and "This" works particularly well to draw attention to the two captives: the skylark and Man. The accentual meter in the second line reinforces the wretchedness of the human condition. No reader could possibly read that line quickly, nor fail to put the full length of the syllable on "dwells." The dash further stresses the length and the low pitch of the last word.

If at first the terms for meter are new and strange, remember that what is most important is not that you mindlessly memorize the terminology but are able to recognize the meter and analyze why the poet has used it in the particular context of the poem. For example, Shakespeare did not want the lyrical fall and rise of the iamb for his witches around the cauldron, so he employs the much more unusual trochee to suggest the gloom and mystery of the heath in *Macbeth*. Many poets will "mix and match" their meter and your task as a student of poetry is to analyze why. Perhaps the poet sets up the regular greeting card meter, rising and falling rhythm, regular end-stopped rhyme. If the poet abruptly changes that pattern, there is a reason. If the poet subtly moves from a disruptive meter into a smooth one, then analyze what is going on in the meaning. If the poet is doing "a good job" as T.S. Eliot suggested, then the rhyme, rhythm, and meter should all work together in harmony to make the poem an integral whole. Answer the test essay questions to practice the points in this section and the integrity of a poem as a single unit will become clearer.

Figurative Language and Poetic Devices

It will be becoming ever more obvious that a poem is not created from mere inspiration. No doubt the initial movement for a poem has something of divine intervention: the ancients talked of being visited by the Muse of Poetry; James Joyce coined the word "epiphany" for the clear moment of power of conception in literature, but then the poet sets to, working at the expression to make it the best it can be.

Perhaps what most distinguishes poetry from any other genre is the use of figurative language—figures of speech—used through the ages to convey the poet's own particular worldview in a unique way. Words have **connotation** and **denotation**, **figurative** and **literal** meanings. We can look in the dictionary for denotation and literal meaning, but figurative language works its own peculiar magic, tapping into shared experiences within the psyche. A simple example involves the word "home." If we free-associated for awhile among a group of twenty students we would find a number of connotations for the word, depending on the way home was for us in our experiences: comforting, scary, lonely, dark, creepy, safety, haven, hell . . . . However, the denotation is quite straightforward: a house or apartment or dwelling that provides shelter for an individual or family. Poets include in their skill various figures of speech to "plug into" the reader's experiences, to prompt the reader to say "I would have never thought of it in those terms but now I see!"

The most important of these skills is perhaps the **metaphor**, which compares two unlike things, feelings, or objects, and the **simile**. Metaphors are more difficult to find than **similes**, which also compare two dissimilar things but always use the words "as if" (for a clause) or "like" (for a word or phrase). Metaphors suggest the comparison, the meaning is implicit. An easy way to distinguish between the two is the simple example of the camel. **Metaphor:** the camel is the ship of the desert. **Simile:** a camel is like a ship in the desert. Both conjure up the camel's almost sliding across the desert, storing up its water as a ship must do for survival of its passengers, and the notion of the vastness of the desert parallels the sea. The metaphor somehow crystallizes the image. Metaphors can be *extended* so that an entire poem consists of a metaphor or unfortunately they can be *mixed*. The latter rarely happens in poetry unless the poet is deliberately playing with his readers and provoking humor.

Start thinking of how many times you use similes in your own writing or speech. The secret is, as Isaac Babel once said, that similes must be "as precise as a slide rule and as natural as the smell of dill." The precision and naturalness coming together perfectly often set up an equation of comparison. A student once wrote "I felt torn apart by my loyalty to my mother and grandmother, like the turkey wishbone at Thanksgiving." We have all experienced divided loyalties. Using the graphic wishbone-tearing idea, something we have all done at Thanksgiving or have seen done, lets us more easily relate to the student's experience. Another student wrote of his friends waiting for the gym class to begin "like so many captive gazelles." Again the visual point of comparison is important but also the sense of freedom in the idea of gazelle– the speed, the grace; juxtaposing that freedom with the word "captive" is a master stroke that makes a simile striking.

The same student went on to an *extended simile* to state precisely and naturally his feelings upon going into a fistfight: "I was like the kid whose parents were killed by the crooked sheriff, waiting for high noon and the showdown that would pit a scared kid with his father's rusty old pistol against the gleaming steel of a matched pair, nestled in the black folds of the sheriff's holsters. I knew there was no way out. Surrounded by friends, I marched out into the brilliant sun, heading for the back fields of the playground, desperately trying to polish the rusty old gun." Although this student was writing in prose, his use of figurative language is poetic. He plugs into readers' movie experiences with the central idea of the showdown at high noon, an **allusion** that involves the reader on the same plane as the writer. The notion of the black holster extends the allusion of the old cowboy films where the "baddies" wore black hats and rode black horses. The use of the word "nestled" provokes some interesting connotations of something soft and sweet like a kitten nestling into something. But then the gun is an implement of destruction and death; maybe "nestles" takes on the connotation of how a snake might curl in the sun at the base of a tree. The metaphor ends with the child going out into the sun. The "rusty gun" in context of the essay was in fact the outmoded ideas and morals his father and old books had inculcated in him. All in all a very clever use of figurative language in prose. If the same concept had been pursued in poetry, the metaphor would have moved more speedily, more subtly—a poet cannot waste words—and of course would have employed line breaks, rhythm, and meter.

Personification is a much easier area than metaphor to detect in poetry. Usually the object that is being personified—referred to as a human with the personal pronoun sometimes, or possessing human attributes—is capitalized, as in this stanza from Thomas Gray's "Ode on a Distant Prospect of Eton College":

> Ambition this shall tempt to rise,
> Then whirl the wretch from high,
> To bitter Scorn a sacrifice,
> And grinning Infamy.
> The stings of Falsehood those shall try,
> And hard Unkindness' altered eye,
> That mocks the tear it forced to flow;
> And keen Remorse with blood defiled,
> And moody Madness laughing wild
> Amid severest woe.

As the poet watches the young Eton boys, he envisions what the years have to offer them, and the qualities he sees he gives human status. Thus Ambition is not only capable of tempting, an amoral act, but also of "whirling," a physical act. Scorn is bitter, Infamy grinning, and so on. Coleridge employs a more visual personification in "The Rime of the Ancient Mariner," in which the sun throws a harsh light on a sailor's transgression against nature:

> . . . the Sun (was) flecked with bars
> (Heaven's Mother send us grace!)
> As if through a dungeon-grate he peered
> With broad and burning face.

More so than with Gray's more formal personification, Coleridge's supplies an image that is precise—we can see the prisoner behind the bars, and what's more this particular prisoner has a broad and burning face . . . of course because he is the sun! The personification brings us that flash of recognition when we can say, "Yes, I see that!"

The word **image** brings us to another important aspect of figurative language. Not a figure of speech in itself, the image plays a large role in poetry because the reader is expected to imagine what the poet is evoking, through the senses. The image can be **literal**, wherein the reader has little adjustment to make to see or touch or taste the image; a **figurative image** demands more from readers, almost as if they have to be inside the poet's imagination to understand the image. Very often this is where students of poetry, modern poetry particularly, find the greatest problems because the poetry of **imagism**, a term coined by Ezra Pound, is often intensely personal, delving into the mind of the poet for the comparison and connection with past memories that many readers cannot possibly share. Such an image is referred to as *free*, open to many interpretations. This concept suits the post-modern poet who feels that life is fragmented, open to multi-interpretations—there is no fixed order. Poets of the Elizabethan and Romantic eras saw the world as whole, steady, *fixed*, exactly the word used for their type of images. Readers of this poetry usually share the same response to the imagery. For example, the second stanza of Keats' "Ode to a Nightingale" sets up the taste imagery of a

> draught of vintage that hath been
> Cooled a long age in the deep-delvéd earth,
> Tasting of Flora and the country green,
> Dance, and Provençal song, and sunburnt mirth!
> O for a beaker of the warm South,
> Full of the true, the blushful Hippocrene,
> With beaded bubbles winking at the brim,
> And purple-stainéd mouth;

Even though Flora and Hippocrene are not names we are readily familiar with, the image of the cool wine, the taste, the look, the feeling evoked of the South and warmth, all come rushing into our minds as we enter the poet's imagination and find images in common.

Blake's imagery in "London" works in a similar way but as readers we have to probe a little harder, especially for the last line of the last stanza:

> But, most thro' midnight streets I hear
> How the youthful Harlot's curse
> Blasts the new-born Infant's tear,
> And blights with plagues the Marriage hearse.

Notice how the "Marriage hearse" immediately sets up a double image. Marriage we associate with happiness and joy; hearse we associate with death and sorrow. The image is troubling. We go back to the previous lines. The harlot curses her new-born—the curse of venereal disease—that child marries and carries the disease to marriage? Or the young man consorting with the harlot passes on the disease to his marriage partner? Marriage then becomes death? The image is intriguing and open to interpretation.

Image in figurative language inevitably leads to symbol. When an object, an image, a feeling takes on larger meaning outside of itself, then a poet is employing a symbol, something which stands for something greater. Because mankind has used symbols for so long many have become stock or conventional: the rose standing for love; the flag standing for patriotism, love of one's country (thus the controversy over flag-burning today); the color yellow standing for corruption (hence Gatsby's Daisy Buchanan—the white-dressed virginal lady with the center core of carelessness); the bird for freedom; the sea for eternity; the cross for suffering and sacrifice. If you are not versed in the Christian tradition, it might be useful to read its symbols. Older poetry dwells on the church and the trials of loving God and loving Woman—the latter also has become a symbol deteriorating over the ages from Eve to the Madonna to Whore.

If the symbol is not conventional then it may carry with it many interpretations, depending on the reader's insight. Some students "get carried away" with symbolism, seeing more in the words than the poets do! If the poet is "doing a good job" the poetry will steer you in the "right" direction of symbolism. Sometimes we are unable to say what "stands for" what, but simply that the symbol evokes a mood; it suggests an idea to you

> Poets tap into *Fast* previous areas of *Facts* experience to re-late their insights, drawing their readers into shared experiences.

that is difficult to explain. The best way to approach symbolism is to understand a literal meaning first and then shift the focus, as with a different camera lens, and see if the poet is saying something even more meaningful. Blake again supplies an interesting example. In his poem "The Chimney Sweeper" he describes the young child's dream of being locked up in "coffins of black." Literally of course coffins are brown wood, the color of mourning is black. Shift the focus then to the young child chimney sweeper, so young he can barely lisp the street cry "Sweep" so it comes out "'weep! 'weep! 'weep! 'weep!" (a symbolic line in itself). Your reading of the Industrial Age's cruelty to children who were exploited as a cheap, plentiful, and expendable labor force will perhaps have taught you that children were used as chimney brushes—literally thrust up the thin black chimneys of Victorian houses and factories, where very often they became trapped, suffocated, sometimes burned to death if fires were set by unknowing owners. Now the black coffins stand for the black-with-soot chimneys the little children had to sweep, chimneys which sometimes became their coffins. The realization of the symbol brings a certain horror to the poem. In the dream an Angel releases the children who then run down "a green plain leaping, laughing . . . /And wash in a river, and shine in the sun." The action is of course symbolic in that in real life the children's movements were restricted, living in monstrous cities where green plains would be enjoyed only by the rich, and totally limited by the size of the chimneys. They were always black with soot. They rarely saw the sun, never mind shone in it! Again the symbolism adds something to the poem. Many students have reacted with tears and anger when *seeing* the symbolism behind such simple lines.

The idea of reading about the Industrial Age brings us to an important part of figurative language, briefly mentioned before: **allusion**. Poets tap into previous areas of experience to relate their insights, to draw their readers into shared experiences. Remember how the student writer alluded to old cowboy movies, the classic *High Noon*. Poets will refer to history, myth, other older poems, plays, music, heroes, famous people. Allusion is becoming more and more difficult for the modern student because reading is becoming more and more a lost art. Core courses in schools have become hotbeds of controversy about what students should know. Fortunately modern poets are shifting their allusions so that contemporary readers can appreciate and join in with their background of knowledge. However, be aware that for the examination in poetry it will be useful to have a working knowledge of, or at least a passing acquaintance with, "oldness." Think of areas of history that were landmarks: the burning of Catharge; Hannibal's elephants; Caesar's greatness; Alexander the Great; the first World War and its carnage of young men; the Second World War and the Holocaust. Think of the great Greek and Roman myths: the giving of fire to the world; the entrance of sin into the world; the labyrinth; the names associated with certain myths: Daedalus, Hercules, the Medusa. You may never have a question on the areas you read but your background for well-rounded college study will already be formulated.

If we now return to more specific figures of speech and other poetic devices, you may feel you can immediately come to grips with these rather than read for background! Alphabetical order may help in your studying:

Alliteration: the repetition of consonants at the beginning of words that are next door to each other or close by. The Hopkins' stanza quoted earlier provides some fine examples: "skylark scanted;" "Man's mounting . . . mean house;" "free fells;" "drudgery, day-labouring-out life's age." Always try to understand the reason for the alliteration. Does it speed or slow the rhythm? Is it there for emphasis? What does the poet want you to focus on?

Apostrophe: the direct address of someone or something that is not present. Many odes begin this way. Keats' "Ode to a Grecian Urn" for example: "Thou still unravished bride of quietness," and "Ode to Psyche:" "O Goddess! hear these tuneless numbers."

Assonance: the repetition of vowel sounds usually internally rather than initially. "Her goodly <u>eyes</u> like sapph<u>i</u>res sh<u>i</u>ning br<u>i</u>ght." Here the poet, Spenser, wants the entire focus on the blue eyes, the crispness, and the light.

Bathos: deliberate anticlimax to make a definite point or draw attention to a falseness. The most famous example is from Pope's "Rape of the Lock": "Here thou, great Anna! whom three realms obey, /Dost sometimes counsel take—and sometimes tea."

The humor in the bathos is the fact that Anna is the Queen of England—she holds meetings in the room Pope describes but also indulges in the venerable English custom of afternoon tea. The fact that <u>tea</u> should rhyme with <u>obey</u> doubles the humor as the elongated vowel of the upper-class laconic English social group is also mocked.

Caesura: the pause, marked by punctuation (/) or not within the line. Sometimes the caesura (sometimes spelled cesura) comes at an unexpected point in the rhythm and gives the reader pause for thought.

Conceits: very elaborate comparisons between unlikely objects. The metaphysical poets such as John Donne were criticized for "yoking" together outrageous terms, describing lovers in terms of instruments, or death in terms of battle.

Consonance: similar to slant rhyme—the repetition of consonant sounds without the vowel sound repeated. Hopkins again frequently uses this as in "Pied Beauty:" "All things counte<u>r</u>, o<u>r</u>iginal, spa<u>r</u>e, st<u>r</u>ange;. . . a<u>d</u>azzle, <u>d</u>im."

Diction: the word for word choice. Is the poet using formal or informal language? Does the poetry hinge on slang or a dialect? If so what is the purpose? Are the words "highfalutin" or low-brow? As always, the diction needs examining and questions like these need answering.

Enjambment: the running-on of one line of poetry into another. Usually the end of lines are rhymed so there is an end-stop. In more modern poetry, without rhyme, often run-on lines occur to give a speedier flow, the sound of the speaking voice or a conversational tone.

Hyperbole: refers to large overstatement often used to draw attention to a mark of beauty or a virtue or an action that the poet disagrees with. Donne's instruction to the woman he is trying to seduce not to kill the flea, by contrasting her reluctance with "a marriage" of blood within a flea, reinforces the hyperbole used throughout the poem:

Oh stay, three lives in one flea spare,
Where we almost, yea, more than married are.

The example is also good for an unexpected caesura for emphasis at the second pause.

Irony: plays an important role in voice or tone, inferring a discrepancy between what is said and what is meant. A famous example is Shelley's "Ozymandias," which tells of the great ruler who thought that he and his name would last forever, but the traveller describes the huge statue in ruins with the inscription speaking truer than the ruler intended: "My name is Ozymandias, king of kings: /Look on my works, ye Mighty, and despair!"

Metonymy: the name for something closely related to it which then takes on a larger meaning. "You can't fight City Hall" has taken on the meaning of fighting against an entire bureaucracy. "You can't go home again" suggests that you can never emotionally return to your roots.

Onomatopoeia: a device in which the word captures the sound. In many poems the words are those in general use: the whiz of fireworks; the crashing of waves on the shore; the booming of water in a underground sea-cave. However, poets like Keats use the device to superb effect in, for example, " To Autumn," when he describes the gleaner sitting by the cider press watching the last "oozings hours by hours" . . . one can hear the last minute drops squeezed from the apples.

Oxymoron: a form of paradox in which contradictory words are used next to each other: "painful pleasure," "sweet sorrow."

Paradox: a situation or action or feeling that appears to be contradictory but on inspection turns out to be true or at least make sense. "The pen is mightier than the sword" at first glance is a contradiction of reality. One can hardly die by being stabbed by a pen . . . but in the larger worldview the words of men, the signing of death warrants, the written issuing of commands to the gas chambers have killed. Or reason has prevailed by men writing out their grievances and as a result lives have been saved. Paradox always opens up the doors to thinking.

Pun: a play on words often for humorous or sarcastic effect. The Elizabethans were very fond of them; many of Shakespeare's comedies come from punning. Much of Donne's sexual taunting involves the use of the pun.

Sarcasm: when verbal irony is too harsh it moves into the sarcastic realm. It is the "lowest form of wit" of course but can be used to good effect in the tone of a poem. Browning's dramatic monologues make excellent use of the device.

Synecdoche: when a part of an object is used to represent the entire thing or vice versa. When we ask someone to give us a hand we would be horrified if they cut off the hand. What we want is the person's help, from all of the body!

Syntax: the ordering of words into a particular pattern. If a poet shifts words from the usual word order you know you are dealing with an older style of poetry (Shakespeare, Milton) or a poet who wants to shift emphasis onto a particular word.

Tone: the voice or attitude of the speaker. Remember that the voice need not be that of the poet's. He or she may be adopting a particular tone for a purpose. Your task is to analyze if the tone is angry, sad, conversational, abrupt, wheedling, cynical, affected, satiric, etc. Is the poet including you in a cozy way by using "you," or is he accusing "you" of what he is criticizing? Is the poet keeping you at a distance with coldness and third person pronouns. If so, why? The most intriguing of voices is Browning's in his **dramatic monologues**: poems that address another person who remains silent. Browning brought this type of poetry to an art. Think of all the variations of voices and attitudes and be prepared to meet them in poetry.

Types of Poetry

Having begun to grasp that poetry contains a great deal more than initially meets the eye, you should now start thinking about the various types of poetry. Of course, when reading for pleasure, it is not vital to recognize that the poem in hand is a sonnet or a villanelle, but for the exam you may well be asked to determine what sort of poem is under scrutiny. Certainly in discussing a poem it is also useful to know what "breed" you are dealing with because the form may dictate certain areas of rhyme or meter and may enhance the meaning.

The pattern or design of a poem is known as **form**, and even the strangest, most experimental poetry will have some type of form to it. Allen Ginsberg's "A Supermarket in California" caused a stir because it didn't read like poetry, but on the page there is a certain form to it. Some poets even try to match the shape of the poem to the subject. Find in anthologies John Hollander's "Swan and Shadow," and Dorthi Charles' "Concrete Cat." Such visual poems are not just fun to look at and read but the form adds to the subject and helps the reader appreciate the poet's worldview. **Closed form** will be immediately recognizable because lines can be counted, shape determined. The poet must keep to the recognized form, in number of lines, rhyme scheme, and/or meter. **Open form** developed from "vers libre," which name some poets objected to as it suggested that there was little skill or craft behind the poem, simply creativity, as the name suggests, gives a freedom of pattern to the poet.

The most easily recognized closed form of poetry is the **sonnet**, sometimes referred to as a **fixed form**. The sonnet always has fourteen lines but there are two types of sonnets, the Petrarchan or Italian, and the Shakespearean or English. The word sonnet in fact comes from the Italian word "sonnetto" meaning a "little song," and Petrarch, the fourteenth century Italian poet, took the form to its peak with his sonnets to his loved one Laura. This woman died before he could even declare his love, and such poignant, unrequited love became the theme for many Elizabethan sonnets. As a young man might telephone a young woman for a date in today's society, the Elizabethan would send a sonnet. The Petrarchan sonnet is organized into two groups: eight lines and six: the **octave** and the **sestet**. Usually the rhyme scheme is abbaabba-cdecde, but the sestet can vary in its pattern. The octave may set up a problem or a proposition, and then the answer or resolution follows in the sestet after a turn or a shift. The Shakespearean sonnet organizes the lines into three groups of four lines: **quatrains** and a **couplet**: two rhyming lines. The rhyming scheme is always abab cdcd efef gg, and the turn or shift can happen at one of three places or leave the resolution or a "twist in the tail" at the end.

Couplet, mentioned earlier, leads us to a closed form of poetry that is very useful for the poet. It is a two-line stanza that usually rhymes with an end rhyme. If the couplet is firmly end-stopped and written in iambic pentameter it is known as an **heroic couplet**, after the use was made of it in the English translations of the great classical or heroic epics such as *The Iliad* and *The Odyssey*. Alexander Pope became a master of the heroic couplet, sometimes varying to the twelve-syllable line from the old French poetry on Alexander the Great. The line became known as the **Alexandrine**. Pope gained fame first as a translator of the epics and then went on to write **mock-heroic** poems like "The Rape of the Lock," written totally in heroic couplets which never become monotonous, as a succession of regularly stepped-out couplets can, because he varied the place of the caesura and masterfully employed enjambment.

Rarely in an exam will you be presented with an **epic** because part of the definition of the word is vastness of size and range. However, you may be confronted with an excerpt and will need to recognize the structure. The translation will usually be in couplets, the meter regular with equal line lengths, because originally these poems were sung aloud or chanted to the beat of drums.

Because of their oral quality, repetition plays an important part, so that if the bard, or singer, forgot the line, the audience, who had heard the stories many times before, could help him out. The subject deals with great deeds of heroes: Odysseus (Ulysses), Hector, and Aeneus, their adventures and their trials; the theme will be of human grief or pride, divided loyalties—but all "writ large." The one great English epic, *Paradise Lost* by Milton, deals with the story of Adam and Eve and the Fall. Adam thus becomes the great hero. The huge battle scenes of *The Iliad* are emulated in the War of the Heavens when Satan and his crew were expelled into Hell; the divided loyalties occur when Adam must choose between obedience to God and love for his wife.

On much simpler lines are the **ballads**, sometimes the earliest poems we learn as children. Folk or popular ballads were first sung as early as the fifteenth century and then handed down through generations until finally written down. Usually the ballads are anonymous and simple in theme, having been composed by working folk who originally could not read or write. The stories—a ballad is a story in a song—revolve around love and hate and lust and murder, often rejected lovers, knights, and the supernatural. As with the epic, and for the same reason, repetition plays a strong part in the ballad and often a repeated refrain holds the entire poem together. The form gave rise to the **ballad stanza**, four lines rhyming abcb with lines 1 and 3 having 8 syllables and lines 2 and 4 having 6. Poets who later wrote what are known as **literary ballads** kept the same pattern. Read Coleridge's "The Rime of the Ancient Mariner" and all the elements of the ballad come together as he reconstructs the old folk story but writes it in a very closed form.

Early poetry dealt with narrative.

Fast Facts

Earlier poetry dealt with narrative. The "father of English poetry," Geoffrey Chaucer, told stories within a story for the great *Canterbury Tales*. The Elizabethans turned to love and the humanistic battle between love of the world and love of God. Wordsworth and Coleridge marked a turning point by not only using "the language of men" in poetry but also by moving away from the narrative poem to the **lyric**. The word comes again from the Greek, meaning a story told with the poet playing upon a lyre. Wordsworth moves from story to emotion, often "emotion recollected in tranquillity" as we saw in "Daffodils." Although sometimes a listener is inferred, very often the poet seems to be musing aloud.

Part of the lyric "family" is the **elegy**, a lament for someone's death or the passing of a love or concept. The most famous is Thomas Gray's "Elegy Written in a Country Churchyard," which mourns not only the passing of individuals but of a past age and the wasted potential within every human being, no matter how humble. Often **ode** and elegy become synonymous, but an ode, also part of the lyric family, is usually longer, dealing with more profound areas of human life than simply death. Keats' odes are perhaps the most famous and most beloved in English poetry.

More specialized types of poetry need mentioning so that you may recognize and be able to explicate how the structure of the poem enhances the meaning or theme. For example, the **villanelle**, a Courtly Love poem structure from medieval times, builds on five three-line stanzas known as **tercets**, with the rhyme scheme aba, followed by a four-line stanza, a **quatrain** which ends the poem abaa. As if this were not pattern and order enough, the poem's first line appears again as the last line of the 2nd and 4th tercets; *and* the third line appears again in the last line of the 3rd and 5th tercets; *and* these two lines appear again as rhyming lines at the end of the poem! The most famous and arguably the best villanelle, as some of the older ones can be so stiff in their pattern that the meaning is inconsequential, is Dylan Thomas' "Do not go gentle into that good night." The poem stands on its own with a magisterial meaning of mankind raging against death, but when one appreciates the structure also, the rage is even more emphatic because it is so controlled. It is a poem well worth finding for "reading for pleasure." In James Joyce's *A Portrait of the Artist as a Young Man*, writing a villanelle on an empty cigarette packet turns the young boy, Stephen Daedalus, who dreams of being an artist, into a poet, a "real" artist.

The most difficult of all closed forms is said to be the **sestina**, also French, sung by medieval troubadours, a "song of sixes." The poet presents six six-line stanzas, with six end-words in a certain order, then repeats those six repeated words in any order in a closing tercet. Find Elizabeth Bishop's "Sestina" or W.H. Auden's "Hearing of Harvests Rotting in the Valleys" and the idea of six images running through the poet's head and being skillfully repeated comes across very clearly. You might even try working out a sestina for yourself.

Perhaps at this stage an **epigram** might be more to your liking and time scale because it is short, even abrupt, a little cynical, and always to the point. The cynical Alexander Pope mastered the epigram, as did Oscar Wilde centuries later. Perhaps at some stage we have all written **doggerel**, rhyming poetry that becomes horribly distorted to fit the rhymes, not through skill but the opposite. In contrast **limericks** are very skilled: five lines using the anapest meter with the rhyme scheme: aabba. Unfortunately they can deteriorate into types such as "There was a young lady from....," but in artful hands such as Shakespeare's (see Ophelia's mad song in *Hamlet*: "And will he not come again?"), and Edward Lear's, limericks display fine poetry. Finally, if you are trying to learn all the different types of closed-form poetry, you might try an **aubade**—originally a song or piece of music sung or played at dawn—a poem written to the dawn or about lovers at dawn—the very time when poetic creation is extremely high!

Although the name might suggest open-form, **blank verse** is in fact closed-form poetry. As we saw earlier, lines written in blank verse are unrhymed and in iambic pentameter. Open-form poets can arrange words on the page in any order, not confined by any rhyme pattern or meter. Often it seems as if words have spilled onto the page at random with a direct address to the readers, as if the poets are cornering them in their room, or simply chatting over the kitchen table. The lines break at any point—the dash darts in and out—the poets are talking to the audience with all the "natural" breaks that the speaking voice will demonstrate. Open-form poets can employ rhyme, but sometimes it seems as if the rhyme has slipped into the poem quite easily—there is no wrenching of the word "to make it rhyme." Very often there is more internal rhyme as poets play with words, often giving the sensation they are thinking aloud. Open-form poetry is usually thought of as "modern," at least post-World War I, but the use of space on the page, the direct address of the voice, and the use of the dash clearly marks Emily Dickinson as an open-form poet, but she lived from 1830-1886.

Satire

Satire, is a *mode* which may be employed by writers of various genres: poetry, drama, fiction, non-fiction. It is more a perspective than a product, a perspective which the reader must try to understand through the critical act. The concept of genre and the concept of mode only come *after* the fact of writing. These concepts offer a convenient ways of describing what readers have already come to understand on the work's own terms.

Satire mainly exposes and ridicules, derides and denounces vice, folly, evil, stupidity, as these qualities manifest themselves in persons, groups of persons, ideas, institutions, customs, or beliefs. While the satirist has many techniques at his disposal, there are basically only two types of satire: gentle or harsh, depending on the author's intent, his audience, and his methods.

The terms **romanticism, realism,** and **naturalism** can help us understand the role of *satire*. Romanticism sees the world idealistically, as perfectible if not perfect. Realism sees the world as it is, with healthy doses of both good and bad. Naturalism sees the world as imperfect, with evil often triumphing over good. The satirist is closer to the naturalist than he is to the romantic or realist, for both the satirist and the naturalist focus on what is wrong with the world, intending to expose the foibles of man and his society. The difference between them lies in their techniques. The naturalist is very direct and does not necessarily employ humor; the satirist is more subtle, and does.

For instance, people plagued with overpopulation and starvation is not, on first glance, material for humor. Many works have treated such conditions with sensitivity, bringing attention to the plight of the world's unfortunate. Steinbeck's *Grapes of Wrath* is such a work. However, Swift's "A Modest

Proposal" takes essentially the same circumstances and holds them up for our amused examination. How does the satirist make an unfunny topic humorous? And why would he do so?

The satirist's techniques—his weapons—include **irony**, **parody**, **reversal** or **inversion**, **hyperbole**, **understatement**, **sarcasm**, **wit**, and **invective**. By exaggerating characteristics, by saying the opposite of what he means, by using his cleverness to make cutting or even cruel remarks at the expense of his subject, the writer of satire can call the reader's attention to those things he believes are repulsive, despicable, or destructive.

Whether he uses more harsh (Juvenalian) or more gentle (Horatian) satire depends upon the writer's attitude and intent. Is he merely flaunting his clever intellect, playing with words for our amusement or to inflate his own sense of superiority? Is he probing the psychological motivations for the foolish or destructive actions of some person(s)? Is he determined to waken an unenlightened or apathetic audience, moving its members to thought or action? Are the flaws which the satirist is pointing out truly destructive or evil, or are they the faults we would all recognize in ourselves if we glanced in the mirror, not admirable but not really harmful to ourselves or society? Is the author amused, sympathetic, objective, irritated, scornful, bitter, pessimistic, mocking? The reader needs to identify the satirist's purpose and tone. Its subtlety sometimes makes satire a difficult mode to detect and to understand.

Irony is perhaps the satirist's most powerful weapon. The basis of irony is inversion or reversal, doing or saying the opposite or the unexpected. Notable poetic satires include Koch's "Variations on a Theme by William Carlos Williams," in which he parodies Williams' "This is Just to Say." Koch focuses on the simplicity and directness of Williams' imagery and makes the form and ideas seem foolish and trivial. In "Boom!," Nemerov takes issue with a pastor's assertion that modern technology has resulted in a concomitant rise in religious activities and spiritual values. Nemerov catalogues the instant, disposable, and extravagant aspects of Americans' lifestyles, which result in "pray as you go . . . pilgrims" for whom religion is another convenience, commercial rather than spiritual.

Some novels, like Dickens' *Hard Times* and Waugh's *The Loved One,* are satires, as is Swift's essay "A Modest Proposal." The challenge for the reader is to understand that satirists are often deliberately writing against their own beliefs. More importantly, the reader must also be able to identify the satirist's target by recognizing the ways in which the satirist questions cultural assumptions and habit. For example, Swift was appalled at the eighteenth century's habit of referring to human beings as "manpower," a degrading custom not unlike considering infants as suitable sources of food.

Satire in drama is also common; Wilde's *The Importance of Being Earnest* is wonderfully funny in its constant word play (notably on the name *Ernest*) and its relentless ridiculing of the superficiality which Wilde saw as characteristic of British gentry. Barrie's *The Admirable Crichton*

Fast Facts

Irony is perhaps the satirist's most powerful weapon.

has a similar theme, with the added assertion that it is the "lower" or servant class which is truly superior—again, the ironic reversal so common in satire. Both of these plays are mild in their ridicule; the authors do not expect or desire any change in society or in the viewer. The satire is gentle; the satirists are amused, or perhaps bemused at the society whose foibles they expose.

Classic novels which employ satire include Swift's *Gulliver's Travels* and Voltaire's *Candide*, both of which fairly vigorously attack aspects of the religions, governments, and prevailing intellectual beliefs of their respective societies. A modern novel which uses satire is Heller's *Catch-22*, which is basically an attack on war and the government's bureaucratic bungling of men and materiel, specifically in WWII. But by extension, Heller is also viewing with contempt the unmotivated, illogical, capricious behavior of all institutions which operate by that basic law: "catch-22." Like Swift and Voltaire, Heller is angry. And although his work, like the other two, has humor and wit, exaggeration and irony, his purpose is more than intellectual entertainment for his readers. Heller hopes for reform.

Heller's attack is frontal, his assault direct. Swift had to couch his tale in a fantastic setting with imaginary creatures in order to present his views with impunity. The audience, as well as the times, also affect the satirist's work. If the audience is hostile, the writer must veil his theme; if the audience is indifferent, he must jolt them with bitter and reviling language if he desires change. If he does not fear reprisals, the satirist may take any tone he pleases.

We can see satire in operation in two adaptations of the biblical story of King Solomon, who settled the dispute between two mothers regarding an infant: Cut the baby in two and divide it between you, he told them. The rightful mother protested, and was promptly awarded the child. The story is meant to attest to the King's wisdom and understanding of parental love, in this case.

However, Twain's Huck Finn has some difficulty persuading runaway slave Jim that Solomon was wise. Jim insists that Solomon, having fathered "'bout five million chillen," was "waseful . . . . *He* as soon chop a chile in two as a cat. Dey's plenty mo'. A chile er two, mo' er less, warn't no consekens to Solermun, dad fetch him!" Twain is ridiculing not only Jim's ingenuousness, as he does throughout the novel; he is also deflating time-honored beliefs about the Bible and its traditional heroes, as he earlier does with the account of Moses and the "bulrushers." While Twain's tone is fairly mild, his intent shows through as serious; Twain was disgusted with traditional Christianity and its hypocritical followers, as we see later in *Huck Finn* when young Buck Grangerford is murdered in the feud with the Shepherdsons: "I wished I hadn't ever come ashore that night to see such things."

A second satiric variation on the Solomon theme appears in Asprin's *Myth Adventures*, in the volume *Hit or Myth*. Skeebe, the narrator, realizes that he, as King pro-tem, must render a decision regarding the ownership of a cat. Hoping to inspire them to compromise, he decrees that they divide the cat between them: "Instead they thanked me for my wisdom, shook hands, and left smiling, presumably to carve up their cat." He concludes that many of the citizens of this realm "don't have both oars in the water," a conclusion very like Huck's: "I never see such a nigger. If he got a notion in his head once, there warn't no getting it out again." The citizens' unthinking acceptance of the infallibility of authority is as laughable as Jim's out-of-hand rejection of Solomon's wisdom because no wise man would "want to live in the mids' er sich a blim-blammin' all de time" as would prevail in the harem with the King's "million wives."

Language and Linguistics

"The meaning of a word," wrote Ludwig Wittgenstein in his *Philosophical Investigations*, "is its use in the language"; and by so writing, he revolutionized the study of language and linguistics. This association of the meaning of a word with the way people use it—as simple and common-sense a notion as that might seem—was a virtually unprecedented move in language philosophy, posing significant challenges to the prominent linguistic theories of the time. Its advantages as a construal of how human beings operate with language are several. To begin with, this approach dispenses with the notion that there is a single, underlying logic to human linguistic practice. Instead of conceiving of language as a monolithic, unified structure functioning according to strict rules, this principle of linguistic analysis allows for the multiple and even inconsistent ways in which people use language. Utterances are no longer seen to boil down to some "deep structure," whereby linguists would simplify or rearrange the grammar of a sentence to show what it "really means." The meaning is, rather, "on the surface," consisting in the various actions which result from the particular words read or spoken.

Meaning Is Use

This transfer of "meaning" from some hidden depth to the surface of an utterance parallels another shift in its location: from the "mind" to the "situation" of an utterance. Previously, it was assumed that meaning must be some sort of mental event or process, taking place in the mind, and the problem of how words meant things to people—how two people in conversation could be sure that they meant the same thing by the same words—remained an inscrutable mystery. The association of meaning with use, however, assures linguists that meaning is a public event, one which can be observed and measured by outward, shareable criteria. Our gaze is now trained on what happens when a person speaks or reads, what actions or consequences follow from a use of words, and how the situation in which they are used changes. This allows us to avoid—in active situations—complicated and perhaps insoluble questions of the speaker's or writer's intention. Intention itself is removed from the mind and is instead seen to be manifested in the situation itself.

A third important consequence of the "meaning is use" assertion is that it avoids the problematic idea of correspondence, which also had frustrated much prior linguistic theory. It formerly was thought that a word had an inherent, one-to-one correspondence with the object it signified, and that the meaning of the word somehow lay in this relationship—as if, for example, the word "chair" had a natural connection to the object we call by that name and that is what "chair" means. The untenability of this notion, as indicated by the fact that different words in different languages are used to refer to the same thing and that the meanings of words sometimes change over the course of time, had already been recognized as early as 1915 by Ferdinand de Saussure in his *Course in General Linguistics*.

Word-Referent Connection

Saussure was one of the first linguists to insist on the idea that the connection between a word and its referent is arbitrary, the result of human conventional practices. He instead proposed that every "sign" consisted of a "signifier" (the word itself) and a "signified" (the idea or object to which the word refers), encouraging the notion in linguistic study that signifiers are detachable from their signifieds but remain in place through sheer force of convention. The trouble with Saussure's model, however, was that it continued to rely on reference as the criterion of meaning. A word, by this way of thinking, means what it refers to. Yet this presumes that all language operates the way nouns do, that all words are merely names for things. While this might be true in some cases, it is inadequate as a total description of linguistic behavior. To what, one might ask, does the word "of" refer? Even if this question had an answer, it is nonetheless obvious that the relationship between the word "of" and what it signifies would be quite a different matter from the relationship between "pug" and what it signifies. Clearly it would be a mistake to adopt this noun-oriented view in order to consider language more generally. The idea of meaning-as-use advocated thus far represents a significant advance beyond Saussure's more limited model.

Situational Meaning

Exactly what is at stake in this approach to linguistic analysis may be illustrated by the following crude but useful example: Suppose John walks into a room in which his roommate Steve is studying and says, "Gee, it's hot in here. Could you open the window, Steve?," whereupon Steve turns away from the book he is reading, says "Sure," opens the window, and resumes his studies. If the question then arose "What did John mean when he said to Steve, 'Could you open the window?'" it could be answered in the following manner. In this context, "Could you open the window?" is a request that Steve perform the action of opening the window. We could, to be sure, imagine other meanings for the sentence; but these other meanings would necessarily depend on other specific situations in which the sentence could be uttered. Suppose, for example, John was questioning Steve's strength or fine motor skills. "Could you open the window?" might then be a question demanding whether or not Steve was actually capable of performing such a task. Alternatively, they might be living in one of those dormitory rooms whose windows do not open sufficiently; John's question in this case might be an appeal to Steve, asking if he knew any possible way to circumvent the dormitory's restriction on air circulation.

The point to these linguistic contortions is that, while other possible meanings for the question "Could you open the window?" can be imagined, each of them depends upon an actual situation in which the words were uttered. It is important to note that, in our original example, when John asked Steve "Could you open the window?," Steve didn't have to translate the sentence into anything else in order to proceed with his action. That is, he didn't take the sentence "Could you open the window?," consider all of its possible meanings, and find the one that matched the situation he was in (as if saying to himself, "Oh, John actually is asking me if I *would* open the window"). Steve didn't have to move from the words of the question itself to any other set of words. Indeed, what would guarantee that the next set of words Steve settled on would be sufficiently clear and that he wouldn't have to move still further to another set of words in order to carry out John's request? This is why it is important to insist that the meaning of the words is "on the surface" and not hidden anywhere in "the mind" or in "deep structures." Steve only needed the question "Could you open the window?" as it stood in order to know what John wanted and to carry it out.

Meaning and Intention

How, it might be asked, can one be certain what John wanted by the question "Could you open the window?" That is, how do we know what John's intention was and how do we know that Steve understood this intention? Surely, one might insist, such processes take place in the mind. One might be led to believe by such a line of reasoning that only John himself could know his intention, that it was private to him and that Steve could only guess what John intended by his question. But this is not at all the case. This is why we must insist that the intention of John's utterance is manifested in the situation. Various factors of the situation work to restrict the possibilities of what "Could you open the window?" means. It was hot in the room; John remarked on his discomfort. So far in their relationship, one might suppose, Steve's strength or fine motor skills have not been called into question. No doubt Steve has opened the window many times before, and they live at a college whose window-opening policies are fairly liberal. All of these factors—and no doubt innumerable others—combine to limit the possibilities of meanings for the sentence in this case. The shared knowledge and assumptions of John and Steve are a reasonable guarantee that John's intentions in uttering these words are clear and evident. This is not to say that there aren't cases in which confusion as to what somebody intends by an utterance cannot arise. No doubt, in certain situations, two or three or even more possible meanings for a given utterance might be available. But it is to say that such confusions can be rectified. John can always elaborate as much as necessary until his intentions are clear. If he couldn't, one might suppose, there would be no guarantee that John himself could know what he intended by the utterance. For how would he be able to explain it, even to himself? The only sensible conclusion one could draw from such an example is that intention, like meaning, is a public event, discernible within a given situation.

How, one might ask, can we be sure Steve understood John's intention? Simple. He opened the window. This was the action which followed from John's utterance, the consequence resulting from the meaning of his question. Like John's intention, Steve's understanding in this situation is a public event, able to measured by outward criteria.

Language as System

Language can be defined as "a system of conventional vocal signs by means of which humans communicate" (Pyles and Algeo, 3). In language, patterns and speech rhythms allow us to construct meaning from the sounds that are uttered. These are organized into meaningful units, known as words. Words can be broken down into individual parts, known as its sound system, or **phonology.** The sounds of a language do not recur randomly; they are arranged into a system. All languages use a grammatical system in order to construct meaning. Within this system, the **morpheme** is the smallest meaningful unit that cannot be divided into smaller meaningful units; the word *flower* is a single morpheme; the word *cornflower* consists of two morphemes. Words can be classified as **parts of speech** (nouns, verbs, adjectives, and adverbs) and are placed in a sentence usually according to syntax, or word order. The meaning of a sentence can change dramatically depending on the order of the words and the inflection, stress, and tempo that the speaker gives the words.

In addition to being oral (spoken) and aural (heard), language can also be written. Although there is some disagreement about the origins of written language, most scholars agree that writing developed from speech about 5,000 years ago. Scholarly theories about the origins of language, speech, and writing, however, are not proven truths; they are informed suggestions designed to stimulate further thought and debate.

Stages of Linguistic Development and Language Acquisition

The "meaning is use" conception of language has extended into many realms of linguistic study, including the basic stages of language development. There is no strict or inherent logic by which children acquire language. In a broad and generalized way, however, the development of language in children can be divided into a number of stages. From two and one-half months onward, the child begins "babbling," pronouncing phonetic sounds without any reference to the surrounding environment. At approximately four months, the child begins to acquire the speech rhythms of the language that surrounds him or her, learning the stresses and tones of this language but still without any specific or meaningful content in his or her utterances. At around eight months the child might be able to repeat words, and at one year, say his or her first word independently. From about eighteen months to three years, the child will gradually develop the capacity for abstract thoughts and the ability to refer to objects in their absence, still predominantly through imitation. Children absorb the language around them and gradually begin to imitate it. The age distinctions are fluid; children may move in and out of various stages at different times.

Adults also pick up new words and new ways of saying previously-acquired words by exposure to their use in different situations. This is most evident in the learning of technical terminologies, ranging from automobile repair to philosophy. Often the sole criteria for assessing the meaning of the new term introduced is by examining how the writer or speaker uses it in the particular situation. In the acquisition of language, then, "use" plays a crucial role.

Standardization of Grammar

While "meaning-as-use" has led to new and valuable insights in the study of language and linguistics, it has also forced the re-conceptualization of teaching practices in challenging ways. For now the grammar, which traditionally was taught in schools as the standard and correct way to speak and write, is seen to be an arbitrary construction—a set of rules not deduced from any logic inherent in language but rather an artificial code of conduct imposed upon it. This discovery has raised complex moral and ethical questions in the linguistic training of people who may not have learned "standard American English" as children before entering the educational system. In addition, it has called into question the efficacy of teaching a standard English, which may have little relationship to the way people in the world actually speak, to speakers of foreign languages. There is, arguably, no one particular standard by which Americans use the English language.

The idea of a standard American English has retained its viability in education and culture only through a major revision of its status. No longer considered the correct or proper way to speak and write, standard English is now conceived of as only one type of language among many, valuable for certain pedagogical uses. In the teaching of English to speakers of foreign languages, standard English can be used as a general, systematic convention by which to begin the process of learning the language. It is a convenience rather than a normative principle—a starting point rather than a goal—providing students with sets of rules with which to grasp the large, bewildering, and inconsistent whole of the language. Equipped with such guidelines, students may then be in a position to cope with the language in all of the various ways in which it is spoken. As is the case with native speakers of English, both children and adults, the only way for students to truly learn any language is to be immersed in it and observe how people are using it in various situations. Standard English provides a general understanding and competence in the language, enabling students to then learn English in all its spoken and written particularity.

Cultural Implications

Somewhat different issues are at stake in the teaching of standard American English to native speakers of the language. Given the cultural, ethnic, and geographic composition of the United States, various forms of English have proliferated among different groups and regions. The imposition of any particular form of English at the expense of others can therefore be seen as an oppressive exercise of power by one group of speakers over the majority. Rather than portray standard English as the proper way to speak and write—implying therefore that other varieties of English are improper or flawed—progressive teachers now recognize its conventional aspect and may teach it as a particular type of discourse for specific purposes. Standard English thus becomes a convenience, a common point of reference among the various types of English. It functions not as a castigating device or exclusionary practice but rather as a means by which members of disparate groups can communicate with one another via certain agreed-upon uses of words.

No one, to be sure, actually or naturally speaks with the fastidiousness and regularity of standard American English. Its function is largely to facilitate certain procedures, such as business or academic writing, by following a set of rules everyone can share. It is, of course, by no means an uncontroversial arrangement; there will no doubt always be disagreement as to which ways of speaking English should be codified as "standard" and which should be excluded from this status. Questions of power relations—for example, whose language does standard English most closely resemble and by whose authority have such decisions been made—will inevitably still arise. But with this reconceptualization of the nature of standard American English has come the belated but growing recognition that the life of the language is not in rigid and stagnant conformity but rather in the diverse and changing employments of words found among particular groups of speakers. The language continues to evolve only through the proliferation of different ways of speaking it, and the exposure of one variety of English to another is potentially a source of great richness. The more possibilities of ways to use words which people possess, the greater the variety and precision with which they can communicate and express themselves will be.

Language Across Disciplines

If the meaning of a word is its use in the language, it follows that the wider a person's exposure to various usages is, the more he or she will be able to comprehend the various linguistic situations with which he or she is confronted. And this is important because, of course, virtually every situation with which we are confronted involves the use of language. From reading a novel to reproducing a physics experiment, from watching television to cooking dinner to learning how to dance, every procedure we perform is dependent upon language. Humans are, with few exceptions, never without language and the importance of linguistic study can thus never be overestimated. Mathematics and perhaps even music can be considered varieties of language.

In a more obvious and practical sense, every profession requires of its members adequate reading and writing skills in order to succeed. The two practices are, moreover, intimately related. Often the difficulty in teaching people good compositional skills stems from the fact that many people do not read extensively. Reading texts is an essential component of writing texts, because the more one reads, the more one witnesses the various uses of language for various purposes. The avid reader is exposed to many more varieties of English usage than the occasional or nonreader, and as we have seen, exposure is crucial to one's capacity to use language. Just as children acquire language from proximity to people using it, just as adults learn new uses of words from listening to other people, so too do active readers increase their linguistic skills relative to the breadth of texts which they encounter. The importance of this point cannot be stressed enough: the best writers are generally the best readers.

Even in intellectual pursuits outside of the humanities, people must rely on strong linguistic capabilities in order to achieve the most effective results possible. Scientific research, for example, is useless unless its results can be expressed cogently and convincingly. No experiment can be successful and accepted into the body of shared knowledge unless its procedures and results are expressed so that they may be followed and verified by other members of the field. Each professional discipline, skilled trade, or academic field depends upon its members' abilities to operate according to shared linguistic principles in order to ensure consistent communication. Just as the various strains of American English can enrich one another through extended contact, one's exposure to the broadest range of linguistic purposes available enables him or her to explore as many subjects and cultivate as many skills as desired.

Early in his career as a philosopher of language, Wittgenstein wrote: "*The limits of my language* mean the limits of my world." We might feel that this statement has a greater resonance than even that learned man intended at the moment he wrote it. For as we have seen, it is not merely the case that one's linguistic skills expand one's horizons and increase one's possibilities for experiencing the world, though both of these are true. It is, above all, language that enables both self and world to exist. The greater and broader our exposure to various uses of language are, the larger and more exciting that world will be.

References

Merleau-Ponty, Maurice. *Consciousness and the Acquisition of Language.* Trans. Hugh J. Silverman. Evanston, IL: Northwestern University Press, 1973.

Wittgenstein, Ludwig. *Tractatus Logico-Philosophicus* (1921). Trans. D. F. Pears and B. F. McGuinness. London: Routledge, 1974. §5.6

Wittgenstein, Ludwig. *Philosophical Investigations.* 3rd ed. Eds. G. E. M. Anscombe and Rush Rhees. Trans. G. E. M. Anscombe. New York: Macmillan, 1958. §43.

Pyles, Thomas and John Algeo, *The Origins and Development of the English Language.* New York: Harcourt Brace Jovanovich, 1982.

History and Social Science Review

From the cradle of civilization to present-day California, our History and Social Science section tells the remarkable story of how humankind has developed and advanced since its earliest days. The migration and settlement of civilizations—their governments, their cultures, their ways of life—are among the wealth of events and ideologies detailed to offer a vivid perspective on our past. Mesopotamia, China, India, Egypt, England, the United States of America, and the state of California are all destinations on our journey through time. We will take you down the Silk Road, through the Protestant Reformation and Renaissance periods, across the Atlantic Ocean to the New World, and on the tracks of the Trans-Continental Railroad.

Because history is the narrative thread linking a chronology of events, written sources are a key component of the record. In the early 21st century C.E., however, the full record still eludes us; after all, not every writing system has its own "Rosetta Stone" to help us unlock its secrets. Nonetheless, new technology enables an increasingly powerful collaboration among historians, anthropologists, archeologists, biologists, and geneticists, allowing them to sift through antiquity to illuminate formerly hidden facets of humankind's story.

Now let's take a look at the task at hand, as you prepare to make a bit of history yourself by becoming a teacher in the Golden State.

In comparison to the other sections of the test, the scope of the CSET: Multiple Subjects History and Social Sciences section is peculiarly both broad and selective. This review includes only those periods and events that you can expect to encounter on the exam, and therefore omits many significant events that fall outside of the CSET's coverage. For example, following the Enlightenment and the French Revolution, history is viewed through the prism of America, returning to Europe and the world at large only as it relates to the emergent United States. A detailed breakdown of the topics to be covered is as follows:

1. World History

a. Ancient Civilizations

Development of ancient cultures, including:

- Mesopotamian
- Egyptian
- Kush
- Hebrew
- Greek
- Indian
- Chinese
- Roman

Understand the intellectual, artistic, religious and social traditions and contributions of these cultures, as well as trading patterns and influences.

b. Medieval and Early Modern Times

Development of medieval and early modern civilizations, including:

- Chinese
- Japanese
- African
- Arabian
- Mesoamerican
- Andean
- European

Understand the decline of the Western Roman Empire and the rise of feudalism in Japan and Europe. Identify the art, architecture and science of Pre-Columbian America. Understand the role of Christianity and its rise in and influence on early and medieval Europe, as well as its expansion into the rest of the world. Understand the development of Islam and its impact on Arabia, Africa, Europe, and Asia. Understand the development of the Renaissance and Scientific Revolution in Europe, and the rise and consequences of early modern capitalism. Understand the evolution of representative democracy from the Magna Carta through the Enlightenment.

2. United States History

a. Early Exploration, the Colonial Era, and the War for Independence

Understand the exploration, settlement, and struggle for control of North America by Europeans during the Colonial Era. Understand the circumstances surrounding relations with Native Americans, including their assistance of and conflict with colonists. Understand the religious and cultural context of early settlers and colonial leaders, and their reasons for the colonization of North America. Understand European colonial policy toward America and the institutionalization of slavery. Understand the consequences of slavery for Europe, America, and Africa. Understand the events leading to the Revolutionary War, France's role, and the philosophy embodied by the Declaration of Independence.

b. The Constitution and the Republic

Understand the tricameral, representative, participatory structure of the U.S. Government. Understand the Articles of Confederation, and the development of the Constitution, including the Bill of Rights. Understand the philosophy embodied in the Constitution, including federalism, and the separation of powers. Understand the development and evolution of political parties and their contrasts and influence. Understand the cultural context of the United States, including regional political affiliations and identities. Understand the context of westward expansion, and government relationships with and policies toward Native Americans and foreign powers. Understand the role of free Blacks and slaves, Native Americans, as well as the Irish and other European immigrants, women, and children in the culture and politics of the United States.

c. Civil War and Reconstruction

Understand the origins and development of the Abolitionist movement, including the roles of women and free Blacks. Understand the opposition to this movement. Understand the social, economic and political context of the Civil War, including the conflict over nullification and secession. Understand the major battles of the Civil War, as well as the relative strengths and weakness of the combatants. Understand the process of Reconstruction, its successes and failures, and the development of Jim Crow laws.

d. Industrialization

Understand the urbanization of America in the 19th century. Understand the influence of new immigrants on the culture, and the rise of nativism in response. Understand the technological aspects of the Industrial Revolution and their impact on the quality of life.

3. California History

a. Pre-Columbian California through the Gold Rush

Understand the relationship between California's geography and its development and history. Understand the geography, culture, economy, and religion of California's Native Americans. Understand the impact of Spanish exploration and colonization, including the role of missions in shaping the culture, economy and development of early California. Understand Mexican rule, and the causes and consequences of the war between the United States and Mexico for control of California. Understand the cultural, economic, social, and political impact of the discovery of gold in California, including the impact of Native Peoples and Mexican nationals.

b. Economic, Cultural, and Political Developments since the 1850's

Understand the Constitution of California, including the reforms of the Progressives (initiative, referendum, and recall). Compare and contrast the Constitution of California with the Constitution of the United States. Understand the patterns of migration to California, including the Dust Bowl migration. Understand the cultural, economic, and social impact of these migrations on the larger environment of California. Understand the federal and state laws that govern the status of immigrants. Understand the context of cultural diversity in California, both historically and today. Understand the geography and development of California's major economic engines, including mining, large-scale farming, entertainment, recreation, aerospace, electronics, and international trade. Understand California's water-delivery system and its relationship to the state's geography.

1. World History

In the most fundamental sense, the difference between pre-history and history is not so great. Human beings in their search to acquire knowledge and to understand how people lived and worked and all of the factors that shaped their lives and beliefs often draw from both written records and from other sources. However, since human beings existed before the development of a written language and records, there is a period of time for which we are dependent upon non-written sources. This entire period before writing is known as pre-history. In the absence of written records, historians who traditionally use the records of a society to understand that culture are dependent upon artifacts excavated by archeologists. The evidence for this early period is fragmentary, only a portion of the stone tools, weapons, human and animal bones, and other artifacts were initially preserved and then discovered and excavated by archeologists.

The earth is estimated to be approximately six billion years old. The earliest known humans, known as hominids, lived in Africa three to four million years ago. Several species of human beings existed or developed but all modern humans are descended from just one group of hominids known as *Homo sapiens sapiens*. *Homo sapien sapiens* is a sub-species of *Homo sapiens* (along with Neanderthals who became extinct) and appeared in Africa between 200,000 and 150,000 years ago.

Historians divide pre-history into three periods. The period from the emergence of the first known hominids, or humans, around 2,500,000 years ago until approximately 10,000 B.C.E. has been designated as the Paleolithic or the old stone age. During this period human beings lived in very small groups of perhaps ten to twenty and were nomadic, constantly moving from place to place. Human beings had the ability to make tools and weapons from stone and the bones of animals they killed. The hunting of large game such as mammoths, which were sometimes driven off cliffs in large numbers, was crucial to the survival of early man who used the meat, fur, and bones of these animals to survive. Early humans supplemented their diets by foraging for food. Human beings took shelter in caves and other natural formations. Early man also painted and drew on the walls of caves. Paintings on the walls of caves in France and northern Spain, created during the pre-historical period, depict scenes of animals such as lions, owls, and oxen. Around 500,000 years ago humans began to use fire, which could provide light and warmth in shelters and caves and also could be used to cook meat and other foods. Human beings developed means of creating fire and improved techniques of producing tools and weapons.

The Mesolithic or "Middle Stone Age" from 10,000 to 7000 B.C.E. marks the beginning of a major transformation known as the Neolithic Revolution. Previously, historians and archeologists thought this change occurred later. Thus they called it the Neolithic Revolution because they thought it took place entirely within the Neolithic or "New Stone Age." It has been demonstrated that beginning in the Mesolithic age, humans domesticated plants and began to shift away from a reliance on hunting large game and foraging. Human beings had previously relied on gathering food where they found it and had moved almost constantly in search of game and wild berries and other vegetation. During the Mesolithic age, humans were able to plant and harvest some crops and began to stay in one place for longer periods of time. Early humans also improved their tool making techniques and developed different kinds of tools and weapons.

During the Neolithic or "New Stone Age," this "revolution" was completed and humans were able to engage in systematic agriculture and also tamed animals. Although humans continued to hunt animals and to supplement their diet with meat and use the skins and bones to make clothing and weapons, there were major changes in society. Human beings became settled and lived in farming villages or towns, the population increased and human beings began to live in much larger communities. A more settled life-style led to a more structured social system and a higher level of organization within societies. It also led to the development of crafts such as the production of pottery and to a rise in trade or exchange of goods between groups. Between 4000 and 3000 B.C.E., writing developed and the towns and villages settled in the Neolithic age developed a more complex pattern of existence. The existence of written records marks the end of the pre-historical period. The beginning of history coincides with the emergence of the earliest societies that exhibit characteristics that enable them to be considered as civilizations. The first civilizations emerged in Mesopotamia and Egypt.

River Valley Civilizations

As humans began to live in increasingly complex societies during the Neolithic period, urban-based cultures began to emerge— around 6000 B.C.E. (Fertile Crescent), 4800 (Nile Delta), 6500 B.C.E. (China) and 2500 B.C.E. (India), usually in the fertile river valley civilizations. Although these cultures varied widely, they all showed certain similar characteristics. All of the early civilizations relied on harnessing the power of the rivers for agriculture, all built some kind of monumental buildings, all had some form of writing, and all were organized within a political and religious framework.

Mesopotamia

Around 6000 B.C.E. Neolithic peoples began moving into the area we call the Fertile Crescent, which is the area around the Tigris and Euphrates Rivers. The two earliest groups in this region, the Akkadians and Sumerians, utilized the potential of the rivers around them. Massive irrigation projects consisting of canals, dikes, drainage ditches, and reservoirs were undertaken. Building and maintaining these projects required an enormous labor force overseen by a strong central government. The early Sumerians discovered that copper, when combined with tin, produced bronze, a stronger metal. Thus, the Sumerians are said to have ushered in the Bronze Age. Bronze Age technology soon spread to Egypt, Europe, and Asia.

Wheeled vehicles, the potter's wheel, and the use of writing in Sumeria, also spread to the Nile and Indus River valleys. The first writing in Mesopotamia was written in clay and was pictographic. Later writing evolved into a system called cuneiform (wedge-shaped), whereby scribes pressed wedge shaped symbols into clay tablets. Sumerian society was hierarchical, with a system of priests, administrators, and kings at the top and slaves at the bottom. We know something about the organization of Sumerian society due to *The Epic of Gilgamesh*, written around 2700 B.C.E. The epic tells the tale of the ruler of Uruk, Gilgamesh, and his friend Enkidu. The pair perform heroic acts but Enkidu eventually offends the gods and dies. The stories explore friendship, morality, immortality, and loyalty. Cuneiform tablets also leave a record of business transactions, taxes, and wages. We know that the Mesopotamians understood multiplication and division and had a calendar based on the moon's phases. The Sumerians also built step-shaped temples known as ziggurats.

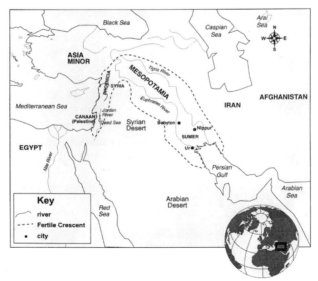

The Fertile Crescent, which is also referred to as the "Cradle of Civilization."

North of Sumeria, the Akkadians, led by King Sargon I (2370–2315 B.C.E.), conquered Sumeria and established an early empire. By 1760 B.C.E., Semitic Amorites, led by King Hammurabi (1792–1750 B.C.E.), brought Mesopotamia under one rule. The Amorites organized the city-states of Sumer and Akkad.

The Babylonians are known for advances in science, math, and astronomy, completing tables for multiplication, division, and square and cube roots. They observed the stars' positions but they thought the sun, moon, and five visible planets were gods with the power to influence their own lives. One of the most significant achievements of the Babylonians was the composition of a written code of laws (the Code of Hammurabi). Hammurabi's law code is the first known written law code which is applied to all those living within the Babylonian empire. All people were subject to this uniform law code. The code itself provides for unequal punishments based on rank and class but all persons within the empire were subject to its provisions. The code set a minimum wage and limited debt slavery to three years.

In 1595 B.C.E. the Hittites, known for their use of iron, invaded Babylon and destroyed Hammurabi's dynasty. The Hittites also used chariots drawn by horses instead of donkeys or oxen. The Hittites themselves were ultimately defeated by the Lydians. The last Lydian king, Croesus, was known for his fabulous wealth.

The earliest Hebrews lived in the area between Mesopotamia and Egypt in the second millennium B.C.E. They were originally a nomadic people but as cities grew and prospered in the region, some Hebrews settled in them. According to Hebrew scripture (the Old Testament of the Bible), Abraham came from Ur but settled in Palestine around 1850 B.C.E. By 1300 B.C.E., the Hebrews left Egypt with Moses and returned to Palestine (for more on the Hebrews see religion section).

Partly as a result of outside pressures, especially invasions by the Philistines, the Israelites (named after Abraham's grandson) joined the 12 tribes into a monarchy. The first king, Saul (r. 1025–1004), died in battle against the Philistines. The next king, David (r. 1004–965), ended the threat posed by the Philistines by restricting their movements. He established a capital at Jerusalem and created ties with the Phoenicians. As Israel united and gained access to ports, it became more prosperous, trading in olive oil and grain. David's son Solomon (r. 965–928) built a temple and palace complex, but after Solomon's death the kingdom split into Israel in the north and Judah in the south and the Israelites once again came under attack from outside forces.

In 722 B.C.E. the Assyrians conquered Israel and scattered the Israelites (the Diaspora). The religious history of the Israelites however is more important than the political history. At a time when the peoples around them believed in a pantheon of gods, the Hebrews (later called the Jews, from Judah) formulated a monotheistic religious tradition. The Hebrew religious code set out a system of moral behavior. Yahweh was omnipotent but also personal. He demanded that his followers worship him alone and entered into covenant with them. Between 1000 and 400 B.C.E. the moral code was set down in scriptures known as the Torah. Because of the Torah and a sense of community, the Jews maintained their beliefs and teachings even in the face of invasion and the Diaspora. Jewish monotheism ultimately influenced both Christianity and Islam.

Egypt

Another early river valley civilization, Egypt, shared many similarities with the Mesopotamians. Egyptian society depended on the annual flooding of the Nile to both irrigate and fertilize their crops. Egyptians were polytheistic and maintained a strong central government to direct building projects, agricultural projects, and religion. Egyptians also had a writing system based on pictographic symbols. Hieroglyphics can be found on the walls of tombs, on art work, and on papyrus scrolls.

Early Egyptian history is generally divided into five periods: 1) the predynastic period 4000–3100 B.C.E. (the approximate date when King Menes united upper Egypt and began creating a kingdom with upper and lower Egypt, 2) the Old Kingdom (2700–2200 B.C.E.), 3) the Middle Kingdom (2050–1570 B.C.E.), 4) the New Kingdom (1570–1090 B.C.E.), and 5) the Third Intermediate period (1090–332 B.C.E.).

Egyptian society was organized hierarchically with the pharaoh (king) having power over all aspects of society. Belief in the pharaoh's divinity led to the construction of pyramids to preserve the bodies of the kings. During the New Kingdom, as the Egyptians threw out the Hyskos ("rulers of foreign lands"), a Semitic people from Western Asia who had assumed power in Egypt between about 1720 and 1570 B.C.E., the Egyptian empire stretched into Western Asia. During this period, the half-sister of Thutmose II (d. 1479 B.C.E.) ruled as co-regent for Thutmose II's child. She claimed to be the designated successor of Thutmose I and in order to establish legitimacy had an oracle proclaim that Amon (a major god) had chosen her to become king.

Another important ruler during the New Kingdom was Akhenaton (originally named Amenhotep IV) who ruled from 1363–1347 B.C.E. Akhenaton proclaimed a form of monotheism where Aton was worshipped above all other gods. However, as Aton's son, the pharaoh also remained a god. Akhenaton's monotheism did not survive him. His younger brother Tutankhamen, returned to the worship of Amon. Under Ramses II (1279–1213 B.C.E.) the Egyptians regained Palestine but faced increasing invasions from Kush and Assyria. By the end of the new kingdom, Egyptian power had waned and Egypt would be dominated by other groups until its conquest by Alexander the Great in 332 B.C.E.

The mighty and predictable Nile River, the significance of the pharaoh as a unifying leader, and Egyptian religion all contributed to the long stretch of Egyptian power and wealth. Religion provided a sense of security for the Egyptians. It was not a separate part of their lives but rather part of their worldview. After the unification of upper and lower Egypt, the Egyptian pharaohs came to be regarded as divine beings. Service to the pharaoh was both a religious and civic duty. Egyptians, like the Mesopotamians, were polytheistic, worshipping a number of gods associated with natural forces. Eventually the Sun God came to have a special role.

The principal gods of Ancient Egypt were Amon and Re. During the Old and Middle Kingdom priests began to combine them into a cult of AmonRe. The cult of Osiris also became an important one. Osiris was associated with the annual flooding of the Nile and with immortality. The Book of the Dead portrays Isis and Osiris watching as the heart of the deceased is weighed against a feather. Those with heavy hearts would not receive immortality. South of Egypt is an area known as Nubia. There is some archeological evidence to suggest that settled agriculture may have appeared first in Nubia rather than in Egypt. And, the first African kingdoms may also have been located in Nubia. Whatever the exact order, it is clear that by the third millennium B.C.E. trade between Egypt and Nubia was occurring. Nubia then evolved into the state of Kush.

The Kingdom of Kush emerged independently of Egypt by 700 B.C.E. The Kushites, known as intermediaries between Egypt and East Africa, eventually became a distinct Sudanic empire. For almost 100 years Kushite kings ruled over Egypt until the Assyrian conquest when the Kushites returned to their Sudanic roots. By the first millennium C.E. Kush had been conquered by Axum, located in modern Ethiopia. Axum's location on the trade route between India and the Mediterranean made it a thriving city.

India

The first civilizations in the Indian subcontinent have been named Harappan civilization. The two main cities archeologists and historians have discovered are Harappa and Mohenjo-Daro. Both are located along the Indus River and both share many of the characteristics of other ancient river valley civilizations. Small farming villages along the river probably date back as far as 6500 or 7000 B.C.E. The walled city of Harappa however was probably built in the third millennium B.C.E. The city had a sophisticated drainage system which carried waste under the streets and outside the city to sewage pits. We do not know as much about Harappan civilization as we do about Egypt and Mesopotamia because although writing has been found on clay seals, it has not yet been deciphered. We do know that Harappans traded as far as Sumer. Historians and archeologists do not agree on what caused the end of this apparently prosperous and advanced civilization. It may have been conquered by the Aryans or the Aryans may simply have moved into an area already severely decaying.

The Aryans, an Indo-European speaking group moved south into northern India between 1500–1000 B.C.E. and ultimately conquered the entire subcontinent. Using the iron plow (probably imported from the Middle East), they cleared the growth along the Ganges River valley and began farming. Much of what we know about the Aryans comes from what is written in the Rig-Veda (one of several Vedas). The Vedas are collections of sacred instructions, which were probably written down from an older oral tradition. The Aryans were led by a Raja (prince) assisted by a council of elders. As the society grew larger and encompassed more territory, the princes became great princes (maharajas). The Aryans were briefly conquered by Alexander the Great who arrived in Northwest India in 326 B.C.E. A new ruler (Chandragupta Maurya—324–301 B.C.E.) founded a new state (the Mauryan) which drove out the remaining Greek forces after the death of Alexander the Great. The reign of Chan dragupta Maurya is described by a work called the Arathustra. The Arathustra, probably written after Chandragupta Maurya's reign, provides an account of government during the time. According to this work, Chandragupta Maurya's government was highly centralized with the army and the police reporting to the king. The empire itself was divided into provinces each ruled by their own governor.

Early China

Sometime around the eighth millennium B.C.E., Chinese people began settling around the rivers and cultivating crops. As in other places, these small villages eventually became more complex. Chinese date the beginning of their civilization to the Xia (Hsia) dynasty, a possibly legendary dynasty, followed by the Shang dynasty around the sixteenth century B.C.E. Archeologists have discovered inscriptions on oracle bones, which are the oldest existing examples of Chinese writing. The Shang king ruled from the capital by utilizing his vast bureaucracy. Territory was divided into provinces ruled by chieftains chosen by the king. The early Chinese believed in supernatural forces. The king was believed to be able to communicate with the gods and the early Chinese believed in an afterlife. They, like the ancient Egyptians, maintained complex tombs. Kings were buried in intricate burial suits and people were sacrificed to be buried with the kings to assist in the afterlife.

In the eleventh century the Shang were overthrown by the Zhou (the longest–lived dynasty in Chinese history, lasting 800 years). The Zhou dynasty (1045–221 B.C.E.) also had a strong king. Under the Zhou the concept of the "mandate of heaven" developed whereby kings were said to rule because of their talents and ties to the gods. The mandate, given by the gods, could also be removed if the king was seen to be unfit or unfaithful. Under the Zhou, large water projects to control rivers and irrigate fields were undertaken. Also during the Zhou dynasty, the manufacture and trade of silk began. Fragments of silk cloth found throughout Central Asia and in the west, as far away as Athens, indicate that by the fifth century B.C.E. the so-called Silk Road had come into existence (see Trade and Migration section). Also in the Zhou period, the "hundred schools" of ancient philosophy originated (see Religion section). Many philosophers such as Confucius and Mencius began to write about and discuss philosophical and metaphysical ideas.

The Rise of Advanced Civilizations

Greece

The Minoans (2600–1250 B.C.E.) lived on Crete. They established a vast overseas trading network and developed several written languages such as Linear A in which symbols stood for entire syllables. Linear A has not yet been completely translated. However, many records using Linear A script have been located. Minoan society was a sophisticated one with vast palace complexes and intricate art and architecture. Some buildings even had indoor plumbing and flush toilets. For reasons which are not entirely clear, Minoan civilization declined around 1400 B.C.E. Most scholars believe that a series of invasions weakened Minoan society. By 1400 B.C.E., Crete had been overtaken by the Mycenaeans. However, by 1100 B.C.E. Mycenaean civilization also collapsed. Invasions, disorders, and declining populations meant that few records have survived and some historians believe that the art of writing itself may have disappeared. Thus, the period from 1100–750 B.C.E is referred to as the Greek Dark Ages.

Writing was reinvented in the eighth century as the Dark Ages ended and the period of Greek city-states began. With the resurrection of writing, some of the important Greek poets and chroniclers began writing. One of the most well-known, because he is said to represent Greek ideals, is Homer whose *Iliad* and *Odyssey* were important in defining for ancient Greek civilization ideas like excellence (arête), courage, honor, heroism, and so on. Hesiod's *Works and Days* summarized everyday life. His *Theogony* recounted Greek myths. Greek religion was based on their writings.

In the archaic period (800–500 B.C.E.) Greek life was organized around the polis (city-state). Oligarchs controlled most of the poleis (city-states) until the end of the sixth century when individuals holding absolute power (tyrants) replaced them. By the end of the sixth century, democratic governments replaced many tyrants.

Sparta, however, developed into an armed camp. Sparta seized control of neighboring Messenia around 750 B.C.E. In 650 B.C.E., the Spartans crushed a revolt and enslaved the Messenians, who outnumbered them ten to one. To prevent future rebellions, every Spartan entered lifetime military service (as hoplites) at the age of seven. Around 640 B.C.E. Lycurgus promulgated a constitution and around 540 B.C.E. Sparta organized the Peloponnesian League.

Athens was the principal city of Attica. Between 1000 and 700 B.C.E., it was governed by monarchs (legendary kings such as Perseus and Theseus). In the eighth century, an oligarchy replaced the monarchy. Draco (621 B.C.E.) first codified Athenian law. His Draconian Code was known for its harshness. Solon (630–560 B.C.E.) reformed the laws in 594 B.C.E. He enfranchised the lower classes and gave the state responsibility for administering justice. The Athenian governing body was the Council of Areopagus, from which archons (leaders) were selected. Growing indebtedness of small farmers and insufficient land strengthened the nobles. Peisistratus (605–527 B.C.E.) seized control and governed as a tyrant. In 527 B.C.E., Cleisthenes led a reform movement that established the basis of Athen's democratic government, including an annual assembly to identify and exile those considered dangerous to the state.

Classical Greece

The fifth century was the high point of Greek civilization and began with the Persian War. At Marathon (490 B.C.E.) the Athenians defeated Darius I's (522–486 B.C.E.) army. Ten years later, Darius's son Xerxes (486–465 B.C.E.) returned to Greece with 250,000 soldiers. The Persians burned Athens, but their fleet was defeated at the Battle of Salamis (480 B.C.E.) and they retreated.

After the Persian War, Athens organized the Delian League. Pericles (495–429 B.C.E.) used League money to rebuild Athens, including construction of the Parthenon and other Acropolis buildings. Athenian dominance, however, spurred war with Sparta.

The Peloponnesian War between Athens and Sparta (431–404 B.C.E.) ended with the defeat of Athens, but weakened Sparta as well. Sparta later fell victim to Thebes, and the other city-states warred among themselves until Alexander the Great's conquest. That conquest unified the Greek city-states in the fourth century B.C.E., which marked the beginning of the Hellenistic Age.

> ***Fast Facts*** The fifth century B.C.E. was the high point of Greek civilization, as a revolution in philosophy occurred.

A revolution in philosophy occurred in classical Athens. The Sophists emphasized the individual and his attainment of excellence through rhetoric, grammar, music, and mathematics. Socrates (470–399 B.C.E.) criticized the Sophists' emphasis on rhetoric and emphasized a process of questioning or dialogues, with his students. Similar to Socrates, his pupil Plato (428–348 B.C.E.) emphasized ethics. His *Theory of Ideas or Forms* said that what we see is but a dim shadow of the eternal Forms or Ideas. Philosophy should seek to penetrate to the real nature of things. Plato's *Republic* described an ideal state ruled by a philosopher king.

Aristotle was Plato's pupil. He criticized Plato, arguing that ideas or forms did not exist outside of things. He contended that it was necessary to examine four factors in treating any object: its matter, its form, its cause of origin, and its end or purpose. Aristotle tutored Alexander the Great and later opened a school, the Lyceum, near Athens.

Greek art emphasized the individual. In architecture the Greeks developed the Doric and Ionian orders. In poetry, Sappho (610–580 B.C.E.) and Pindar (522–438 B.C.E.) wrote lyric poems. In tragedy, Aeschylus (525–456 B.C.E.) examined the problem of hubris, most notably in his Orestia trilogy: *Agamemnon, The Libation Bearers,* and *The Eumenides*. Sophocles (496–406 B.C.E.) used irony to explore the fate of Oedipus in *Oedipus Rex*.

Euripides (484–406 B.C.E.) is often considered the most modern tragedian because he was so psychologically minded. In comedy, Aristophanes (450–388 B.C.E.) was a pioneer who used political themes. The New Comedy, exemplified by Menander (342–292 B.C.E.), concentrated on domestic and individual themes.

The Greeks were the first to develop the study of history. They were skeptical critics, intent on banishing myth from their works. Herodotus (460–400 B.C.E.), called the "father of history," wrote *History of the Persian War*. Thucydides (460–400 B.C.E.) wrote *History of the Pelopennesian War*. The Greeks pioneered the study of metaphysics, ethics, politics, rhetoric, and cosmology.

The Hellenistic Age and Macedonia

The Macedonians were a Greek people who were considered semi-barbaric by their southern Greek relatives. They never developed a city-state system and had more territory and people than any of the poleis. In 359 B.C.E. Philip II became king. To finance his state and secure a seaport, he conquered several poleis and in 338 B.C.E., Athens fell. In 336 B.C.E., however, Philip was assassinated.

Philip's son, Alexander the Great (356–323 B.C.E.), killed or exiled rival claimants to his father's throne. He established an empire that included Syria and Persia and extended to the Indus River Valley. However, his troops threatened to mutiny in 325 B.C.E. So he would not have to depend on the questionable loyalty of his Macedonian troops, Alexander married a Persian princess and ordered eighty of his generals to do likewise. At the time of his death, Alexander had established seventy cities and a vast trading network.

With no succession plan, Alexander's realm was divided among three of his generals. Seleucus I established a dynasty in Persia, Mesopotamia, and Syria; Ptolemy I controlled Egypt, Palestine, and Phoenicia; and Lysimachus governed Asia Minor and Macedonia. Several Greek poleis rebelled against Macedonia and formed the Achaean and Aetolian leagues, the closest the Greeks ever came to national unity until modern times. Nevertheless, by 30 B.C.E. all of the successor states had fallen to Rome.

Rome

The traditional founding date for Rome is 753 B.C.E. Between 800 and 500 B.C.E., Greek tribes colonized southern Italy, bringing their alphabet and religious practices to Roman tribes. In the sixth and seventh centuries, the Etruscans expanded southward and conquered Rome. Late in the sixth century (the traditional date is 509 B.C.E.), the Romans expelled the Etruscans and established an aristocratically–based republic in place of the monarchy (the rebellion was supposedly marked by the rape of Lucretia, a Roman matron, by an Etruscan).

In the early Republic, power was in the hands of the patricians (wealthy landowners). A Senate composed of patricians governed. The Senate elected two consuls to serve one-year terms. Roman executives had great power (the imperium). They were assisted by two quaestors, who managed economic affairs. The consuls' actions were supposed to be approved by the Senate and then by the Assembly, which represented all the people, but in practice consuls in early times had near-despotic power.

Between 509 and 264 B.C.E., Rome conquered Italy through a mixture of diplomatic guile and brute force. It then turned its attention to Carthage, a powerful trading outpost. In the three Punic Wars (264–146 B.C.E.), Rome defeated Carthage to gain control of the Mediterranean.

The First Punic War (264–241 B.C.E.) began when Carthage tried to dominate eastern Sicily. After its defeat, Carthage relinquished its interest and paid war reparations to Rome. The Second Punic War (218–201 B.C.E.) saw Carthage try to expand into Spain. Carthage's General Hannibal (247–183 B.C.E.) led 26,000 troops and sixty elephants across the Alps into Italy. He defeated the Romans at Cannae in 216 B.C.E. The Roman Publius Cornelius Scipio (d. 211 B.C.E.) defeated Carthage in a series of battles in Italy and Africa. The final Roman victory, in the Battle of Zama (202 B.C.E.), led to Carthage's surrender in 201 B.C.E. Carthage was reduced to a minor state. Macedonia allied with Carthage in the Third Punic War (149–146 B.C.E.). Macedonia's defeat brought Greek slaves, culture, and artifacts into Rome. In 146 B.C.E., the Romans burned Carthage and, according to legend, salted the earth to keep anything from growing again.

Rome's expansion and contact with Greek culture disrupted the traditional agrarian basis of life. Tiberius Gracchus (163–133 B.C.E.) and Gaius Gracchus (153–121 B.C.E.) promoted the cause of the common people. They called for land reform and lower grain prices to help small farmers. They were opposed by the Optimates (best men). Although Tiberius was assassinated, Gaius continued his work, assisted by the Equestrians. After several years of struggle, Gaius committed suicide. Power passed into the hands of military leaders for the next eighty years. General Marius (157–86 B.C.E.) defeated Rome's Germanic invaders. A revolt of Rome's allies (the Social War) broke out in 90 B.C.E., although Sulla (138–78 B.C.E.), Marius's successor, restored order by granting citizenship to those who could not meet property qualifications. During the 70s and 60s, Pompey (106–48 B.C.E.) and Julius Caesar (100–44 B.C.E.) emerged as the most powerful men. In 73 B.C.E. Spartacus led a slave rebellion, which General Crassus suppressed.

In the 60s, Caesar helped suppress Cataline, who had led a conspiracy in the Senate. In 60 B.C.E. Caesar convinced Pompey and Crassus, two important Romans, to form the so-called "First Triumvirate," which was an informal political alliance. When Crassus died in 53 B.C.E., Caesar and Pompey fought for leadership. In 49 B.C.E. Caesar crossed the Rubicon, the stream separating his province from Italy, and a civil war followed in which Caesar ultimately defeated Pompey. Caesar reformed the tax code and eased burdens on debtors. He instituted the Julian calendar, which remained in use until 1582. The Assembly under Caesar had little power.

In 47 B.C.E. the Senate proclaimed Caesar as dictator, and later named him dictator for life. Two Roman politicians, Brutus and Cassius, believed that Caesar had destroyed the Republic. They formed a conspiracy and on March 15, 44 B.C.E. (The Ides of March), Caesar was assassinated in the Theatre of Pompey. His eighteen-year-old great-nephew and adopted son, Octavian, came to power after a struggle against more powerful rivals.

In literature and philosophy, Plautus wrote Greek-style comedy. Cato the younger was an important advocate of the Roman Republic and an opponent of Caesar. Catullus was the most famous lyric poet. Lucretius's *Order of Things* described Epicurean atomic metaphysics, while arguing against the immortality of the soul. Cicero, the great orator and stylist, defended the Stoic concept of natural law. His *Orations* described Roman life and religion as family centered and more civic minded than Greek religion.

The Roman Empire

Octavian (63 B.C.E.–14 C.E.), named as Caesar's heir, did not have enough power to control the state. He formed the Second Triumvirate in 43 B.C.E. with Mark Anthony (Caesar's lieutenant) and Lepidus, governor of the western provinces, to run the Republic and punish Caesar's assassins. The armies of Brutus and Cassius were defeated at Philippi in 42 B.C.E. The triumvirs divided the state, with Anthony getting Egypt and the east, Lepidus getting Africa, and Octavian getting Rome and the western provinces. Lepidus soon lost his position and Octavian went to war with Anthony and Cleopatra, queen of Egypt. Octavian's army triumphed at Actium, in western Greece (31 B.C.E.), and Anthony and Cleopatra fled to Egypt, where they committed suicide (30 B.C.E.).

Octavian held absolute control while maintaining the appearance of a republic. When he offered to relinquish his power in 27 B.C.E., the Senate gave him a vote of confidence and a new title, "Augustus." Augustus ruled for 44 years (31 B.C.E.–14 C.E.). He introduced many reforms, including new coinage, new tax collection, fire and police protection, and land for settlers in the provinces.

Between 27 B.C.E. and 180 C.E., Rome's greatest cultural achievements occurred under the Pax Romana (Roman Peace). The period between 27 B.C.E. and 14 C.E. is called the Augustan Age. Vergil (70–19 B.C.E.) wrote the *Aeneid*, a poetic account of Rome's rise. Horace (65–8 B.C.E.) wrote the lyric *Odes*. Ovid (43 B.C.E.–18 C.E.) published the *Ars Amatoria*, a guide to seduction, and the *Metamorphoses*, about Greek mythology. Livy (57 B.C.E.–17 C.E.) wrote a narrative history of Rome based on earlier accounts. The Silver Age lasted from 14–180 C.E. Writings in this period were less optimistic. Seneca (5 B.C.E. to 65 C.E.) espoused Stoicism in his tragedies and satires. Juvenal (50–127 C.E.) wrote satire; Plutarch's (46–120 C.E.) *Parallel Lives* portrayed Greek and Roman leaders; and Tacitus (55–120 C.E.) criticized the follies of his era through his history of the earlier empire.

Stoicism was the dominant philosophy of the era. Epictetus (60–120 C.E.), a slave, and Emperor Marcus Aurelius were its chief exponents. In law, Rome made lasting contributions. It distinguished three orders of law: civil law (jus civile), which applied to Rome's citizens; law of the people (jus gentium), which merged Roman law with the laws of other peoples of the Empire; and natural law (jus naturale), governed by reason.

In science, Ptolemy, an Alexandrian, and Galen worked in the provinces. Pliny the Elder's (23–79 C.E.) *Natural History* was widely known in the Middle Ages. In architecture, the Colosseum and Pantheon were constructed. The Romans also developed the use of concrete as a building material.

After the Pax Romana, the third century was a period of great tumult for Rome. Marcus Aurelius's decision to name his son Commodus as his successor (r. 180–192), rather than the most talented governor, provoked vicious infighting. Commodus was ultimately strangled. Three emperors governed in the next ten years. Civil war was nearly endemic in the third century. Between 235 and 284 C.E., 26 "barracks emperors" governed, taxing the population heavily to pay for the Empire's defense.

Rome's frontiers were attacked constantly. The Sassanids, a Persian dynasty attacked Mesopotamia in 224 C.E. and took Emperor Valerian hostage in 259 C.E.. By 250 C.E., the Germanic Goths had captured Rome's Balkan provinces. In the fifth century the Huns under Attila (406–453 C.E.) swept in from Central Asia, driving out the Visigoths and other Germanic tribes before them. In 378, the Visigoths defeated Emperor Valens in the Battle of Adrianople. In 410 the Visigoths under Alaric (370–410 C.E.) looted Rome. Emperors Diocletian (r. 285–305 C.E.) and Constantine (r. 306–337 C.E.) tried to stem Rome's decline. Diocletian divided the Empire into four parts, moved the capital to Nicomedia in Asia Minor. Constantine moved the capital to Constantinople.

Some historians argue that the rise of Christianity was an important factor in Rome's decline. Jesus was born around 4 B.C.E. and began preaching and ministering to the poor and sick at the age of 30. The Gospels provide the fullest account of his life and teachings. Saul of Tarsus (10–67 C.E.), later called Paul, transformed Christianity from a small sect of Jews who believed Jesus was the Messiah into a world religion. Paul, a Hellenized Jew, had a conversion experience in 35 C.E. Early followers of Jesus believed that Christianity was a part of Judaism, and continued to follow Jewish law. Paul taught that Christians were justified by their faith in Jesus, and need no longer to follow Jewish law. Paul won followers through his missionary work. He also shifted the focus from the early followers' belief in Jesus's imminent return to concentration on personal salvation. His *Epistles* (letters to Christian communities) laid the basis for the religion's organization and sacraments.

The Pax Romana allowed Christians to move freely through the Empire. But, in this new era, many Romans felt confused and alienated, and thus drawn to the new religion. And unlike many mystery religions, Christianity included women. By the first century, the new religion had spread throughout the Empire. Generally, the Romans tolerated other religions, including Christianity, but there were short, sporadic persecutions, reaching an apex under Diocletian.

Around 312 C.E., Emperor Constantine converted to Christianity and ordered toleration in the Edict of Milan (ca. 313 C.E.). In 391 C.E., Emperor Theodosius I (r. 371–395 C.E.) proclaimed Christianity as the Empire's official religion. By the second century, the church hierarchy had developed. Eventually, the Bishop of Rome came to have preeminence based on the interpretation that Jesus had chosen Peter as his successor.

The Byzantine Empire

Emperor Theodosius II (r. 408–450 C.E.) divided his empire between his sons, one ruling the East, the other the West. After the Vandals sacked Rome in 455 C.E., Constantinople was the undisputed leading city of the Empire. In 476, the Ostrogoth king, Odoacer, forced the last emperor in Rome, Romulus Augustulus (r. 475–476) to abdicate. In 527, Justinian I (483–565) became emperor in the East and reigned with his controversial wife, Theodora until 565. The Nika revolt broke out in 532 and demolished the city. It was crushed by General Belisarius in 537 after 30,000 had died in the uprising. However, Justinian's campaigns to win back the western lands failed. Justinian's lasting contribution to history comes not however from his conquests but through his codification of Roman law. Justinian took the mass of written laws, senate decisions, legal commentaries, and edicts and authorized a jurist to compile all of these into a systematic compilation of law. The first part of this, the *Corpus Iuris*

Civilis (The Body of Civil Law) was completed in 529. Later they were supplemented by the Digest, a summary of the writings of Roman jurists and the Institutes, a summary of the most important principles of Roman law. Justinian's law code, derived from Roman law and written in Latin, became the basis for many of the legal systems in Europe.

The Crusaders further weakened the state. In 1204, Venice contracted to transport Crusaders to the Near East in return for the Crusaders capturing and looting Constantinople. The Byzantines were defeated in 1204. Though they drove out the Crusaders in 1261, the empire never regained its former power. In 1453, Constantinople fell to the Ottoman Turks.

As Greek and then Roman culture became dominant in the West, large empires also flourished in the East. Although many differences existed between East and West the two were not cut off from one another. Archaeologists have discovered fragments of Chinese porcelain on African tombs, pieces of Chinese silk in Athenian tombs, and Greek artifices in the East.

Trade and Migration in the Ancient World

Since early times, the sea routes along the Mediterranean and the land routes that reached out from the sea and extended across continents have served as a conduit not only for trade but also for a migration of peoples, ideas, philosophies, and disease. Early peoples did not live in isolation from a greater milieu.

Trade before the classical era could be extremely dangerous since there were no regulations on long distance trade, and roads and bridges were scarce. However, beginning with the Greeks, and especially after the establishment of Alexander the Great's empire, the frequency and possibility of long distance trade increased. Archaeologists have found coins, jewelry, and other artifacts which indicate the presence of Greek communities in Persia and Bactria during the Hellenistic era.

The Silk Road

As people became more familiar with geography, modes of travel and sea routes, they began to sail from the Mediterranean to the Indian Ocean. Regular trade routes linked the Red Sea between India and Arabia in the East and the Mediterranean in the west. Part of the Silk Road carried caravan traffic between China and the Roman Empire. The main road went from the Chinese capital of Chang'an to the Taklamakan desert. The road then split into several branches to avoid the main part of the desert. The roads then reconnected at a city in the western most corner of China before traveling to Bactria, northern India, and northern Iran. The road connected several ports on the Caspian Sea and the Persian Gulf.

This giant trading network also had sea routes, which crossed through the South China Sea into the Indian Ocean and the Arabian Sea and branched off into the Persian Gulf and Red Sea.

A wide variety of goods traversed these complicated trading routes. Silk (mostly from China), spices such as cloves, nutmeg, mace, pepper, cinnamon, and cardamon (from Southeast Asia, China, and India), textiles (from India and Central Asia), and horses (from Central Asia) traveled west. Glassware, decorative items, perfumes, textiles, pottery, olive oil, wine, and gold traveled east.

Although a great deal or merchandise crossed the wide expanse of the Silk Road, few people or individual merchants traveled the entire routes. Rather, trade was handled by a variety of intermediaries. And, although trade was the purpose of the silk roads, many other things were exchanged as well. Diseases and pathogens traveled freely along the Silk Road with the animals and people crossing it. And, missionaries and religious ideas and philosophies also traveled extensively on the Silk Road.

Trade routes linked India and Arabia in the East with the Mediterranean in the West.

Fast Facts

Disease also traveled quickly along the Silk Road and other trade routes. The most disastrous disease of the Middle Ages was the bubonic plague. The bubonic plague (Black Death) is a disease affecting the lymph glands which causes death quickly. Conditions in Europe encouraged the quick spread of this disease during the fourteenth century. There was no urban sanitation, and streets were filled with refuse, excrement, and dead animals. Living conditions were overcrowded with families often sleeping in one room or one bed. Poor nutrition was rampant. Carried by fleas on rats, the plague was brought from Asia to Europe in 1347 by merchants. The Black Plague probably began in India, infected Mongol armies attacking cities on the Black Sea in 1346, and then spread to

Italian merchants who brought the disease back to Western Europe. The plague affected all of Europe by 1350 and killed perhaps 25 million people—about a third of the population. The plague killed very rapidly (within two or three days) bringing horrible symptoms to the sufferer. Victims developed large boils, black blotches on their skin, and a horrible body odor. Cities were often evacuated during the plague as frightened residents sought refuge elsewhere. This, however, only served to spread the plague to new regions.

By 1000 C.E., the Silk Road trade routes could also connect with caravan traders in the Sahara. By 1100, the trans-Saharan trade route was well-established and gold, slaves, and other tropical items traversed the desert.

Rise of World Religions

The earliest religions were all polytheistic (belief in many gods). The early civilizations of Egypt, Mesopotamia, and India each worshipped numerous gods who were often identified with forces of nature, celestial bodies, or plants and animals that were important to these civilizations. Although many of these early religions remained significant for some time, the first millennium B.C.E. witnessed the beginnings of religions and philosophies that would in time come to be adopted throughout much of the world.

Hebrews

The Hebrews were a Semitic speaking people whose history is later written down as the Hebrew Bible. The Hebrews were a nomadic people, organized into a clan structure and said to be descended from the patriarch Abraham who migrated from Mesopotamia to Palestine. According to the Hebrew Bible, they lived in Palestine until a drought forced them to move to Egypt where they lived for many years until being enslaved by the Pharaoh. They were then led out of slavery in Egypt by Moses around the first half of the thirteenth century B.C.E. According to this account, they wandered in the desert for many years before re-entering Palestine and coming into conflict with the Philistines. There is not enough archeological evidence to definitively support this story which tells us what the Israelites had come to believe about themselves and their history by the time it is written down centuries later. However, by 1000 B.C.E., the Israelites had emerged as a group of people organized into twelve tribes with Saul as their king (r. 1025–1004 B.C.E.). After Saul's death, David (r. 1004–965 B.C.E.) brought the Israelites together, defeated the Philistines, took over Palestine, and made Jerusalem the capital. Under David, the Kingdom of Israel was united. David's son Solomon (r. 965–930 B.C.E.) further expanded royal power and is best known for his construction of the temple in Jerusalem. However, after Solomon's death, the northern and southern tribes split into the Kingdom of Israel with a capital at Samaria and the Kingdom of Judah with the capital at Jerusalem. As Assyrian power rose, the power of Israel declined. Israel itself was taken over by 722 B.C.E. and many Israelites were dispersed to other parts of the Assyrian empire. These "lost tribes" merged with other peoples and lost their distinct identity. Despite the fall of the early Jewish kingdom (tenth century B.C.E.), the Jews retained their faith under several successive regimes (Babylonian, Archaemenid, Alexandrian, Seleucid, and Roman). The Jews who remained monotheistic were often persecuted under these regimes as they were largely polytheistic and often worshiped the king as divine.

Judah survived under the Assyrians but as the Assyrians were conquered by the Chaldeans, Jerusalem was destroyed as well in 586 B.C.E., and many Jews were sent into exile—the so-called Babylonian captivity. However, the Chaldeans were conquered by the Persians and the Judeans were allowed to return and rebuild. The people of Judah eventually became known as Jews. The Israelites themselves were not an especially important people politically or militarily. However, the monotheism that eventually developed among them and their laws was different and important.

The Israelite's religion came to be very different from all other religions of the time. They worshipped only one god who was omnipotent and they did not worship forces of nature such as the sun, the moon, rivers, or trees. The Jews eventually recorded their history and beliefs in the Hebrew Bible. This written source served not only as a document of faith but also as a law code. The most important aspect of this law was the covenant between Yahweh (God) and his chosen people. In the covenant, the Israelites promised to obey Yahweh and in return, Yahweh promised to take care of his people. "Now if you obey me fully and keep my covenant, then out of all nations you will be my treasured possession" (Exodus 19:1–8). The covenant also set out specific standards of moral behavior.

Hinduism

Vedic religions (from the Veda—ancient religious texts dating from 1,500 to 500 B.C.E.) were polytheistic. Priests called Brahmins knew the ritual, prayers, and technology of sacrifice (which they derived from the Rig Veda). Jainism, Buddhism, and then Hinduism all challenged and adapted the older Vedic traditions and ultimately transformed them into something new which used the old texts. Under Hinduism, the Brahmin priests retained their high status even when sacrifices became less common. The names and personalities of some gods also changed. Vishnu and Shiva became central gods in the new religion.

Hinduism maintained many gods (perhaps as many as 300 million). Nonetheless, all gods are seen as manifestations of one divine force which underpins the universe.

The ideal life cycle for a Hindu follows: 1) the young man becomes a student and studies the sacred texts, 2) he marries, has children, and acquires material goods, 3) when he has grandchildren he leaves his home and meditates, and 4) he abandons his own identity and waits for death. A person who passes through these stages will be able to achieve liberation from worldly issues at the end of his life.

Buddhism

During the time that Israel was under Persian control, new philosophies and religions were springing up in the East. Gautama Buddha was born around 566 B.C.E. to a wealthy ruling family. Despite his wealth, marriage, and the birth of a son, at the age of 30, he left home dissatisfied, and wandered and meditated, seeking enlightenment. While meditating beneath a tree for 49 days, he found enlightenment and became known as a Buddha (the Enlightened One). When he left the tree he gave a sermon at the Deer Park near Benares preaching the middle path. For Buddha, all suffering is caused by desire. The way to end suffering is to end desire. The way to end desire is to follow the eightfold path (right views, right aspirations, right speech, right conduct, right livelihood, right effort, right mindfulness, and right meditation) which describes the way one must live in order to achieve Nirvana. While Buddhism shares some key beliefs such as the idea of Nirvana and the belief in multiple gods with Hinduism, it rejects the strict caste system and denies the existence of an individual soul. As with other major religions, Buddhism changed over time. Immediately after Buddha's death his disciples gathered to compile his teachings. Other councils were held later which established the canons of Buddhism. However, despite some shared beliefs, several different types of Buddhism emerged.

Buddha preached that pain was caused by desires and that pain could be alleviated by detaching from material things and by following the eightfold path to reach Nirvana. In the original Theravada Buddhism, the achievement of Nirvana was an indescribable tranquil state one could realize when freed from desire. But Gautauma taught that the world was soulless and that the world soul preached in the Upanishads is an illusion.

This type of Buddhism however was difficult for many people to understand and a new interpretation (Mahayana–the Great Vehicle) developed. In this version believers could achieve Nirvana with the help of compassionate beings. The Theravada School became known as the Hinaya (Lesser Vehicle) because it did not allow as many people to achieve Nirvana. By the first century

B.C.E. statues and images of Buddha came to be worshipped and honored. Mahayanans also developed the idea that Buddha was not merely a man but rather the earthly expression of a great spiritual being.

A third version of Buddhism is known as Jainism. Jainism was founded by Mahavira (Great Hero). Born in 540 B.C.E., Mahavira was also born into a wealthy family.

Zoroastrianism

The elites of ancient Persia practiced a religion known as Zoroastrianism. In the early sixth century B.C.E. a prophet named Zoroaster (Zarathustra) began preaching a monotheistic religion. This god, Ahura Mazda, represented goodness, light, and truth. He was opposed by another power, Ahriman (darkness and evil). Zoroaster preached a final judgment day whereby all living beings would be consigned to either darkness (Ahriman) or light (Ahura Mazda). Zoroastrianism may have influenced the early Christians and almost certainly influenced the Mahayana Buddhist cult of Maitreya. Although Zoroastrianism did not spread widely, it did survive the fall of the Persian Empire and small Zoroastrian communities remain today in parts of Iran and India.

Confucianism

In China as in Ancient Greece, philosophy flourished. The era between 600–300 B.C.E. in China has been called the era of a Hundred Schools. At the same time that the books of the Hebrew Bible were being codified and while famous Greek philosophers were writing, Chinese philosophers also were contemplating moral, political, and theological ideas.

The most famous of these Chinese philosophers is Confucius (551–479 B.C.E.). His Chinese name, K'ung Fu-tzu was Latinized by Jesuit missionaries. After Confucius's death, his sayings were compiled by his disciples into a book called the Analects.

For Confucius, a moral society was ruled by hierarchical relationships, especially those between family members. Confucius felt that the best government was one filled with well educated and conscientious people, i.e. men of talent vs. those of noble birth. The Confucian belief in the importance of government selecting people of talent is later reflected in the Chinese civil service examination system. Confucius' disciples studied poetry and history. However, Confucianism was not a religion per se. Confucius thought that questions about religion, an afterlife and spirits, were beyond the capacity of human reason. His philosophy was of an ethical nature. For Confucius, finding the way (dao) was the most important aspect of life. Each person must discover their individual duty and fulfill it.

Confucius' most famous disciple was Mencius (372–289 B.C.E.). Mencius traveled around China advocating Confucian values. Mencius believed the state should be moral and that the head of state should be a moral leader.

Daoism

Another group of philosophers, the Daoists, criticized Confucian ideals. According to tradition, the founder of Daoism was a wise man, Laozi, who lived during the sixth century B.C.E. But the classic Daoist work, Daodejing (Classic of the Way and of the Virtue) was undoubtedly written by more than one person.

The main concept of Daoism is the idea of dao (the way). The dao can be the cosmos, an eternal and unchanging principle, but it can also be a passive force. It does nothing and yet accomplishes everything. Thus, living in harmony with dao meant retreating from the physical world. Daoists strive to live simply in harmony with nature.

Islam

Islam was founded by Muhammad (570–632). Muhammad grew up in Mecca with his uncle who participated in the caravan trade. In 610 Muhammad meditated and received a proclamation from the angel Gabriel. As Muhammad came to understand that he was hearing the voice of God, he began sharing his revelations. His revelations called on people to proclaim that one god had created the universe and everything in it. That god would judge them at the end of time and those who had not sinned would go to paradise and the sinful would go to hell. Because all people were called to submit themselves to God and accept Muhammad as the last of God's messengers, those who submitted became known as Muslims (one who makes submission). Muslims were called to practice the Five Pillars of Islam: 1) avow that there is only one god (Allah) and Muhammad is his prophet 2) pray five times a day, 3) fast during Ramadan, 4) pay alms to the poor, and 5) make a pilgrimage to Mecca at least once during one's lifetime.

After Muhammad's death, dissention broke out regarding this succession. Abu Bakr was immediately proclaimed the caliph (successor) but Abu Bakr did not have Muhammad's power to receive revelations or the power to govern. Abu Bakr did orchestrate those who had heard Muhammad's revelations and who had acted as secretaries and scribes for him to gather his revelations into a book. This book, the Quran, was compiled around 650. The Quran is regarded as the word of God.

After the assassination of the third caliph, Uthman in 656, civil war broke out over the succession of the caliphate. One group in this civil war became known as the Shi'ites. Shi'ites believe that Ali should have been the successor to Muhammad and that the office of caliph is a secular rather than religious one. Those Muslims who believe that the first three caliphs after Muhammad were properly chosen became known as Ahl al-Sunna wa'l-Jama'a (Sunni). Sunnis consider the caliphs to be both secular and religious leaders.

Civilizations in the Middle Ages

Japan

Feudalism in Japan began with the arrival of mounted nomadic warriors from throughout Asia during the Kofun Era (300–710 C.E.). Some members of these nomadic groups formed an elite class and became part of the court aristocracy in the capital city of Kyoto, in western Japan. During the Heian Era (794–1185), a hereditary military aristocracy arose in the Japanese provinces, and by the late Heian Era, many of these formerly nomadic warriors had established themselves as independent land owners, or as managers of landed estates (shoen) owned by Kyoto aristocrats. These aristocrats depended on these warriors to defend their shoen and in response to this need, the warriors organized into small groups called bushidan. Members of these groups were often related by either blood or ties of personal loyalty, and were given rewards in the form of booty or land in return for service to the landowners.

As the years passed, these warrior clans grew larger, and alliances formed among them, led by imperial descendants who moved from the capital to the provinces. By the twelfth century, local warrior chieftains were serving as liaisons between Kyoto and the provinces, and giving military support to the factions that were locked in a constant struggle for wealth and power. At this time, the dominant clans were the Taira (or Heike) and the Minamoto (or Genji) and in the bloody Taira-Minamoto War (1180–1185) the Taira were defeated.

After this victory, Minamoto no Yorimoto forced the emperor to award him the title of shogun, which is short for "barbarian subduing generalissimo." He used this power to found the Kamakura Shogunate which survived for 148 years. This was the first of the three feudal governments, or bakfu, which directly translates means "tent government," but is usually translated as shogunate. Under the Kamakura Shogunate, many vassals were appointed to the position of jitro or land steward, or the position of provincial governors (shugo) to act as liaisons between the Kamakura government and local vassals.

By the fourteenth century, the shugo had augmented their power enough to become a threat to the Kamakura, and in 1333 lead a rebellion that overthrew the shogunate. After his crushing defeat of the Kamakura, Ashikaga Takauji founded the second bakfu, which would bear his name. Under the Ashikaga Shogunate, the office of shogun was made hereditary, and its powers were greatly extended. These new shogun turned their vassals into aggressive local warriors called kokujin, or jizamurai. Following this move, the Ashikaga shoguns lost a great deal of their power to political fragmentation, which eventually lead to the Onin War (1467–1477) and the Sengoku, or Warring States Era (1467–1568).

By the middle of the sixteenth century, the feudal system had evolved considerably. At the center of this highly evolved system was the daimyo, a local feudal lord who ruled over one of the many autonomous domains. Some daimyo were descendants of the shogun families, and others were simply opportunistic warriors who took advantage of political unrest to seize power by force. More than 100 daimyo once ruled the fragmented Japan and saw their relationships to their vassals as nothing short of patriarchal.

Far-reaching alliances of daimyo were forged under the national unifiers Oda Nobunaga, Toyotomi Hideyoshi, and Tokugawa Ieyasu, who together founded the Tokugawa Shogunate, the final and most unified of the three shogunates. Under the Tokugawa, the daimyo were considered direct vassals of the shoguns, and were kept under strict control. The warriors were gradually transformed into scholars and bureaucrats under the bushido or code of chivalry, and the principles of Neo-Confucianism. A merchant class or chonin gained wealth as the samurai class began to lose power, and the feudal system effectively ended when power was returned to the emperor under the Meiji Restoration of 1868, abolishing all special privileges of the samurai class.

Sub-Saharan Kingdoms

The Nok were a people that lived in the area now known as Nigeria. Artifacts indicate that they were peaceful farmers who built small communities consisting of houses of wattle and daub. They made jewelry of iron and tin, and beads have been found, indicating an interest in beauty and decoration. Perhaps the most revealing artifacts are the terra cotta figurines they left behind. These nearly life-sized figurines of people and animals show great skill on the part of the Nok.

The people referred to as the Ghana lived about 500 miles from what we now call Ghana. The Ghana traded with Berber merchants, offering these traders gold from deposits found in the south of their territory. Muslim influence in Ghana grew between 1054 and 1076 C.E. and for a century the country flourished under this new religion. Well-constructed stone houses replaced the older wooden ones and Muslim mosques appeared. In the 1200s, the Mali Kingdom conquered Ghana and the civilization mysteriously disappeared.

The people known as the Mali lived in a huge kingdom that mostly lay on the savanna bordering the Sahara Desert. The city of Timbuktu, built in the thirteenth century, was a thriving city of culture where traders visited stone houses, shops, libraries, and mosques. Although the religion of the kingdom was Islamic, the royal leaders and their subjects were reluctant to give up their belief in royal magic. In the fourteenth century, questions of succession to the throne weakened the kingdom, but the country did thrive for 400 years.

The Songhai lived near the Niger River and gained their independence from Mali in the early 1400s. The major growth of the empire came after 1464 under the leadership of Sunni Ali, who devoted his reign to warfare and expansion of the empire. Sunni Ali also professed to be Muslim but ruled as a magician king claiming the right to rule through his heritage. His successor was a devout Muslim who put Muslims in high government positions. In the 1500s, people from Morocco came to find gold and salt deposits near Songhai territory, and the Songhai were forced to flee east of the Niger.

The Bantu peoples, numbering about 100 million, lived across large sections of Africa. Bantu societies consisted of tiny chiefdoms, starting in the third millennium B.C.E., and each group developed its own version of the original Bantu language. Instead of one Bantu people, they divided and re-divided into a great number of distinct societies sharing some common forms of government and religious belief. Chiefs evolved into kings and some were buried with considerable worldly goods made of copper, iron, and ivory. The city of Great Zimbabwe, a walled city built of stone, was a major trading center providing gold and ivory to Swahili merchants. The Bantu fashioned bells, fine pottery, bark, and raphi and, in some areas, cotton cloth.

Civilizations of the Americas

The great civilizations of early America were agricultural and foremost of these was the Mayan in Yucatan, Guatemala and eastern Honduras. The Maya developed a highly integrated society with elaborate religious observances for which they built stone and mortar pyramid temples faced with carved stone. The Maya also developed an elaborate calendar, a system of writing, and the mathematical concept of zero. Astronomy, engineering, and art were highly advanced. Mayan priests used the calendar to commemorate the erection of stone monuments and kept elaborate historical scrolls.

Mayan history is divided into three parts, the Old Empire, Middle Period, and the New Empire. During the period known as the New Empire, the Mayans built the city of Chichen Itza with its famous well in which human victims were sacrificed. By the time the Spanish conquerors arrived, most of the Mayan religious centers had been abandoned and their civilization had deteriorated seriously, perhaps due to the wide gulf between the majority of the people who were peasants and the priests and nobles.

Farther north in Mexico there arose a series of advanced cultures that derived much of their substance from the Maya. Such peoples as the Zapotecs, Totanacs, Almecs, and Toltecs evolved a high level of civilization. By 500 B.C.E. agricultural peoples had begun to use a ceremonial calendar and had built stone pyramids on which they performed religious observances. Their script was partly alphabetic and their codices dealt with history, religion, and secular affairs. Building in stone was characteristic of Mexican culture. The greatest site of the formative period of Mexican history is at San Juan, Teotihuacan, which consists of more than a hundred pyramids arranged around a long plaza and was never finished.

The Aztecs then took over Mexican culture. A major feature of their culture was human sacrifice in repeated propitiation of their chief god. Aztec government was centralized, with an elective king and a large army. Like their predecessors, they were skilled builders and engineers, accomplished astronomers and mathematicians. They built the famous city of Tenochtitlan, with 300 or more pyramids, palaces, plazas, and canals and its population perhaps numbered five million.

Andean civilization was characterized by the evolution of beautifully made pottery, intricate fabrics, and flat-topped mounds called huacas.

On the Andean plateaus, various highland cultures learned to cut stone and build palace structures, and in some cases stone pyramids. Andean cultural achievement reached a climax in the Chimu period, in which the various Andean cultures were welded into the Chimu Empire early in the common era.

The Incas, a tribe from the interior of South America who termed themselves "Children of the Sun," controlled an area stretching from Ecuador to central Chile. Sun worshippers, they believed themselves to be the vice-regent on earth of the sun god. The Inca were all powerful; every person's place in society was fixed and immutable; the state and the army were supreme. Although not so advanced in scholarship as the Mayans and Aztecs, the Incas had a well developed system of roads and were very advanced politically. They were at the apex of their power just before the Spanish conquest.

In North America, two major groups of mound builders are known as the Woodland and Mississippian peoples. The Woodland peoples lived in the Great Lakes and northern Mississippi area and built burial mounds of several varieties from 500 B.C.E. to 1000 C.E. The Mississippian peoples lived in the middle and southern Mississippi area. They built flat-topped mounds as sub-structures for wooden temples dating from 500 C.E.

In the southwestern U.S. and northern Mexico, two varieties of ancient culture can be identified, the Anasazi and the Hohokam. The Anasazi developed adobe architecture. They worked the land extensively, had a highly developed system of irrigation, and made cloth and baskets. The Hohokam built separate stone and timber houses around a central plaza. Neither peoples developed a written language.

Europe

Between 486 and 1050 C.E. Europe saw the growth of many different ethnic groups. Following Roman withdrawal from the West, much of Europe was occupied by Germanic tribes. The northern tribes became the Vikings and Norsemen. The eastern tribes (Vandals, Burgundians, and Goths) settled east of the Elbe River. The Saxons and Lombards dominated the western tribes. In Eastern Europe and Russia, the Slavs were the dominant group.

Nomadic tribes from the Central Asian steppes had invaded Europe and pushed Germanic tribes into conflict with the Roman Empire. The Huns invaded in the fourth Century, and led by Attila (406–453) again in the fifth. In 410 C.E., the Visigoths sacked Rome, followed by the Vandals in 455 C.E. In 476 the Ostrogoth king forced the boy emperor Romulus Augustulus to abdicate, ending the Roman Empire in the west.

The Frankish Kingdom was the most important medieval Germanic state. Under Clovis I (481–511) the Franks finished conquering Gaul in 486 CE. Clovis converted to Christianity and founded the Merovingian dynasty. Pepin's son Charles, known as Charles the Great or Charlemagne (r. 758–814), founded the Carolingian dynasty. He defeated the Lombards in northern Italy, declaring himself their king, and pushed the Muslims out of northern Spain. He converted the Saxons to Christianity and helped put down a revolt of Roman nobles in 799 C.E. In 800 C.E., Pope Leo III named Charlemagne Holy Roman Emperor. In the Treaty of Aix-la-Chapelle (812), the Byzantine emperor recognized Charles's authority in the West.

The Holy Roman Empire was intended to reestablish the Roman Empire in the West. Charles vested authority in 200 counts, who were each in charge of a county. Charles's son, Louis the Pious, succeeded him. On Louis's death his three sons vied for control of the Empire. After Louis II the German and Charles the Bald had sided against Lothair I, the three eventually signed the Treaty of Verdun in 843 C.E. This gave Charles the Western Kingdom (France), Louis the Eastern Kingdom (Germany) and Lothair the Middle Kingdom, a narrow strip of land running from the North Sea to the Mediterranean.

Fast Facts Manorialism and feudalism developed during the early Middle Ages.

In the ninth and tenth centuries, Europe was threatened by attacks from the Vikings in the North, the Muslims in the South, and the Magyars in the East. The Vikings occupied England, leaving only Wessex under control of the English king Alfred (r. 871–899 C.E.). King Alfred fought back and drove the invaders into an area called the Danelaw for which he earned the name "the Great." Viking invasions left France divided into small principalities. Danish Vikings seized control of Normandy and Brittany at the end of the ninth century. Under the leadership of William the Conqueror, the Normans conquered England in 1066 C.E. by his victory at the Battle of Hastings.

The Saxon king Otto I stopped the Magyar advance in the East and made the Saxons the most powerful group in Europe. In 962, Otto was crowned Holy Roman Emperor. Rome's collapse ushered in the decline of cities, a reversion to a barter economy from a money economy, and a fall in agricultural productivity with a shift to subsistence agriculture.

Manorialism and feudalism developed in this period. Manorialism refers to the economic system in which large estates, granted by the king to nobles, strove for self-sufficiency. Large manors might incorporate several villages. The lands surrounding the villages were usually divided into long strips, with common land inbetween. Ownership was divided among the lord and his serfs (also called villains). The lord's property was called the demesne.

Feudalism describes the decentralized political system of personal ties and obligations that bound vassals to their lords. Serfs were peasants who were bound to the land. They worked on the demesne three or four days a week in return for the right to work their own land. In difficult times the nobles were supposed to provide for the serfs.

The Catholic church was the only institution to survive the Germanic invasions intact. The power of the popes grew in this period. Gregory I was the first member of a monastic order to rise to the papacy. He is considered one of the four church fathers (along with Jerome, Ambrose, and Augustine). He advanced the ideas of penance and purgatory. He centralized church administration and was the first pope to rule as secular head of Rome.

Literacy nearly disappeared in Western Christendom during the early Middle Ages. Monasteries preserved the few remnants of antiquity that survived the decline. Outside the monasteries the two most important literary works of the period were *Beowulf* and the Venerable Bede's *Ecclesiastical History of the English People*.

The High Middle Ages began in 1050 C.E. Europe was poised to emerge from five centuries of decline. Inferior to the Muslim and Byzantine empires in 1050 C.E., by 1300 C.E. the Europeans had surpassed them. Between 1000 and 1350, the population grew from 38 million to 75 million. Agricultural productivity grew, aided by new technologies such as heavy plows and a slight temperature rise which produced a longer growing season. Horses were introduced into agriculture in this period, and the three-field system replaced the two-field system of farming.

As new lands came into cultivation, nobles needed an incentive to get serfs to move. Enfranchisement, or freeing of serfs, grew in this period, and many other serfs simply fled their manors for the new lands. Enfranchisement progressed most rapidly in England, and most slowly in Russia and Eastern Europe.

Charlemagne's grandson, Louis the German, became Holy Roman Emperor under the Treaty of Verdun. Under the weak leadership of his descendants, the dukes in Saxony, Franconia, Swabia, Bavaria, and the Lorraine eroded Carolingian power. The last Carolingian died in 911. The German dukes elected the leader of Franconia to lead the German lands. He was replaced in 919 by the Saxon dynasty, which ruled until 1024. Otto became Holy Roman Emperor in 962. His descendants governed the Empire until 1024 when the Franconian dynasty assumed power, reigning until 1125.

A dispute over lay investiture (in which monarchs chose the high church officials of their realm) between Pope Gregory VII (pope 1073–1085) and Emperor Henry IV came to a head in 1077 when the pope forced Henry to beg forgiveness for appointing church leaders. In revenge, Henry captured Rome in 1083 and sent the pope into exile. The dispute dragged on until 1122 when the Concordat of Worms gave the emperor the right to grant secular, but not religious authority to German bishops.

When the Franconian line died out in 1125, the Hohenstaufen family (Conrad III, r. 1138–1152) won power over a contending family. The Hapsburg line gained control of the Empire in 1273.

The Romans abandoned their last outpost in England in the fourth century. Around 450 the Jutes, Angles, and Saxons occupied different parts of the country. Danes began invading in the eighth century. Alfred the Great defeated the Danes in 878. In 959 C.E., Edgar the Peaceable became the king of all England. William stripped the Anglo-Saxon nobility of its privileges and instituted feudalism. He ordered a survey of all property of the realm, which was recorded in the Domesday Book (1086). His descendants, William II and Henry I, continued to centralize the kingdom. Henry created the Office of the Exchequer to monitor receipt of taxes.

Nineteen years of civil war followed Henry's death. In 1154 his grandson Henry II was crowned king, founding the Plantagenet dynasty. Henry inherited Brittany from his mother. His reign was controversial, marked by a power struggle with the pope (during which Henry supposedly had Thomas Becket murdered) and his son's revolt. In 1189 Richard the Lionhearted succeeded his father and spent most of his reign fighting on Crusade and in France.

Richard's brother, John I, became king upon his brother's death in 1199. In 1215 the English barons forced John to sign the Magna Carta Libertatum, acknowledging their "ancient" privileges. Magna Carta established the principle of a limited English monarchy, monitored by the barons. Henry III reigned from 1216–1272. In 1272 Edward I became king. His need for revenue led him to convene a parliament of English nobles, which would act as a check upon royal power.

France and the Capetian Dynasty

The creation of a strong national monarchy was slower in France than in England. Hugh Capet founded the dynasty in 987 but it had little power until 1108 when Louis the Fat subdued his most powerful vassals. Louis's grandson Philip Augustus defeated King John of England to win large territories in western France. Philip's son, Louis VIII, conquered most of southern France during his prosperous three year reign. His grandson Philip IV ("The Fair") involved France in several wars. Philip also summoned a parliament, the Estates General, but it did not develop into a counterweight to royal power. In 1328, the Capetian dynasty ended with the death of Charles IV. Since Edward III, king of England, had a claim to the French throne, the succession sparked the Hundred Years' War between England and France.

Spain under the Muslims

In 710, the Muslims conquered Visigothic Spain. Under the Muslims, Spain enjoyed a stable, prosperous government. The caliphate of Cordoba became a center of scientific and intellectual activity. Internal dissent caused the collapse of Cordoba and the division of Spain into more than 20 Muslim states in 1031.

The Reconquista (1085–1340) wrested control of Spain from the Muslims. Rodrigo Diaz de Bivar, known as El Cid, was the most famous of its knights. The small Christian states of Navarre, Aragon, Castile, and Portugal organized the Reconquista. Each had a *cortes*, an assembly of nobles, clergy, and townspeople. The fall of Cordoba in 1234 completed the Reconquista, except for the small Muslim state of Granada.

Most of Eastern Europe and Russia had never been under Rome's control, and they were cut off from Western influence by the Germanic invasions. Poland converted to Christianity in the tenth century and after 1025 was dependent on the Holy Roman Empire. In the twelfth and thirteenth centuries, powerful nobles divided control of the country.

The Crusades

The Crusades attempted to liberate the Holy Land from "infidels." There were seven major crusades between 1096 and 1300. Urban II called Christians to the First Crusade with the promise of a plenary indulgence (exemption from punishment in purgatory). Younger sons who would not inherit their father's lands were attracted by the prospect of travelling to foreign lands.

Several months later, the organized Crusaders reached the Holy Land, capturing Jerusalem in 1099. They established four feudal Crusader states: Edessa, Antioch, Tripoli, and Jerusalem. The success of the First Crusade sparked a movement of pilgrims to the Levant and the organization of several religious and military orders to aid the pilgrims, including the Knights of St. John (Hospitalers), the Templars, and the Teutonic Knights. The Second Crusade (1147–1149) attempted to recapture Edessa and failed.

In 1187 the Muslim leader Saladin captured Jerusalem, sparking the Third Crusade, which failed to dislodge the Muslims, though Richard the Lionheart negotiated the right of Christian pilgrims to visit shrines in Jerusalem.

In the Fourth Crusade (1202–1204) the Crusaders never reached the Holy Land. They had hired the Venetians to transport them to Jerusalem in payment for which they agreed to loot Constantinople, which fell to them in 1204. The Crusaders then established the Latin kingdom of Constantinople, but it was recaptured by the Byzantine emperor's troops 57 years later.

In the Fifth Crusade (1228–1229), the Holy Roman Emperor Frederick II negotiated what the Crusaders could not win by force: control of Jerusalem and Nazareth. In the Sixth Crusade (1248–1254) Louis IX tried unsuccessfully to capture Egypt. In 1270 Louis IX died outside of Tunis in the Seventh Crusade. In 1291 Acre, the last Christian enclave in the Holy Land fell.

The Crusades helped to renew interest in the ancient world. But thousands of Jews and Muslims were massacred as a result of the Crusades, and relations between Europe and the Byzantine Empire collapsed.

Philosophy and the Arts in Europe

Charlemagne mandated that bishops open schools at each cathedral and founded a school in his palace for his court. The expansion of trade and the need for clerks and officials who could read and write spurred an 1179 requirement that each cathedral set aside enough money to support one teacher. The first universities opened in Italy at Bologna and Salerno, which became respective centers for legal and medical studies. Others followed, notably in Paris, Salamanca, and Oxford.

Scholasticism was an effort to reconcile reason and faith, and to instruct Christians on how to make sense of the pagan tradition. Peter Abelard (1097–1142) was a controversial proponent of Scholasticism both for his love affair with Heloise, niece of the canon of Notre Dame, and for his views. In *Sic et Non* (*Yes and No*), Abelard collected statements from the Bible and church leaders that contradicted each other. Abelard believed that reason could resolve the apparent contradictions between the two authorities, but the church judged his views as heretical.

Thomas Aquinas, whose doctrines remained influential in church teachings for some time, believed that there were two orders of truth. The lower, reason, could demonstrate propositions such as the existence of God, but on a higher level, some of God's mysteries such as the nature of the Trinity must be accepted on faith. Aquinas viewed the universe as a great chain of being, with humans midway on the chain, between the material and the spiritual. His *Summa Theologica* helped to incorporate the scientific approach of Aristotle with Catholic doctrine.

Latin was the language used in universities. Groups of satirical poets called Golliards also wrote in Latin. But the most vibrant works were in the vernacular. The *chansons de geste* were long, epic poems composed between 1050 and 1150. Among the most famous are the *Song of Roland*, the *Song of the Nebelungs*, the *Icelandic Eddas,* and *El Cid*. The *fabliaux* were

Fast Facts

All of Europe was devastated by the Black Death during the late Middle Ages (1300–1500).

short stories, many of which ridiculed the clergy. Boccaccio and Chaucer belonged to this tradition. The works of Dante, the greatest medieval poet, synthesized the pagan and Christian traditions, both in form and in content.

In this period, polyphonic (more than one melody at a time) music was introduced. In architecture, Romanesque architecture (rounded arches, thick stone walls, tiny windows) flourished between 1000 and 1150. After 1150 Gothic architecture, which emphasized the use of light, came into vogue because new building techniques, such as the peaked arch and the flying buttress, permitted thinner walls, larger windows, and taller buildings.

The Late Middle Ages

The Middle Ages exist chronologically between the classical world of Greece and Rome and the modern world. The papacy and monarchs, after exercising much power and influence in the high Middle Ages, were in eclipse after 1300. During the late Middle Ages (1300–1500), all of Europe suffered from the Black Death. While England and France engaged in destructive warfare in northern Europe, in Italy the Renaissance had begun by around 1400.

The governments of medieval Europe did not have the control over their lands that we associate with modern governments. Toward the end of the period, monarchs began to assert their power and control. The major struggle of the period, between England and France, was the Hundred Years' War (1337–1453).

The English king, Edward III, had a claim to the French throne through his mother, a princess of France. Thus, France faced a succession crisis. The English king was the vassal of the French king for the duchy of Aquitaine, and the French king wanted control of the duchy; this was the event that started the fighting. Additionally, French nobles sought opportunities to gain power at the expense of the French king. England also exported its wool to Flanders, which was coming under the influence of the king of France. Finally, kings and nobles shared the values of chivalry which portrayed war as a glorious and uplifting adventure.

The war was fought in France, though the Scots (with French encouragement via the Auld Alliance) invaded northern England. A few major battles occurred—Crecy (1346), Poitiers (1356), and Agincourt (1415). The war nonetheless consisted largely of sieges and raids. Eventually, it became one of attrition; the French slowly wore down the English. Technological changes during the war included the use of English longbows, the increasingly expensive plate armor of knights, and gunpowder weapons.

Joan of Arc (1412–1431), an illiterate peasant girl who said she heard voices of saints, rallied the French army for several victories. Joan's victories led to Charles VII being crowned king at Rheims, the traditional location for enthronement. Joan was later captured by the Burgundians, allies of England, and sold to the English, who tried her for heresy (witchcraft). She was burned at the stake at Rouen.

As a result of the war, England lost all of its continental possessions, except Calais. French farmland was devastated by the war, and England and France both expended great sums of money. Population, especially in France, declined though both countries struggled. Both countries also suffered internal disruption as soldiers plundered and local officials left to fight the war. Trade everywhere was disrupted and England's wool trade with the Low Countries slumped badly. To cover these financial burdens, heavy taxation was inflicted on the peasants.

A series of factional struggles led to the deposition of Richard II in 1399. The Hundred Years' War ended with England finally stretched beyond its resources; it was evicted from Guyenne in 1453 and thus had its French territories pared down to Calais. The English nobility continued fighting each other in the War of the Roses (1450–1485), choosing sides in the dynastic struggle between the Lancastrians or Yorkists.

Literature also came to express nationalism as it was written in the language of the people instead of in Latin. Geoffrey Chaucer, the first of the great English poets, was inspired by Italian authors, particularly Bocaccio; his best known work is the unfinished *Canterbury Tales.* François Villon in his *Grand Testament* emphasized the ordinary life of the French with humor and emotion.

The New Monarchs

Nobles claimed various levels of independence under feudal rules or traditions. Forming an assembly provided some sort of a meeting forum for nobles. Furthermore the core of royal armies consisted of nobles. Many of the higher clergy of the church were noble-born. Additionally, some towns had obtained independence during times of trouble. Church and clergy saw the pope as their leader. The defeat of the English in the Hundred Years' War and of the Duchy of Burgundy in 1477 removed major military threats. Trade was expanded, fostered by the merchant Jacques Coeur (1395–1456). Louis XI (1461–1483) demonstrated ruthlessness in dealing with his nobility as individuals and collectively in the Estates General.

The marriage of Isabella of Castile and Ferdinand of Aragon created a united Spain. The Muslims were defeated at Granada in 1492. Navarre was conquered in 1512.

A government organization called the Mesta encouraged sheep farming. An alliance with a group of cities and towns, the Hermandad, was formed to oppose the nobility. Finally, reform and control of the church was enacted through the Inquisition.

Renaissance, Reformation, and Enlightenment

Renaissance (1300–1600)

The Renaissance emphasized new learning, including the rediscovery of much classical material and new art styles.

Italian city-states such as Venice, Milan, Padua, Pisa, and especially Florence were the home to many Renaissance developments, which were limited to the rich elite. Jacob Burkhardt's *The Civilization of the*

Renaissance in Italy (1860) popularized the study of the period and argued that it was a strong contrast to the Middle Ages. Subsequent historians have often found more continuity with the Middle Ages.

Humanists, as both orators and poets, were inspired by and imitated works of the classical past. The literature was more secular and wide ranging than that of the Middle Ages. Dante (1265–1321) was a Florentine writer who spent much of his life in exile after being on the losing side in political struggles in Florence. His *Divine Comedy*, describing a journey through hell, purgatory, and heaven, shows that reason can only take people so far and that God's grace and revelation must be used. Dealing with many other issues and with much symbolism, this work is the pinnacle of medieval poetry.

Petrarch (1304–1374), who wrote in both Latin and Italian, encouraged the study of ancient Rome, collected and preserved work of ancient writers, and produced much work in the classical literary style. He is best known for his sonnets, including many expressing his love for a married woman named Laura, and is considered the father of humanism. Boccaccio (1313–1375) wrote *The Decameron* a collection of short stories in Italian which were meant to amuse, not edify, the reader.

Artists also broke with the medieval past in both technique and content. Renaissance art sometimes used religious topics, but often dealt with secular themes or portraits of individuals. Oil paints, chiaroscuro, and linear perspective produced works of energy in three dimensions.

Michelangelo's *Creation of Man*, which he painted on the Sistine Chapel, Rome, Italy.

Several artists became associated with the new style or art. Leonardo da Vinci (1452–1519) produced numerous works, including *The Last Supper* and *Mona Lisa*, as well as many mechanical designs, though few were ever constructed. Raphael, a master of Renaissance grace and style, theory and technique represented these skills in the *School of Athens*. Michelangelo, a universal man, produced masterpieces in architecture, sculpture (*David*), and painting (the Sistine Chapel). His work was a bridge to a new, non-Renaissance style called Mannerism.

Renaissance scholars were more practical and secular than medieval ones. Manuscript collections enabled scholars to study the primary sources and to reject all traditions which had been built up since classical times. Also, scholars participated in the lives of their cities as active politicians.

Leonardo Bruni (1370–1444), a civic humanist, served as chancellor of Florence, where he used his rhetorical skills to rouse the citizens against external enemies. He also wrote a history of his city and was the first to use the term humanism. Machiavelli (1469–1527) wrote *The Prince*, which analyzed politics from the standpoint of expediency rather than faith or tradition. His work advocated the acquisition and maintenance of power by any means.

The Reformation

The Reformation destroyed Western Europe's religious unity and introduced new ideas about the relationships between God, the individual, and society. Its course was greatly influenced by politics and led, in most areas, to the subjection of the church to the political rulers.

Earlier threats to the unity of the church had been made by the works of John Wycliffe and John Hus. The abuses of church practices and positions upset many people. Likewise, Christian humanists had been criticizing abuses. Personal piety and mysticism, which were alternative approaches to Christianity and did not require the apparatus of the institutional church and the clergy, appeared in the late Middle Ages.

Martin Luther (1483–1546)

Martin Luther was a miner's son from Saxony in Central Germany. At the urgings of his father, he studied for a career in law. While traveling he underwent a religious experience that led him to become an Augustinian friar. Later he became a professor at the university in Wittenberg, Saxony.

Luther to his personal distress could not reconcile the problem of the sinfulness of the individual with the justice of God. How could a sinful person attain the righteousness necessary to obtain salvation? He wondered. During his studies of the Bible, especially of Romans 1:17, Luther came to believe that personal efforts—good works such as a Christian life and attention to the sacraments of the church – could not "earn" the sinner salvation, but that belief and faith were the only way to obtain grace. By 1515, Luther believed that justification by faith alone and that the scriptures are the sole source of faith.

Indulgences, which had originated in connection with the Crusades, involved the cancellation of the penalty given by the church to a confessed sinner. Indulgences had long been a means of raising money for church activities. In 1517, the pope was building the new cathedral of St. Peter in Rome. Also, Albrecht, archbishop of Mainz, had purchased three church positions (simony and pluralism) by borrowing money from the banking family, the Fuggers. A Dominican friar, John Tetzel, was authorized to preach and sell indulgences, with the proceeds going to build the cathedral and repay the loan. The popular belief was that "As soon as the coin in the coffer rings, the soul from purgatory springs," and Tetzl had much business. On October 31, 1517, Luther, with his belief that no such control or influence could be had over salvation, nailed 95 theses, or statements, about indulgences to the door of the Wittenberg church and challenged the practice of selling indulgences. At this time, he was seeking to reform the church, not divide it.

In 1519, Luther presented various criticisms of the church and was driven to say that only the Bible, not religious traditions or papal statements, could determine correct religious practices and beliefs. In 1521, Pope Leo X excommunicated Luther for his beliefs. In 1521, Luther appeared in the city of Worms before a meeting (diet) of the important figures of the Holy Roman Empire, including the Emperor, Charles V. He was again condemned. At the Diet of Worms Luther made his famous statement about his writings and the basis for them: "Here I stand, I can do no other." After this, Luther could not go back; the break with the pope was permanent.

Frederick III of Saxony, the ruler of the territory in which Luther resided, protected Luther in Wartburg Castle for a year. Frederick never accepted Luther's beliefs, but protected him because Luther was his subject. The weak political control of the Holy Roman Emperor contributed to Luther's success in avoiding the pope's and the Emperor's penalties.

Other Reformers

Anabaptist (derived from a Greek word meaning to baptize again) is a name applied to people who rejected the validity of child baptism and believed that such children had to be rebaptized when they became adults.

Anabaptists sought to return to the practices of the early Christian church which was a voluntary association of believers with no connection to the state. Anabaptists adopted pacifism and avoided involvement with the state whenever possible. Today, the Mennonites, founded by Menno Simons (1496–1561) and the Amish are the descendents of the Anabaptists.

In 1536, John Calvin (1509–1564), a Frenchmen, arrived in Geneva, a Swiss city-state which had adopted an anti-Catholic position. He left after his first efforts at reform failed. Upon his return in 1540, Geneva became the Center of the Reformation. Calvin's Institutes of the Christian Religion (1536), a strictly logical analysis of Christianity, had a universal appeal. Calvin brought knowledge of organizing a city from his stay in Strasbourg, which was being led by the reformer Martin Bucer (1491–1551). Calvin emphasized the doctrine of predestination (God knew who would obtain salvation before those people were born) and believed that church and state should be united.

Calvinism triumphed as the majority religion in Scotland, under the leadership of John Knox (1514–1572) and in the United Provinces of the Netherlands. Puritans in England and New England also accepted Calvinism.

Reform in England

England underwent reforms in a pattern different from the rest of Europe. Personal and political decisions by the rulers determined much of the course of the Reformation there. Henry VIII (1509–1547) married Catherine of Aragon, the widow of his older brother. By 1526 Henry became convinced that he was unable to produce a legitimate son to inherit his throne because he had violated God's commandments (Leviticus 18:16, 20:21) by marrying his brother's widow.

Soon, Henry fell in love with Anne Boleyn and decided to annul his marriage to Catherine in order to marry Anne. Pope Clement VII, who had the authority necessary to issues such an annulment, was, after 1527, under the political control of Charles V, Catherine's nephew. Efforts by Cardinal Wolsey (1473–1530) to secure the annulment ended in failure and Wolsey's disgrace. Thomas Cranmer (1489–1556), named archbishop in 1533, dissolved Henry's marriage. Henry married Anne Boleyn in January 1533. In 1536, Thomas More was executed for rejecting Henry's leadership of the English church. Protestant beliefs and practices made little headway during Henry's reign, as he accepted transubstantiation, enforced celibacy among the clergy, and otherwise made the English church conform to most Catholic practices.

Under Henry VIII's son, Edward VI (1537–1553), who succeeded to the throne at the age of ten, the English church adopted Calvinism. Clergy were allowed to marry, communion by the laity expanded, and images were removed from churches. The doctrine included justification by faith, the denial of transubstantiation, and only two sacraments.

From 1553–1558, England was ruled by Queen Mary I, daughter of Henry VIII. An ardent Catholic, Mary sought to restore the Roman church in England. In 1554, Mary wed Philip II, heir to the Spanish throne, creating fear and suspicion among many who were anti-Catholic and anti-Spanish. Mary pursued a policy of carefully dismantling a number of the religious reforms undertaken by her brother and father, although she was met with fierce resistance along the way. Mary came to be known by the vivid moniker "Bloody Mary" in the wake of mass executions of Protestants who refused to acquiesce to her attempts to reintroduce Catholicism in England. Mary's own mental and physical condition was fragile, and her husband, upon ascending to the Spanish throne, was largely absent from England. She lapsed into depression and became delusional. Her death in 1558 cleared the way for her sister who had no intention of continuing Mary's Catholic program.

Under Elizabeth I (1558–1603), who was Henry VIII's daughter and half-sister to Edward and Mary, the church in England adopted Protestant beliefs again. The Elizabethan Settlement required outward conformity to the official church, but rarely inquired about inward beliefs. Some practices of the church, including ritual, resembled the Catholic practices. Catholicism remained, especially among the gentry, but could not be practiced openly. Some reformers wanted to purify (hence Puritans) the church of its remaining Catholic aspects. The resulting church, Protestant in doctrine and practice but retaining most of the physical possessions, such as buildings, and many of the powers, such as church courts, of the medieval church, was called Anglican.

The Counter-Reformation

The Counter-Reformation brought changes to the portion of the Western Church, which retained its allegiance to the pope. Some historians see this as a reform of the Catholic Church, similar to what Protestants were doing, while others see it as a result of the criticisms of Protestants. Ignatius of Loyola (1491–1556), a former soldier, founded the Society of Jesus in 1540 to lead the attack on Protestantism. Jesuits, as the order's followers are known became the leaders of the Counter Reformation. By the 1540s Jesuits, including Francis Xavier (1506–1552), traveled to Japan as missionaries.

Popes resisted reform efforts, fearing what a council of church leaders might do to papal powers. The Sack of Rome in 1527, when soldiers of the Holy Roman emperor captured and looted Rome, was seen by many as a judgment of God against the lives of the Renaissance popes. In 1534, Paul III became pope and attacked abuses while reasserting papal leadership.

The Wars of Religion (1560–1648)

The approximate period of 1560–1648 witnessed continuing warfare, primarily between Protestants and Catholics. Though religion was not the only reason for the wars—occasionally Catholics and Protestants were allies—it was the dominant cause. In the latter half of the sixteenth century, the fighting was along the Atlantic seaboard between Calvinists and Catholics; after 1600 the warfare spread to Germany, where Calvinists, Lutherans, and Catholics fought.

The Catholic Crusade

The territories of Charles V, emperor of the Holy Roman Empire, were divided in 1556 between Ferdinand, Charles's brother, and Philip II (1556–1598), Charles's son. Ferdinand received Austria, Hungary, Bohemia, and the title of Holy Roman Emperor. Philip received Spain, Milan, Naples, the Netherlands, and the New World. Both parts of the Hapsburg family cooperated in international matters.

Philip was a man of severe personal habits, deeply religious, and a hard worker. Solemn (it is said he only laughed once in his life, when the report of the St. Bartholomew's Day Massacre reached him) and reclusive (he built the Escorial outside Madrid as a palace, monastery, and eventual tomb), he devoted his life and the wealth of Spain to making Europe Catholic. It was Philip, not the pope, who led the Catholic attack on Protestants.

The gold and silver of the New World flowed into Spain, especially following the opening of the silvers mines at Potesi in Peru. Spain dominated the Mediterranean following a series of wars led by Philip's half-brother, Don John, against Muslim (largely Turkish) forces. Don John secured the Mediterranean for Christian merchants with a naval victory over the Turks at Lepanto off the coast of Greece in 1571. Portugal was annexed by Spain in 1580 following the death of the king without a clear successor. This gave Philip the only other large navy of the day as well as Portuguese territories around the globe. Calvinism was spreading in England, France, the Netherlands, and Germany. Calvinists supported each other, often disregarding their countries' borders.

England and Spain

England was ruled by two queens, Mary I (reigned 1553–1558) who married Philip II, and then Elizabeth I (reigned 1558–1603), while three successive kings of France from 1559 to 1589 were influenced by their mother, Catherine de Medici (1519–1589). Women rulers were a novelty in European politics. Monarchs attempted to strengthen their control and the unity of their countries, a process which nobles often resisted. Mary I was the daughter of Henry VIII and Catherine of Aragon. Mary sought to make England Catholic. She executed many Protestants, earning the nickname "Bloody Mary" from opponents. To escape persecution, many English went into exile on the Continent in Frankfurt, Geneva, and elsewhere, where they learned more radical Protestant ideas. Mary married Philip II, king of Spain, and organized her foreign policy around Spanish interests. They had no children. Elizabeth I, a Protestant, achieved a religious settlement between 1559 and 1563 which left England with a church governed by bishops and practicing Catholic rituals, but maintaining Calvinist doctrine. Though suppressed by Elizabeth's government, Puritans were not condemned to death.

Catholics participated in several rebellions and plots. Mary, Queen of Scots had fled to England from Scotland in 1568, after alienating the nobles there. In Catholic eyes, she was the legitimate queen of England. Several plots and rebellions to put Mary on the throne led to her execution in 1587. Elizabeth was formally excommunicated by the pope in 1570. In 1588, as part of his crusade and to stop England from supporting the rebels in the Netherlands, Philip II sent the Armada, a fleet of more than 125 ships, to convey troops from the Netherlands to England as part of a plan to make England Catholic. The Armada was defeated by a combination of superior naval tactics and a wind which made it impossible for the Spanish to accomplish their goal. A peace treaty between Spain and England was signed in 1604, but England remained an opponent of Spain.

The Thirty Years' War

Calvinism was spreading throughout Germany. The Peace of Augsburg (1555), which settled the disputes between Lutherans and Catholics, had no provision for Calvinists. Lutherans gained more territories through conversions and often took control of previous church-states—a violation of the

Peace of Augsburg. A Protestant alliance under the leadership of the Calvinist ruler of the Palatinate opposed a Catholic League led by the ruler of Bavaria. Religious wars were common.

Not all issues pitted Protestants versus Catholics. The Lutheran ruler of Saxony joined the Catholics in the attack on Elector Palatine Frederick at White Mountain, and Albrecht of Wallenstein, the leading general for the Holy Roman Emperor Ferdinand, was a Protestant. The Thirty Years' War (1618–1648), the result of a cauldron of issues including religious conflict, trade rivalries, and territorial disputes, brought great destruction to Germany, leading to a decline in population of perhaps one-third, or more, in some areas. Germany remained divided and without a strong government until the nineteenth century. After 1648, warfare, though often containing religious elements, would not be executed primarily for religious goals. The Catholic crusade to reunite Europe failed, largely due to the efforts of the Calvinists. The religious distribution of Europe has not changed significantly since 1648. Nobles, resisting the increasing power of the state, usually dominated the struggle. France, then Germany, fell apart due to the wars. France was reunited religiously in the seventeenth century. Spain began a decline which ended its role as a great power of Europe.

The Growth of the State and the Age of Exploration

In the seventeenth century, the political systems of the countries of Europe began dividing into two types, absolutist and constitutionalist. England, the United Provinces, and Sweden moved towards constitutionalism, while France was adopting absolutist ideas. Overseas exploration, begun in the fifteenth century, expanded. Governments supported such activity in order to gain wealth and to preempt other countries.

England

The English church was a compromise of Catholic practices and Protestant beliefs and was criticized by both groups. The monarchs, after 1620, gave leadership of the church to men with Arminian beliefs, a modified Calvinist creed that deemphasized predestination. Arminius (1560–1609), a Dutch theologian, had shifted the emphasis in Calvinist beliefs—if only slightly—away from absolute predestination. English Arminians also stressed the role of ritual in church services and sought to enjoy the "beauty of holiness," which their opponents viewed as too Catholic. William Laud (1573–1645), Archbishop of Canterbury, accelerated the growth of Arminianism.

Opponents to this shift in belief were called Puritans, a term that covered a wide range of beliefs and people. To escape the church in England, many Puritans began moving to the New World, especially Massachusetts. Both James I and Charles I made decisions, which, to Puritans, favored Catholics too much.

In financial matters, inflation and Elizabeth's wars left the government short of money. Contemporaries blamed the shortage on the extravagance of the courts of James I and Charles I. James I sold titles of nobility in an effort to raise money, annoying nobles with older titles. The monarchs lacked any substantial source of income and had to obtain the consent of a Parliament to levy a tax.

Parliament met only when the monarch summoned it. Though Parliaments had existed since the Middle Ages, there were long periods of time between parliamentary meetings. Parliaments consisted of nobles and gentry, and a few merchants and lawyers. The men in a Parliament usually wanted the government to remedy grievances as part of the agreement to a tax. In 1621, for the first time since the Middle Ages, the power to impeach governmental servants was used by a Parliament to eliminate men who offended its members.

James I ended the war with Spain and avoided any other entanglements. The Earl of Somerset and then the Duke of Buckingham served as favorites for the king, doing much of the work of government. Charles I inherited both the English and Scottish thrones at the death of his father, James I. Like his father, he claimed a "divine right" theory of absolute authority for himself as king and sought to rule to rule without Parliament. That rule also meant control of the Church of England. Henrietta Maria, a sister of the King of France and a Catholic, became his queen. Charles stumbled into wars with both Spain and France during the late 1620s. A series of efforts to raise money for the wars led to confrontations with his opponents in Parliament. A "forced loan" was collected from taxpayers with the promise it would be repaid when a tax was voted by a Parliament. Soldiers were billeted in subjects' houses during the wars. People were imprisoned for resisting these royal actions. In 1626, the Duke of Buckingham was nearly impeached. In 1628, Parliament passed the Petition of Right, which declared royal actions involving loans and billeting illegal.

Charles ruled without calling a Parliament during the 1630s. A policy of "thorough"–strict efficiency and much Central government activity—was followed, which included reinstating many old forms of taxation. In August 1642, Charles abandoned all hope of negotiating with his opponents and instead declared war against them. Charles's supporters were called Royalists or Cavaliers. His opponents were called Parliamentarians or Roundheads, due to many who wore their hair cut short. This struggle is called variously the Puritan Revolution, the English Civil War, or the Great Rebellion. Charles was ultimately defeated. His opponents had allied with the Scots, who still had an army in England. Additionally, the New Model Army with its general, Oliver Cromwell (1599–1658), was made up of common people, mostly volunteers, who could attain rank through merit rather than by aristocratic birth. The New Model Army became a cauldron of radical political ideas.

France

The regions of France had long had a large measure of independence, and local parliaments could refuse to enforce royal laws. The centralization of all government proceeded by replacing local authorities with intendants, civil servants who reported to the king. As a result of the Edict of Nantes, the Huguenots had separate rights and powers. All efforts to unify France under one religion faced both internal resistance from the Huguenots and the difficulty of dealing with Protestant powers abroad. By 1650 France had been ruled by only one competent adult monarch since 1559. Louis XIII came to the throne at age of nine and Louis XIV at the age of five. The mothers of both kings, Maria de' Medici and Anne of Austria, governed until the boys were of age. Both queens relied on chief ministers to help govern: Cardinal Richelieu and Cardinal Mazarin (1602–1661). Henry IV relied on the Duke of Sully (1560–1641), the first of a series of strong ministers in the seventeenth century. Sully and Henry increased the involvement of the state in the economy, acting on a theory known as mercantilism. Monopolies on the production of gunpowder and salt were developed.

Louis XIII reigned from 1610 to 1643 but Cardinal Richelieu became the real power in France. Foreign policy was difficult because of the problems of religion. The unique status of the Huguenots was reduced through warfare and the Peace of Alais (1629), when their separate armed cities were eliminated. The nobility was reduced in power through constant attention to the laws and the imprisonment of offenders.

Cardinal Mazarin governed while Louis XIV (r. 1643–1715) was a minor. During the Fronde, from 1649 to 1652, the nobility controlled Paris, drove Louis XIV and Mazarin from the city and tried to run the government. Noble ineffectiveness, the memories of the chaos of the wars of religion, and the overall anarchy convinced most people that a strong king was preferable to a warring nobility. The Fronde had little impact. Louis XIV saw the need to increase royal power and his own glory and dedicated his life to these goals. He steadily pursued a policy of "one king, one law, one faith."

Portugal

Prince Henry the Navigator (1394–1460) supported exploration of the African coastline, largely in order to seek gold. Bartholomew Dias (1450–1500) rounded the southern tip of Africa in 1487. Vasco da Gama (1460–1524) reached India in 1498 and, after some fighting, soon established an empire in the Spice Islands after 1510.

Spain

Christopher Columbus (1451–1506), seeking a new route to the East Indies, "discovered" the Americas in 1492. Sailing under the Spanish flag, the Portuguese sailor Ferdinand Magellan (1480–1521) circumnavigated the globe in 1521–1522. Conquests of the Aztecs by Hernando Cortes (1485–1547), and the Incas by Francisco Pizarro (ca. 1476–1541), enabled the Spanish to send much gold and silver back to Spain.

Other Countries

In the 1490s the Cabots, John (1450–1498) and Sebastian (ca. 1483–1557) explored North America, and after 1570, various Englishmen, including Francis Drake (ca. 1540–1596) fought the Spanish around the world. Jacques Cartier (1491–1557) explored parts of North America for France in 1534.

Samuel de Champlain and the French explored the St. Lawrence River, seeking furs to trade. The Dutch established settlements at New Amsterdam and in the Hudson River Valley. The Dutch founded trading Centers in the East Indies, the West Indies, and southern Africa. Swedes settled on the Delaware River in 1638.

Bourbon, Baroque, and the Enlightenment

Through the Treaty of Paris (1763) France lost all possessions in North America to Britain. (In 1762 France had ceded to Spain all French claims west of the Mississippi River and New Orleans.) France retained fishing rights off the coast of Newfoundland and two sugar-producing islands of Martinique and Guadeloupe in the West Indies. Spain ceded the Floridas to Britain in exchange for the return of Cuba.

France entered the French-American Alliance of 1778 in an effort to regain lost prestige in Europe and to weaken her British adversary. In 1779, Spain joined France in the war, hoping to recover Gibraltar and the Floridas. Rochambeau's (1725–1807) and Lafayette's (1757–1834) French troops aided Washington at Yorktown.

With the Treaty of Paris (1783) Britain recognized the independence of the United States of America and retro ceded the Floridas to Spain. Britain left France no territorial gains by signing a separate and territorially generous treaty with the United States.

Economic Developments

There were several basic assumptions of mercantilism: 1) wealth is measured in terms of commodities, especially gold and silver, rather than in terms of productivity and income-producing investment; 2) economic activities should increase the power of the national government in the direction of state controls; 3) since a favorable balance of trade was important, a nation should purchase as little as possible from nations regarded as enemies. The concept of the mutual advantage of trade was not widely accepted; 4) colonies existed for the benefit of the mother country, not for any mutual benefit that would be gained by economic development.

Absentee landlords and commercial farms replaced feudal manors, particularly in England. Urbanization, increased population, and improvement in trade stimulated the demand for agricultural products. The design of farm implements improved. Drainage and reclamation of swamp land was expanded. Experiments with crops, seeds, machines, breeds of animals, and fertilizers were systematically attempted.

The construction of canals and roads was of fundamental importance. The major rivers of France were linked by canals during the seventeenth century. Thomas Newcomen in 1706 invented an inefficient steam engine as a pump. James Watt, between 1765 and 1769 improved the design so that the expansive power of hot steam could drive a piston. Later, Watt translated the motion of the piston into rotary motion. The steam engine became one of the most significant inventions in human history. It was no longer necessary to locate factories on mountain streams where water wheels were used to supply power. Its portability meant that both steamboats and railroad engines could be built to transport goods across continents. Ocean-going vessels were no longer dependent on winds to power them.

At the same time, textile machines revolutionized that industry. John Kay introduced the flying shuttle in 1733. James Hargreaves patented the spinning jenny in 1770. Richard Arkwright perfected the spinning frame in 1769. Samuel Crompton introduced the spinning mule in 1779. Edward Cartwright invented the power loom in 1785.

Bourbon France

Louis XIV (r. 1643–1715) was vain, arrogant, and charming. The king had hours of council meetings and endless ceremonies and entertainments. He aspired to be an absolute ruler. The king believed in royal absolutism, where the most effective government was one in which the king had unquestioned authority. Louis XIV deliberately chose his chief ministers from the middle class in order to keep the aristocracy out of government. No members of the royal family or the high aristocracy were admitted to the daily council sessions at Versailles, where the king presided personally over the deliberations of his ministers. Council orders were transmitted to the provinces by intendants, who supervised all phases of local administration (especially courts, police, and the collection of taxes). Additionally, Louis XIV nullified the power of French institutions that might challenge his centralized bureaucracy. Louis XIV never called the Estates General. His intendants arrested the members of the three provincial estates who criticized royal policy, and the parlements were too intimidated by the lack of success of the Frondes to offer further resistance. Control of the peasants who comprised 95 percent of the French population was accomplished by numerous means. Some peasants kept as little as 20 percent of their cash crops after paying the landlord, the government, and the church. Peasants also were subject to the corvée, a month's forced labor on the roads. People not at work on the farm were conscripted into the French army or put into workhouses. Finally, rebels were hanged or forced to work as galley slaves.

Under Louis XV (r. 1715–1774), French people of all classes desired greater popular participation in government and resented the special privileges of the aristocracy. All nobles were exempt from certain taxes. Many were subsidized with regular pensions from the government. The highest offices of the government were reserved for aristocrats. Promotions were based on political connections rather than merit. Life at Versailles was wasteful, extravagant, and frivolous. There was no uniform code of laws and little justice, and the king had arbitrary powers of imprisonment. Government bureaucrats were often petty tyrants, many of them merely serving their own interests. The bureaucracy became virtually a closed class. Vestiges of the feudal and manorial systems taxed peasants excessively compared to other segments of society. A group of intellectuals called the philosophes gave expression to these grievances as discontent grew. When Louis XV died, he left many of the same problems he had inherited from his great grandfather Louis XIV. Corruption and inequity in government were even more pronounced. Ominously, crowds lined the road to St. Denis, the burial place of French kings and cursed the king's casket just as they had his predecessor.

Louis XVI (r. 1774–1792) was the grandson of Louis XV. He married Marie Antoinette (1770), daughter of the Austrian Empress Maria Theresa. Louis XVI was honest, conscientious, and sought genuine reforms, but he was indecisive and lacking in determination. He antagonized the aristocracy when he sought fiscal reforms. One of his first acts was to restore judicial powers to the French parlements. When he sought to impose new taxes on the undertaxed aristocracy, the parlements refused to register the royal decrees. In 1787, he granted toleration and civil rights to French Huguenots (Protestants). In that same year, the king summoned the Assembly of the Notables, a group of 144 representatives of the nobility and higher clergy. Louis XVI asked them to tax all lands, without regard to privilege of family; to establish provincial assemblies; to allow free trade in grain; and to abolish forced labor on the roads. The Notables refused to accept these reforms and demanded the replacement of certain of the king's ministers. The climax of the crisis came in 1788 when the king was no longer able to achieve either fiscal reform or new loans. He could not even pay the salaries of government officials. By this time one-half of the government revenues went to pay interest on the national debt (at eight percent). For the first time in 175 years, the king called for a meeting of the Estates General (1789). The Estates General formed itself into the National Assembly and the French Revolution was under way.

England, Scotland, and Ireland

One of the underlying issues in the English Civil War (1642–1649) was the constitutional issue of the relationship between the king and Parliament. Could the king govern without the consent of Parliament, or go against the wishes of Parliament? In short, the question was whether England was to have a limited constitutional monarchy, or an absolute monarchy as in France and Prussia.

The theological issue focused on the form of church government England was to have—whether it would follow the established Church of England's hierarchical, Episcopal form of church government, or acquire a Presbyterian form. The Episcopal form meant that the king, the Archbishop of Canterbury, and the bishops of the church would determine policy, theology, and the form of worship and service. The Presbyterian form of polity allowed for more freedom of conscience and dissent among church members. Each congregation would have a voice in the life of the church, and a regional group of ministers or "presbytery," would attempt to ensure "doctrinal purity." The political implications for representative democracy were present in both issues. That is why most Presbyterians, Puritans, and Congregationalists sided with Parliament and most Anglicans and Catholics sided with the king. The Parliament in effect bribed the king by granting him a tax grant in exchange for his agreement to the Petition of Rights in 1628. It stipulated that no one should pay any tax, gift, loan, or contribution except as provided by an act of Parliament; no one should be imprisoned or detained without due process of law; all were to have the right to the writ of habeas corpus; there should be no forced billeting of soldiers in the homes of private citizens; and martial law was not to be declared in England.

In the midst of a stormy debate over theology, taxes, and civil liberties, the king sought to force the adjournment of Parliament. But when he sent a message to the Speaker ordering him to adjourn, some of the more athletic members held him in his chair while the door of the House of Commons was locked to prevent the entry of other messengers from the king. That famous date was March 2, 1629. A number of resolutions passed. Concessions towards Catholicism or Arminianism were to be regarded as treason. Whoever advised any collection of taxes without consent of Parliament would be guilty of treason. Whoever should pay a tax levied without the consent of Parliament would be considered a betrayer of liberty and guilty of treason.

A royal messenger was allowed to enter the Commons and declare the Commons adjourned, and a week later Charles I dissolved Parliament—for eleven years. Puritan leaders and leaders of the opposition in the House of Commons were imprisoned by the king, some for several years.

The established Church of England was the only legal church under Charles I, a Catholic. Archbishop of Canterbury William Laud (1573–1645) sought to enforce the king's policies vigorously. Arminian clergymen were to be tolerated, but Puritan clergymen silenced. Criticism was brutally suppressed. Several dissenters were executed. The Scots invaded northern England. Charles called a Great Council of Lords, who arranged a treaty with the Scots to leave things as they were.

The king was cornered—he had no money, no army, and no popular support. He summoned the Parliament to meet in November 1640. The Commons immediately moved to impeach one of the king's principal ministers, Thomas Wentworth, Earl of Strafford (1593–1641). With mobs in the street and rumors of an army en route to London to dissolve Parliament, a bare majority of an underattended House of Commons passed a bill of attainder to execute the earl. Fearing mob violence as well as Parliament itself, the king signed the bill and

Fast Facts The House of Commons passed a series of laws to strengthen its position and to protect civil and religious rights.

Strafford was executed in 1641. Archbishop William Laud was also arrested and eventually tried and executed in 1645.

The House of Commons passed a series of laws to strengthen its position and protect civil and religious rights. The Triennial Act (1641) provided that no more than three years should pass between Parliaments. Another act provided that the current Parliament should not be dissolved without its own consent. Various hated laws, taxes, and institutions were abolished: the Star Chamber, the High Commission, and power of the Privy Council to deal with property rights. Ship money, a form of tax, was abolished and tonnage duties were permitted only for a short time. The courts of common law were to remain supreme over the king's courts. The Commons was ready to revoke the king's power over the Church of England, but there was disagreement over what form the state church would take: Episcopal, Presbyterian, or congregational. Puritans were in the majority. The Grand Remonstrance listed 204 clauses of grievances against the king and demanded that all officers and ministers of the state be approved by Parliament. In 1641 a rebellion began in Ireland. Irish Catholics murdered thousands of their Protestant neighbors. The Commons voted funds for an army, but it was unclear whether Parliament or the king would control the army.

Men began identifying themselves as Cavaliers if they supported the king or Roundheads if they supported Parliament. The king withdrew to Hampton Court and sent the queen to France for safety. In March 1642, Charles II went to York, and the English Civil War began. Charles put together a sizeable force with a strong cavalry and moved on London, winning several skirmishes. He entered Oxford, but was beaten back from London. Oxford then became his headquarters for the rest of the war.

Oliver Cromwell (1599–1658), a gentlemen farmer from Huntingdon, led the parliamentary troops to victory, first with his cavalry, which eventually numbered 1,100 and then as lieutenant general in command of the well-disciplined and well-trained New Model Army. He eventually forced the king to flee. During the Civil War, under the authority of Parliament, the Westminster Assembly convened to write a statement of faith for the Church of England that was Reformed or Presbyterian in content. Ministers and laymen from both England and Scotland participated for six years and wrote the Westminster Confession of Faith, still a vital part of Presbyterian theology. When the war ended, Parliament ordered the army to disband without receiving the pay due them. The army refused, and in 1647 Parliament sought to disperse them by force. The plan was to bring the Scottish army into England and use it against the men who had won the war.

The army refused to obey Parliament and arrested the king when he was brought across the border. In August the army occupied London and some of their leaders wrote an "Agreement of the People," to be presented to the

House of Commons. It called for a democratic republic with a written constitution and elections every two years, equal electoral districts, and universal manhood suffrage, freedom of conscience, freedom from impressments, equality before the law, and no office of king or House of Lords. On the night of November 11, 1647, the king escaped from Hampton Court and went to the Isle of Wight. He had made a secret agreement with the Scots that he would establish Presbyterianism throughout England and Scotland if they would restore him to his throne. The Second Civil War followed in 1648 but it consisted only of scattered local uprisings and the desertion of part of the English fleet.

The Scots invaded England, but were defeated by Cromwell at Preston, Wigan, and Warrington in the northwest of England. After these victories, the English army took control. London was again occupied. The army arrested 45 Presbyterian members of Parliament, excluded the rest, and admitted only about 60 Independents, who acted as the "Rump Parliament." The army then tried Charles Stuart, formerly king of England, and sentenced him to death for treason. He was beheaded on January 30, 1649. The execution of the king particularly shocked the Scots, because the English had specifically promised not to take the king's life when the Scots delivered him into English hands.

After the execution of the king, Parliament abolished the office of king and the House of Lords. The new form of government was to be a Commonwealth, or Free State, governed by the representatives of the people in Parliament. Many large areas of the country had no representatives in Parliament. Parliament was more powerful than ever because there was neither king nor House of Lords to act as a check. This commonwealth lasted four years between 1649 and 1653. Royalists and Presbyterians both opposed Parliament for its lack of broad representations and for regicide. The army was greatly dissatisfied that elections were not held, as one of the promises of the Civil War was popular representation. Surrounded by foreign enemies, the Commonwealth became a military state with a standing army of 44,000. The North American and West Indian colonies were forced to accept the government of the Commonwealth. When it became clear that Parliament intended to stay in office permanently, Cromwell agreed to serve as Lord Protector from 1653–1659, with a Council of State and a Parliament. Some degree of religious toleration, except for Catholics and Anglicans, was permitted by Cromwell's protectorate. The new Parliament restored the monarchy from 1660–1688, but the Puritan Revolution clearly showed that the English constitutional system required a limited monarchy. Parliament in 1660 was in a far stronger position in its relationship to the king than it ever had been before. Under the Convention Parliament of 1660, Royalists whose lands had been confiscated by the Puritans were allowed to recover them through the courts. Manorialism was largely abolished.

The leaders of Parliament were not willing to sacrifice the constitutional gains of the English Civil War and return to absolute monarchy. Two events in 1688 goaded them to action. In May, James II reissued the Declaration of Indulgence with the command that it be read on two successive Sundays in every parish church. On June 10, 1688, a son was born to the king and his queen, Mary of Modena. As long as James was childless by his second wife, the throne would go to one of his Protestant daughters, Mary or Anne. The birth of a son, who would be raised Roman Catholic, changed the picture completely.

A group of Whig and Tory leaders, speaking for both houses of Parliament, invited William and Mary to assume the throne of England. William III was stadtholder of Holland and Mary was the daughter of James II by his Protestant first wife, Anne Hyde. They were both in the Stuart dynasty. On November 5, 1688, William and his army landed at Torbay in Devon. King James offered many concessions, but it was too late. He finally fled to France. William assumed temporary control of the government and summoned a free Parliament. In February 1689, William and Mary were declared joint sovereigns, with administration given to William. The English Declaration of Rights (1689) declared the following:

1) The king could not be a Roman Catholic.

2) A standing army in time of peace was illegal without Parliamentary approval.

3) Taxation was illegal without Parliamentary consent.

4) Excessive bail and cruel and unusual punishments were prohibited.

5) Right to trial by jury was guaranteed.

6) Free elections to Parliament would be held.

The Toleration Act (1689) granted the right of public worship to Protestant Nonconformists, but did not permit them to hold office. The Act did not extend liberty to Catholics or Unitarians, but normally they were left alone. The Trials for Treason Act (1696) stated that a person accused of treason should be shown the accusations against him and should have the advice of counsel. They also could not be convicted except upon the testimony of two independent witnesses. Freedom of the press was permitted, but with very strict libel laws. Control of finances, including military appropriations, was to be in the hands of the Commons. There would no longer be uncontrolled grants to the king. The Act of Settlement in 1701 provided that should William, or later Anne, die without children (Queen Mary had died in 1694) the throne should descend, not to the exiled Stuarts, but to Sophia, Electress Dowager of Hanover, a granddaughter of

King James I or to her Protestant heirs. Judges were made independent of the Crown. Thus, England declared itself a limited monarchy and a Protestant nation. Following the Act of Settlement in 1701 and Queen Anne's death in 1714, the House of Hanover inherited the English throne in order to ensure that a Protestant would rule the realm. The Hanover dynasty order of reign was a follows: George I (1714–1727), George II (1727–1760); George III (1760–1820); George IV (1820–1830); William IV (1830–1837); and Queen Victoria (1837–1901).

The Scientific Revolution and Scientific Societies

The scientific revolution of the sixteenth and seventeenth centuries came about as a result of the confluence of many different ideas and because of a handful of great scientists. Renaissance studies of language and of math and science drew on the earlier achievements of the Greeks. Thus, the revolution in science drew upon Greek ideas of astronomy and medicine, the ideas of Aristotle, Ptolemy (an astronomer), and curiosity about the universe around them. Scientists universally believed they were studying and analyzing God's creation, not an autonomous phenomenon known as "Nature." There was no attempt, as in the nineteenth and twentieth centuries, to secularize science. Nonetheless, the new discoveries in astronomy and science would challenge traditional religious views and lead to philosophical questions about the nature of the universe. The question of the extent of the Creator's involvement in creation was an issue of the eighteenth century, but there was universal agreement among scientists and philosophers as to the supernatural origin of the universe.

Astronomy in the sixteenth century was built around Ptolemy's view of the universe. In the Ptolemaic view, the universe was a series of spheres with a fixed and motionless earth at the center. Around the earth, the sphere, made up of a crystalline substance, moved in circles. Beyond these heavenly bodies in Ptolemy's fixed universe was the sphere of God (Heaven).

Nikolai Copernicus (1473–1543) disputed this earth centered Ptolemaic universe in his work *On the Revolutions of the Heavenly Spheres* (published in May 1543). Copernicus' universe was centered around a motionless sun. Copernicus' system was still extremely complex and still failed to accurately describe the universe (partly because it still relied on circular orbits for the stars and planets). Nonetheless, the move to a sun-centered theory raised significant questions.

Johannes Kepler (1571–1630) built upon Copernicus' work and arrived at his three laws of planetary motion (published in 1609). These laws confirmed Copernicus' sun-centered theory but claimed that the orbits were elliptical rather than circular. Kepler's laws eliminated the idea of crystalline spheres and of uniform planetary motion, essentially destroying the ancient Ptolemaic system.

Galileo Galilei (1564–1642), a mathematicician, is best known for his creation of the telescope. Once the telescope was developed, the stars and the heavens could be directly observed. Galileo thus discovered the mountains and craters on the moon, the moons of Jupiter, and other previously unknown stars. These discoveries and the discovery that other planets appeared to be composed of a substance similar to that of earth rather than of some celestial and heavenly substance, threatened church doctrine and Galileo soon found himself facing the Inquisition. When Galileo published *Dialogue on the two Chief World Systems: Ptolemaic and Copernican* (1632) he was condemned by the Inquisition, forced to recant his ideas, and placed under house arrest for the rest of his life.

The problems which Kepler, Brahe, and Galileo had raised would not be definitively solved until Isaac Newton's publication of *The Mathematical Principles of natural Philsophy* (1687), often known as *Principia.* In this work, Newton sets out his three now famous laws of motion: 1) every object continues in a state of rest unless deflected by a force, 2) the rate of change of motion of an object is proportional to the force acting upon it, and 3) to every action there is an equal and opposite reaction. Newton also explore the laws of gravity and shows elliptical orbits for the planets around the sun. For Newton, although God was absolutely present in all of creation, his universe was a mechanistic one run by mathematical laws.

The Enlightenment

Note ➤ The Enlighten-ment fostered **a belief in the existence of God as a rational explanation of the universe and its form, while the "Counter Enlight-enment" encompassed diverse and disparate groups who disagreed with the fun-damental assumptions of the Enlightenment and pointed out its weaknesses.**

The mathematical and scientific discoveries of the Scientific Revolution, profoundly influenced the intellectuals of the eighteenth century. This became known as the age of the Enlightenment. In the past, some kind of a religious perspective had always been central to Western civilization. The philosophical starting point for the Enlightenment was the belief in the autonomy of man's intellect apart from God. The most basic assumption was faith in reason rather than faith in revelation. The "Enlightened" claimed for themselves, however, a rationality they were unwilling to concede to their opponent.

The Enlightenment fostered a belief in the existence of God as a rational explanation of the universe and its form; "God" was a deistic Creator who made the universe and then was no longer involved in its mechanistic operation. That mechanistic operation was governed by "natural law." Rationalists stressed deductive reasoning or mathematical logic as the basis for their epistemology (source of knowledge). They started with "self-evident truths," or postulates, from which they constructed a coherent and logical system of thought. Rene Descartes (1596–1650) sought a basis for logic and thought. He found it in man's ability to think. "I think, therefore I am" was his most famous statement. That statement cannot be denied without thinking. Therefore, it must be an absolute truth that man can think. His proof depends upon logic alone.

Benedict de Spinoza (1632–1677) developed a rational pantheism in which he equated God and nature. He denied all free will and ended up positing an impersonal, mechanical universe.

Gottfried Wilhelm Leibniz (1646–1716) worked on symbolic logic and calculus, and invented a calculating machine. He too, had a mechanistic world and life view and thought of God as a hypothetical abstraction rather than a persona.

Empiricists stressed inductive observation–the "scientific method"–as the basis for their epistemology.

John Locke (1632–1704) pioneered the empiricist approach to knowledge and stressed the importance of environment in human development. He classified knowledge as 1) according to reason, 2) contrary to reason, or 3) above reason. Locke believed reason and revelation were not only complementary but also from God.

David Hume (1711–1776) was a Scottish historian and philosopher who began by emphasizing the limitations of human reasoning and later became a dogmatic skeptic.

The people of the Enlightenment believed in absolutes. They believed in absolute truth, absolute ethics, and absolute natural law. And they believed optimistically that these absolutes were discoverable by man's rationality. It was not long, of course, before one rationalist's "absolutes" clashed with those of another.

The Enlightenment set forth a closed system of the universe in which the supernatural was not involved in human life, in contrast to the traditional view of an open system in which God, angels, and devils were very much a part of human life on earth.

The "Counter-Enlightenment" is a comprehensive term encompassing diverse and disparate groups who disagreed with the fundamental assumptions of the Enlightenment and pointed out its weaknesses. Roman Catholic Jansenism in France argued against the idea of an uninvolved or impersonal God. Hasidism in Easter European Jewish communities, especially in the 1730s, stressed a religious fervor in direct communion with God.

Radical ideas about society and government were developed during the eighteenth century in response to the success of the "scientific" and "intellectual" revolutions of the preceding two centuries. Armed with new scientific knowledge of the physical universe, as well as new views of the human capacity to detect "truth," social critics assailed existing modes of thought governing political, social, religious, and economic life. Then years of upheaval in France (1789–1799) further shaped modern ideas and practices. The modern world that came of age in the eighteenth century was characterized by rapid, revolutionary changes which paved the way for economic modernization and political centralization throughout Europe. The Enlightenment itself was influenced by the scientific method, which involved identifying a problem or question, forming a hypothesis, making observations, conducting experiments, interpreting results with mathematics, and drawing conclusions.

While they came from virtually every country in Europe, most of the famous social activists of the Enlightenment were French, and France was the center of this intellectual revolution. Francois Marie Arouet (1694–1778), better known as Voltaire, was one of the most famous philosophes. Denis Diderot (1713–1784) served as editor of *The Encyclopedia*, the bible of the Enlightenment period. This twenty-eight-volume work was a compendium of all new learning. Baron de Montesquieu (1689–1755) authored the *Spirit of the Laws* (1748) in which the separation of the powers theory was found. Montesquieu believed such a separation would keep any individual (including the king) or group (including the nobles) from gaining total control of the government. Jean-Jacques Rousseau (1712–1778) wrote the *Social Contract* (1762) in an attempt to discover the origin of society, and to propose that the composition of the ideal society was based on a new kind of social contract.

The major assumptions of the Enlightenment were as follows:

1) Human progress was possible through changes in one's environment, i.e., better people, better societies, better standard of living.

2) Humans were free to use reason to reform the evils of society.

3) Material improvement would lead to moral improvement.

4) Natural science and human reason would discover the meaning of life.

5) Laws governing human society would be discovered through application of the scientific method of inquiry.

6) Inhuman practices and institutions would be removed from society in a spirit of humanitarianism.

7) Human liberty would ensue if an individual became free to choose what reason dictated was good.

Many Enlightenment thinkers and philosophes were also Deists. Deism rejected traditional Christianity by promoting an impersonal God who did not interfere in the daily lives of the people.

Political theorists such as John Locke (1632–1704) and Jean Jacques Rousseau (1712–1778) believed that people were capable of governing themselves, either through a political (Locke) or social (Rousseau) contract forming the basis of society. However, most philosophes opposed democracy, preferring a limited monarchy that shared power with the nobility. During the Enlightenment, traditional mercantilist economic theory gradually came under fire, first by the physiocrats in France who proposed a "laissez-faire" (nongovernmental interference) approach to the economy and then by Adam Smith (1723–1790) who advocated free trade, free enterprise, and the law of supply and demand. Many philosophes believed that human progress and liberty would ensue as absolute rulers became "enlightened." The rulers would still be absolute, but would use their power benevolently, as reason dictated. Most of the philosophes opposed democracy. According to Voltaire, the best form of government was a monarchy in which the rulers shared the ideas of the philosophes and respected the people's rights. Such an "enlightened" monarchy would rule justly and introduce reforms. Voltaire's and other philosophes' influence on Europe's monarchs produced the "enlightened despots" who nonetheless failed to bring about lasting political change. Some famous "despots" included Frederick the Great of Prussia (r. 1740–1786), Catherine the Great of Russia (r. 1762–1796), and Joseph II of Austria (r. 1765–1790).

Causes of the French Revolution

The increased reliance on science and reason brought about by the Scientific Revolution and the philosophical thought of the Enlightenment, each contributed to the French and American Revolutions. The rising expectations of "enlightened" society were demonstrated by the increased criticism directed toward government inefficiency and corruption, and toward the privileged classes. The clergy (First Estate) and nobility (Second Estate), representing only two-percent of the total population of 24 million, were the privileged classes and were essentially tax exempt. The remainder of the population (Third Estate) consisted of the middle class, urban workers, and the mass of peasants, who bore the entire burden of taxation and the imposition of feudal obligations. As economic conditions worsened in the eighteenth century, the French state became poorer, and totally dependent on the poorest and most depressed sections of the economy for support at the very time this tax base had become saturated.

The mode of absolute government practiced by the Bourbon dynasty was wed to the "Divine Right of Kings" philosophy. This in turn produced a government that was irresponsible and inefficient, with a tax system that was unjust and inequitable and without any means of redress because of the absence of any meaningful representative assembly. The legal system was chaotic with no uniform or codified laws. As France slid into bankruptcy, Louis XVI summoned an Assembly of Notables (1787) in the mistaken hope they would either approve his new tax program or consent to removing their exemption from payment of taxes. They refused to agree to either proposal. Designed to represent the three estates of France, this ancient feudal body had only met twice, once at its creation in 1302 and again in 1614. When the French parlements insisted that any new taxes must be approved by this body, King Louis XVI reluctantly ordered it to assemble at Versailles by May 1789. Each estate was expected to elect its own representatives. As a gesture to the size of the Third Estate, the king doubled the number of its representatives. However, the Parlement of Paris decreed that voting in the Estates General would follow "custom and tradition," with each estate casting a vote as a unit. Therefore the First and Second Estates with similar interests to protect, would control the meeting despite the increased size of the Third Estate.

Election fever swept over France for the very first time. The election campaign took place in the midst of the worst subsistence crisis in eighteenth-century France, with widespread grain shortages, poor harvests, and inflated bread prices. Finally, on May 5, 1789, the Estates General met and argued over whether to vote by estate or individual. Each estate was ordered to meet separately and vote as a unit. The Third Estate refused and insisted that the entire assembly stay together.

The French revolution broke out when the third estate broke away from the National Assembly and were locked out of their meeting place by Louis XVI.

2. United States History

The New World that Columbus and other explorers discovered in the late fifteenth and early sixteenth centuries was neither recently formed nor recently settled. It had actually been settled between 15,000 and 35,000 years ago. As in other areas of the world, these peoples formed communities but did not immediately develop a written language. The lack of any kind of written record makes interpreting this pre-historical past more difficult. Archeologists and anthropologists working in North and South America have unearthed the remains of these early communities, and it is upon this evidence that the earliest theories about the origins, movement, and lifestyle of these people are based. It is important to remember that there is not one universally accepted theory regarding the earliest history of the people who settled North and South America. It is also important to remember that by the time Europeans came into contact with the indigenous peoples of the Americas, over 2,000 distinct cultures and hundreds of distinct languages existed. It is therefore necessary to trace not just the origins but also the developments, impacted by various factors such as the environment, that took place prior to the arrival of the Europeans. This will provide us with an understanding of the various Indian cultures and societies and the impact that contact with Europeans had upon them.

The Great Ice Age

During the Great Ice Age, which lasted over two million years, so much water was frozen that sea levels dropped drastically. One consequence of this was that a land mass between Siberia and Alaska known as Beringia, now covered in water, was exposed and formed a bridge between the Asian and American continents. This land bridge was exposed during three separate periods: the earliest was from 70,000 to 45,000 years ago, the second was from about 22,000 to 12,500 and the last was approximately 11,000 to 8,000 years ago. It is thought that several groups migrated along this path during at least two different periods and there is strong evidence that people migrated across Beringia during the second period. These earliest people followed and hunted large game animals, such as mammoths, which found the climate and conditions in Beringia suitable to their needs.

About 9,000 years ago changes in environmental conditions and ultimately the ending of the Ice Age had a number of consequences. The resulting warmer temperatures led to the development of different climates in different regions of the Americas, the loss of large areas of grassland, and the melting of water, which once again covered areas such as Beringia, thus cutting off the Americas from the other continents. Many large animals such as mammoths, mastodons, and horses became extinct and the nomadic big game hunters who had survived largely by killing and using the meat, skin, and bone of these animals were forced to accommodate the loss of such prey by making changes in their lifestyle.

Changes in Hunting and the Development of Agriculture

Archeologists refer to the period from approximately 9,000 to 3,000 B.C.E., when humans shifted away from a reliance strictly on hunting and towards a more diverse lifestyle, as the archaic period. It is necessary to review general trends that occurred during this period before turning to the distinct cultures that developed in various regions and that were in existence when the Europeans arrived. One of the changes was the development of additional types of tools made from various materials. Previously, hunters had relied on the effective "Clovis" points, named after the site in Mexico where they were first discovered. They were made by chipping away flakes from the bones of large animals that had been killed. These points were an advance over earlier stone arrow points and proved more reliable and more effective. The shift away from big game hunting, however, gave early man the time as well as the need to develop a vast array of other tools other than hunting spears from other materials such as wood. The increased amount of time that was produced by not having to constantly track and kill large animals also led to the development of artwork and ornate baskets and other crafts. Population also increased as early people spent more time in each place, although they continued to be nomadic.

The impact of environmental conditions and the introduction of farming techniques and crops, such as maize, had a tremendous impact in the Americas and led to the emergence of the distinct cultures mentioned earlier. It is not possible to describe in depth the 2,000 cultures that had developed by the time the explorers arrived. Instead some indication of specific trends and cultures that existed in various regions and climates just prior to the arrival of the Europeans will be provided.

Indian Cultures Just Prior to the Arrival of the Europeans

In the Southwest region of North America severe restrictions were imposed by the aridity of the climate and the fact that nothing could be planted in vast areas of the desert. The cultivation of plants was possible, however, along the banks of the several rivers that flow from the mountains through the southwest toward the Gulf of Mexico or the Gulf of California. These rivers also provided water for irrigation and farming, and Indian farmers had been growing crops in this manner for about 3,000 years prior to contact with European explorers. The Indians cultivated crops such as corn, beans, sunflowers, and cotton.

They lived in settlements spread across the desert at intervals of approximately one mile and trading networks extended across the entire southwest. Each settlement had a headman who managed irrigation matters, but a council of adult men made decisions with unanimous consent being required. Ceremonies were an integral part of life and the most important ceremonies focused on bringing rain. One ceremony required everyone present to drink cactus wine until intoxicated, as this ceremony was thought to both purify the individual and also to bring rain for the community.

Native Communities in the South and Southwest

One group of Indians living in the Southwest, the Anasazis, lived a few hundred miles north of the area, known as the "Four Corners," where modern-day Arizona, New Mexico, Utah, and Colorado connect. Around the first century C.E., the Anasazis–or "ancient outsiders"–began to settle down and cultivate crops. A change in the climate during the eighth century C.E. presented them with a new challenge. Instead of reverting to a nomadic lifestyle they found ways to improve their farming techniques and also implemented a system of terraced fields that were irrigated by a sophisticated canal system. In addition to farming, the Anasazis hunted and around 500 C.E. they benefited from the introduction of a more effective bow and arrow. Although the Anasazis were very skilled at basket making and pottery, it is their architectural achievements that have received the most attention. The Anasazis built and lived in complexes of apartments that had a central plaza, along with areas for storage and religious ceremonies. One of these complexes, named *Pueblo Bonito* by the Spanish, was completed in the twelfth century and contains more than 650 connected rooms. Only a few of the more than 25,000 communities have been excavated but it is already clear that the Anasazis had a communication system consisting of signaling stations in the mountains and distributed food and resources over an extended network. Although the Anasazis continued to develop more complex irrigation systems and other techniques to counter the dry conditions, these measures were not enough to sustain them through a prolonged drought that occurred in the thirteenth century. The impact of the subsequent crop failures and attacks by bands of Athapascan migrants (the ancestors of the Navajos and Apaches) on the Anasazis contributed to the decline of this community.

It is thought that the cliff dwellings built at Mesa Verde, Colorado, during the fourteenth and fifteenth centuries, and later used by the Pueblo people, may have been constructed to defend the Anasazis from their enemies. The Anasazis abandoned these dwellings, however, and left the Four Corners area. There is evidence to suggest that they settled along the Rio Grande and intermarried with the local population leading to the emergence of the Pueblo people. The Pueblo culture inherited architectural knowledge and also farming and religious practices from the Anasazis. The Pueblo people spoke several different languages but they had a common code of behavior regulating personal conduct that was enforced by matrilineal clans and societies of both a religious and a political nature. The Pueblo were able to produce harvests of corn and squash because these plants were drought-resistant and could be cultivated using dry farming techniques.

Conditions in the South were less harsh and more favorable to human settlement. The winters are short and the climate is mild compared to other areas. Furthermore, this region has a broad fertile plain of rich soil that makes cultivation easier and less dependent upon irrigation techniques. There are also a number of rivers that provide opportunities for travel, fishing, and hunting. In the Mississippi Valley, a number of cultures thrived at different time periods. In the mid–1200s at a place archeologists have named Cahokia (near modern-day St. Louis), there was an urban center of approximately 30,000 people. There are no written records to tell us about life at Cahokia, but archeologists have unearthed the remains of a flourishing civilization. Cahokia had a huge earthwork pyramid built as a temple to the gods. The pyramid was built on top of fifteen acres and was as tall as a ten-story building. The Indian chiefs and the priests of Cahokia lived in residences built on the top of the pyramid while the rest of the population of Cahokia lived in houses along the riverbank and worked either in shops along the river bank or in the fields. Fields of corn, beans, and pumpkins covered the surrounding countryside as far as one could see while standing atop of the pyramid. Pottery, clay sculptures, and metal objects were produced at Cahokia and were traded long distances along trading routes that reached the Great Lakes and even as far as the Atlantic coast. The civilization at Cahokia declined and disappeared in the fourteenth century. When the Europeans arrived, they came into contact with various peoples who continued some of the same patterns of life as had existed at Cahokia. Most of the peoples in the Mississippi valley were decimated by disease almost immediately after contact with Europeans and thus little is known about them as well.

The Natchez farmers of the lower Mississippi delta, however, survived into the eighteenth century, and thus considerably more is known about their culture. The ruler of the Natchez was known as the Great Sun. He lived on a ceremonial mound in his village capitol and when he went out among his subjects he was carried upon a litter. The wives and servants of the chief preceded the litter and swept its path clean. Natchez society was divided into classes. The members of one class, the nobles, served as advisors to the Great Sun and were appointed to serve as peace and war chiefs of the villages. The majority of the Natchez people–known as the "Stinkards"–was subordinate to the ruler and the nobles. The Natchez considered the act of warfare to elevate the status of the individual and the state, thus the state was drawn into a number of conflicts. They also practiced public torture and human sacrifice. The Natchez, along with other Mississippian cultures, were organized into confederacies consisting of several farming towns, with the most powerful confederacies living along the floodplains. However, these highly organized confederacies, such as the Natchez, proved more vulnerable to conquest by the Europeans than the more loosely organized tribes of the continental interior, such as the Cherokees.

Native Communities in the Northeast

The Iroquois inhabited Ontario and upstate New York for at least 4,500 years before the arrival of Europeans and were among the first people in that area to rely more on cultivation of crops than on fishing and hunting. The Iroquois lived in an area featuring mountain highlands, great rivers, lakes, and valleys and also coastal plains and wooded areas. In the coastal areas and the river valleys, the growing season lasted long enough to produce a crop of maize and from around 500 C.E., maize farming became the dominant economic pursuit. The Iroquois had a matrilineal line of descent, and it was also women who planted and harvested the corn, beans, squash, and sunflowers that fed and supported the community. The community was organized into fifty longhouses, each containing an extended family and wooden walls were usually constructed around a village to protect it from attack. Population growth and also persistent violence and war led to the creation of the Iroquois Confederation. This confederacy outlawed warfare among member nations but encouraged violence against neighboring groups that were outside the Confederation. The Confederation was also modeled on the longhouse system. Each nation occupied a separate area but was linked by descent from a common mother and women played important roles in choosing male leaders or chiefs who would represent them in the Confederation. The Iroquois Confederation came to be extremely significant during the period of European colonization. In addition to the tribes that spoke Iroquois and formed the Confederation, there were at least fifty different cultures created by people who all spoke a common language. These people all spoke Algonquian and they shared some other characteristics. Unlike the Iroquois, the Algonquians were hunters and foragers who lived in bands with only loose family affiliations. The Algonquians were patrilineal, lived in smaller villages and houses, and had fewer fortifications. The Algonquians also relied more on hunting and fishing than on the cultivation of crops, and the bow and arrow and fishing spear were their most important tools. Some of the Algonquian-speaking tribes, such as the Chippewas and the Crees, came to be involved in the fur trade that developed in that region.

Beginnings of European Exploration

Europeans were largely unaware of the existence of the American continent despite the fact that a Norse seamen, Leif Eriksson, had sailed within sight of the continent in the eleventh century. There were a few other explorers who ventured nearly as far as America as well. Prior to the fifteenth century, Europeans had little desire to explore nor were they ready to face all of the challenges involved in a long sea voyage. Just as developments led to changes and conflict in North America that produced an increasing number of distinct cultures and systems, developments in Europe were about to make possible the great voyages that led to contact between Europe and the Americas. In the fifteenth and sixteenth centuries, technological devices such as the compass and astrolabe freed and motivated explorers from some of the constraints that had limited early voyages. There were three primary factors—god, gold, and glory—that led to increased interest in exploration and eventually to a desire to settle in the newly discovered lands.

Although Europeans, such as Italians, participated in overland trade with the east and sailed through the Mediterranean and beyond, it was the Arabs who played the largest part in such trade and who benefited the most economically. Prince Henry "the Navigator," the ruler of Portugal, sponsored voyages aimed at adding territory and gaining control of trading routes in order to increase the power and wealth of Portugal. Prince Henry also wanted to spread Christianity and prevent the further expansion of Islam in Africa. Prince Henry the Navigator brought a number of Italian merchant traders to his court at Cape St. Vincent and they sailed subsequently in Portuguese ships down the western coast of Africa. The initial voyages were extremely difficult due to the lack of navigational aids and the lack of any kind of maps or charts. Europeans had charted the entire Mediterranean Sea, including harbors and the coastline, but they had no knowledge or maps of the African coast. The first task of the explorers was to create accurate charts of the African shoreline they encountered along their voyages. The crews on these initial voyages did not encounter horrible monsters or boiling water, which rumors had said existed in the ocean beyond Cape Bojador, which was the farthest point Europeans had previously reached. They did discover, however, that there were strong southward winds that made it easy to sail out of the Mediterranean but difficult to return. It was firmly believed that Africa and China were joined by a southern continent, eliminating any possibility of an eastern, maritime route to the Indian Ocean. Prince Henry, however, sent ships along the coast of Africa because he believed that it was possible to sail east through the Atlantic and reach the Indian Ocean.

Technical Innovations Aiding Exploration

One of the reasons that the explorers sailing from Portugal sailed along the coast was so that they would not lose sight of land. By the thirteenth century, the compass, borrowed from China, was being used by explorers to determine direction, but it was more difficult to determine the relative position from the North and South Poles and therefore from anything else, such as known landmasses. In the Northern Hemisphere, one could determine relative north-south position, or latitude, by calculating the height of the Pole Star from the horizon. South of the equator the Pole Star cannot be seen and until around 1460, captains had no way to determine their position if they sailed too far south. The introduction of the astrolabe allowed sailors to calculate their latitude south of the equator, although longitude (relative east-west position) remained unknown until the eighteenth century

Along with navigational aids, improvements in shipbuilding and in weaponry also facilitated exploration. Unlike the Mediterranean, it was not possible to use ships propelled only by oarsmen in the Atlantic due to the high waves and stronger currents and winds. Europeans had initially used very broad sails on ships that went out into the Atlantic, but these ships were heavy and were often stranded by the absence of favorable tailwinds upon which they were dependent. The Portuguese borrowed from Arab and European shipbuilding techniques and developed a ship known as the Caravela Redondo. This ship proved to be more worthy of long voyages because it combined square rigging for speed with lateen sails that were more responsive and easier to handle. This ship was adopted by other European states, as was the practice of mounting artillery and other weapons on exploration vessels.

Main Factors of European Exploration

As the Portuguese began to trade and explore along the coast of Africa, they brought back slaves, ivory, gold, and knowledge of the African coast. It looked as though the Portuguese might find a route to the Indian Ocean and was also clear that the voyages sponsored by Prince Henry were benefiting Portugal in a number of ways. Other European states also wanted to increase their territory and wealth, as well as establish trade routes to the east. Although the desire for control of trade routes and wealth was a primary motive in launching voyages of exploration, it was not the only motivation.

Europe in the fifteenth and sixteenth centuries, despite the increase in dissenting views, was still extremely religious. The Catholic Church continued to exert a tremendous influence and some Christians were motivated to go on voyages of discovery in order to conduct missionary activities and to spread the word of God. After the beginning of the Reformation, many Lutherans, Calvinists, and other groups who had left the Catholic Church emigrated from Europe in the hopes of settling where they would be free from religious persecution or violent conflicts. Younger sons of families in Europe might be able to secure a prominent position in the church but were not often able to find lucrative opportunities at home, because inheritance of lands and wealth was also usually limited to the eldest son. The voyages of exploration, therefore, were a means of securing fame and fortune and of obtaining opportunities that would not be available otherwise. Other individuals sponsored or participated in voyages in the hopes of gaining either wealth or increased opportunities. God and gold were two motivating factors and the third was glory. Although fame and fortune were often not primary factors, a number of individuals were motivated by the possibility of adventure and by their desire to explore uncharted territory. These three factors—gold, god, and glory—operated on both an individual and a state level, due to the fact that kings and heads of states were as interested in spreading their faith and increasing the wealth and prestige of their states.

Fast Facts

Three main factors influenced European exploration on both an individual and state level: gold, god, and glory.

Portugal was the first European state to establish sugar plantations and did so on an island off the West coast of Africa, importing slaves from Africa to labor there. This was the beginning of the slave trade, but it was initially far less extensive and intense than during the later period of the slave trade when Spain and England became involved. In an attempt to maintain control of the slave trade and of the Eastern routes to India, the Portuguese appealed to the Pope who ruled in their favor and forbade the Spanish and others to sail south and east in an attempt to reach India or Asia. When Ferdinand and Isabella married and united the two largest provinces in Spain—Castile and Aragon—they not only began the process of uniting all of Spain but they also agreed to sponsor Christopher Columbus in his voyage of exploration. Only the heads of states had the necessary resources and could afford the risk involved in sponsoring a major voyage across the oceans of the world, but most monarchs were unwilling to take such a risk. Columbus was an Italian explorer looking for a sponsor, who had approached Ferdinand and Isabella after being turned down by the English government. He convinced the Spanish monarchs that a Western route to the Indian Ocean existed and that it would be possible to make the voyage.

However, Columbus had miscalculated the distance of the voyage from Europe to Asia. His estimate of the circumference of the earth was much less than it should have been for an accurate calculation, and no Europeans were aware of the existence of the American continents. One of the reasons that Ferdinand and Isabella were willing to support Columbus was due to the previous agreements that prevented all states but Portugal from sailing east to reach India. Therefore, the only chance for a Spanish expedition to India and to participate in trade and exploration existed in the discovery of a Western route to India.

European Contact with the Americas

In 1492, Columbus sailed from Spain with three ships, the Nina, the Pinta, and the Santa Maria, and ninety men, landing initially in the Bahamas after a ten-week voyage. He reached Cuba on his second trip and then in 1498, during his third trip, he reached the mainland and sailed along the northern coast of South America. Columbus originally thought he had reached India and thus referred to the people he encountered in the Bahamas and on his second landing in Cuba as "Indians." There is a considerable debate centered around the issue of whether or not he realized, either during his third voyage and at a later point prior to his death, that he had landed not in India but in an entirely unknown continent that lie between Europe and Asia. There is also a debate as to whether or not Columbus, who died in obscurity despite his fame for having discovered America, should be given credit for this discovery since it had now been demonstrated that earlier explorers had reached the American continent. However, since it is Columbus's voyage that led to extensive exploration and settlement of the Americas, it is accurate to state that he led to the discovery of the New World by Europeans. Nevertheless, the name for the New World does not stem from Columbus but was derived from the name of a merchant from Florence, Amerigo Vespucci. Amerigo Vespucci took part in several voyages to the New World and then wrote a series of descriptions that not only gave Europeans an image of this "New World" but also spread the idea that the discovered lands were not a part of Asia or India. The newly discovered continents become known as the Americas after Vespucci who popularized the image and the idea that they were continents separate from those that were previously known.

Another result of Columbus's voyages was the increased focus of Spain on exploration and conquest. It was a Portuguese navigator, Vasco da Gama, who crossed the Isthmus of Panama and came to another ocean, which separates the American continents from China. The Spanish sponsored another Portuguese sailor, Ferdinand Magellan, who discovered a strait at the southern end of South America that provided access to the ocean west of the Americas. Magellan named this ocean the "Pacific" because it was much calmer than the strait through which he had sailed to reach it. Later, he reached the Philippines and met his death in a conflict with the natives. Magellan's voyage, nevertheless, was the final stage of the process whereby Europeans completed the first known circumnavigation of the globe. Although the Spanish were at first eager to find a route around the Americas so that they could sail on towards their original goal, the treasures of the Far East, they began to consider that the Americas might be a source of untapped wealth.

From Exploration to Conquest and Settlement in the New World

The Spanish claimed all of the New World except Brazil, which had been given to the Portuguese by a papal decree. The first Spanish settlements were founded on the islands of the Caribbean Sea. It was not until 1518 that Hernando Cortez, who had been appointed by Spain as a government official in Cuba, led a small military expedition against the Aztecs in Mexico. Cortez and his men failed in their first attack on the Aztec capital city, Tenochtitlan, but were ultimately successful. A combination of factors allowed this small force of approximately 600 soldiers to overcome the extensive Aztec empire. The Spanish were armed with rifles and with bows, which provided an advantage over Aztec fighters armed only with spears. However, weapons and armor were not the main reason that the Spanish were able to overcome the military forces of the natives. The Aztec ruler, Montezuma, allowed a delegation, which included Cortez, into the capitol city because the description of the Spanish soldiers in their armor and with feathers in their helmets was similar to the description in Aztec legend of messengers who would be sent by the chief Aztec god, Quetzcoatl. The members of Cortez's expedition exposed the natives to smallpox and other diseases that devastated the native population. Finally, the Spanish expedition was also able to form alliances with other native tribes who had been conquered by the Aztecs and who were willing to cooperate in order to defeat the Aztecs and thus break up their empire. Twenty years after Cortez defeated the Aztecs, another conquistador, and expedition led by Francisco Pizarro, defeated the Incas in Peru. Pizarro's expedition enabled the Spanish to begin to explore and settle South America.

The Conquistadors, or conquerors, were funded by Spain and were the first to explore some areas of the Americas, but they were only interested in defeating the natives in order to gain access to gold, silver, and other wealth. Spain established mines in the territory it claimed and produced a tremendous amount of gold and silver. In the 300 years after the Spanish conquest of the Americas in the sixteenth century, these mines produced ten times more gold and silver than the total produced by all of the mines in the rest of the world. Just as

Fast Facts

The Spanish claimed all of the New World except Brazil, which had been given to the Portuguese by a papal decree.

Spain had come to view the New World as more than an obstacle to voyages towards India, it began over time to think that it might be possible to exploit this territory for more than just mining.

It had been the Conquistadors who had made it possible for the Spanish to settle the New World, but they were not responsible for forming settlements nor were they appointed to oversee Spanish colonies in the New World. Instead, Spain sent officials and administrators from Spain to oversee settlements after they begin to form. Spanish settlers came to the New World for a variety of reasons. Some went in search of land to settle or buy, priests and missionaries went to spread Christianity to the natives, and others went looking for opportunities that were not available to them in Europe. By the end of the sixteenth century, Spain had established firm control over the several islands in the Caribbean, Mexico, southern North America, as well as in the territory currently within the modern states of Chile, Argentina, and Peru.

Spanish Settlements in the New World

The first permanent settlement established by the Spanish was the predominantly military fort of St. Augustine, located in Florida. In 1598, Don Juan de Onate led a group of 500 settlers North from Mexico and established a colony in what is now New Mexico. Onate granted encomiendas to the most prominent Spanish individuals who had accompanied him. The encomienda system established by the Spanish in Mexico and parts of North America consisted of the granting of the right to exact tribute and/or labor from the native population, which was allowed to continue to live on the land in exchange for the services it provided. Spanish colonists founded Santa Fe in 1609 and by 1680 there were about 2,000 of them living in New Mexico. These colonists were largely involved in raising sheep and cattle on large ranches and lived among approximately 30,000 Pueblo Indians. The Spanish crushed a major revolt that threatened to destroy Santa Fe in 1680. To a large degree, the revolt was provoked by attempts to prevent the natives—both those who had converted to Catholicism and those who had not—from performing religious rituals that pre-dated the Spanish arrival. The Spanish were driven from Santa Fe but returned in 1696 crushing the Pueblos and seizing their land. Although the Spanish ultimately crushed this revolt they began to change their policies toward the natives who continued to significantly outnumber the Spanish settlers.

The Spanish continued to try to Christianize and civilize the native population, but they also began to allow the Pueblos to own land. In addition, they unofficially tolerated native religious rituals, although Catholicism continued officially to condemn all such practices. By 1700, the Spanish population in New Mexico increased and reached about 4,000 while the native population had decreased to about 13,000 and intermarriage between natives and Spaniards increased. Nevertheless, disease, war, and migration resulted in the steady decline in the Pueblo population. New Mexico had become a prosperous and stable region, but it was still relatively weak and was fairly isolated as the only major Spanish settlement north Mexico.

Impact of European-American Contact

The impact of Europeans upon the New World, both before and after the arrival of the English and French, cannot be underestimated. The most immediate impact was the spread of disease, which decimated the native population. In some areas of Mexico, 95 percent of the native population died as a result of contact with Europeans and the subsequent outbreaks of diseases, such as smallpox. In South America the native population was devastated not just by disease, but by deliberate policies instituted to control and in some cases to eliminate native peoples. While most diseases were passed from the Europeans to the natives, syphilis was passed from the natives to the Europeans and was carried back to Europe.

Plants and animals were also exchanged between the European and American continents. Europeans brought over animals to the new world and they took plants such as potatoes, corn, and squash back to Europe where introduction of these crops led to a explosion of the European population. In addition to the plants and animals that Europeans brought to the New World they also began to bring slaves from Africa to work in the New World. The decimation of the native population and the establishment of large plantations led to a shortage of workers and Europeans began to transport slaves from Africa to the New World to fill this shortage.

European Settlement and Development in North America

Although King Henry VIII of England sponsored a voyage by John Cabot to try and discover a northwest passage through the New World to the Orient in 1497, the English made no real attempt to settle in the New World until nearly a century later. By the 1600s the English became interested in colonizing the New World for a number of reasons. Many in England were induced to emigrate overseas due to an increase in the English population and using land that was once utilized for the growth foodstuffs as land for pasturing of sheep in order to meet the increased demand for wool. The opportunity to obtain land and other opportunities that were becoming scarcer in England was one motive for emigration from England. Others in England were motivated by the religious turmoil that had engulfed England after the beginning of the Protestant Reformation. In addition to converts to Lutheranism and Calvinism, there were groups such as the Puritans, who were so named because they called for reforms to "purify" the church. Mercantilism also provided a motive for exploration and for the establishment of colonies. According to mercantile theories, an industrialized nation needed an inexpensive source of raw materials and markets for the finished products. Colonies were a way to obtain both raw materials and to guarantee a market for industrial goods.

The French and the Dutch were also motivated by economic and other reasons to explore and establish colonies in the New World. The year after the first English settlement occurred in 1608, the French established a colony at Quebec. The French, overall, had far fewer settlers travel to the New World, but were still able to exercise a tremendous influence through the establishment of strong ties with the natives. The French were able to create trading partnerships and a vast trading network and often intermarried with the local native population. The Dutch financed an English explorer, Henry Hudson, who claimed for Holland the territory that is now New York. The Dutch settlements along the Hudson, Delaware, and Connecticut rivers developed into the colony of New Netherlands and established a vast trading network that effectively separated the English colonies of Jamestown and Plymouth from one another.

One of the reasons that English settlements began to become more prominent after 1600 was due to fate of the Spanish fleet, the invincible Armada, which had been launched against and defeated by the English in 1588. The changing power balance on the seas encouraged the English to increase their exploration and attempted colonization of the Americas.

The first few colonies founded by the English in America did not flourish. Sir Humphrey Gilbert, who had obtained a six-year grant giving him the exclusive rights to settle any unclaimed land in America, was planning to found a colony in Newfoundland but a storm sank his ship and instead Sir Walter Raleigh was awarded a six-year grant. Raleigh explored the North American coast, naming the territory through which he traveled as "Virginia" in honor of the virgin-queen Elizabeth I of England and convinced his cousin, Sir Grenville, to establish a colony on the island of Roanoke. Roanoke was off the coast of what later became North Carolina. The first settlers lived there for a year while Sir Grenville returned to England for supplies and additional settlers. However, when Sir Francis Drake arrived in Roanoke nearly a year later and found that Sir Grenville had not yet returned, the colonists left on his ship and abandoned the settlement. In 1587, Raleigh sent another group of colonists to Roanoke but a war with Spain broke out in 1588 and it kept him from returning until 1590. When Raleigh returned, the colonists had vanished. A single word, "Croatan," carved into a tree, could have referred to a nearby settlement of natives. This suggested a number of possibilities in regard to the missing settlers, although conclusive proof of their fate was never found.

Beginnings of English Colonization

In 1606, King James I of England granted a charter for exploration and colonization to the Virginia Company. This marked the beginning of ventures sponsored by merchants rather than the crown directly. The charter of the Virginia Company had two branches. James I gave one branch to the English city of Plymouth, which had the right to the northern portion of territory on the eastern coast of North America, and the other branch—the London branch of the company—was given the right to the southern portion.

Jamestown Settlement

There were still considerable difficulties in founding and maintaining a permanent settlement in North America. The Plymouth Company failed to establish a lasting settlement. The company itself ran out of money and the settlers that had gone to the New World gave up and abandoned the Sagadahoc colony that they had established in Maine. The London Company decided to colonize the Chesapeake Bay area and the company sent three ships with about 104 sailors to this area in 1607. These ships sailed up a river, which they named the James in honor of the English king, and they established the fort and the permanent settlement of Jamestown. The London company and the men who settled Jamestown were hoping to find a northwest passage to Asia, gold, silver, or to be able to find lands capable of producing valuable goods, such as grapes, oranges, or silk. The colony at Jamestown did not allow the settlers to accomplish any of those things and its location on the river, which became contaminated every spring, led to the outbreak of diseases such as typhoid, dysentery, and malaria. Over half of the colonists died the first year and by the spring of 1609 only a third of the total number of colonists who had joined the colony were still alive.

The survival of the colony initially was accomplished largely due to the efforts of Captain John Smith. Smith was a soldier who turned the focus from exploration to obtaining food. Initially Smith was able to buy and obtain corn from local Indians who were led by Powhatan and his twelve-year-old daughter

> ### Fast Facts
> Over half the colonists died the first year and by the spring of 1609 only a third of the total number of colonists who had joined the colony were still alive.

Pocahontas. Smith also forced all able men in the colony to work four hours a day in the wheat fields that had been planted. Attempts by the London Company to send additional settlers and supplies encountered troubles and were delayed. Thomas Gates and some 600 settlers, who left for Jamestown in 1609, ran aground on Bermuda and had to build a new ship. Although some new settlers did arrive in Jamestown, disease continued to shrink the population and Smith was seriously injured and returned to England. Smith's departure deprived the colony of its most effective and resourceful leader. It was not long after Smith left that the colonists provoked a war with Powhatan, who was beginning to tire of their demands for corn. Powhatan realized that the settlers intended to stay indefinitely and might challenge the Indians for control of the surrounding territory.

Gates finally arrived with only 175 of the original 600 settlers in June of 1610. He found only 60 colonists who had survived the war with the Indians and the harsh winter of 1610, during which they had minimal food and other resources. Gates decided to abandon Jamestown and was sailing down the river with the surviving colonists on board when he encountered the new governor from England, Thomas West, Baron de la Warr. Gates and de la Warr returned to Jamestown, imposed martial law, responded to Indian attacks, and survived a war with the Indians from 1609–1614. Although the war did not end until 1614 when the colonists were able to negotiate a settlement by holding Powhatan's daughter Pocahontas hostage, the situation in Jamestown began to improve in 1610. Some of the settlers were sent to healthier locations, and in 1613 one of them, John Rolfe, married Pocahontas. In 1614, a mild strain of tobacco was introduced to the colony, which gave the colony a crop it could sell for cash.

Two new charters issued by the crown allowed Virginia to extend its borders all the way to the Pacific and made the London Company a joint-stock company. Changes in the company led to a new treasurer who tried to reform Virginia. Sir Edwin Sandy encouraged settlers in Virginia to try to produce grapes and silkworms and to diversify the economy in other ways. Sandy also replaced martial law with English common law. The colonists established a council to make laws, and settlers were given the right to own land. By 1623, 4,000 additional settlers had arrived in Virginia. Attempts to produce and sell crops other than tobacco, however, failed and the arrival of large numbers of new colonists provoked renewed conflict with the Indians who launched a major attack and killed 347 colonists in March of 1622. Investors in the London Company withdrew their capital and appealed to the king, and a royal commission visited the colony. As a result of this investigation, the king declared the London Company bankrupt and assumed direct control of Virginia in 1624. Virginia became the first royal colony, and the crown appointed a governor and a council to oversee its administration.

Two trends continued after the Crown assumed control. The first was continued conflict with the Indians. As a result of war and raids, the Indians in the area immediately around Jamestown had been killed or driven out by 1632. The second trend was the yearly influx of thousands new settlers and a high death rate in the colony. Despite the high mortality rate, the population of the colony began gradually to increase. The expansion of tobacco production led to a demand for labor and thousands of the young men who came were indentured servants. In exchange for their passage to America and food and shelter during their terms of service, these men were bound to work for their master for four or five years. After this time they gained their freedom and often a small payment to help them become established. Most of these men were not able to participate in the running of the colony even after they became free, although some were able to acquire land. In 1634, Virginia was divided into counties and justices were appointed to each with the right to fill all other positions. Thus these positions tended to be dominated by individuals from the same wealthy families. Most of the counties became Anglican and the colony continued to elect representatives to its House of Burgesses, an assembly that had been formed and met with the governor to discuss issues of Common Law. The king, however, refused to recognize the colony's House of Burgesses. After 1660, the colony became even more dominated by the wealthiest 15 percent of the population, and these individuals and their sons served as justices and were elected to the House of Burgesses.

Founding of Maryland

The Maryland colony later resembled the one in Virginia, but its early history was quite different. George Calvert, the first Lord of Baltimore, wanted to establish a colony for Catholics and also as a real estate investment designed to produce a profit. Although the crown granted Calvert's request for a charter, he died before the end of the negotiations, and so it was his son, Cecilius, who received the charter in 1632. The second Lord Baltimore, Cecilius, appointed his brother Leonard to be governor of the colony. Leonard and approximately 300 colonists sailed for America in 1634 on two ships called the "Ark" and the "Dove." They established a settlement on a bluff overlooking one of the tributaries that flows into the Potomac River. The settlers benefited from local Indians, who provided the colonists with shelter and food.

Despite the Catholic values of the Calverts, they realized that the colony would only survive if they could attract thousands of settlers and so they allowed Protestants to join the settlement. When the Catholics became a minority group among the population, the Calverts passed the "Act Concerning Religion" in 1649 that proclaimed religious toleration. However, conflict plagued the colony for years, as this act did not prevent conflict between the Catholics and Protestants. The Calverts also agreed to establish a representative assembly, which was formed in 1635, but the proprietor Lord Baltimore retained the right to grant large estates. The colony was dominated by this distinct upper class that had been given huge land grants even after a severe shortage of labor led to a change in the way in which land was granted. After 1640, each male settler was eligible to receive 100 acres of land for himself, another 100 for his wife, and another 50 for every child in his family. Maryland began to resemble Virginia more closely as it turned to the production of tobacco, largely because Maryland dealt with the need for labor by recruiting indentured servants and later by importing slaves toward the end of the seventeenth century.

Conflict in the Colonies and with Natives

Sir William Berkeley became the royal governor of Virginia in 1642, at the age of thirty-six, and served nearly continuously until 1670. The colonists sent an expedition across the Blue Ridge Mountains and defeated an Indian uprising in 1644. This defeat led to a treaty that ceded most of the territory east of the mountains to the colonists while at the same time restricting their expansion by establishing a boundary beyond which westward expansion was forbidden. The dramatic increase in the population of Virginia, however, which was more than four times larger in 1660 than it had been in 1640 (increasing from 8,000 to 40,000) made it increasingly unlikely that the colonists would permanently honor this agreement. By 1652, three counties had been established in the territory reserved for Indians and conflict with the natives was becoming inevitable; in 1675, fighting broke out.

Conflict in Virginia, however, was not limited to the Indians and the colonists, but also serious disputes among the colonists themselves. The right to vote for delegates to the House of Burgesses had been a right exercised by all white men, but by 1670 it was restricted to white men who owned land. This restriction and the infrequent holding of elections allowed the established landowners to dominate the entire colony. The growing population in the newly settled lands in the West or the backcountry resented the dominance as well as specific decisions made by the elite.

Bacon's Rebellion

Nathaniel Bacon owned a farm in the West and became the leader of a rebellion against the colonial government. Bacon resented the fact that he could not participate in the fur trade controlled by Berkeley and the fact that Berkeley attempted to prevent the settlers from expanding further into Indian territory. Bacon demanded that the governor send forces when fighting with the Indians broke out in 1675. When the governor refused, Bacon offered to do so and then organized an army of backcountry men to fight the Indians. Berkeley declared Bacon and his forces to be rebels and during the subsequent conflict, known as Bacon's Rebellion, the backcountry militia fought against forces sent by

Berkeley. Ultimately Bacon died of dysentery after burning much of Jamestown and Berkeley was able to regain control. Despite earlier reluctance, the Indians were forced to sign a treaty that opened new lands to white settlement. The elites in Virginia supported an increasing turn away from indentured servants and toward slave labor in part because of the unrest that had been caused by the newly-freed but landless former indentured servants.

The Puritans and the Plymouth Colony

The Puritans were a group of Separatists who migrated from England and founded the first enduring settlement in New England. The Puritans had initially settled in Holland where they were not persecuted for their religious beliefs, but they were employed in very low paying jobs. Their children grew up embracing Dutch customs and beliefs rather than those of their English parents. A group of the Separatists in Holland decided to travel to America and create a stable community to spread their religious ideas as well as raise their children according to their own traditions and customs.

Fast Facts **The Mayflower set sail from Plymouth, England, with 35 Pilgrims and 67 others on board and landed at Plymouth Rock on December 21, 1620.**

The Mayflower set sail from Plymouth, England, in 1620 with 35 Pilgrims and 67 others on board. The ship landed in Cape Cod much farther north than intended and in an area outside the control of the London Company. Before landing in an area that was designated as "Plymouth" on a map drawn earlier by John Smith, individuals on board the Mayflower signed the Mayflower Compact establishing a government and agreeing to abide by decisions voted on by a majority of the settlers. The Pilgrims landed at Plymouth Rock on December 21, 1620 and like earlier settlers in the New World they endured a very difficult first year. The winter was hard and half the colonists died the first year. The assistance of local Indians, who taught the settlers how to fish and plant corn, was one factor in the survival of the colonists. Later, the settlers and the Indians held a joint feast of celebration after the first harvest. Ultimately, the local Indians were devastated by the spread of European diseases. The land on which the Pilgrims settled was not suitable for agricultural pursuits but the colonists were able to sell furs and fish for a profit. The population of the Plymouth colony grew to 300 and the colonists elected William Bradford as their governor

In England the death of James I led to even more repressive policies toward the Puritans. His son and successor Charles I imprisoned many Puritans for their beliefs and dissolved Parliament to eliminate any opposition to his policies. Despite such policies a group of Puritan merchants was able to obtain a grant of land in New England and they acquired a charter from the king allowing them to create the Massachusetts Bay Company. The Massachusetts

Bay Company was a joint stock company but the owners who wanted to create a Puritan colony bought out the rights of the other owners, including those who preferred to stay in England, and elected John Winthrop to serve as Governor. They sailed from England in 1630. This voyage was unique because with 1,000 people it marked the largest single migration during the seventeenth century and because the charter of the Massachusetts Bay Company accompanied the colonists. Since the colonists had purchased and taken the charter with them to the New World, they did not have to answer to anyone in England. The size of this migration led to the establishment of several settlements including the port city of Boston, Charlestown, Newtown (later renamed Cambridge), Dorchester, Watertown, Concord, Sudbury, and others). Winthrop and other colonists wanted to establish a model city that other communities could see and attempt to copy. The Pilgrims did not escape the consequences of harsh winters—200 settlers died the first winter—but the presence of a large number of families provided a sense of security and additional settlers as well as co-operation with the natives allowed the colony to survive and to grow.

Some English colonists began to migrate from the original settlements to the surrounding areas. Some individuals left because they did not want to abide by the strict rules of the church-dominated government, while others left to search for more fertile land on which to farm. The Connecticut River valley was very attractive because it was isolated from the settlements in Massachusetts Bay and because of the fertile soil. Thomas Hooker left the Bay and established the town of Hartford in 1635. He and members of two other towns created their own colony with similar laws, which were detailed in the Fundamental Orders of Connecticut, to the Massachusetts Bay Colony but they allowed more of the adult men in the community to vote and hold office. Another community in New Haven drew up a constitution that established a Bible-based constitution that was even stricter than that of Massachusetts Bay. New Haven was an independent colony until 1662 when a royal charter handed control of New Haven over to Hartford.

Founding of Rhode Island, New Hampshire, Maine

Roger Williams, a minister in Salem, Massachusetts, founded another English colony called Rhode Island. Although Williams was a dedicated Separatist, he believed and proclaimed in public that the land occupied by the colonists was the property of the natives. The colony decided to deport him but he fled and after taking refuge with an Indian tribe he created the town of Providence. In 1644, he was able to obtain a charter from Parliament. Williams created a government that was separate from the church and Rhode Island practiced religious toleration.

Another member of the community in Massachusetts, Anne Hutchinson, provided further impetus for migration. Hutchinson disputed the claim that all of the current members of the clergy were in fact the "elect" and therefore invested with spiritual authority. She also challenged ideas regarding the proper role of women. Hutchinson began to declare her ideas publicly and the elite in the colony organized and convicted her of heresy and sedition and banished her from the colony in 1638. Hutchinson settled near Providence and later moved to New York where she died in 1643 during an Indian uprising.

New Hampshire and Maine were established in 1629 by individuals who were the proprietors of the colonies, but initially few people were willing to settle in these areas. After Hutchinson was banished, one of her followers, John Wheelwright settled in New Hampshire and other colonists followed. This influx of settlers led to the designation of New Hampshire as a separate colony in 1679 while Maine remained part of Massachusetts until 1820.

Conflict between the colonists and the natives continued to occur and in 1675, the bloodiest and most prolonged conflict began, known as King Philip's War. An Indian chief who was referred to as King Philip by the settlers (his own people called him Metacomet), rose up against the English settlers and killed over a thousand people living in towns in Massachusetts. Only a year later, in 1676, the colonists were able to effectively fight the Indians. The colonists had allied themselves with a group of Mohawk who killed Metacomet, leading to a virtual collapse of the coalition of Indian tribes he had formed and the defeat by the colonists of the uprising. Although both the colonists and the Indians began to use the new flintlock rifles and the Indians constructed forts, the English had a greater number of weapons and were growing in number while the Indians continued to be divided into various tribes or nations and to be reduced in number by disease and war.

Resurgence of English Colonial Activity

The charter given to Lord Baltimore for Maryland in 1632 proved to be the last issued, and therefore Maryland was the last English colony established in North America for almost thirty years. The English Crown did not issue any additional charters during this period because of unrest in England. The dismissal of Parliament by Charles I and his attempts to rule absolutely led to a crisis and eventually to a Civil War. Charles I was forced to call a meeting of Parliament in 1640, eleven years after he dismissed it, in order to request new taxes. Parliament refused and when he dismissed and recalled it again, parliament responded, in 1642, by organizing a military force. Civil war broke out and the king was defeated. Oliver Cromwell, leader of the largely Puritan parliamentary forces beheaded the king and assumed the position and title of Protector. Cromwell ruled in an absolute manner and resentment built up against him. When he died in 1658 and his son was unable to maintain order, Charles II, the heir of the executed King Charles I, achieved the "restoration" of the monarchy. Charles II gave several of his most loyal supporters grants of land in the new world. He issued charters for the colonies of Carolina, New York, New Jersey, and Pennsylvania.

A series of charters issued between 1663 and 1665 gave the rights, in form of joint titles, to a vast section of land from Virginia to Florida, including all territory west to the Pacific Ocean, to eight individuals or proprietors. The proprietors retained estates for themselves and distributed the rest in a headright system, and the territory of Carolina was named in deference to King Charles. Many of the owners lost interest after the initial idea of attracting settlers from within the existing colonies was unsuccessful, but Anthony Ashley Cooper convinced them to finance expeditions from England.

Foundations of the Carolina Colony

In 1690, settlers who had come over from England founded the city that would become Charleston. Cooper was influenced by John Locke and the two drew up the Fundamental Constitution for Carolina in 1669. This Constitution divided the territory into counties of equal size and also provided for a stratified society dominated by the aristocrats who owned large estates. Despite a constitution based upon these ideas, the society envisioned by Locke and Cooper, who had become the Earl of Shaftesbury, did not become a reality. Instead Carolina was plagued by tensions between the northern and southern regions that had distinctively different economies and social customs. The north was dominated by small farmers while the south, especially the area around Charleston, was dominated by the wealthy planters who established a hierarchical social system that favored the aristocratic planters. The death of Lord Shaftesbury and the inability of the other proprietors to maintain control enabled the colonists to seize control in 1719, and then ten years later the king divided the region into the two royal colonies of North and South Carolina.

Founding of New York and New Jersey

Conflict between England and the Netherlands spread to the New World after Charles II granted his brother James, the duke of York, all the territory between the Connecticut and Delaware rivers in 1664. The Dutch had already claimed this area and there was a brief struggle between the two countries. By 1674, the English had permanently captured the capitol of the Dutch colony of New Netherlands and renamed the territory New York. James was now in control of the territory. Since there were large numbers of Dutch, Scandinavians,

Germans, French, and Africans living within the territory, James did not impose Catholicism on these settlers nor did he create representative assemblies. James allowed some of the Dutch landowners to keep their lands and granted large estates to a number of his own supporters. The colony was dominated by a diverse group of individuals including Dutch landowners, wealthy English landlords, and the duke's political appointees. The population in New York grew from approximately 7,000 to an estimated 30,000 by 1685. James gave a large section of land south of New York to two of his political supporters who held proprietary interests in Carolina. One supporter sold his interests and the other, Sir George Carteret, named the territory New Jersey. New Jersey was divided into two distinct territories, East and West, until 1702 when the two halves were reunited, but religious and ethnic differences between the two regions persisted long after 1702. New Jersey did not develop a class of large landowners nor was the government able to exercise complete control over the diverse population.

Settling Pennsylvania

Pennsylvania was founded by members of the Society of Friends, an English Protestant sect. This society, which came to be known as the Quakers, came about in the mid-seventeenth century and was founded by George Fox. The Quakers had no formal church government and they believed that all people could cultivate divine qualities within themselves and attain salvation. The refusal of Quakers to participate in or take sides during conflicts incurred resentment in England and the Quakers began to emigrate to the Americas. A few settled in already established colonies but for the majority, America offered the opportunity to found their own colony. The conversion of several wealthy and important individuals in English society enabled them to carry out this goal. William Penn converted to Quakerism and he and George Fox began work to create a colony. They received a charter for a vast tract of land between New York and Maryland after the death of Penn's father, because the crown had owed the elder Penn a large sum of money. The only condition placed on the grant was that the territory had to be named Pennsylvania in honor of William Penn's father. William Penn recruited settlers, planned the colony carefully, and benefited from the fertile soil and mild climate. All of these factors enabled Pennsylvania to become one of the most prosperous colonies. Penn had sailed to the New World in 1682 and founded a city he named Philadelphia, which meant "the city of brotherly love" in Greek. While Penn managed to avoid conflicts with natives, who were paid money in compensation for the land occupied by colonists, a number of settlers objected to the tremendous amount of power held by Penn. Penn finally agreed, shortly before departing to England in 1701, to allow a Charter of Liberties to be created. This document established a representative assembly that limited the proprietor and also stated that the lower counties of the colony could have a separate assembly. The lower three counties did establish an assembly and in 1703 they became a separate colony, known as Delaware.

During the seventeenth century and well into the eighteenth century, the Spanish continued to exercise control over vast territories in the Americas. The Spanish considered the greatest threat to be the French, as they had sponsored explorations down the Mississippi and claimed the territory of Louisiana. The Spanish fortified their position, fearing French expansion, although the Spanish represented a threat to the growing English presence on the eastern seaboard of North America. The Spanish had claimed parts of Florida and were moving into the western areas of this territory, northward into Georgia, and were looking even farther north in the direction of Carolina. During the eighteenth century, there were tensions and conflict broke out primarily between the Spanish and the English but also between the Spanish and the French. English pirates attacked Spanish settlements and the English attempted to convince the Indians in Florida to rise up against the missions. The Spanish offered to give freedom to the African slaves of Carolina settlers if they converted to Catholicism. The Spanish organized one hundred slaves from Carolina and formed them into a military unit that was given the task of defending the northern border of New Spain. Florida ultimately came under the control of the British, but only after the Seven Years' War (1757–1763), also known as "The French and Indian War."

Founding the Georgia Colony

Georgia was the last English colony to be founded in North America. General James Oglethorpe and several other trustees were given the task of overseeing this colony. Georgia was founded to provide a military barrier or buffer zone between South Carolina and Spanish Florida. Oglethorpe and others, however, were appalled by the number of English citizens in prison due to debts and thought the colony could provide an opportunity for the poorer population of England. Oglethorpe himself led the expedition to Georgia and built a fortified town in 1773. The colony excluded Catholics and slaves, as it was feared that the former might join with the Catholic Spanish forces and the later might disrupt internal order. The trustees also regulated trade with the Indians in order to avoid being dependent upon them during a conflict. Although a few people were released from debtors prison and sailed to Georgia, most of the colonists were poor tradesmen and artisans or people who had been persecuted for their religious beliefs. Many of the settlers came from Scotland, Switzerland, and Germany and of the colonies founded by England Georgia had the lowest number of English settlers. Oglethorpe not only set up the colony as a defensible military settlement but he also exercised almost complete control, although his constant regulation of the colony produced resentment. After the threat from the Spanish had been reduced, Oglethorpe was unable to maintain this control and Georgia, like other colonies, elected a legislature and reduced restrictions on the colonists. Although the population in Georgia grew slowly, it began to resemble South Carolina in its development.

Attempts at Stronger Control of the Colonies

The crown had exercised only slight control over the colonies including those of which it had taken direct control and the colonies themselves remained separate. The increasing size and commercial success of the colonies, however, began to attract the attention of England. The English government passed a series of acts in an attempt to regulate colonial trade and obtain a more favorable trading situation for England. Parliament passed a law prohibiting Dutch ships from continuing their contact with the colonies in the 1650s.

The Navigation Acts

The Navigation Acts, passed in 1660, 1663, and 1673, further restricted trade by and with the colonies. The act passed in 1660 stated that only English ships could trade with the colonists and the colonists could only sell tobacco and other goods produced in the colonies to England or its other territories. The act passed in 1663 required that all goods being sent from Europe to the Colonies had to be conducted by English ships and had to pass through England to pay taxes on the shipment. The act passed in 1673 created taxes or duties on coastal trade between the colonies and provided for the appointment of customs officials who enforced the Navigation Acts. The king recognized that the largely independent colonial governments, with the exception of Virginia, were unlikely to enforce these new regulations. King James II began to take steps in 1679 to gain control over a central area in the English New World in order to be able to effectively enforce regulations imposed by England. The king first separated New Hampshire from Massachusetts and appointed a governor for New Hampshire. King James II then accused Massachusetts of violating the Neutrality Acts and revoked its charter. Charles II, who succeeded him on the throne, combined the government of Massachusetts with that of the rest of the New England colonies, and later New York and New Jersey, and created the Dominion of New England. Increasing interference and control by the crown produced tension and resentment in the colonies, which were used to regulating their own affairs and exercising rights in their colonial assemblies.

James II also tried to exercise more absolute control in England and to restore Catholicism as the official faith. These actions led to a revolt in England in 1688, when Parliament invited James's Protestant daughter Mary and her husband, William of Orange, who ruled the Netherlands, to become the joint monarchs of England. James II fled to France and the bloodless revolution not only resulted in the rule of William and Mary but it also firmly established the role of Parliament and the limitations of the monarch's power in England. When the news of the "Glorious Revolution" in England reached the Dominion of New England, colonists overthrew the unpopular governor appointed by the crown, Sir Edmund Andros. The new monarchs in England abolished the New England Dominion but in 1691 they combined Massachusetts with Plymouth and made it a single royal colony. The new charter gave the crown the right to appoint the governor and it made church membership instead of property a requirement for voting and holding office. The revolution in England had had repercussions in British North America as well as in England. Initially, the colonists representative bodies were restored but the desire of the crown to unify and exercise greater control over the British colonies did not disappear and the colonial governments were set up in a way that would allow attempts to exercise such control from above.

Growth of the Slave Trade

The shortage of labor in the southern colonies and the drop in the number of people coming to the colonies as indentured servants forced the colonists to search for other sources of labor. Although the colonists used African servants and slaves almost immediately upon settling the New World, the slave trade and the slave population in English North America remained small in the first half of the seventeenth century. Towards the end of the seventeenth century increasing numbers of slaves from Africa became available and the demand for them in North America further stimulated the growth of the transatlantic slave trade. By the nineteenth century millions of Africans had been forcibly taken from their native land and sold into perpetual slavery. Slaves were brought to the coast and sold where the Europeans had established forts in Africa after which they were packed into the lower region of ships as closely together as possible for the long journey to the Americas. Slaves were kept chained together, given only enough food and water to keep them alive, and were unable to wash themselves. Many slaves died during the "Middle Passage" and those who survived were then sold to work on plantations in the Caribbean, Brazil, or North America. It was only after 1697 that large numbers of slaves began to be sold to the English colonies and by 1760 approximately a quarter of a million slaves were present in the colonies and concentrated in the south. Slave labor replaced indentured servitude and a race-based system of perpetual slavery developed. Colonial assemblies began to pass "slave codes" in the eighteenth century. These codes identified all non-whites or dark skinned people as slaves, made their condition permanent, and legalized slavery in British North America.

Development of Trade Networks

American merchants who participated in trading activities were at a disadvantage since they had almost no gold or silver and their paper currency was not usually accepted as payment for goods. American merchants were also unable to plan in advance because they did not know what they would find in foreign ports and often had to trade goods at several different ports in order to find a commodity they could sell for a profit. Despite these obstacles the colonists did continue to trade with each other and also began to establish trade with West Indies. The British colonists in North America traded rum, agricultural products, meat and fish to Caribbean islands, which offered sugar, molasses, and sometimes slaves in return. England also participated in this trade, taking products from North America to Africa to trade for slaves, then taking these slaves to the Caribbean in exchange for sugar and molasses, and then finally trading these items back to the colonists. This triangular trade, however, was not the dominant or only exchange of goods taking place during this period; in fact, a complex system of trading routes and exchange of goods was taking place. The colonists were also sending raw materials to England in exchange for industrial goods and the colonists continued, even after the Navigation Acts forbade it, to trade with the French, Spanish, and Dutch West Indies.

While trade and demand for material goods was growing in the colonies, tension and religious revivals were also taking place. Puritan New England experienced strain and tensions in the 1680s and 1690s. Population growth and the tendency to divide land among all sons rather than just leaving it to the eldest resulted in a shortage of land and young men began to leave their communities in search of greater opportunities. The rise of commercial activity also changed the community and produced tension.

Salem Witch Trials

During this period of increasing tensions, several communities held witchcraft trials. In Salem, Massachusetts, a group of young girls accused servants from West India and then older members of the community, mostly women, of exercising powers given to them by Satan. Other towns also experienced turmoil and charged residents with witchcraft. In Salem, nineteen people were killed before the trials ended in 1692 when the girls admitted their stories were not true. The witchcraft trials illustrate the highly religious nature of the New England society, but they also suggest that individuals who do not conform to societal expectations are at risk. Most of the women accused were older, either widows or unmarried women who did not have children, and who were outspoken and often critical of their community. Some of these women had

Library of Congress

An accused witch is taken to be hanged during Salem Witch Trials.

acquired property despite the accepted views and limitations regarding women's role in society.

Religion in the Colonies and the Great Awakening

The religious nature of colonial settlers did not lead to the kind of religious intolerance or persecution that had plagued Europe since the Reformation. Conflict between different religious groups did break out occasionally, but British North America enjoyed a far greater degree of religious toleration than anywhere else. One of the reasons this toleration existed was due to the number of different religious groups that had emigrated to North America, and the fact that in all colonies, except for Virginia and Maryland, the laws establishing the Church of England as the official faith of the colony were ignored. Even among the Puritans, differences in religious opinion led to the establishment of different denominations. While religious toleration was often achieved, Protestants still tended to view Roman Catholics as their rivals and as a threat. In Maryland, where the largest concentration of them lived (about 3,000), Catholics were actually persecuted. Jews were more uniformly persecuted. Jews could not vote or hold office in any of the colonies and it was only in Rhode Island that they were able to practice their religion openly. The other main trends in addition to toleration were the tendency of communities to spread westward, the rise of cities, and a perceived as well as real decline in religious piousness.

This sense of the weakening of religious authority and faithfulness led to the Great Awakening. The Great Awakening refers to a period beginning in the 1730s in which several well-known preachers traveled through British North America giving speeches and arguing for the need to revive religious piety and closer relationships with God. The main message of the preachers emphasized that everyone has the potential, regardless of past behavior, to reestablish their relationship with God. This message appealed to many women and to many younger sons of landowners who stood to inherit very little. The most well-known preacher during this period was Jonathon Edwards. Edwards denounced some currently held beliefs as doctrines of easy salvation. Edwards gave sermons at his church in Northampton about the absolute sovereignty of God, predestination, and salvation by grace alone. The Great Awakening further divided religion in America by creating distinctions between New Light or revivalists, Old Light or traditional doctrines or religious groups, and new groups that incorporated elements of both. The various revivalists or New Light groups did not agree on every issue. Some of the revivalists denounced education and learning from books while others saw education as a means of furthering religion and founded schools.

During the same period that some individuals were stressing a need for renewed spiritual focus, others were beginning to embrace the ideas of the Enlightenment. The Scientific Revolution had demonstrated the existence of natural laws that operated in nature and enlightened thinkers began to argue that man had the ability to improve his own situation through the use of rational thought and acquired knowledge. Intellectuals of the Enlightenment shifted the focus from God to man and introduced the idea of progress, arguing that man could improve his own situation and that individuals should make decisions on how to live rather than just having faith in God and waiting for a better life upon death and salvation. Enlightenment thought had a tremendous impact among the North American colonists, who began to found more schools, to encourage the acquisition of knowledge, and to become more interested in gaining scientific knowledge. The colleges that had been established in North America taught the scientific theories held by Copernicus, who argued that planets rotated around the sun not the earth, and Newton, who introduced the key principles of physics (gravity). The colonists did not just learn European theories. Colonists themselves, such as Benjamin Franklin, began to carry out their own experiments and form their own theories. Franklin experimented with electricity and was able to demonstrate in 1752 by use of a kite, that electricity and lightning were the same. Scientific theories also led to inoculations against smallpox. Puritan theologian Cotton Mather convinced the population of Boston to allow themselves to be injected with a mild case of smallpox in order to build up their resistance to the disease and make it unlikely that they would contract it again. Leading theologians and scientists spread European scientific ideas and developed their own theories and applications using the knowledge they had acquired.

Differentiation in the Colonies

All of the colonies grew more separate and farther removed from the customs and control of England during the period from 1650 to 1750. The colonies were also developing in ways distinctively different from each other. The greatest differences were between the northern colonies and the southern colonies. The north had small farms and more commerce, while large plantations and a large slave population dominated the south. The colonies, however, did continue to share some characteristics, for instance the Great Awakening had an impact in all of the colonies and a large number of the white settlers in all of British North America remained devoted to some religion. The majority of white colonists accepted and reflected the belief that Native Americans and African Americans were inferior to the colonists and that they were justified in forcing the natives off the land and in depriving African Americans of their freedom.

The Colonies in the Eighteenth Century

War broke out in North America between the British and the French in the 1750s. This conflict was an extension of a larger conflict between Great Britain and France. Colonists in British North America refer to the conflict as the French and Indian War. The French were in control of the entire Mississippi River including present day Louisiana, and also the territory west to the Rocky Mountains and south to the Rio Grand. The French had established a series of forts, trading posts, and missions in this territory. The French had also created a greater network of trading routes, but had less colonists in North America than did the British. New Orleans was founded in 1718 and the French, as did the British colonists, developed a plantation system in the area around Louisiana. The support and assistance of Native Americans would be an important factor in the struggle for North America. While both the British and the French were aware of this fact, by the time the conflict spread to North America the French had already established better ties with the natives and the British were unable to alter this situation. The British could offer the natives more money or goods and more desirable goods in exchange for their assistance, but various native groups held the French in much higher esteem. Unlike the British, the French traders and settlers had not forced out or displaced native tribes and they had intermarried with the natives and adopted some of their customs. The French were far more tolerant of Indian customs and even converted many natives to Catholicism without challenging or denouncing their traditional values or beliefs. Neither the British nor the French had been able to establish ties with the five Indian member-nations of Iroquois Confederacy. This Confederation dominated the Ohio Valley and the surrounding regions. The Iroquois refused to take sides during the French and Indian War and were able to continue to trade with both sides, playing each against the other and enabling the Iroquois to continue to maintain control of the Great Lakes region.

The French and Indian War

The conflict that broke out in the 1750s between the French and the British in the New World was partly a result of earlier conflicts that had unsettled the tentative balance in the New World. As a result of tensions and earlier fighting, the governor of Virginia sent a militia force under the command of a young colonel, George Washington, into the Ohio Valley. Washington built a stockade, named Fort Necessity, fairly close to the French position on the site of what is now Pittsburgh. The French attacked Fort Necessity and forced Washington to surrender, beginning the French and Indian War.

There were three phases of fighting during the French and Indian War. The first phase lasted from the attack on Fort Necessity in 1754 through 1756 and was characterized by the limited nature of the war, which did not extend beyond the North American continent. The second phase of the war occurred during 1756–1757 and was marked by the beginning of the Seven Years' War (in 1757). During this phase, the war spread to the West Indies, India, and Europe but most of the fighting continued to be in North America where the British made little progress. In order to assist the British military effort, the British secretary of state, William Pitt, began to direct the war effort and to issue orders to the colonists. Pitt authorized British commanders to forcibly enlist colonists to serve and to seize needed supplies from the colonists. These measures led to a struggle between the colonists and the British authorities that seriously hindered the war effort. Pitt responded by relaxing most of the offensive measures, an act that marked the beginning of the final phase of the war in 1758. Pitt also sent additional troops to the colonies and the colonists began to aid the war effort once again, which led the British beginning to have some military success.

The fall of Quebec in September of 1759 to British forces was a significant step towards bringing the war to a close. The French army officially surrendered in 1760 but the Peace of Paris that ended the war was not signed until 1763. This treaty ceded some French territory in India and Canada to the British as well as all French territory in North America east of the Mississippi. The French gave New Orleans and their claims to the territory west of the Mississippi to Spain. The French and Indian War expanded Great Britain's territory in North America and was a profound defeat for the Indian tribes in the Ohio Valley. In particular, the outcome of the war was a defeat for those native groups that had sided with the French. However, the result of the war also led to an increase in tensions between the British and the colonists.

The Colonies and the Coming American Revolution

Many members of the British government were angered by the failure of the colonists to fight the French effectively during the French and Indian War and felt that the colonists should shoulder more of the financial burden incurred during a war that largely benefited the colonies. England began to try to assert increased authority in the colonies. This desire for increased control stemmed partly from resentment over the fact that the colonists continued to defy the Navigation Acts and traded with the French and other nations and partly out of a desire to tax the colonists. George III, who became king in 1760, took an extremely hard line toward the colonists and was unable to establish and maintain a stable government. The king made George Grenville prime minister in 1763 and it was Grenville who began to try to compel the colonists to pay increased taxes and to obey the laws of England. The British also issued a proclamation in 1763 which forbade settlers to advance beyond the mountains that lay just to the west of the eastern colonies. This proclamation improved relations between the British and the natives but provoked the colonists who wanted to be able to emigrate westward. This declaration proved completely ineffective at restricting or halting the advance into native territory.

> **Two measures enacted by England outraged the colonists:** **Fast Facts**
> - **permanently stationing regular British troops in the North American colonies and requiring the colonists to provide troops with shelter and provisions;**
> - **the passing of various acts, such as the Sugar Act and the Stamp Act, which raised taxes or duties on specific goods.**

Grenville later enacted two measures that outraged the colonists. One was his decision to permanently station regular British troops in the North American colonies and to require, under the provisions of the Mutiny Act of 1765, the colonists to provide the British troops with shelter and help to supply their provisions. The British increased their presence in the colonies by sending both soldiers and ships. This presence, as well as that of royal officials, helped enforce the Navigation Acts more effectively. Furthermore, the British imposed restrictions on manufacturing in the colonies in order to continue to have a market for their own industrial goods. The other unpopular measure was the passing of various acts that raised taxes or duties on specific goods. The

Currency Act, passed in 1764, forbade the colonial assemblies from printing their own money and the Sugar Act, passed in that same year, raised the duty on sugar. The Stamp Act that would be passed in 1765 imposed a tax on every printed item such as newspapers, deeds, and pamphlets produced in the colonies.

The colonists were not able effectively to resist these measures immediately, because there were still deep divisions within such colonies as Pennsylvania and North Carolina and among the thirteen colonies. A more unified resistance began to emerge, however, as a direct result of Grenville's policies. The restrictions on expansion westward, printing currency, manufacturing, and the Stamp Act combined to produce resentment among colonists in the north and in the south and among a majority of the colonists. In particular, the Stamp Act was universally opposed not because the tax itself was so burdensome but because it represented a raise in taxes and not the regulation of commerce. The colonists asserted that they could only be taxed with the consent of their assemblies while the British maintained that all British subjects were represented indirectly by Parliament and were bound to obey all laws and taxes enacted by that body. Various individuals and colonies began to protest and in October of 1765 the Stamp Act Congress, with delegates from nine colonies, met in New York and denied the right of the British government to tax the colonies except by consent of the representative bodies in the colonies. In Boston, men belonging to the "Sons of Liberty," a protest group that had just been formed, burned stamps and harassed stamp agents. Unrest broke out in other cities as well and citizens such as Thomas Hutchinson, who were viewed as loyal British aristocrats, were attacked or had their houses burned. The crisis only passed when Great Britain repealed the Stamp Act in 1766 due to pressure not from the American colonists but from British merchants whom the colonists had boycotted in protest of the unpopular Sugar and Stamp Acts. The British Parliament passed a Declaratory Act reaffirming the right of Parliament to enact and enforce any and all laws without the consent of local assemblies, but this act was simply ignored by the colonists who considered the repeal of the Stamp Act as a victory.

A new British government was formed and led by William Pitt but Charles Townshend exercised real authority. Townshend responded to the refusal of the New York assembly to vote to provide the British troops stationed there with provisions by disbanding the New York assembly. Townshend also established new taxes on goods imported from Great Britain, including lead, paint, paper, and tea. He hoped to avoid incurring the anger of all colonists by disbanding only the New York assembly and by taxing only external transactions and imports from overseas. The colonists, however, viewed the new taxes as violating their principle of no taxation without representation and realized that the suspension of the New York assembly had implications for all colonial assemblies. Townshend also established a new board of customs commission that effectively prevented smugglers from doing trade in the harbor of Boston, although they continued to trade with other colonial ports. The colonists in Boston organized a boycott against the British and the prime minister who came to power in 1770 (Townsend had died in 1767) repealed all the Townshend duties except for the tax on tea.

The "Boston Massacre"

An incident in Boston occurred in March of 1770 between British soldiers and a mob of dockworkers or "liberty boys." The crowed began to pelt the sentries with rocks and snowballs and the British captain, Thomas Preston, lined his men up to protect the customs house in Boston. The British soldiers fired into the crowd and killed five people. Although it is unclear what exactly provoked their fire, local newspapers and resistance leaders referred to the incident as the "Boston Massacre." Samuel Adams was one of the individuals who was outraged over the incident in Boston and who began to argue that Britain was morally corrupt. In 1772, Adams also suggested that a committee be formed in order to make public specific grievances against England and to proclaim the misdeeds of the British. The "Boston Massacre" had provoked considerable sympathy for the victims and outrage against the British and the continued enforcement of the Navigation Acts continued to provoke further resentment. The colonists circulated pamphlets describing grievances, giving speeches, and discussing such issues at local taverns.

The Tea Act and "Boston Tea Party"

As a result of the near financial failure of Britain's East India Company, which had large stocks of tea that it was unable to sell in Britain, the government passed the Tea Act of 1773. This act allowed the company to export and sell the tea in the colonies without paying any taxes or duties. This act meant that the company could undersell colonial merchants and effectively dominate the tea market in British North America. This act actually made tea available at a lower price, but the colonists initiated a boycott against British tea. According to the colonists, the continued existence of the Townshend Act and the exemption granted to the East India Company further violated American rights including their right to no taxation without representation. This tea boycott was able to gain support among a large section of the population, including a large number of women who formed "The Daughters of Liberty" group. On December 16, 1773, local citizens dressed as Mohawk Indians, went aboard three East India Company ships, and threw chests of tea into the harbor. Other colonies effectively prevented the East India Company from landing and unloading their shipments of tea.

The British responded to the "Boston Tea Party" by passing four acts in 1774. These acts closed the port of Boston, reduced the powers of self-government in Massachusetts, stated that royal officers could be tried in other colonies or in Britain, and provided for the stationing or quartering of troops by the colonists. These Coercive Acts, known as the Intolerable Acts in the American colonies, galvanized support for Massachusetts among the other colonies. The colonists opposed to British actions, in all colonies, were able to unify and to form various kinds of organizations. Virginia established a committee of inter-colonial correspondence that made it possible for all of the colonies to cooperate effectively.

The War for Independence

Fast Facts

The Declaration of Independence first described the theory that governments have the obligation to protect the life, liberty, and the pursuit of happiness of their citizens.

The First Continental Congress met in 1774 and delegates from all of the colonies except Georgia attended. The decisions made at this congress meeting included rejection of a proposal that would have united all of the colonies under British rule, and approval of or voting on a list of grievances addressed to the king. The congress also agreed to accept a proposal to carry out military preparations due to the threat of a British attack on Boston, and agreed to form a "Continental Association" to oversee enforcement of a series of boycotts. The last resolution of the Congress was an agreement to meet again the following year. In Britain, Lord North and the British Parliament passed a measure that would have allowed the colonial assemblies to actually assign taxes upon the demand of parliament but this concession came too late and did not appease moderate colonists in part because war had already broken out by the time it was declared.

The defensive measures approved by the Continental Congress had resulted in the training of a number of individuals in Massachusetts who were to be prepared to fight on a minute's notice. General Thomas Gage, the British commander in Boston, was reluctant to take action or even to arrest the leaders of the rebel movement such as Sam Adams, due to the size of his forces. The information that the minutemen were storing a large amount of ammunition in Concord convinced him to act and he marched his regiment towards Concord. The colonists, however, were not caught unaware because they had been expecting a British action of this nature and William Dawes and Paul Revere were given the task of alerting the colonists. Having issued the warning as planned, a group of minutemen were waiting for the redcoats (British soldiers) in Lexington and the first shots of the American Revolution were fired. Several minutemen were killed immediately and they were not able to prevent the British advance, but as the British marched, local farmers and colonists fired shots, and by the end of the day the British had lost more soldiers than the colonists. By the time the British reached Concord most of the ammunition had been moved to another location.

The Second Continental Congress met in Philadelphia three weeks after the battles of Lexington and Concord. All of the representatives present, Georgia did not have a delegate present, voted to support the conflict with Britain but some of the colonists wanted to fight for independence while others wanted only to force the British to make some concessions and address colonial grievances. It was the refusal of the British, in the first year of the war, to make any concessions as well as their blocking of colonial ports, hiring of German mercenaries, and attempting to recruit Indians to fight that alienated additional colonists and convinced many that independence was the only real solution. In a pamphlet titled "Common Sense" by Thomas Paine, a recent immigrant from England, he argued that it was only common sense to break away from a political system that allowed such abuses against its own citizens to occur. This pamphlet, costly encounters with British troops, and British governmental actions resulted in the rapid growth of support for complete independence in 1776.

The Continental Congress was also coming to the conclusion that a complete break with England was necessary and appointed a committee to draw up a resolution stating this sentiment. Thomas Jefferson, assisted by Benjamin Franklin and John Adams, wrote the Declaration of Independence. The declaration first described the theory that governments have the obligation to protect the life, liberty, and the pursuit of happiness of its citizens and then went on to list the specific ways in which the British king and parliament had failed to uphold this duty. Therefore, according to the declaration, the United Colonies had no option but to dissolve their ties to Great Britain and set up an independent government of their own.

One of the difficulties in fighting the British was the lack of a centralized authority, therefore the Continental Congress had to request money or taxes from each of the colonies or states. Since states were reluctant to impose new taxes and since few colonists could afford to buy bonds or finance the war effort the Congress had to issue paper or continental money that was not backed by gold or silver and had little value. Inflation increased at a rapid rate and it was only the ability to obtain loans from foreign nations that enabled the colonists to finance the war. Militias were raised by each state and each state retained control of their militia until the Continental Congress created a Continental Army with a single commander, George Washington, in June of 1775. The conflict with Britain divided American society and forced individuals to choose between supporting the revolution or remaining loyal to the English crown and parliament.

Outbreak of the American Revolution

Emmanuel Leutze, *Washington Crossing the Delaware*

The war of independence can be divided into three phases. The initial phase from 1775 to the spring of 1776 consisted mainly of skirmishes since the colonists were not prepared to fight a major conflict and the British were not yet aware that it would be necessary to fight such a conflict. The main fighting during this period took place in Boston where the Battle of Bunker Hill (fought on Breed's Hill) took place on June 17, 1775. Despite serious losses of their own, the Patriots were able to inflict significant losses on the British before withdrawing and continued to launch attacks on the British forces in this area. The British decided that it was too difficult to defend their position in Boston and in March of 1776 they moved their forces, along with hundreds of loyalists, to Halifax, Nova Scotia. The British forces reorganized quickly and established a new base in New York. Meanwhile, the colonists crushed a loyalist uprising in the south and two patriot generals attacked Quebec. These events convinced the British that they were not just dealing with an uprising in Boston but a much greater conflict against all of the colonies.

Early Course of the War

The British sent General William Howe, hundreds of ships, and 32,000 soldiers to New York in order to defeat the colonists. This launched the second phase of the war (1776–1778) during which time the British had the opportunity to crush the rebellion. Howe offered the colonists the option of surrendering and receiving a pardon instead of fighting a costly and potentially futile battle against superior British forces. The Continental army under

Washington's command consisted of only about 19,000 soldiers few of whom were as well-trained or equipped as the British troops. The American forces suffered a series of defeats and had to retreat. In 1776, Washington launched an attack on Christmas night against Hessian forces (German troops hired by Britain) camped on the Delaware River. The Hessians were taken by surprise and Washington defeated them, occupied Trenton, and forced British troops to withdraw from Princeton. Even though Washington could not defend either Trenton or Princeton and had to retreat, he had won two battles and withdrew with most of his original force still intact.

Howe captured Philadelphia in 1777, but the rebellion did not collapse as he had hoped. Furthermore, Howe's failure to move his troops north to meet up with forces under the command of Burgoyne, the original plan, left Burgoyne to carry out a campaign with only his own troops. After two defeats and an attack that prevented a detachment of British soldiers from obtaining necessary supplies, Burgoyne was surrounded at Saratoga and forced to surrender in October of 1777.

Two important events occurred after the defeat of the British at Saratoga. The first event was an offer by Lord North to give the colonists complete home rule within the British empire and the second, partly a result of the British settlement offer, was the official recognition of the United States as a legitimate state by the French government. The French had already provided supplies and financial assistance, but had been reluctant to recognize officially the U.S. without any signs that the U.S. could defeat the British in battle. Saratoga provided such evidence and the French who hoped that a prolonged war would weaken the British empire, not only formally recognized the U.S. but also began to provide substantial military assistance

Allied Victory and British Defeat

During the third and final phase, the war expanded into a conflict in which France, Spain, and the Netherlands joined the colonists in fighting the British and the British employed a new strategy in North America. The British tried to gain the support of loyalists and slaves in the south and began a military campaign in the south that lasted from 1778 through 1781, but the amount of support they hoped to gain from the campaign never materialized. The Patriot forces were more familiar with southern territory and were hard to distinguish from the local population. This phase of the war was characterized by new kinds of warfare and an increased support for and participation in the revolutionary cause. The British suffered several setbacks during this period although they were able to capture Savannah, Georgia, and Charleston, South Carolina. The Patriots had greater success during this period than previously, but also suffered setbacks and disillusionment.

In the fall of 1780, one of the leading American generals, Benedict Arnold, became convinced that the Americans could not win and transferred information regarding the American stronghold of West Point to the British. His betrayal was discovered and the stronghold did not fall, although he fled to the British camp. The unconventional tactics of the American forces and mistakes by the British forced British General Cornwallis to retreat to the north. Cornwallis was subsequently ordered to take up a defensive position at Yorktown where the American and French forces descended upon him and forced him to surrender on October 17, 1781. Two days later, the entire British army of more than 7,000 also surrendered. This defeat led the British to open negotiations to end the war.

The Americans had agreed to negotiate a joint treaty with the French rather than make a separate peace with the British. The refusal of the French to end the war until the British surrendered Gibraltar to the Spanish threatened to prolong the war indefinitely and thus the Americans proceeded to negotiate with the British. Benjamin Franklin, who had been sent to France upon the outbreak of war to try and gain their support, was able to pacify the French representative and avoid a break in American-French relations despite the failure of the Americans to honor their original promise to the French. The treaty between the United States and Britain was signed on September 3, 1783 and according to the treaty, Britain recognized the independence of the United States and ceded a vast territory to the new nation.

Impact of the American Revolution

The American Revolution had a profound impact. Those colonists who supported the revolution may not have all benefited equally under the laws established by the new nation but its establishment represented a victory for their cause. Those colonists who had remained loyal to the British government found themselves in a very different situation. Many had been harassed or arrested during the revolution and after the British were defeated nearly 100,000 fled the country. Some remained abroad while others were able to return after the war and become a part of the American community. The Indian tribes also suffered a profound blow when the French and the British, both of whom had placed some restrictions on the expansion of settlements into Indian territory, were replaced as the dominant force in North America by the United States of America. The Anglican Church ceased to be the official religion of Maryland and Virginia and the Quakers, whose pacifism had prevented them from supporting the war, were weakened by the resentment that this position had stirred up.

Development of the New Nation and the Constitution

The Declaration of Independence had stated two primary beliefs and principles of the delegates who had approved it. The first was the idea that the government should be both created by and responsible to the people. The second was the idea that all men were created equal and entitled to certain rights and privileges. The declaration stated these fundamental ideas and also illustrated the conflict between the ideals of the founding fathers and the reality of the newly formed nation that sanctioned the removal and killing of Native Americans and the enslavement of African Americans.

All of the states except for Connecticut and Rhode Island, which just deleted references to the king, drew up new constitutions. These initial constitutions, however, proved unworkable and by the late 1770s most states began to revise their constitutions. The new constitution written by Massachusetts reflected the changes being made in many of the state constitutions. There were two key differences between these and the earlier documents. The first was the fact that the later documents were written by state legislatures and could be amended by them whereas Massachusetts created a constitutional convention that met specifically for the purpose of creating the new constitution. The other change was a strengthening of the executive branch of government. The colonists thought that the power exercised by the crown had been one of the causes of the corruption and abuses. This had severely limited the powers of governors and governors were forbidden from holding a seat on the legislature while serving as governor. Later constitutions provided that the general population would elect governors, stated that they were to receive a fixed salary that could not be adjusted by the legislature, and gave them increased power to appoint people to positions and to veto legislation.

The Continental Congress had reflected the earlier ideas regarding the need to limit executive authority and the desire to ensure state rights by enacting the Articles of Confederation in 1777. The Congress was given the authority as well as the responsibility to conduct war, foreign policy, and borrow and issue money. The authority of the Congress was severely limited though; it did not have the power to regulate trade, draft troops, or levy taxes. Aside from the powers granted to Congress, however, the

Fast Facts According to the Constitution, all power stemmed from the people.

government was relatively weak and the powers of the president were limited to presiding over sessions of Congress. All thirteen states had to approve any amendments to the Articles of Confederation and there were disagreements about representation, but the Articles were approved and went into effect in 1781. They remained in effect until 1789, but they did not provide the government with the ability to regulate interstate commerce or to make the states enforce legislation that they did not support.

By the 1780s, it was recognized not just among leading advocates of governmental reform such as Alexander Hamilton, but among a number of individuals and groups, that the Articles of Confederation and the inability of the government to impose taxes were problematic. Hamilton and James Madison attended a meeting in Annapolis that approved a proposal for a convention of special delegates to meet in Philadelphia the next year. Only five states had sent delegates to Annapolis and there was little evidence to suggest that more states would send representatives, but a rebellion convinced Washington to support the convention. The convention that met in Philadelphia in 1787 included representatives from every state except Rhode Island. Washington was elected to preside over the sessions and James Madison, as well as the other members of the Virginia delegations, had written a proposal that shaped both the convention as well as the new written constitution. The delegates voted, after a brief debate, to accept a government based upon the idea of a national government that had an executive, a judicial, and a legislative branch, but the convention quickly divided over specific proposals and issues. Key disputes over how the legislature should be set up as well as over the continuation of the slave trade were finally settled by the Great Compromise. A committee including Benjamin Franklin had suggested a type of legislature that included aspects designed to appeal to different groups. The acceptance of this proposal prevented the constitutional convention from collapsing and in 1787 the convention produced the Constitution that is still the basis of our government.

There were several principal ideas incorporated into this new document. According to the Constitution, all power stemmed ultimately from the people. If the people were the highest authority then it followed that powers could be divided between the state and federal government without having to designate one as supreme over the other. One of the other vital aspects of the Constitution was the separation of powers and the system of checks designed to keep any one branch of government from becoming too powerful. Instead of revising the Articles of Confederation, the convention had written a new constitution. Although all states except Rhode Island immediately elected delegates to ratifying conventions, most of which met in early 1788, there was by no means universal support for the new document. Washington, Franklin, and others who supported the adoption of the new constitution began to call themselves Federalists while their opponents were named Anti-federalists. In addition to having the advantage of the support of several well-known figures and political philosophers, such as

James Madison, who could make eloquent arguments, the Federalists were also better organized. The Anti-federalists who had some prominent supporters, such as Henry and Sam Adams, argued that the Constitution failed to uphold some of the basic rights for which the revolution had been fought. They argued that the Constitution would increase taxes, weaken the states, favor the wealthy, and diminish individual liberty. They objected in particular to the absence of a bill of rights or any written guarantee of certain basic rights and freedoms for all citizens.

Several states ratified the Constitution in 1788, but Virginia and New York were deeply divided. The new Constitution was only enacted after these two states had ratified it, by narrow margins, because it was understood that a new government would not work unless it had the support of most of the states. The deciding factor in ratification in New York and Virginia was the argument that a bill of rights could be introduced or added to the Constitution in the form of amendments.

The Constitution of the United States

Here is an overview of the Constitution of the United States of America:

Preamble

"We the People of the United States, in Order to form a more perfect Union, establish Justice, insure domestic Tranquility, provide for the common defense, promote the general Welfare, and secure the Blessings of Liberty to ourselves and our Posterity, do ordain and establish this CONSTITUTION for the United States of America."

Article I

All legislative powers are given to a Federal Congress which will consist of a Senate and a House of Representatives. The creation of an upper house with equal representation and a lower house with proportional representation was achieved as a result of the "Great Compromise." This article indicates that to be eligible to be elected to the House of Representatives an individual must be at least 25 years of age and must have been a citizen of the United States for at least seven years. The number of seats that each state has in the House was designated by the Constitution for the original thirteen colonies. The constitution states that in the future the number of Representatives will be determined proportionally by determining the population of each state, including indentured servants, excluding Indians and counting 3/5ths of the slave population of a state towards its total population in the census to determine seats in the House. (We currently reapportion seats following the national census, which is conducted every ten years.) The Constitution also states that all states must have at least one representative. Representatives will be elected every two years. The House of Representatives has the sole right to impeach the President of the United States.

In order to be eligible to serve as a Senator an individual must be at least thirty years old and must have been a citizen of the United States for at least nine years. Every state shall have two senators to be elected for six year terms. The terms shall be staggered so that a third of the Senate will be elected every two years. The Vice President of the United States is the President of the Senate but will only have a vote when the Senate is equally divided. The Senate has the sole right to try and convict a President who has been impeached and to vote as to whether or not the President shall be removed from office.

In addition to the powers specifically granted to Congress, the necessary and proper clause (elastic clause) expands the power of Congress. Congress can make all laws necessary and proper for enumerated powers. The right of Congress to makes laws that deal with issues not directly stated in the powers given to Congress was upheld by the Supreme Court when it ruled on *McCulloch* vs. *Maryland* (1819). McCulloch was the bank manager of the Baltimore branch of the 2nd Bank of the United States. Maryland tried to make the bank pay state taxes, as the bank was not chartered by the state of Maryland. McCulloch refused to pay the tax after losing in Maryland's State Supreme Court, and the case went before Supreme Court. Maryland was challenging federal authority by arguing that Congress was not given the right to charter a bank. Chief Justice Marshall wrote the opinion of the Supreme Court, in which the Maryland law was struck down in a unanimous decision. The Court ruled that the creation of a national bank was constitutional because the creation of the bank was necessary and proper in order to carry out other powers that were specifically granted to Congress.

Prohibited or denied powers:

Congress cannot pass bills of attainder, a law that declares a person or a group of people guilty of some crime and convicts them without a trial. Congress may not suspend habeas corpus except in times of war or crisis, and it cannot pass ex post facto laws. Ex post facto laws attempt to convict a person for an act committed before the law was passed making the said act illegal.

Article II

Executive:

The constitution states that in order to be eligible to be elected President, an individual must be a natural born citizen, at least forty years old, and has to have been a resident of the United States for at least fourteen years. This article establishes the term of President as four years but places no limit on how many times a person may be re-elected. The President and Vice-President are not elected directly by popular vote, instead each state chooses electors who will cast votes after the popular election has taken place. The number of electors for each state equals the states representation in Congress (House and Senate seats combined). Each party picks a slate of electors and then whichever party carries the popular vote in that state sends their electors to vote in their respective state Capitols. However, electors are not required to vote for the candidate of their party. Also, if there is a dispute over who carried the vote within a state then the state legislator picks which slate goes. Originally the person with highest number of votes was elected President, and the person with the second highest number of votes was Vice-President. This created problems and could lead to a President and Vice-President of different political parties. An amendment was passed that states Presidential and Vice-Presidential candidates will be indicated on tickets of their respective political affiliation.

Upon being elected, and before beginning to carry out his duties, the President must take the following oath, "I do solemnly swear that I will faithfully execute the Office of President of the United States, and will, to the best of my Ability, preserve, protect, and defend the Constitution of the United States." The President is Commander-in-Chief of the military and has the power to make treaties. All treaties, however, have to be ratified by a two-thirds vote of the Senate. The President can make some executive agreements that do not require the approval of Congress. The President also nominates and appoints, with the consent of the Senate, ambassadors, and Supreme Court justices. The cabinet, or group of advisors consulted by the President, is not mentioned in the constitution and was created later. The President may fill any vacancies that may arise during a congressional recess without congressional approval. These appointments stand until the end of next session at which time an election must be held. If the President is impeached or dies while in office, the Vice-President becomes President. He can be impeached for high crimes and misdemeanors.

The President is charged to report "from time to time" on the State of the Union. This report began as a letter to Congress and has progressed to a speech made before a joint session of Congress and the media.

Article III

Judicial Branch:

There are no specific requirements in regard to age or citizenship for individuals to be eligible to be appointed as justices. The constitution states that judicial power shall be vested in one Supreme Court and such inferior courts as Congress deems necessary. The constitution does not indicate how many courts or justices there should be; it is left up to Congress to establish courts and appoint justices as necessary. Supreme Court and other federal justices are appointed for life and can only be removed if they fail to maintain "good behavior." Justices have to be approved in a rigorous appointment process and essentially any behavior, during their time on the bench, with the exception of serious crimes or treason is considered "good behavior." Justices can be impeached and removed for high crimes. The constitution also prohibits Congress or the Federal government from reducing or failing to pay justices after they are appointed and for so long as they are serving on the court. In certain cases, including those involving treason, ambassadors, or cases between states, the case will go directly to the Supreme Court for trial. In all other cases, the accused has the right to a jury trial. In cases that are reviewed by the Supreme Court, after being appealed, the Supreme Court ruling shall be final. This article also states that Treason against the United States consists of levying war against the United States or giving comfort and aid to the enemy and it requires two witnesses to Treason unless there is a confession.

Article IV

This article addresses Federal obligations to the states and state obligations to one another. This article includes the full "faith and credit" clause. It requires that "full faith and credit" shall be given in each state, which means that legal documents valid in one state—wills, marriage licenses, death certificates, adoption papers—must be valid in other states. According to this section of the constitution every citizen must have equal rights under the law in every state and all areas under U.S. jurisdiction. It also requires states to extradite suspects back to the state where the crime was believed to have been committed for trial under that state's legal system. If a state refuses to abide by the jurisdiction requirements, Federal troops can be sent into that state to remove the suspect. New states can be admitted to the Union but new states cannot be formed within the territory of an existing state nor can the boundaries of any state be changed unless this change is approved by the legislatures of the states involved as well as by Congress. The Federal government must make sure that each state has a republican or constitutional form of government and must provide for the defense of each state against invasion or domestic unrest.

Article V

This article states that, when two-thirds of both houses think it is necessary, amendments can be attached to the constitution. It requires that each state call a convention and that nine of the thirteen states, or two-thirds, have to ratify amendments in order for them to become part of the constitution. This article also states that no amendments can be proposed prior to 1808, and excludes certain sections of the constitution from being altered by amendment. In addition it prohibits any state from being denied equal representation in the Senate without its consent.

Article VI

This article, the best supremacy clause, is constantly being invoked by the Supreme Court. This clause insures that when a state law and a federal law come into conflict with one another, the state law must yield.

Article VII

Article seven indicates that nine of the thirteen states must ratify the Constitution in order for it to be approved. Under the Articles of Confederation, unanimous consent was required for ratification. The Founding Fathers did not want the same problems with ratifying the Constitution and thus set a lower bar in regard to approving the Constitution. This article also contains the signatures of all of the delegates to the convention.

Amendments

The first ten amendments are listed as articles and were voted on and ratified together and are an exception to no amendments prior to 1808 because they are allowed by the fifth article of the Constitution. These articles were a necessary addition in order to gain support for the constitution among those who thought that the Federal Government was given too much power and that the rights of citizens had to be protected. The first ten articles or amendments are known as the Bill of Rights.

I – Congress is forbidden to make any law that restricts freedom of religion, free speech, freedom of the press, or the right of individuals to assemble peaceably or petition the government to respond to grievances. (1791)

II – The right of the people to keep and bear arms in a regulated militia is protected and cannot be infringed upon by the government. (1791)

III – The government is forbidden from housing or quartering soldiers in the house of a private citizen, in peace or war, without the consent of the owner. (1791)

IV – This amendment protects the rights of individuals by forbidding their property or house to be searched except where there is probable cause and a search warrant has been issued. (1791)

V – No person shall be deprived of life, limb, or property without due process of law. Nor can anyone be forced to testify or otherwise incriminate themselves. A person may only be held or punished if they have been tried and indicted, except for cases of military personnel during a time of war. It also states that no person can be tried twice for the same crime, a provision known as double jeopardy. A person may, however, be tried separately on criminal and on civil charges. (1791)

VI – This article guarantees the right, in criminal cases, to a speedy and public trial by an impartial jury. It also requires that persons be informed of the charges against them, be able to confront the witnesses against them, and be provided with counsel and be able to call witnesses on their behalf. (1791)

VII – This amendment specifically guarantees the right to a jury trial. It states that in civil suits where the amount is in excess of twenty dollars, the right to trial by jury will apply and no decision by a jury shall be overturned by any court of the United States except according to the rules of common law. (1791)

VIII – Excessive bails or fines cannot be imposed upon individuals and cruel and unusual punishments cannot be imposed. (1791)

IX – This amendment indicates that citizens have rights beyond those stated in the Constitution and that the specific listing of certain rights in the Constitution cannot be used to deny or abridge other rights retained by the people. (1791)

X – Any powers not directly delegated to the Federal government or prohibited by it are reserved for the states or for the people. This is the source of "reserved" powers, the bulk of powers granted to the states. (1791)

XI – This amendment prohibits individuals from suing states. (1798)

XII –States that distinct ballots will be cast for President and Vice-President by the Electors following the popular vote in the presidential election. Also proscribes the manner, time, and place the electors shall meet and vote and when that vote shall be counted. If the electors fail to elect a president by a majority of the vote, the election goes to the House of Representatives. The House may choose from the top three candidates from the Electoral College. (1804)

Amendments XIII-XIV are called the "Reconstruction" or Civil War Amendments, passed in quick succession following the end of the Civil War, primarily dealing with issues regarding newly-freed slaves.

XIII – Bans slavery and involuntary servitude except as punishment for a crime for which one has been convicted. (1865)

XIV – Is the first time the Constitution addresses citizenship. Clearly defined citizenship and stated that: "All persons born or naturalized in the United States, and subject to the jurisdiction thereof are citizens of the United States and of the State wherein they reside." It is significant that this amendment confers state "citizenship" as well as national citizenship, as some Southern states were reluctant to confer all rights and privileges to recently freed slaves.

This amendment repeats the 5th Amendment's protection against "life, liberty, or property without due process of law," this time applying to the states rather than the federal government and extends "equal protection" of the laws, which becomes one of the focal points of the modern civil rights movements in the 1960's.

This amendment allows for reapportionment of the seats in the House of Representatives following a census, counting all persons, except for untaxed Native Americans. It voids the three-fifths clause in Article I regarding population counts. (1868)

XV – Stated that the right of U.S. citizens to vote cannot be denied "on account of race, color, or previous condition of servitude," clearing the way for African-American men (former slaves) 21 years and older to vote. Many Southern states searched for ways to get around the amendment, breaking the spirit of the law with literacy tests, poll taxes, and grandfather clauses. (1870)

XVI – Permits Congress to pass legislation allowing for the collection of an income tax, which was up until this point, unconstitutional. (1913)

XVII – This amendment came about as part of the Progressive Movement in America and provides for the direct popular election of Senators. Senators were originally elected by their respective state legislatures. (1913)

XVIII – Bans the production, sale, and transport of alcohol. This Amendment was repealed by the XXI Amendment in 1933. (1919)

XIX – States that a citizen cannot be denied the right to vote based on sex, and thus grants women the right to vote. (1920)

Fast Facts

The 18th Amendment would eventually be repealed by the 21st Amendment in 1933, making the 18th Amendment the only repealed amendment in the Constitution.

XX – This amendment changes the inauguration date from March 4th to January 20th in order to eliminate the "lame-duck" session of Congress, which was the session just after the November election and before the new President assumed office. (1933)

XXI – Repeals the eighteenth amendment. Alcohol becomes legal again. This is the only article that repeals an earlier amendment. (1933)

XXII – Individuals elected to the Presidency are limited to serving two terms or ten years. Individuals who became President while serving as Vice-President, due to the death or removal of the President, and served more than two years of a predecessor's term, can only be elected for one additional term. (1951)

XXIII – This article states that the District of Columbia shall have electoral votes. (1961)

XXIV – Indicates that poll taxes cannot be used to deny the right to vote to any citizen, effectively making poll taxes illegal. (1964)

XXV – This article outlines the order of succession to the Presidency and provides guidelines for presidential disability.

XXVI – Extends the vote to individuals who are eighteen years of age (changes the previous requirement, which was twenty-one years of age). (1971)

XXVII – This establishes procedures for Congressional pay increases. (1992)

Powers Reserved for the Federal Government

_ regulate foreign commerce

_ regulate interstate commerce

_ mint money

_ regulate naturalization and immigration

_ grant copyrights and patents

_ declare and wage war and declare peace

_ admit new states

_ fix standards for weights and measures

_ raise and maintain an army and a navy

_ govern Washington D.C.

_ conduct relations with foreign powers

_ universalize bankruptcy laws

Powers Reserved for State Governments

_ conduct and monitor elections

_ establish voter qualifications within the guidelines established by the constitution

_ provide for local governments

_ ratify proposed amendments to the Constitution

_ regulate contracts and wills

_ regulate intrastate commerce

_ provide for education for its citizens

_ levy direct taxes

_ maintain police power over public health and safety

_ maintain integrity of state borders

Powers Shared by State and Federal Governments (The Concurrent Powers)

_ taxing, borrowing, and spending money

_ controlling the militia

_ acting directly on individuals

Washington's Administration

The first elections were held and the new constitution went into effect in 1789 with George Washington as the first president. The first Congress drew up twelve amendments, ten of which were ratified by the states, and became the "bill of rights."

Fast Facts

The first elections were held and the new constitution, which included the "bill of rights," went into effect in 1789 with George Washington as the first president.

The Constitution had authorized Congress to set up a Supreme Court as well as any inferior courts that it deemed necessary. The Judiciary Act of 1789, passed by Congress, set up a Supreme Court with six members and a system of lower courts including courts of appeal and district courts. The Supreme Court was given the right to make the final decision in all cases determining whether or not specific state laws were constitutional. The exact number and nature of the Federal Courts was not the only issue left unresolved by the Constitution. A number of other issues, which were also not specifically addressed in the document, created problems for the first government.

The disagreement between those who favored a strong centralized federal government, known as Federalists, and those who wanted the United States to remain rural and agricultural with power being vested primarily in the state governments, known as Republicans, continued. The Federalists, represented primarily by Alexander Hamilton were able to dominate the government for the first twelve years after its creation. Hamilton recommended that bonds be exchanged and various debts and certificates issued during and after the Revolution and that state debts from the revolutionary period also be assumed and paid by the federal government. Hamilton thought that these measures would gain the support of wealthy individuals and encourage them to lend money to the new government since the bonds they were issued would only be redeemable if the new government succeeded. Hamilton also wanted to establish a national bank and to enact two kinds of taxes to increase revenue. He wanted an excise tax on alcoholic beverages and a tariff on imports. Most members of Congress supported the idea of paying off previously issued certificates but they disagreed over whether the individuals who currently held the certificates, many of whom were speculators and who had paid very little to the original owners for the certificates, should be paid full price for them. In the end Congress agreed to pay whomever held the certificates the full amount rather than giving some of the money to the original owners. Congress also agreed to assume state debts, but this was far more controversial and it was only passed after a compromise was reached. This compromise stipulated that if the state of Virginia and other states who had small debts agreed that the federal government would repay all state debt, then the capitol of the United States would be constructed on the banks of the Potomac River, which divided Maryland and Virginia. Despite the protests of small farmers who converted part of their crop into whiskey, Hamilton also won the approval of Congress for the excise tax and a tariff was passed in 1792, although it was not as high as Hamilton had proposed.

The Constitution had avoided mentioning political parties, which were viewed as undesirable by many of the founding fathers, but the domination of the government by the Federalists' led to the organization of an opposing faction. This faction called itself the Republicans and was formed not long after the Constitution had passed. Ultimately, political parties would become an integral part of the American system of government. Neither the Federalists nor the Republicans referred to themselves as parties and neither formally recognized the other, but the beginning of the party system can be traced to their increasing activities in the 1790s. Regional economics continued to divide the country and the Federalists drew more support from commercial centers in the northeast while the Republicans attracted most of their members from rural areas in the southern and western areas of the nation. Washington was convinced to run for a second term as president, in part because he was viewed as non-partisan, but in reality he favored the Federalists' view. The new government was effectively able to exercise authority in regard to territorial expansion and diplomacy, unlike the government created by the Articles of Confederation.

Farmers and settlers in the western territory were not inclined to support the new Federal government any more than they had the original one. In fact, in 1794, farmers in Massachusetts refused to pay the excise tax on whiskey and harassed tax collectors. Hamilton convinced Washington to take action instead of allowing the state of Pennsylvania to settle the "Whiskey Rebellion." Washington led a force of 15,000 into Pennsylvania and the rebellion fell apart. The Federal government managed to gain the loyalty of the population in the west through a combination of the threat and use of force and accepting new states into the union. A number of ordinances were issued between 1784 and 1787 and the provisions for settlement in the west led to serious border conflicts with the Native Americans. The government was given the right to regulate trade between the United States and the Indians and was also supposed to uphold all treaties signed previously with Indian tribes. Nevertheless, the status of native tribes was not clearly defined and failure to resolve this issue, as well as national expansion, led to significant conflicts in the future.

The new nation also found itself at odds with the Great Britain and France. The United States tried to stay neutral during a war between the two European Nations but when the British began seizing U.S. ships engaged in trade with French colonies, the U.S. created and sent a delegation to Britain. The head of the Supreme Court, John Jay, negotiated the "Jay Treaty." This treaty stated that the U.S. was sovereign over the entire North American northwest and provided for compensation for seized shipping, but it also stirred up controversy and opposition. The U.S. also signed treaties with Spain. The Pinckney Treaty allowed the U.S. to send ships down the Mississippi and allowed them to dock in New Orleans and transfer their goods to ships headed for the ocean. This treaty also set the north border of Spanish territory at the thirty-first parallel and required the Spanish authorities to prevent Indians from making raids across the border. These treaties improved relations with Spain and Britain, but unresolved issues with France stemming from the outbreak of the French Revolution in 1789 caused French-American relations to deteriorate.

It was necessary for the U.S. to send a commission to France since authorities refused to receive the U.S. minister and French officials representing the foreign minister Talleyrand refused to meet with the commission unless they received a bribe and the U.S. promised to loan money to France. The official refused and published an account of the incident, known as the X,Y.Z affair since the French officials were listed in that manner. The United States then carried on an unofficial war with France and in 1789 Congress created the department of the Navy. The capture of eighty-five French ships by the U.S. Navy, and also cooperation between the Americans and the British, convinced the French to end the conflict. The new head of the French government, Napoleon Bonaparte, received a U.S. delegation in 1800 and signed a treaty resolving the key issues of contention and providing for commercial relations.

Adams's Administration

The Federalist, John Adams, won the election of 1796 and the Federalists were able to increase their representatives in Congress as a result of the conflict with France. Congress passed the Alien Act that made it more difficult for foreigners to become citizens and allowed the president to take stronger action against alien residents. Congress also passed the Sedition Act that allowed the government to prosecute anyone who engaged in sedition against the government. These acts were an attempt to increase Federalist control and reduce the opposition to their policies. Adams signed the laws but was very cautious and prevented the laws from being used to persecute the Republicans, but the broad language of the laws (which referred only to sedition), meant that in theory the laws could be used against a wide variety of individuals charged with "libelous or treasonous acts." The Alien Act discouraged further immigration and some foreigners left the United States, while the Sedition Act was used to prosecute ten Republican newspaper editors who had criticized the Federalist government. Leading Republicans protested these acts and looked for a way to overturn them. Serious disputes and divisions led to an incident in the House of Representatives in which Mathew Lyon (Vermont: Republican) spit in Roger Griswold's eye (Connecticut: Federalist). Griswold then attacked Lyon with his cane and Lyon fought back with a pair of tongs resulting in a brawl on the floor of Congress in 1798.

The Election of 1800 and Jefferson's Administration

The bitter differences that led to the brawl in Congress also had an impact on the Election of 1800. Adams and Jefferson were again the candidates for the presidency in 1800. When the Republicans carried New York, it appeared that Jefferson had won but the result was a tie between Burr, the vice-presidential nominee, and Jefferson. Electors were instructed to vote for two persons. The electors did not vote for a presidential and a vice-presidential candidate and unless one elector refrained from voting for the second person, a tie would result. The Federalist Congress had the right to decide the outcome of the election between the two candidates, but considered Burr too risky and therefore voted for Jefferson. The Congress also passed an act reducing the number of Supreme Court justices by one, increasing the number of federal judgeships, and appointing loyal Federalists to these positions. Despite the Federalists efforts to keep control of the judicial branch of government, the Republicans came to power with Jefferson as president and a Republican majority in Congress. The change in government would later be referred to as the "Revolution of 1800."

Jefferson and the Republicans wanted to reverse the direction in which the United States had been going while the Federalists were in power. Jefferson had a distinct vision for the United States. This vision was founded upon the idea of a nation of small, independent farmers and severe limits on industrialization and urbanization to avoid the conditions in Europe. The Republicans were also determined to limit the powers of the federal government and to uphold the independent status and power of the states. Despite their majority in Congress and Jefferson's position as president, they could prevent neither the urbanization nor industrialization of the U.S. and Jefferson himself expanded the powers of the federal government by taking action in regard to several key issues.

Marbury vs. Madison

A dispute that occurred as the Jefferson administration came into power fundamentally altered the role of the judiciary by confirming their power to review laws passed by Congress. In 1803, the Supreme Court ruled in the case of Marbury vs. Madison. Marbury was one of the judges appointed by Adams just before he left office and although Adams had appointed Marbury, his letter of commission had not been delivered. Jefferson's secretary of state, James Madison, refused to deliver his letter. Marbury sued and requested that the court force Madison to carry out his duty and deliver the letter. An earlier act, the Judiciary Act of 1789, granted the Supreme Court the power to compel officials to carry out certain duties, such as delivering letters of commission. This act seemed to indicate that the decision would be made in favor of Marbury, but the court ruled that Congress had exceeded its authority and that Congress could not expand the powers of the judiciary that were delegated by the Constitution. By declaring that the Supreme Court did not have the power exercise authority over government officials and compel them to uphold the duties of their job, the court seemed to be weakening its authority. In fact, while giving up the minor power to force officials to carry out certain acts, the court had indicated that it had a far more important power, namely the power to declare an act of Congress invalid. The power of the Supreme Court to review and nullify acts of Congress had been advocated by the Federalists but it was only after Marbury vs. Madison that this power became the foundation of the Supreme Court's check on the other two branches of government.

Louisiana Purchase

A number of decisions and events during Jefferson's tenure as president had profound and lasting effects on the United States. The Jefferson administration immediately ceased to enforce the Alien and Sedition Acts and released a number of individuals previously convicted. In April of 1803, an American delegation sent to meet with Napoleon, negotiated an agreement to purchase the trans-Mississippi territory for 15 million dollars. Jefferson's interpretation of the Constitution and his belief in limitations on the power of the government did not allow him to purchase the land without the approval of Congress. Because Jefferson was in favor of westward expansion and the acquisition of land for farmers, he listened to his advisors. According to his advisors, the treaty-making powers of the president included the right to purchase land. Congress then authorized the purchase of the territory retroactively and allocated the money for the payment to France. The territory of the United States had been effectively doubled overnight by this purchase. Meriwether Lewis (1774–1809) and William Clark (1770–1838) led an expedition to explore the newly purchased territory in 1804. During their two-year trip they kept a journal of their explorations, and collected a vast amount of scientific, in addition to, geographical information.

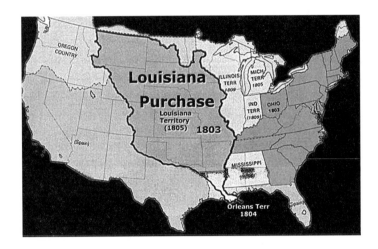

Thomas Jefferson purchased the Louisiana Teritory from France in 1803;
the U.S. took formal possession of the whole territory in 1804.

Twelfth Amendment

The Twelfth Amendment was also passed in an attempt to avoid a recurrence of the tie vote during the 1800 election. This amendment was ratified in 1804 and stated that electors would cast one vote for the presidential candidate and one vote for the vice presidential candidate. The importation of slaves was abolished in 1808.

American Cultural and Religious Developments

The period of the Republican's dominance of government witnessed an increase in opportunities for education and the nation's literary and artistic life began to reflect less the influence of European ideas and become more distinctive. Washington Irving, and other writers, recounted adventures of American figures and increased the popularity of American literature. The Republican aim, however, of establishing a nationwide public school system that would provide free education to both girls and boys was not realized. Both public schools for children and universities remained dependent upon private donations and were, to a large degree, only accessible by white men from wealthy families.

The American Revolution had weakened traditional religion, and by the 1790s there were complaints about the decline in piety. Religious authorities also denounced the new "rational" religious doctrines that incorporated scientific attitudes. Deism, which had originated among enlightened philosophers in France, spread to the United States. According to Deism, God existed but after creating the earth God withdrew from it and was no longer directly involved in human affairs. The efforts of conservative religious authorities to counter the spread and impact of these kinds of ideas led to the Second Great Awakening. The fundamental message of the Second Great Awakening was that individuals must reject rationalism, reaffirm their relationship with God, and adopt a more active form of piety. This movement attracted a large number of female followers and also had an impact on African-Americans and natives. A group of black preachers emerged who taught that salvation was available to all and some African-Americans interpreted this message into one preaching for equality in this life. One black preacher, Gabriel Proser created a plan for slaves to rebel and attack the city of Richmond, Virginia. Although whites discovered this plan and prevented the rebellion, religious revivalism continued to create racial unrest in the South. Native Americans also embraced this message and some transformed themselves, giving up alcohol and gambling. Handsome Lake, a Seneca who had converted and gained special status within his tribe, encouraged Christian missionaries to become active within Indian tribes and supported male and female roles in Indian society similar to those in white society. However, he also denounced individualism and called for a revival of traditional Indian ways and the reestablishment of communal practices.

Some industries and inventions led to changes in the United States during this period, but overall the U.S. remained rural and agricultural. Despite a grand design plan drawn up by the French architect, Pierre L'Enfant, throughout most of the nineteenth century, Washington, D.C., remained a small provincial city. Most members of Congress and other members of the government lived elsewhere and only stayed in Washington, D.C., briefly during sessions of the legislature.

Madison's Administration

War between Great Britain and Napoleonic France caused Britain to take measures that brought it into conflict with the United States. The British, who had a hard time recruiting sailors and had a high rate of desertion, asserted the right to stop and search American merchant vessels and to reimpress any deserters. The British stopped American ships and seized many citizens, some naturalized and some native-born, and forced them to serve in the British Navy.

When an American naval frigate, the Chesapeake, refused to let the British search it, the British commander opened fire, boarded the ship, and ultimately seized four men. The British government denounced the commander's actions, offered compensation for those killed and wounded during the incident, and promised to return three of the four men who had been seized. The British maintained, however, that they did have the right to search American ships in an effort to recover deserting seamen. Congress passed an act that Jefferson proposed in 1807, the Embargo Act, which forbade American ships to sail to any foreign port. Although this act was not strictly enforced, it still led to a serious economic recession. Madison, the Republican candidate won the 1808 election but opposition to the act was so strong that Jefferson approved a bill calling for the end of his "peaceable coercion" policy and Congress passed the Non-Intercourse Act in 1809, just before Madison assumed the presidency. The Non-Intercourse Act allowed American ships to sail for other ports and to carry on trade with all nations except Britain and France. This act expired after one year and instead of renewing the Non-Intercourse Act, Congress passed Macon's Bill No. 2, which allowed commercial trade with all countries but specified that the president could cut off trade with Britain or France, if one country continued violating neutral shipping and the other did not. French concessions that led to the blockade only of Britain convinced the British to repeal the blockade of Europe but tensions continued to build between the Americans and the British.

Westward Expansion and Conflict

The British also became involved in the renewed conflict between Americans and natives in the Northwest territory, leading to a further deterioration of relations between Britain and America. Jefferson's solution to the Indian problem was to state that they could either become part of white society as settled farmers or they could migrate west of the Mississippi. Jefferson appointed William Henry Harrison, in 1801, as governor of the Indian Territory and Harrison began to use any and all means to enforce Jefferson's policy. Initially there was little resistance because separate Indian tribes did not have the ability to oppose the Americans by themselves. The rise of an Indian later known as Tecumseh, or "the Prophet," who preached a return to the superior values of native culture, began to unite tribes. A religious revival spread through many tribes and then, under the leadership of Tecumseh's brother Shooting Star, a joint military action was planned. When Tecumseh left to try to gain further support among other tribes, Harrison attacked and the Battle of Tippecanoe occurred, weakening the confederacy Tecumseh had built even as a number of Indian warriors continued to fight. During this conflict, British agents in Canada had encouraged and helped supply the conflict, which aroused bitter feelings against the British and led Harrison and others to begin to advocate the annexation of Canada.

Expansion into Florida also provided a motive for war with Britain. American settlers seized the Spanish fort at Baton Rouge and wanted to expand into all of Spanish Florida. The settlers were subject to raids from Indians living in Spanish territory, but they also wanted control of rivers in Spanish Florida that would provide them access to ports in the Gulf of Mexico. Spain was allied with Britain and thus a war with Britain might provide the opportunity to seize all of Spanish Florida. By 1810, there was considerable support for war with Britain. Henry Clay of Kentucky and John Calhoun became the leaders of the "War Hawks," or the group of young congressmen who advocated war against the British. President Madison would have preferred a peaceful solution but in the end he approved war on June 18, 1812.

War of 1812

The British, who were still fighting Napoleon, had tried to avoid open conflict and were not prepared to begin major operations against the Americans when the war of 1812 began. It was only after Napoleon's disastrous campaign in Russia and his defeat in 1814 that the British were able to send troops as well as naval forces to support their war effort against the Americans. The United States was able to invade Canada and burn the capitol, although the major victories of the United States in the first years of the war were against Indian tribes. Tecumseh, who had joined the British forces, was killed in a major battle in the northwest and a series of victories against tribes in the southwest also occurred. These victories did not weaken the Americans and after the arrival of the British armada in 1814, the British launched a major campaign.

The British captured and destroyed parts of Washington D.C. and then marched on Baltimore. The Americans occupied Fort McHenry and had sunk several ships in the harbor, forcing the British to bombard the fort from a distance. Francis Scott Key, who was a Washington lawyer, was observing the bombardment aboard a British ship. He wrote a poem recording the fact that "by the dawn's early light" he could still see the flag of the fort flying and set it to the tune of an English drinking song. This song, known as "The Star-Spangled Banner," would become the official national anthem in 1831.

The Americans were able to thwart a larger British naval and land force attempting to land in New York at the Battle of Plattsburgh. Andrew Jackson, who had been made a major general due to his earlier victories, faced the British at New Orleans. The British landed a veteran force at New Orleans and began to advance northward, but Jackson was waiting with a mixed force of volunteers and regular army troops. Jackson's forces were protected behind the earthwork fortifications they had dug and they managed to inflict serious casualties on the British (700 dead, 1,400 wounded, 500 captured) while suffering only 8 killed and 13 wounded. The Battle of New Orleans was a victory for the Americans, although it actually occurred several weeks after the Peace Treaty had been signed, unbeknownst to the combatants.

Fast Facts
Francis Scott Key wrote "The Star-Spangled Banner," a poem set to the tune of an English drinking song, which became the official national anthem in 1831.

The United States had experienced a number of defeats during the war and opposition to it increased as the war continued. The opposition became focused around the Federalists, who were the minority party in the United States but were still able to capture the majority of votes in New England. Those opposed to governmental policies began to discuss the idea of seceding and forming their own nation. A convention met in Hartford, Connecticut, and many of the representatives from the New England States were fairly moderate. The result of this convention was a report that hinted at secession and proposed several constitutional amendments in an attempt to protect New England from the growing influence of other areas, such as the south. The delegates at the New England convention thought that the stress of the war effort, and the recent defeats, would force the Republicans to agree to their demands in order to maintain support in New England for the war effort. The victory at New Orleans and then the news of the peace treaty reached New England after the convention's report was released and this victory not only invalidated the attempt to force concessions on the Republicans but also cast the convention's representatives in an unfavorable light.

Treaty of Ghent

British and American diplomats met in Ghent, Belgium, and negotiated a peace via the Treaty of Ghent. John Quincy Adams and Henry Clay were members of the American delegation and they agreed to give up the American demand that would have required the British to renounce impressments and cede Canada to the U.S. The British in turn gave up their demand for the creation of an Indian buffer state in the Northwest and the treaty was signed on Christmas Eve 1814. The final treaty did little, except to end the war, although both sides were already willing to end the war. The British had fought a long costly war against Napoleon and the war of 1812 produced undesirable consequences in the U.S. and the Americans assumed the end of the European war would put an end to British violations in regard to American commercial shipping. The Americans and British also signed a commercial treaty in 1815, and in 1817 they signed the Rush-Bagot Agreement. This agreement called for a mutual disarmament in the Great Lakes region and although it did not occur immediately, the border between Canada and the United States would become in time the longest unfortified border in the world.

Expansion and Economic Growth of the U.S.

Between 1812 and the outbreak of the Civil War in 1861, the United States changed to a significant extent. In addition to westward expansion and conquest of the Native Americans in the name of Manifest Destiny, the U.S. also experienced the Era of Good Feelings, economic industrialization, and recession. Two trends emerged during this period, expansion of the United States demonstrated by the addition of several new states and the continuation of conflict with the Indians, and increasing tensions and conflict between the northern and southern regions of the country.

In the aftermath of the war of 1812, Congress created the charter for the Second Bank of the United States. The charter held by the First Bank had expired and a number of problems emerged including the problem of determining the value of bank notes issued by various banks and valued at different amounts. Congress also passed a tariff protecting the industries that had been stimulated by the war from foreign competition. The 1816 tariff effectively limited competition on cotton cloth, a consequence that elicited the objection of farmers who would have to pay higher prices for manufactured goods. A bill allowing the use of government funds to accomplish internal improvements, however, was vetoed by Madison on his last day in office, and so state governments and businesses continued to build their own transportation networks.

Expansion westward and Manifest Destiny began to emerge. There were a number of factors that led to the mass movement to the western United States. A growth in the population and the shortage of land in the east were two such factors. The governmental support of the movement and the government's policy of resettling the Indians also led to increased settlement. As the border continued to shift farther and farther west, those people living on the edge of the border often moved into the new territory, relocating on a regular basis. Even before American settlers moved into Texas, California, and other areas in the far west, traders and fur trappers began to carry on trade with these areas that were under the control of Mexico. The American Fur Company, owned by John Jacob Astor, expanded operations from the Great Lakes area all the way to the Rockies. Fur trappers in the early period bought furs from the Indians but as time went by they began to set their own traps. These trappers were almost all young single men and were often the first whites to set foot in western areas. Many of them entered into sexual relations with native and Mexican women, who often helped them skin and prepare the furs. Andrew and William Ashley founded the Rocky Mountain Fur Company in 1822. The Ashley brothers then found men who would go and live permanently in the Rockies. These men then exchanged the fur and skins they prepared for the supplies that were sent by the Ashleys. The arrival of the supply train became a huge gathering for the mountain men many of whom lived most of the year in isolation.

"Era of Good Feelings" and the Panic of 1819

The period following the end of the war of 1812 became known as the "Era of Good Feelings." James Monroe faced little opposition from the candidate of the considerably weaker Federalist Party and was elected president in 1816. The economy was expanding, the nation was migrating westward, and Monroe attempted to forge a government and a nation that was unified rather than divided into parties and factions. He appointed John Quincy Adams, a former Federalist from New England, to the important office of secretary of state and he toured the country in an attempt to encourage goodwill and cooperation. Even in New England, where the Hartford Convention had met in the recent past, large and enthusiastic crowds received him. Monroe was reelected in 1820 and the Federalist Party for all intents and purposes had disappeared.

While many positive trends occurred, this period also witnessed a severe economic crisis. The land boom that was a result of easy credit offered by many private banks as well as the national bank was followed by the Panic of 1819. In 1819, the Bank of the United States, under new management, restricted credit, called in loans, and foreclosed on mortgages. These policies led to the collapse of a number of state banks and six years of depression followed. Some individuals saw this depression as a warning that rapid economic and territorial expansion would threaten the stability of the United States, but the majority of Americans were committed to the expansion.

In addition to economic problems, the expansion of the United States was also causing a national crisis over the issue of whether or not slavery would be allowed in the new territories when they were admitted to the union. Missouri applied for statehood in 1819. Slavery existed in Missouri but Representative James Tallmadge, Jr., of New York introduced an amendment that would have prohibited an increase in the number of slaves in Missouri and called for the gradual emancipation of those slaves already in this territory. Maine also applied for statehood as a new and free state. A compromise was reached when the Senate agreed to combine the proposals and admit Maine as a free state and

Missouri as a slave state. This comprise, known as the Missouri Compromise, included an amendment that prohibited slavery in all of the Louisiana Purchase territory north of the thirty-sixth parallel. This compromise eased tensions for a while and was viewed by both sides as an agreeable settlement to this matter, but the underlying issues were not permanently resolved.

The Monroe Doctrine

The foreign policy legacy of President Monroe that culminated in 1823 was largely a result of the efforts and ideas of John Quincy Adams. This "Monroe Doctrine," as it came to be known thirty years later, stated that European powers should cease to consider the American continent as a place for possible colonization. It also stated that the United States had no intent to intervene in European affairs. The Monroe Doctrine had little impact upon European policy and would have been difficult for the United States to enforce had there been a serious challenge to the doctrine, but it did illustrate the view of the United States in regard to the Western Hemisphere.

The Election of 1824

The Era of Good Feelings was followed in the late 1820s by a period of renewed factionalism and the rise of a new opposition party. In 1824 candidates began to receive nominations from state legislatures and mass meetings rather than the previous system of nomination by the caucuses of the two parties in Congress. There were four presidential candidates in the 1824 election, namely John Quincy Adams, William H. Crawford of Georgia, Henry Clay (the Speaker of the House of Representatives), and Andrew Jackson. Henry Clay advocated the "American System" which would have created an internal market for factory and farm products by strengthening the national banks, raising higher tariffs, and allotting money for internal development. Jackson received more popular and electoral votes than any of the other candidates, but he did not receive a majority. The twelfth amendment, passed after the contested election of 1800, stipulated that if no candidate received a majority of the votes, the House of Representatives would decide which of the three candidates with the largest number of electoral votes would become President. Clay, who was Speaker of the House, was not among the top three but he did have a tremendous amount of influence in the House of Representatives. Since Crawford was seriously ill at the time, Jackson and Adams were the two choices. Clay viewed Jackson as a dangerous opponent and so he endorsed Adams who was elected by the House. Jackson's supporters, already outraged by the fact that Jackson lost despite the fact that he received more votes than anyone else, were outraged when Adams named Clay as his secretary of state. In light of the fact that many previous secretaries of state had later been elected president, it appeared that Clay might have supported Adams on the condition that Adams appoint Clay as secretary of state. This "corrupt bargain," produced a considerable amount of resentment and Adams was unable to obtain support for a number of measures resembling Clay's "American System." Adams did sign the tariff bill of 1828, but southerners denounced this tariff and duties that had been added to the original bill upset the New England citizens who had originally supported the bill.

The Election of 1828

The 1828 election marked the beginnings of the two-party system in American politics. John Quincy Adams led the National Republicans and was able to gain the support of most former Federalists. Andrew Jackson and his followers called themselves the Democratic Republicans and appealed to a diverse segment of the population, all of whom opposed "economic aristocracy." During the 1828 election, a number of personal attacks and attempts to discredit the opponent occurred. For example, Adams's followers called Jackson a murderer and passed out a handbill naming several men Jackson had shot in cold blood. Jackson had legally executed the men, all of whom had been court-martialed and sentenced to death for deserting. Jackson received a majority of votes and won the election in 1828 but Adams had won in New England and several other states. Jackson's proponents stated that privilege had been overthrown and that a new era, the "era of the common man," had begun.

Jacksonian Democracy

Democracy in the United States had never translated into voting or political rights or even representation for all Americans. A number of individuals were unable to vote due to restrictions that only allowed property owners or taxpayers or both to vote. Beginning in the 1820s, some older states, who were concerned about the large number of people moving westward, begin to reduce or eliminate voting requirements. In Rhode Island, where half of the people were barred from voting, Thomas Dorr and a group of his followers formed a People's Party. The Dorrites (followers of Dorr) drafted a new constitution for Rhode Island and set up a government with Dorr as governor. The existing or old government declared Dorr and his followers to be rebels and began to imprison them. The Dorrites attempted to seize the arsenal but were defeated. Although this rebellion failed, it did compel the government of Rhode Island to create a new constitution that greatly expanded suffrage. While suffrage was steadily expanded, a large number of people could not vote, including slaves in the south, some free African-Americans in the north and in the south, and no women in any state. Furthermore, ballots were often verbal or spoken and thus it was possible to intimidate or persuade voters. Still, while only 27 percent of white adult males had voted in 1824, 58 percent voted in the election of 1828, and by 1840 nearly 80 percent of adult white males voted. Electors, some of whom had been chosen by the legislature, were chosen by the people in every state except South Carolina by 1828.

Jackson argued that the government should offer "equal protection and equal benefits." He also maintained that government offices were the property of all Americans and thus permanent office holders were denying opportunities to others and creating a self-serving bureaucracy. While Jackson claimed to represent all Americans, he clearly was also motivated by the desire to reward his own followers with positions in the government. Jackson upheld the "spoils system" and it became an accepted aspect of party politics. Jackson tried to reduce the power of the federal government in some ways, such as through his economic program, but he also wanted to assert and maintain the supremacy of the Union. One of the challenges to the supremacy of the federal government was the nullification theory advocated by vice-president John C. Calhoun.

Nullification Theory

Calhoun was faced by growing dissatisfaction in South Carolina in regard to the tariff of 1816, which was blamed for economic problems and encouraged calls for secession from the Union. In response to these challenges, Calhoun began to argue that the federal government was a creation of the states and therefore the ultimate power to decide whether or not laws were constitutional resided with the states and not the federal government or the courts. According to Calhoun, a state could hold a special convention and declare a federal law null and void. The nullification doctrine, and the use of it to nullify the 1828 tariff, attracted a lot of support within South Carolina. This doctrine would lead to a crisis and would also weaken Calhoun's political position.

Martin Van Buren had been elected as governor of New York, but had resigned this position in order to become Jackson's secretary of state. In addition to becoming part of the official cabinet, Van Buren became part of the president's circle of unofficial friends and advisors, known as the "Kitchen Cabinet." Jackson would ultimately support Van Buren as a candidate for President. The nullification crisis erupted in 1832 when another tariff bill was passed by Congress. The legislature summoned a convention and nullified the tariffs of 1828 and 1832. Jackson insisted that nullification was not only illegal but also treasonous. Jackson proposed a bill that would authorize the president to use military force to make sure that laws of Congress were obeyed. Open conflict seemed likely, but Henry Clay achieved a compromise by proposing a bill that would gradually lower the tariff so that by 1842 it would be as low as it had been in 1816. The bill in regard to tariffs and the Force Act were both passed by Congress on March 1, 1833, and Jackson signed them both. In South Carolina the convention met again and repealed the nullification of the tariff bills but in order to send a message to the federal government it nullified the Force Act.

Removal of the Indians

Andrew Jackson was determined to force the Native Americans to migrate farther westward. A few individuals, such as Thomas Jefferson, viewed the Indians as "noble savages" with an inherent dignity of their own but most white settlers considered them to be savage and uncivilized. Settlers wanted to obtain valuable Indian land and some wanted a cessation to violence that threatened their homes and families. Fox Indians, under Black Hawk, fought a war with settlers from 1831–1832 in an effort to undo a treaty giving up tribal lands that they considered invalid. The Black Hawk War convinced many whites that the only solution to the Indian problem was to force all Indians to migrate westward and during the conflict many Indians who were trying to surrender or retreat were slaughtered.

Even more than the Black Hawk War, the issue of the "Five Civilized Tribes," the Cherokee, Creek, Seminole, Chickasaw, and Choctaw, still living in the South demanded the attention of the government in the 1830s. Jackson was determined to force these tribes to resettle and he refused to abide by a court decision issued by John Marshall, which stated that the government had no right to negotiate with tribal representatives. In 1835, the government was able to sign an agreement with a small group of Cherokees that gave the tribe's land to the state of Georgia in exchange for five million dollars and a reservation west of the Mississippi. Most of the 17,000 Cherokee refused to accept the terms of the treaty but Jackson ordered General Winfield Scott to relocate the Indians forcibly. Many of the 17,000 were forced on a long march from Georgia all the way to what is now Oklahoma. Thousands perished along the way due to disease, winter conditions, and as a result of the march itself. Between 1830 and 1838, most Indians belonging to the "Five Civilized Tribes" were forced to relocate to Indian Territory. Survivors from the original march remembered it as "the trail where we cried" or the "Trail of Tears."

Support and Opposition to Jackson

Jackson's removal of the Indians, his attempts to crush the Bank of the United States, and his response to the nullification process led to an anti-Jacksonian faction that named themselves the Whigs. The Whigs in England attempted to limit the power of the king and the American Whig party wanted to reduce Jackson's use of power. Democrats supported westward expansion, honest workers, and small farmers, while the Whigs favored expanding the power of the federal government in order to promote commercial and industrial growth but were concerned about supporting westward expansion. Support for the Whig party was strongest among manufacturers in the northeast, plantation owners in the South, and rising merchants and farmers in the West. The Whigs managed to elect some officials to government positions and in 1839 supported William Henry Harrison, who won the presidential election. Harrison, however, died one month after taking office and John Tyler became President. The Whig party lost the White House in the 1844 election and began to decline. The Whigs had achieved some successes but were a relatively short-lived party that had united out of opposition to Jacksonian Democracy.

Changes in Industry and Agriculture

Between 1820 and 1850, the U.S. economy underwent a number of changes including the initial phase of industrialization. This beginning phase of the Industrial Revolution had a considerable impact. This transformation was a result of a growing population, new technologies that spurred the development of industry, and the development of mass production methods. The changes in the economy increased the wealth of a few individuals, created a new middle class, and increased the gap between the wealthiest and the poorest individuals in American society. In addition to economic change, there were also changes in society and the structure and behavior of families. The changes in the role of women and the changes in popular culture led to increased differences between northern and southern values and societies.

Tobacco became less important in the upper South and was replaced by other crops. Most of these other crops, such as sugar and long-staple cotton, could not have entirely replaced tobacco and supported the economy. Southerners had begun to plant fields of short-staple cotton, which could be grown in a variety of climates, but it was so difficult to process that only small amounts could be processed. The invention of the cotton gin allowed the seeds to be removed quickly and enabled large amounts of short-staple cotton to be processed. The growing demand for cotton that accompanied the growth of the textile industry in Britain made cotton a valuable commodity and it became the main crop in the South. Southern politicians said that cotton was King. Cotton production also encouraged settlement in the lower South and the sale of slaves to the Southwest became an important part of the economy in the upper South. The South became an area of large plantations and small farms and did not develop either a significant banking system, a major transportation system, or a large manufacturing sector. This made the South dependent upon activities and services of northern bankers, merchants, and manufacturers.

Society in the South

Southern white society was dominated by a relatively small planter class. In 1860, only about 383,637 of the almost 8 million whites owned slaves. Wealthy southern whites adopted an elaborate system of "chivalry," which obligated men to respond to insults to their honor by dueling. The elaborate social structure of the South may have favored wealthy aristocrats, but it also made it clear that even the poorest white sharecropper was far superior to the African slaves. Therefore, even poor whites had a reason to support and uphold the social system created by the plantation owners. Furthermore, wealthy whites held office, owned local stores, rented land to poorer whites, and were therefore able to exert a considerable amount of influence over all of white society.

Women in the South were also firmly subordinated to the dominant class, in this case, men. As in the North, women were supposed to stay at home and their primary activities centered on being wives and mothers. The additional emphasis placed upon the special status of women and the need to protect their honor further reduced their influence. According to George Fitzhugh, in the 1850s, "women like children, have but one right, and that is the right to protection. The right to protection involves the obligation to obey." Most of the "educational" opportunities for women in the South were centers that taught women how to be good wives and mothers. Women in the South had a higher birth rate than women in the north, although a higher rate of infant mortality in the South meant that they did not always have larger families. Women living on farms, as opposed to large plantations, were not as restricted in their activities. They would often engage in agricultural activities or oversee slaves in addition to spinning, weaving, and carrying out other tasks for which they were ideally suited. Women living on large plantations were more isolated and had few duties either within or outside the home. These women often had servants and few responsibilities, and more leisure time, but there were few acceptable activities for them to pursue. Southern women also had to deal with the issue of male slave-owners who had sexual relations with their slaves and children produced by these activities.

Slavery in the U.S.

Slavery in the Southern United States was indeed a distinctive system and by the mid-nineteenth century it was one of only a small number of areas where slavery continued to exist. In the South, slave codes forbade slaves to own property, to leave the plantation or farm without permission, to be out after dark, or to congregate after dark. Furthermore, very harsh penalties were applied to whites who taught slaves how to read or write and slaves who refused to carry out their master's orders or who rebelled. The slave codes did not recognize African-American marriages and defined slavery as perpetual and characterized anyone with even a trace of African blood as a slave.

Fast Facts

In the South, slave codes forbade slaves to:
- **own property**
- **leave the plantation or farm without permission**
- **be out or congregate after dark**

In practice, these laws were not evenly enforced and some African Americans did acquire property, married, and some even gained their freedom. Conditions varied, to a considerable degree, between regions and according to the character and behavior of individual slave-owners. Slaves in all areas, however, enjoyed few rights, worked long hours, and for most freedom was not a viable goal. Slaves also experienced extremely harsh conditions, whipping and deprivation of food and other punishments were designed to control slaves and to insure their obedience. Even when slaves had adequate food, it was a monotonous diet consisting mainly of cornmeal, salt pork, and molasses. Fresh meat and poultry were infrequent additions to meals and slaves themselves had a variety of roles just as they were treated in a variety of ways.

Household servants were not engaged in hard physical labor and on large plantations, cooks, nursemaids, and butlers developed closer ties with the master and his family. Female household slaves were more likely to encounter sexual advances or demands from the male head of household. Sometimes white southern women would punish female slaves with beatings or increased workloads out of frustration because they were unable to challenge their husbands directly. Field slaves, both male and female, worked long hours engaged in difficult or tedious tasks and had to work in all kinds of conditions. Some slaves might be appointed to oversee other slaves in the field and were usually given either additional food or some other privilege. At harvest time, slaves would be expected to work harder and for longer periods. Female slaves often were responsible for preparing meals and caring for any children who were not sold or separated from them in addition to working in the field. The number of slave families, either parents and children, or siblings, or husband and wives, broken up by the internal slave trade is disputed. The internal slave trade continued to flourish long after the importation of slaves had been banned and thousands of slaves were sold by their masters and went to live with new owners. What percentage of the total slave population was sold and how many of the slaves sold were separated from other slave family members is somewhat difficult to estimate, but it is clear that thousands of slaves were separated and these separations had a tremendous impact upon African Americans. After the Civil War, hundreds of slaves wrote letters and published ads trying to track down family members who had been sold and with whom they had lost touch.

By the 1830s, new laws made the system more rigid and it was difficult, and in some areas virtually impossible, for slaves to obtain their freedom. A few slaves, mostly in the North, were able to establish communities and to live in relative peace and stability but most free blacks faced discrimination in both the North and the South.

Slaves in the South resisted slavery in a number of ways. Passive resistance was extremely common in the south. Slaves feigned illness, slowed down work production, and sabotaged machinery. At the other extreme, some slaves rebelled and attempted to lead armed uprisings. Actual slave revolts were not very common but the fear of them had a great impact upon society in the South.

Despite increasing restrictions and attempts to control the slave population, slaves did develop and maintain a distinct culture of their own. A number of slaves continued to practice voodoo and other traditional African practices, often combining them with elements of Christianity. African Americans also often incorporated singing and dancing into their services. Officially African Americans attended white churches where they were segregated and sat in the back of churches but they often held unofficial or secret services.

Newly arrived slaves often had as much difficulty communicating with each other as they did with whites, since a number of languages and dialects were spoken in Africa. Slaves developed a simple common language and even after they acquired greater knowledge of English they retained some words from the simple language they had developed. African Americans developed their own particular kind of music that retained elements of African rhythm and they began to create songs with political or implied messages as well.

Increasing Contrast Between North and South Before 1860

Significant differences between the North and the South became more pronounced in the decades just prior to 1860. The South remained an agricultural economy but many individuals migrated into the Deep South and cotton became king. The owners of large plantations, a small percentage of the total population in the South, dominated political, economic, and social life. The differences between the North and the South were in part due to the different climates, natural resources, and a reflection of different values and cultures. Slavery came to symbolize these differences and many northerners came to oppose the extension of slavery and some opposed the institution itself.

Rapid changes were taking place in the antebellum period, the period just prior to the Civil War, and new literary and cultural movements were having an impact. American writers, artists, and intellectuals were influenced by European ideas such as the Romantic Movement. These individuals were responsible for the advent of a distinctly American culture that emphasized personal liberation and the need to give individuals the freedom to discover and express their own divinity. This emphasis on personal freedom inevitably denounced the enslavement of millions of African Americans. These ideas gave rise first to an anti-slavery movement and then to an abolitionist movement, or a call for the immediate emancipation of all slaves. The growing demand to free slaves led to further tensions between the North and the South.

Continuation of Westward Expansion

Manifest Destiny had become a popular idea by the 1840s, in part because it had been widely advocated by newspapers, which were increasingly less expensive and more available. This Manifest Destiny, approved by God and a natural historical development, was the expansion of the United States over a vast area. The exact boundaries or extent of this destiny were debated. Some Americans thought the United States should expand to include a greater area of the Western territory while others proposed an "empire of liberty" that would include Mexico, Canada, as well as islands in the Caribbean and the Pacific. Texas and Oregon were two areas in which Americans were interested and had already began to settle. A few leading figures such as Henry Clay warned that territorial expansion would necessarily create controversy and conflict over the issue of slavery but most of the nation was caught up in the grand vision of Manifest Destiny and the vision of a Great American nation encompassing a vast territory stretching from the East to the West Coast.

Many individuals began long overland journeys in covered wagons. Some settled in the old frontier areas just west of the Mississippi while others continued on a much longer and hard trip all the way to Oregon and later California. Wagon trains faced a number of obstacles. They had to carry all provisions for the trip, cross flooded rivers, withstand attacks from hostile Indians, and cross mountain passes. Settlers headed to California and Oregon usually joined an organized excursion, which might have a guide, rather than setting out on their own. These trips were hard on both men and women who often had to abandon their traditional role as wives and mothers in order to help repair wagons, defend the wagons against Indian attacks, and help clear land to build a home and to plant crops.

California Gold Rush

In 1848, gold was discovered in California causing a major "rush" to settle the area. Initially, it was primarily men who abandoned homes, farms, and jobs in order to seek gold in California. The society they created reflected the absence of large numbers of women and families. The migration to California created job opportunities in the areas from which the settlers had moved and it led to the rapid growth of California. Most of the men who settled there were unable to find enough gold to make a profit but many stayed and by 1856 San Francisco had a population of 50,000 people. The growth of California and its application for statehood would also have implications for the entire United States.

American Involvement in Texas

In Texas, where many Americans had settled when the Mexican government offered cheap land in 1824, there were twice as many Americans as Mexicans by 1830. A large number of these settlers were white southerners who had established cotton plantations and taken slaves with them into Texas. The Mexican government banned further American settlement in 1830, but additional Americans immigrated to the area and the Americans began to challenge the authority of the Mexican government.

General Santa Anna seized power in Mexico and increased the power of the central government, thus reducing the power of state governments and of Texas. Fighting between the Americans and Mexicans broke out and the American settlers in Texas proclaimed their independence from Mexico. Santa Anna led a large army into Texas where he destroyed an American garrison at the Alamo Mission in San Antonio. The defenders included one of the most well-known frontiersmen, Davy Crockett. The American positions at the Alamo and at Goliad were inherently incapable of withstanding a large assault and their defeat appeared to signal the crushing of the American rebellion.

Another Texan, Sam Houston, was able to keep a force together and rallied support by referring to the Alamo. In 1836, he defeated the Spanish forces at the battle of San Jacinto and captured Santa Anna. The Mexican dictator signed an agreement giving Texas independence. A number of Mexicans who had settled in Texas, known as tejanos, had fought on the side of the Americans. Even though the tejanos had fought alongside Americans, they were still feared and distrusted and they were subsequently expelled from the newly-formed republic. Sam Houston became the first President of the Republic of Texas and sent a delegation to Washington, D.C., to inquire about joining the Union. President Jackson blocked the annexation of Texas and even delayed recognizing the republic because he feared that admitting a large slave state would upset the balance between the North and the South in a Union already plagued by sectional divisions. Texas was encouraged to apply for admission to the Union by President Tyler in 1844, but was again denied admission due to the efforts of northern senators.

The Events Leading to the Civil War

The Civil War emerged out of a complex series of events and an unwillingness or inability to achieve compromise. The period immediately following the war of 1812 witnessed a high tide of nationalism and unity but just underneath the surface lurked issues such as federal versus state rights, which had never been truly resolved. Furthermore, the expansion of the United States created several new issues and a series of crises occurred during the 1850s.

As the nation expanded westward, the questions of whether or not slavery would be permitted in the western territories and new states admitted to the Union and who had the authority or right to make the decision regarding the expansion of slavery emerged. These issues reached a critical point in 1849. California adopted a constitution that prohibited slavery and applied for statehood in 1849. Some members of Congress were unwilling to admit California as a free state and were concerned about other issues, such as the movement to end slavery in the District of Columbia and the emergence of personal liberty laws in the north. These laws barred courts and police from returning runaway slaves to the south.

Furthermore, there were several other territories such as New Mexico, Oregon, and Utah, all of which had applied for statehood. The Union had fifteen free and fifteen slave states in 1849 but the admission of these states depending on their status might completely upset this balance. Southern representatives brought up the idea of secession while state legislatures in the North passed resolutions demanding that slavery be prohibited in the western territories.

Compromise of 1850 and Popular Sovereignty

The Compromise of 1850 was a result of complex negotiations as well as various deals and efforts by individuals such as Henry Clay and Stephen Douglas. This compromise admitted California to the Union as a free state, formed territorial governments in the rest of the area acquired from Mexico without restrictions on slavery, the abolition of the slave trade but not slavery itself in the District of Columbia, and a new and more effective Fugitive Slave Law. The debates and negotiations that would ultimately lead to the Compromise also introduced the idea of popular sovereignty. Popular sovereignty would allow the individuals living within a territory or state to decide for themselves, as opposed to the decision being made in Congress, whether or not they would allow slavery.

The Compromise averted the immediate crisis and attempted to resolve some aspects of the slavery issue in regard to the newly acquired territories but it did not resolve the fundamental underlying problems. The Compromise itself also stirred up resentment much of it centered around the Fugitive Slave Act. Northerners resented the new act that enabled Southerners to travel freely within the North and seize individuals they claimed were fugitives including some free African Americans and a number of escaped slaves who had been living in the North for several months and in some cases years. The South was angered by northern attempts to prevent the Fugitive Slave Act from being enforced by the passage of state laws that barred the deportation of slaves, despite the federal act authorizing southern agents to retrieve runaway slaves.

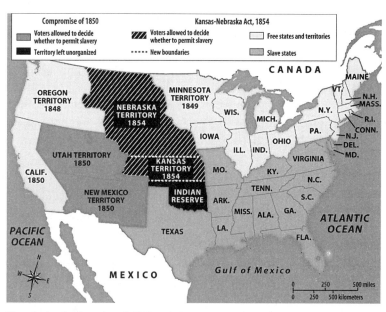

Though the Compromise of 1850 and the Kansas-Nebraska Act of 1854 followed the principle of popular sovereignty, allowing residents to determine whether theirs would be a slave or free state, the tragic result was to exacerbate tensions between North and South that would ultimately lead to Civil War.

Kansas-Nebraska Act

Stephen Douglas from Illinois created a proposal that led to further conflict. Douglas was aware that if a transcontinental railroad, which had obtained considerable support, were constructed so that it ran through Illinois it would provide considerable advantage to his state. Douglas wanted to quickly organize and admit the territory north of the 36–30 line into the Union in order to strengthen his argument that the railroad should be built in the North. The resulting Kansas-Nebraska Act, which had been modified several times in order to gain the support of southern senators while retaining support in the North, proved to be a source of immediate and considerable consequences.

The Kansas-Nebraska Act divided the area into two territories, Kansas and Nebraska, and included a provision stating that the territorial legislatures would decide the issue of slavery and a clause that expressly repealed the Missouri Compromise. This bill divided the Democratic and Whig parties and led to the rise of a new organization, the Republican Party. The Republicans gained support and become a major force in American politics. This bill threatened the stability of the entire Union and thousands of pro-slavery and anti-slavery advocates crossed the border into Kansas where bitter struggles led to the designation of the territory as "bleeding Kansas." Increasingly bitter sentiments in the North and South, as well as a series of compromises that seemed to undermine the spirit of negotiation by overturning early agreements, further divided the country.

Anti-Slavery and Abolitionist Movements

The anti-slavery movement had been divided into those who opposed the expansion of slavery and the abolitionists who called for the immediate end to slavery. In the decade prior to the Civil War many individuals who had been opposed only to the expansion of slavery or indifferent to the plight of slaves began to join or support the abolitionist movement.

A number of factors increased anti-slavery sentiment and further deepened the gap between northern and southern views. One factor was the Underground Railroad, a network of contacts that assisted and hid slaves who were fleeing to the North.

The efforts of Northerners to free slaves angered white southerners and the stories and testimonies of escaped slaves increased sympathy and support for African Americans in the North. Harriet Beecher Stowe wrote *Uncle Tom's Cabin* based on observations of slave-holding communities in Kentucky. This work, published initially as a series of articles, was widely circulated in the North and portrayed the brutality and oppressive nature of slavery in a way that made it more real and more objectionable to white individuals in the North.

Dred Scott Decision

In 1857, a Supreme Court ruling known as the Dred Scott decision provoked outrage in the North. Upon the death of his master, a slave who had accompanied and lived with his master in territories that prohibited slavery sued the master's widow for his freedom. The Supreme Court was divided and issued a series of rulings; however, two basic ideas or statements emerged. The first was the statement by the Chief Justice Roger Taney that indicated that slaves were not citizens and therefore had no right to due process of law and could not bring a suit in federal court. Furthermore, Congress did not have the right to pass laws depriving citizens of their property, including slaves according to this ruling, and therefore the Missouri Compromise had been unconstitutional.

This ruling did not prevent individual states from passing anti-slavery laws or measures and enforcing them but it did make it clear that the federal government could not act or enforce such laws due to the designation of slaves as property. This ruling seemed to weaken the ability of any state to prohibit slavery since the federal government would not intervene and it caused outrage in the North, while southerners considered it to be a major step forward since it upheld their argument that slaves were property.

The Election of 1860

The last incident that divided the Union and the one that provoked the secession crisis was the election of Abraham Lincoln in the 1860 Presidential election. The deep divisions within the major parties and the United States generally led to the election of Lincoln, who received only 40 percent of the popular vote.

Lincoln had engaged Stephen A. Douglas in a number of debates during the Illinois senate race and although he lost he gained considerable attention. Lincoln had little political experience and was opposed to the expansion of slavery. The South viewed Lincoln as an abolitionist and a direct threat to the southern way of life. Immediately following the election of Lincoln, South Carolina began to discuss secession from the Union. Southern states had long maintained that they had the right to nullify acts of Congress and even withdraw voluntarily from the Union without approval from the federal government if they had sufficient cause or grievances.

It did not take long for South Carolina to pass a bill of secession and six other states followed its lead and voted themselves out of the Union (Mississippi, Florida, Alabama, Georgia, Louisiana, and Texas). These six states would join together to form the Confederate States of America or the Confederation. Jefferson Davis was chosen to be the President of this new "nation." President Buchanan just prior to leaving office told Congress that states did not have the right to secede but that the federal government did not have the right to use force to prevent them from leaving the Union. Attempts to negotiate failed, and the situation remained unresolved when Lincoln arrived in Washington, D.C. for his inauguration. Lincoln immediately made it clear that he considered acts of secession to be insurrection and stated that the federal government would take all actions necessary, including force, to protect federal forts and property in the south and to put an end to insurrection.

The Civil War and Reconstruction

Fort Sumter and the Outbreak of War

National attention turned to Fort Sumter, a federal fort in South Carolina that was occupied by loyal federal troops and surrounded by a hostile local population. Lincoln sent an expedition with supplies, after stating that he would not attempt to send ammunition or additional troops unless the supply ships encountered resistance. General Beauregard, the officer in command of Confederate forces in Charleston, was ordered by the Confederate government to seize the fort. The Confederates demanded the surrender of the fort and when the Union commander, Anderson, refused, they shelled the fort for thirty-six hours after which the Union commander surrendered. On April 12, 1861, the first shots had been fired in a bloody struggle that would determine the fate of the nation. Lincoln responded by calling for the states to provide 75,000 volunteers. Four slave states that had initially remained in the Union, Virginia, Arkansas, Tennessee, and North Carolina, refused to respond to this call for militia forces and instead seceded from the Union. The four remaining slave states, (Maryland, Delaware, Kentucky, and Missouri) all of which lie on the border between the Union and the Confederacy, took on additional significance. The Border States all remained in the Union for the duration of the war, but only as a result of tremendous pressure exerted by the Union as well as the presence of federal troops in some areas.

Advantages of the Confederacy and the Union

The North enjoyed at least five advantages over the South. It had greater financial resources and it had a far greater industrial base and manufacturing capability. The North also had a far greater population and immigrants continued to arrive in the North during the conflict. Moreover, the North retained control of the U.S. Navy and thus was able to command the sea and blockade the South. Finally, the North had a better transportation system, as nearly two-thirds of all rail lines that had been constructed were in the North.

The South had some advantages as well. The South was vast in size, making it difficult to conquer. Its troops were fighting on their own territory and they were motivated by their cause and by the need to defend their homes and their families. Moreover, the South was also on the defensive militarily, giving them a slight advantage as well.

At the outset of the war, the South drew a number of highly qualified senior officers, men like Robert E. Lee, Joseph Johnston, and Albert Johnston from the U.S. Army. By contrast the Union command structure was already set when the war began. Winfield Scott, who had fought in the Mexican war, was at the top of the command structure. Scott wanted to slowly strangle the South—The Anaconda Plan—by blockading Southern ports and cutting off Southern trade along the Mississippi. Though Jefferson Davis had extensive military and political experience, Lincoln was much superior to Davis as a war leader, showing firmness, flexibility, great political skill, and a grasp of strategy.

Early Progress of the War

Impatience with Scott's plan led to a Union advance towards the Confederate capitol at Richmond. At a creek called Bull Run near the town of Manassas Junction, Virginia, just southwest of Washington D.C., the Union army met a Confederate force under generals Beauregard and Joseph Johnston on July 21, 1861. The Confederates won the battle, in part due to a failure of the Union army to effectively coordinate its movements, and the Union army was forced to retreat in confusion back to Washington. The Confederacy failed to follow up its advantage. It was a bloody battle, foreshadowing the high casualty rate and setting the scene for a prolonged conflict. General Scott was replaced with McClellan but although McClellan had been nicknamed "little Napoleon" for his exploits prior to the Civil War he adopted a very cautious strategy.

The campaigns during 1861–1862, illustrated the superior military leadership of the South. Lincoln would change the commander in charge of the

Northern army several times, eventually promoting Grant who would lead the Union to victory. The Union lost several battles but it was able to mobilize and raise greater armed forces and industrial production also increased. The South won a series of victories but the blockade was effectively reducing the ability of the South to supply its forces. Both sides enacted policies aimed at the British and French observers of the war. The South hoped that European demand for cotton would persuade the British and French to intervene on behalf of the South. The British gave the South belligerent rights but neither foreign power would intervene unless it became clear that the South could win the war.

Battle of Antietam

The battle of Antietam, which began on September 17, 1862, was the bloodiest battle in the American Civil War. During the first day of the battle there were 10,000 combined casualties, most of the men were killed fighting over a 20-acre cornfield that changed hands fifteen times. Union commanders again failed to destroy Lee's armies by pressing their slight advantage and pursuing the Confederate forces who had to cross a river in order to retreat. Total casualties from the battle of Antietam were 12,000 for the Union and nearly 11,000 Confederates or 1 in every 4 confederate soldiers engaged. After claiming the battle of Antietam as a "victory," Lincoln issued the preliminary Emancipation Proclamation.

The Emancipation Proclamation

The Emancipation Proclamation did not effectively free any slaves, since it stated that only slaves in areas of rebellion against the government would be freed, but it did reduce the possibility that the British would intervene since the North was now fighting, at least in part, to abolish slavery. The British had initiated the end to the slave trade and popular opinion in Britain began to favor the North in a struggle that was now not just about governments and national politics but also about individual freedom.

The War Turns Against the South

As the war dragged on, the greater population and material advantages of the North became a significant factor. The blockade and Union victories that gave them control of the Mississippi allowed Union forces to divide the South in half and to interrupt their trade and supply lines. The Union had a better Navy and in addition to blocking Southern ports, also shelled land forts and took part in joint army and navy actions. The one battle between the newly constructed Union ironclad, The Monitor, and the Confederate ironclad, The Virginia, also demonstrated the superiority of the Union Navy even though neither side actually won the battle between the two ships.

Furthermore, several key Confederate officers, such as Stonewall Jackson and Johnston, were severely injured or killed. The replacement of the largely ineffective McClellan only made an impact when he was permanently removed from command of the army in favor of Grant. After 1863, the Union was able to go on the offensive and to invade the South. Vicksburg and Gettysburg were besieged and ultimately fell to the Union. Lincoln's speech at Gettysburg stressed the honor of the dead on both sides and the need to bind up the wounds of a nation. This conciliatory attitude, as well as his determination to readmit the southern states as quickly as possible, would be reflected in his 10 percent plan.

The final Union campaign consisted of a series of coordinated offensives in the South. Sherman's "March to the Sea," created a path of destruction and aroused bitter feelings in the South that would not end with the war. The final Confederate collapse was only a matter of time. Grant cut off all supplies to Lee and the Army of Northern Virginia, which had withdrawn to the area around Richmond and on April 9, 1865, Lee surrendered at Appomattox Court House.

Consequences of the Civil War

The Civil War had killed 360,000 Union soldiers and 260,000 Confederate soldiers. Almost two-thirds of these casualties were from disease or infection rather than battle wounds. The war had also demonstrated the importance of being able to draft large numbers of soldiers, and to organize and use them effectively. Superior logistics, transportation, and communication systems had played a role in the Northern victory. The economic impact on the South was enormous. The Civil War had divided families as well as the country into two opposing camps. It had left 620,000 Americans dead and thousands of others had been wounded and many returned home with amputated limbs. Most of the destruction had occurred in the South where cities and entire areas had been destroyed and where many people were homeless and without means to support themselves. The end of the war also brought about the end of slavery. The end of the Civil War did not signify the end of conflict within the United States. At the end of the war, there were a number of issues facing the North. What should be done with the southern states that had seceded? What kind of policies should be implemented in terms of readmitting the South to the Union and should the South be occupied by the military or allowed to immediately resume control over its own affairs. The Emancipation Proclamation and the freeing of approximately four million slaves presented another challenge to the nation in 1865. The issues faced by the nation were further exacerbated by a conflict between the Executive and Legislative branch over what policies should be implemented.

Ending Slavery

There were serious debates concerning the end of slavery. Some advocates noted that freed slaves would have no resources and those in the South were sure to face continued discrimination. These individuals thought that federal policy needed to go beyond setting slaves free and attempt to provide them with means to support themselves. Few people were willing to support the idea of seizing and redistributing all land in the South, but some did advance the suggestion that all African Americans be given forty acres and a mule. In the end, no effort was made to provide for the economic support of former slaves. In 1865, Congress did, however, create the Freedman's Bureau to provide some food, clothing, and education to slaves and also to arbitrate disputes involving slaves and their former owners.

Readmitting Southern States to the Union

Lincoln proposed a 10 percent plan to restore legal governments in the seceded states. Lincoln's plan stipulated that southerners, except for high-ranking rebel officials, could take an oath promising future loyalty to the Union and acknowledge the end of slavery. When the number of people who had taken this oath within any one state reached ten percent of the number who had been registered to vote in that state in 1860, a loyal state government could be formed. Only those who had taken the oath would be able to vote or participate in the government. Tennessee, Arkansas, and Louisiana met the requirements and formed loyal governments, and were approved by Lincoln for readmission but Congress, dominated by radical Republicans, refused to recognize these states. Thaddeus Stevens of Pennsylvania was among the Republican representatives who believed that Lincoln's plan did not adequately punish the South, restructure southern society, and that it might lead to a rapid decline in the influence of the Republicans in Congress since former Confederate States would be rapidly readmitted to the Union.

Debate Over Dealing with the South

The Radicals developed their own plan for restoring the Union. The Wade-Davis bill required a majority of individuals who had been alive and registered to vote in 1860 to swear an "ironclad" oath stating that they were loyal and had never been disloyal. Under these terms, no confederate state could have been readmitted unless African Americans were given the vote. Until a majority of individuals able to vote took the oath, the state could not send representatives to the federal congress. The Wade-Davis bill reached Lincoln's desk before his assassination and he killed it with a pocket veto. When Andrew Johnson became President, upon Lincoln's death, the radical Republicans thought he would be harder on the South or at least easier to control.

Although Johnson was a southerner and had owned slaves, he was not a member of the plantation aristocracy and prior to becoming president he stated that if he ever had the opportunity he would make the southern aristocracy pay dearly. As president he failed to follow through on this course of action and instead came out in support of Lincoln's 10 percent plan and a more lenient peace for the defeated southern states. He obeyed the letter of the law in regard to reconstruction acts but he violated the spirit of Congressional Acts designed not just to bring the South back into the Union, but to punish them for having seceded from it.

Thirteenth and Fourteenth Amendments

The Thirteenth Amendment, officially ending slavery, had already been passed. After Johnson's succession to the Presidency, Congress passed a Civil Rights Act and extended the authority of the Freedman's Bureau. Johnson vetoed both bills, claiming they were unconstitutional but Congress overrode the vetoes. Congress approved the Fourteenth Amendment and sent it to the states for ratification in June of 1866. The Fourteenth Amendment defined citizenship and forbade any states to deny various rights to citizens. Any state that denied the vote or other rights to eligible citizens, including African Americans, would have their representation in Congress reduced. The amendment also prohibited the paying of any Confederate debts and made former Confederates ineligible to hold public office.

Impeachment of Johnson

Congress also passed the Tenure of Office Act. This act forbade Johnson from dismissing cabinet members without the permission of Congress. Congress was attempting to protect the last radical Republican cabinet member, Secretary of War Edwin M. Stanton. Johnson dismissed Stanton, in violation of the Tenure of Office Act in 1867 in order to test the constitutionality of the act. Before the matter could be taken up in court, Congress responded by impeaching Johnson. The House of Representatives voted articles of impeachment against Johnson. Once the President was accused of acts for which he could be removed from office, the matter went to the Senate for trial. The Senate needed a two-thirds majority in order to convict and remove Johnson from office and the final count was one vote less than required. Johnson remained in office but offered little resistance to the radical Republicans during his last months in office.

The Election of 1868 and the Fifteenth Amendment

The Republican convention in 1868 formulated a platform that endorsed radical reconstruction and nominated Ulysses S. Grant for president. Grant had an impressive military record but no political experience and naively trusted matters to a number of corrupt individuals. A number of scandals emerged during Grant's tenure as president. Meanwhile, Congress passed the Fifteenth Amendment that specifically gave African-American men the vote. Women such as Elizabeth Cady Stanton, who had been agitating for the vote for women since the Seneca Falls Convention in 1848, bitterly denounced the reconstruction amendments that upheld the disenfranchisement of women. During radical reconstruction, the South was occupied by federal forces and during this period African Americans were able to exercise voting rights. Two African Americans were also elected to Congress from southern states ruled over by republican governments during radical reconstruction.

The Compromise of 1877

While the Radical Republicans passed a number of acts and amendments granting rights to African Americans, they were unable to effectively enforce these acts in all areas in the South. Furthermore, the Compromise of 1877, which ended reconstruction, also effectively led to the end of the few opportunities that existed for former slaves in the South. The Democratic candidate in the election of 1877 was one electoral vote short of the required number for victory and twenty electoral votes from southern states with republican governments were disputed. The Republican candidate, Hayes, would need all the disputed votes in order to win the election. Hayes was awarded all of the votes by a commission created to decide the election but the Democrats protested. The Compromise of 1877 stipulated that Hayes would become President but it also stated that all federal troops would be withdrawn from the South and that the South would be granted federal funds to build railroads and other projects.

The Consequences of Reconstruction

Reconstruction had effectively ended. The struggle between the President and Congress and between the North and the South had finally ended but the impact of both the war and the efforts to restore the Union would continue to exert an influence on the development of the United States. The Union had been preserved, but at what cost and to what extent was the nation that emerged after 1877 fundamentally different from the one that had gone to war in 1861?

The abolition of slavery led to real changes in the lives of former slaves, but it did not end their economic dependence on southern whites nor did it end discrimination in the South. African Americans after the Civil War were able to legally marry and divorce, and hundreds published letters and ads seeking loved ones from whom they had been separated as a result of the internal slave trade. African Americans immediately began to form their own schools and churches. The restrictions that forbade slaves from learning to read and write in the old slave codes were now nullified and former slaves realized the importance of education especially for children. Former slaves also began to leave white churches and form their own church communities, which often had distinctive elements such as music or dance as a part of the service. African Americans also gained control over their time and their movements but in terms of their economic status, little changed as a result of their emancipation. The failure of the government to provide former slaves with land or other economic opportunities meant that many blacks ended up renting land, or sharecropping, from their former masters.

Jim Crow Laws segregated whites from African Americans.

Fast Facts

White southerners could no longer exercise complete control over former slaves. For instance many African American males refused to allow their wives to work for whites, but they could demand a large portion of their crop as rent payment. Whites could also charge African Americans high prices for seed and other supplies that had to be purchased from stores owned by whites. In addition to economic inequalities, former slaves also faced campaigns of terror and intimidation designed to keep them in their place in society and to persuade them not to try and exercise their right to vote. The Klu Klux Klan was formed and began to intimidate, beat, and lynch African Americans. Southern States also introduced Jim Crow Laws that segregated whites from African Americans. And it was not just in the South that African Americans encountered discrimination and hostility, although the worst abuses took place in the South. All in all, reconstruction was a mixed bag but in terms of achieving equality within the United States, it was clearly a failure.

The Acceleration of Industrialization

Between 1860 and 1894, the United States moved from the fourth-largest manufacturing nation to the world's leader through capital accumulation, natural resources, especially in iron, oil, and coal. Industrialization was also advanced by an abundance of labor supplemented by massive immigration, railway transport, and communications. The telephone was introduced by Alexander Graham Bell in 1876. The development of the modern steel industry introduced by Andrew Carnegie and the discovery of electrical energy by Thomas Edison further stimulated industrial growth. A few individuals such as John D. Rockefeller, who came to control 95 percent of all U.S. oil refineries by 1877, became extremely wealthy but the mass of workers who were employed by the rising number of factories had a difficult time earning enough to feed and clothe their families. Conditions in factories were often appalling, and the rise of the Union movement was partly a response to the dangerous working conditions, low pay, and lack of job security. Despite the drawbacks, industrialization did enable the United States to emerge as a major power.

3. California History

The history of California must be understood in the context of its distinct geography. The state's extreme isolation, extraordinary climate, rich natural resources, and striking geographic diversity have consistently and significantly shaped human action and interaction in the region. California's oceans, deserts, and mountains sheltered the region and its native people from foreign stimulation and conquest for centuries. Its Mediterranean conditions ultimately provided more incentive to migrants than gold ever did. Its rich soils, as well as valuable mineral deposits, especially gold and oil, have been vital not only to the state's economic growth, but also to the economic development of the entire United States. Finally, its varying landscapes have offered some of the most beautiful scenery in the world, as well as unparalleled opportunities for recreation. Very few regions offer its inhabitants the chance to surf in the morning and ski in the afternoon. Regional diversity, however, has also spurred perpetual conflicts between those regions which have water in excess and those which do not.

Such conflicts were practically non-existent before the region was "discovered" by Europeans. In the years before Spanish conquest, approximately three hundred thousand native people lived within the present boundaries of the state. For North America, however, even this population was relatively dense. Indeed, if settlement by families was a criteria for civilization, as Old World inhabitants would later claim, then California prior to European invasion was one of the most civilized places in the trans-Mississippi West. For most California Indians, however, family ties were much more than autonomous household units. They formed a network of kinship that influenced, if not defined, every political, social and economic transaction in their society. While these relationships varied with tribe and locality, anthropologists have elaborated general life and value systems for the region's indigenous people.

California Indians occupied the coastal, central, and northwestern parts of the state. In these areas several *rancherias* (villages) that recognized a single chief formed a tribelet. In turn, several tribelets formed a tribe. Over thirty diverse tribes thrived in the region. Chiefs (who were occasionally women) almost always came from the wealthiest families, and thus inherited their elite positions. Their principal duties included governing the hunting and gathering activities on tribal land, and overseeing a fair distribution of goods. They also arranged public feasting and ceremonial food exchanges to ameliorate and refine relations with neighboring people. To further secure these relations, which were critical during times of war and famine, chiefs often took several wives from various *rancherias*. Diplomatic polygamy provided kinship links that maintained prosperity and limited conflicts surrounding poaching and blood feuds.

Kinship Patterns

Kinship patterns were not merely critical components of Indian leadership. They also suffused the daily lives of ordinary people. Familial association delineated where an individual could hunt or gather and with whom he or she could engage in trade. In the Northwest, where a premium was placed on wealth and status, the owner of a resource could rent, sell or grant operational rights to another family to secure an advantageous marriage. The theft of such resources demanded retribution in the form of enslavement or material compensations. As a result, malefactors lost both wealth and status for their families.

Some tribes supplemented blood relations with moieties that connected them to special totem animals such as the eagle or coyote. Children belonged to their father's moiety and were forbidden to kill their totemic affiliations. Since a wide range of commonly hunted animals were moieties, this arrangement regulated hunting. Moreover, since individuals had to marry someone from another moiety, the custom also regulated blood ties. Throughout California, then, kinship determined the nature of hunting and trading and removed naked self interest from such transactions.

Arrival of Missionaries

These Indian life ways were completely reconstructed by Spanish imperialists seeking wealth and advantage for themselves and their country. Although Spanish sailors had visited California as early as 1542 during Juan Rodriguez's fatal search for the Northwest Passage, the Empire made its first serious effort to establish missions, presidios, and towns in the late eighteenth century. In 1769, Fra Junipero Serra founded a string of missions which would eventually stretch from San Diego to San Francisco. Because Spanish missionaries encountered less opposition from the Indians of California than other areas in the Southwest, and because of the state's mild climate and rich resources, these missions were the best administered and most prosperous in the world. The missionaries wielded a vast amount of control over land and livestock. They baptized nearly 54,000 Indians and instructed them in a wide variety of new skills. Indian weavers, brick makers, blacksmiths, farmers, shepherds, and *vaqueros* (cowboys) became the keystone of the California economy. Unlike the Anglo social order, which had no place at all for the region's natives, Spanish colonialists, and later, Mexican societies depended on the labor of Indians.

Nevertheless, while the Franciscans insisted that their missions were essentially humanitarian endeavors, this wholesale transformation of Indian life yielded horrifying and catastrophic consequences. Under the mission system, the neophytes (as baptized Indians were called) owned neither their labor nor its fruits. They were slaves, who were subjected to the almost absolute authority of the priests. Neophytes who refused to work, fled, or posed other discipline problems faced severe physical punishment and public humiliation. During the mission period, the California Indian population declined from 72,000 to 18,000. This death toll, whole primarily attributed to disease introduced form Europe, stemmed from harsh social discipline, poor sanitation, and lack of medical care in the missions.

Independence for the Southwest

Indian discontent was only a small part of the internal instability that confronted New Spain. By the early nineteenth century, Mexico began to demand its freedom from European rule. For California, as well as New Mexico and Texas, the revolution that resulted meant independence from Spain and an ambiguous territorial status within the new nation of Mexico. Upheaval also dismantled the mission system. Despite significant resistance from the Catholic Church, determined liberals in the Mexican government ordered the secularization of the California missions and the redistribution of their holdings. This policy sprang partly from sincere desires not only to eliminate the economic privileges of the church, but also to liberate the Indians from the stern discipline of the priests. However, secularization also arose from the machinations of the *californio* elite, the *gente de razon* ("the people of reason"), who desired access to the missions' vast holdings. Ultimately, while liberal attacks on the mission intended to create economic equality, they succeeded in creating great economic inequality. Between 1830 and 1846, eight million acres of land were delivered to less than eight hundred grantees.

A remarkably rigid hierarchy divided *californio* society. Occupying its highest rung were the large ranchers, Spanish soldiers, and Spanish Franciscans who received the bulk of the mission holdings. As their giant *ranchos* came to dominate the landscape, many of them attained a status akin to the great barons of Europe to the surrounding villages of dependent laborers. These villages were occupied by Mexicans, who lacked both the lineage and the wealth to make the often dubious, but always critical, claim to "pure Spanish blood." While Mexican villagers deferred to the authority of the *gente de razon* and paid them tribute, they were able to maintain a large degree of autonomy through their access to large plots of communal land. At the bottom of the hierarchy lay the Indians, who continued to provide the bone and sinew of the Hispanic economy. Ranchers forced Indians to work for them sometimes with impunity, but primarily by advancing them goods, liquor, and money in a way that coerced them into life-long debt peonage.

From Californio to Anglo

The passage from *californio* to Anglo dominance, while swift, was an uneven, and multifaceted process that began with California's early integration into the American economy. Because Mexico could not provide a merchant marine or an internal market for cattle and cattle hides, the *californios'* primary staples, the region was easily steered into an American orbit. The 1830s American adventurers and entrepreneurs soon attained a critical presence in the social complex of California as they facilitated the area's vast exports of hides and tallow (cattle fat used to make candles) into the United States.

The American expansionist agenda became much more direct in the next decade, when President Polk deliberately provoked war with Mexico. In 1845, the American annexation of Texas had triggered a crisis with the Mexican government, which had never formally recognized the independence of its lost province. When Polk received word of a minor skirmish on the Texas-Mexican border, he immediately seized the incident as a pretext for war, and artfully proclaimed that Mexico had "invaded our territory and shed American blood on American soil." By 1847, American armies had conquered Mexico City and the

Mexican government lay in collapse. In February of the next year, the two countries negotiated the Treaty of Guadeloupe Hidalgo which granted the United States Texas, New Mexico, and California for the sum of $15 million.

Contrary to the posturing of Polk, the U.S. was hardly engaged in a defensive struggle against the significantly weaker country of Mexico. The Mexican War was fundamentally a war of conquest. Polk, along with large sectors of American society, was convinced that expansion was the key to both economic stability and sectional harmony. He was also fueled by the racist, imperialist doctrine of manifest destiny, which, "by divine right," decreed the entire continent to the U. S.

While the 1848 treaty promised the *californios* citizenship and the "free enjoyment of liberty and property," such "enjoyment" was hardly theirs to have. Even as the document was being negotiated, the Gold Rush was spelling out dire consequences for the rancheros. Upon arriving, many newcomers began squatting upon californio land, killing the cattle and cultivating crops. Even more deleterious were the actions of land speculators who legally and illegally purchased and enclosed both the estates of the *gente de razon* and large plots of communal land. While state land laws validated many Spanish and Mexican land grants, litigation costs money and time, two resources the californios simply did not have. By the time the commissioners and courts legitimated their claims, squatters, moneylenders, tax-collectors, and attorneys drained the rancheros of their possessions. In the span of a single generation, *californios* were made politically powerless in a region they had lived in their entire lives. Confronted with various forms of violence and disenfranchisement, many Mexicans withdrew into insulated *barrios*, where they could retain the traditions of the past and establish new cultural imperatives for the future.

The Gold Rush

The Gold Rush migrations dramatically transformed the largely Indian and Hispanic West. How many migrants came is uncertain, but the non-Indian population of California increased from about 14,000 in 1848 to 223,856 in 1852. As the gateway to California's gold country, late nineteenth century San Francisco emerged as the social and economic capital of Western America. On the eve of the Civil War, the population of the "Queen City" (as the city was known to many of its inhabitants) was the ninth largest in the United States. The lure of gold, moreover, produced the most cosmopolitan, multinational population in the world. By the late nineteenth century, the "foreign-born" comprised almost 60 percent of the city's inhabitants. During that time, Chinese, Italian, and Irish immigrants established ethnic enclaves that would become permanent features of San Francisco's cityscape.

Most of the gold seekers were lucky to leave California "in the pink," as boom soon turned to bust. The mines quickly populated, while mining, itself, became less an individual adventure than a business run by a few large operators. Unable to find their fortune in the "diggings" many immigrants had little choice but to fill the rising demand for cheap, expendable labor. To a large extent the early history of Northern California's working class is the history of immigrant families

Gold miners searching for gold during the Gold Rush of California.

The need for labor came from San Francisco's booming maritime and railroad industries, which were critical to the city's transformation from a mining encampment to a real metropolis. Significantly, the city's vast system of wharves and warehouses facilitated the export of wheat, northern California's new cash crop. The economic promise of this crop prompted the federal government to dispose of public lands in the great Central Valley. Much of this land was obtained by large bonanza farmers who raised wheat for the world markets. Large scale wheat production, while notorious for its labor exploitation, effectively subsidized industry in San Francisco and the rest of the Bay area. Wheat was exchanged for pig iron and scrap steel, the indispensable raw material for the Bay area's increasingly important metal industry. Most importantly, wheat was exchanged for British coal, one of the few energy sources that the region lacked.

The Trans-Continental Railroad

California's full integration into the national and international market, however, demanded a transportation system capable of transporting heavy loads over the long distances at a cost that would ensure a profit at the journey's end. Towards this end, the construction of the transcontinental railroad and its constituent feeder lines was indispensable. Because they were so expensive to build, railroads required extensive capital from distant financiers in New York and in Europe, as well as from gargantuan federal, state, and county subsidies. Railroad corporations, both desperate and greedy, resorted to a previous system of financing that invited fraud from promoters, speculators, politicians, and bankers. To combat skepticism among potential investors, railroads promised high returns on their securities, and they "watered" the face value of their stocks so that they far exceeded their actual value. To secure federal grant and loans, they established large slush funds for purposes of bribery. To obtain cheap labor, they contracted over 10,000 Chinese workers, who were paid appallingly low wages for a job involving long hours, rickety equipment, dynamite, and long winters in the Sierras.

The Central Pacific Railroad was particularly deft in manipulating stock and corrupting public officials. While T.D. Judah, an engineer, created the Central Pacific he was ultimately squeezed out by the ruthless, cutthroat tactics of Leland Stanford, Collis P. Huntington, Mark Hopkins, and Charles Crocker. Together, these four men turned a modest investment of $60,000 into a virtual empire. They established their own separate construction company, and voted themselves construction contracts that paid them $90 million for work that cost them only $32.2 million. By 1876, the "Big Four" (as Stanford, Huntington, Hopkins, and Crocker came to be known) secured a monopoly over rail transportation in California. Their success created the Southern Pacific (S.P.) the notorious "Octopus," which became far and away the dominant economic power on the west coast. So large, so influential, so necessary to the livelihood of hundreds of thousands of Californians, the S.P. extended its "tentacles" into almost every sphere of society. Not until the early 1900s would federal and state policy regulate the excesses of the S.P. monopoly. The railroad nevertheless primed California for its global prominence in the twentieth century.

Despite the remarkable and far-reaching transformations that took place in the next century, the Gold Rush *mystique* died hard in the "Golden State." If a common theme pervades the wheat boom, the citrus boom, the oil boom, the motion picture and entertainment boom, the real estate boom, and the silicon chip boom, it is a "get-rich-quick" myth that has never disappeared from the state. If another common theme exists, it is the idea that anything is possible in California; it is the idea that people can invent new roles for themselves if they don't like the ones they have. Clearly such ambitions spurred the movement of millions of California migrants, including African Americans fleeing repression in the South, dust bowl migrants seeking farmland during the depression, and disgruntled youth in the 1960s seeking refuge in San Francisco's flourishing counterculture. While the myths and yearning behind the so-called "California dream" have earned their share of derision from many of the state's detractors, the dream clearly invoked the real longings and aspirations of the people who migrated there.

The Rise of Los Angeles

Californian's quest for fast fortunes and their ability to "defy reality" found expression in the growth of Los Angeles, a tiny Spanish pueblo smack in the middle of an empty, semi-arid coastal plain. The region was isolated; it contained no dominant industry, no natural harbors, no navigable rivers, and no dependable water supply. Indeed, the fact that the city materialized at all suggests its leaders were remarkably bold visionaries or remarkably talented con artists. One thing was certain: the city was extraordinarily oligarchic. Precisely because Los Angeles lacked the essential infrastructure required for sustaining a large city, gargantuan land owners, developers, speculators, and boosters realized they would

> ◀ ***Fast Facts***
>
> **Los Angeles began as a tiny Spanish pueblo smack in the middle of an empty, semi-arid coastal plain.**

have to create those attributes themselves. Only the state's richest men, working in tandem with the municipal and federal government, could have provided the overhead necessary for a transportation system, a man-made port, and an extensive hydraulic complex. What made Los Angeles unique to the American urban experience, was that its elite made their gigantic investments far in advance of demand. The Owens Valley water was tapped and the Los Angeles Harbor was constructed not to satisfy a large population, but, rather, to lure one into Southern California.

Boosterism, corporate growth, the aggressive expansion of municipal services, and the federal government thus came together in an extraordinary fashion. Once Los Angeles overcame its natural handicaps, it underwent an expansion unparalleled among American metropolises. In a few short years, San Francisco conceded its position as the economic center of the great Southwest. By 1930, L.A. stood fourth in population, second in size, and ninth in manufacturing. The city was the world's largest oil port. It was one of the world's leading agricultural regions. It maintained the biggest tourist industry in the nation. Even more critical to Southern California's incredible growth were the contemporaneous automobile and entertainment revolutions, two industries that continued to increase, even through the Great Depression.

While unevenly distributed, sustained growth had been the general rule since 1890. Accordingly, Californians were ill-prepared for the long, debilitating depression that occurred in the 1930s. By 1934, more than 1,250,000 people—about one-fifth of the whole population of the state—depended on public relief. In the face of dramatic economic decline, California's long tradition of social violence found renewed vigor in the bitter struggles between labor and employers. Especially volatile were the state's agricultural regions, where ill-fed migratory workers were forced to watch food crops rot and burn because harvesting and marketing costs could not be generated. Growers, who had always been able to block collective action, had to hire armed vigilantes to violently crush unions of grape pickers in Lodi, cotton pickers in the southern San Joaquin Valley, and vegetable pickers in the Imperial Valley. This violence, however, was not limited to the state's hinterland. In San Francisco, traditionally a bastion for organized labor, the governor called out the National Guard to clearaway 5,000 striking maritime workers. Sixty-four people were injured (thirty-one of them shot), and two strikers were killed. In retaliation, nearly all the unions in the Bay Area joined in a general strike. These kinds of conflicts found further expression in the Democratic gubernatorial nomination of Upton Sinclair.

Sinclair's extremely controversial End Poverty in California (EPIC) campaign espoused a socialist agenda that promised to put all the unemployed to work in state-aided cooperative enterprises. A thoroughly frightened Republican Party forged an extensive, costly mud-slinging campaign to ensure victory. In the end, Republican Frank Merriam garnered 1,138,620 votes to Sinclair's 87,957.

While California's dominant Anglo society quarreled amongst itself, whites from all sectors often found unity in their opposition against a perceived racial "other"—especially in time of extreme stress. Just as the Chinese were targeted in the depression of the 1870s, Mexican immigrants became popular scapegoats for the depression of the 1930s. While state-sponsored programs enthusiastically recruited Mexican agricultural laborers during World War I, both political parties in California expressed resentment and suspicion of "aliens" on relief during the depression. In response, state and federal government initiated forced repatriations/deportation programs that depopulated Mexican communities across the Southwest. Racial scapegoating intensified during World War II, when xenophobic servicemen, flushed with general anxiety about the war, provoked the notorious Zoot Suit riots of 1943. For six full days, mobs of white sailors, soldiers, and civilians ran rampant into the Los Angeles barrios and violently attacked scores of young Mexican Americans. The most flagrant wartime episode of Anglo-American bigotry, however, was the virtual imprisonment of over 100,000 Japanese and Japanese Americans. While their "relocation" was based upon the argument of "military necessity," not one shred of evidence of Japanese sabotage was ever detected.

World War II, nevertheless, revitalized California's economy. From 1940–1946, the federal government pumped over $35 billion into the state to create or expand military installations and new defense industries. As personal income in California soared to more than three times its prewar figure, ships in the north and airplanes in the south became the state's most important products. There was now a desperate shortage of labor. Necessity induced employers to draw upon new pools of labor groups that had been previously excluded from the "work force" or confined to the least desirable jobs. In the 1940s, women comprised at least one-third of the workforce in the war industries of the Pacific

Coast. Public policy turned 180 degrees, as state-sponsored "bracero" programs enlisted the labor of 200,000 Mexicans (and provided incentive for an additional 800,000 to "illegally" cross the border). The migration of African Americans spurred the most striking minority addition to the work force. Blacks did not attain full equality in the western workplace, but they made significant gains.

In the postwar years, California has constituted a kind of barometer for American political culture. The anti-communist fervor in the 1950s found vigorous expression in California, a region which owed much of its growth to military expansion. Conservative Presidents Richard Nixon and Ronald Reagan, both native sons of the state, built their political careers on cold war hysteria. They both played important roles in the stormy controversies that surrounded the Hollywood industry and the University of California, two prominent targets of the House Un-American Activities Committee. At the other end of the spectrum, California was also at the forefront of the social radicalism that occurred in the 1960s. The Berkeley campus inspired militant student rebellions across the country. San Francisco was the virtual capital of counterculture. In Southern California, riots in Watts forced the federal government to reexamine the plight of African Americans. Yet, while the social and political temperament of the state frequently ventured into the extremes, the state had also come to define a general middle-class lifestyle that Americans nationwide aspired to: an ideal embodied by single family houses, surrounded by landscaped lawns and isolated from business districts. Indeed, Southern California's notorious urban sprawl stemmed from its inhabitants' unprecedented quest for suburban privatism.

Socio-economic Tensions

The demographic and economic explosions in postwar California have generated repercussions that threatened to undermine the vitality and influence of the state. In Southern California especially, physical dispersion has meant segregation and social schisms. The more affluent districts in Los Angeles County have incorporated themselves as independent cities, and have used their new powers to zone out poor people and put forth policy tailored to middle-class property owners. As national manufacturing plants have declined and relocated, the poorer, more urban districts, have suffered unemployment, drug use, and gang violence. The county's sprawling, fragmented landscape is thus marked by dispersed pockets of sheltered suburbs and inner-city slums. Although the City of Los Angeles boasts one of the most ethnically diverse regions in the world, it has failed dramatically to become a true multicultural city. An almost Third World economy in East Los Angeles and the South Central district has created as much tension among Asians, Mexicans, and African Americans as it has solidarity. The pressures of urban blight erupted most recently in 1992, after a jury acquitted Los Angeles police officers for excessively beating black motorist Rodney King. The riots that ensued destroyed more property and cost more lives than any other American urban disturbance since the 1863 New York Draft Riots.

Limited natural resources also promise a rough future ahead. California's vast hydraulic systems constitute the most ambitious attempt ever on the planet to create a civilization out of semi-arid desert. The inability of these systems to sustain themselves, however, will force the state's inhabitants to substantially alter the way they have traditionally dealt with their precious water resources. Problems of salinization and heavy metal contamination will not go away, and the inevitable silting over of dams and canals will require enormous expenditures. Other forms of environmental degradations, including ocean, air, and land pollution will also make Californians, as well as Americans, question their tenacious belief that growth and progress are one and the same. The fact that many areas in the Southwest and Pacific Northwest owe their expansion to people fleeing California suggests that this self-reflection is already occurring.

Works Consulted

Kimberly Arvanigian. Lecturer, Political Science. California State University, Fresno.

Jerry Bentley and Herbert Ziegler. *Traditions and Encounters: A Global Perspective on the Past.* Boston: McGraw-Hill, 2003.

Alan Brinkley. *The Unfinished Nation: A Concise History of the American People.* Boston: McGraw-Hill, 2004.

Richard Bulliet, Pamela Crossley, Daniel Headrick, Steven Hirsch, Lyman Johnson, David Northrup. *The Earth and Its Peoples: A Global History.* Boston: Houghton Mifflin Company, 2001.

William Duiker and Jackson Spielvogel. *The Essential World History.* Wadsworth/ Thomson Learning, 2002.

John Mack Faragher, Mari Jo Buhle, Daniel Czitrom, Susan Armitage, eds. *Out of Many: A History of the American People.* Englewood Cliffs, New Jersey: Prentice Hall, 1994.

Andrew Rolle. *California: A History.* Wheeling, Illinois: Harlan Davidson, Inc., 1998.

Science
Review

Science is systematized knowledge derived from observation and study. Knowledge you will derive from the study of this section includes the properties of matter, heat transfer, structure of living organisms, the solar system and universe, and the composition of the Earth. After carefully studying and analyzing the data of this section, you will conclude you are prepared to perform well when taking the science portion of the CSET.

Structure and Properties of Matter

Structure

Matter is anything that takes up space and has mass. At a fundamental microscopic level, matter is made up of atoms or molecules, the atoms themselves being made up of even smaller particles called neutrons, electrons, and protons. The neutrons and protons make up most of the mass of atoms and are located in the atomic nucleus at its center. Electrons have little mass and can be thought of as orbiting the nucleus like planets circling a sun. Electrons have a negative charge equal and opposite to a positive charge on the proton. Since atoms are neutral (unless ionized), the number of electrons and protons is equal. Electrons, however, determine the chemical properties of the atom, because it is the electrons that enter into bonding (see below). Molecules are made up of atoms combined in definite proportions.

At the macroscopic level, **matter can exist in four distinct states: solid, liquid, gas, and plasma**. Matter can be further classified as mixtures, elements, compounds, or solutions. Elements consist of only one type of atom; an example would be a bar of pure iron. Compounds consist of matter that is made up of atoms that are chemically combined with one another in definite weight proportions. An example of a compound would be water, which is oxygen and hydrogen combined in the ratio of two hydrogen molecules to one oxygen molecule. Mixtures are matter that is made up of one or more types of molecules, not chemically combined and without any definite weight proportions. An example would be milk, which is a mixture of water and butterfat particles. Solutions are homogeneous mixtures, e.g., mixtures where the substances are distributed evenly. An example of a solution would be sea water.

> *Fast Facts* Matter can exist in four distinct states: Solid, liquid, gas, and plasma.

Mixtures can be separated by either physical or chemical means. Physical means are usually employed for mixtures. An example would be straining the butterfat from milk to make skim milk. Other means used for solutions include evaporation. An example of the former would be the separation of salt from sea water by means of evaporation and recondensation.

Properties of Matter

Physical Properties

All matter has physical, thermal, electrical, and chemical properties. The physical properties of matter include **color, density, hardness, and conductivity**. **Color** is the human eye's response to light either reflected or emitted by matter. **Density** is the amount of mass that is contained in a unit volume by a given substance. **Hardness** is the resistance to penetration offered by a given substance. **Conductivity** is a substance's ability to transmit heat (thermal) or current (electrical).

Thermal Properties

When heated or cooled, matter undergoes phase changes. Phase change means that a substance changes state. The most common progression of phase changes observed, when hosting a substance, is solid to liquid to gas. When cooling, the reverse progression of gas to liquid to solid is ordinarily seen. In a phase change the chemical properties of the matter remain unchanged: the substance still has the same chemical formulation after the change. Energy (heat) is invoked in every phase change with an input of heat required to move to less-ordered states and a release of heat involved in moving to more-ordered states. An example of the former is the conversion of water to steam. An example of the latter is heat being released by snowflakes upon conversion from water vapor.

Electrical Properties

Matter can be classified as either a conductor or non-conductor. Conductors have a (relatively) high number of free electrons, while non-conductors do not. Free electrons are loosely bound electrons that can wander from atom to atom within the material, belonging to no particular atom. These free electrons are also referred to as valence electrons. Conduction occurs when battery terminals are connected across a material object, causing the free electrons to flow as a current through the object. The direction of flow is towards the positive battery terminal as it attracts the negative electrons, while the negative terminal repels them. In general, metals are good conductors and non-metals are not, because metals have abundant free electrons.

Chemical Properties

Matter can react with other types of matter when chemically combined. A product is chemically combined reactants that, along with any heat energy, can either be liberated (exothermic) or absorbed (endothermic). The resulting product is composed of molecules having atoms bonded together in various ways, such as ionic or covalent bonds. These terms refer to how outer or valence electrons bond between the two different elements.

The location of a substance in the periodic table determines how it will react to another substance. Atomic structure is related to the properties and arrangement of elements in the periodic chart. Elements are classified into groups, periods, and families. It is from these groupings that matter is classified and its behavior is studied, based on the ability of an element to combine or react with other elements. In general, elements from the same groups will not react, while elements from different groups may. The more separated the groups, the more likely the possibility for reaction.

Solution Characteristics

A large class of solutions can be broadly classified as either acids or bases.

Acid/water solution properties include (1) conducting electrically, (2) reacting strongly with metals, (3) changing blue litmus to pink and (4) reacting with base solutions to form a neutralizing salt.

Base/water solution properties Include (1) conducting electrically, (2) changing red litmus paper to blue, (3) reacting with acid solutions to form a neutralizing salt and (4) feeling slippery with strong solutions caustic to the skin.

Principles of Motion and Energy

Motion Descriptors

The parameters (or terms) of position, displacement, speed, velocity, and acceleration, all have very specific definitions and are used to describe motion.

Position

Position refers to location of an object. Often, position is given with reference to a coordinate system along some axis. For example, we can say that an object is 2 m to the right of an origin and on the x axis, or that it is 5 m to the left of an origin on the x axis. For the former case, the object coordinate would be +2 m and for the latter it would be –5 m.

Displacement

Displacement refers to how far an object has moved. In general, displacement is the signed number difference in start and end position. For example, if an object (moving in a straight line along some axis) has an initial position of –2 m and its final position is 7 m, then we can say that its displacement is 7 – (–2) = 9 m.

Speed

Speed is the time-rate of displacement. To find the average speed over some time t we divide the displacement by the time. For example, if the displacement of 9 occurs over a time period of 4.5 seconds, the average speed over that interval of time is 9/(4.5) m/s = 2 m/s.

Velocity

Velocity is a speed with a specified direction. Using the above example, we can specify velocity as 2 m/s to the right. An opposite velocity would be 2 m/s to the left. An alternative representation for the former is +2 m/s and for the latter is –2 m/s. Here the + and – are used, respectively, to signify rightward and leftward. Direction may also be specified by an angle or by an arrow (vector). Angle specification is usually with respect to a reference direction taken as 0 degrees. Use of a vector shows not only velocity direction, but its sense. The arrowhead indicates which way along the vector length the object is moving.

Acceleration

Acceleration is the rate of velocity change. To find the average acceleration over some time t we divide the change in velocity by the time. For example, if the starting velocity is 6 m/s to the right along some axis and the final velocity 12 m/s to the right over a 3 second time, the acceleration is (12 – 6)/3 = 6/3 = 2 m/s/s to the right. (Alternatively, the + sign for the answer signifies "to the right" since the + sign on the initial and final velocity was taken to mean "to the right" in the first place.

Energy

Energy is the ability to do work. "Work" is the force applied to an object which is moved some distance. Energy comes in many forms and work is often accomplished using simple machines.

Energy exists in three states: potential, kinetic, and activation energies. An object possessing energy because of its motion has kinetic energy. The energy that an object has as the result of its position or condition is called potential energy. The energy necessary to transfer or convert potential energy into kinetic energy is called activation energy.

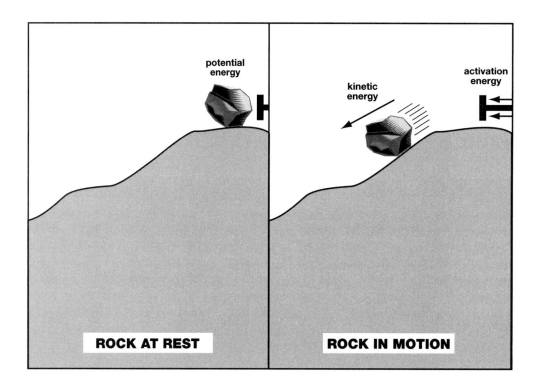

Force

Force is defined as either a push or pull on an object. If the force is unbalanced, the object will accelerate. A good example of an unbalanced force is the thrust provided by a rocket engine moving the rocket upward at ever increasing speeds from a launch pad. If, however, the net force is balanced on an object, the object will not accelerate. It will either remain still or continue to move at a constant speed.

Work

Work is defined as exerting a force on an object over a distance. If you lift a heavy ball from the floor to a table top, you have done work. Note that both a force and a displacement are involved if you try to lift the ball but can not; no work was done, though a considerable force was exerted. Alternatively, if a body is displaced with no force acting on it, no work is done either. An example of this situation is a spent rocket in space. While the rocket may be continuously moving, no force acts on it, so no work is done. Quantitatively, work is the product of the force acting in the direction of movement and the displacement.

Energy Sources

Energy is available in many forms including **heat**, **light**, **solar radiation**, **chemical**, **electrical**, **magnetic**, and **sound**. When you turn the lights on in your car, chemical energy stored in the battery is converted into electrical energy (current flowing in the circuitry), which is then converted into both heat and light in the head-lamp filament. Solar radiation is used in some parts of the world to heat water by flowing cold water through pipes exposed to the sun. Here solar radiation is converted to heat, which raises the water temperature. Lightning strikes produce thunder, because some of the electrical energy in the lightning strike sets up vibrations in the air, which are then converted into sound.

Machines in general are used to either multiply force and/or change direction of force. Simple machines include the lever, ramp, and pulley. For perfect (frictionless) machines, the work done by the user is equal to the work done by the machine. A good example of a lever is the nail puller on a hammer. The user exerts a small force at a large distance, while the hammer exerts a larger (multiplied) force over a short distance. Pulleys change the direction of a form enabling a user to pull down in order to move an object up. Ramps enable users to push horizontally to move objects upward with relatively small amounts of applied force as compared to direct lifting.

Conservation of Energy

In the process of energy conversion, all energy is conserved. This is a fundamental law of science that means energy never disappears; it just changes its form. A good example of energy conservation is lifting a heavy object from floor to table top. Work is done and is stored as potential energy when the object is placed on the table top. However, the potential energy can be recovered by pushing the object off of the table. The potential energy is then converted to kinetic energy (energy of motion) and work that was done is recovered. For this ideal simple system, the energy recovered (kinetic) is equal to the energy stored (potential). However, for non-ideal (real) systems, the recovered energy is always less than the stored energy. This is usually attributable to losses of one type or another (often friction). Nevertheless, it is always true that energy is conserved; stored or potential energy is always the sum of recovered energy plus losses, if any.

Heat and Temperature

Heat is a form of energy. **Temperature**, however, is a measure of aggregate atomic or molecular activity within an object. To illustrate the difference, consider the example of a pot of water on a stove where heat energy is transferred to the water. The effect of heating the water is to put its molecules into ever increasing vibratory motion. If heated sufficiently, the vibratory motion is strong enough to break intermolecular bonds and the water is thereby converted into steam and boils away. Note that adding heat is the cause of increasing temperature, not the other way around.

Temperature Measurement Systems

There are a number of devices used to measure temperature. Among them are thermometers, thermocouples, and optical methods, all of which are explained below.

Thermometers: The common mercury and alcohol thermometers both rely on expansion properties of the fluids. When heated to a given temperature, each fluid will expand an exact amount. Within the thermometer tubes, the fluids are constrained to expand or contract along the tube length and within a very small diameter. Markings alongside the tubes denote the temperature for each and every expansion amount

Thermocouples: When dissimilar metals are joined together, a small electrical signal is produced. If the joined metals are wires, then one can measure the signal using an instrument known as a voltmeter connected to the wires. However, if the junction of the wires is heated to a particular temperature, the electrical signal will change in a predictable way. Thus, for every signal there is a corresponding temperature. In this way thermocouples can be used to measure temperatures by associating the measured signal with a corresponding temperature.

Optical Methods: When certain solids (often metals) are heated to elevated temperatures, they begin to glow. At first a dull red is observed, but as temperatures increase a mix of colors is observed, starting with a yellowish white and then (at even higher temperatures) becoming blueish white. The colors are due to increasing electron vibration within the atoms of the heated substance. The stronger the vibration (lots of heating) the bluer the emitted light. The weaker the vibration (not much heating) the redder the emitted light. Optical pyrometers utilize this property of heated objects to determine object temperature. (In practice, objects produce a mixed spectrum of color similar to that of the sun, but the optical pyrometer manages to separate out the strongest color within the spectrum. From this information, it deduces the temperature in much the same way as is done with the thermocouple.) Note that optical methods offer the advantage of being able to measure temperatures remotely thereby eliminating the need for physical contact with the object. This is the way astronomers deduce the temperature of distant stars.

> *Fast Facts*
>
> **Three common methods used to measure temperature are thermometers, thermocouples, and optical methods.**

Heat Transfer

The transfer of heat is accomplished in three different ways: **conduction**, **convection** and **radiation**.

Conduction: If two objects differing in temperature are placed in contact, heat will flow from the hotter object to the cooler object. A good example is the automobile cooling system. Heat from the engine interior is transferred to a liquid coolant that circulates from the engine to the car radiator and then back. When the coolant reaches the radiator, heat is again conductivity transferred from the water to the radiator, which then transfers the heat to the air by means of radiation.

Radiation: Heat transfer can occur in a vacuum where there is no possibility of conduction. In this instance, heat is radiated from the object into space. A common example is heated iron. A hand held near the iron can sense the heat (actually infrared radiation) that is emitted. Stars transfer enormous amounts of heat (and light) energy by means of radiation into the surrounding vacuum of space.

Convection: This type of heat transfer involves heating and circulation of a substance that changes its density when heated. A good example is the heating of air over land near coastal areas leading to the influx of sea breezes from off shore. The heated air inland expands and thereby decreases in density. This in turn causes the air to rise, creating a decreased pressure inland.

Cooler air off shore then rushes into the low pressure area, while the rising, heated air is cooled and made dense again at higher altitudes. The net effect is to create a circulation of air where heated inland air is replaced by cooler off-shore air. The heated inland air rises, cooling and decreasing in density, and eventually sinks back down through the atmosphere only to repeat the process again. Convective processes are also important in heat exchanges taking place beneath the earth's crust involving magma and volcanoes.

Light Sources

Light sources can be either mixtures of multiple wavelengths or a single wavelength. ("Wavelength" in this context means color.) Generally, a source that produces a mixture of colors is termed polychromatic or a white light source, while single color sources are termed monochromatic.

An example of a white light source is the incandescent light bulb. Heating the filament by application of power causes it to glow white, indicating that the entire spectrum of visible colors is being mixed to produce white light.

An example of a monochromatic light source is the laser. The red light scanners used in supermarkets use laser light. The light is produced by exciting the lasing material with some sort of activation energy (often a pulse of ordinary light) followed by the relaxation of the excited atoms back to what is termed the ground state. Accompanying the relaxation is the emission of laser light, which is all the same color (wavelength).

An interesting example involving both polychromatic and monochromatic sources is the fluorescent light. Fluorescent tubes contain small amounts of mercury vapor, which under electrical stimulation emit monochromatic ultraviolet light. However, the insides of the fluorescent tubes are coated with a phosphor which emits white light when excited by the ultraviolet. Thus, the monochromatic ultraviolet produced by the mercury vapor excites the phosphor, which in its turn produces white or polychromatic light.

Light/Matter Interaction

There are three principal modes of **light/matter interaction**. These include **vision**, **photosynthesis**, and **photoemission**.

Vision: Light in the visible spectrum interacts with the rods and cones of the human eye, producing electrical signals which the brain interprets as color.

Photosynthesis: the process by which chlorophyll-containing organisms—green plants, algae, and some bacteria—capture energy in the form of light and convert it to chemical energy.

Photoemission: When light interacts with certain types of materials (usually the alkali metals or combinations thereof), the possibility of photoemission exists. When photoemission occurs, electrons are emitted by the illuminated material. The wavelength (color) of the light is important because there is a cutoff color: any color in the spectrum that is blue-wards of the cutoff color will produce emission while any color that is red-ward will not. The explanation for why this is so involves conservation of energy; the bluer the light, the more energetic it is while the redder the light, the less energetic it is. A practical example of photoemission is the TV camera, where light images are converted to electron images.

Waves

Broadly speaking, **waves** can be categorized as either **transverse** or **longitudinal**. In transverse waves, the wave disturbance (amplitude) is perpendicular or transverse to the direction of propagation. In longitudinal waves, wave disturbances are parallel to the direction of propagation. Wave energy can be thought of as disturbances making their way through mediums at speeds that depend on the medium. Note, however, that electromagnetic waves are unique: they require no medium for transmission and can readily propagate through a vacuum.

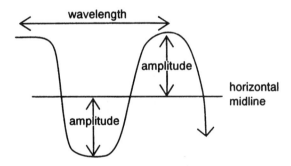

An example of a transverse wave is the wave produced when a rock is tossed into a still pond. The circular wave fronts travel outward from the splash center, with the disturbance (ripple or wave crest) transverse to the direction of movement. Light or electromagnetic radiation is also a transverse wave.

An example of both is the waves produced by seismic shock (earthquakes). One component is p-waves that cause building structures to be shaken up and down. A second component is s-waves that cause building structures to be shaken right and left. Both travel along the ground at different speeds, but each has its wave disturbance (amplitude) in different directions.

Wave Phenomena

Waves can be **reflected** or **refracted**. Reflection occurs when all or part of a wave incident on a material surface (in effect) bounces off the surface and is redirected. Refraction occurs when all or part of a wave penetrates the surface. Note that the reflected ray angle with a normal to the surface is equal to the incident ray angle with the surface. For refracted rays this is not true, as the angle made by the refracted ray will depend on material type and density.

An example of reflection is the image seen in plane mirrors: someone viewing your image will see you behind the mirror at exactly the same distance if he/she looks along a reflected angle that is equal to the incident angle. An example of refraction is the swimming pool bottom appearing closer than it really is. Light waves coming from the bottom of the pool encounter a water/air interface which produces refraction. The effect of changing the direction of the waves is to fool the eye into seeing the pool bottom as being closer than it really is.

Life Science

Structure Of Living Organisms And Their Functions (Physiology And Cell Biology)

Cellular Biology

A **cell** is the fundamental unit of all living organisms. Some cells are complete organisms, such as the unicellular bacteria and protozoa; others, such as nerve, organ, and muscle cells, are parts of multi-cellular organisms. Although they may differ widely in appearance and function, all cells have an internal substance called cytoplasm and a surrounding membrane. Each cell contains genetic material deoxyribonucleic acid (DNA), having coded instructions for the behavior and reproduction of the cell, and the chemical apparatus for translation of these instructions into protein.

Cells are composed primarily of the elements oxygen, hydrogen, carbon, and nitrogen. These are the constituents that make up most organic compounds. Among organic compounds in a cell are proteins, nucleic acids, lipids, and polysaccharides (carbohydrates). Water makes up most of the cell, because water is a favorable environment for biochemical reactions.

Generalized Animal Cell

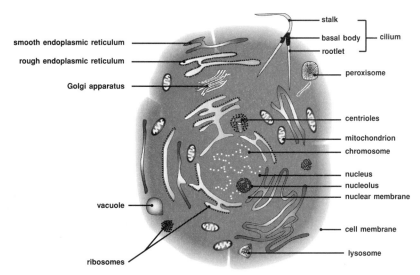

Generalized Plant Cell

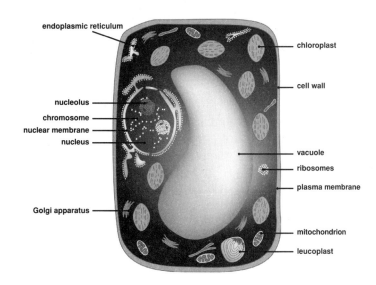

Within an animal cell, mitochondria are important agents where the products of the enzymatic breakdown, or metabolism, convert into energy in the form of the molecule adenosine triphosphate (ATP). This process consumes oxygen and is termed aerobic respiration. Plants in contrast have mitochondria and similar organelles called chloroplasts. Chloroplasts contain chlorophyll, used in converting light into ATP. This process is called photosynthesis. Photosynthesis is the process by which chlorophyll-containing organisms convert light energy to chemical energy.

A chemical equation illustrating photosynthesis in algae and green plants is

$$CO_2 + 2H_2O + light \rightarrow (CH_2) + H_2O + H_2O$$

In this formula H_2O represents water that is oxidized; CO_2 is carbon dioxide; and CH_2 is a product hydrocarbon.

Organ Systems in Humans

Musculoskeletal System

The human skeleton consists of more than 200 bones held together by connective tissues called ligaments. Movements are effected by contractions of the skeletal muscles, to which the bones are attached by tendons. Muscular contractions are controlled by the nervous system.

Nervous System

The **nervous system** has two divisions: the **somatic**, allowing voluntary control over skeletal muscle, and the **autonomic**, or involuntary, controlling cardiac and glandular functions.

Voluntary movement is caused by nerve impulses arising in the brain, carried by cranial or spinal chord nerves connecting to skeletal muscles. Involuntary movement occurs in direct response to outside stimulus. Involuntary responses are called reflexes. Various nerve terminals called receptors constantly send impulses to the central nervous system. There are three types of receptors:

- **Exteroceptors**: pain, temperature, touch, and pressure receptors

- **Interoceptors**: internal environment receptors

- **Proprioceptors**: movement, position, and tension receptors.

Each of the above receptors routes nerve impulses to specialized areas of the brain for processing.

Circulatory System

Blood in the **circulatory system** is pumped by the heart, passing through the right chambers of the heart and through the lungs where it acquires oxygen. From there it is pumped back into the left chambers of the heart. Next, it is pumped into the main artery, the aorta, which branches into increasingly smaller arteries. Beyond that, blood passes through tiny, thin-walled structures called capillaries. In the capillaries, the blood gives up oxygen and nutrients to tissues, absorbing from them carbon dioxide metabolic waste product. Finally, blood completes the circuit by passing through small veins, joining to form increasingly larger vessels until it reaches the largest veins which return it to the right side of the heart.

Immune System

The body defends itself against foreign proteins and infectious microorganisms by means of a complex dual system that depends on recognizing a portion of the surface pattern of the invader. **Lympthocytes** and **antibody molecules** are generated to destroy the invader molecules.

Respiratory System

Respiration is carried on by the expansion and contraction of the lungs. In the lungs, oxygen enters tiny capillaries where it combines with hemoglobin in the red blood cells and is carried to the tissues. At the same time, carbon dioxide passes through capillaries into the air contained within the lungs. Inhaling draws air into the lungs that is higher in oxygen and lower in carbon dioxide; exhaling forces air from the lungs that is high in carbon dioxide and low in oxygen.

Digestive and Excretory Systems

The energy required for sustenance of the human body is supplied by food. After fragmenting by chewing and mixing with saliva, digestion begins. Chewed food passes down the gullet into the stomach, where the process is continued by the gastric and intestinal juices. Thereafter, the mixture of food and secretions makes its way down the alimentary canal by peristalsis, rhythmic contractions of the smooth muscle of the gastrointestinal system.

Plant/Animal Comparisons

Plants are multi-cellular green organisms their cells containing eukaryotic (nucleated) protoplasm held within cell walls composed primarily of cellulose. The most important characteristic of plants is their ability to photosynthesize, e.g., to make their own food by converting light energy. The animal kingdom is also multicellular and eukaryotic, but its members differ from the plants in deriving nutrition from other organic matter, by ingesting food rather than absorbing it.

Living and Nonliving Components in Environments (Ecology)

Ecology is the study of the relationship of plants and animals to their physical and biological environment. The physical environment includes light, heat, solar radiation, moisture, wind, oxygen, carbon dioxide, nutrients in sod, water, and atmosphere. The biological environment includes organisms of the same kind as well as other plants and animals.

A useful way of thinking is in terms of **ecosystems**, thereby considering each locale or habitat as an integrated whole.

There are four major parts of ecosystems:

- producers (green plants)

- consumers (herbivores and carnivores)

- decomposers (fungi and bacteria)

- nonliving, or abiotic, components, consisting of dead organic matter and nutrients in the soil and water.

Inputs to ecosystems include solar energy, water, oxygen, carbon dioxide, nitrogen, and other elements and compounds. Outputs from an ecosystem include the heat of respiration, water, oxygen, carbon dioxide, and nutrient losses. The main input is solar energy.

Ecosystems function with energy input from the sun and through nutrients, which are continuously recycled. Light energy is used by plants, which photosynthetically convert it to carbohydrates and other carbon compounds. This energy is then further transferred by a series of steps involving eating and/or being eaten. Each step in the transfer involves several feeding levels: plants, herbivores (plant eaters), two or three levels of carnivores (meat eaters), and decomposers. Plant and animal matter not used in the grazing food chain, such as fallen leaves, twigs, roots, tree trunks, and the dead bodies of animals, support the decomposers. Bacteria, fungi, and animals that feed on dead material become the energy source for higher feeding levels. In this way nature makes maximum use of energy originally stored by plants.

Ecosystems function with energy input from the sun and through nutrients, which are continuously recycled.

Fast Facts

Imbalances

In any ecosystem, outputs must be balanced by inputs or the ecosystem will fail. Nutrients can be input or output from a system by various means. Rain can bring nutrients to a system while runoff from the rain can leach nutrients from the ecosystem. Crops can deplete nutrients, necessitating fertilization for nutrient replacement. In extreme cases, input imbalances can completely destroy ecosystem equilibrium by polluting it. An example would be acid rain in a forest, which retards plant growth by destroying the acid-base balance in the soil, while also killing fish with acidified runoff in nearby bodies of water.

Habitat and Niche

Ecosystems provide **habitat**, e.g., the place where particular plants or animals live. Within habitats, organisms occupy different niches. A **niche** is the functional role of a species in a community. For example, an African lioness lives in an African game preserve habitat. Its niche, in part, is preying upon other animals.

Population Growth Rates

Populations have a **birth rate** and a **death rate**. The major agent of population growth is births, and the major agent of population loss is deaths. If births exceed deaths, a population increases; and conversely, it decreases. If births equal deaths in a given population, its size remains the same, and it is said to have zero population growth.

When introduced into a favorable environment with abundant resources, a small population may undergo geometric, or exponential growth. Populations that exponentially continue to grow, however, eventually reach the upper limits of resources. Such populations then decline sharply because of some catastrophic event such as starvation, disease, or competition from other species.

Other populations tend to grow exponentially at first, and then their growth slows as the population increases, leveling off as the limits of their environment or carrying capacity are reached. Through various regulatory mechanisms, such populations maintain an equilibrium between their numbers and available resources.

Community Interactions

Major influences on population growth involve population interactions. These include competition, predation, and coevolution, as follows:

Competition

When a shared resource is scarce, organisms **compete**, and those that are more successful survive. Within some plant and animal populations, all individuals may share the resources in such a way that none obtains sufficient quantities to survive as adults or to reproduce. Among other plant and animal populations, dominant individuals claim access to the scarce resources and others are excluded. Individual plants tend to claim and hold onto a site until they lose vigor or die. These prevent other individuals from surviving by controlling light, moisture, and nutrients in their immediate areas.

Predation

Predation is the consumption of one living organism, plant, or animal, by another. While it serves to move energy and nutrients through the ecosystem, predation may also regulate population and promote natural selection by weeding the unfit from a population.

Coevolution

Coevolution is the joint evolution of two unrelated species that have a close ecological relationship, that is, the evolution of one species depends in part on the evolution of the other. Coevolution is also involved in predator-prey relations. Over time, as predators evolve more efficient ways of capturing or consuming prey, the prey evolves ways to escape predation.

Life Cycle, Reproduction and Evolution (Genetics and Evolution)

Life Cycle

Every higher organism has an average life span, defined and limited by species survival. This is thought to be true because (1) if an adult plant or animal were to live indefinitely after it has procreated it would deplete nutrients or food supplies, jeopardizing population survival, and (2) immortality would impede or arrest the process of natural selection, the mechanism by which a species adapts to environmental changes.

Theories on Life-Span Limits

Most biologists agree that an organism's **life span** is determined and limited by the laws of natural selection. However, no single theory is prevalent which explains the mechanisms by which a species replaces one generation with the next. There are three competing theories as follows:

- **Error theory**: aging is caused by the accumulation of small flaws in genetic information passed on as the body cells reproduce.

- **Cell rate theory**: cells taken from humans and other mammals and grown in the laboratory have been found to die before reaching 50 transfers of daughter cells to a new culture medium. This fact suggests that the rate at which individual cells age defines not only the average life span of a species, but also that of the species' sexes (females commonly outlive males).

- **Immune theory**: the body of an organism slowly loses its ability to defend itself from harmful organisms that invade from without and cellular anomalies that subvert from within. In humans, the thymus gland, which plays a main role in the immune system by generating antibodies, diminishes to a fraction of its original bulk and function by a person's 50th year. Proponents of the immune theory believe that the entire immune system loses its ability to distinguish friend from foe within the body and attacks the body's own tissues, producing what are called autoimmune diseases.

Reproduction

Reproduction is a process whereby living plant or animal cells or organisms produce offspring.

Animal Propagation

In almost all animal organisms, reproduction occurs during or after the period of maximum growth. Reproduction in animals can be further subdivided into asexual and sexual as follows:

Asexual animal propagation: Most single-celled organisms reproduce by a process known as fission, in which the parent organism splits into two or more daughter organisms, thereby losing its original identity. Also, there are instances where cell division results in the production of buds that arise from the body of the parent and then later separate to develop into a new organism identical with the parent. Reproductive processes such as those cited above, in which only one parent gives rise to the offspring, are scientifically classified as asexual reproduction. The offspring produced are identical with the parent

Sexual animal propagation: Reproduction here is governed by sperm uniting with ova for fertilization. Primary means are insemination (vertebrates by means of copulation) and cross fertilization (ova and sperm deposited in water at some distance from each other as by fish).

Plant Propagation

Individual plants have growth limitations imposed by inherited characteristics and environmental conditions; if the plant grows excessively, any number of reproductive processes may be simulated. However, in plants, reproduction may be either sexual or asexual as follows:

Asexual plant propagation: Also known as vegetative reproduction, it is the method by which plants reproduce asexually, e.g., without the union of cells or nuclei of cells, producing individuals that are genetically identical to the parent. Vegetative reproduction takes place either by fragmentation or by special asexual structures. An example of fragmentation is growing new plants from cuttings.

Sexual plant propagation: Sexual propagation involves seeds, produced by two individuals, male and female in practically all instances. Most plant propagation is, in fact, from seed, including all annual and biennial plants. Seed germination begins when a sufficient amount of water is absorbed by the seed, precipitating biochemical changes whereupon cell division is initiated.

Evolution (Genetics and Evolution)

Evolution is defined as the complex of processes by which living organisms originated on earth and have been diversified and modified through sustained changes in form and function.

Darwin reasoned that, in nature, species with qualities that made them better adjusted to their environments or gave them higher reproductive capacities would tend to leave more offspring.

Thus, such individuals were said to have higher fitness. Because more individuals are born than survive to breed, elimination of the less fit (natural selection) should occur, leading to a population that is well adapted to environmental habitats. According to Darwin, evolution proceeds by the natural selection of well-adapted individuals over a span of many generations. However, Darwin's work preceded that of Mendel and others and thereby did not benefit from having knowledge of the role genetics plays in the evolution process.

After Mendel's genetic discoveries, mutations were thought to be the only source of genetic variation with many geneticists believing that evolution was driven by the random accumulation of favorable mutational changes. Natural selection as defined above was reduced to a minor role by mutationists whose ideas held sway well into the 1930s.

Still later, during the establishment of what has been termed the "synthetic theory of evolution," scientific understanding was greatly expanded in 1953, when James Watson and Francis Crick demonstrated that genetic material is composed of two nucleic acids, deoxyribonucleic acid (DNA) and ribonucleic acid (RNA). Mutations (in light of these discoveries) were then seen to be changes in gene position that can affect the function of the protein derived from the gene. Natural selection in this view now operates to favor or suppress a particular gene according to how strongly its protein product contributes to the reproductive success of the organism.

Today, evolution is a widely accepted context within which many branches of life science continue to advance their understanding.

Earth and Space Science

The Solar System and the Universe (Astronomy)

Solar System

The **solar system** is defined as the Sun and its nine orbiting planets. The Sun is composed of essentially hydrogen and is very massive with a mass 750 times the amount of all the planets combined. Planet names in order from the Sun are Mercury, Venus, Earth, Mars, Jupiter, Saturn, Uranus, Neptune, and Pluto. The innermost planets of Mercury, Venus, Earth, and Mars are composed mostly of rocky-metallic material, while the outermost planets of Saturn, Uranus, Neptune, and Pluto are composed mostly of hydrogen, helium, and ices of ammonia and methane. Jupiter is a gas giant exception, composed largely of hydrogen, and is best thought of as a half-formed sun. Many of the planets have satellite moons, including Earth (1), Mars (2), Jupiter (8), Pluto (2), or other distinguishing features (Saturn's rings), significant atmospheres (Earth and Venus), or the giant red spot on Jupiter. Distances from the Sun can be expressed in terms of AU or astronomical units, with the Sun-Earth distance taken as AU=1. In terms of AU, the closest planet is Mercury with AU = 0.39 and furthest is Pluto AU = 39.4.

Comets and Asteroids

There are bodies much smaller than the planets that also have orbits about the Sun. Innumerable **asteroids** lie in a belt between Mars and Jupiter and orbit into the same rotational sense as the rest of the planets. Sizes of asteroids range from the largest, Cares (having a diameter of about 1000 km), to others too small to have any perceptible gravity. Their composition is generally carbonaceous or rocky-metallic.

Comets differ greatly from asteroids in their composition having significant amounts of ices and water. Also a comet's period (time taken to orbit the sun) can vary considerably. Comets have been described by the astronomical community as "dirty snowballs." Comet orbits are generally more acutely elliptical than that of planets or asteroids and when approaching the Sun they exhibit tails or comas that are the result of their ice being boiled or sublimated off by heating. For purposes of analyses, comets are described in terms of their nucleus, head (or coma), and tail. The nucleus is the small, solid body from which an extended atmosphere is developed as the comet nears the Sun. The coma is the boiled-off atmosphere that surrounds the nucleus. The tail is the long streamers of gas and dust that are swept away from the sun.

> *Fast Facts*
>
> Comets have been described by the astronomical community as "dirty snowballs."

Earth's Rotation and the Time of Day

Because the Earth rotates once upon its axis every 24 hours, the time of day varies from point to point on its surface. For example, when it is sunrise at one point on Earth, approximately halfway round the Earth it is also sunset. So, at a given instant of time at one point on Earth it is sunset (6:00 p.m.), at another point diametrically opposite the first point it is sunrise (6:00 a.m.) and halfway in between it is 12:00 p.m. or 12:00 a.m., depending on which hemisphere one chooses. To facilitate the obvious need for time zones, the Earth is gridded with latitude and longitude lines. Longitude lines run from pole to pole and there are 360 of these around the Earth in one degree increments. Every hour a given location on the Earth's surface rotates through 15 degrees of longitude.

Position of the Sun in the Sky

For all practical purposes the Sun is fixed in position. However, the daily west to east rotation of the earth appears to make the Sun "rise" and "fall" in the sky each day. It rises above the eastern horizon at dawn, when the line of sight from an observer to the Sun is first made clear by the rotation of the Earth. It sets below the western horizon at dusk, when the line of sight from an observer to the Sun is last made clear by the rotation of the earth. Thus, throughout the day the Sun is seen to rise steadily higher in the sky as the west to east rotation of the Earth continually alters a viewer's line of sight.

In longer (seasonal) periods the Sun is seen to change its position in another way. In the northern hemisphere, as winter approaches, the sun is seen to sink towards the southern horizon. Later, when winter wanes and summer approaches, the Sun is seen to rise higher above the southern horizon. The low point is on the first day of winter (December 21) and the high point is on the first day of summer (June 21). (Halfway in between these two dates are the equinoxes which mark the beginning of spring and fall). This motion too is apparent and is due to the Earth being tilted on its axis and thereby pointing either away or towards the Sun at different times of the year (Equivalently different positions along Earth's orbital path around the Sun). In winter, the north pole of the earth points away from the Sun, causing it to appear lower (or further south) to observers in the northern hemisphere. In summer, the north pole of the Earth points towards the Sun, causing it to appear higher (or further north) to observers in the northern hemisphere. Note that the tilting of the Earth's axis also accounts for the difference in length of days from season to season with the effect being more pronounced at higher latitudes. Note also that for the southern hemisphere that the same process occurs, but with opposite seasonal phasing.

Stars, Sun, and Galaxies

The **Sun** of our solar system is a medium sized star and is only one of billions of stars in our Milky Way galaxy, itself a spiral galaxy. The Andromeda Nebula Galaxy, first studied in 1612, resembles the Milky Way. It is the nearest galaxy that northern hemisphere observers can see. Galaxies are large collections of stars which are composed of not just stars but also hydrogen, dust particles, and other gases. They are located millions to billions of light-years from the earth. **Galaxies** are classified as to their appearance. Irregular systems have no special form or symmetry. Spiral systems resemble a large pinwheel with arms extending from the dense central core. Elliptical systems appear round with spiral arms.

The universe itself is composed of countless galaxies; its age is estimated to be about 18 billion years.

Stars are essentially large masses of hydrogen, which have been pulled together under the influence of gravity. With sufficient amounts of hydrogen and gravitational pressure, fusion is initiated in the star's interior, which causes the star to glow with visible fight. (Fusion is the process of liberating energy by fusing hydrogen to form helium.) As such, stars represent the most abundant mass-type in the universe: plasma. Depending on the amount of hydrogen mass involved, stars undergo an evolutionary cycle which can involve a vast army of forms including red giants, novas, supernovas, neutron stars, white dwarfs, and others.

The Structure and Composition of the Earth (Geology)

Mineral Characteristics

Minerals are the most common form of solid material found in the Earth's crust. Even soil contains bits of minerals that have broken away from its rock source. Minerals are dug from the Earth and are used to make a variety of products. To be considered a mineral the element must be found in nature and must never have been a part of any living organism. Atoms, making up the element or substance, must be arranged in regular patterns to form crystals. Examples of minerals include quartz, calcite, and mica.

Rock Types

The hard, solid part of the Earth's surface is called **rock**. Rock may be exposed from its soil cover when highways are cut through hillsides or mountain regions. River channels or shorelines frequently cut through rock beds. Some mountain chains expose rock beds when weathering exposes the rock base. Rocks are useful in many ways as granite (igneous), marble (metamorphic), or limestone (sedimentary). They can be used in buildings, dams, highways, or the making of cement. Metals like aluminum, iron, lead and tin are removed from rock that is comas.

Landform Characteristics

The formation of deserts, mountains, rivers, oceans, and other landforms can be described in terms of geological process. Deserts are often formed where natural geographical barriers (rain shadows for example) prevent rain. Mountains are formed by colliding plates. Rivers form at low elevations where rainfall is collected and then is carried off into the oceans. Deltas or estuaries at river mouths are formed by accumulated sediment that is washed down the rivers.

Rock Formation

Igneous rocks are called fire rocks and are formed either underground or above ground. Underground, they are formed when the melted rock deep within the earth, called magma, becomes trapped in small pockets. As these pockets of magma slowly cool underground, the magma becomes igneous rocks. Igneous rocks are also formed when volcanoes erupt, causing the magma to rise above the earth's surface. When magma appears above the earth, it is called lava. Igneous rocks are formed as the lava cools above

Metamorphic rocks are rocks that have "morphed" into another kind of rock. These rocks were once igneous or sedimentary rocks. They were heated under tons of pressure, and this caused them to change. Examinations of metamorphic rock samples show flattening of some of the grains in the rock.

Sedimentary rocks are formed over thousands or even millions of years. They are formed when little pieces of earth are broken down and worn away by wind and water. These little bits of our earth are washed downstream where they settle to the bottom of rivers, lakes, and oceans. Layer after layer of eroded earth is deposited on top of each. These layers are pressed down more and more through time until the bottom layers slowly turn into rock.

Soil Processes

Rock is the parent material for soil. Rock under the action of both mechanical and chemical weathering is broken down into smaller bits. Mechanical weathering includes the effects of heating/cooling and water freezing into ice and expanding. Chemical weathering involves chemical breakdown of the rocks mineral material under the action of acids which transform its mineral composition. During the weathering process, four components are released:

- minerals in solution (cations and anions), the basis of plant nutrition.

- oxides of iron and alumina (sesquioxides $Al2O3$, $Fe2O3$).

- various forms of silica (silicon-oxide compounds).

- stable wastes as very fine silt (mostly fine quartz) and coarser quartz (sand). These have no nutritious value for plants.

The final stage in the process is the combining of silica and oxides to form various clays, whose mineral content is crucial to plant nutrition. The resulting admixture of sand, slit, and clay is termed "loam."

Layers of the Earth

The Earth consists of five parts: the first, the **atmosphere**, is gaseous; the second, the **hydrosphere**, is liquid; the third, fourth, and fifth, the **lithosphere**, **mantle**, and **core**, are largely solid. The atmosphere is the gaseous envelope that surrounds the solid body of the planet. (The atmosphere itself can be subdivided into troposphere, stratosphere, and mesosphere.) Although the atmosphere has a thickness of more than 1100 km (more than 700 mi.), about half its mass is concentrated in the lower 5.6 km (3.5 mi.). The lithosphere, consisting mainly of the cold, rigid, rocky crust of the Earth, extends to depths of 100 km (60 mi). The hydrosphere is the layer of water that, in the form of the oceans, covers approximately two-thirds of the surface of the Earth. The mantle and core are the heavy interior of the Earth, making up most of the Earth's mass.

Plate Tectonics

Plate tectonics is a relatively new theory that has revolutionized the way geologists think about the Earth. According to the theory, the surface of the Earth is broken into large lithospheric plates. The size and position of these plates change over time. The edges of these plates, where they move against each other, are sites of intense geologic activity such as earthquakes, volcanoes, and mountain building. Plate tectonics is a combination of two earlier ideas, continental drift and sea-floor spreading. Continental drift is the movement of continents over the Earth's surface and their change in position relative to each other. Sea-floor spreading is the creation of new oceanic crust at mid-ocean ridges and movement of the crust away from the mid-ocean ridges.

Mountain and Volcano Formation

A **volcano** is a mountain that shoots out magma which eventually hardens into lava. It also blasts out ash, sometimes creating rivers of lava.

Volcanoes are found all over the world; for example, the Pacific Ocean, the Hawaiian islands, and the southeastern border of Asia.

Volcanoes are created when two tectonic plates collide, form a mountain, and blow their tops.

Volcanoes are composed of fiery igneous rock, ash, and many different kinds of layers of dirt and mud that have hardened from previous eruptions.

Evidence for Plate Tectonics

Among the classes of evidence for continental drift and the underlying plate tectonics:

1. The shapes of many continents are such that they look like they are separated pieces of a jig-saw puzzle. For example, the east coast of North and South America relative to the shape of the west coast of Africa and Europe fit together.

2. Many fossil comparisons along the edges of continents that look like they fit together suggest species similarities that would only make sense if the two continents were joined at some point in the past.

3. There is a large amount of seismic, volcanic, and geothermal activity along plate boundaries compared to sites far from boundaries.

4. There are ridges, such as the Mid-Atlantic Ridge, where plates are separating due to lava welling up from between the plates as they pull apart. Likewise, there are mountain ranges being formed where plates are pushing against each other (e.g., the Himalayas, which are still growing).

Effects of Plate Tectonics on Climate
Geography and Distributions of Organisms

Plate tectonics affects the climate system through three major mechanisms as follows:

- Altering the distribution of continental land masses: the distribution of the continents has changed dramatically over geologic time. For example, just 165 million years ago there was only one super-continent, Pangea and one super-ocean, Panthalassa. Antarctica, today an ice-covered continent with life only at its maritime fringe, hasn't always been centered at the south pole, and extensive coal beds indicate a much more temperate climate in the past.

- Changing continental elevations: Colliding continental land masses are thrust upward, thereby forcing elevations upwards.

- Varying the atmospheric concentration of carbon dioxide: increased tectonic activity leads to increasing volcanism, which in turn leads to more greenhouse gases in the atmosphere, thereby altering the climate by raising temperatures.

The Earth's Atmosphere (Meteorology)

Day-by-day variations in a given area constitute weather, whereas climate is the long-term synthesis of such variations. Besides the effects of solar radiation, however, climate is also influenced by the complex structure and composition of the atmosphere and by the ways in which it and the ocean transports heat.

All weather is due to heating from the sun. The sun emits energy at an almost constant rate, but a region receives more heat when the sun is more directly overhead and when there are more hours of sunlight in a day. The overhead sun of the tropics makes this area much warmer than the poles, and in summer more overhead sun and long days make a given region much warmer than in winter.

All weather is due to heating from the sun. *Fast Facts*

Ocean Effects on Atmosphere

The surface currents of the ocean are characterized by currents that are kept in motion by prevailing winds, the direction of which is altered by the rotation of the earth. The best known of these currents is probably the Gulf Stream in the North Atlantic.

The **Hydrologic Cycle** is a series of movements of water above, on, and below the surface of the earth. This cycle consists of four distinct stages: storage, evaporation, precipitation, and runoff. It is the means by which the sun's energy is used to transport, via the atmosphere, stored water from the oceans to the land masses. Stored water is transported by means of evaporation, then precipitation, followed by unconsumed runoff and back into storage.

Air movement in the atmosphere is governed by differences of pressure. In general, air masses at the poles can be characterized as having high pressures and low moisture content. Air masses near the equators can be characterized as having low pressures and high moisture content. (Heating decreases the density of air at the equator and increases it at the poles.) Wind flow tendency is, therefore, from high to low pressure regions, although the picture is complicated by the rotation of the earth.

The Earth's Water (Oceanography)

Various bodies of water are studied in **oceanography**, including rivers, lakes, oceans, and estuaries. These can be described as follows:

Rivers: A river is a large, flowing body of water that usually empties into a sea or ocean.

Estuary: An estuary is where a river meets the sea or ocean.

Ocean: An ocean is a large body of salt water that surrounds a continent. Oceans cover more than two-thirds of the Earth's surface.

Lake: A lake is a large body of water surrounded by land on all sides. Very large lakes are often called seas.

Tides

The word **tides** is a generic term used to define the alternating rise and fall in sea level with respect to the land, produced by the gravitational attraction of the moon and the sun. Additional nonastronomical factors such as configuration of the coastline, local depth of the water, ocean-floor topography, and other hydrographic and meteorological influences may play an important role in altering the range, interval, and times of arrival of the tides.

Planning and Conducting Experiments

In planning experiments, one is generally attempting to test a hypotheses. A **hypotheses** is an educated guess that states there is some measurable relationship between two quantifiable variables. The outcome of the test in a well-designed experiment answers questions suggested by the hypotheses in a clear and unambiguous way. In planning and conducting the experiment one must (a) identify relevant variables, (b) identify equipment and apparatus to be used to measure and record the variables, (c) eliminate or suppress any other factors that could influence measured variables, and (d) decide on a means of analyzing the data obtained.

Principles of Experimental Design

In conducting experiments, it is imperative that questions raised by the hypotheses are testable and the data recorded is sufficiently accurate and repeatable.

1. Formulation of Testable Questions:

An example of a testable question might be, "Does mass have an influence on acceleration for bodies subjected to unbalanced forces?" This question is testable because it identifies specific variables (Force, Mass, and Acceleration) that can be measured and controlled in any experiment that seeks to establish a connection. Thus, testable questions must specify variables that are subject to both measurement and control.

2. Evaluation of Data

Reliability of data obtained in any experiment is always a concern. At issue is reproducibility and accuracy. In general, data must be reproducible not only by the experimenter but others using the same apparatus. If results cannot be reproduced, then results are suspect. Accuracy is often limited by measurement instruments. Any reported numerical result must always be qualified by the uncertainty in its value. A typical example might be a voltage readout on a meter-scale as 3.0 volts. If the meter has a full scale reading of 10 volts and meter accuracy is 3 percent, then the actual value could be anywhere between 2.7 volts and 3.3 volts.

Data Representation

Data is often represented in graphical form, where raw data is plotted. The independent (controlled) variable is usually associated with the x-axis and the dependent variable is usually associated with the y-axis. Graphs can either be linear (graph as straight lines) or non-linear. Often, equations can be fitted to graphs obtained for purposes of finder analyses. Use of a graphing calculator and specialized software can facilitate both the data collection and data representation in graphical form.

Note that x-y plots are not the only means of data representation. Charts, diagrams, and tables are also often used to display results.

Scientific Vocabulary

The following terms are useful and form an indispensable part of the vocabulary used in scientific experimentation

Observation: The act of sensing some measurable phenomenon.

Organization: Relating parts to a coherent whole.

Experimental: Testing the effect of an independent variable on a dependent variable in a controlled environment.

Inference: Deducing a conclusion from a measurement or observation that is not explicit to either. Example: We can infer that a classroom of 30 students has 16 girls, if we know that there are 14 boys. Here the inference is done my means of subtracting 14 from 30.

Prediction: Stating the outcome of an experiment in advance of doing it. An example would be predicting that a plot of velocity vs. time for a freely falling object will be a straight line.

Evidence: Data or observations that are relevant factors in testing hypotheses.

Opinion: An explanation of phenomena that may or may not be supported by evidence.

Hypothesis: An educated guess as to the relationship between two variables, which is subject to testing and verification.

Theory: Systematically organized knowledge that explains scientific phenomena.

Law: A statement of observable behavior based on consistent experience. Example: The law of gravity.

Scientific Tools and Their Use

A variety of tools or instruments are used in scientific experimentation. These include microscopes, graduated cylinders, scales, voltmeters, ammeters, meter sticks, and micrometers. In general, these are devices which enable measurements such as mass volume, length, and voltage. Inherent to their proper use is recognition of limitations on accuracy and precision. Precision concerns have to do with the number of places that can be reliably read from any measurement device. As an example, a meter stick is generally good to 3-place precision, the first two places being determined by scale markings and the third place determined by the estimated position between scale markings.

Interpretation of Experimental Results

Sometimes experimental work involves measurements which do not directly yield the desired variable value, but which can be interpreted or reduced to provide the desired value. Here, the experimental approach is indirect An example is the measurement of acceleration of gravity, or g, a fundamental gravitational constant. One common method is to measure displacement vs. time for a falling body. The resulting graph is then reduced (interpreted) to yield a plot of velocity vs. time. This plot in turn is then reduced (interpreted) to yield a plot of acceleration vs. time, from which the acceleration of gravity "g" can be read. Inherent to each of the reductions was finding the slope (rise/run) at various points, which is a mathematical technique, enabling interpretation of the results.

Communicating Experimental Results

Experimental results are usually formatted into a report of some kind. Report essentials normally include statements of purpose (objective), methods used, experimental set-up (including instrumentation), results (raw data and reduced data), error analysis, and conclusions. Such reports are logically organized and make abundant use of figures, charts, graphs, and other graphic aids to support narrative account of what was accomplished.

In addition to reports, oral presentations are sometimes required to communicate results. In most cases, graphics also used in reports will form a core of visuals that are supported by oral explanatory narrative.

Preparing for Investigative Activity

Preparation for doing experimental work usually involves researching the literature to determine what may or may not have been done in a particular field of interest. Researching includes both print and electronic resources (WWW), where various approaches and associated outcomes can be surveyed. Survey results can be useful in (a) suggesting refinements in procedures and techniques and (b) avoiding blind alleys of inquiry.

Chapter 5

Mathematics Review

Add clear, concise concepts and information together and divide them into well organized categories to reach the solution to your problem — the mathematics review section, which will help you multiply the number of questions you answer correctly on the CSET. Number systems, percents, algebraic expressions, geometry, measurements, and elementary statistics are all topics discussed in this successful equation. The formulas, functions, and concepts presented are equivalent to those you will find on the test and are an absolute value to your test-taking experience.

Arithmetic

Real Numbers

Most of the numbers used in algebra belong to a set called the **real numbers**, or **reals**. This set, denoted IR, can be represented graphically by the real number line.

Given a straight horizontal line extending continuously in both directions, we arbitrarily fix a point and label it with the number zero. In a similar manner, we can label any point on the line with one of the real numbers, depending on its position relative to zero. Numbers to the right of zero are called positive, while those to the left are called negative. Value increases from left to right, so that if a is to the right of b, it is said to be greater than b.

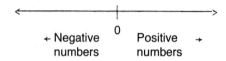

Integers

If we divide the number line into equal segments called unit lengths, we can then label the boundary points of these segments according to their distance from zero. For example, the point 2 lengths to the left of zero is –2, while the point 3 lengths to the right of zero is +3. (The + sign is usually assumed, so +3 is written as 3.) The number line now looks like this:

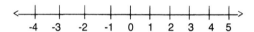

These boundary points represent the subset of the reals known as the **integers**, denoted Z. Some subsets of Z are the natural numbers or positive integers, the set of integers starting with 1 and increasing, $Z^+ = N = \{1, 2, 3, 4, \ldots\}$; the whole numbers, the set of integers starting with zero and increasing, $W \{0, 1, 2, 3, \ldots\}$; the negative integers, the set of integers starting with –1 and decreasing: $Z = \{-1, -2, -3, \ldots\}$; and the prime numbers, the set of positive integers greater than 1 that are divisible only by 1 and themselves: $\{2, 3, 5, 7, 11, \ldots\}$.

The following are properties of integers:

Commutative property: $a + b = b + a.$
Example: $2 + 3 = 3 + 2.$

Associative property: $(a + b) + c = a + (b + c).$
Example: $(2 + 3) + 4 = 2 + (3 + 4).$

Distributive property: $a(b + c) = ab + ac.$
Example: $2(3 + 4) = (2 \times 3) + (2 \times 4)$
$2 \times 7 \quad\;\; = 6 + 8$
$14 \qquad\;\; = 14.$

Additive identity: $a + 0 = a$.
Example:　　　$2 + 0 = 2$.

Multiplicative identity: $a \times 1 = a$.
Example:　　　$2 \times 1 = 2$.

Rationals

One of the main subsets of the reals is the set of **rational numbers**, denoted Q. This set is defined as all the numbers that can be expressed in the form a/b, where a and b are integers, $b \neq 0$. This form is called a fraction or ratio; a is known as the numerator, b the denominator.

Example: $\dfrac{-7}{5}, \dfrac{8}{6}, \dfrac{9}{-3}, \dfrac{5}{100}$

Note: the integers can all be expressed in the form a/b.

Example: $2 = \dfrac{2}{1}, -3 = \dfrac{6}{-2}, -5 = \dfrac{-5}{1}$

Irrationals

The complement of the set of rationals is the **irrationals**, whose symbol is Q'. For now, they are defined as the set of real numbers that cannot be expressed as the quotient of two integers.

Example: $\dfrac{a}{b}, b \neq 0$.

Absolute Value

The **absolute value** of an integer is the measure of the distance of the integer from zero. Since the measure of distance is always positive, absolute value is always positive (e.g., $|-3| = 3$, $|3| = 3$). The absolute value of a real number A is defined as follows:

$$|A| = \begin{cases} A \text{ if } A \geq 0 \\ -A \text{ if } A < 0 \end{cases}$$

e.g. $|5| = 5$, $|-8| = -(-8) = 8$.

Absolute values follow the given rules:

A) $|-A| = |A|$

B) $|A| \geq 0$, equality holding only if $A = 0$

C) $\left|\dfrac{A}{B}\right| = \dfrac{|A|}{|B|}$, $B \neq 0$

D) $|AB| = |A| \times |B|$

E) $|A|^2 = A^2$

Absolute value can also be expressed on the real number line as the distance of the point represented by the real number from the point labeled 0.

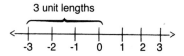

So $|-3| = 3$ because -3 is 3 units to the left of 0.

Prime and Composite Numbers

When two whole numbers are multiplied, they yield a **product**. These two whole numbers can be called **factors** or **divisors** of the product. (An exception to this is zero. Zero can be a factor, but not a divisor, since division by zero is undefined.)

Example: $2 \times 3 = 6$. 2 and 3 are factors or divisors of the product 6.

Example: $0 \times 3 = 0$. 3 is a factor and divisor of the product 0, but 0 is only a factor of the product 0, since $0 \div 0$ is undefined.

A **prime number** is a whole number that has only two different whole number factors, 1 and the number itself.

Example: 5 is a prime number, because it has only two different factors, and 5.

A **composite number** is a whole number that has three or more whole number factors.

Example: 6 is a composite number, because it has four different factors– 1, 2, 3, and 6.

Even and Odd Numbers

Even numbers are whole numbers that have 2 as a factor.

Example: 6 is an even number, since $2 \times 3 = 6$.

Odd numbers are whole numbers that do not have 2 as a factor.

Example: 5 is an odd number, since 2 is not a factor of 5.

Place Value

Our numeration system uses the *Hindu-Arabic numerals* (0, 1, 2, 3, 4, 5, 6, 7, 8, 9) to represent numbers.

Our numeration system follows a **base 10 place-value scheme**. As we move to the left in any number, each place value is ten times the place value to the right. Similarly, as we move to the right, each place value is one-tenth the place value to the left.

Example: In the number 543.21, the place value of the 5 (100's) is ten times the place value of the 4 (10's). The place value of the 1 ($^1/_{100}$'s) is one-tenth the place value of the 2 ($^1/_{10}$'s).

Powers and Roots of Whole Numbers

Exponents and Bases

When a number is multiplied by itself a specific number of times, it is said to be **raised to a power**. The way this is written is $a^n = b$ where a is the number or **base**, n is the **exponent** or **power** that indicates the number of times the base is to be multiplied by itself, and b is the product of this multiplication.

In the expression 3^2, 3 is the base and 2 is the exponent. This means that 3 is multiplied by itself 2 times and the product is 9.

$$3^2 = 3 \times 3 = 9$$

When the base has an exponent of 2, the base is said to be *squared*. When the base has an exponent of 3, the base is said to be *cubed*.

An exponent can be either positive or negative. A negative exponent implies a fraction. Such that, if *n is* a positive integer

$$a^{-n} = \frac{1}{a^n}, \, a \neq 0. \text{ So, } 2^{-4} = \frac{1}{2^{-4}} = \frac{1}{16}.$$

An exponent that is zero gives a result of 1, assuming that the base is not equal to zero.

$$a^0 = 1, \, a \neq 0.$$

An exponent can also be a fraction. If *m* and *n* are positive integers,

$$a^{\frac{m}{n}} = \sqrt[n]{a^m}.$$

The numerator remains the exponent of a, but the denominator tells what root to take. For example,

(1) $4^{\frac{3}{2}} = \sqrt[2]{4^3} = \sqrt{64} = 8.$

(2) $3^{\frac{4}{2}} = \sqrt[2]{3^4} = \sqrt{81} = 9.$

If a fractional exponent were negative, the same operation would take place, but the result would be a fraction. For example,

(1) $27^{-\frac{2}{3}} = \dfrac{1}{27^{\frac{2}{3}}} = \dfrac{1}{\sqrt[3]{27^2}} = \dfrac{1}{\sqrt[3]{729}} = \dfrac{1}{9}.$

The Basic Laws of Exponents are

1) $b^m \times b^n = b^{m+n}.$
Example: $2^5 \times 2^3 = 2^{5+3} = 2^8.$

2) $b^m \div b^n = b^{m-n}.$
Example: $2^5 \div 2^3 = 2^{5-3} = 2^2.$

3) $(b^m)^n = b^{m \times n}.$
Example: $(2^5)^3 = 2^{5 \times 3} = 2^{15}.$

Roots

Consider again the expression 5^3. If we carry out the implied multiplication, we get $5^3 = 5 \times 5 \times 5 = 125$. Five is called the cube root of 125, since $5^3 = 125$. In general, when a base is raised to a power to produce a given result, the base is called the **root** of the given result.

If the power for the base is 2, the base is called the square root. If the power for the base is 3, the base is called the *cube root*. In general, if $b^n = p$, then b is the *nth root* of p.

Examples: Since $4^2 = 16$, 4 is the square root of 16.
Since $2^3 = 8$, 2 is the cube root of 8.
Since $3^5 = 243$, 3 is the 5th root of 243.

Scientific Notation

A real number expressed in **scientific notation** is written as a product of a real number n and an integral power of 10; the value of n is $1 \leq n \leq 10$.

e. g.

Number	Scientific Notation
1) 1956.	1.956×10^3
2) .0036	3.6×10^{-3}
3) 59600000.	5.96×10^7

Arithmetic Operations and Integers

Integers are **signed numbers** preceded by either a "+" or a "–" sign. If no sign is given for the integer, one should infer that the integer is positive (e.g., 3 means +3). Integers to the **left of zero** are **negative** and integers to the **right of zero** are **positive**.

Addition

When **two integers are added**, the two integers are called **addends**, and the result is called the **sum**, as illustrated in the following:

$$5 \quad + \quad 3 \quad = \quad 8$$
(addend)   (addend)   (sum)

or

$$
\begin{array}{r}
5 \\
+\,3 \\
\hline
8
\end{array}
$$

(addend)
(addend)
(sum)

When adding two integers, one of the following two situations might occur:

Situation 1: Both integers have the same sign. In this case, add the absolute values of the two addends and give the sum the same sign as the addends.

Examples: 2 + 3 = 5, and
−2 + (−3) = −5.

Situation 2: The two integers have different signs. In this case, subtract the addend with the smaller absolute value from the addend with the larger absolute value. The sum gets the sign of the addend with the larger absolute value.

Examples: −2 + 5 = 3, but
2 + (−5) = −3.

Subtraction

In a subtraction sentence, the top or first number in the subtraction is the **minuend**, the bottom or second number is the **subtrahend**, and the result is the **remainder** or **difference**. These quantities are demonstrated in the following figure:

5	−	3	=	2
(minuend)		(subtrahend)		(remainder)

or   5   (minuend)
         − 3   (subtrahend)
           2   (remainder)

When subtracting two integers, change the sign of the subtrahend and add the resulting two integers, following the procedures given above.

Example: 5 − 3 = 2, but
5 − (−3) = 5 + (+3) = 5 + 3 = 8.

Multiplication

When **multiplying two integers**, the two integers are called **factors**, and the result is called the **product**, as illustrated in the following:

$$5 \times 3 = 15$$
(factor) (factor) (product)

or $\quad$ 5 $\quad$ (factor)
$\quad \underline{\times 3}$ $\quad$ (factor)
$\quad$ 15 $\quad$ (product)

When multiplying two integers, multiply the absolute values of the factors. If the factors have the **same sign**, the product is **positive**; if the factors have **different signs**, the product is **negative**. If either factor is zero, the product is zero.

Example: $3 \times 5 = 15$ and $(-3) \times (-5) = 15$, but
$(-3) \times 5 = -15$ and $3 \times (-5) = -15$.

Division

When **dividing two integers**, the number being divided is the **dividend**, the number being divided into another integer is the **divisor**, and the result is the **quotient**, as illustrated in the following:

$$10 \div 2 = 5$$
(dividend) (divisor) (quotient)

When dividing two integers, divide the absolute values of the dividend and divisor. The sign of the quotient can be obtained by following the same procedures given above in the multiplication section.

Example: $10 \div 2 = 5$ and $(-10) \div (-2) = 5$, but
$(-10) \div 2 = (-5)$ and $10 \div (-2) = (-5)$.

Arithmetic Operations and Common Fractions

A **common fraction** is a number that can be written in the form $\dfrac{a}{b}$, where a and b are whole numbers. In the expression $\dfrac{a}{b}$, the dividend a is called the **numerator** and the divisor b is called the **denominator**.

Example: In the expression $\dfrac{3}{4}$, 3 is the numerator and 4 is the denominator.

A common fraction may not have zero as a denominator, since division by zero is **undefined**.

A fraction is in **lowest terms** if the numerator and denominator have no common factors.

Example: $\dfrac{1}{2}, \dfrac{3}{4}$ and $\dfrac{5}{6}$ are in lowest terms, since the numerator and denominator of each have no common factors.

$\dfrac{2}{4}, \dfrac{9}{21}$ and $\dfrac{20}{24}$ are *not* in lowest terms, since the numerator and denominator of each have common factors.

Fractions are **equivalent** if they represent the same number.

Example: $\dfrac{8}{16}, \dfrac{4}{8}, \dfrac{2}{4}$ and $\dfrac{5}{10}$ are equivalent fractions, since each represents $\dfrac{1}{2}$.

A **mixed numeral** is a number that consists of an integer and a common fraction.

Example: $5\dfrac{3}{4}$ is a mixed numeral since it consists of the integer 5 and the common fraction $\dfrac{3}{4}$.

An **improper fraction** is a common fraction whose numerator is larger than its denominator. A mixed numeral can be expressed as an improper fraction by multiplying the denominator of the common fraction part times the integer part and adding that product to the numerator of the common fraction part. The result is the numerator of the improper fraction. The denominator of the improper fraction is the same as the denominator in the mixed numeral.

Example: $5\dfrac{3}{4} = \dfrac{23}{4}$, since $(4 \times 5) + 3 = 23$, and 4 was the denominator of the common fraction part, $\dfrac{23}{4}$ is an improper fraction, since the numerator 23 is larger than the denominator 4.

Addition

In order to **add two fractions**, the denominators of the fractions must be the same; when they are, they are called **common denominators**. The equivalent fractions with the smallest common denominator are said to have the **lowest common denominator**.

Example: $\dfrac{3}{8} + \dfrac{2}{8} = \dfrac{5}{8}$, but

$\dfrac{3}{8} + \dfrac{1}{4} = \dfrac{3}{8} + \dfrac{2}{8} = \dfrac{5}{8}$. Note that while 16, 24, 32, and so forth, could have been used as common denominators to obtain equivalent fractions, the lowest common denominator, 8, was used to generate like denominators.

The procedures regarding the addition of signed numbers given in the addition section also apply for the addition of common fractions.

Subtraction

The procedures given for the addition of common fractions together with the procedures for subtraction of signed numbers form the basis for the subtraction of common fractions.

Example: $\dfrac{3}{8} - \dfrac{2}{8} = \dfrac{1}{8}$, but

$$\dfrac{3}{8} - \dfrac{1}{4} = \dfrac{3}{8} - \dfrac{2}{8} = \dfrac{1}{8}$$

As also suggested:

$$\dfrac{3}{8} - \left(-\dfrac{2}{8}\right) = \dfrac{3}{8} + \dfrac{2}{8} = \dfrac{5}{8} \text{ and}$$

$$\dfrac{3}{8} - \left(-\dfrac{1}{4}\right) = \dfrac{3}{8} + \dfrac{1}{4} = \dfrac{3}{8} + \dfrac{2}{8} = \dfrac{5}{8}$$

Multiplication

To **multiply two common fractions**, simply find the product of the two numerators and divide it by the product of the two denominators. Reduce the resultant fraction to lowest terms.

Example: $\dfrac{2}{3} \times \dfrac{9}{11} = \dfrac{18}{33} = \dfrac{6}{11}$.

Division

To find the **reciprocal** of a common fraction, exchange the numerator and the denominator.

Examples: The reciprocal of $\dfrac{2}{3}$ is $\dfrac{3}{2}$.

The reciprocal of $\dfrac{21}{4}$ is $\dfrac{4}{21}$.

To **divide two common fractions**, multiply the fraction which is the dividend by the reciprocal of the fraction which is the divisor. Reduce the result to lowest terms.

Examples: $\dfrac{4}{9} \div \dfrac{2}{3} = \dfrac{4}{9} \times \dfrac{3}{2} = \dfrac{12}{18} = \dfrac{2}{3}$.

$\dfrac{7}{8} \div \dfrac{21}{4} = \dfrac{7}{8} \times \dfrac{4}{21} = \dfrac{28}{168} = \dfrac{1}{6}$.

In addition, the procedures regarding the division of integers given above apply for the division of common fractions.

ARITHMETIC OPERATIONS AND DECIMAL FRACTIONS

As discussed above, our numeration system follows a base 10 place value scheme. Another way to represent a fractional number is to write the number to include integer powers of ten. This allows us to represent **decimal fractions** as follows:

$\dfrac{1}{10} = 10^{-1} = 0.1$ (said "one-tenth")

$\dfrac{1}{100} = 10^{-2} = 0.01$ (said "one-hundredth")

$\dfrac{1}{1000} = 10^{-3} = 0.001$ (said "one-thousandth"), and so forth.

Examples: 3.14 is said "three and fourteen hundredths."

528.5 is said "five hundred twenty-eight and five-tenths."

Addition

To **add decimal fractions**, simply line up the decimal points for each decimal numeral to be added, and follow the procedures for the addition of integers. Place the decimal point in the sum directly underneath the decimal point in the addends.

Examples:

```
  89.8        32.456
 152.9      6561.22
+  7.21     +   2.14
-------     ---------
 249.91     6595.816
```

Subtraction

To **subtract decimal fractions**, place zeros as needed so that both the minuend and the subtrahend have a digit in each column.

Examples:

$$
\begin{array}{r}
152.9 \\
-7.21 \\
\end{array}
\rightarrow
\begin{array}{r}
152.90 \\
-7.21 \\
\hline
145.69 \\
\end{array}
$$

$$
\begin{array}{r}
32.456 \\
-2.14 \\
\end{array}
\rightarrow
\begin{array}{r}
32.456 \\
-2.140 \\
\hline
30.316 \\
\end{array}
$$

Multiplication

To **multiply decimal fractions**, follow the procedures given in the multiplication of integers section and then place the decimal point so that the total number of decimal places in the product is equal to the sum of the decimal places in each factor.

Examples: (3.14) (0.5) = 1.570, and
(89.8) (152.9) = 13730.42

Division

To **divide decimal fractions**,

1) move the decimal point in the divisor to the right, until there are no decimal places in the divisor,

2) move the decimal point in the dividend the same number of decimal places to the right, and

3) divide the transformed dividend and divisor as given above.

4 The number of decimal places in the quotient should be the same as the number of decimal places in the transformed dividend.

Examples: 15.5 ÷ 0.5 → 155 ÷ 5 = 31, and
32.436 ÷ 0.06 → 3243.6 ÷ 6 = 540.6

Percent

Percent is another way of expressing a fractional number. Percent always expresses a fractional number in terms of $\frac{1}{100}$'s or 0.01's. Percents use the "%" symbol.

Examples: $100\% = \frac{100}{100} = 1.00$, and

$25\% = \frac{25}{100} = 0.25$.

As shown in these examples, a percent is easily converted to a common fraction or a decimal fraction. To convert a decimal to a common fraction, place the percent in the numerator and use 100 as the denominator (reduce as necessary). To convert a percent to a decimal fraction, divide the percent by 100, or move the decimal point two places to the left.

Examples: $25\% = \frac{25}{100} = \frac{1}{4}$ and
$25\% = 0.25$.

Similarly, $125\% = \frac{125}{100} = 1\frac{25}{100} = 1\frac{1}{4}$ and
$125\% = 1.25$.

To convert a **common fraction to a percent**, carry out a division of the numerator by the denominator of the fraction to three decimal places. Round the result to two places. To convert a **decimal fraction to a percent**, move the decimal point two places to the right (adding 0's as place holders, if needed) and round as necessary.

Examples: $\frac{1}{4} = 1 \div 4 = 0.25 = 25\%$, and

$\frac{2}{7} = 2 \div 7 \cong 0.28 = 28\%$.

If one wishes to find the **percentage** of a known quantity, change the percent to a common fraction or a decimal fraction, and multiply the fraction times the quantity. The percentage is expressed in the same units as the known quantity.

Example: To find 25% of 360 books, change 25% to 0.25 and multiply times 360, as follows: $0.25 \times 360 = 90$. The result is 90 books.

(Note: The known quantity is the **base**, the percent is the **rate**, and the result is the **percentage**.)

Algebra

ALGEBRAIC EXPRESSIONS

An **algebraic expression** is an expression using letters, numbers, symbols, and arithmetic operations to represent a number or relationship among numbers.

A **variable**, or unknown, is a letter that stands for a number in an algebraic expression. **Coefficients** are the numbers that precede the variable to give the quantity of the variable in the expression.

Algebraic expressions are comprised of **terms**, or groupings of variables and numbers.

An algebraic expression with one term is called a **monomial**; with two terms, a **binomial**; with three terms, a **trinomial**; with more than one term, a **polynomial**.

Examples: $2ab - cd$ is a binomial algebraic expression with variables a, b, c, and d, and terms $2ab$ and $(-cd)$. 2 is the coefficient of ab and -1 is the coefficient of cd.

$x^2 + 3y - 1$ is a trinomial algebraic expression using the variables x and y, and terms x^2, $3y$, and (-1);

$z(x - 1) + uv - wy - 2$ is a polynomial with variables z, x, u, v, w, and y, and terms $z(x - 1)$, uv, $(-wy)$, and (-2).

As stated above, algebraic expressions can be used to represent the relationship among numbers. For example, if we know there are 10 times as many students in a school as teachers, if S represents the number of students in the school and T represents the number of teachers, the total number of students and teachers in the school is $S + T$.

If we wished to form an algebraic sentence equating the number of students and teachers in the school, the sentence would be $S = 10T$. (Note that if either the number of students or the number of teachers were known, the other quantity could be found.)

Simplifying Algebraic Expressions

Like terms are terms in an algebraic expression that are exactly the same; that is, they contain the same variables and the same powers.

Examples: The following are pairs of like terms:
x^2 and $(-3x^2)$, abc and $4abc$, $(x - 1)$
and $(x - 1)^2$.
The following are not pairs of like terms:
x and $(-3x^2)$, abc and $4a^2bc$, $(x - 1)$ and $(x^2 - 1)$.

To simplify an algebraic expression, combine like terms in the following order:

1) simplify all expressions within symbols of inclusion (e.g., (), [], {}) using steps 2-4 below;

2) carry out all exponentiation;

3) carry out all multiplication and division from left to right in the order in which they occur;

4) carry out all addition and subtraction from left to right in the order in which they occur.

Factoring Algebraic Expressions

When two numbers are multiplied together, the numbers are called factors and their result is called the product. Similarly, algebraic expressions may be the product of other algebraic expressions.

In **factoring algebraic expressions**, first remove any monomial factors, then remove any binomial, trinomial, or other polynomial factors. Often one may find other polynomial factors by inspecting for the sum and difference of two squares; that is, $x^2 - y^2 = (x + y)(x - y)$.

Examples: $2a + 2b = 2(a + b)$
$4x^2y - 2xy^2 + 16x^2y^2 = 2xy(2x - y + 8xy)$
$x^2 - 4 = (x + 2)(x - 2)$
$4a^2 - 16b^2 = 4(a^2 - 4b^2) = 4(a + 2b)(a - 2b)$

In **factoring polynomials**, one often uses what is called the **"FOIL"** method (First, Outside, Inside, Last).

Examples: $x^2 + 3x - 10 = (x - 2)(x + 5)$
$6y^2 - y - 2 = (2y + 1)(3y - 2)$
$ab^2 - 3ab - 10a = a(b^2 - 3b - 10) = a(b + 2)(b - 5)$

Solving Linear Equations

To **solve a linear equation**, use the following procedures:

1) isolate the variable; that is, group all the terms with the variable on one side of the equation (commonly the left side) and group all the constants on the other side of the equation (commonly the right side);

2) combine like terms on each side of the equation;

3) divide by the coefficient of the variable;

4) check the result in the original equation.

Problem: Solve $3x + 2 = 5$ for x.
Solution: $3x + 2 = 5$ (add –2 to both sides)

$3x = 3$ (multiply by $\frac{1}{3}$)

$x = 1$

Problem: Solve $a + 3a = 3a + 1$ for a.
Solution: $a + 3a = 3a + 1$ (add $-3a$ to both sides)
$a = 1$

Problem: Solve $3(y - 2) + 5 = 3 + 5y$ for y.
Solution: $3(y - 2) + 5 = 3 + 5y$ (simplify)
$3y - 6 + 5 = 3 + 5y$ (combine like terms)
$3y - 1 = 3 + 5y$ (add 1 to both sides)
$3y = 4 + 5y$ (add $-5y$ to both sides)

$-2y = 4$ (multiply by $-\frac{1}{2}$)

$y = -2$

Slope

A **slope** is the tangent of the angle between a given straight line and the x-axis of a system of coordinates.

The formula used for determining the slope of a line is

$$\frac{(y_2 - y_1)}{(x_2 - x_1)}$$

Example: What is the slope of a line containing points (3, 1) and (5, 6)?
In this case, $3 = x_1$, $5 = x_2$, $1 = y_1$, $6 = y_2$. Therefore,

$$\text{slope} = \frac{6 - 1}{5 - 3} = \frac{5}{2}$$

The slope of the line is $\frac{5}{2}$.

Example: Line A contains the points (–1, 4) and (4, 6). Line B contains the points (5, 2) and (–3, 3). Are the two lines parallel?

$$\text{Line A} = \frac{6-4}{4-(-1)} = \frac{2}{5} \quad \text{Line B} = \frac{-3-2}{-3-5} = \frac{-5}{-8} = \frac{5}{8}$$

Parallel lines have the same slope. Since the slope of Line A does not equal the slope of Line B, the lines cannot be parallel.

Two lines are perpendicular if the slope of one line (m) equals the negative reciprocal of the other $\left(\dfrac{-1}{m}\right)$.

Example: Line A slope = $\dfrac{3}{4}$ Line B slope = $\dfrac{-4}{3}$

These two lines are perpendicular because the slope of Line B $\left(\dfrac{-4}{3}\right)$ is the negative reciprocal of Line A $\left(\dfrac{3}{4}\right)$.

Graphing Linear Equations

Example: Find three pairs of coordinates that the line below passes through.
$y = 3x + 7$

Pick three arbitrary values for x.
0, 1, 2
Substitute each value for x in the equation to obtain y.
Make a chart to log the values.

x	y
0	7
1	10
2	13

$y = 3(0) + 7 = 7$
$y = 3(1) + 7 = 10$
$y = 3(2) + 7 = 13$

Rewrite each set of coordinates.
(0, 7), (1, 10), (2, 13)
The correct answers are (0, 7), (1, 10), and (2, 13). However, there are many possible answers. Any answer is valid if the coordinates make the equation true.

Example: Graph the equation $\frac{1}{4}y = \frac{1}{2}x - 1$.

Put the equation in *y* slope–intercept form.

$$\frac{1}{4}y = \frac{1}{2}x - 1$$
$$y = 2x - 4$$

Choose two arbitrary values of *x*. Log the values in a chart. Use the values of *x* to obtain values for *y*.

x	y
0	−4
2	0

Use the *x* and *y* values to form coordinates. Note that there are many different possible coordinates. However, the graph should look the same.
(0, −4) and (2, 0)

Use the coordinates to graph the line.

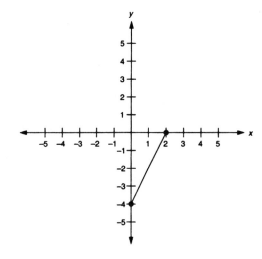

Solving Inequalities

The equivalence properties of integers given in the integers section and the procedures for solving linear equations given in solving linear equations are used **to solve inequalities**. In addition, the following properties of inequalities should be noted:

If $x < y$ and $z > 0$, then $zx < zy$.
If $x > y$ and $z > 0$, then $zx > zy$.
If $x < y$ and $z < 0$, then $zx > zy$.
If $x > y$ and $z < 0$, then $zx < zy$.

In other words, if both sides of an inequality are **multiplied by a positive number**, the **sense of the inequality remains the same**. If both sides of an inequality are **multiplied by a negative number**, the **sense of the inequality is reversed**.

Examples: Since $3 < 5$ and 2 is positive,
$(2)(3) < (2)(5)$ or $6 < 10$.
But since $3 < 5$ and -2 is negative,
$(-2)(3) > (-2)(5)$ or $-6 > -10$.

The above properties are also demonstrated in the following problems:

Problem: Find the values of y for which $2y > y - 3$.
Solution: $2y > y - 3$ (add $-y$ to both sides)
$y > -3$

Problem: Find the values of x for which $x > 4x + 1$.
Solution: $x > 4x + 1$ (add $-4x$ to both sides)

$-3x > 1$ (multiply by $-\dfrac{1}{3}$)

$x < -\dfrac{1}{3}$

Graphing Inequalities

Example: Graph the inequality $-y > x + 5$.

Put the inequality in *y* slope-intercept form.

$-y > x + 5$

$y < -x - 5$

Choose two arbitrary values of *x*. Log the values in a chart. Use the values of *x* to obtain values for *y*. This will solve the inequality $y < -x - 5$.

x	y
0	-5
-5	0

Use the *x* and *y* values to form coordinates. Note that there are many different possible coordinates. However, the graph should look the same.

(0, -5) and (-5, 0)

Use the coordinates to graph the line. Notice that a dashed line connects the points. The points along the line do not satisfy the inequality. Only the points in the shaded region satisfy the inequality.

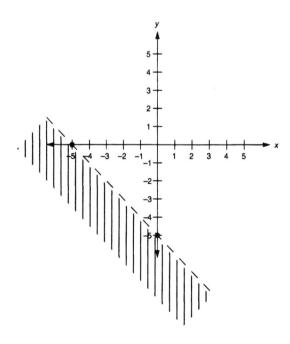

Evaluating Formulas

Formulas are algebraic sentences that are frequently used in mathematics, science, or other fields. Examples of common formulas are $A = l \times w$, $d = r \times t$, and $C = \left(\dfrac{5}{9}\right)(F - 32°)$. To **evaluate a formula**, replace each variable with the given values of the variables and solve for the unknown variable.

> Example: Since $A = l \times w$, if $l = 2$ ft. and
> $w = 3$ ft.,
> then $A = 2$ ft. $\times 3$ ft. $= 6$ sq. ft.

> Example: Since $d = r \times t$, if $r = 32$ m/sec^2 and
> $t = 5$ sec.,
> then $d = (32$ m/sec$) \times 5$ sec. $= 160$ m.

> Example: Since $C = \left(\dfrac{5}{9}\right)(F - 32)$, if $F = 212°$,
>
> then $C = \left(\dfrac{5}{9}\right)(212° - 32°) = 100°$.

Relations and Functions

A **relation** is any set of ordered pairs. The set of all first members of the ordered pairs is called the **domain** of the relation and the set of all second members of the ordered pairs is called the **range** of the relation.

> Example: Find the relation defined by $y^2 = 25 - x^2$ where the domain D = {0, 3, 4, 5}.

Solution: x takes on the values 0, 3, 4 and 5. Replacing x by these values in the equation $y^2 = 25 - x^2$ we obtain the corresponding values of y:

Hence the relation defined by $y^2 = 25 - x^2$ where x belongs to D = {0, 3, 4, 5} is

{(0,5),(0,–5),(3,4),(3,–4),(4,3),(4,–3),(5,0)}.

The domain of the relation is (0,3,4,5). The range of the relation is (5, –5, 4, –4, 3, –3, 0).

A function is a relation in which no two ordered pairs have the same first member. Example:

$$X = \{1, 2, 3, 4, 5, 6, 7, 8\} \text{ and } Y = \{2, 4, 6, 8\}$$

A function with domain X and range Y could be given by:

x	$y^2 = 25 - x^2$	y
0	$y^2 = 25 - 0$ $y = \sqrt{25}$ $y = \pm 5$	± 5
3	$y^2 = 25 - 3^2$ $y^2 = 25 - 9$ $y^2 = 16$ $y = \sqrt{16}$ $y = \pm 4$	± 4
4	$y^2 = 25 - 4^2$ $y^2 = 25 - 16$ $y^2 = 9$ $y = \sqrt{9}$ $y = \pm 3$	± 3
5	$y^2 = 25 - 5^2$ $y^2 = 25 - 25$ $y^2 = 0$ $y = 0$	0

$$\{(1,2),(2,2),(3,4),(4,4),(5,6),(6,6),(7,8),(8,8)\}$$

You can see above that every member of the domain is paired with one and only one member of the range. Then this relation is called a function and is represented by $y = f(x)$, where $x \, \varepsilon X$ and $y \, \varepsilon Y$. If f is a function that takes an element $x \, \varepsilon \, X$ and sends it to an element $y \, \varepsilon \, Y$, f is said to map x into y. We write this as f:$x \rightarrow y$. For this reason, a function is also called a mapping.

Given f:$x \rightarrow y$, we can also say that y is a function of x, denoted $f(x) = y$, "f of x equals y." In this function, y is called the dependent variable, since it derives its value from x. By the same reasoning, x is called the independent variable.

Another way of checking if a relation is a function is the vertical line test: if there does not exist any vertical line which crosses the graph of a relation in more than one place, then the relation is a function. If the domain of a relation or a function is not specified, it is assumed to be all real numbers.

A relation R from set A to set B is a subset of the Cartesian Product A × B written a e b with a ε A and b ε B.

Let R be a relation from a set S to itself. Then

A) R is said to be reflexive if and only if sRs for every S ε S.

B) R is said to be symmetric if $s_iRs_j \rightarrow s_jRs_i$ where s_i, s_j ε S.

C) R is said to be transitive if s_iRs_j and s_jRs_k implies s_iRs_k.

D) R is said to be anti-symmetric if s_1Rs_2 and s_2Rs_1 implies $s_1 = s_2$.

A relation R on S × S is called an equivalence relation if R is reflexive, symmetric, and transitive.

Properties of Functions

If f and g are two functions with a common domain then the sum of f and g, written $f + g$, is defined by:

$$(f + g)(x) = f(x) + g(x).$$

The difference of f and g is defined by

$$(f - g)(x) = f(x) - g(x).$$

The quotient of f and g is defined by

$$\left(\frac{f}{g}\right)(x) = \frac{f(x)}{g(x)} \text{ where } g(x) \neq 0.$$

Example: Let $f(x) = 2x^2$ with domain $D_f = R$ (or, alternatively, C) and $g(x) = x - 5$ with $D_g = R$ (or C). Find (a) $f + g$, (b) $f - g$, (c) fg, (d) $\dfrac{f}{g}$.

(a) $f + g$ has domain R (or C) and

$$(f + g)(x) = f(x) + g(x) = 2x^2 + x - 5$$

for each number x. For example, $(f + g)(1) = f(1) + g(1) = 2(1)2 + 1 - 5 = 2 - 4 = -2$.

(b) $f - g$ has domain R (or C) and

$$(f - g)(x) = f(x) - g(x) = 2x^2 - (x - 5) = 2x^2 - x + 5$$

for each number x. For example, $(f - g)(1) = f(1) - g(1) = 2(1)^2 - 1 + 5 = 2 + 4 = 6$.

(c) fg has domain R (or C) and

$$(fg)(x) = f(x) \bullet g(x) = 2x^2 \bullet (x - 5) = 2x^3 - 10x^2$$

for each number x. In particular, $(fg)(1) = 2(1)^3 - 10(1)^2 = 2 - 10 = -8$.

(d) $\dfrac{f}{g}$ has domain R (or C) excluding the number $x = 5$ (when $x = 5$, $g(x) = 0$ and division by zero is undefined) and

$$\left(\frac{f}{g}\right)(x) = \frac{f(x)}{g(x)} = \frac{2x^2}{x - 5}$$

for each number $x \neq 5$. In particular, $\left(\dfrac{f}{g}\right)(1) = \dfrac{2(1)^2}{1 - 5}$

$$= \frac{2}{-4} = -\frac{1}{2}.$$

If f is a function then the inverse of f, written f^{-1} is such that:

$$(x,y) \; \varepsilon \; f \Longleftrightarrow (y,x) \; \varepsilon \; f^{-1}.$$

The graph of f^{-1} can be obtained from the graph of f by simply reflecting the graph of f across the line $y = x$. The graphs of f and f^{-1} are symmetrical about the line $y = x$.

The inverse of a function is not necessarily a function.

Example: Show that the inverse of the function $y = x^2 + 4x - 5$ is not a function.

Solution: Given the function f such that no two of its ordered pairs have the same second element, the inverse function f^{-1} is the set of ordered pairs obtained from f by interchanging in each ordered pair the first and second elements. Thus, the inverse of the function

$$y = x^2 + 4x - 5 \text{ is } x = y^2 + 4y - 5.$$

The given function has more than one first component corresponding to a given second component. For example, if $y = 0$, then $x = -5$ or 1. If the elements $(-5, 0)$ and $(1, 0)$ are reversed, we have $(0, -5)$ and $(0, 1)$ as elements of the inverse. Since the first component 0 has more than one second component, the inverse is not a function (a function can have only one y value corresponding to each x value).

A function $f : A \rightarrow B$ is said to be one-to-one or injective if distinct elements in the domain A have distinct images, i.e. if $f(x) = f(y)$ implies $x = y$. For an example: $y = f(x) = x^2$ defined over the domain $\{ x \ \varepsilon \ R \mid x \geq 0 \}$ is an injection or an injective function.

A function $f : A \rightarrow B$ is said to be a surjective or an onto function if each element of B is the image of some element of A. i.e. $f(A) = b$. For instance, $y = x^3 \sin x$, is a surjection of a surjective function.

A function $f : A \rightarrow B$ is said to be bijective or a bijection if f is both injective and surjective. f is also called a one-to-one correspondence between A and B. An example of such function would be $y = x$.

Quadratic Equations

A second degree equation in x of the type $ax^2 + bx + c = 0$, $a \neq 0$, a, b and c real numbers, is called a **quadratic equation**.

To solve a quadratic equation is to find values of x which satisfy $ax^2 + bx + c = 0$. These values of x are called solutions, or roots, of the equation.

A quadratic equation has a maximum of 2 roots. Methods of solving quadratic equations:

A) Direct solution: Given $x^2 - 9 = 0$.

We can solve directly by isolating the variable x:

$x^2 = 9$

$x = \pm 3.$

B) Factoring: given a quadratic equation $ax^2 + bx + c = 0$, a, b, $c \neq 0$, to factor means to express it as the product $a(x - r_1)(x - r_2) = 0$, where r_1 and r_2 are the two roots.

Some helpful hints to remember are:

a) $r_1 + r_2 = -\dfrac{b}{a}.$

b) $r_1 r_2 = \dfrac{c}{a}.$

Given $x^2 - 5x + 4 = 0$.

Since $r_1 + r_2 = \dfrac{-b}{a} = \dfrac{-(-5)}{1} = 5$, the possible solutions are (3,2), (4,1) and (5,0). Also $r_1 r_2 = \dfrac{c}{a} = \dfrac{4}{1} = 4$; this equation is satisfied only by the second pair, so $r_1 = 4$, $r_2 = 1$ and the factored form is $(x - 4)(x - 1) = 0$.

If the coefficient of x^2 is not 1, it may be easier to divide the equation by this coefficient and then factor.

Given $2x^2 - 12x + 16 = 0$

Dividing by 2, we obtain:

$$x^2 - 6x + 8 = 0$$

Since $r_1 + r_2 = \dfrac{-b}{a} = 6$, the possible solutions are (6, 0), (5, 1), (4, 2), (3, 3). Also $r_1 r_2 = 8$, so the only possible answer is (4,2) and the expression $x^2 - 6x + 8 = 0$ can be factored as $(x - 4)(x - 2)$.

C) Completing the Squares:

If it is difficult to factor the quadratic equation using the previous method, we can complete the squares.

Given $x^2 - 12x + 8 = 0$

We know that the two roots added up should be 12 because $r_1 + r_2 = \dfrac{-b}{a} = \dfrac{-(-12)}{1} = 12$. The possible roots are (12,0), (11,1), (10,2), (9,3), (8,4), (7,5), (6,6).

But none of these satisfy $r_1 r_2 = 8$, so we cannot use (B).

To complete the square, it is necessary to isolate the constant term,

$$x^2 - 12x = -8.$$

Then take $\dfrac{1}{2}$ coefficient of x, square it, and add to both sides

$$x^2 - 12x + \left(\frac{-12}{2}\right)^2 = -8 + \left(\frac{-12}{2}\right)^2$$

$$x^2 - 12x + 36 = -8 + 36 = 28.$$

Now we can use the previous method to factor the left side: r1 + r2 = 12, r1r2 = 36 is satisfied by the pair (6, 6), so we have:

$$(x - 6)^2 = 28.$$

Now extract the root of both sides and solve for x.

$$(x - 6) = \pm\sqrt{28} = \pm 2\sqrt{7}$$

$$x = \pm 2\sqrt{7} + 6$$

So the roots are: $x = 2\sqrt{7} + 6$, $x = -2\sqrt{7} + 6$.

Quadratic Formula

Consider the polynomial:

$ax^2 + bx + c = 0$, where $a \neq 0$.

The roots of this equation can be determined in terms of the coefficients a, b, and c as shown below:

$$x = \frac{-b \pm \sqrt{b^2 - 4ac}}{2a}$$

where $(b^2 - 4ac)$ is called the **discriminant** of the quadratic equation.

Note that if the discriminant is less than zero ($b^2 - 4ac < 0$), the roots are complex numbers, since the discriminant appears under a radical and square roots of negatives are complex numbers, and a real number added to an imaginary number yields a complex number.

If the discriminant is equal to zero ($b2 - 4ac = 0$) the roots are real and equal.

If the discriminant is greater than zero ($b2 - 4ac > 0$) then the roots are real and unequal. Further, the roots are rational if and only if a and b are rational and ($b2 - 4ac$) is a perfect square; otherwise the roots are irrational.

Example: Compute the value of the discriminant and then determine the nature of the roots of each of the following four equations:

$$4x^2 - 12x + 9 = 0,$$

$$3x^2 - 7x - 6 = 0,$$

$$5x^2 + 2x - 9 = 0,$$

and $x^2 + 3x + 5 = 0.$

A) $4x^2 - 12x + 9 = 0,$

Here a, b, c are integers,

a = 4, b = –12, and c = 9.

Therefore,

$b^2 - 4ac = (-12)^2 - 4(4)(9) = 144 - 144 = 0$

Since the discriminant is 0, the roots are rational and equal.

B) $3x^2 - 7x - 6 = 0$

Here a, b, c are integers,

a = 3, b = –7, and c = –6.

Therefore,

$b^2 - 4ac = (-7)^2 - 4(3)(-6) = 49 + 72 = 121 = 11^2.$

Since the discriminant is a perfect square, the roots are rational and unequal.

C) $5x^2 + 2x - 9 = 0$

Here a, b, c are integers,

a = 5, b = 2, and c – 9

Therefore,

$$b^2 - 4ac = 2^2 - 4(5)(-9) = 4 + 180 = 184.$$

Since the discriminant is greater than zero, but not a perfect square, the roots are irrational and unequal.

D) $x^2 + 3x + 5 = 0$

Here a, b, c are integers,

a = 1, b = 3, and c = 5

Therefore,

$$b^2 - 4ac = 3^2 - 4(1)(5) = 9 - 20 = -11$$

Since the discriminant is negative the roots are imaginary.

Algebra Word Problems

A general procedure for solving problems was suggested by **Polya**. His procedure can be summarized as follows:

1)   Understand the problem.

2)   Devise a plan for solving the problem.

3)   Carry out the plan.

4)   Look back on the solution to the problem.

When taking the mathematics section of the CSET, you can use this procedure by translating the word problem into an algebraic sentence, then follow the procedures for solving an algebraic sentence. Find a variable to represent the unknown in the problem. Look for key synonyms such as "is, are, were" for "=", "more, more than" for "+", "less, less than, fewer" for "−", and "of" for "x."

Problem: The sum of the ages of Bill and Paul is 32 years. Bill is 6 years older than Paul. Find the age of each.

Solution: If p = Paul's age, then Bill's age is $p + 6$. So that $p + (p + 6) = 32$. Applying the methods from above, we get $p = 13$. Therefore, Paul is 13 and Bill is 19.

Problem: Jose weighs twice as much as his brother Carlos. If together they weigh 225 pounds, how much does each weigh?

Solution: If c = Carlos' weight, then Jose's weight is $2c$. So $c + 2c = 225$ pounds. Applying the methods above, we get $c = 75$. Therefore, Carlos weighs 75 pounds and Jose weighs 150 pounds.

Problem: Julia drove from her home to her aunt's house in 3 hours and 30 minutes. If the distance between the houses is 175 miles, what was the car's average speed?

Solution: As noted above, distance = rate × time. Since we know

$$d = 175 \text{ mph and } t = 3\frac{1}{2} \text{ hr., then } 175 \text{ mph} = r \times 3\frac{1}{2}$$

hr. Solving for the rate (r), we get $r = 50$ mph.

(It is strongly suggested that individuals who feel they need additional practice in solving word problems using the above procedures seek out additional practice problems in a standard high school first-year algebra textbook.)

Measurement and Geometry

Perimeter and Area of Rectangles, Squares, and Triangles

Perimeter refers to the measure of the distance around a figure. Perimeter is measured in linear units (e.g., inches, feet, meters). **Area** refers to the measure of the interior of a figure. Area is measured in square units (e.g., square inches, square feet, square meters).

The **perimeter of a rectangle** is found by adding twice the length of the rectangle to twice the width of the rectangle. This relationship is commonly given by the formula $P = 2l + 2w$, where l is the measure of the length and w is the measure of the width.

> Example: If a rectangle has $l = 10$ m and $w = 5$ m,
> then the perimeter of the rectangle is given by
> $P = 2(10 \text{ m}) + 2(5 \text{ m}) = 30$ m.

The **perimeter of a square** is found by multiplying four times the measure of a side of the square. This relationship is commonly given by the formula, $P = 4s$, where s is the measure of a side of the square.

> Example: If a square has $s = 5$ feet,
> then the perimeter of the square is given by
> $P = 4(5 \text{ feet}) = 20$ feet.

The **perimeter of a triangle** is found by adding the measures of the three sides of the triangle. This relationship can be represented by $P = s_1 + s_2 + s_3$, where s_1, s_2, and s_3 are the measures of the sides of the triangle.

> Example: If a triangle has three sides measuring
> 3 inches, 4 inches, and 5 inches,
> then the perimeter of the triangle is given by
> $P = 3 \text{ inches} + 4 \text{ inches} + 5 \text{ inches} = 12$ inches.

Area of Rectangles, Squares, and Triangles

The **area of a rectangle** is found by multiplying the measure of the length of the rectangle by the measure of the width of the triangle. This relationship is commonly given by $A = l \times w$, where l is the measure of the length and w is the measure of the width.

> Example: If a rectangle has $l = 10$ m and $w = 5$ m,
> then the area of the rectangle is given by
> $A = 10 \text{ m} \times 5 \text{ m} = 50 \text{ m}^2$.

The **area of a square** is found by squaring the measure of the side of the square. This relationship is commonly given by $A = s^2$, where s is the measure of a side.

> Example: If a square has $s = 5$ ft.,
> then the area of the square is given by
> $A = (5 \text{ ft}^2) = 25 \text{ ft}^2$.

The **area of a right triangle** is found by multiplying $\frac{1}{2}$ times the product of the base and the height of the triangle. This relationship is commonly given by $A = \frac{1}{2} bh$, where b is the base and h is the height.

> Example: If a triangle has a base of 3 in. and a height of 4 in.,
> then the area of the triangle is given by
> $$A = \frac{1}{2} (3 \text{ in.} \times 4 \text{ in.}) = \frac{1}{2} (12) = 6 \text{ in}^2.$$

Circles

A **circle** is a set of points in the same plane equidistant from a fixed point called its **center**. The **radius of a circle** is a **line segment** drawn from the center of the circle while the **diameter** is a straightline segment passing through the center of a circle or sphere and meeting the circumference at each end.

radius

diameter

The diameter is an example of a **chord** which is a line segment joining any two points on a circle. A line which intersects a circle in two points is called a **secant**. A **tangent of a circle** is a line which has one and only one point of intersection with a circle. Their common point is called a **point of tangency**.

chord

secant

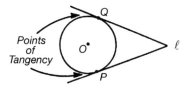

A portion of a circle is called an **arc**. An arc whose end points lie on the **extremeties** of a diameter of a circle is called a **semicircle** and its measure is 180°. An arc which is greater than a semicircle is called a **major arc** while an arc less than 180° is called a **minor arc**. A **quadrant** is an arc whose measure is 90°. **Congruent arcs** are arcs which have equal degree measures and lengths. The **midpoint** of an arc is the point that divides the arc into two congruent arcs.

semicircle

major arc

minor arc

$\overset{\frown}{AC} \cong \overset{\frown}{CB}$
midpoint of arc

Different types of circles include **congruent circles**, which are defined as circles with congruent radii, and **concentric circles**, which have the same center and unequal radii. **Tangent circles** are circles which are in a plane and tangent to the same line at the same point.

congruent circles

concentric   internally
circles   tangent

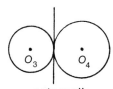
externally
tangent

The **measure of the diameter of a circle** is twice the measure of the radius.

The number π (approximately 3.14) is often used in computations involving circles.

The **circumference of a circle** is found by multiplying π times the diameter (or twice the radius). This relationship is commonly given by $C = \pi \times d$, or $C = 2 \times \pi \times r$.

The **area of a circle** is found by multiplying π by the square of the radius of the circle. This relationship is commonly given by $A = \pi \times r^2$.

Example: If a circle has a radius of 5 cm, then
$C = \pi \times 10$ cm $= 3.14 \times 10$ cm ≈ 31.4 cm, and
$A = \pi \times 5^2 \approx 3.14 \times 5^2 = 78.50$ cm^2.

Spheres

A **sphere** is the set of points in space at a given distance from a given point, called the **center** of the sphere. The distance from a given point to a sphere is the length of the line segment with endpoints that are the given point and the point of intersection of the sphere with the line that passes through the center of the sphere and the given point.

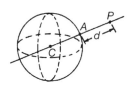

A **great circle** of a sphere is any circle lying on the sphere and having the same radius as the sphere. Any circle on the sphere with radius less than the radius of the sphere is called a **small circle** of the sphere. A radius of a sphere is a line segment joining the center and any point of the sphere. A diameter of a sphere is a segment passing through the center and having its endpoints on the sphere. The diameter of a sphere is twice as long as the radius of the sphere.

Congruent spheres are spheres with congruent radii. A tangent to the sphere is any line which is perpendicular to a radius of a sphere at the outer extremity of the radius.

Volume of Cubes and Rectangular Solids

Volume refers to the measure of the interior of a three-dimensional figure.

A **rectangular solid** is a rectilinear (right-angled) figure that has length, width, and height. The volume of a rectangular solid is found by computing the product of the length, width, and height of the figure. This relationship is commonly expressed by $V = l \times w \times h$.

Example: The volume of a rectangular solid with
$l = 5$ cm, $w = 4$ cm, and $h = 3$ cm is given by
$V = 5$ cm $\times 4$ cm $\times 3$ cm $= 60$ cm^3.

A **cube** is a rectangular solid, the length, width, and height of which have the same measure. This measure is called the **edge** of the cube. The volume of a cube is found by cubing the measure of the edge. This relationship is commonly expressed by $V = e^3$.

Example: The volume of a cube with $e = 5$ cm is given by $V = (5$ cm$)^3 = 125$ cm^3.

Angle Measure

An **angle** consists of all the points in two noncollinear rays that have the same **vertex**. An angle is commonly thought of as two "arrows" joined at their bases.

Two angles are **adjacent** if they share a common vertex, share only one side, and one angle does not lie in the interior of the other.

Angles are usually measured in **degrees**. A circle has a measure of 360°, a half circle 180°, a quarter circle 90°, and so forth. If the measures of two angles are the same, then the angles are said to be **congruent**.

An angle with a measure of 90° is called a **right angle**. Angles with measures less than 90° are called **acute**. Angles with measures more than 90° are called **obtuse**.

If the sum of the measures of two angles is 90°, the two angles are said to be **complementary**. If the sum of the measures of the two angles is 180°, the two angles are said to be **supplementary**.

If two lines intersect, they form two pairs of **vertical angles**. The measures of vertical angles are equivalent; that is, vertical angles are congruent.

Properties of Triangles

Triangles are three-sided polygons.

If the measures of two sides of a triangle are equal, then the triangle is called an **isosceles triangle**. If the measures of all sides of the triangle are equal, then the triangle is called an **equilateral triangle**. If no measures of the sides of a triangle are equal, then the triangle is called a **scalene triangle**.

The sum of the measures of the angles of a triangle is 180°.

Problem: Find the measures of the angles of a right triangle, if one of the angles measures 30°.

Solution: Since the triangle is a right triangle, a second angle of the triangle measures 90°. We know the sum of the measures of a triangle is 180°, so that, $90° + 30° + x° = 180°$. Solving for $x°$, we get $x° = 60°$. The measures of the angles of the triangle are 90°, 60°, and 30°.

The Pythagorean Theorem

In a right triangle, the side opposite the 90° angle is called the **hypotenuse** and the other two sides are called the **legs**. If the hypotenuse has measure c and the legs have measures a and b, the relationship among the measures, known as the **Pythagorean Theorem**, is given by

$$c^2 = a^2 + b^2.$$

Problem: Find the length of the hypotenuse of a triangle if the measure of one leg is 3 cm and the other leg is 4 cm.

Solution: By the Pythagorean Theorem, $c^2 = 3^2 + 4^2$, so that $c^2 = 9 + 16$, $c^2 = 25$. Taking the square root of both sides, we get $c = 5$ cm.

Properties of Parallel and Perpendicular Lines

If lines have a point or points in common, they are said to **intersect**.

Lines are **parallel** if they do not intersect.

Lines are **perpendicular** if they contain the sides of a right angle.

If a third line intersects two other lines, the intersecting line is called a **transversal**.

Two lines crossed by a transversal form eight angles. The four angles that lie between the two lines are called **interior angles**. The four angles that lie outside the two lines are called **exterior angles**.

The interior angles that lie on the same side of the transversal are called **consecutive interior angles**. The interior angles that lie on opposite sides of the transversal are called **alternate interior angles**. Similarly, exterior angles that lie on the same side of the transversal are called **consecutive exterior angles**, and those that lie on opposite sides of the transversal are called **alternate exterior angles**.

An interior angle and an exterior angle that have different vertices and have sides that are on the same side of the transversal are called **corresponding angles**.

Properties of Parallel Lines

The following are true for parallel lines:

Alternate interior angles are congruent. Conversely, if alternate interior angles are congruent, then the lines are parallel.

Interior angles on the same side of the transversal are supplementary. Conversely, if interior angles on the same side of the transversal are supplementary, then the lines are parallel.

Corresponding angles are congruent. Conversely, if corresponding angles are congruent, then the lines are parallel.

Properties of Perpendicular Lines

If two lines are perpendicular, the four angles they form are all right angles.

If two lines are perpendicular to a third line, the lines are parallel.

If one of two parallel lines is perpendicular to a third line, so is the other line.

Coordinate Geometry

The rectangular coordinate system is used as a basis for coordinate geometry. In this system, two perpendicular lines form a plane. The perpendicular lines are called the **x-axis** and the **y-axis**. The coordinate system assigns an **ordered pair** of numbers (x, y) to each point in the plane. The point of intersection of the two axes is called the origin, O, and has coordinates (0,0).

As shown in the figure below, the x-axis has positive integers to the right and negative integers to the left of the origin. Similarly, the y-axis has positive integers above and negative integers below the origin.

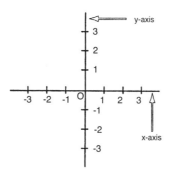

The distance between any two points in the coordinate plane can be found by using the **distance formula**. According to the distance formula, if P_1 and P_2 are two points with coordinates (x_1, y_1) and (x_2, y_2) respectively, then the distance between P_1 and P_2 is given by

$$P_1 P_2 = \sqrt{(x_2 - x_1)^2 + (y_2 - y_1)^2}$$

Problem: Compute the distance between the points A and B with coordinates (1,1) and (4, 5) respectively.

Solution: Using the distance formula,

$$AB = \sqrt{(4-1)^2 + (5-1)^2}$$
$$= \sqrt{3^2 + 4^2}$$
$$= \sqrt{9 + 16}$$
$$= \sqrt{25}$$
$$= 5$$

Graphs

To **plot** *a point* on a graph, first plot the x-coordinate, then plot the y-coordinate from the given ordered pair.

Problem: Plot the following points on the coordinate plane: A (1, 2), B (2, 1), C (−2, −1).

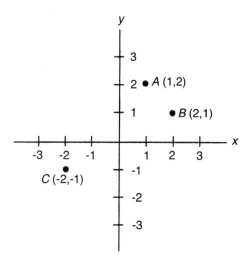

The Metric System

The **metric system of measurement** is closely related to the base 10 place value scheme. The prefixes commonly used in the metric system are:

Prefix	Meaning
kilo-	thousand (1000)
deci-	tenth (0.1)
centi-	hundredth (0.01)
milli-	thousandth (0.001)

The basic unit of linear measure in the metric system is the **meter**, represented by m. The relationship among the commonly used linear units of measurement in the metric system is as follows:

1 kilometer (km)	=	1000 m
1 meter (m)	=	1.0 m
1 decimeter (dm)	=	0.1 m
1 centimeter (cm)	=	0.01 m
1 millimeter (mm)	=	0.001 m

The basic unit of measurement for mass (or weight) in the metric system is the **gram**, represented by g. The relationship among the commonly used units of measurement for mass in the metric system is as follows:

1 kilogram (kg)	=	1000 g
1 gram (g)	=	1.0 g
1 milligram (mg)	=	0.001 g

The basic unit of measurement for capacity (or volume) in the metric system is the **liter**, represented by L or l. The most commonly used relationship between two metric units of capacity is

1 liter (l)	=	1,000 milliliters (ml)
1 deciliter (dl)	=	100 ml; 10 cl
1 centiliter (cl)	=	10 ml

The U.S. System of Measurements

Linear Measure

12 inches (in.)	=	1 foot (ft.)
3 feet	=	1 yard (yd.)
1,760 yards	=	1 mile
5,280 feet	=	1 mile

Area Measure

144 square inches	=	1 sq. ft.
9 square feet	=	1 sq. yd.
4,840 square yards	=	1 acre
640 acres	=	1 square mile

Cubic Measure

1,728 cubic inches	=	1 cubic foot
27 cubic feet	=	1 cubic yard

Metric / U.S. Conversions

Linear Measure

1 centimeter	=	.3937 inches
1 foot	=	.3048 meter
1 inch	=	2.54 centimeters
1 kilometer	=	.621 mile
1 meter	=	39.37 inches; 1.094 yards
1 mile	=	1.609 kilometers
1 yard	=	.9144 meter

Area Measure

1 square centimeter	=	.155 square inch
1 square foot	=	929.030 square centimeters
1 square inch	=	6.4516 square centimeters
1 square kilometer	=	.386 square mile
1 square meter	=	10.764 square feet; 1.196 square yards

Cubic Measure

1 cubic centimeter	=	.061 cubic inch
1 cubic inch	=	16.387 cubic centimeters
1 cubic meter	=	1.308 cubic yards
1 cubic yard	=	.765 cubic meter
1 liter	=	61.024 cubic inches

Statistics, Data Analysis, and Probability

Elementary Statistics

Mean

The **average**, or **mean**, of a set of numbers can be found by adding the set of numbers and dividing by the total number of elements in the set.

Example: The mean of 15, 10, 25, 5, 40 is
$$\frac{15+10+25+5+40}{5} = \frac{95}{5} = 19.$$

Median

If a given set of numbers is ordered from smallest to largest, the **median** is the "middle" number; that is, half of the numbers in the set of numbers is below the median and half of the numbers in the set is above the median.

Example: To find the median of the set of whole numbers 15, 10, 25, 5, 40, first order the set of numbers to get 5, 10, 15, 25, 40. Since 15 is the middle number (half of the numbers are below 15, half are above 15), 15 is called the median of this set of whole numbers. If there is an even number of numbers in the set, the median is the mean of the middle two numbers.

Mode

The **mode** of a set of numbers is the number that appears most frequently in the set.

Example: In the set 15, 10, 25, 10, 5, 40, 10, 15, the number 10 appears most frequently (three times); therefore, 10 is the mode of the given set of numbers.

Range

The **range** of a set of numbers is obtained by subtracting the smallest number in the set from the largest number in the set.

Example: To find the range of 15, 10, 25, 5, 40, find the difference between the largest and the smallest elements of the set. This gives $40 - 5 = 35$. The range of the given set is 35.

Definition of Standard Deviation

The **standard deviation** of a set x_1, x_2, ..., x_n of n numbers is defined by

$$s = \sqrt{\frac{\sum\limits_{i=1}^{n} \left(x_1 - \bar{x}\right)^2}{n}} = \sqrt{\overline{(x - \bar{x})^2}}$$

The sample standard deviation is denoted by s, while the corresponding population standard deviation is denoted by s.

For grouped data, we use the modified formula for standard deviation. Let the frequencies of the numbers x_1, x_2, ..., x_n be f_1, f_2, ..., f_n respectively. Then

$$s = \sqrt{\frac{\Sigma f_i \, (x_i - \bar{x})^2}{\Sigma f_i}} = \sqrt{\frac{\Sigma f \, (x - \bar{x})^2}{\Sigma f}}$$

Often, in the definition of the standard deviation the denominator is not n but $n - 1$. For large values of n, the difference between the two definitions is negligible.

Example:

We find the standard deviation for the data shown below. The height of 100 students was measured and recorded.

Height (inches)	Class Mark x	x^2	Frequency f	fx^2	fx
60 – 62	61	3,721	7	26,047	427
63 – 65	64	4,096	21	86,016	1,344
66 – 68	67	4,489	37	166,093	2,479
69 – 71	70	4,900	26	127,400	1,820
72 – 74	73	5,329	9	47,961	657
			$\Sigma f = 100$	$\Sigma fx^2 = 453,517$	$\Sigma fx = 6,727$

We apply the formula

$$s = \sqrt{\frac{\Sigma fx^2}{\Sigma f} = \left(\frac{\Sigma fx}{\Sigma f}\right)^2}$$

Hence

$$s = \sqrt{4,535 - 4,525} = 3.16.$$

Elementary Probability

The likelihood or chance that an event will take place is called the **probability** of the event. The probability of an event is determined by dividing the number of ways the event could occur by the number of possible events in the given sample. In other words, if a sample space S has n possible outcomes, and an event E has m ways of occurring, then the probability of the event, denoted by $P(E)$, is given by

$$P(E) = \frac{m}{n}$$

It should be noted that $0 \leq P(E) \leq 1$.

Problem: What is the probability of getting "heads" on the toss of a coin?

Solution: Since the number of possible outcomes in the toss of a coin is 2 and the number of ways of getting "heads" on a coin toss is 1, $P(head) = \frac{1}{2}$

Problem: What is the probability of drawing an ace from a standard deck of playing cards?

Solution: Since the number of aces in a standard deck is 4 and the number of cards in a standard deck is 52, $P(ace) = \frac{4}{52} = \frac{1}{13}$.

Physical

Education

Review

The Physical Education review section offers a perspective on the importance of maintaining a healthy mind and body as well as demonstrating how the two work in conjunction. Armed with a balanced diet of information on every page, our section will train your mind with a circuit of content including cardiovascular fitness, nutrition, team sports, and the role of athletics. Preparing your mind through study will leave you in great shape to succeed come test day.

Benefits of Diet and Exercise

One of the primary reasons for the teaching of physical education is to instill a willingness to exercise. To that end, it is important to understand the benefits in participating in a lifelong program of exercise and physical fitness.

Fortunately, it is not difficult to find justification for exercising and maintaining a consistently high level of fitness. The benefits of a consistent program of diet and exercise are many. Improved cardiac output, improved maximum oxygen intake, and improvement of the blood's ability to carry oxygen are just a few of these benefits. Exercise also lowers the risk of heart disease by strengthening the heart muscle, lowering pulse and blood pressure, and lowering the concentration of fat in both the body and the blood. It can also improve appearance, increase range of motion, and lessen the risk of back problems associated with weak bones and osteoperosis.

Principles of Cardiovascular Fitness

Cardiovascular fitness, or aerobic capacity, is the ability of the entire body to work together efficiently—to be able to do the most amount of work with the least amount of effort. Cardiovascular fitness is composed of four basic components: strength and power, endurance, movement speed and flexibility, and agility. Training is required to develop consistent aerobic capacity, and training is comprised of several principles. To begin, a warm-up is essential. An effective warm-up will increase body temperature and blood flow, as well as guard against strains and tears to muscles, tendons, and ligaments. A good warm-up consists of stretching exercises, calisthenics, walking, and slow jogging.

While exercising, a student must be aware of his or her body's adaptations to the demands imposed by training. Some of these adaptations are improved heart function and circulation, improved respiratory function, and improved strength and endurance. All of these adaptations lead to improved vigor and vitality. In order to affect these adaptations, the students must exert themselves to a far greater degree than their normal daily activities. This exertion is referred to as overload. Despite what this term suggests, it does not imply that trainers should work beyond healthy limits. However, it does imply that they must push themselves in order to see results. The rate of improvement and adaptation is directly related to the frequency, intensity, and duration of training.

In addition to regular training, you must gear your students' training toward those adaptations that are important to them. This is known as specificity. Performance improves when the training is specific to the activity being performed. That is to say, certain activities will have more effect on cardiovascular health than overall muscle tone and appearance, and vice versa. Therefore, you should always try to maintain a balance in your exercise.

Fast Facts

Cardiovascular fitness is the ability of all parts of the body to work together efficiently.

The body thrives on activity and, therefore, the axiom "use it or lose it" certainly holds true. Lack of activity can cause many problems, including flabby muscles, a weak heart, poor circulation, shortness of breath, obesity, and a degenerative weakening of the skeletal system. It is important to note, however, that when many people begin a program of exercise, they expect to see results immediately. More often than not, this is not the case. Individual response to exercise varies greatly from person to person. This can be affected by heredity, age, general cardiovascular fitness, rest and sleep habits, an individual's motivation, their environmental influences, and any handicap, disease or injury that may impede the body's adaptation to training. The sum of all these factors is an individual's potential for maximizing their own cardiovascular fitness. Unfortunately, very few people live up to this full potential.

Finally, a good program of exercise always ends with a cooling off period. Very much like the warm-up, and just as essential, the same low-impact exercises used during a warm-up may be used to cool off after a period of intense exertion. Without cooling off, blood will pool and slow the removal of waste products. With this basic introduction in mind, let's look at some more specific forms of exercise and the positive effects they have on the body.

Aerobic Exercise

Aerobic exercise involves both muscle contraction and movement of the body. Aerobic exercise requires large amounts of oxygen and when done regularly will condition the cardiovascular system. Some aerobic exercises are especially suited to developing aerobic training benefits, with a minimum of skill and time involved. Examples of good aerobic activities are walking, running, swimming, rope skipping, and bicycling. These activities are especially good in the development of fitness because all of them can be done alone and with a minimum of special equipment. In order to be considered true aerobic conditioning, an activity must require a great deal of oxygen, it must be continuous and rhythmic, it must exercise major muscle groups and burn fat as an energy source, and it must last for at least 20 minutes at an individual's target heart rate. You may determine your target heart rate by subtracting 80% of your age from 220.

Interval training is also a good way to develop fitness. This type of exercise involves several different aerobic activities performed at intervals to comprise one exercise session. If a student learns about interval training, he or she will be better able to create his or her own fitness program. All the above mentioned activities provide examples of methods of interval training.

Low-Impact Aerobics

For some people, low-impact aerobics may have some advantages over traditional, or high-impact aerobics. Because low-impact aerobic exercise is easier to perform, it is an option for all ages and levels of fitness. It is easier to monitor your heart rate, and there is less warm up and cool down required. Because one foot is on the ground at all times, there is less chance of injury. In all other respects, such as duration and frequency, low-impact aerobic exercise is identical to high-impact.

Anatomy and Physiology

Anatomy describes the structure, position, and size of various organs. Because our bones adapt to fill a specific need, exercise is of great benefit to the skeletal system. Bones that anchor strong muscles thicken to withstand the stress. Weight-bearing bones can develop heavy mineral deposits while supporting the body. Because joints help provide flexibility and ease of movement, it is important to know how each joint moves. Types of joints are ball and socket (shoulder and hip), hinge (knee), pivot (head of the spine), gliding (carpal and tarsal bones), angular (wrist and ankle joints), partially moveable (vertebrae), and immovable (bones of the adult cranium).

Muscles are the active movers in the body. In order to properly teach any physical education activity, the functions and physiology of the muscles must be understood. Since muscles move by shortening or contracting, proper form should be taught so the student can get the most out of an activity. It is also important to know the location of each muscle. This knowledge will help in teaching proper form while doing all physical education activities. Understanding the concept of antagonistic muscles, along with the related information concerning flexors and extensors, is also vital to the physical educator. Imagine trying to teach the proper form of throwing a ball if you do not understand the mechanics involved. Knowledge of anatomy and physiology is also necessary to teach proper techniques used in calisthenics as well as all physical activities. Some physical education class standbys are frequently done improperly or done when the exercise itself can cause harm. Examples of these are squat thrusts, straight leg sit-ups, straight leg toe touches, straight leg push-ups for girls, and double leg lifts.

Sports and Games

Individual, dual, and team sports all have a prominent place in a successful physical education curriculum. Since one of the attributes of a quality physical education program is its carry over value, it is easy to justify the inclusion of these activities in a curriculum. That is not to say that "rolling out the ball" is enough to create learning situations through the use of sports and games. Learning the rules and keeping score supplies a framework for goals and learning how to deal with both victory and defeat. Examples of some sports and games that are useful to achieve the aforementioned goals are as follows:

Team Sports

Volleyball—6 players, two out of three games. Winner scores twenty-five points with a margin of two.

Basketball—5 players. Most points at the end of the game wins.

Softball—9 or 10 players. Most runs at the end of seven innings wins.

Field hockey—11 players. Most goals wins.

Soccer—11 players. Most goals wins.

Flag football—9 or 11 players (can be modified to fit ability and size of the class). Six points for a touchdown, one or two for a point after, and two for a safety.

Dual Sports

Tennis—Either doubles or singles. Four points–fifteen, thirty, forty, and game. Tie at forty–deuce. Winner must win by a margin of two. Remember, love means zero points in tennis.

Badminton—Either doubles or singes. Winner in doubles 15 points, singles 21 by a margin of two.

Table tennis—Either doubles or singles. 21 points by a margin of two.

Shuffleboard—Either singles or doubles. 50, 75, or 100 points. Determined by participants before the game begins.

Individual Sports

Swimming—Very good for cardiovascular conditioning and can be done almost anywhere there is water.

Track and field—Scoring varies with event.

Bowling—Scoring is unique and good math skills are encouraged.

Weight training—No scoring involved but the benefits are many. Muscles are toned and strengthened through the use of weight training. Either weight machines or free weights can be used. It is important for students to learn the proper techniques and principles of weight training so they can reap the benefits while avoiding injury. When weight training, participants must consider the concept of muscular balance—this is equal strength in opposing muscle groups. All opposing groups (antagonistic muscles), i.e., triceps and biceps, hamstrings and quadriceps, need to be equal or body parts may become improperly aligned. The responsibility of the physical educator is to teach accurate information about the human body as well as teach ways to prevent injury and achieve efficiency in movement. Understanding that abdominal strength is important to lower back strength can help students create an exercise program to help avoid back injuries.

Gymnastics—Includes tumbling. Excellent activity for developing coordination and grace. Also requires strength, which is developed by the activities done. This training can begin at a very early age with tumbling activities and progress to gymnastics.

Golf—A fantastic carry over activity that can be taught on campus, at the golf course, or both. Requires coordination, concentration, and depth perception.

Rhythmics—Includes ball gymnastics and other activities that may require music. Rhythmics can be taught in early elementary physical education, enabling students to develop music appreciation as well as spatial awareness.

Dance—Can be done either individually or with a partner. Dance is especially good at developing spatial awareness and the ability to follow instructions. Dance instruction should begin in elementary school. Basic steps are walk and/or skip and are suitable to teach to first and second graders. Skip, slide, and/or run are suitable for second and third graders. The more difficult step-hop can be taught to grades three through six. The ability to dance can also aid in the development of social skills and teamwork. Dance also provides an excellent framework for multicultural education. Many dances are indigenous to certain cultures, and students can learn about different races and cultures while learning dances. Having the class walk through the dances without the music and then adding the music is effective. The instructor must be careful not to teach too many steps before the dance is tried with the music. Most students enjoy dance in spite of themselves.

Adaptive Physical Education

Public Law 94-142 provides the legal definition for the term "handicapped children." It includes children who have been evaluated as being mentally impaired, deaf, speech impaired, visually handicapped, emotionally disturbed, orthopedically impaired, multi-handicapped, having learning disabilities or having other health impairments (anemia, arthritis, etc.). P.L. 94-142 states that these children need special education and services. The challenge in teaching physical education to handicapped children is tailoring activities to fit each child. For example, blind or partially sighted students can participate in weight lifting, dance, and some gymnastic and tumbling activities. These students can also participate in some other activities with modifications. A beeper ball can be used for softball; a beeper can be used for archery. If a beeper is not available for archery, the teacher can put the student in position and assist in aiming. Many games and activities can be modified for the handicapped. Sometimes all it takes is a little ingenuity to change activities so handicapped students can enjoy participating.

There are many students who are only temporarily disabled who will benefit from adaptive physical education. Examples of temporary disabilities are pregnancy, broken bones, and recovery from surgery and disease. It is very important when teaching the handicapped and temporarily handicapped not to have a very large class. The optimum class size for handicapped students is less than ten with fifteen being the absolute maximum.

Health and Diet

Along with exercise, a knowledge of and participation in a healthy lifestyle is vital to good health and longevity. What constitutes good nutrition, the role of vitamins, elimination of risk factors, and strategies to control weight are all part of a healthy lifestyle.

Good Nutrition

Complex carbohydrates should comprise at least half of the diet. This is important because these nutrients are the primary and most efficient source of energy. Examples of complex carbohydrates are: vegetables, fruits, high-fiber breads, and cereals. Fiber in the diet is very important because it promotes digestion, reduces constipation, and has been shown to help reduce the risk of colon cancer. Another benefit of complex carbohydrates is that they are high in water content, which is vital to the functioning of the entire body.

Proteins should comprise about one-fifth of the diet. It is a food that builds and repairs the body. Sources of protein are beans, peas, lentils, peanuts, and other pod plants. Another source is red meat, which unfortunately contains a great deal of saturated fat.

There are two categories of fat: unsaturated, which is found in vegetables, and saturated, which comes from animals or vegetables. Cocoa butter, palm oil, and coconut oil are saturated fats that come from vegetables. Unsaturated vegetable fats are preferable to saturated fats because they appear to offset the rise in blood pressure that accompanies too much saturated fat. These fats may also lower cholesterol and help with weight loss. Whole milk products contain saturated fat, but the calcium found in them is vital to health. For this reason, most fat limiting diets suggest the use of skim milk and low fat cheese.

Research indicates a link between high fat diets and many types of cancer. Diets high in saturated fats are also dangerous because fats cause the body to produce too much low-density lipoprotein in the system. Cholesterol, a substance only found in animals, is of two different kinds, LDL (low-density lipoproteins) and HDL (high-density lipoproteins). Some cholesterol is essential in order for the body to function properly. It is vital to the brain and is an important component in the creation of certain hormones. The body produces cholesterol in the liver. Excess cholesterol found in the blood of so

> **Fast Facts**
>
> **Along with exercise, a knowledge of, and participation in, a healthy lifestyle is vital to good health and longevity.**

many people usually comes from cholesterol in their diet rather than from internal production. LDL cholesterol encourages the build up of plaque in the arteries. HDLs do just the opposite. LDL cholesterol can be controlled through proper diet, and HDL cholesterol levels can be raised by exercise. Triglycerides are another form of fat found in the blood that are important to monitor because high triglycerides seem to be inversely proportional to HDLs.

Vitamins

Vitamins are essential to good health. One must be careful, however, not to take too much of certain vitamins. Fat soluble vitamins, A, D, E, and K, will be stored in the body, and excessive amounts will cause some dangerous side effects. The remaining vitamins are water soluble and are generally excreted through the urinary system and the skin when taken in excess. A brief synopsis of the vitamins and minerals needed by the body follows:

Vitamin A: Needed for normal vision, prevention of night blindness, healthy skin, resistance to disease, and tissue growth and repair. Found in spinach, carrots, broccoli and other dark green or yellow orange fruits and vegetables; also found in liver and plums.

Vitamin D: Promotes absorption of calcium and phosphorous, and normal growth of healthy bones, teeth, and nails. Formed by the action of the sun on the skin. Also found in halibut liver oil, herring, cod liver oil, mackerel, salmon, and tuna, and is added to many milk products.

Vitamin E: Protects cell membranes, seems to improve elasticity in blood vessels, also may prevent formation of blood clots and protect red blood cells from damage by oxidation. Found in wheat germ oil, sunflower seeds, raw wheat germ, almonds, pecans, peanut oil, and cod liver oil.

Thiamin/B1: Functioning of nerves, muscle growth, and fertility. Also, production of energy, appetite, and digestion. Found in pork, legumes, nuts, enriched and fortified whole grains, and liver.

Riboflavin/B2: Aids in the production of red blood cells, good vision, healthy skin and mouth tissue, and production of energy. Found in lean meat, dairy products, liver, eggs, enriched and fortified whole grains, and green leafy vegetables.

Niacin/B3: Promotes energy production, appetite, digestive and nervous system, healthy skin, and tongue.

Pyridoxine/B6: Red blood cell formation and growth. Found in liver, beans, pork, fish, legumes, enriched and fortified whole grains, and green leafy vegetables.

Vitamin B12: Healthy nerve tissue, energy production, utilization of folic acid, and aids in the formation of healthy red blood cells. Found in dairy products, liver, meat, poultry, fish, and eggs.

Vitamin C: Promotes healing and growth, resists infection, increases iron absorption, and aids in bone and tooth formation/repair. Found in citrus fruits, cantaloupe, potatoes, strawberries, tomatoes, and green vegetables.

Minerals

Sodium: Normal water balance inside and outside cells. Blood pressure regulation and electrolyte and chemical balance. Found in salt, processed foods, bread, and bakery products.

Potassium: Volume and balance of body fluids. Prevents muscle weakness and cramping, important for normal heart rhythm and electrolyte balance in the blood. Found in citrus fruits, leafy green vegetables, potatoes, and tomatoes.

Zinc: Taste, appetite, healthy skin, and wound healing. Found in lean meat, liver, milk, fish, poultry, whole grain cereals, and shellfish.

Iron: Red blood cell formation, oxygen transport to the cells, and prevents nutritional anemia. Found in liver, lean meats, dried beans, peas, eggs, dark green leafy vegetables, and whole grain cereals.

Calcium: Strong bones, teeth, nails, muscle tone, and prevents osteoporosis and muscle cramping. Helps the nerves function and the heart beat. Found in milk, yogurt, and other dairy products, and dark leafy vegetables.

Phosphorous: Regulates blood chemistry and internal processes, strong bones and teeth. Found in meat, fish, poultry, and dairy products.

Magnesium: Energy production, normal heart rhythm, nerve/muscle function, and prevents muscle cramps. Found in dried beans, nuts, whole grains, bananas, and leafy green vegetables.

Elimination of Risk Factors

Another aspect of physical education concerns awareness and avoidance of the risks that are present in our every day lives. Some risk factors include being overweight, smoking, using drugs, having unprotected sex, and stress. Education is the key to minimizing the presence of these risk factors. Unfortunately, because of the presence of peer pressure and the lack of parental control, the effect of education is sometimes not enough.

Weight Control Strategies

Statistics show that Americans get fatter every year. Even though countless books and magazine articles are written on the subject of weight control, often the only place a student gets reliable information about diet is in a classroom. For example, it is an unfortunate reality that fat people do not live as long, on average, as thin ones. Being overweight has been isolated as a risk factor in various cancers, heart disease, gall bladder problems, and kidney disease. Chronic diseases such as diabetes and high blood pressure are also aggravated by, or caused by, being overweight.

Conversely, a great many problems are presented by being underweight. Our society often places too much value on losing weight, especially on women. Ideal weight as well as a good body fat ratio is the goal when losing weight. A study done at the Cooper clinic shows a correlation between body fat and high cholesterol. Exercise is the key to a good body fat ratio. Exercise helps to keep the ratio down thus improving cholesterol levels, and helps in preventing heart disease.

In order to lose weight, calories burned must exceed calories taken in. No matter what kind of diet is tried, this principle applies. There is no easy way to maintain a healthy weight. Here again, the key is exercise. If calorie intake is restricted too much, the body goes into its starvation mode and operates by burning fewer calories. Just a 250-calorie drop a day combined with a 250-calorie burn will result in a loss of one pound a week. Crash diets, which bring about rapid weight loss, are not only unhealthy but also are not very effective. Slower weight loss is more lasting. Aerobic exercise is the key to successful weight loss. Exercise speeds up metabolism and causes the body to burn calories. Timing of exercise will improve the benefits. Exercise before meals speeds up metabolism and has been shown to suppress appetite. Losing and maintaining weight is not easy. Through education, people will be better able to realize that losing weight is hard work and is a constant battle.

First Aid

First aid is the immediate, temporary care of an injured or ill person. Occasionally during physical education classes, injuries and illnesses can occur. For this reason, a basic knowledge of first aid is important for physical education teachers.

Fractures—Any break in a bone is a fracture. Fractures can be *simple*—a break in the bone, *comminuted* or shattered—many breaks in the bone, or *compound*—a break in the bone and the skin. First aid: immobilize, use ice to control swelling, and seek medical aid. In the case of a compound fracture, it is important to stop the bleeding.

Shock—Traumatic shock is a severe compression of circulation caused by injury or illness. Symptoms include cool clammy skin and a rapid weak pulse. First aid: minimize heat loss and elevate the legs without disturbing the rest of the body. Seek medical help.

Sprain—An injury to a joint caused by the joint being moved too far or away from its range of motion. Both ligaments and tendons can be injured. Ligaments join bone to bone and tendons join muscle to bone. First aid: R.I.C.E.—rest, ice, compression, and elevation.

Strain—A muscle injury caused by overwork. First aid: use ice to lessen the swelling, some heat after can be beneficial. Opinion on the value of heat varies.

Dislocation—A joint injury in which bone ends are moved out of place at the joints and ligaments holding them are severely stretched and torn. First aid: immobilize and seek medical help. Some people advocate "popping" the dislocation back into place, but this can be risky for both the injured person and person giving the first aid (liability).

Heat exhaustion—Symptoms include, cold clammy skin, nausea, dizziness, and paleness. First aid: not as severe as heat stroke but must be treated by increasing water intake, replacing salt, and getting out of the heat.

Heat stroke—High fever, dry skin, and may be unconscious. First aid: attempt to cool off gradually, get into the shade, and seek medical attention immediately.

CPR—Cardiopulmonary Resuscitation. First-aid technique used to provide artificial circulation and respiration. Remember: A=airway, B=breathing, C=circulation. Check the airway to make sure it is open, and check breathing and circulation.

Heart attack—Symptoms may include any or all of the following: shortness of breath, pain in the left arm, pain in the chest, nausea, and sweating. First aid: elevate the head and chest, give CPR if indicated, and seek medical assistance.

Seizures—Generally caused by epilepsy. First aid: clear the area so victim is not injured during the seizure, do not place anything in the mouth, and seek medical help after the seizure if necessary.

Movement Education

Movement education is the process by which a child is helped to develop competency in movement. It has been defined as learning to move and moving to learn. Movement competency requires the student to manage his or her body. This body management is necessary to develop both basic and specialized activities. Basic skills are needed by the child for broad areas of activity that are related to daily living and child's play. Specialized skills are required to perform sports and have very clear techniques. Basic skills must be mastered before the child can develop specialized ones. The child controls his or her movement during nonlocomotor (stationary) activities, in movements across the floor or field, through space, and when suspended on an apparatus. To obtain good body management skills is to acquire, expand, and integrate elements of motor control. This is done through wide experiences in movement, based on a creative and exploratory approach. It is important that children not only manage the body with ease of movement but also realize that good posture and body mechanics are important parts of their movement patterns.

Perceptual motor competency is another consideration in body management. Perceptual motor concepts that are relevant to physical education include those that give attention to balance, coordination, lateral movement, directional movement, awareness of space, and knowledge of one's own body. Basic skills can be divided into three categories, locomotor, nonlocomotor, and manipulative skills. A movement pattern might include skills from each category.

Locomotor Skills

Locomotor skills are moving the body from place to place: walking, running, skipping, leaping, galloping, and sliding. Skills that move the body upward, such as jumping or hopping, are also locomotor skills.

Nonlocomotor Skills

Nonlocomotor skills are done in place or with very little movement from place to place. Examples of nonlocomotor skills are bending and stretching, pushing and pulling, raising and lowering, twisting and turning, and shaking and bouncing.

Manipulative Skills

Manipulative skills are skills used when the child handles a play object. Most manipulative skills involve using the hands and the feet, but other parts of the body may be used as well. Hand-eye and foot-eye coordination are improved with manipulative objects. Throwing, batting, kicking, and catching are important skills to be developed using balls and beanbags. Starting a child at a low level of challenge and progressing to a more difficult activity is an effective method for teaching manipulative activities. Most activities begin with individual practice and later move to partner activities. Partners should be of similar ability. When teaching throwing and catching, the teacher should emphasize skill performance, principles of opposition, weight transfer, eye focus, and follow-through. Some attention should be given to targets when throwing because students need to be able to catch and throw to different levels. Reaching is a "point-to-point" arm movement that is very common in our daily activities. In fact, reaching and grasping are typically used together to serve a number of purposes like eating, drinking, dressing, or cooking. The reaching/grasping task requires an "eye-hand" coordination and control of movement timing for a successful attempt.

Specialized Skills

Specialized skills are related to various sports and other physical education activities such as dance, tumbling, gymnastics, and specific games. To teach a specialized skill, the instructor must present and use explanation, demonstration, and drill. Demonstration can be done by other students provided the teacher monitors the demonstration and gives cues for proper form. Drills are excellent to teach specific skills but can become tedious unless they are done in a creative manner. Using game simulations to practice skills is an effective method to maintain interest during a practice session.

Teachers must also remember to use feedback when teaching a skill or activity. Positive feedback is much more conducive to skill learning than negative feedback. Feedback means correcting with suggestions to improve. If a student continually hits the ball into the net while playing tennis, he or she is aware that something is not right. The teacher should indicate what the problem is and tell the student how to succeed in getting the ball over the net.

 *Fast Facts*

Movement education enables the child to make choices of activity and the method they wish to employ. Teachers can structure learning situations so the child can be challenged to develop his or her own means of movement. The child becomes the center of learning and is encouraged to be creative in carrying out the movement experience.

Movement education enables children to make choices of activity and the methods they wish to employ.

In this method of teaching, the child is encouraged to be creative and progress according to his/her abilities. The teacher is not the center of learning, but suggests and stimulates the learning environment. Student-centered learning works especially well when there is a wide disparity of motor abilities. If the teacher sets standards that are too high for the less talented students, they may become discouraged and not try to perform.

Basic movement education attempts to develop the children's awareness not only of what they are doing but how they are doing it. Each child is encouraged to succeed in his or her own way according to his or her own capacity. If children succeed at developing basic skills in elementary school, they will have a much better chance at acquiring the specialized skills required for all sports activities.

Psychological and Social Aspects of Physical Education

Physical education is a very important part of a student's elementary school education. It is not only an opportunity to "blow off steam," but it is also an arena of social interaction. One psychological aspect of physical education is the enhancement of self-esteem. Often students who have limited success in other classes can "shine" in physical education. This does not happen automatically; it is up to the teacher to create situations that enable students to gain self-esteem. Teachers must also be careful not to damage self-esteem. An example of a potentially damaging situation occurs during the exercise of choosing members of a team. Teachers should not have the captains chosen and then choose the teams in front of the whole class. Nothing is more demeaning than to be the last person chosen. A better method is for the teacher to select the captains (this is also a very good way to separate the superstars: have the six best athletes be the captains). The captains then go to the sidelines and pick the teams from a class list. The teacher can then post or read the team lists after mixing up the order chosen so no one knows who were the first and last picked.

From a developmental perspective, considerable research evidence suggests that children's participation in exercise or sports would result in a number of long-term benefits, including the improvement of self-esteem or self-confidence for social interactions, and the development of sport leadership, sportsmanship, and motivation for participating in lifetime physical activities.

Gender Equity

It is important to choose both girls and boys as captains so the girls do not feel left out. Lack of gender equity can contribute to serious self-esteem problems for girls. Frequently, girls are ignored in co-ed classes even when they have good skills. If students have been in co-ed classes for a long period of time, gender equity seems to be less of a problem, but it still exists. Teachers can, through example, foster an atmosphere of fairness. Teachers' attention to students has been proven to effect self-esteem and self-confidence.

Another method to enhance self-esteem is to use students, whenever possible, to demonstrate skills. When students are used to demonstrate, classmates will realize that they too may possess that skill. As they demonstrate, students can give cues and suggestions to improve performance. Most students enjoy being involved in demonstrations so the instructor should be careful to use as many students as possible. The teacher must not abdicate his or her authority, but provide direction and examples of proper form when teaching skills.

Social Interaction

Being a member of a team provides many opportunities for social interaction. The team concept emulates life situations. Team members can practice leadership and followership skills. Students can learn to win and lose gracefully when playing any sport. Another concept teamwork teaches is that everyone makes his or her own contributions to the team.

Physical education will also provide many opportunities to develop social skills. Both same-sex classes and co-ed classes provide many opportunities for social interaction. Getting along with others is a valuable skill that can be promoted by physical education. If teachers create an atmosphere of equal treatment to all students, it will be easier for all to coexist. Teachers who have "pets" and exclude others in the class because of gender or behavior spoil the atmosphere of the class. If students don't feel that they are worthy of the teacher's attention, their self-esteem will suffer. The physical education class can provide tremendous benefits to students, but it takes a skilled teacher to create situations to provide those benefits.

Chapter 7

Human Development Review

The Human Development section offers theories relating to growth and maturation and the effect nature has on each. Jean Piaget, Erik Erikson, and Abraham Maslow are among the psychologists mentioned. Other topics include environmental and emotional factors, learning styles, metacognition, and study strategies. Learning the content of the CSET certainly is a learning process, and this section will provide the right environment to help you achieve successful results on the test.

This portion of the CSET is unlike the others in that it seeks to assess your understanding of the developmental needs of your students rather than the subject matter that you will be responsible to teach.

In order for teachers to successfully teach students of all ages and in all disciplines, it is necessary that teachers understand learners. Benjamin Bloom (1976) has suggested that students' cognitive entry skills and intelligence (or IQ) account for about 50 percent of what students achieve academically; 25 percent can be attributed to the quality of instruction students receive; and 25 percent can be attributed to affective characteristics of the students. Those affective characteristics include such things as the learner's personality, self-concept, locus of control, attitudes, level of anxiety, and study habits. Therefore, although it is important that teachers acquire and utilize effective teaching techniques and provide quality instruction to students, it can be argued that it is even more important in terms of educational outcomes that teachers understand cognitive and affective factors that influence student performance.

The traditional view of education saw the learner as a **tabula rasa**, a blank slate, upon which the teacher wrote knowledge. In this model, the student was assumed to be an empty vessel; he or she came into the classroom knowing nothing. It was the teacher's responsibility, as the expert, to impart knowledge or to fill the empty vessel.

Today, cognitive psychologists have corrected this faulty notion. Educators now recognize that students bring to the classroom an array of personal characteristics and experiences upon which they base their present knowledge. Those characteristics and experiences may or may not be congruent to the teacher's background; nonetheless, they constitute a knowledge base for the learner. Therefore, the teacher's role is to activate the learner's prior knowledge and help the student connect new information with what is known already. Thus, in today's educational model, the student is seen as an active learner who brings much to the classroom.

The effective teacher, then, must go beyond assuming the role of a "sage on the stage." The effective teacher must be more than just an expert who has mastered a discipline or body of knowledge. The effective teacher must be a facilitator of learning; an effective teacher empowers students to learn for and by themselves. The effective teacher, in other words, is a "guide by the side" of students, assisting them in the process of learning and enhancing that process for students.

The importance of teachers' having a basic understanding of the principles of human development in its many dimensions: physically, mentally, emotionally, and socially, cannot be overstated. It is also important that teachers appreciate a dynamic and interactive view of human development. This approach to understanding human development is one that recognizes that human beings do not develop in a vacuum. People exist in an environment that, friendly or unfriendly, supportive or nonsupportive, evokes and provokes reactions from individuals; moreover, it is not a one-way street with the environment doing all the driving. People also act in certain ways to shape and form their environment. There is a constant interaction or interplay between people and their environments. Thus, effective teachers must be sensitive to and knowledgeable of both personal characteristics of students and characteristics of their environment.

Student Development and Maturation

A teacher does not have to be an expert in anatomy and physiology to see the physical changes that accompany students' growth and maturity. The preschool child has trouble grasping pencils or crayons in a manner to facilitate handwriting; however, even most two-year olds can grasp crayons sufficiently to make marks on papers and, thus, enjoy the creative excitement of art.

Physiological changes play a significant role in the development of children as they increase their control of bodily movements and functions and refine their motor skills. Their ability to engage in simple to complex classroom and playground activities increases as they develop. Classroom and playground activities must be adjusted and adapted in order to be developmentally appropriate for the skill levels of the children.

As students enter junior high or begin their secondary education, they again experience important physiological changes with the onset of puberty. With puberty comes changes in primary sexual characteristics and the emergence of secondary sexual characteristics. In addition to bodily characteristics, there is a change in bodily feelings, and there is an increase in sex drive.

Girls, on average, reach maturational milestones before boys. Physical changes may cause embarrassment to both females and males when they draw unwelcome attention; moreover, these changes almost always create some discomfort as adolescents find the body they were familiar and comfortable with to be quite different, sometimes seemingly overnight.

David Elkind has noted two developmental characteristics of adolescence that share a relationship to the physiological changes accompanying maturation. These two characteristics are the **imaginary audience** and the **personal fable**. First, adolescents, preoccupied with their own physiological changes, often assume that others are equally intrigued by these changes in appearance and behavior; they may feel that others are staring at them, watching their every move, scrutinizing their behavior for one misstep or their appearance for any flaws. If everyone is watching, then it's imperative to be, to act, and to look just right. In today's culture, that means wearing the right clothes and having all the right brand names and status symbols. Because of adolescents' sensitivity to attention (especially the wrong kind of attention, that is, not fitting in, not being "right"), it is especially important that teachers of this age group be aware of the *imaginary audience* phenomenon and be sensitive to social interactions in the classroom. It, indeed, is important that teachers not contribute to creating unwanted attention or to stigmatizing or stereotyping students.

Personal fable refers to the belief that "My life is different from everyone else's; therefore, no one can understand how I feel or what I think. No one has ever felt or thought what I feel and think." This out-of-focus view tends to support both a feeling of isolation (which may be precipitated by the changing sensations from a body that is undergoing biological changes) and a willingness to engage in risky behaviors (thinking that only others have car accidents when they drive dangerously—"It won't happen to me"—or, only other girls get pregnant when they have unprotected sexual relations—"It won't happen to me.").

In sum, these two characteristics of adolescence are examples of how physical changes accompany and, perhaps even evoke, emotional and cognitive changes as individuals grow and mature. Both phenomena of *imaginary audience* and *personal fable* have emotional features (fear of rejection, fear of isolation, fear of difference, shame, guilt from increased sexual feelings, frustration, and so forth) and both describe a feature of adolescent cognitive ability: the ability to think about one's self as an object of one's own and of other's thoughts. The developmental epistemologist Jean Piaget explained that this way of thinking represents the cognitive stage of formal operations.

Cognition is a term commonly used to refer to all the processes whereby knowledge is acquired; the term can be used to cover very basic perceptual processes, such as smell, touch, sound, and so forth, to very advanced operations, such as analysis, synthesis, and critical thinking.

Theories of Cognitive Development

Until his death in 1980, Jean Piaget was a predominant figure in the field of cognitive psychology. It is safe to postulate that perhaps no other single individual has had greater influence on educational practices than Piaget. Basically, his theory of cognitive development is based on the notion that cognitive abilities (or one's ability to think) are developed as individuals mature physiologically, and they have opportunities to interact with their environment. Piaget described these interactions as the **equilibration of accommodation** and **assimilation cycles** or processes. In other words, when individuals (who, according to Piaget, are innately endowed with certain cognitive predispositions and capabilities) encounter a new or novel stimulus, they are brought into a state of **disequilibrium**.

That is a way of saying that they are thrown off balance; they do not know or understand that which is new or unfamiliar. However, through the complementary processes of **accommodation** (or adjusting prior knowledge gained through former experiences and interactions) and **assimilation** (fitting together the new information with what has been previously known or understood), individuals come to know or understand that which is new. Once again, individuals are returned to a state of **equilibrium** where they remain until the next encounter with something unfamiliar. For Piaget, this is how learners learn.

Piaget also predicted that certain behaviors and ways of thinking characterize individuals at different ages. For this reason, his theory is considered a **stage theory**. Stage theories share the common tenet that certain characteristics will occur in predictable sequences and at certain times in the life of the individual.

According to Piaget, there are four stages of cognitive development, beginning with the **sensorimotor** stage (describing individuals from birth to around the age of two). The second stage, **preoperational** (describing cognitive behavior between the ages of two and seven) is characterized by egocentrism, rigidity of thought, semilogical reasoning, and limited social cognition; some cognitive psychologists have observed that this stage seems to describe how individuals think more in terms of what they can't do than what they can do. This stage describes the way that children in preschool and kindergarten go about problem-solving; also, many children in the primary grades may be at this stage in their cognitive development.

The next two stages, however, may be most important for elementary and secondary school teachers since they describe cognitive development during the times that most students are in school. The third stage, **concrete operations**, is the beginning of operational thinking and describes the thinking of children between the ages of seven and eleven. Learners at this age begin to decenter. They are able to take into consideration viewpoints other than their own. They can perform transformations, meaning that they can understand reversibility, inversion, reciprocity, and conservation. They can group items into categories. They can make inferences about reality and engage in inductive reasoning; they increase their quantitative skills, and they can manipulate symbols if they are given concrete examples with which to work. This stage of cognitive development is the threshold to higher level learning for students.

Finally, **formal operations** is the last stage of cognitive development and opens wide the door for higher ordered, critical thinking. This stage describes the way of thinking for learners between the ages of eleven and fifteen, and for Piaget, constitutes the ultimate stage of cognitive development (thus also describing adult thinking). Learners at this stage of cognitive development can engage in logical, abstract, and hypothetical thought; they can use the scientific method, meaning they can formulate hypotheses, isolate influences, and identify cause-and-effect relationships. They can plan and anticipate verbal cues. They can engage in both deductive and inductive reasoning, and they can operate on verbal statements exclusive of concrete experiences or examples. These cognitive abilities characterize the highest levels of thought.

Another theoretical approach to understanding human development is offered by Erik Erikson, another important stage theorist, who described psychosocial development. For each of eight stages, he identified a developmental task explained in terms of two polarities. For the purposes of this discussion, only those stages describing school-age individuals will be included.

According to Erikson, preschoolers and primary-school aged children must be able to function in the outside world independently of parents; when children are able to do this, they achieve a sense of **initiative**; when children are not able to move away from total parental attachment and control, they experience a sense of **guilt**. Thus, this stage of psychosocial development is the stage of initiative versus guilt. The child's first venture away from home and into the world of school has considerable significance when viewed in light of this theory; it is imperative that teachers assist students in their first experiences on their own, away from parental control.

Erikson's next stage of development is one involving a tension between **industry and inferiority**. For example, if the child who enters school (thus achieving initiative) acquires the skills (including academic skills such as reading, writing, and computation, as well as social skills in playing with others, communicating with others, forming friendships, and so forth) that enable her or him to be successful in school, then the child achieves a sense of industry; failure to achieve these skills leads to a sense of inferiority.

Most methods for assessing the developmental level of children's language has focused on "length of utterance" as measured by the number of words. Brown (1973) proposed using "mean length of utterance" (MLU), with the count to be based on the number of morphemes (a unit of meaning, which would be 3 for "unhappily"). By using MLUs, Brown found that language progressed along fairly orderly stages. While Brown did not, others have assigned approximate ages to each of the five stages. Advanced stages are marked by containing longer and more complex utterances.

Erikson (1972) considered children's play to be a vital mechanism in the representation and solution of social conflicts. Vygotsky (1978) considered play activity to promote a child's ability to "behave beyond his average age…as though he were a head taller than himself" (Saltz & Saltz, 1986). These qualities of play apply to both growth toward cognitive complexity as well as to emotional growth and awareness of others (Youngblade & Dunn, 1995).

Identity Achievement and Diffusion

Around the time students enter junior high, they begin the developmental task of achieving **identity**. According to Erikson, the struggle to achieve identity is one of the most important developmental tasks and one that creates serious psychosocial problems for adolescents. For example, even the individual who has successfully achieved all the important developmental milestones (such as initiative and industry) now finds him- or herself in a state of flux: Everything (body, feelings, thoughts) is changing. The adolescent starts to question, "Who am I?" Erikson believed that if adolescents find out what they believe in, what their goals, ideas, and values are, then they attain identity achievement; failure to discover these things leads to identity diffusion.

By the time many students reach high school, they are entering a stage of young adulthood, for Erikson, a psychosocial stage characterized by the polarities of **intimacy and isolation**. Individuals at this stage of development begin to think about forming lasting friendships, even marital unions. Erikson would argue that many psychosocial problems experienced by young adults have their origin in the individual's failure to achieve identity during the preceding stage; the young man or woman who does not know who he or she really is cannot achieve true intimacy.

For the classroom teacher, knowledge of psychosocial stages of human development can result in greater effectiveness. For example, the effective teacher realizes the importance of helping students to achieve skills necessary to accomplish crucial developmental tasks. According to Erikson's theory, teachers of elementary school-aged learners would do well to focus on teaching academic and social skills, helping students to gain proficiency in skills that will enable learners to be productive members of society. On the other hand, secondary school teachers would do well to keep in mind, as they engage students in higher-ordered thinking activities appropriate to their stage of cognitive development, that students have pressing psychological and social needs in their struggle to achieve identity and to attain intimacy.

By understanding key principles of human development in its multiple dimensions, effective teachers provide students with both age-appropriate and developmentally appropriate instruction. This, in sum, is the best instruction. It is instruction that addresses all the needs of students, their physical, emotional, and social needs, as well as their cognitive (or intellectual) needs.

Stage theories of development (Erikson, Piaget) have heavily influenced research on moral development. Kohlberg, Levine, and Hewer's (1983) work speaks of six levels of development of the moral decision-making of the child. The (progressive, sequential) stages parallel those of Piaget's cognitive developmental outline.

A telling critique of both Piaget's, but especially Kohlberg's work, has been leveled by Carol Gilligan (1982). Gilligan notes that the research done on these theories has largely been conducted by men on male subjects. This has led to distortions when applied to females, Gilligan contends. Often, the interpretations have cast women in a negative light. Her argument centers not on the stage concept, but on the bases for changes to be more cognitive for men while more based on a sense of self for women. Later research has built on, and clarified, Gilligan's distinction.

The preceding discussion on human development emphasized primarily the characteristics of learners or what may be considered internal factors. Internal factors, beyond the general characteristics that humans share as they grow and mature, also include factors such as students' personality characteristics, their self-concept and sense of self-esteem, their self-discipline and self-control, their ability to cope with stress, and their general outlook on life.

External factors are those things outside the student personally but which impact on the student. They include the home environment and family relationships, peer relationships, community situations, and the school environment. In other words, external factors constitute the context in which the student lives and learns.

Maslow's Hierarchy of Needs

Abraham Maslow's **hierarchy of human needs** is a model applicable to many diverse fields, including education, business and industry, health and medical professions, and more. Maslow identified different levels of individuals' needs in a hierarchical sequence, meaning that lower level needs must be satisfied before individuals could ascend to higher levels of achievement. He identified the fulfillment of basic physiological needs as fundamental to individuals' sense of well-being and their ability to engage in any meaningful activity. Simply stated, students' **physiological needs** (to have hunger and thirst satisfied, to have sleep needs met, to be adequately warm, and so forth) must be met before students can perform school tasks. Today's schools provide students with breakfast and lunch when needed, and great effort and expense are often directed towards heating and cooling school buildings.

Maslow's second level of need concerned **safety**. Again, students must feel safe from harm and danger before they are ready to learn. Today, schools often are equipped with metal detectors to increase students' sense of safety. In some schools, guards and security officers patrol the halls.

The third level of need, according to Maslow's theory, is the need for **affiliation** or the need to belong and to be accepted by others. Although this need may, at first glance, seem less related to the student's environment, it does, indeed, refer to the student's social environment. Students need the opportunity to develop social relationships and to establish friendships among their peers. In essence, Maslow, through his theory, determined that environmental factors are important in education.

Another significant principle of human development arises from a long debate between those experts who believed that innate characteristics (those the individual is born with) play the most important role in determining who the individual will become and what he or she will do versus those who believed that environmental characteristics are most important. This argument is referred to in the literature as the **nature versus nurture** debate.

Nature and Nurture

After experts on both sides of the argument stated their positions, the conclusion seemed to be that both **nature** (the internal variables) and **nurture** (the environment) play equally important roles in determining the outcome of individuals' growth and maturation. Again, it is important to remember the interaction of the individual with her or his environment, recalling that this view is the **dynamic** view of human development.

Heritability studies appear to demonstrate that both nurture and nature contribute to the child's trait makeup. However, the amount each contributes to any given trait cannot be precisely stated (no exact number or weight can be assigned).

A finding from those studies that stands out is that siblings are quite "unlike." Correlations between siblings on a wide variety of traits are remarkably low. Despite the above, another strong finding is the degree to which parenting can impact the child (Maccoby, 2000). Focus of future research needs to be on the interaction of the traits.

Before proceeding, teachers would do well to understand that perception plays an important role for learners to the extent that perception creates our individual reality. The world as we know it is a result of our selective perception. We cannot attend to all events and variables in our environment. We select certain events and variables to notice, to attend to, and these phenomena that we observe form our perceptions; thus, we create our own reality. External and internal phenomena grab our attention and shape reality for each of us.

Thus, it is one thing for teachers to be aware of and sensitive to the students' environment; it is, however, impossible for teachers to see, feel, and understand the individual's environment in exactly the same way that it is seen, felt, and understood by the student.

Carol Tavris, a social psychologist and author of the book, *Anger the Misunderstood Emotion*, notes that emotion plays a significant role in students' perceptions. For example, guilt is an emotion aroused by thoughts such as, "I should study or my parents will kill (be disappointed in) me." This is easily contrasted with the emotion of fear generated by the thought, "I should study or I will be a failure in life." Furthermore, guilt and fear can be compared to the emotion of anger that is prompted by thoughts such as, "Why should I study when my teacher is out to get me?" Today's student often sees the teacher as an enemy, not as an authority figure or a friend. Tavris has identified anger as a primary emotion experienced by many students today and one that plays a significant role in shaping their academic perceptions, which, in turn, forms their reality of classroom experiences.

Explaining further, Tavris observes that unfulfilled expectations lead to anger. For example, if a student is led to believe (by teachers, school administrators, their peers, or by parents and siblings) that attending class is somehow irrelevant to academic achievement, then the student who is frequently absent still has the expectation of being successful. The student's perception is that absenteeism is compatible with academic achievement. If, because of absenteeism, the student fails to master essential elements of the curriculum and does not succeed, then the student will feel anger, the appropriate and anticipated emotion.

Anger, however, can be diffused by addressing perceptions, correcting false impressions, and establishing appropriate and realistic expectations. To illustrate, if all those significant individuals to the student emphasize the importance of class attendance, then students acquire the correct perception (in this case) that attendance is important for academic achievement and that absenteeism leads to academic failure.

For the sake of illustration only, let's consider what might happen if the teacher stresses attendance and the parents do not. In this case, the best route for the teacher to take is to show empathy for the student's dilemma. The teacher can acknowledge how difficult it is for the student to attend class when the parents are not supporting attendance, but the teacher also must seek to empower the student to make choices and to take responsibility for her or his own behavior.

In the situation described here, the student undergoes stress because of conflicting messages, and stress is faced by students and faculty alike. In fact, in the above example, the teacher is stressed too in that the teacher faces the conflict between supporting the parents of the student and supporting that which is in the best educational interests of the student.

Stress is the product of any change; both negative and positive changes produce stress. Environmental, physiological, and psychological factors cause stress. For example, environmental factors such as noise, air pollution, and crowding (among others) create stress; physiological factors such as sickness and physical injuries create stress; and, finally, psychological factors such as self-deprecating thoughts and negative self-image cause stress. In addition to the normal stressors that everyone experiences, some students are living in dysfunctional families; some students are dealing with substance abuse and addictions; and some are experiencing sexual abuse. There are numerous sources of stress in the lives of students.

Since life is a stressful process, it is important that students and faculty learn acceptable ways to cope with stress. The first step in coping with stress is to recognize the role that stress plays in our lives. A teacher might lead a class through a brainstorming activity to help the students become aware of the various sources of stress affecting them. Next, the teacher could identify positive ways of coping with stress such as the importance of positive self-talk, physical exercise, proper nutrition, adequate sleep, balanced activities, time-management techniques, good study habits, and relaxation exercises.

Students who are stressed often become angry rather easily; however, students are not just angry. They experience a wide range of emotions, and may be sad, depressed, frustrated, afraid, and, on the positive side, happy and surprised. Effective teachers realize that students' emotions, as explained in this section and the preceding section on human development, play a significant role in students' classroom performance and achievement. Thus, effective teachers seek to create a classroom environment supportive of students' emotional needs. They have appropriate empathy and compassion for the emotional conflicts facing students, yet their concern is tempered by a realistic awareness of the importance of students attaining crucial academic and social skills that will grant them some control over their environment as they become increasingly independent and, eventually, must be prepared to be productive citizens.

The ability to make moral judgments and to react (behave) in a moral fashion depends on the child's ability to empathize, correctly assess another's point of view—especially when the other person is in discomfort (Hoffman, 1987).

The capacity to experience and express empathy increases with development of understanding of self and others, and especially with the development of language (Martin & Clark, 1982). Early school-age children are likely to view external events as causes of emotional reactions, but with further growth can recognize internal states ("sad because her tummy aches") (Fabes et al., 1997).

Empathy can promote opportunities for moral teachings. It can also assist in recruiting a child's willingness to give aid or assistance. And empathy can be used to generate remorse for causing another person's discomfort (Batson et al., 1997).

Effective teachers recognize the effects of students' perceptions on the learning process and the effects of many environmental factors; as a result, they plan instruction to enhance students' self-esteem and to promote realistic expectations. It is important that teachers be able to differentiate positive and negative environmental factors, maximizing the positive variables and minimizing the negative ones. The teacher has the primary responsibility of creating a classroom environment that recognizes the different environmental factors affecting each student and that encourages each learner to excel, and to achieve her or his personal best. Effective teachers work hard at creating learning environments in which all students are ready to learn—where students feel safe, accepted, competent, and productive.

Effective teachers also realize that students bring to the classroom a variety of characteristics, both personal and social, that create within the classroom a microcosm reflective of American society at large. Indeed, America has long held to the notion of being a "melting pot" whereby members of various racial, ethnic, religious, and national origin groups have contributed to the wealth of our culture.

Ethnocentrism is a sociological term used to describe the natural tendency of viewing one's own cultural or familial way of doing things as the right, correct, or best way. Because ethnocentrism is a natural tendency, all people are likely to engage in ethnocentric thinking and behaviors at times.

Some social critics have pointed out that ethnocentrism has played a notable role in American education. They assert that educational institutions often have been guilty of assuming a Eurocentric viewpoint, that is, solely recognizing the contributions of European writers, artists, scientists, philosophers, and so forth, at the expense of those from other cultures. These critics have also noted that the contributions of men often are disproportionately recognized over like achievements of women (Sadker & Sadker, 1994).

In fact, David and Myra Sadker (1994) have found that teachers, both male and female, at all grade levels, are more likely to call on male than female students, are more likely to give positive reinforcement to males' correct responses than to those of females, and to provide coaching or instructional help to males when their responses are incorrect than to females. Their research has led them to conclude that teachers are usually unaware of gender bias in their teaching, but that such bias is pervasive in American schools. Their research also has persuaded them that bias can be eliminated once teachers become sensitive to its debilitating effects on students.

The point made here is that ethnocentrism, in any form, can be damaging because it is exclusive rather than inclusive. Eurocentric and other ethnocentric perspectives are equally limited in that they narrowly focus attention on one set of ideas at the neglect of others. Therefore, effective teachers will wisely expend a degree of effort in avoiding ethnocentric thinking and behaviors. Effective teachers will attempt to include all students in all classroom activities. The race, ethnicity, religion, national origin, and gender of learners will be viewed as strengths that enable students to learn with and from each other.

Historically speaking, educational experiments have demonstrated the importance of teachers' avoiding bias and ethnocentric thinking. The *Hawthorne effect,* or the phenomenon whereby what teachers expected became reality, was demonstrated when teachers were told that some students in their classes were extremely intelligent whereas others were extremely slow or mentally retarded. In fact, all students had normal range intelligence. Nonetheless, at the end of the experiment, all students who had been identified to the teachers as being extremely intelligent had made significant academic progress and were not only at the top of their class, but also performing at the top on national achievement tests. Those students who had been identified as retarded had made no progress at all; in fact, they had lost previously made gains. Thus, it was demonstrated that teachers' expectations for students often become self-fulfilling prophecies.

Because multiculturalism and/or cultural diversity can be a controversial issue with many sides to consider, a reasonable approach to diversity for the classroom teacher is to distinguish between cultural diversity and learning diversity and to focus on diversity in learning. This approach transcends cultural boundaries and recognizes that all people have distinct learning preferences and tendencies. Furthermore, this approach acknowledges that all preferences and tendencies are equally valid and that each style of learning has strengths. The teacher who understands learning styles can validate all students in the class.

Environmental Factors

Many factors play a role in determining a student's learning style. Among those most often cited in the research literature on learning style are environmental, emotional, sociological, physiological, and psychological factors (Dunn & Dunn, 1993). Although there are several different models for understanding learning differences and many good instruments for assessing learning styles, the Dunn and Dunn (1993) model is one widely used in public schools with versions suitable for students in elementary and secondary classrooms. It will serve as the basis for the following discussion.

Environmental factors include students' reactions to such stimuli as sound, light, temperature, and room design. Do students prefer to study and learn with or without sound, with bright or soft lights, in warm or cool rooms, with standard classroom furniture or alternative seating? Classroom teachers observe that some students are easily distracted by any noise and require absolute quiet when studying or working on assignments. On the other hand, some students seem to learn best when they can listen to music. Some researchers have found evidence that students who prefer sound learn best when classical or instrumental music is played in the background.

Light is another environmental factor with students' preferences for light appearing to be basically inherited. Family members often exhibit the same preference. Some students prefer bright, direct illumination while others prefer dim, indirect lighting.

Temperature and design are two other environmental factors affecting learning style. Some students will prefer warmer temperatures whereas others will prefer cooler temperatures. Finally, some students will prefer to sit in straight-backed chairs at desks while others may prefer to sit on soft, comfy chairs or to sit or recline on the floor.

Although traditional classrooms are structured to provide quiet, brightly illuminated study and work areas with straight-backed chairs and desks, classroom teachers will observe that this environment meets the needs of only some of the learners in the class. An effective teacher will take into consideration the learning styles of all students and experiment with different room designs and study centers, and create different environments in the classroom. Although classroom temperature may seem to be beyond the control of the teacher, students can be advised to dress in layers so that they can remove outer garments when they are too warm and put on more layers when they are too cool.

Emotional Factors

According to Rita and Kenneth Dunn, **emotional factors** include motivation, persistence, responsibility, and structure. To explain, some students are motivated intrinsically: they undertake and complete tasks because they see the value in doing so. Other students are motivated extrinsically: They undertake and complete tasks because they desire to please others or to earn good marks. In regard to persistence, some students, when they undertake assignments, become totally and completely engaged in their work; they seem to lose track of time and can work for long periods without interruption or without feeling fatigued. Other students seem to work in short spurts of energy, needing to take frequent breaks.

When it comes to responsibility, some students are nonconforming, always doing the unexpected (and sometimes unwanted), whereas other students are conforming, always following the rules. Structure refers to whether or not students need detailed and precise instructions. Some students have lots of questions about how assignments should be done, and they desire detailed, step-by-step instructions on each phase of the assignment. Other students, however, seem to work from general concepts and are usually eager to begin assignments, often beginning their work before the directions have been given.

Sociological factors include whether or not students are social learners—preferring to work in pairs or in groups—or whether they are independent learners—preferring to work alone. Another sociological factor is whether or not students work best under the close guidance and supervision of an authority figure, be it teacher or parent, or whether they work best with a minimum of adult guidance and are best left primarily on their own to do their work.

Physiological factors include students' preferences for food or drink while they study, what time of day they learn best, their mobility needs, and their perceptual strengths. Briefly, some students may need to eat or drink in order to effectively and efficiently learn. Rita Dunn says that to make sure that students do not abuse this privilege, she allows them to eat only carrot or celery sticks (cooked so that the snacks will not crunch when eaten by students) and to drink water. This way, she is certain that only students who really need intake when they are learning will take advantage of this concession.

Some students may learn best early in the morning, some later in the morning, some in early afternoon, and some later in the afternoon. Researchers have found that merely manipulating the time of day that certain students take tests can significantly affect their test performance.

Mobility needs refer to the fact that some students need to move around when they study, whereas other students can sit still for longer periods of time. Although all of these factors are important, and a growing body of literature tends to support the idea that these factors play a significant role in increasing students' performance and in increasing teachers' effectiveness with students, perhaps one of the most important elements in understanding learning style is to identify students' perceptual strengths. Perceptual strengths refer to students' learning modalities, such as whether they are visual, auditory, tactile, or kinesthetic learners. Basically, these perceptual modalities refer to whether students learn best by seeing, hearing, or doing.

Some students can be given a book or handout to read and then perform a task well based on what they have read. These students tend to have visual (iconic or semantic) perceptual strength. Other students are visual learners, too, but they tend to learn best from images. These are the students who seem to recall every event, even minor details, from films, videos, or classroom demonstrations.

Although evidence indicates that less than fifteen percent of the school-age population is auditory (Dunn, 1993), much of the classroom instruction takes the form of teachers telling students information. Most students do not learn auditorially. Therefore, these students must be taught how to listen and learn from oral instructions and lectures.

Teachers who rely on telling students the information that is important would do well to remember that females are more likely to learn auditorially than males. Teachers should also keep in mind that whether or not students benefit from lectures is likely to depend on several other elements as well as whether or not the students are auditory learners, such as whether or not the students like the teacher, whether or not they think the information being presented is important, or whether or not they think that listening to the teacher will help them to achieve their goals (Baxter-Magolda, 1992).

On the other hand, there are students who do not seem to benefit much from lectures, textbook assignments, or visual aids. These students' perceptual strengths are tactile and kinesthetic. They learn from movement and motion, from being able to touch, handle, and manipulate objects. Often these students may have been identified as having learning disabilities. Sometimes they have been relegated to shop or cooking classes or have found their success in athletics, music, or art. Interestingly, many of the "hands on" skills that often identify a student for a career as an auto mechanic are also important skills for mechanical engineers and surgeons.

Learning Styles

The obvious benefit of knowing whether or not students are **auditory**, **visual**, **tactile**, or **kinesthetic** learners is not simply to cater to the learners' preferences or strengths. The significance is that once strengths are identified, then teachers can teach students to use those strengths in situations that are not easy or natural. For example, students who are not auditory learners (but tactile and kinesthetic) must learn responsibility for their own learning; they must learn to become involved in lecture classes. Becoming involved means that they learn to take copious notes, participate in class discussions, ask questions, and answer questions posed by the teacher.

Visual learners must sit where they can see what's going on in class, where they can see the teacher and the board. They need opportunities to draw pictures, to diagram, to take good notes, to create mind maps, and to use flashcards. They must be taught how to visualize the abstract concepts they are being taught, and they need opportunities to practice all these techniques.

For visual learners who learn best by reading, teachers can provide adequate opportunities to read in class. Students need to learn specific note-taking methods, and reading and comprehension strategies. They also can be taught to use supplemental readings, to use the library effectively, and to use workbooks.

Auditory learners need to learn attention-directing activities. They can learn to use audiocassettes as learning aids. They can learn to ask questions in class and to participate in class discussions. They must be taught how to summarize and paraphrase—especially how to state in their own words the concepts they are trying to master. They may need the teacher to repeat or to restate ideas. Students must learn to pay close attention to verbal cues such as voice tone and inflection. Reciting what they have heard (or read) is an important strategy for auditory learners as is finding someone to whom they can explain ideas they have acquired. It may be helpful for auditory learners to work on some assignments with students who are visual learners (Nolting, 1993).

Tactile, kinesthetic learners may benefit from study groups, discussion groups, role-playing situations, lab settings, computer activities, learning games, and by using flashcards and other manipulatives. They must get involved in class by asking questions and participating in discussions. They learn best when they can convert what they are learning into real-life, concrete experiences; for example, they may learn fractions by cutting a pizza into slices. Often, they need to work math problems immediately after being shown examples to check their understanding. They often need to move around while they are studying, reviewing ideas while exercising, or doing chores. Many times, they do their best work when they are using tools such as computers, calculators, or even their fingers.

When classroom teachers assess students' learning styles and then begin to teach to empower students to learn more effectively and perform tasks with greater proficiency, the result is that students also learn a tremendous lesson about diversity. They learn that not everyone learns in the same way, but that everyone can achieve. The products of learning can meet the same high standards although the processes for learning may be different for different students.

This is a rich lesson for students and faculty alike. It tells students that it is okay to be different; in fact, everyone is different. It tells students that it is okay to be the way they are. Apart from their race, ethnicity, religious beliefs, national origin, or gender, they are special, and they are good. They can learn. This may be one of the most important lessons that students ever learn and one that all teachers can be proud and eager to teach.

It is one thing for teachers to have command of their subject matter. It is a given that English teachers will be able to write well, that math teachers will be able to compute and calculate, that science teachers will know and understand science, and so forth. However, it is something else—and something at least as important—that teachers know how to teach.

When teachers understand learners, that is, when teachers understand developmental processes common to all learners, and how environmental features and learning styles, varied and diverse, affect learning, then teachers are better able to design and deliver effective instruction. Although there may be some intuitive aspects to teaching (and it seems that some people were born to teach), teaching skills can be acquired through processes of introspection, observation, direct instruction, self-evaluation, and experimentation.

How teachers teach should be directly related to how learners learn. Theories of cognitive development describe how learners learn new information and acquire new skills. There are many theories of cognitive development, two of which will be included in this review; they are (a) the Piagetian (or Neo-Piagetian) theory and (b) the information processing theory.

Piagetian theory (including Neo-Piagetian theory) describes learning in discrete and predictable stages. Therefore, teachers who understand this theory can provide students with developmentally appropriate instruction. This theory also describes learners moving from simpler ways of thinking to more complex ways of problem-solving and thinking. For teachers, there are many important implications of this theoretical perspective. For example, teachers must create enriched environments that present learners with multiple opportunities to encounter new and unfamiliar stimuli—be they objects or ideas. Teachers must also provide learners with opportunities to engage in extended dialogue with adults; according to Piaget's theory, conversational interactions with adults are a key component in cognitive development, especially the acquisition of formal operations (or higher-ordered thinking skills). Moreover, it is important that adults (and teachers in particular) model desired behaviors; teachers must reveal their own complex ways of thinking and solving problems to students.

On the other hand, information processing theories of human development take a different approach to describing and understanding how learners learn. Based on a computer metaphor and borrowing computer imagery to describe how people learn, information processing theories begin by determining the processing demands of a particular cognitive challenge (or problem to solve) necessitating a detailed task-analysis of how the human mind changes external objects or events into a useful form according to certain, precisely specified rules or strategies, similar to the way a computer programmer programs a computer to perform a function. Thus, information processing theories focus on the process, how the learner arrives at a response or answer.

A brief analysis of one information processing theory will serve to illustrate this point. Sternberg's (1985) triarchic theory of intelligence is a theory taking into account three features of learning. Those three features are (a) the mechanics or components of intelligence (including both higher ordered thinking processes, such as planning, decision making and problem solving, and lower-ordered processes, such as making inferences, mapping, selectively encoding information, retaining information in memory, transferring new information in memory, and so forth); (b) the learner's experiences; and (c) the learner's context (including the adaptation to and the shaping and selecting of environments).

According to Sternberg, learners' use of the mechanics of intelligence is influenced by learners' experiences. To illustrate, some cognitive processes (such as those required in reading) become automatized as a result of continued exposure to and practice of those skills. Learners who come from homes where parents read and where there are lots of different reading materials tend to be more proficient readers; certainly, learners who read a lot become more proficient readers. Those learners who are exposed to reading activities and who have ample opportunities to practice reading have greater skill and expertise in reading; and in a cyclical manner, students who have skills in reading like to read. Conversely, those who lack reading skills don't like to read. Students who don't like to read, don't read; thus, their reading skills, lacking practice, fail to improve.

An information processing approach acknowledges that not only are individuals influenced by their environments and adapt to those environments, individuals also are active in shaping their own environments. In other words, a child who wants to read but who has no books at home may ask parents to buy books, or may go to the library to read or check out books to read at home.

Information processing theory is of interest to educators because of its insistence on the idea that intelligent performance can be facilitated through instruction and direct training. In sum, intelligent thinking can be taught. Sternberg has urged teachers to identify the mental processes that academic tasks require and to teach learners those processes; he challenges teachers to teach learners what processes to use, when and how to use them, and how to combine them into strategies for solving problems and accomplishing assignments.

Teachers who wish to follow Sternberg's advice might choose to begin teaching by identifying **instructional objectives**, that is, what should students be able to do as a result of instruction. Second, teachers would analyze the objectives in terms of identifying the **instructional outcomes,** those being the tasks or assignments that students can perform as a result of achieving the instructional objectives. Third, teachers would analyze instructional outcomes in terms of the **cognitive skills** or mental processes required to perform those tasks or assignments. After following these three steps and identifying instructional objectives, instructional outcomes, and cognitive skills involved, the teacher is ready to conduct a **preassessment** (or pretest) to determine what students already know.

Instruction is then based on the results of the preassessment with teachers focusing on teaching directly the cognitive skills needed in order for students to perform the task(s). Following instruction, teachers would conduct a **post-assessment** (or post-test) to evaluate the results of instruction. Further instruction would be based on the results of the post-assessment, that is, whether students had achieved expected outcomes and whether teachers had achieved instructional objectives.

Regardless of which theoretical perspective is adopted by teachers, and, at times, teachers may find themselves taking a rather eclectic approach and borrowing elements from several theoretical bases, it is helpful for teachers to consider if they are structuring their classrooms to satisfy learners' needs or merely their own needs as teachers. Furthermore, if the teachers' goal is to increase teaching effectiveness by facilitating learners' knowledge and skill acquisition, then teachers will engage continuously in a process of self-examination and self-evaluation.

Metacognition

Self-examination and self-evaluation are both types of **metacognitive** thinking. **Metacognition** is a term used to describe what, how, and why people know what they know when they know it. In short, it is thinking about thinking and knowing about knowing. Cognitive psychologists describe metacognition as a characteristic of higher ordered, mature, and sophisticated thinking. Generally speaking, as learners achieve higher levels of cognitive skills, they also increase their metacognitive skills. Therefore, not only should teachers engage in metacognitive thinking, they should model that thinking for their students and encourage them to develop metacognitive skills.

Metacognition can be understood in terms of (a) **metacognitive knowledge** and (b) **metacognitive control** (Flavell, 1987). Basically, metacognitive knowledge is what learners need to know and metacognitive control is what learners need to do. Metacognitive control, therefore, is in the hands of the learner. Teachers cannot control learners' behavior although they can encourage and admonish. The best that teachers can do is help learners expand their metacognitive awareness and knowledge.

Awareness can be increased by talking about metacognition. Flavell has explained that there are three kinds of metacognitive knowledge, those three kinds being (a) **person knowledge**, (b) **task knowledge**, and (c) **strategy knowledge**.

Person knowledge falls into one of three categories: (a) **intraindividual knowledge**, (b) **interindividual knowledge**, and (c) **universal knowledge**. First, **intraindividual knowledge** is what the learner knows or understands about him- or herself. Therefore, it is important that learners have opportunities to learn about themselves, about their interests, abilities, propensities, and so forth. For this reason (among others), it is important that learners have opportunities to learn about their own learning style and their perceptual strengths. It is also helpful for them to have opportunities to examine their personalities, values, and goals.

Furthermore, in a model that recognizes the dynamic nature of instruction, that is, one that recognizes that the learner also knows certain things and can contribute to the classroom, the teacher realizes that she or he is a learner, too. Teachers, then, can benefit from examining their own learning style, perceptual strengths, personalities, values, and goals. Moreover, it can be extremely beneficial for teachers to consider their own instructional style.

Instructional Style Assessment

One instrument that assesses instructional style, the Instructional Style Inventory (Canfield & Canfield, 1988), identifies instructional styles in four general categories (although there also can be combinations of different styles). The four categories are **social**, **independent**, **applied**, and **conceptual**. Briefly stated, the social style is one that describes the teacher who values classroom interactions, who stresses teamwork and group work; the independent style describes the teacher who emphasizes working alone and is likely to rely on self-paced, individualized, and programmed instruction; the applied style is one that stresses real-world experiences and avoids lecture and preparatory reading, but focuses on practicums and site visits, and so forth; finally, the conceptual style is one describing the teacher who is language-oriented and likes highly organized materials and tends to depend on lectures and readings.

Returning to the discussion on metacognitive knowledge, the second kind of person knowledge is **interindividual knowledge**, how learners are alike and how they are different. Again, this is another reason why the recognition of diversity brought about by studying learning styles can inform learners and improve their cognitive performance. As they learn about their own learning style, learners also observe that their classmates have some similarities and some differences when it comes to the various elements or factors in determining learning style. Interindividual knowledge is increased as students realize that there are many different ways to learn.

Finally, the third kind of personal knowledge is **universal knowledge**, the knowledge that there are degrees of understanding. Examples are the realization that short-term memory is fallible and has limited capacity, that people can make mistakes, that it is easier to remember things if they are written down, that memory work requires repetition, and so forth. To examine students' understanding of universal knowledge, teachers might ask students to identify what they know about learning, for example, by asking students to write down on notecards what they know about how people learn things or by brainstorming the question in class.

The second broad category of metacognitive knowledge, according to Flavell, is **task knowledge**. Task knowledge includes several different variables, such as whether information is interesting or boring, or if it is new or familiar, or if it is easy or difficult. Task knowledge enables learners to plan appropriately for undertaking tasks (for example, if something is hard to learn, then it may take more time, more concentration, and more effort) and tells them how to go about accomplishing the task (for example, if the task requires memory, then a memory strategy is needed).

Specific tasks relevant to academic disciplines can be identified by classroom teachers; however, there are academic tasks that are generally applicable to all content areas. These academic tasks include what are broadly referred to as study skills, but that are foundational skills for all learning. They include such tasks as time management, directing attention, processing information, finding main ideas, studying, and taking tests, among others (Weinstein, Schulte, & Palmer, 1988).

Flavell's final category of metacognitive knowledge is **strategy knowledge**, which takes into account how learners can best accomplish particular tasks and how they can be reasonably certain that they have reached their cognitive goals. Strategy knowledge also equips learners to monitor their cognitive activities and to gain confidence in their abilities. To illustrate, if the task is to find main ideas, then learners need strategies for finding main ideas. Strategies for this task include learning (a) to preview or survey reading assignments (reading headings, words in bold print; looking at illustrations and graphic aids); (b) to ask questions (What is this about?, Who is this about?, When did it happen?, Where did it happen?, How did it happen?, Why did it happen?); and (c) to read the first and last sentences in each paragraph (knowing that the first and last sentences in paragraphs are most likely to be topic sentences).

Study Strategies

If the task is to study, then learners need specific strategies for studying. These strategies can include, among others, (a) outlining, mapping, or summarizing text (from books or notes); (b) marking text (using margins for notetaking and summarizing); (c) participating in group review sessions; (d) comparing notes with a friend, tutor, or teacher; (e) getting extra help (from a tutor, teacher, or parent); and (f) going to the library (to get additional information from alternative sources). Of course, strategies such as outlining can be further delineated into specific steps for various kinds of outlines.

Obviously, there is an interaction between person, task, and strategy knowledge. For example, if the task is studying, then a visual learner who learns well by reading (individual characteristic) might choose to go to the library to find an alternative source of information (strategy characteristic); in this example, there is a three-way interaction involving task, individual, and strategy.

Although teachers willingly expend considerable energy teaching students about tasks, they often erroneously assume that students will automatically or tacitly acquire learning strategies. However, the fact is that many students do not acquire these strategies and that even those who may learn some strategies would benefit from direct instruction in the use of specific learning strategies. The research literature indicates that the use of think-aloud protocols, spontaneous private speech, skimming, rereading, context clues, error-detection, grouping skills, and examination/evaluation skills (distinguishing between conceptual versus superficial features, or between major themes and minor details and between decoding and comprehension, between verbatim recall and recall for gist) can significantly enhance learners' performance.

Teachers who incorporate an understanding of the role played by metacognition (especially in teaching middle-school and older students) into their instruction will find that they are preparing their students well for a lifetime of learning. Flavell (1979) explained that metacognition is necessary for the oral communication of information, oral persuasion, oral comprehension, reading comprehension, writing, language acquisition, attention, memory, problem-solving, social cognition, self-control, and self-instruction. It is hard to imagine a task that one might do that wouldn't require metacognition.

A recent critique of education in America includes the observation that the movement to teach basic academic skills in America's schools may have resulted in more students performing well on tests of basic skills; however, thinking skills, not just basic skills, are needed in the real world of jobs, families, and citizenship. To better prepare students for the real world, teachers need to focus on the *process* of learning, teaching students *how to think and learn*. Teaching metacognitive awareness and fostering the development of metacognitive knowledge are steps in the right direction.

Students often say that they like teachers who can motivate students when, in fact, teachers are not responsible for students' motivation. Motivation is a student's responsibility; motivation comes from within the student. However, effective teachers will help students develop self-discipline, self-control, and self-motivation. These skills of self-management can be taught, yet they require a great deal of effort and practice in order for students to gain true proficiency.

When students say that they like or want teachers who motivate them, they are probably referring to some characteristics that teachers possess that are attractive and interesting to learners. So, while it is true that teachers are not responsible for students' motivation, it is also true that teachers can influence motivation, and that teachers can promote and/or inhibit motivation in the classroom by their attitudes and their actions.

One researcher has offered three principles to guide teachers that will lead to greater effectiveness in the classroom (Baxter-Magolda, 1992). Interestingly, each of these principles leads to empowering students and, thus, are motivational in nature.

The first principle is to *validate students as knowers*. This principle is based on the idea of the active learner who brings much to the classroom (the dynamic view of human development). How can teachers validate students? Baxter-Magolda suggests that teachers display a caring attitude towards students. This means that it's appropriate for teachers to take an interest in students, to learn about their likes and dislikes, their interests and hobbies, both in school and outside school. This also means that it's okay for teachers to show enthusiasm and excitement for their classes, not only the subject-matter they teach, but the students they teach as well. It also means, as Carol Tavris (1994) noted, that it's good for teachers to show empathy for students' emotional needs.

Baxter-Magolda also recommends that teachers question authority by example and let students know that they, as teachers, can also be questioned. This means that teachers model critical-thinking skills in the classroom. Teachers can question authority when they examine and evaluate readings—whether from textbooks or other sources. Teachers can question authorities when they teach propaganda techniques, exposing advertising claims and gimmicks. Teachers can question authority when they discuss the media and how so-called news sources shape and form public opinion. There are numerous opportunities for teachers in dealing with current affairs and public opinion to question authority and inculcate in their students critical thinking and higher ordered reasoning skills.

Also, when teachers allow students to question them, teachers are acknowledging that everyone is a learner. Everyone should participate in a lifelong process of continuous learning. It is no shame or disgrace for the teacher to admit that sometimes he or she doesn't know the answer to every question. This gives the teacher the opportunity to show students how adults think, how they have a level of awareness (metacognition) when they don't know something, and about how they go about finding answers to their questions. Teachers who admit that they don't have all the answers thus have the opportunity to show students how answers can be found and/or to reveal to students that there are no easy answers to some of life's most difficult questions.

Third, to validate students as knowers, teachers can value students' opinions, ideas, and comments. Teachers' affirmations include smiles and nods of approval, positive comments (such as, "That's a good answer."), and encouraging cues (such as, "That may seem like a reasonable answer, but can you think of a better answer?" or "Can you explain what you mean by that answer?"). Validating students as knowers also means supporting students' voices, that is, giving them ample opportunities to express their own ideas, to share their opinions, and to make their own contributions to the classroom. These opportunities can include times of oral discussion as well as written assignments.

Jointly Constructed Meaning

Another principle in Baxter-Magolda's guidelines for teaching effectiveness is for teachers and students to recognize that learning is a process of **jointly constructing meaning**. To explain, Baxter-Magolda says that it is important for teachers to dialogue with students (also an important concept in Piagetian theory) and that teachers emphasize mutual learning. Also in agreement with Piagetian principles, Baxter-Magolda recommends that teachers reveal their own thinking processes as they approach subjects and as they analyze and understand new subjects and as they solve problems and reach decisions. She further advises that teachers share leadership and promote collegial learning (group work), acknowledging that individual achievement is not the sole purpose or focus for learning. By allowing students to collaborate, they also will learn significant lessons directly applicable to work situations where most accomplishments are the result of team efforts, not the sole efforts of individuals.

Baxter-Magolda's final principle for teachers is to *situate learning in the students' own experiences.* She suggests that this be done by letting students know that they are wanted in class, by using inclusive language (avoiding ethnic and cultural bias and stereotyping, instead using gender-neutral and inclusive language), and focusing on activities. Activities are important for motivation because they give learners things to do, to become actively involved in, arousing their attention and interest, and giving them an outlet for their physical and mental energy. Activities can have an additional positive benefit in that they can serve to connect students to each other, especially when students are given opportunities to participate in collaborative learning (the way things happen in the "real world") and to work in groups. Finally, in situating learning in students' own experiences, it is important to consider the use of personal stories in class, as appropriate (that is, without violating anyone's right to privacy and confidentiality). Moreover, teachers can share personal stories that allow them to connect with students in a deeper and more personal way.

The child psychologist, Harvard professor, and author of numerous scholarly and popular books, Robert Coles, wrote in 1993 of his experiences teaching in a Boston inner-city high school. He told of his disillusionment and his struggle to claim students' respect and attention so that he could teach them. Finally, there was a classroom confrontation, followed by a self-revelation (that being to show his students what he was like as a person). He shared some of his thoughts and feelings about loneliness. He told about his own boyhood experiences of visiting museums with his mother and what she taught him about art. In the end, he, too, had a revelation; he concluded that when teachers share what we have learned about ourselves with our students, we often can transcend the barriers of class and race. A teacher can change a "me" and a "them" (the students) into an "us." Building camaraderie this way then becomes an optimal starting point for teaching and learning (Coles, 1993). Dr. Coles' experience was that telling his story to the class was a step towards helping his students claim some motivation of their own.

When students assume responsibility for their own motivation, they are learning a lesson of personal empowerment. Unfortunately, although personal empowerment is probably one of the most important lessons anyone ever learns, it is a lesson infrequently taught in classrooms across the country.

Empowerment has at least four components, one of which is self-esteem. A good definition of self-esteem is that it is my opinion of me, your opinion of you. It is what we think and believe to be true about ourselves, not what we think about others and not what they think about us. Self-esteem appears to be a combination of self-efficacy and self-respect as seen against a background of self-knowledge.

Self-efficacy, simply stated, is one's confidence in one's own ability to cope with life's challenges. Self-efficacy refers to having a sense of control over life or, better, over one's responses to life. Experts say that ideas about self-efficacy get established by the time children reach the age of four. Because of this early establishment of either a feeling of control or no control, classroom teachers may find that even primary grade students believe that they have no control over their life and that it makes no difference what they do or how they act. Therefore, it is all the more important that teachers attempt to help all students achieve coping skills and a sense of self-efficacy.

Control, in this definition of self-efficacy, can be examined in regard to external or internal motivators. For example, external motivators include such things as luck and the roles played by others in influencing outcomes. Internal motivators are variables within the individual. To explain, if a student does well on a test and is asked, "How did you do so well on that test?," a student who relies on external motivators might reply, "Well, I just got lucky," or "The teacher likes me." If the student failed the test and is asked why, the student dependent on external motivators might answer, "Well, it wasn't my lucky day," or "The teacher doesn't like me," or "My friends caused me to goof off and not pay attention so I didn't know the answers on the test." A student who relies on internal motivators and who does well on a test may explain, "I am smart and always do well on tests," or "I studied hard and that's why I did well." On the other hand, even the student who relies on internal motivators can do poorly on tests and then may explain, "I'm dumb and that's why I don't do well," or "I didn't think the test was important and I didn't try very hard." Even though students have similar experiences, in regard to issues of control, what is important is how students explain their experiences. If students have external motivators, they are likely to either dismiss their performance (success or failure) as matters of luck or to credit or blame the influence of others. If students have internal motivators, then they are likely to attribute their performance to either their intelligence and skills (ability) or their effort.

Students who have external motivators need help understanding how their behavior contributes to and influences outcomes in school. Students need clarification as to how grades are determined and precise information about how their work is evaluated. Students who have internal motivators but low self-esteem (such as thinking, "I'm dumb") need help identifying their strengths and assets (something that can be accomplished when students are given information about learning styles). Self-efficacy can be enhanced.

Another factor in empowerment is self-respect. Self-respect is believing that one deserves happiness, achievement, and love. Self-respect is treating one's self at least as nicely as one treats other people. Many students are not aware of their internal voices (which are established at an early age). Internal voices are constantly sending messages, either positive or negative. Psychologists say that most of us have either a generally positive outlook on life, and our inner voice sends generally positive messages ("You're okay," "People like you," "Things will be all right," and so forth) or a generally negative outlook on life, and an inner voice sending negative messages ("You're not okay," "You're too fat, skinny, ugly, stupid," and so forth).

Many students need to become aware of their inner voice and how it can be setting them up for failure. They need to learn that they can tell their inner voice to stop sending negative messages, and that they can reprogram their inner voice to be kinder, gentler, and to send positive messages. However, it does require effort, practice, and time to reprogram the inner voice.

Two tools that can help students in the reprogramming process are affirmations and visualizations (Ellis, 1991). Affirmations are statements describing what students want. Affirmations must be personal, positive, and written in the present tense. What makes affirmations effective are details. For example, instead of saying, "I am stupid," students can be encouraged to say, "I am capable. I do well in school because I am organized, I study daily, I get all my work completed on time, and I take my school work seriously." Affirmations must be repeated until they can be said with total conviction.

Visualizations are images students can create whereby they see themselves the way they want to be. For example, if a student wants to improve his or her typing skills, then the student evaluates what it would look like, sound like, and feel like to be a better typist. Once the student identifies the image, then the student has to rehearse that image in her or his mind, including as many details and sensations as possible. Both visualization and affirmation can restructure attitudes and behaviors. They can be tools for students to use to increase their motivation.

Finally, the fourth component of empowerment is self-knowledge. Self-knowledge refers to an individual's strengths and weaknesses, assets and liabilities; self-knowledge comes about as a result of a realistic self-appraisal (and can be achieved by an examination of learning styles). Achieving self-knowledge also requires that students have opportunities to explore their goals and values.

The teacher must reflect continuing optimism for positive change. It is true that adolescent behavior can often be predicted by earlier patterns of behavior. But, many adolescent problem behaviors are not persistent into adulthood and will be resolved. These include "substance abuse, unemployment, and delinquency" (Steinberg & Morris, 2001, p. 86).

Students who know what their goals and values are can more easily see how education will enable them to achieve those goals and values. Conversely, students cannot be motivated when they do not have goals and values, or when they do not know what their goals and values are. In other words, without self-knowledge, motivation is impossible. Therefore, teachers who follow Baxter-Magolda's guidelines for effective instruction and who teach their students about personal empowerment are teachers who realize the importance of motivation and who set the stage for students to claim responsibility for their own successes and failures. Such teachers help students to become motivated to make changes and to accomplish more.

Abuse and Neglect of Children: Factors of Risk and Treatment

The same set of correlated systems that help understand the correlates of the risk of abuse and neglect of children also illuminate the areas in which the antidotes may be found—the child, the family, the community, and the society. (The sources for what follows are Mrazek & Mrazek, 1987; Tzeng, Jackson, & Karlson, 1996; Chalk & King, 1998; and Black, 2000. Further, it must be emphasized that all that follows is based on relational data—no cause-and-effect connections may be scientifically established.)

Children certainly are not the cause of neglect/abuse inflicted on them. But, there are increased risks between a child's characteristics and abuse/neglect. These risk factors include age (young are more likely neglected, older abused), being female (more likely to suffer sexual abuse), or being a child with disabilities leads to more risk for abuse.

Families with the following characteristics all increase the risks of neglect/abuse for children: having existing substance abuse issues, having a history of abuse, having family members who themselves experienced abuse, and having poor parenting/communication skills.

The community that has high rates of unemployment, poverty, crime, or violence is at risk to have more children that experience abuse/neglect. Societal factors that are associated with increased abuse/neglect include an acceptance of violence (in music, games, films, etc.), legal definitions of abuse/neglect that are overly narrow, and a religious or political climate that encourages nonintervention into families that are at risk.

The consideration of factors that promote protection from abuse/neglect which are inherent in the child include personality dimensions (internal locus of control, good social skills, easy temperament, positive disposition), good health, good peer relationships, and above-average intelligence.

The family/parent factors that are associated with reduced incidence of abuse/neglect include household rules and parental monitoring of child, extended family support systems, higher parental education, and family expectations of pro-social behaviors.

The community and societal factors associated with reduced abuse/neglect include accessible social and health services, adequate housing opportunities, good schools, and adults in the community (outside of family) who are available to serve as mentors and role models for children of the community.

References

Batson, C., Polycarpou, M., Harman-Jones, E., Imhoff, H., Mitchener, E., Bednar, L., Klein, T., and Highberger, L. (1997). Empathy and attitudes: Can feeling for a member of a stigmatized group improve feelings toward the group? *Journal of Personality and Social Psychology*, *72*, 105–118.

Black, M. (2000). The roots of child neglect. In R. M. Reece (Ed.), *Treatment of child abuse*; *Common mental health, medical and legal practitioners*. Baltimore, MD: Johns Hopkins University Press.

Brown, R. (1973). *A first language: The early stages*. Cambridge, MA: Harvard University Press.

Chalk, R., and King, R. (1988). *Violence in families*: *Assessing prevention and treatment programs*. Washington, D.C.: National Academy Press, 41–50.

Erikson, E. (1972). Play and actuality. In M. W. Piers (Ed.), *Play and development* (pp. 127–167). New York: Norton.

Fabes, R., Eisenberg, N., Nyman, M., and Michealieu, Q. (1991). Young children's appraisals of others' spontaneous emotional reactions. *Developmental Psychology*, *27*, 858–866.

Gilligan, C. (1982). *In a different voice*: *Psychological theory and women's development*. Cambridge, MA: Harvard University Press.

Hoffman, M. (1987). The contribution of empathy to justice and moral judgment. In N. Eisenberg and J. Strayer (Eds.), *Empathy and its development* (pp. 47–80). Cambridge: Cambridge University Press.

Kohlberg, L., Levine, C., and Hewer, A. (1983). *Moral stages*: *A current formulation and response to the critics*. Basel, Switzerland: S. Karger.

Maccoby, E. E. (2000). Parenting and its effects on children: On reading and misreading behavior genetics. *Annual Review of Psychology*, *57*, 1–27.

Martin, G. and Clark, R. (1982). Distress in crying in neonates: Species and peer specificity. *Developmental Psychology, 18*, 3–9.

Mrazek, P., and Mrazek, D. (1987). Resilience in child maltreatment victims: A conceptual exploration. *Child Abuse and Neglect*, *11*, 357–366.

Piaget, J., and Inhelder, B. (1969). *The psychology of the child.* New York: Basic Books.

Saltz, R., and Saltz, E. (1986). Pretend play training and its outcomes. In G. Fein and M. Rivking (Eds.), *The young child at play: Reviews of research* (Vol. 4, pp. 155–173). Washington, D.C.: National Association for the Education of Young Children.

Steinberg, L., and Morris, A. (2001). Adolescent development. In *Annual Review of Psychology, 52*, 83–110.

Tzeng, O., Jackson, J., and Karlson, H. (1991). *Theories of child abuse and neglect: Differential perspective, summaries, and evaluations.* New York: Praeger Press.

Vygotsky, L. (1978). *Mind in society.* Cambridge, MA: Harvard University Press.

Youngblade, L., and Dunn, J. (1995). Individual differences in young children's pretend play with mother and sibling: Links to relationships and understanding of other people's feelings and beliefs. *Child Development*, *66*, 1472–1492.

Visual and Performing Arts Review

In the Visual and Performing Arts section, you will have the opportunity to admire and learn of great performances given by the giants of the art and music worlds and of the stage. Preparing for the Visual and Performing Arts section of the test with this review will help you deliver a great performance on the CSET.

The Visual and Performing Arts section of the CSET focuses on the four major disciplines of the arts: visual arts, dance, music, and drama. Each of the disciplines is addressed directly in both historical and comparative contexts. The test questions may require you to blend knowledge of more than one of the artistic disciplines; however, they usually are more concerned with a general understanding of aesthetic principles than names and dates of specific artists, works of art, etc.

Aesthetic Perception and Creative Expression

The visual and performing arts have served to express humanity's basic spiritual beliefs and the need to organize its environment from prehistoric times to the present. Seventeen thousand years ago, before cities and settled villages, Paleolithic people at Lascaux (modern France)—and at Altimira (modern Spain) about 2,000 years later—produced realistic animal paintings on cave walls in an attempt to capture the essences of the creatures they hunted and encountered. The urge to create art existed even earlier in the Paleolithic period, and numerous small female figures (now called Venuses) and carved weapons dating from perhaps as early as 30,000 B.C.E. have been discovered in Europe. Megalithic structures, such as Stonehenge in England, and monuments of ancient civilizations, such as the Egyptian pyramids, were precisely calculated architectural forms that answered sophisticated needs of astronomical calculation, paid homage to the mysteries and power of the sun and stars, and attempted to master the passage to the afterlife. Tribal people throughout history have used dance and music to control their environment, communicate with animals, and comprehend the unseen world, as well as to merely celebrate; they have also produced masks, weavings, textiles, pottery, and jewelry of harmonious form and color and complex abstract patterns.

Beginning with the first great civilized society, the Sumerians in Mesopotamia more than 5,000 years ago, the peoples of the world have continued on a consistent path in the area of fine, applied, and performing arts. Visual fine art has come to mean a self-conscious creation of aesthetically sophisticated works, usually by one individual, in an attempt to further knowledge, expand style and technology, and create beauty. Applied art is practical and often evolves directly from the needs, culture, and tastes of a community; crafts and decorative art, utilitarian or commercial objects in which quality of technique is primary, are examples. Increasingly, the lines between fine art and craft have become blurred, so that it is no longer necessary to arbitrarily enthrone a work of art merely because it is, for example, a painting rather than a piece of pottery or jewelry. In the performing arts, folk dance and music are a natural outgrowth of a community's recreational, entertainment, celebratory, and ritualistic needs. The great masterpieces of ballet, opera, and classical music each represent the conscious manipulation of form and idea in a new way to create an individualistic work, usually for the purposes of an audience's edification and amusement.

Venus of Willendorf
c. 25,000–20,000 B.C.E. Stone Museum of Natural History, Vienna.

All of the arts on all levels may be judged as either successful or not, as good or mediocre, and have a beauty and legitimacy that operates on an aesthetic level and arises from its culture.

The visual and performing arts basically encompass the categories of sculpture, painting and graphics, architecture, dance, music, and theater. Each of these has its own rules and requirements and aesthetic appeal, its own distinct way of satisfying a basic human means of expression.

Sculpture is concerned with molding shapes in three-dimensional forms. Sculptures may be cast—molten metals poured into molds to create cast-bronze figures—and such works would include ancient Greek statues of warriors, equestrian monuments of the Italian Renaissance, Auguste Rodin's *Thinker*, and Frederic Bartholdi's enormous Statue of Liberty. They may also be carved—from wood, stone, or marble—shaped from clay, or in the twentieth century, welded together from metal pieces.

Painting is a two-dimensional means of re-creating reality or arranging abstract forms in color on a flat surface. Surfaces have traditionally been walls, wooden panels, canvas, paper and parchment, even decorative objects such as vases. The color is usually applied with a brush, using pigments mixed with media such as linseed oil or water. Types of painting include watercolor, oil, tempera, and acrylic; for frescoes, pigments are applied directly over wet plaster to seal in the art on a wall or ceiling. Other two-dimensional art, in color or black and white, are **drawing**—with graphite (pencil), ink applied by pen or brush, and chalk or crayons—and **printmaking**. In etching, woodcuts, lithographs, and the many variations on these methods, multiple copies of a drawing are made by creating either a raised or recessed surface (metal, wood, or stone) that takes ink and pressing paper against the surface.

Architecture is the conscious organization of space and form to provide a structure for living, working, worshipping, or for other residential or civic needs. Great architecture has always been intimately connected with new technologies and building materials, as well as with the immediate cultural needs of a community, city, or nation. Gothic cathedrals, for example, soar to the heavens with massive vertical elements to reflect the religious devotion of medieval Europe. The simple shapes and unadorned facades of many twentieth-century buildings reveal a fascination with the era's ease of using such materials as glass, steel, and concrete and a rejection of what was considered the overly decorated architecture of the previous century.

> **The great masterpieces of ballet, opera, and classical music each represent the conscious manipulation of form and idea.**
>
> *Fast Facts*

Dance is an art form based on physical movement and expression—by humans singly, or in couples or groups. Folk and tribal dancing are often related to communal celebration or religious ritual. Dance created to entertain an audience by one person may be choreographed and worked out in strict steps and gestures, such as in ballet or musical theater.

Music is the arrangement of sounds for voice and musical instruments, and, like dance, requires training and repetitive practice. For most of history, music has been an outgrowth of a community's or an ethnic group's need to celebrate, and has often been linked to story-telling or poetry. Traditional instruments have been indigenous variations on drums, horns, pipes (such as flutes), and hollow boxes fitted with vibrating strings (such as lyres or lutes). In Europe, a system of musical notation developed during the Middle Ages and the use of notation (written symbolic indications of pitch and duration of tones) is a convenient way to distinguish "art" (or classical, or complexly composed) music from folk and ethnic music. Since the seventeenth century, orchestral instruments of the West have multiplied to include pianos, saxophones, clarinets, cellos, and in our own era, electronic synthesizers.

Theater is the performance, for the sake of an audience's education or entertainment, of a story, usually of drama, comedy, or some combination thereof. The West's tradition of theater originated chiefly with the ancient Greeks—the tragedies of Aeschylus and Sophocles, the comedies of Aristophanes—and many feel reached its high point in the late sixteenth and early seventeenth centuries in England with the plays of William Shakespeare, who is revered throughout the world for his mastery of the form. Theater requires vocal declamation, acting, costumes, sometimes masks, usually a scenic backdrop or constructed set, and poetic expression. Music is often an integral part of the performance as well. Theater may be said to encompass all the art forms, since a theatrical production of ballet, opera, or musical drama/comedy can include all the disciplines, employing set decoration, costuming, dance, song, and instrumental music.

Cultural Heritage

Artistic expression in dance, theater, music, and the visual arts has undergone many stylistic changes in the passing centuries of the world's civilizations. It can be affected by the era's spirit, by evolving economic and social changes, and by religion. The form the art takes, and the way it fits into the lives of a people, depends on its geographical source and the ethnic group from which it originates. For example, one form of dance in Europe by the seventeenth century evolved into the sophisticated high-art form of ballet, which is both entertaining and cerebral. In India, four types of dance are considered classical, but these have very different forms and purposes than European ballet. Even within a society, the representations and needs of an art form change with the cultural forces of an age. While the religious-symbolic paintings, sculptures, and manuscript illuminations of the Middle Ages saw no need to relate human beings realistically to each other in size, or place them in a natural-looking environment or realistic space, the Renaissance artists, seeing humans as the center of the universe and seeking rational knowledge, depicted a world of visual beauty, of perfectly observed persons in perfectly proportioned environments.

In theater, twentieth-century drama may emphasize psychological portraits of individuals and realistic dialogue. But the ancient Greeks sought to portray—using masks and chorus (a group of dancer-singers) commentary on the main action—great themes of fate, honor, and pride. In the tradition of Japanese Noh plays, which originated in the fifteenth century and derive from Zen Buddhism, five plays separated by three comic interludes are marked by stylized acting, masks, mime, and folk dance.

In music, the system of tonal scales and preferences is often unique to a culture: for example, the Chinese prefer the pentatonic scale of five notes, while the West has primarily used a scale of seven notes (eight with the repeated first note for an octave). Indian musical pieces are often built upon *ragas* (meaning "mood" or "color"), which are melodic patterns of five to seven tones. Indian compositions feature repetitive patterns and use scales whose octaves have twenty-two intervals, or steps.

Architecture is related to the most basic needs of a society and the technology and materials available to a culture or in a geographic location. Because the ancient Egyptians needed grandeur in their funerary monuments and they were able to master the complicated calculations to perfectly cut and arrange huge stones, the magnificent pyramids were created. Architecture is the measure of the prevailing philosophy of an age. The Renaissance architects, for example, sought to express their rediscovery of ancient humanism and the search for knowledge, as well as their newfound joy in earthly life and beauty, through the application of perfect proportions, the use of classical engineering techniques, and by perfecting of the art of dome construction.

Historical Survey

Visual Arts

Paleolithic people in Europe painted animal pictures on the cave walls at Lascaux and Altimira about 15,000 to 13,000 B.C.E. Some examples of even older art, dating from 30,000 to 20,000 B.C.E., are the various "Venuses"— small stylized stone carvings of women as symbols of fertility, found in modern France, Italy, and Austria. The artists of the ancient civilizations of Sumer, Babylon, and Assyria were skilled in carving even the hardest rocks, such as granite and basalt, into narratives of battles and historical records. Egyptian statues, like their architectural monuments the pyramids, were often of colossal size, to further exalt the power of the society's leaders and gods. The art of ancient Greece has its roots in the Minoan civilization on the island of Crete, which flourished about 2500–1400 B.C.E. The palace at Knossos is known for characteristic wall paintings revealing a people enamored of games, leisure, and the beauty of the sea. The mainland Greeks of the classical period, about a thousand years later, were fascinated by physical beauty. Their Olympian gods were fashioned in the human image, and a universe of perfection, guided by a master plan, was recreated in their idealized and gracefully proportioned sculptures, architecture, and paintings. In the Hellenistic period, these various objects came to be appreciated as art for their beauty alone.

The culture of Rome excelled in engineering and building, whose purpose it was to efficiently organize a vast empire and provide an aesthetic environment for private and public use. The Romans built temples, roads, bath complexes, civic buildings, palaces, and aqueducts. One of the greatest of their artistic and engineering accomplishments was the massive-domed temple of all the gods, the Pantheon, which is today one of the most perfectly preserved of all classical-period buildings.

The early Christian period era borrowed the basilica form of Roman architecture for its churches, particularly evident in churches in the town of Ravenna in northeastern Italy. The seventh-century church of San Vitale echoes the mosaic mastery of the eastern Roman, or Byzantine, empire in Constantinople (which flourished as a center of civilization for a thousand years after the decline of Rome). Its grandiose apse mosaic depicts Emperor Justinian and Empress Theodora.

The Romanesque style of art and architecture was preeminent from about 800 to 1200. By then many local styles, including the decorative arts of the Byzantines, the Near East, and the German and Celtic tribes, were contributing to European culture. Common features of Romanesque churches are round arches, vaulted ceilings, and heavy walls that are ornately decorated—primarily with symbolic figures of Christianity, the realism of which had become less and less important as they were subordinated to the message.

Gothic art flourished in Europe for the next 300 years. The cathedrals in this style are some of the purest expressions of an age. They combine a continued search for engineering and structural improvement with stylistic features that convey a relentless verticality, a reach toward heaven, and the unbridled adoration of God. Soaring and airy, these cathedrals were constructed using such elements as flying buttresses and pointed arches and vaults, and were decorated by a profusion of sculptures and stained-glass windows that were, for the worshippers, visual encyclopedias of Christian teachings and stories.

The Italian Renaissance's roots are found as early as the 1300s, when the painter Giotto began to compose his figures into groups and depict expressive human gestures. During the fifteenth century, art, architecture, literature, and music were invigorated. Renaissance artists developed new forms and revived classical styles and values, with the belief in the importance of human experience on Earth. Great sculptors approached true human characterization and realism. Lorenzo Ghiberti created the bronze doors of the

View from the Apse of San Vitale, Ravenna, Italy, 526 B.C.E.–47 C.E.

Florence Baptistry (early fifteenth century) and Donatello produced *Gattamelata*, the first equestrian statue since the Roman era.

Architecture, in the hands of Filippo Brunelleschi and Leon Battista Alberti, revived the Greek elements and took a scientific, ordered approach, one similarly expressed in painting, with the emphasis on the calculated composition of figures in space known as perspective. The Renaissance artists sought to produce works of perfect beauty and engaged in a constant search for knowledge, most often portraying religious subjects and wealthy patrons. The stylistic innovations of such fifteenth-century painters as Masaccio, Paolo Uccello, Fra Angelico, Piero della Francesca, Andrea Mantegna, and Sandro Botticelli were built upon in the High Renaissance of the next century.

Art became more emotional and dramatic, color and movement were heightened, compositions were more vigorous, and there were increased references to classical iconography and the pleasures of an idyllic golden age. These aspects can be seen in Michelangelo's magnificent Sistine Chapel frescoes and his powerful sculptures of *David* and *Moses,* Leonardo's *Mona Lisa,* Raphael's *School of Athens* fresco, and the increasingly dramatic and colorful works of the Venetian and northern Italian masters Titian, Correggio, Giorgione, and Bellini. The northern European Renaissance also emphasized a renewed interest in the visible world, and works by Albrecht Durer, Lucas Cranach, Matthias Grunewald, and Albrecht Altdorfer reveal an emphasis on the symbolism of minutely observed details and accurate realism based on observation of reality rather than prescribed rules.

> ▸ *Fast Facts*
>
> **Renaissance artists sought to produce works of perfect beauty and engaged in a constant search for knowledge.**

Presaged by the works of the Venetian artist Tintoretto (the radiating *Last Supper*) and El Greco in Spain (*View of Toledo; The Immaculate Conception*), the baroque period of the seventeenth century produced artists who added heightened drama to the forms of Renaissance art. Caravaggio (*The Calling of Saint Matthew; The Conversion of Saint Paul*) and the sculptor Gianlorenzo Bernini (*Saint Teresa in Ecstasy*) in Italy; the Flemish masters Peter Paul Rubens (*Marie de Medici Lands at Marseilles)* and Jacob Jordaens portrayed figures in constant motion, draperies of agitated angles, and effects of lighting and shadow that amplified emotional impact and mystery.

In this spirit followed such painters of court life and middle-class portraiture as Velazquez, Rembrandt, Anthony Van Dyck, and Frans Hals. Rembrandt used expressive brushwork and mysterious light contrasts to enliven genre painting and portraiture, particularly of groups. Rembrandt's influence has remained potent, since his art appears to impart universal truths, and sections of his compositions glow with a mysterious inner light often unrelated to realistic effects (*The Night Watch,* many self-portraits).

The art of the early eighteenth century is often called rococo. Painters like Jean-Antoine Watteau (*Embarkation for Cythera*), Giambattista Tiepolo (frescoes of the Wurzberg Residenz), Francois Boucher, and Jean-Honore Fragonard, often for decorative wall and ceiling schemes, turned the agitated drama of the baroque into light, pastel-toned, swirling compositions that seem placed in an idyllic land of a golden age. In the seventeenth and eighteenth centuries, European artists also responded to middle-class life and everyday objects and created genre paintings (Jan Vermeer, Adriaen van Ostade, Jean-Baptiste Chardin). Jean-Baptiste Greuze in France and William Hogarth in England endowed their everyday subjects with a wealth of narrative detail that aimed to impart a specific moral message.

Such narrative art combined in the nineteenth century with romantic literature—Goethe, Byron, Shelley, Scott, Wordsworth, and others—and political events to produce works with a political point of view or a story to tell, in a variety of styles. Jacques-Louis David used a severe classical sculptural style (neoclassical) in his paintings to revive classical art and ennoble images of the French Revolution and Napoleon's empire (*The Death of Marat; The Oath of the Horatii; Napoleon in His Study*). Neoclassical sculpture revived the aloof severity and perfection of form of ancient art (Jean-Antoine Houdon, Antonio Canova, Bertel Thorvaldsen, Horatio Greenough)—a style also reflected in Thomas Jefferson's architectural designs for his Monticello home and the University of Virginia.

The Spanish painter Francisco de Goya commented powerfully on political events in his painting *May 3, 1808*. In France, Eugene Delacroix (*The Death of Sardanapalus; Liberty Leading the People*) and Theodore Gericault (*The Raft of the Medusa*) imbued subjects from literature, the Bible, exotic lands, and current events with dramatic and heroic intensity. The grandeur and transcendence of nature, the emotional reaction to inner dreams and metaphysical truths of romanticism are seen in the work of such mystical artists as England's William Blake, Henry Fuselli, and John Martin, and America's Thomas Cole. Caspar David Friedrich in Germany and the English Pre-Raphaelites (William Holman Hunt, John Everett Millais, Dante Gabriel Rossetti, Ford Madox Brown, Arthur Hughes, and others) endowed their keenly observed, minutely detailed works with a romantic spirit of poetic yearning and literary references, and accurately re-created the natural world in brilliantly colored landscapes.

In the first half of the nineteenth century, landscape painting in England reached a zenith with the works of Constable and Turner. Turner's awe-inspiring landscapes form a bridge between the spirit of romanticism and the expressionistic brushwork and realism of the Barbizon School in France, whose chief painters were Charles Daubigny and Jean-Baptiste-Camille Corot. Beginning with Barbizon, the French painters of the nineteenth century concentrated more and more on the reporterlike depiction of everyday life and the natural environment in a free, painterly (gesture and brushwork) style.

The realist pioneers were Gustave Courbet (*The Stone Breakers; A Burial at Ormans*), Jean-Francois Millet (*The Sower; The Angelus*), and Honoré Daumier (*The Third-Class Carriage*). Renowned as a political caricaturist, Daumier's chief medium was the lithograph and paved the way for the stylistic and subject innovations of the Impressionists. Traditional means of composing a picture, academic methods of figure modeling, of color relations, and accurate and exact rendering of people and objects, were rejected in favor of an art that emphasized quickly observed and sketched moments from life, the relation of shapes and forms and colors, the effects of light, and the act of painting itself.

Beginning with Edouard Manet (*Le Déjeuner sur l'Herbe; Olympia*) in the 1860s, French artists continually blurred the boundaries of realism and

The Death of Marat
Jacques Louis David, 1793. Royal Museums of Fine Arts, Brussels.

abstraction, and the landscapes and everyday-life paintings of such Impressionist artists as Claude Monet, Camille Pissarro, Auguste Renoir, Alfred Sisley, and Edgar Degas gave way to the more experimental arrangements of form and color of the great Postimpressionists—Paul Gauguin, Vincent Van Gogh, Georges Seurat, and Toulouse-Lautrec. Auguste Rodin produced powerful sculptures with the freedom of Impressionist style.

Greatly influenced by Japanese art and particularly the flattened space, distinctive shapes, and strong colors of Japanese woodblock prints, artists from Manet and Degas to the American Impressionist Mary Cassatt, from Toulouse-Lautrec to the Nabis (Edouard Vuillard, Pierre Bonnard, and Maurice Denis) used paintings, pastels, and lithography to further break down the boundaries between representational art and abstraction. The new freer form of art, centered around the personality of the artist and celebrating personal style and the manipulation of form and color, in the late nineteenth and early twentieth centuries evolved in a number of directions.

Some artists turned inward to explore mystical, symbolic, and psychological truths: Symbolists, Expressionists, and exponents of art nouveau, such as Odilon Redon, Jan Toorop, Edvard Munch (*The Scream*), James Ensor (*The Entry of Christ into Brussels*), Gustav Klimt (*The Kiss*), Ernst Kirchner, and Max Pechstein. Others pursued formal innovations, among them Paul Cézanne, Henri Matisse, Pablo Picasso, Georges Braque, and Juan Gris. Picasso's Cubism (*Les Demoiselles d'Avignon*) seemed the most direct call for the total destruction of realistic depiction; his use of African and Oceanic tribal art, and his emphasis on taking objects apart and reassembling them—thus showing a subject's multiplicity of aspects and dissolving time and space—led to similar experiments by Fernand Leger, Marcel Duchamp, the sculptors Alexander Archipenko and Jacques Lipchitz, and the Italian Futurist Umberto Boccioni (*Unique Forms of Continuity in Space*).

Pure abstraction, with little or no relation to the outside world, was approached in the more emotional, expressionistic, and color-oriented paintings of Wassily Kandinsky, Roger Delauney, and Paul Klee. More cerebral arrangements of abstract geometrical shapes and colors were the mark of Kasimir Malevich, Piet Mondrian, and the Bauhaus School of Design in Germany, whose stripped-down, simplified, and usually geometrically oriented aesthetic influenced architecture, industrial and commercial design, sculpture, and the graphic arts for half a century.

Fast Facts ➤ **A new, freer form of art, appearing in the late nineteenth and early twentieth centuries, evolved in a number of directions.**

In architecture can be seen the most obvious results of this new tradition, from the simplified, sleek structures of Le Corbusier and Walter Gropius to the boxlike glass skyscrapers of Philip Johnson. The pioneering giant of twentieth-century architecture was Frank Lloyd Wright, whose rejection of eclectic decorative styles of the previous century's architecture and use of new engineering techniques paralleled the Bauhaus aesthetic. From the early 1900s, Wright's buildings (the Robie House, Fallingwater, and Tokyo's Imperial Hotel) exhibited a personal and bold originality, based on a philosophy of "organic architecture," a belief that the form of a structure should be dictated by its natural surroundings, purpose, and building materials.

Inspired by the psychoanalytic writings of Sigmund Freud and Carl Jung, the subconscious and the metaphysical became another important element in art, especially in the work of the Surrealist artists Salvador Dali (*The Persistence of Memory*), Giorgio de Chirico, Max Ernst, Rene Magritte, Joan Miro, and Yves Tanguy. Important sculptors who manipulated abstract shapes and were influenced by tribal arts in the twentieth century include Constantin Brancusi, Henry Moore, Hans Arp, and Alberto Giacometti; Alexander Calder created floating

Shop Block, The Bauhaus.
Walter Gropius. 1925–1926, Dessau, Germany.

assemblies called mobiles, and Louise Nevelson made constructions and wall sculptures from scraps of everyday objects.

Obsession with self and with abstraction also led to the major American art movement after World War II, known as Abstract Expressionism. The chief proponents of this style were Clifford Still, Jackson Pollock, Willem de Kooning, and Robert Motherwell. Other Americans took this movement into the area of color-field painting, a cooler, more reserved formalism of simple shapes and experimental color relationships. Artists in this movement include Mark Rothko, Barnett Newman, Joseph Albers, and Ad Reinhardt.

Other important trends in American art in the twentieth century were reflective of a democratic and consumer society. The muralists and social realists between the wars created art that was physically interesting and whose subjects were accessible to the average person. John Sloan, George Bellows, Edward Hopper, Thomas Hart Benton, Grant Wood, and John Stuart Curry were among those who celebrated the American scene in paintings, and frequently in murals for public buildings and through widely available fine prints. The great Mexican muralists, who usually concentrated on political themes—Diego Rivera, Jose Clemente Orozco, and David Siqueiros—brought their work to the public both in Mexico and in the United States. The icons of American popular culture found their way, in the movement known as Pop Art, into canvases by Andy Warhol, Robert Indiana, Larry Rivers, Jasper Johns, Roy Lichtenstein, and Robert Rauschenberg.

Three Flags
Jasper Johns, 1958. Collection of Mr. and Mrs. Burton Tremaine, Meriden, CT.

Music

In the ancient world, Egyptian, Sumerian, and Hebrew cultures used song and such instruments as lyres, harps, drums, flutes, cymbals, and trumpets. The ancient Greeks accompanied the recitation of poetry with the stringed lyre, and Athenian drama was accompanied by the *aulos* or double-piped oboe (an instrument used in the worship of Dionysus), and choral songs were heard between recited passages.

In the early Christian era, plainsong, or unaccompanied religious chant, was codified and arranged, with early forms of music notation, by Pope Gregory the Great (late sixth century). This is the origin of Gregorian chant. By the twelfth and thirteenth centuries, the important form of polyphony, upon which the distinctive art music of the West is based, enabled supportive melodies to be added to the main chant. The basic form of music notation, representing pitch through the use of a staff, was invented by the Italian Benedictine monk Guido d'Arezzo. Throughout the later Middle Ages both religious and secular polyphonic music was composed, and melodies and rhythms became more diversified: new musical forms included the ballade, the rondeau, and the virelai of the troubadours. The first polyphonic setting of the Catholic mass was composed by Guillaume de Machaut in the fourteenth century.

During the Renaissance, the spirit of humanism and rationalism pervaded polyphonic music, technical problems of composition were eagerly resolved, and music began to be seen as a mark of culture. More and more emphasis was placed upon secular music and dance and instrumental music ensembles, as well as on increasingly complex combinations of voices and instruments. Major composers were Giovanni da Palestrina, Josquin des Pres, Orlando di Lasso, William Byrd, and Giovanni Gabrieli.

Baroque music of the seventeenth and early eighteenth centuries employed a greater complexity of contrapuntal, or multimelodic, form, and the beginnings of harmony, the use of colorful instrumental ensembles, and great drama and emotion. The new dramatic forms became popular entertainment, particularly the operas of Claudio Monteverdi (*The Coronation of Poppea*). Other innovative forms included the oratorio, the cantata, the sonata, the suite, the concerto, and the fugue. The great works of baroque music were composed by Dietrich Buxtehude, Johann Pachelbel, Alessandro Scarlatti, Antonio Vivaldi (*The Four Seasons*), Henry Purcell, Jean Phillipe Rameau, George Frederic Handel (*The Messiah; Israel in Egypt*), and Johann Sebastian Bach (Brandenberg concertos; *Saint Matthew Passion*).

The greatest composers of the classical period of the latter half of the eighteenth century, marked by clarity of form, logical thematic development, and strict adherence to sonata form, were Franz Joseph Haydn and Wolfgang Amadeus Mozart. Mozart's structurally exquisite works approach perfection of form while adding to music inventive melodic diversity. Mozart wrote 41 symphonies, as well as such innovative operas as *The Marriage of Figaro* and *The Magic Flute*. The German composer Ludwig van Beethoven (Fifth and Ninth symphonies, *Moonlight* and *Pathetique* sonatas) ushered in the romantic school of symphonic music. His symphonies and piano sonatas, concertos, and string quartets explode with dramatic passion, expressive melodies and harmonies, and complex thematic development.

Much of the romantic music that followed was less formal and more expressive, often associated with grandiose concepts and literary themes, and increasingly more colorful instrumentally. Art songs, piano concertos and sonatas, and symphonic poems (which seek to paint a musical picture or tell a story) became important forms for romantic composers. These included Fredric Chopin (mainly piano music, some of which he called nocturnes), Hector Berlioz (*Symphonie Fantastique; Les Troyans*), Franz Liszt (*Mephisto Waltz,* piano concertos), Richard Strauss (*Also Sprach Zarathustra, Don Juan*, the operas *Salome* and *Elektra*), and Felix Mendelssohn (four symphonies, incidental music to *A Midsummer Night's Dream*). Other important symphonic composers of the nineteenth century were Robert Schumann, Johannes Brahms, Peter Ilich Tchaikovsky, and Gustav Mahler.

Throughout the century, musical development continued in the direction of a greater richness of harmony, a more varied use of musical instruments and orchestral color, and a greater use of chromaticism (the freedom to use tones not related to the key of the composition).

Other important influences in nineteenth-century music include the use of ethnic influences or folk melodies and music of a nationalistic vein, as well as of popular song—often linked to composers who were outstanding melodists and harmonic innovators—pieces such as this were written by Giacomo Rossini (*The Barber of Seville; William Tell*), Georges Bizet (*Carmen*), Giuseppe Verdi (*Aida; La Traviata*), Giacomo Puccini (*La Boheme; Tosca*), the American Louis Moreau Gottschalk (*A Night in the Tropics; The Banjo*), and the Russians—Mikhail Glinka (*A Life for the Tsar*), Alexander Borodin (*Prince Igor, In the Steppes of Central Asia*), Modest Mussorgsky (*Boris Gudonov, A Night on Bald Mountain*), and Nicholas Rimsky-Korsakov (*Russian Easter Overture, Sherherazade*).

One of the great innovators in opera, Richard Wagner, sought to create a new form of music drama, using continuous music and relentless, swirling harmonies to underlie massive spectacle and recitative, or sung dialogue. Mussorgsky and Wagner's idiomatic and chromatic harmonies greatly influenced the French "impressionist" composers Claude Debussy (*La Mer; Prelude to the Afternoon of a Faun; Children's Corner Suite*) and Maurice Ravel (*Rhapsodie Espagnole; Mother Goose Suite; Tombeau de Couperin*), who for the most part eschewed the traditional larger forms and wrote emotional, dramatic, and colorful tone pictures and sonatas, using oriental tonalities and free rhapsodic forms.

The concert music of the twentieth century increasingly endeavored to enlarge the boundaries of rhythm, form, and harmony, seemingly parallel to the direction in the visual arts away from traditional structure and melodic-harmonic connections with listeners and toward more personal or intellectual experiments in abstraction. Thus, Igor Stravinsky may be seen as the musical equivalent of Picasso, as a composer who, during the years before World War I, broke apart rhythms and introduced radical harmonies in works like *The Rite of Spring* and *Petrushka,* which set the stage for further trends away from traditional ideas of tonality and harmony. Francis Poulenc (*Les Biches*) and Stravinsky sought to use the new rhythms and harmonies in more structurally clear, and less orchestrally dense, neoclassical pieces. The Austrian composers Arnold Schoenberg, Anton von Webern, and Alban Berg employed a new, twelve-tone system, which was a highly intellectualized method of composing music without a fixed key and by establishing an arbitrary "tone row."

Ethnic and popular influences continued to exert an important pull in the creation of twentieth-century music. Folk music was a major element in the works of the English composers Ralph Vaughan Williams and Gustav Holst, of the Hungarian composers Béla Bartók and Zoltan Kodaly, and often in the music of

Stravinsky and the Soviet Union's Sergei Prokofiev and Aram Khachaturian. Ragtime, blues, jazz, and other popular folk, dance, and commercial music provided material for some of the most innovative and exciting work in twentieth-century music: Stravinsky's *Ragtime for Eleven Instruments* and *A Soldier's Tale;* Ravel's *Les Enfants et Les Sortileges* and Piano Concerto in G; Darius Milhaud's *La Creation du Monde* and *Le Boeuf sur le Toit;* Kurt Weill's *Threepenny Opera;* Erik Satie's *Parade;* George Gershwin's *Rhapsody in Blue* and *Porgy and Bess;* and many pieces by Poulenc, Paul Hindemith, Leonard Bernstein, and Bohuslav Martinu. Composers after World War II continued to employ the intellectual methods of Schoenberg and to experiment with tape-recorded sound (Edgard Varese) and conceptual music based on indeterminacy or chance (John Cage). Since the 1970s, American music has seen a return to romanticism, reflected in the renewed interest in the music of Samuel Barber and David Diamond and in the lush scores of David Del Tredici (*Final Alice).* The minimalists, whose work is built upon gradual shifts of consistently repeated melodies and harmonies, include Philip Glass (*Einstein on the Beach)* and John Adams (*Nixon in China).*

Dance, Theater, Opera, Popular Musical Theater, and Ethnic/Folk Traditions

Tribal people believe that through imitative dance they can gain knowledge of the mysterious powers of nature and influence the unseen world. Most dancing of this kind is communal. Dances of the ancient civilizations were often reserved for priests and religious rituals. But even the pharaohs of ancient Egypt enjoyed dancing as spectacle, and the ancient Greeks held dancing in high esteem, establishing many different styles for different purposes: the *gymnopedia,* for example, was a vigorous dance for athletic young men, and the *dithyramb* was a processional dance employing poetry and narrative, from which Greek drama arose. Romans enjoyed dancing as entertainment and pioneered the use of pantomime.

During the Middle Ages, the common folk enjoyed dancing, much of it related to fertility or seasonal rituals such as Maypole and wedding dances. The frenzied dance of death was the popular response to the spread of the plague in Europe, and dances in parades and pageants were also popular. Secular dance with more formalized steps and forms became important among the upper classes after the Renaissance period. Stylized and formalized dances included the pavanne, the galliard, the sarabande, the gigue, the minuet, the gavotte, and the chaconne.

Among Western and non-Western cultures alike the folk traditions of the performing arts often link the disciplines of dance, theater, and music. Ethnic dance with the longest and most sophisticated tradition is the classical dance of India, of which there are four main schools. Kathakali is the most theatrical of the Indian dances: actor-dancers perform stories based on mythological tales, and extensive use is made of costumes, masks, drums, makeup, and shouts.

Bharata Natyam, of southern India, is the oldest form, whose principles were described in Hindu scriptures 2,000 years ago. It requires extensive body movements, complex rhythms for the feet, and complex facial movements and hand gestures. Kathek is the Moslem-influenced dance of northern India, which values virtuosity and emotional expression. Manipuri dancing is strictly religious, and one of the annual village dance festivals is a ballet of the creation of the world. Indian dance has exerted great influence over the court and temple dances of Indonesia, Thailand, Japan, and other Asian countries.

The folk traditions of the performing arts often link the disciplines of dance, theater, and music.

Fast Facts

Dance is primarily linked with theatrical entertainments in China (the opera) and Japan. Japanese Kabuki theater employs masks, singing, and dancing in a highly stylized manner, and the Noh plays of Japan are dance-dramas with stylized scenery and acting. In Indonesia, the Javanese *gamalen,* an orchestra of tuned percussion instruments consisting of up to eighty pieces, is played softly to accompany song and gentle dancing, and powerfully for heroic dances. Native American tribal dances are essentially ritualistic (such as the ghost dance of the Paiutes), but the hoop and eagle dances of the western Indian peoples are theatrical and intricate.

Folk dancing for pure recreation is also an important tradition, and in the West among the most significant dances are the Scottish Highland fling, the Italian tarantella, the American Virginia reel and square dances, and the Argentine tango. Popular American social dancing, usually requiring two persons, in the twentieth century has adopted many Latin American dances, including the rhumba, mambo, and tango, and is related to both popular songs and jazz-band arrangements—first spread through sales of sheet music, then records, and often derived from musical theater and films.

The importance of social dancing and the continual interest in new popular dance steps was essentially begun by the American dance team of Irene and Vernon Castle in the period during and after World War I. Popular dances have included the Charleston, the jitterbug, the fox trot, the twist, and, increasingly after the 1950s, other youth-oriented dances related to rock music.

Self-consciously created dance, as a form of theater and as ballet, has been used alone or as part of a larger production. Ballet has origins in both the ancient Roman pantomime and the Italian *commedia dell'arte.* France led the way in establishing the essentials of the classical ballet, beginning with the founding of the Royal Academy of Dancing in Paris in 1661. France created a theatrical tradition of opera ballets, and dance rules and steps were strictly formalized.

Into the nineteenth century it was nearly impossible for an acceptable opera not to include a ballet section. In Italy the ballet was affiliated with the opera company at La Scala in Milan, and in Russia academies of ballet in Moscow and St. Petersburg won worldwide fame. By the end of the nineteenth century, significant ballets were being composed by Tchaikovsky (*Swan Lake; The Nutcracker*). It was another Russian, Sergei Diaghilev, who made ballet one of the most important independent art forms of the twentieth century. Diaghilev, who was essentially a producer, brought together such great choreographers and dancers as Michael Fokine, Leonide Massine, and Vasilav Nijinsky with composers such as Stravinsky, Prokofiev, Debussy, Poulenc, and Satie. One of Diaghilev's greatest Ballet Russe choreographers, George Balanchine, became the most important American choreographer, director of the New York City Ballet, after World War II. The traditional elements of ballet were enlarged by the use of more abstract patterns, nontraditional steps and forms, greater individual expression, less virtuosic display, greater athleticism, and more incorporation of folk/popular-dance elements. Pioneering choreographers in the first half of the twentieth century include Isadora Duncan, Ruth St. Denis, Ted Shawn, Martha Graham, Agnes De Mille, and Jerome Robbins.

Agnes De Mille and Jerome Robbins were the leading figures of ballet-dance as used in American musical theater. Their folk- and jazz-inflected dances added significantly to the ballet idiom and revolutionized the American musical—De Mille with Rodgers and Hammerstein's *Oklahoma* and Robbins with Leonard Bernstein's *West Side Story.*

Music and theater have always been linked, and the traditions of opera, operetta, and musical comedy/drama in Europe and America have produced enduring theatrical masterpieces: the operas of Rossini, Verdi, Puccini, Bizet, Wagner, Weill, and Gershwin; the operettas of Gilbert and Sullivan (*The Pirates of Penzance; The Mikado; Patience*), Johann Strauss, Jr. (*Die Fledermaus*), Jacques Offenbach (*Tales of Hoffmann*), and Franz Lehar (*The Merry Widow*); and the musical comedies (a term loosely applied; musical theater is more accurate) of Jerome Kern (*Show Boat*), Richard Rodgers (*Carousel; Oklahoma; The King and I*), George Gershwin (*Strike Up the Band; Of Thee I Sing*), Leonard Bernstein (*On the Town; West Side Story*), and Stephen Sondheim (*Follies; Sweeney Todd*).

Drama and comedy have sought without music to portray humanity's deepest passions and most universal concerns, and simply to amuse or entertain. Medieval drama was primarily religious, with the stylized mystery and miracle plays often presented in cathedrals and monasteries. Most theatrical performances in Europe until the sixteenth century took place in booths or courtyards or an outside open area. The great plays of Shakespeare and his contemporaries were presented in theaters, but these were merely stages set against the side of a building with spectators gathered around the stage on three sides in the yard or in galleries, with no provisions for scenery. Over the next hundred years, theaters were gradually enclosed and a separated stage, demarcated by a proscenium opening, hosted theatricals with elaborate scenery and even indoor lighting. Molière in the seventeenth century and Beaumarchais in the eighteenth wrote comedies of manners and farces; the latter's *Barber of Seville* and *Marriage of Figaro* were adapted for operas by Rossini and Mozart, respectively.

Similar plays, with somewhat more realism and characters reflecting the interests and values of the middle class, were written in the nineteenth century by Oscar Wilde (*The Importance of Being Earnest; Lady Windemere's Fan*), George Bernard Shaw (*Pygmalion*), and Anton Chekov (*The Cherry Orchard*). Drama became more psychological and sought to reveal truths about real people and their inner and interpersonal conflicts with the dramas of August Strindberg (*Miss Julie*) and Henrik Ibsen (*A Doll's House*). Great American twentieth-century playwrights include Eugene O'Neill (*Long Day's Journey into Night; The Iceman Cometh*), Tennessee Williams (*The Glass Menagerie; A Streetcar Named Desire*), and Arthur Miller (*Death of a Salesman; The Crucible*).

Critical Judgment

In addition to understanding the history of the visual and performing arts, it is important to be able to confront a work and judge its aesthetic merits—regardless of whether we specifically recognize it from memory. Questions one may ask are: A) What is the purpose of the work? Religious? Entertainment? Philosophical? Emotional? Didactic? Pure form? Social or political commentary? B) To what culture does it belong, and to what geographical region and time period—and how does it reflect these? C) Is its origin and/or function

In addition to understanding the history of the visual and performing arts, it is important to be able to confront a work and judge its aesthetic merits.

popular or commercial? Does it derive organically from the needs or celebratory functions of a community, or is it a self-conscious artistic creation of one individual? and D) What style is it in? For example: Is this music baroque, classical, or romantic? Is it influenced by ethnic or popular music? Often after answering such questions, one may even be able to determine the specific artist—by putting all the clues together as in a detective story.

In looking at a work of visual art, in order to judge its quality—whether it is or isn't good art—we need to assess: A) whether it succeeds in its purpose; B) if the artist has spoken with a unique voice—regardless of style—or could this artwork just as easily be the work of someone else? C) if the style is appropriate to the expressed purpose of the work; D) if the work is memorable and distinctive; and E) if the artist has used all the technical elements available to the particular discipline with accomplished skill.

Although such basic questions as these can be applied in evaluating all good art, it is important to remember that beyond these kinds of questions there are other criteria that apply only to certain art forms, for certain purposes, in certain cultures. For example, it is inappropriate to look for the use of perspective of the Western-realist tradition in Japanese or Chinese art. In music, the improvisitory style and variation forms of American jazz, and other musical vocabulary unique to jazz (as played by such musician/composers as Duke Ellington and King Oliver) allows its quality to be judged on equal but different terms than a symphony by Beethoven. In Islamic art, the beauties of manuscripts, textiles, and architectural decoration are normally limited to exquisite patterns, beautiful script for texts, and stylized naturalistic forms for ornamentation; in the religious tradition, the realistic representation of human figures is purposely avoided.

The intensity of the Hindu religious feeling in India, the workings of the universe, the endless cycles of rebirth, the goal of the ultimate blissful union with the divine, especially the intense experience of erotic love—all are embodied in Kandarya Mahaveda and other temples at Khajuraho. The profusion of sculptures rising up the temple walls at Khajuraho occupy the senses and mind in ways similar to the religious instruction afforded by the profusion of sculptural and stained-glass stories and images of the European Gothic cathedrals, such as Rheims, Chartres, and Naumberg.

In opera, the masterful works by Puccini and Weill succeed on very different levels, and were created using different styles and for different purposes. While Puccini's *La Bohème, Tosca, Madama Butterfly,* and *La Fanciulla del West* are affecting melodramas of the highest order, with ravishing music serving drama and emotion in a perfect union, Kurt Weill's and Bertolt Brecht's *Threepenny Opera* and *The Rise and Fall of the City of Mahagonny* excoriate the excesses of modern societies built on greed and bloated bourgeois values—by using oblique satire and austerely constructed music that incorporates jazz rhythms and harmonies and popular-music-type melodies. Similarly, style and purpose are served brilliantly by the naturalism and accurate depiction of observed nature in the works of such masters as Rembrandt, Gainsborough, Van Dyck, Courbet, and Renoir.

Just as successful and affecting are the personal, mystical vision of William Blake appropriately expressed in his watercolors and hand-colored prints of symbolic, contorted figures. And just as aesthetically brilliant are the agitated woodcuts and paintings depicting the psychological introspection and emotional turmoil of expressionist artists such as Edvard Munch, Oskar Kokoschka, Egon Schiele, and Max Beckman.

CSET

**California Subject Examinations
for Teachers: Multiple Subjects**

Practice Test 1

Answer Sheet

53–56 are Constructed-Response questions. See sample essays in Detailed Explanation of Answers section.

Subtest I:

Reading, Language & Literature; History & Social Science

1. Ⓐ Ⓑ Ⓒ Ⓓ	14. Ⓐ Ⓑ Ⓒ Ⓓ	27. Ⓐ Ⓑ Ⓒ Ⓓ	40. Ⓐ Ⓑ Ⓒ Ⓓ
2. Ⓐ Ⓑ Ⓒ Ⓓ	15. Ⓐ Ⓑ Ⓒ Ⓓ	28. Ⓐ Ⓑ Ⓒ Ⓓ	41. Ⓐ Ⓑ Ⓒ Ⓓ
3. Ⓐ Ⓑ Ⓒ Ⓓ	16. Ⓐ Ⓑ Ⓒ Ⓓ	29. Ⓐ Ⓑ Ⓒ Ⓓ	42. Ⓐ Ⓑ Ⓒ Ⓓ
4. Ⓐ Ⓑ Ⓒ Ⓓ	17. Ⓐ Ⓑ Ⓒ Ⓓ	30. Ⓐ Ⓑ Ⓒ Ⓓ	43. Ⓐ Ⓑ Ⓒ Ⓓ
5. Ⓐ Ⓑ Ⓒ Ⓓ	18. Ⓐ Ⓑ Ⓒ Ⓓ	31. Ⓐ Ⓑ Ⓒ Ⓓ	44. Ⓐ Ⓑ Ⓒ Ⓓ
6. Ⓐ Ⓑ Ⓒ Ⓓ	19. Ⓐ Ⓑ Ⓒ Ⓓ	32. Ⓐ Ⓑ Ⓒ Ⓓ	45. Ⓐ Ⓑ Ⓒ Ⓓ
7. Ⓐ Ⓑ Ⓒ Ⓓ	20. Ⓐ Ⓑ Ⓒ Ⓓ	33. Ⓐ Ⓑ Ⓒ Ⓓ	46. Ⓐ Ⓑ Ⓒ Ⓓ
8. Ⓐ Ⓑ Ⓒ Ⓓ	21. Ⓐ Ⓑ Ⓒ Ⓓ	34. Ⓐ Ⓑ Ⓒ Ⓓ	47. Ⓐ Ⓑ Ⓒ Ⓓ
9. Ⓐ Ⓑ Ⓒ Ⓓ	22. Ⓐ Ⓑ Ⓒ Ⓓ	35. Ⓐ Ⓑ Ⓒ Ⓓ	48. Ⓐ Ⓑ Ⓒ Ⓓ
10. Ⓐ Ⓑ Ⓒ Ⓓ	23. Ⓐ Ⓑ Ⓒ Ⓓ	36. Ⓐ Ⓑ Ⓒ Ⓓ	49. Ⓐ Ⓑ Ⓒ Ⓓ
11. Ⓐ Ⓑ Ⓒ Ⓓ	24. Ⓐ Ⓑ Ⓒ Ⓓ	37. Ⓐ Ⓑ Ⓒ Ⓓ	50. Ⓐ Ⓑ Ⓒ Ⓓ
12. Ⓐ Ⓑ Ⓒ Ⓓ	25. Ⓐ Ⓑ Ⓒ Ⓓ	38. Ⓐ Ⓑ Ⓒ Ⓓ	51. Ⓐ Ⓑ Ⓒ Ⓓ
13. Ⓐ Ⓑ Ⓒ Ⓓ	26. Ⓐ Ⓑ Ⓒ Ⓓ	39. Ⓐ Ⓑ Ⓒ Ⓓ	52. Ⓐ Ⓑ Ⓒ Ⓓ

53–56 are Constructed-Response questions. See sample essays in Detailed Explanation of Answers section.

Subtest II:

Science; Mathematics

1. Ⓐ Ⓑ Ⓒ Ⓓ	14. Ⓐ Ⓑ Ⓒ Ⓓ	27. Ⓐ Ⓑ Ⓒ Ⓓ	40. Ⓐ Ⓑ Ⓒ Ⓓ
2. Ⓐ Ⓑ Ⓒ Ⓓ	15. Ⓐ Ⓑ Ⓒ Ⓓ	28. Ⓐ Ⓑ Ⓒ Ⓓ	41. Ⓐ Ⓑ Ⓒ Ⓓ
3. Ⓐ Ⓑ Ⓒ Ⓓ	16. Ⓐ Ⓑ Ⓒ Ⓓ	29. Ⓐ Ⓑ Ⓒ Ⓓ	42. Ⓐ Ⓑ Ⓒ Ⓓ
4. Ⓐ Ⓑ Ⓒ Ⓓ	17. Ⓐ Ⓑ Ⓒ Ⓓ	30. Ⓐ Ⓑ Ⓒ Ⓓ	43. Ⓐ Ⓑ Ⓒ Ⓓ
5. Ⓐ Ⓑ Ⓒ Ⓓ	18. Ⓐ Ⓑ Ⓒ Ⓓ	31. Ⓐ Ⓑ Ⓒ Ⓓ	44. Ⓐ Ⓑ Ⓒ Ⓓ
6. Ⓐ Ⓑ Ⓒ Ⓓ	19. Ⓐ Ⓑ Ⓒ Ⓓ	32. Ⓐ Ⓑ Ⓒ Ⓓ	45. Ⓐ Ⓑ Ⓒ Ⓓ
7. Ⓐ Ⓑ Ⓒ Ⓓ	20. Ⓐ Ⓑ Ⓒ Ⓓ	33. Ⓐ Ⓑ Ⓒ Ⓓ	46. Ⓐ Ⓑ Ⓒ Ⓓ
8. Ⓐ Ⓑ Ⓒ Ⓓ	21. Ⓐ Ⓑ Ⓒ Ⓓ	34. Ⓐ Ⓑ Ⓒ Ⓓ	47. Ⓐ Ⓑ Ⓒ Ⓓ
9. Ⓐ Ⓑ Ⓒ Ⓓ	22. Ⓐ Ⓑ Ⓒ Ⓓ	35. Ⓐ Ⓑ Ⓒ Ⓓ	48. Ⓐ Ⓑ Ⓒ Ⓓ
10. Ⓐ Ⓑ Ⓒ Ⓓ	23. Ⓐ Ⓑ Ⓒ Ⓓ	36. Ⓐ Ⓑ Ⓒ Ⓓ	49. Ⓐ Ⓑ Ⓒ Ⓓ
11. Ⓐ Ⓑ Ⓒ Ⓓ	24. Ⓐ Ⓑ Ⓒ Ⓓ	37. Ⓐ Ⓑ Ⓒ Ⓓ	50. Ⓐ Ⓑ Ⓒ Ⓓ
12. Ⓐ Ⓑ Ⓒ Ⓓ	25. Ⓐ Ⓑ Ⓒ Ⓓ	38. Ⓐ Ⓑ Ⓒ Ⓓ	51. Ⓐ Ⓑ Ⓒ Ⓓ
13. Ⓐ Ⓑ Ⓒ Ⓓ	26. Ⓐ Ⓑ Ⓒ Ⓓ	39. Ⓐ Ⓑ Ⓒ Ⓓ	52. Ⓐ Ⓑ Ⓒ Ⓓ

Answer Sheet (cont.)

40–42 are Constructed-Response questions. See sample essays in Detailed Explanation of Answers section.

Subtest III:

Physical Education; Human Development; Visual and Performing Arts

1. Ⓐ Ⓑ Ⓒ Ⓓ	14. Ⓐ Ⓑ Ⓒ Ⓓ	27. Ⓐ Ⓑ Ⓒ Ⓓ
2. Ⓐ Ⓑ Ⓒ Ⓓ	15. Ⓐ Ⓑ Ⓒ Ⓓ	28. Ⓐ Ⓑ Ⓒ Ⓓ
3. Ⓐ Ⓑ Ⓒ Ⓓ	16. Ⓐ Ⓑ Ⓒ Ⓓ	29. Ⓐ Ⓑ Ⓒ Ⓓ
4. Ⓐ Ⓑ Ⓒ Ⓓ	17. Ⓐ Ⓑ Ⓒ Ⓓ	30. Ⓐ Ⓑ Ⓒ Ⓓ
5. Ⓐ Ⓑ Ⓒ Ⓓ	18. Ⓐ Ⓑ Ⓒ Ⓓ	31. Ⓐ Ⓑ Ⓒ Ⓓ
6. Ⓐ Ⓑ Ⓒ Ⓓ	19. Ⓐ Ⓑ Ⓒ Ⓓ	32. Ⓐ Ⓑ Ⓒ Ⓓ
7. Ⓐ Ⓑ Ⓒ Ⓓ	20. Ⓐ Ⓑ Ⓒ Ⓓ	33. Ⓐ Ⓑ Ⓒ Ⓓ
8. Ⓐ Ⓑ Ⓒ Ⓓ	21. Ⓐ Ⓑ Ⓒ Ⓓ	34. Ⓐ Ⓑ Ⓒ Ⓓ
9. Ⓐ Ⓑ Ⓒ Ⓓ	22. Ⓐ Ⓑ Ⓒ Ⓓ	35. Ⓐ Ⓑ Ⓒ Ⓓ
10. Ⓐ Ⓑ Ⓒ Ⓓ	23. Ⓐ Ⓑ Ⓒ Ⓓ	36. Ⓐ Ⓑ Ⓒ Ⓓ
11. Ⓐ Ⓑ Ⓒ Ⓓ	24. Ⓐ Ⓑ Ⓒ Ⓓ	37. Ⓐ Ⓑ Ⓒ Ⓓ
12. Ⓐ Ⓑ Ⓒ Ⓓ	25. Ⓐ Ⓑ Ⓒ Ⓓ	38. Ⓐ Ⓑ Ⓒ Ⓓ
13. Ⓐ Ⓑ Ⓒ Ⓓ	26. Ⓐ Ⓑ Ⓒ Ⓓ	39. Ⓐ Ⓑ Ⓒ Ⓓ

CSET

Practice Test 1

Subtest I:

Reading, Language & Literature;
History & Social Science

Practice Test 1: Subtest I
Reading, Language & Literature; History & Social Science

DIRECTIONS: This test consists of two sections: multiple-choice and constructed-response questions. The former is composed of 52 multiple-choice questions and the latter is composed of four questions, that involve written responses. You may work on the questions in any order, keeping in mind that when taking the actual test you will have one five-hour test session in which to complete the subtest(s) for which you are registered.

Multiple-Choice Questions

Reading, Language & Literature

QUESTIONS 1–5 are based on the following excerpt from *The Rape of the Lock* by Alexander Pope. Read the poem carefully before choosing your answers.

1	One speaks the glory of the British Queen,
	And one describes a charming Indian screen;
	A third interprets motions, looks, and eyes;
	At every word a reputation dies.
5	Snuff, or the fan, supply each pause of chat,

With singing, laughing, ogling, and all that.
Meanwhile, declining from the noon of day,
The sun obliquely shoots his burning ray;
The hungry judges soon the sentence sign,
10   And wretches hang that jurymen may dine;

1.   The last two lines suggest that this society

    (A)   takes pride in its justice system.

    (B)   speedily administers justice for humanitarian reasons.

    (C)   sentences the wrong people to death.

    (D)   sentences people for the wrong reasons.

2.   Lines 1–6 suggest that this society

    I.   indulges in gossip that slanders the Queen.

    II.   engages in serious discussions about affairs of state.

    III. engages in gossip that ruins reputations.

    (A)   I and III.   (C)   II only.

    (B)   III only.   (D)   I, II, and III.

3.   The juxtaposition in lines 1 and 2 suggests that the people

    (A)   talk of trivia.

    (B)   revere the monarchy and Indian screens equally.

    (C)   are Imperialists.

    (D)   are Royalists.

4.   The word "obliquely" (line 8) in this context could mean or functions as all of the following EXCEPT:

    (A)   perpendicularly.

    (B)   at a steep angle.

    (C)   a pun on hidden meanings.

    (D)   a pun on stealth.

5. The change in voice from the first half of the excerpt into the second is best described as one from

 (A) light to dark.

 (B) critical to amused.

 (C) sarcastic to light-hearted.

 (D) amused to sadness.

QUESTIONS 6–13 are based on the following passage, which is taken from *Martin Chuzzlewit* by Charles Dickens. Read the passage carefully before choosing your answers.

"What is he, then?"

"Why, I'll tell you what he is," said Mr. Jonas, apart to the young ladies, "he's precious old, for one thing; and I an't best pleased with him for that, for I think my father must have caught it of him. He's a strange old chap, for another," he added in a louder voice, "and don't understand any one hardly, but him!" He pointed to his honoured parent with the carving-fork, in order that they might know whom he meant.

"How very strange!" cried the sisters.

"Why, you see," said Mr. Jonas, "he's been addling his old brains with figures and book-keeping all his life; and twenty years ago or so he went and took a fever. All the time he was out of his head (which was three weeks) he never left off casting up; and he got to so many million at last that I don't believe he's ever been quite right since. We don't do much business now though, and he an't a bad clerk."

"A very good one," said Anthony.

"Well! He an't a dear one at all events," observed Jonas; "and he earns his salt, which is enough for our look-out. I was telling you that he hardly understands any one except my father; he always understands him, though, and wakes up quite wonderful. He's been used to his ways so long, you see! Why, I've seen him play whist, with my father for a partner; and a good rubber too; when he had no more notion what sort of people he was playing against, than you have."

6. From this passage it can be inferred that Mr. Jonas is all of the following EXCEPT:

 (A) irritated that the old clerk understands hardly anyone except the father.

 (B) unconcerned about hurting the old clerk's feelings.

 (C) worried that the old clerk might make a serious error.

 (D) intent upon impressing the sisters.

7. If the old clerk is not "quite right" in the head, then why is he kept on as an employee?

   (A) Mr. Jonas will not go against his father's wishes.

   (B) Mr. Jonas does not want to offend the ladies.

   (C) Mr. Jonas reveres people of the older generation.

   (D) Mr. Jonas is somewhat afraid of the "strange old chap."

8. As used in the passage, the word "precious" means

   (A) very.   (C) beloved.

   (B) of high value.   (D) very overrefined in behavior.

9. What has made the old clerk not "quite right" in the head?

   (A) going a bit deaf in his old age.

   (B) working with numbers and bookkeeping all his life.

   (C) working sums and figures in his fever.

   (D) having to put up with Mr. Jonas' abuse.

10. The sentence "He an't a dear one at all events" can best be interpreted to mean which of the following?

   (A) Mr. Jonas does not like the old clerk.

   (B) The customers of the business do not like the old clerk.

   (C) Sometimes the clerk creates serious problems.

   (D) His wages do not cost the company very much money.

11. All of the following are things Mr. Jonas dislikes about the clerk EXCEPT that he is:

   (A) old.

   (B) a bit strange.

   (C) a good whist player.

   (D) not always aware of who is around him.

12. What is the meaning of "he got to so many million at last"?

   (A) He irritated countless customers.

   (B) He had trouble keeping up with the high figures.

(C) He became quite advanced in years.

(D) He thought the three weeks was a million days.

13. A reasonable description of the old man is that he

(A) knows what he is doing when it is something he has been accustomed to doing.

(B) only pretends to be deaf and addled in order to irritate Mr. Jonas.

(C) can do only the simplest of tasks, although he would like to be able to do more.

(D) can do anything he wants to do, but only chooses to do what pleases him.

14. Which of the following, according to current linguistic theories, is the best definition of the meaning of a word?

(A) Its general, dictionary definition.

(B) Its use in a particular situation.

(C) Its referent (the object to which it refers).

(D) Its thought or corresponding idea in the mind.

15. Saussure's major breakthrough in linguistics was his insistence that

(A) there is an inherent, one-to-one correspondence between a word and its referent.

(B) the meaning of a word is subject to change over the course of time.

(C) there are different words for the same referent in different languages.

(D) the connection between a word and its referent is an arbitrary convention.

16. Which of the following best describes the acquisition of language by children?

(A) A logical process by which a child learns to express his or her thoughts

(B) A series of imitative stages occurring in a necessary succession, where each advance is built on the previous one

(C) A series of imitative stages occurring in a rough, overlapping sequence, including possible regressions

(D) A random developmental sequence indivisible into stages

17. Adults acquire new words and expressions primarily through

(A) casual explanation from peers.

(B) formal instruction in school.

    (C)   exposure to their use.

    (D)   use of a dictionary or thesaurus.

18.   The intention of an utterance is

    (A)   private, available only to the speaker of the utterance.

    (B)   public, measurable by various outward criteria.

    (C)   unknowable to either the speaker or the listener of the utterance.

    (D)   translatable into the "deep structure" of the utterance.

19.   The best way to judge whether or not an intention has been fulfilled is by

    (A)   observing the actions that follow from the utterance.

    (B)   consulting the speaker of the utterance for confirmation.

    (C)   asking the listener of the utterance if he or she understood the intention.

    (D)   consulting the rules of standard American English.

Read the passage below; then answer questions 20 and 21.

[1] Henry Wadsworth Longfellow's "The Village Blacksmith" is a direct descendent of the emblem poem. [2] Although the basic emblem format existed as early as medieval times, its popularity reached its greatest heights in the seventeenth century. [3] Poet Francis Quarles's (1592-1644) book *Emblems, Divine and Moral* (1635) was the best-selling book of the century. [4] Emblem poetry consisted of a picture, illustrating some "moral or divine truth," which might be a proverb, psalm, or any terse quote of scripture. [5] The picture was followed by a relevant scriptural citation. [6] The poem would then culminate with a concluding epigram. [7] Then, a poem of approximately 40 to 50 lines would further elaborate on the scripture.

20.   Which of the following changes of a sentence could best improve the syntax of the passage?

    (A)   Sentence 1: "The Village Blacksmith" epitomizes the best poetry of the American seventeenth century.

    (B)   Sentence 2: Although the basic emblem format dated to medieval times, its popularity peaked in the seventeenth century.

(C) Sentence 3: What emblem poetry symbolized was exemplified by a careful blend of an illustration of some "moral or divine truth" that might have been rooted in a proverb, psalm or biblical citation.

(D) Sentence 4: The illustration was followed by some sort of excerpt from the Bible.

21. Which of the following changes could best improve the logical flow of the passage?

(A) Move Sentence 5 so that it follows Sentence 1.

(B) Move Sentence 5 so that it follows Sentence 7.

(C) Move Sentence 6 so that follows Sentence 7.

(D) Move Sentence 4 so that it follows Sentence 6.

QUESTIONS 22–26 refer to the following passage.

1   The house of fiction has in short not one window, but a million—a number of possible windows not to be reckoned, rather; every one of which has been pierced, or is still pierceable, in its vast front, by the need of the individual vision and by the pressure of the individual will. These apertures, of dissimilar shape and size, hang so, 5 all together, over the human scene that we might have expected of them a greater sameness of report than we find. They are but windows at the best, mere holes in a dead wall, disconnected, perched aloft; they are not hinged doors opening straight upon life. But they have this mark of their own that at each of them stands a figure with a pair of eyes, or at least with a field-glass, which forms, again and again, for 10 observation, a unique instrument, insuring to the person making use of it an impression distinct from every other. He and his neighbours are watching the same show, but one seeing more where the other sees less, one seeing black where the other sees white, one seeing big where the other sees small, one seeing coarse where the other sees fine. And so on, and so on; there is fortunately no saying on what, for the 15 particular pair of eyes, the window may <u>not</u> open; "fortunately" by reason, precisely, of this incalculability of range. The spreading field, the human scene, is the "choice of subject"; the pierced aperture, either broad or balconied or slitlike and low-browed, is the "literary form"; but they are, singly or together, as nothing without the posted presence of the watcher—without, in other words, the consciousness of the artist. Tell 20 me what the artist is, and I will tell you of what he has *been* conscious. Thereby I shall express to you at once his boundless freedom and his "moral" reference.

22. The phrase "they are not hinged doors opening straight upon life" (lines 7–8) implies that

(A) fiction does not directly mirror life.

(B) works of fiction are windows, not doors.

    (C)   fiction presents twisted versions of life.

    (D)   fictional works are not easily created.

23.   What is the antecedent of "they" in line 6?

    (A)   Windows (line 6).

    (B)   Apertures (line 4).

    (C)   Holes (line 6).

    (D)   Need (line 3) and pressure (line 4).

24.   The shifts in point of view from "we" (lines 5–6) to "he" (line 11) to "I" (line 20) has which of the following effects?

    (A)   The shifts indicate the speaker's distinguishing himself/herself from the critics who inhabit the house of fiction.

    (B)   The shifts symbolize the speaker's alienation from the genre.

    (C)   The movement from group to individual parallels the movement from the group "house of fiction" (line 1) to individual "figure with a pair of eyes" (lines 8–9).

    (D)   The movements separate the readers from the authors.

25.   Which of these phrases contains an example of antithesis?

    (A)   "These apertures, of dissimilar shape and size, hang so, all together, over the human scene" (lines 4–5).

    (B)   "They are but windows at the best, mere holes in a dead wall, disconnected, perched aloft; they are not hinged doors" (lines 6–7).

    (C)   "…at each of them stands a figure with a pair of eyes, or at least with a field-glass" (lines 8–9).

    (D)   "…one seeing more where the other sees less, one seeing black where the other sees white, one seeing big where the other sees small, one seeing coarse where the other sees fine" (lines 12–14).

26.   Which of the following does the speaker consider to be the most important element in the "house of fiction"?

    (A)   The "figure with a pair of eyes" (line 9).

    (B)   The "apertures" (line 4).

    (C)   The "hinged doors" (line 7).

    (D)   The "human scene" (line 5).

History and Social Science

27. Which observation does not correctly describe California's unique geography?

    (A) Its isolation kept it free from European settlement, even after centuries of European settlement on the Pacific coast.

    (B) Its large population and industrial centers are located in arid and semi-arid environments.

    (C) Its semi-tropical, Mediterranean climate has been a perpetual source of attraction since people first entered the region.

    (D) Its long, navigable rivers facilitate the movement of produce to the state's multiple ports.

28. The demise of the California missions can ultimately be traced to

    (A) Mexican independence.

    (B) low productivity and the inability of the missions to sustain themselves.

    (C) imperial policies that recalled the Franciscans back to Spain.

    (D) the desires of missionaries to seek out "virgin" territories elsewhere.

29. What made Los Angeles especially attractive to many immigrants from 1890–1910 was

    (A) the city's large, natural harbor capable of facilitating an international trade.

    (B) the city's bountiful and dependable water supply from the Los Angeles river.

    (C) the city's booming wheat industry.

    (D) None of the above.

30. In announcing the Emancipation Proclamation, Lincoln's immediate purpose was to

    (A) free black slaves in all of the slave states.

    (B) free black slaves in only the border slave states that had remained loyal to the Union.

    (C) let the Southern states know that whether or not they chose to secede from the Union, slavery would not be tolerated by his administration once he took office.

    (D) rally Northern morale by giving the war a higher moral purpose than just perserving the Union.

31. In its decision in the case of *Dred Scott v. Sanford*, the U.S. Supreme Court held that

    (A) separate facilities for different races were inherently unequal and therefore unconstitutional.

    (B) no black slave could be a citizen of the United States.

    (C) separate but equal facilities for different races were constitutional.

    (D) Affirmative Action programs were acceptable only when it could be proven that specific previous cases of discrimination had occurred within the institution or business in question.

32. In coining the phrase "Manifest Destiny," journalist John L. O'Sullivan meant that

    (A) the struggle for racial equality was the ultimate goal of America's existence.

    (B) America was certain to become an independent country sooner or later.

    (C) it was the destiny of America to overspread the continent.

    (D) America must eventually become either all slave or all free.

33. Thomas Paine's pamphlet *Common Sense* was significant in that it

    (A) emotionally aroused thousands of colonists to the abuses of British rule, the oppressiveness of the monarchy, and the advantages of colonial independence.

    (B) rallied American spirit during the bleak winter of 1776, when it appeared that Washington's forces, freezing and starving at Valley Forge had no hope of surviving the winter, much less defeating the British.

    (C) called for a strong central government to rule the newly independent American states and foresaw the difficulties inherent within the Articles of Confederation.

    (D) asserted to its British readers that they could not beat the American colonists militarily unless they could isolate New England from the rest of the American colonies.

34. Abraham Lincoln took the Union into war against the Confederate States of America with the stated purpose of

    (A) protecting federal installations in Confederate territories.

    (B) freeing the slaves and abolishing slavery from American soil.

    (C) preserving the Union.

    (D) punishing the South for ts arrogance, rebelliousness, and the enslavement of blacks by Southern slaveholders.

35. The greatest significance of the U.S. Supreme Court's decision in *Marbury v. Madison* was that it

    (A) claimed for the first time that the Supreme Court could issue directives to the president.

    (B) claimed that the Supreme Court alone was empowered to say what the Constitution meant.

    (C) claimed for the first time that the Supreme Court could declare an act of Congress to be unconstitutional.

    (D) was openly defied by President Thomas Jefferson.

36. The term "Trail of Tears" refers to

    (A) the Mormon migration from Nauvoo, Illinois, to what is now Utah.

    (B) the forced migration of the Cherokee tribe from the southern Appalachians to what is now Oklahoma.

    (C) the westward migration along the Oregon Trail.

    (D) the migration into Kentucky along the Wilderness Road.

37. The Silk Road did NOT connect to which of the following countries

    (A) China   (C) Iran

    (B) Greece   (D) India

38. The overall strategic policy of the Union to destroy the Confederacy through a combination of constant pressure and slowly wearing down the South's ability to wage war was called

    (A) the Nutcracker Plan.   (C) the Squeeze Plan.

    (B) the Anaconda Plan.   (D) the Attrition Plan.

39. During the late seventeenth century, Austria confronted several decades of almost continuous warfare on two fronts against

    (A) Italy and Prussia.

    (B) England and Russia.

    (C) France and the Ottoman Empire.

    (D) Prussia and the Ottoman Empire.

40. The characteristics of fascism include all of the following EXCEPT:

    (A) totalitarianism.   (C) romanticism.

    (B) democracy.   (D) militarism.

41. The industrial economy of the nineteenth century was based upon all of the following EXCEPT:

    (A) the availability of raw materials.

    (B) an equitable distribution of profits among those involved in production.

    (C) the availability of capital.

    (D) a distribution system to market finished products.

42. Oscar Wilde's *The Picture of Dorian Gray* and Thomas Mann's *Death in Venice*

    (A) are examples of the romantic literature that dominated the literary scene at the turn of the twentieth century.

    (B) embodied a new symbolist direction in literature that addressed themes previously ignored.

    (C) emphasized a new sense of realism in literature.

    (D) were representative of a literary movement known as expressionism.

43. The response of the Catholic Church to the Reformation was delayed because

    (A) the papacy feared the remnants of the Conciliar Movement within the church itself.

    (B) Rome wanted to coordinate its policy with secular Catholic leaders.

    (C) church leaders thought that the opposition would self-destruct.

    (D) the situation did not appear to be that serious from the Roman perspective.

44. The key issue that prevented the American colonists from resolving their problems with England without open rebellion was

    (A) the sovereignty of King George III over the colonies.

    (B) the sovereignty of Parliament's edicts over colonies.

    (C) the stationing of British soldiers on American soil.

    (D) American desire for total independence from Britain.

45. Among the non-French intellectuals who participated in the Enlightenment were all of the following EXCEPT:

    (A) Edward Gibbon.   (C) Benjamin Franklin.

    (B) David Hume.   (D) Leopold von Ranke.

46. "Jim Crow" laws were laws that

    (A) effectively prohibited blacks from voting in state and local elections.

    (B) restricted American Indians to U.S. government reservations.

    (C) restricted open-range ranching in the Great Plains.

    (D) established separate segregated facilities for blacks and whites.

47. Colonies such as the Carolinas were known as "restoration colonies" because

    (A) their creation was mainly due to the restoration of the Stuarts to the English throne.

    (B) they were created as places to send criminals to restore them to civilized behavior and give them a chance to lead decent, honest lives.

    (C) their creation was mainly due to the restoration of the power of English Parliment over the king.

    (D) their creation was an attempt to restore the supremacy of the Anglican Church in the colonies.

48. Which of the following is used to effect the release of a person from improper imprisonment?

    (A) A writ of mandamus

    (B) A writ of habeas corpus

    (C) The Fourth Amendment requirement that police have probable cause in order to obtain a search warrant

    (D) The Supreme Court's decision in *Roe vs. Wade*

49. When a member of the House of Representatives helps a citizen from his or her district receive federal aid to which that citizen is entitled, the representative's action is referred to as

    (A) casework.   (C) lobbying.

    (B) pork barrel legislation.   (D) logrolling.

50. Which of the following statements most accurately compares political parties in the United States with those in other Western democracies?

    (A) Parties in the United States exert a greater influence over which candidates run for office.

    (B) Parties are much more centralized in the United States.

    (C) There are usually more political parties in other Western democracies.

    (D) Party members in the national legislature are much freer to vote against the party line in other Western democracies.

51. Which artistic form is Renaissance figure Michelangelo NOT well known for?

    (A) Sculpting   (C) Architecture

    (B) Writing   (D) Painting

52. Which of the following Indian tribes was NOT a member of the "Five Civilized Tribes"?

    (A) Seminole   (C) Cherokee

    (B) Seneca   (D) Chickasaw

Constructed-Response Questions

Constructed-Response Directions

Prepare a written response for each constructed-response assignment. Read each assignment carefully before you begin to write. Think about how you will organize what you plan to write.

Scoring of responses to CSET: Multiple Subjects constructed-response assignments is based on the following criteria.

PURPOSE: the extent to which the response addresses the constructed-response assignment's charge in relation to relevant CSET content specifications.

SUBJECT MATTER KNOWLEDGE: the application of accurate subject matter knowledge as described in the relevant CSET content specifications.

SUPPORT: the appropriateness and quality of the supporting evidence in relation to relevant CSET content specifications.

The assignments are intended to assess subject matter knowledge and skills, not writing ability. Your responses, however, must be communicated clearly enough to permit a valid judgment of your knowledge and skills. Your responses should be written for an audience of educators in the field.

You may wish to write each of your responses to the CSET: Multiple Subjects Subtest I practice test constructed-response assignments and ask a mentor, advisor, or teacher to help evaluate them. Sample responses are provided for these assignments following the detailed answers section of the Subtest I practice test.

53. Discuss the challenge that a non-native speaker of English encounters in the language acquisition process?

54. Write an essay on the poem below. In your essay, take into consideration the following: verse and meter, figurative language, form, poetic devices, central argument of the poem, and tone.

> 1   Love is not all: it is not meat nor drink
>   Nor slumber nor a roof against the rain;
>   Nor yet a floating spar to men that sink
>   And rise and sink and rise and sink again;
> 5   Love cannot fill the thickened lung with breath,
>   Nor clean the blood, nor set the fractured bone;
>   Yet many a man is making friends with death
>   Even as I speak, for lack of love along.
>   It well may that in a difficult hour,
> 10 Pinned down by pain and moaning for release,
>   Or nagged by want past resolution's power,
>   I might be driven to sell your love for peace,
>   Or trade the memory of this night for food.
>   It well may be. I do not think I would.

55. During the Civil War, the federal government increased its power. Give at least five examples of how the central government expanded its power in the North during the Civil War.

56. Give a definition of and describe the relationship between the following:

a) Jim Crow laws

b) *Plessy vs. Ferguson*

CSET

Practice Test 1

Subtest II:

Science
Mathematics

Practice Test 1: Subtest II
Science
Mathematics

DIRECTIONS: This test consists of two sections: multiple-choice and constructed-response questions. The former is composed of 52 multiple-choice questions and the latter is composed of four questions that involve written responses. You may work on the questions in any order, keeping in mind that when taking the actual test you will have one five-hour test session in which to complete the subtest(s) for which you are registered.

Multiple-Choice Questions

Science

1. Which of the following defines a salt?

    (A)   One of the reactant products of an acid and base

    (B)   One of the reactant products of a base and water

    (C)   One of the reactant products of an acid and water

    (D)   Reactant product of a phase transformation

2. Atomic number for neutral (un-ionized) atoms as listed in the periodic table refers to

    (A) the number of neutrons in an atom.

    (B) the number of protons in an atom.

    (C) the number of electrons in an atom.

    (D) Both B and C.

3. Which of the following is a phenomenon involving the physical properties of a substance?

    (A) Corrosion of iron   (C) Rocket engine ignition

    (B) Burning of wood   (D) Melting of ice

4. Isotopes of a given element contain

    (A) more electrons than protons with equal numbers of neutrons.

    (B) more protons than electrons with equal numbers of neutrons.

    (C) differing numbers of neutrons.

    (D) unequal numbers of protons and electrons and equal numbers of neutrons.

5. Newton's Second Law of Motion states that "the summation of forces acting on a body is equal to the product of mass and acceleration." Which of the following is a good example of the law's application?

    (A) Decreased friction between surfaces by means of lubrication

    (B) Potential energy stored in a compressed spring

    (C) A rocket lifting off at Cape Canaveral with increasing speed

    (D) Using a claw hammer to pull a nail out with multiplied force

6. Which of the following is most likely to contain the greatest thermal energy?

    (A) The Pacific Ocean with an average temperature of 50°F

    (B) A 1 g sample of molten metal at 2000°F

    (C) A bucket of water at 75°F

    (D) Lake Michigan at an average temperature of 50°F

7. A small mass is fired straight upwards with some initial velocity. Which of the following graphs would best represent a plot of velocity (*y*-axis) vs. time (*x*-axis) over the time it takes to reach its high point?

(A)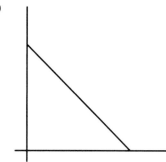

(C)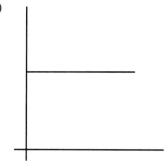

(B)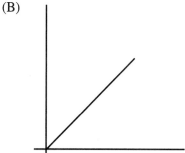

(D)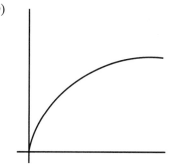

8. A plastic rod is charged by means of rubbing it with a silk cloth. The charging action involves the

    (A) transfer of electrons from one body to the other.

    (B) transfer of protons from one body to the other.

    (C) transfer of neutrons from one body to the other.

    (D) transfer of atoms from one body to the other.

9. Two charged bodies are brought near to one another. The force each experiences is repulsive. The charge on each body is, therefore,

    (A) equal and opposite in polarity.

    (B) not necessarily equal and opposite in polarity.

    (C) equal with same polarity.

    (D) not necessarily equal with same polarity.

10. Which cellular component is responsible for the regulation of exchanges of substances between a cell and its environment?

    (A) The endoplasmic reticulum   (C) The cytoplasm

    (B) The cell nucleus   (D) The cell membrane

11. Genetic information that needs to move out of the nucleus cannot leave by way of the DNA; therefore, it is carried out by the

    (A) tRNA.   (C) tDNA.

    (B) mDNA.   (D) mRNA.

12. A nucleotide consists of

    (A) sugar, protein, and uracil.

    (B) sugar, phosphate group, and nitrogenous base.

    (C) starch, nitrogenous base, and a sugar.

    (D) protein, starch, and a sugar.

13. Humans have 46 chromosomes in their body cells. How many chromosomes are found in the zygote?

    (A) 2   (C) 23

    (B) 10   (D) 46

14. The order of skin layers from the outside of the body proceeding inward is

    (A) stratum corneum, layer of Malpighi, dermis.

    (B) stratum corneum, layer of Malpighi, epidermis.

    (C) dermis, layer of Malpighi, stratum corneum.

    (D) dermis, stratum corneum, layer of Malpighi.

15. Human body temperature regulation via the skin involves

    (A) respiration.   (C) perspiration.

    (B) transpiration.   (D) sensation.

16. Darwin's original theory of natural selection asserts that

    (A) all organisms have descended with modification from a common ancestor.

    (B) random genetic drift plays a major role in speciation.

(C)   species characteristics are inherited by means of genes.

(D)   speciation is usually due to gradual accumulation of small genetic changes.

17.   The following reaction describes photosynthesis: $CO_2 + H_2O \rightarrow$ glucose + oxygen. It is the means by which

(A)   plants produce light energy.

(B)   plants convert light energy into energy useful in internal processes.

(C)   plants directly consume light energy as food.

(D)   plants warm the atmosphere.

18.   Photosynthesis is a

(A)   reduction process where oxygen is reduced by a coenzyme.

(B)   reduction process where hydrogen is oxidized by a coenzyme.

(C)   reduction process where hydrogen is reduced by a coenzyme.

(D)   reduction process where oxygen is oxidized by a coenzyme.

19.   The lunar period is nearest in length to

(A)   24 hours.   (C)   365 days.

(B)   30 days.   (D)   1 week.

20.   A supernova normally occurs when

(A)   a star first initiates fusion.

(B)   galaxies collide.

(C)   the end of a star's lifetime nears, with its nuclear fuel exhausted.

(D)   a wandering comet plunges into the stars interior.

21.   The most important factor in Earth's seasonal patterns is the

(A)   distance from the sun to the Earth.

(B)   Earth's rotation period of 24 hours.

(C)   tilting of the Earth's axis.

(D)   moon and associated tides.

22. Metamorphic rocks are

    (A) derived from igneous rocks.

    (B) unrelated to igneous rocks.

    (C) a type of sedimentary rock.

    (D) a type of rock not found on this planet.

23. Which of the following is considered to be evidence for plate tectonics?

    (A) Continental coastline "fit"

    (B) Identical fossil evidence at fit locations

    (C) Intense geological activity in mountainous regions

    (D) All of the above

24. Sea floor spreading is characterized as

    (A) plate spreading with upwelling magma forming ridges.

    (B) plate collisions with associated ridge formation.

    (C) plate spreading with no ridge formation.

    (D) plate collisions with no ridge formation.

25. Igneous rocks are formed by

    (A) magma cooling in underground cells and pockets.

    (B) magma ejected aboveground as lava, which cools.

    (C) layers of sediment collecting and compacting at the bottom of lakes and seas.

    (D) both (A) and (B).

26. In descending order of abundance, what is the composition of the Earth's atmosphere?

    (A) Oxygen, nitrogen, carbon dioxide, trace gases

    (B) Nitrogen, oxygen, carbon dioxide, trace gases

    (C) Nitrogen, carbon dioxide, oxygen, trace gases

    (D) Carbon dioxide, oxygen, nitrogen, trace gases

Mathematics

27. Simplify the following expression: $6 + 2(x - 4)$.

   (A) $4x - 16$ (C) $2x - 2$

   (B) $2x - 14$ (D) $-24x$

28. If six cans of beans cost $1.50, what is the price of eight cans of beans?

   (A) $.90   (C) $1.60

   (B) $1.00   (D) $2.00

29. Bonnie's average score on three tests is 71. Her first two test scores are 64 and 87. What is her score on test three?

   (A)   62   (C)   74

   (B)   71   (D)   151

30. In the figure below, what is the perimeter of square *ABCD* if diagonal *AC* = 8?

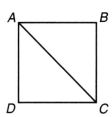

   (A)   32   (C) $4\sqrt{2}$

   (B)   64   (D) $16\sqrt{2}$

31. If $2x^2 + 5x - 3 = 0$ and $x > 0$, then what is the value of x?

   (A) $-\dfrac{1}{2}$ (C)   1

   (B) $\dfrac{1}{2}$ (D) $\dfrac{3}{2}$

32. A jar contains 20 balls. These balls are labeled 1 through 20. What is the probability that a ball chosen from the jar has a number on it that is divisible by 4?

   (A) $\dfrac{1}{20}$ (C) $\dfrac{1}{4}$

   (B) $\dfrac{1}{5}$ (D)   4

33. According to the chart, in what year were the total sales of Brand X televisions the greatest?

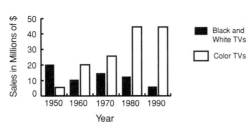

Sales of Brand X Televisions

(A) 1950

(B) 1960

(C) 1970

(D) 1980

34. How many odd prime numbers are there between 1 and 20?

(A) 7

(B) 8

(C) 9

(D) 10

35. Two concentric circles are shown in the figure below. The smaller circle has the radius $OA = 4$, and the larger circle has the radius $OB = 6$. Find the area of the shaded region.

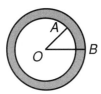

(A) 4π

(B) 16π

(C) 20π

(D) 36π

36. Solve the following inequality for x: $8 - 2x \le 10$.

(A) $x \le 1$

(B) $x \ge -9$

(C) $x \le -1$

(D) $x \ge -1$

37. In the figure shown below, $l_1 \parallel l_2$, $\triangle RTS$ is an isosceles triangle, and the measure of $\angle T = 80°$. Find the measure of $\angle OPR$.

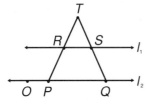

(A) 50°

(B) 80°

(C) 130°

(D) 105°

38. What is the midpoint of $\overline{MN}$ in the figure below?

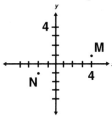

(A) (−4, 2)

(C) $\left(-\dfrac{3}{2}, 1\right)$

(B) (0, 0)

(D) (1, 0)

39. Linda bought a jacket on sale at a 25% discount. If she paid $54 for the jacket, what was the original price of the jacket?

(A) $72.00

(C) $54.00

(B) $67.50

(D) $40.50

40. In the number 72104.58, what is the place value of the 2?

(A) Thousands

(C) Ten-thousands

(B) Millions

(D) Tenths

41. Mrs. Wall has $300,000. She wishes to give each of her six children an equal amount of her money. Which of the following methods will result in the amount that each child is to receive?

(A) $6 \times 300,000$

(C) $300,000 \div 6$

(B) $6 \div 300,000$

(D) $6 - 300,000$

42. Bob wants to bake some cupcakes. His recipe uses $2^2/_3$ cups of flour to produce 36 cupcakes. How many cups of flour should Bob use to bake 12 cupcakes?

(A) $\dfrac{1}{3}$

(C) 1

(B) $\dfrac{8}{9}$

(D) $1\dfrac{2}{9}$

43. Ricky drove from Town A to Town B in 3 hours. His return trip from Town B to Town A took 5 hours because he drove 15 miles per hour slower on the return trip. How fast did Ricky drive on the trip from Town A to Town B?

(A) 25.5 mph

(C) 37.5 mph

(B) 32 mph

(D) 45 mph

44. Which of the following inequalities represents the shaded region in the figure below?

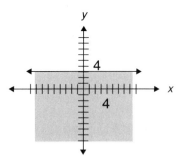

(A) $x \geq 2$

(B) $x \leq 2$

(C) $y \geq 2$

(D) $y \leq 2$

45. Round the following number to the nearest hundredths place: 287.416.

(A) 300

(B) 290

(C) 287.42

(D) 287.41

46. If $a = b^3$ and $a = \dfrac{1}{8}$, what is the value of b?

(A) $\dfrac{1}{512}$

(B) $\dfrac{1}{8}$

(C) $\dfrac{3}{8}$

(D) $\dfrac{1}{2}$

47. In a barn there were lambs and people. If we counted 30 heads and 104 legs in the barn, how many lambs and how many people were in the barn?

(A) 10 lambs and 20 people

(B) 16 lambs and 14 people

(C) 18 lambs and 16 people

(D) 22 lambs and 8 people

48. If two lines, l_1 and l_2, which lie in the same plane, are both perpendicular to a third line, l_3, in the same plane as the first two, what do you definitely know about l_1 and l_2?

(A) l_1 and l_2 are perpendicular.

(B) l_1 and l_2 are parallel.

(C) l_1 and l_2 intersect.

(D) l_1 and l_2 are skew.

49. What is $\dfrac{1}{2} + \dfrac{1}{3}$?

(A) $\dfrac{1}{5}$ (C) $\dfrac{1}{6}$

(B) $\dfrac{2}{5}$ (D) $\dfrac{5}{6}$

50. Which of the following sets is graphed below?

(A) $\{x \mid x \geq -1\}$ (C) $\{x \mid x \leq -1\}$

(B) $\{x \mid x > -1\}$ (D) $\{x \mid x < -1\}$

51. According to the graph, during how many months was supply greater than demand?

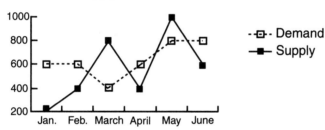

(A) 0   (C) 2

(B) 1   (D) 3

52. What is the greatest common divisor of 120 and 252?

(A) 2   (C) 6

(B) 3   (D) 12

Constructed-Response Questions

Constructed-Response Directions

Prepare a written response for each constructed-response assignment. Read each assignment carefully before you begin to write. Think about how you will organize what you plan to write.

Scoring of responses to CSET: Multiple Subjects constructed response assignments is based on the following criteria:

PURPOSE: the extent to which the response addresses the constructed-response assignment's charge in relation to relevant CSET content specifications.

SUBJECT MATTER KNOWLEDGE: the application of accurate subject matter knowledge as described in the relevant CSET content specifications.

SUPPORT: the appropriateness and quality of the supporting evidence in relation to relevant CSET content specifications.

The assignments are intended to assess subject matter knowledge and skills, not writing ability. Your responses, however, must be communicated clearly enough to permit a valid judgment of your knowledge and skills. Your responses should be written for an audience of educators in the field.

You may wish to write each of your responses to the CSET: Multiple Subjects Subtest II practice test constructed-response assignments and ask a mentor, advisor, or teacher to help evaluate them. Sample responses are provided for these assignments following the detailed answers section of the Subtest II practice test.

53. Use the diagram shown to complete the exercise that follows.

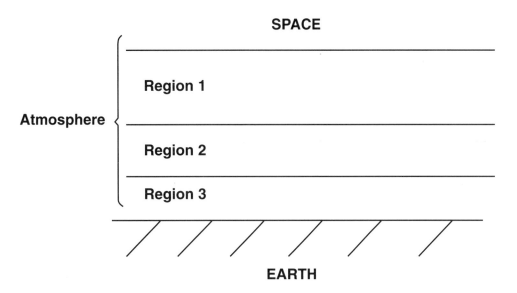

SPACE

Atmosphere {
Region 1

Region 2

Region 3

EARTH

The diagram above shows three regions of the Earth's atmosphere above the Earth's surface. Using your knowledge of Earth and atmospheric science, respond to the following questions:

1. What are the names of Regions 1, 2, and 3?

2. List major differences in each region, taking into account factors such as temperature, weather, density, ionization, and composition.

3. Which gas in atmospheric composition is most important in the greenhouse effect? Describe its role in the process.

54. Use the diagram shown to complete the exercise that follows.

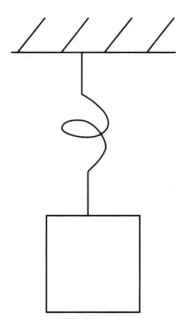

A block of a certain mass is connected to a spring as shown. The system is set into vibration by pulling down on the mass and releasing it.

Using your knowledge of motion and energy, respond to the following questions.

1.   Briefly define potential and kinetic energy and specify which parts of the system are associated with each.

2.   When the block is at its high point, what is the block's kinetic energy?

3.   When the block is halfway between the high point and low point, what is the block's kinetic energy?

4.   Where will block speed be maximum and zero? Why?

5.   How will the sum of potential and kinetic energy at the high point compare with the sum at the low point? Why?

55. The following is a list of yearly salaries for Company A:

    $20,000

    $20,000

    $25,000

    $32,000

    $33,000

    $90,000

    $95,000

The median salary for Company A is $32,000.
The mean salary for Company A is $45,000.

Why is the median salary, rather than the mean salary, a better indication of the average salary of this company?

56. A child's kite is on top of a straight pine tree. A ladder is placed against the tree and touches the kite. The ladder forms a 45° angle with the flat ground. The base of the tree is 4 feet away from the base of the ladder.

With only this information, how can you determine the height of the tree?

CSET

Practice Test 1

Subtest III:
Physical Education
Human Development
Visual and Performing Arts

Practice Test 1: Subtest III

Physical Education
Human Development
Visual and Performing Arts

> DIRECTIONS: This test consists of two sections: multiple-choice and constructed-response questions. The former is composed of 39 multiple-choice questions and the latter is composed of three questions, that involve written responses. You may work on the questions in any order, keeping in mind that when taking the actual test you will have one five-hour test session in which to complete the subtest(s) for which you are registered.

Multiple-Choice Questions

Physical Education

1. The handicapping conditions represented by Public Law 94-142 includes children defined as

    I.   Mentally retarded

    II. Hard of hearing

    III. Learning disabled

(A) I and II.

(C) III only.

(B) I only.

(D) I, II, and III.

2. Most children with a history of epileptic seizures

(A) can take part in physical education programs with nonepileptics.

(B) may participate in limited activities, depending on the type of seizure experienced.

(C) may experience minor motor seizures during physical activity.

(D) will have an abnormal increase in heart rate and blood pressure during physical activity.

3. Activities that develop gross motor-visual skills almost always involve the use of a

(A) ball.

(C) trampoline.

(B) balance beam.

(D) exercise mat.

4. A volleyball game scores for

(A) 12 points, and the serving team must win by 1 point.

(B) 11 points, and the serving team must win by 1 point.

(C) 25 points, and the serving team must win by 2 points.

(D) 14 points, and the serving team must win by 2 points.

5. Exercise systems commonly used to develop muscular strength include

I.   Weight training

II. Interval training

III. Isometric training

IV. Isokinetic training

(A) I, II, and III.

(C) I and II.

(B) I, III, and IV.

(D) III and IV.

6. During prolonged exercise in the heat, fluid balance is reestablished by

(A) consuming salt tablets.

(C) drinking water.

(B) taking vitamins.

(D) taking mineral supplements.

7. Most of the calories in an athlete's diet should be derived from

   I.   Fats

   II. Carbohydrates

   III. Proteins

   (A) I and II.   (C) II only.

   (B) I only.   (D) III only.

8. Of the following, which test does NOT measure muscular strength and endurance in children?

   (A) Pull-ups   (C) Grip strength test

   (B) Flexed arm hang   (D) Sit and reach test

9. Dance steps most appropriate for younger children (grades 1–2) are

   (A) walk and/or skip. (C) skip and slide.

   (B) run and/or skip.   (D) skip and step-hop.

10. Which of the following minerals is not known to prevent muscle cramping?

    (A) Calcium   (C) Potassium

    (B) Magnesium   (D) Sodium

11. The "E" in the acronym R.I.C.E., a treatment process for sprains, represents

    (A) exercise.   (C) evaluation.

    (B) elevation.   (D) expose.

12. To complete an effective aerobic workout, exercise should be performed at an individual's target heart rate for a minimum of

    (A) 15 minutes.   (C) 30 minutes.

    (B) 20 minutes.   (D) 45 minutes.

13. What percentage of a diet should be composed of carbohydrates?

    (A) 20%   (C) 40%

    (B) 25%   (D) 50%

Human Development

QUESTIONS 14–16 refer to the following passage.

Miss Sharp's fourth-grade class is studying a unit entitled "Discoveries" in social studies and science. Miss Sharp has prepared four learning centers for the class. In Learning Center #1 students use information from their science and social studies textbooks to prepare a time line of discoveries that occurred between 1800 and 1990. In Learning Center #2 students use a variety of resource materials to research one particular discovery or discoverer they have selected from a prepared list. Each student then records what they learned about this discovery or discoverer on an individual chart that will later be shared with the whole class. In Learning Center #3 students add small amounts of five different substances to jars of water and record the results over a period of five minutes. In Learning Center #4 students write a description of the need for a new discovery to solve a problem or answer a question. Then students suggest several possible areas of research that may contribute to this new discovery.

14. Miss Sharp introduces the learning centers by explaining the purpose of each center and giving directions for each activity. Next, she divides the class of 22 into four groups and assigns each group to a different center. After 20 minutes, some students are completely finished with one center and want to move on, but other students have only just begun working. What would be the best solution to this situation?

   (A) Each learning center should be revised so that the activities will require approximately the same amount of time to complete.

   (B) Students who finish one center early should be given additional work to complete before moving to the next center.

   (C) Students should be permitted to move from center to center as they complete each activity as long as no more than six students are working at each center.

   (D) Students should be permitted to work through the activities in each center as quickly as possible so that the class can move on to the next unit.

15. Which of the following would be the most appropriate concluding activity for the Discoveries unit?

   (A) Students should have a class party celebrating the birthday of Marie Curie, Jonas Salk, and Thomas Edison.

   (B) Each student should be required to prepare a verbal report detailing what they learned about an important medical discovery.

   (C) Each student should take a multiple-choice test containing questions related to each learning center.

(D) Each student should design a concluding activity, or select one from a prepared list, that reflects what they learned about a discovery they studied.

16. In selecting resource materials for Learning Center #2, Miss Sharp carefully chooses materials that present information about a variety of discoveries made by both men and women from several different countries. Her purpose in making these selections is most probably to ensure that materials

(A) are challenging but written at the appropriate reading level.

(B) demonstrate the diversity of individuals who have made discoveries.

(C) contain information about discoveries included in the textbook.

(D) will be of interest to the majority of the students.

17. The stage of development within which a child can reliably demonstrate conservation of mass and number is the _____ stage.

(A) preoperational   (C) operational

(B) sensorimotor   (D) concrete

QUESTIONS 18–19 refer to the following passage.

The fourth-grade students in Mrs. Alvarez's class are studying Native Americans. Mrs. Alvarez wants to strengthen her student's ability to work independently. She also wants to provide opportunities for the students to use a variety of print and media resources during this unit of study. Mrs. Alvarez plans to begin the unit by leading the class in a brainstorming session to formulate questions to guide their research about Native Americans.

18. Which of the following criteria should guide Mrs. Alvarez as she leads the brainstorming session?

(A) The questions should emphasize the factual content presented in the available print materials.

(B) The questions should emphasize higher order thinking skills, such as comparison, analysis, and evaluation.

(C) The questions should reflect the interest of the students.

(D) The questions should include all of the fourth-grade objectives for this unit.

19. Mrs. Alvarez has collected a variety of print and media resources for the students to use in their research. Which of the following will probably be the best way to motivate students to research the questions they have prepared?

    (A) The teacher should assign two to three questions to each student so that all the questions are covered.

    (B) The teacher should allow individual students to select the questions they would like to research.

    (C) The teacher should select three key questions and assign them to all the students.

    (D) The teacher should assign one topic to each student, then provide the students with additional information.

20. In which of Piaget's stages of cognitive development will a child realize that when a volume of water is poured from a tall, narrow beaker to a wide beaker, the volume remains the same even though it reaches a lower level?

    (A) Preoperational   (C) Concrete operational

    (B) Sensorimotor   (D) Latency

QUESTIONS 21–24 refer to the following passage.

Mrs. Gettler teaches 26 third graders in a large inner city school. About one-third of her students participate in the ESL program at the school. Mrs. Gettler suspects that some of the students' parents are unable to read or write in English. Four of the students receive services from the learning resource teacher. At the beginning of the year, none of the students read above 2.0 grade level, and some of the students did not know all the letters of the alphabet.

21. Which of the following describes the instructional strategy that is most likely to improve the reading levels of Mrs. Gettler's students?

    (A) An intensive phonics program that includes drill and practice work on basic sight words.

    (B) An emergent literacy program emphasizing pattern books and journal writing using invented spelling.

    (C) An instructional program that closely follows the third-grade basal reader.

    (D) All the students should participate in the school's ESL program and receive services from the learning resource center.

22. Mrs. Gettler is selecting books for the classroom library. In addition to student interest, which of the following would be the most important considerations?

    (A) The books should have a reading level that matches the students' independent reading ability.

    (B) The books should only have a reading level that is challenging to the students.

    (C) The books should include separate word lists for student practice.

    (D) A classroom library is not appropriate for students at such a low reading level.

23. Which of the following individual and small group learning centers is suitable for Mrs. Gettler's class?

    I.   A post office center where students can write letters to friends and family.

    II. A restaurant center where students read menus, write food orders, and pay the bill with play money.

    III. A weather center where students record current conditions, including temperature, cloud cover and wind direction, and prepare graphs of weather patterns.

    IV. A science center where students record the results of experiments with combining liquids such as bleach, vinegar, cooking oil, food coloring, and rubbing alcohol.

    (A) I only.   (C) I, II, and III.

    (B) I and II.   (D) II, III, and IV.

24. Mrs. Gettler realizes that an individual's preferred learning style contributes to that individual's success as a student. Mrs. Gettler wants to accommodate as many of her students' individual learning styles as possible. Which of the following best describes the way to identify the students' learning styles?

    (A) Mrs. Gettler should record her observations of individual students' behaviors over a period of several weeks.

    (B) Each of the students should be tested by the school psychologist.

    (C) Mrs. Gettler should administer a group screening test for identifying learning styles.

    (D) Mrs. Gettler should review the permanent file of each student and compare the individual's previous test scores with classroom performance

25. If, during a child's development, the amount of frustration and anxiety concerning movement to the next stage becomes too great, development may come to a halt. The individual is then said to have become

    (A) dependent.   (C) fixated.

    (B) passive.   (D) regressive.

26. Maslow would contend that a person must first satisfy _____ needs before satisfying _____ needs.

    (A) cognitive ... attachment   (C) aestetic ... esteem

    (B) attachment ... esteem   (D) safety ... biological

Visual and Performing Arts

27. The great ziggurat at Ur was produced by a Mesopotamian civilization known as the

    (A) Egyptians.   (C) Assyrians.

    (B) Sumerians.   (D) Babylonians.

28. Flying buttresses, pointed arches, and stained glass windows are characteristic of which historic style of architecture?

    (A) Romanesque   (C) Renaissance

    (B) Byzantine   (D) Gothic

29. Jackson Pollock's *Lucifer* of 1947 is an example of which post-World War II artistic movement?

    (A) Fauvism   (C) Cubism

    (B) Futurism   (D) Abstract Expressionism

30. Use the reproduction below of Caravaggio's *The Conversion of St. Paul* to answer the question that follows.

Caravaggio, *The Conversion of St. Paul*

This work exhibits all of the following characteristics EXCEPT:

(A) a contrast of deep shadows and bright highlights.

(B) a sense of drama.

(C) a preference for soft contours and loose brushwork.

(D) a strongly foreshortened figure.

31. A printmaking process that involves the use of a limestone block is

(A) lithography.   (C) etching.

(B) engraving.   (D) woodcutting.

32. The costumed characters pictured below would be most appropriate for which of the following plays?

(A) Ibsen's *A Doll's House*   (C) Shaw's *Pygmalion*

(B) Shakespeare's *Twelfth Night*   (D) Aristophanes' *The Birds*

33. Which of the following is a complementary color pair?

   (A) Blue and green.

   (C) Red and green.

   (B) Yellow and red.

   (D) Purple and red.

QUESTIONS 34–35 are based on the following works of art.

(A)

(B)

(C)

(D)

(A) Alexander Archipenko, *Woman Combing Her Hair,* Museum of Modern Art, New York

(B) Henry Moore, *Reclining Figure,* Detroit Institute of Art

(C) *Venus of Willendorf,* Naturhistorisches Museum, Vienna

(D) Henri Matisse, *Back I,* Tate Gallery, London

34. Which of the above figures seems to best embody the compositional principles of Cubism?

35. Which of the above may have served as a Paleolithic fertility idol?

36. Use the illustration below of a Buddhist burial mound in India to answer the question that follows.

Completed in the first century C.E., structures like this one are among the most important ancient architectural monuments of southern Asia. They are called

(A) pagodas.   (C) mastabas.

(B) stupas.   (D) mandorlas.

37. "Form Follows Function" is an expression coined by

(A) Frank Lloyd Wright.   (C) Le Corbusier.

(B) Louis Sullivan.   (D) Mies van der Rohe.

38. Use the reproduction below of *Nude Descending a Staircase, No. 2*, to answer the question that follows.

This painting was created by

(A) Marcel Duchamp.

(B) Pablo Picasso.

(C) Georges Braque.

(D) Piet Mondrian.

39. In a perspective drawing, the lines that appear to be perpendicular to the picture plane and which intersect at the vanishing point are called

(A) epigones.

(B) orthogonals.

(C) hatchings.

(D) imagines.

Constructed-Response Questions

Constructed-Response Directions

Prepare a written response for each constructed-response assignment. Read each assignment carefully before you begin to write. Think about how you will organize what you plan to write.

Scoring of responses to CSET: Multiple Subjects constructed-response assignments is based on the following criteria:

PURPOSE: the extent to which the response addresses the constructed-response assignment's charge in relation to relevant CSET content specifications.

SUBJECT MATTER KNOWLEDGE: the application of accurate subject matter knowledge as described in the relevant CSET content specifications.

SUPPORT: the appropriateness and quality of the supporting evidence in relation to relevant CSET content specifications.

The assignments are intended to assess subject matter knowledge and skills, not writing ability. Your responses, however, must be communicated clearly enough to permit a valid judgment of your knowledge and skills. Your responses should be written for an audience of educators in the field.

You may wish to write each of your responses to the CSET: Multiple Subjects Subtest III practice test constructed-response assignments and ask a mentor, advisor, or teacher to help evaluate them. Sample responses are provided for these assignments following the detailed answers section of the Subtest III practice test.

40. Briefly describe two ways in which teachers can enhance students' self-esteem in the context of physical education.

41. Briefly describe two different styles of learning and ways in which a teacher must adapt to these styles.

42. Briefly describe ways in which theater can be said to encompass all the artistic disciplines.

Answer Key

Subtest I:

Reading, Language & Literature; History & Social Science

1.	(D)	14.	(B)	27.	(D)	40.	(B)
2.	(B)	15.	(D)	28.	(A)	41.	(B)
3.	(B)	16.	(C)	29.	(D)	42.	(B)
4.	(A)	17.	(C)	30.	(D)	43.	(A)
5.	(D)	18.	(B)	31.	(B)	44.	(B)
6.	(C)	19.	(A)	32.	(C)	45.	(D)
7.	(A)	20.	(B)	33.	(A)	46.	(D)
8.	(A)	21.	(C)	34.	(C)	47.	(A)
9.	(C)	22.	(A)	35.	(C)	48.	(B)
10.	(D)	23.	(B)	36.	(B)	49.	(A)
11.	(C)	24.	(C)	37.	(B)	50.	(C)
12.	(B)	25.	(D)	38.	(B)	51.	(B)
13.	(A)	26.	(A)	39.	(C)	52.	(B)

Subtest II:

Science; Mathematics

1.	(A)	14.	(A)	27.	(C)	40.	(A)
2.	(D)	15.	(C)	28.	(D)	41.	(C)
3.	(D)	16.	(A)	29.	(A)	42.	(B)
4.	(D)	17.	(B)	30.	(D)	43.	(C)
5.	(C)	18.	(C)	31.	(B)	44.	(D)
6.	(A)	19.	(B)	32.	(C)	45.	(C)
7.	(A)	20.	(C)	33.	(D)	46.	(D)
8.	(A)	21.	(C)	34.	(A)	47.	(D)
9.	(D)	22.	(A)	35.	(C)	48.	(B)
10.	(D)	23.	(D)	36.	(D)	49.	(D)
11.	(D)	24.	(A)	37.	(C)	50.	(A)
12.	(B)	25.	(D)	38.	(D)	51.	(C)
13.	(D)	26.	(B)	39.	(A)	52.	(D)

Answer Key (cont.)

Subtest III:

Physical Education; Human Development; Visual and Performing Arts

1.	(D)	14.	(C)	27.	(B)
2.	(A)	15.	(D)	28.	(D)
3.	(A)	16.	(B)	29.	(D)
4.	(C)	17.	(D)	30.	(C)
5.	(B)	18.	(C)	31.	(A)
6.	(C)	19.	(B)	32.	(B)
7.	(C)	20.	(C)	33.	(C)
8.	(D)	21.	(B)	34.	(A)
9.	(A)	22.	(A)	35.	(C)
10.	(D)	23.	(C)	36.	(B)
11.	(B)	24.	(A)	37.	(B)
12.	(B)	25.	(C)	38.	(A)
13.	(D)	26.	(B)	39.	(B)

Practice Test 1: Subtest I
Detailed Explanations of Answers

Multiple-Choice Section

1. **D**

The prisoners are speedily sentenced because the judges and the jurymen are hungry and want to go home for supper as the day ends—the prisoners may be guilty, but the wrong reasons determine their sentences (D). No doubt the people do believe in the system, but the sarcasm of the piece suggests that this society uses the system for personal selfish benefits—certainly not a humanitarian society.

2. **B**

The society depicted is shallow and trivial, engaging in chatty conversations that everyone takes seriously. Serious as the discussions may be, they possibly involve extramarital affairs rather than affairs of state (C, D)—such gossip ruins reputations (B). The gossiping involves the Queen, but it is not revealed that she is slandered (which would involve maliciousness), which, if you hadn't already done so, eliminates (D) along with (A).

3. **B**

The question wants you to analyze the clash or conflict of two very different concepts in conversation: the glory of the Queen in one breath and a fire screen (or room divider) in another. The juxtaposition is not so much to suggest trivia or seriousness (the Queen's glory is serious but the furniture is not), but that this society holds both in equal reverence (B). No real evidence is given that the people are Royalists or Imperialists.

4. **A**

There is a clever use of the language in this one adverb. It stands for the angle of the sun as it declines at a steep angle but also for the hidden meanings behind the word as it refers to this society: the deceit, the amorality. It certainly does not mean that the sun is at a perpendicular angle (A).

5. **D**

The move is light to dark in the physical movement of the day but not specifically in the voice. On analysis you will find the "coming down" of mood from amusement at the chat of the day—the trivia—to a sadness of the effect of the hunger of the court officials, a hunger that sends men to the gallows. The answer is (D).

6. **C**

Evidence in the passage indicates the old clerk is still a good records keeper. Mr. Jonas observes that he "an't a bad clerk," to which Anthony adds, "A very good one." Mr. Jonas is obviously unconcerned about hurting the old clerk's feelings (B) as he says terribly rude things in front of his father and the old clerk. Mr. Jonas says the clerk is "old," and he is not "pleased with him for that." Mr. Jonas' irritation with the old man shows through when he points out the clerk's inability (A) to hear no one but Mr. Jonas' father. Perhaps Mr. Jonas is trying to impress the young ladies (D) as he addresses them "apart."

7. **A**

Mr. Jonas' father is described in the passage as "honoured parent." This wording might be taken ironically, and perhaps is humorous given the way he speaks in front of his parent, but Mr. Jonas goes on to say how the two old men are used to each other. As it would probably upset Mr. Jonas' father to do without his longtime companion, (A) is the logical conclusion. Choice (C) is a possible option, but "revere" is too strong a word given the tone Mr. Jonas uses. Mr. Jonas is more concerned with impressing than offending the young ladies (B), and there is no evidence to support (D).

8.

Although "precious" can mean all of the definitions listed as possible answers, "very old" is the best meaning for "precious old" because the rest of the passage details the old clerk's eccentricities brought on by the passing of time. Choices (B) and (C) may apply to the way Mr. Jonas' father feels about the clerk, but they do not fit Mr. Jonas' feelings. Nowhere in the passage is (D) discussed.

9.

When the old clerk took a fever "twenty years ago or so," he was delirious for three weeks. The entire time he had fever, he "never left off" running figures in his head, and the figures eventually became so high that his brain became addled. Choice (B) may have contributed to the clerk's problem, but it is not the immediate cause. Choice (A) is incorrect as the fever happened many years before he grew deaf. Choice (D) may have contributed, but there is no evidence in the passage to indicate it.

10.

During the conversation between Mr. Jonas and Anthony about the clerk's worth as a worker, Mr. Jonas comments, "He an't a dear one" and then explains how he "earns his salt." The idiom "earns his salt" means he "earns his wages," so "dear" can be taken to mean "expensive" in this context: the old clerk does not have to be paid much but he earns his pay. Although (A) may be true, it is not the meaning in this context. There is no evidence to support (B) or (C).

11.

The clerk's being a good whist player seems to strike a bit of admiration in Mr. Jonas because the old man can play well even when he "had no more notion what sort of people he was playing against, than you have." Even though he seems to be amazed at the old clerk's whist game, Mr. Jonas seems irritated the old man is unaware of anyone else but the "honoured parent" (D). Mr. Jonas speaks disparagingly of the clerk's age (A) and strangeness (B).

12.

During his fever, the old clerk added numbers for three weeks. The numbers mounted steadily into "so many million at last." Choice (D) is a possibility, but evidence in the passage does not indicate this probability. The fever happened before (C) became a factor. Choice (A) has no evidence to support it.

13. **A**

The old clerk seems sharp enough dealing with accustomed things—clerking, whist, responding to Mr. Jonas' father—but he has difficulties with responding to new people and situations.

There is no evidence (B) is correct: The passage references a problem he has with understanding what is being said, not hearing it. Keeping books and playing whist are not "the simplest of tasks" (C). What the old clerk "would like" (C) to do or is pleased (D) to do is not a consideration in this passage. It seems as if the old man's mind is permanently afflicted; Mr. Jonas says of him after the fever, "I don't believe he's ever been quite right since."

14. Ⓑ

According to current linguistic theories, use is the criterion by which the meaning of a word may be measured. The meaning of any particular word or utterance is context-bound, changing from situation to situation and dependent on the specific circumstances of that situation. Meaning thus conceived is a public event, which people can observe and assess; choice (B) is correct. A general, dictionary definition of a word is inadequate to explain the meaning of a word, because it only applies to one particular type of situation. Even if a dictionary offers several possible meanings for a word, it doesn't provide any method by which to select from these possibilities to assess the meaning of a word in a particular situation; choice (A) is incorrect. Words are sometimes used to refer to objects, but this is by no means the only way in which they are used, thus (C) is not the best choice. Thoughts or ideas "in the mind" are not visible, and we could never be sure that what occurs in the speaker's mind when he or she utters a word is the same as what occurs in the listener's mind; choice (D) is not correct.

15. Ⓓ

Saussure was one of the first linguists to propose that there was no particular or logical connection between a word and what it refers to. While the connection between a word and its referent is arbitrary, it is nonetheless held in place by conventional practice; words are thus not used at random by each speaker of a language but rather according to the ways previous speakers have used them; choice (D) is correct. Choices (B) and (C), while both correct statements in and of themselves, were not discoveries of Saussure's, but rather generally available empirical information that he used in order to arrive at his conclusion. Neither (B) nor (C) is the best answer. The notion that a word has an inherent, one-to-one correspondence with its referent, choice (A), is the prior linguistic theory against which Saussure made his claim of arbitrariness. Choice (A) is incorrect.

16. Ⓒ

According to the studies of Maurice Merleau-Ponty, there are a number of generally discernible stages in childhood language development. While warning against the danger of insisting too heavily on artificial divisions, Merleau-Ponty nonetheless recognized several particular stages in the child's acquisition of language, based on increasingly sophisticated operations of imitation. He also allowed for the possibility of temporary regression in these stages, in addition to that of precocious advancement where the child suddenly manifests a linguistic capacity previously absorbed but hitherto undisplayed. Choice (C) is the correct answer. The conception of the acquisition of language as a child's learning to express his or her thoughts is an incoherent notion, because it necessarily presupposes a prior language in which the child is having such thoughts; choice (A) is therefore incorrect. As Merleau-Ponty's study indicates, the child's acquisition of language is able to be divided roughly into successive stages, avoiding either extreme of a strict series of stages each logically dependent on the previous one, or of a chaotic, undefinable development. Both extremes, choice (B) and choice (D), are not correct.

17. **C**

Merleau-Ponty, as we have seen in the article above, denies that there is a radical distinction between the way children learn language and the way adults continue to expand their linguistic repertoire. As children learn language by being surrounded by it, so too do adults acquire new verbal possibilities primarily by dint of their exposure to them. Choice (C) is therefore correct. It is only rarely that adults find it necessary to interrupt a conversational sequence for explanation of a specific unfamiliar term or phrase; hence, (A) is not the best answer. Similarly, even in technical or academic situations, the meaning of a new term or expression is generally established by the use a given writer or speaker is making of it; thus, (B) is not the correct choice. The use of a dictionary or thesaurus, choice (D), is generally not an effective means of learning language, as such reference books cannot tell you how the new linguistic item in question is used in its various, particular applications. Choice (D) is not correct.

18. **B**

Like meaning, the intention of an utterance is "on the surface," manifested within the particular situation and measurable by outward criteria pertinent to the situation. Choice (B) is thus correct. Intention is not a private act occurring in the mind of a speaker; if one couldn't express one's intentions verbally to another person, one wouldn't be able to articulate them to oneself. Therefore, choice (B) is correct. For the same reason, choice (A) cannot be correct. If intentions were unknowable, it would make no sense to speak of intentions at all; hence, choice (C) is incorrect. Finally, the notion that intention is public and "on the surface" contradicts previous linguistic theories of "deep structure," which maintained that one must translate a given sentence into another set of words in order for its intention to be clear. The problem with such a notion is that there is nothing to guarantee the adequacy of the translation and thus we are involved in an infinite regress. If the intention of an utterance cannot be made clear by the utterance itself, it is unlikely another set of words would possess such clarity. Choice (D) is therefore incorrect.

19. **A**

Because intention is a public event, measurable by outward criteria, the best way to judge whether or not a given intention has been fulfilled is to observe the actions that follow from it. Choice (A) is therefore correct. Both choices (B) and (C) attempt to remove intention from what is publicly observable and to locate it in the mind, either of the speaker or the listener. Neither (B) nor (C) can be the correct choice. Consulting the rules of standard American English, choice (D) would similarly focus our attention away from the situation itself to an abstract concept of language. But because an intention is manifested in the given situation of the utterance, it would be impossible to consider in the abstract, by a set of rules not bound to any particular set of circumstances. Choice (D) is thus incorrect.

20. **(B)**

The correct answer is (B), as the revised sentence is more concise. The other choices are either off-topic (A), prolix (C), or unhelpful (D).

21. **(C)**

The correct answer is (C). The use of the term "culiminate" is the key clue. Every other choice would actually upset the logical organization of the passage.

22. **(A)**

A door that would open "straight upon life" would directly reveal life: fictional works are not such doors and do not strictly imitate life (A). (A) is a better answer than (B) because (B) interprets the phrase literally, not as the metaphor it is. (C) is incorrect because it relies upon a misinterpretation of "not...opening straight." There are no contextual references to the making of fiction (D).

23. **(B)**

"Apertures" (openings) precedes "they" and is synonymous with its predicate "windows" (B). (A) and (C) are incorrect because they follow "they" and are its predicates. "Need" and "pressure" (D) describe the formation of the windows, not the windows themselves.

24. **(C)**

The shift in point of view from "we" to "he" to "I" mimics the description of fiction that moves from building/genre housing all authors to each watcher at a window with an individual perspective (C). (A) is incorrect because the "house of fiction" contains authors, not their critics. The speaker neither affirms nor denies that he/she is a writer of fiction, making (B) incorrect. The use of "we" draws readers in and allies them with, rather than alienating them from, the speaker's perspective (D).

25. **(D)**

Choice (D), with its parallel pairs of contrasting words, exemplifies antithesis. There are no such contrasts in the other four choices. Shape and size (A), windows and doors (B), eyes and field-glass (C) are not opposites.

26. **A**

The speaker states that human scene/choice of subject and window/literary form are nothing without the "consciousness of the artist" (line 19). (B) and (D) are consequently incorrect. Hinged doors (C) are dismissed because they do not have the same function as the windows.

27. **D**

The answer is (D). While California has a number of rivers for white-water rafting, none of them is used for commerce. Therefore, (A), (B), and (C) are incorrect.

28. **A**

The answer is (A). Mexican liberals who controlled the new government demanded the secularization of the missions. The missions were highly productive (B), and the Franciscans had no intention of abandoning them (D). Moreover, by "pacifying" the natives, missionaries were an integral part of Spanish imperial policy (C) and supported by the crown.

29. **D**

The answer is (D). Los Angeles had no natural harbor (A), no dependable water supply (B), and no industry. Wheat was extracted in northern California (C). Los Angeles's growth sprung from the efforts of boosters and land speculators, who shrewdly used their great wealth, as well as municpal and federal subsidies, to build the necessary infrastructure in advance of demand.

30. **D**

Lincoln's immediate purpose in announcing the Emancipation Proclamation was to rally flagging Northern morale. Lincoln waited until after a major Union victory, at Antietam in 1862, so he couldn't be charged with making the announcement as an act of desperation. He recognized that the costs of the war had reached a point where preserving the Union would not be a powerful enough reason to motivate many Northerners to continue the war. Framing the war as a war against slavery would mobilize powerful abolitionist forces in the North and perhaps create an atmosphere of a "holy crusade" rather than one of using war to resolve a political conflict.

While the Emancipation Proclamation had the announced purpose of freeing the slaves, Lincoln himself indirectly stated that freeing the slaves was a means to a greater end, preserving the Union. In a statement released before the Emancipation Proclamation, Lincoln asserted, "If I could save the Union without freeing any slave I would do it, and if I could save it by freeing all the slaves I would do it...What I do about slavery, and the colored race I do because I believe it helps to save the Union."

31. (B)

In the 1857 case Dred Scott v. Sanford, *the Supreme Court held that no black slave could be a citizen of the United States. It was in the 1954 case* Brown v. Topeka Board of Education *that the court held separate facilities for the races to be unconstitutional (A). The reverse (C) was the court's holding in the 1896 case* Plessy v. Ferguson. *Affirmative Action was limited (D) in the 1970s and 1980s.*

32. (C)

O'Sullivan spoke of America's "manifest destiny to overspread the continent." The idea that America must eventually become either all slave or all free (D) was expressed by Lincoln in his "House Divided" speech and was called by William H. Seward the "Irresponsible Conflict." Racial equality (A) was still not a popular idea when O'Sullivan wrote in the first half of the nineteenth century. By that time, of course, America was already an independent country (B).

33. (A)

Thomas Paine wrote several pamphlets before and during the American Revolution. Common Sense *was the most significant because it carefully documented abuses of the British parliamentary system of government, particularly in its treatment of the American colonies. Paine portrayed a brutish monarchy interested only in itself and pointedly argued how independence would improve the colonies' long-term situation. His argument was directed at the common man, and it struck a chord unlike anything previously written in the colonies. Its publication in 1774 was perfect in reaching the public at just the moment that their questions and concerns regarding British rule were peaking. The answers provided in Paine's essays were pivotal in the subsequent behavior of many colonists who, until that time, had been unsure of what they believed regarding independence and British rule.*

Answer (B) is incorrect. Paine wrote another essay called American Crisis *during the winter of 1776. THIS essay, not* Common Sense, *helped rally American spirits during that long, demoralizing winter.*

Answers (C) and (D) are incorrect. Paine wrote to an American, not a British audience. He also wrote Common Sense *well before American independence was achieved.*

34. (C)

Lincoln firmly believed that the Southern states did not have the constitutional right to secede from the Union. He only went to war when Southerners attacked Fort Sumter, and then he mobilized Union forces to put down "a state of insurrection" in the Southern states. Throughout the war Lincoln repeatedly emphasized that his purpose in warring with the South was to preserve the Union of which he felt the Southern states were an integral part.

35. **C**

Marbury v. Madison *asserted for the first time the Supreme Court's right to declare an act of Congress unconstitutional. It did not, however, go so far as to claim that the Supreme Court alone was empowered to say what the Constitution meant (B). In the decision of this case, Chief Justice John Marshall wisely avoided issuing a directive (A) that President Thomas Jefferson would have defied (D) had it been issued.*

36. **B**

The term "Trail of Tears" is used to describe the relocation of the Cherokee tribe from the southern Appalachians to what is now Oklahoma. The migration of Mormons from Nauvoo, Illinois, to the Great Salt Lake in Utah (A), the westward movements along the Oregon Trail (C), and, much earlier, the Wilderness Road (D), all took place and could at times be as unpleasant as the Cherokees' trek. They were, however, voluntary and therefore did not earn such sad titles as the "Trail of Tears."

37. **B**

(B) is the correct answer. The Silk Road was a transcontinental trade route that branched out over a vast area, including (A) western China, (C) northern Iran, (D) northern India, and eventually the Sahara.

38. **B**

The Anaconda Plan envisioned the Union wrapping itself around the Confederacy like a giant boa constrictor, or anaconda, and slowly squeezing the life out of the Confederacy. The plan emphasized the Union's greatest area of superiority over the Confederacy, its large, well-equipped navy. The plan called for the Union navy to blockade Confederate ports along the Atlantic and Gulf coasts and to seize those ports whenever the opportunity arose. This would deny the Confederates the ability to import desperately needed goods or export cotton for badly needed cash. It would also open the door for potential Union land invasions anywhere along the thousands of miles of Confederate coastline, forcing the Confederates to spread out their forces wastefully. Secondly, the plan called for combined land and naval operations along the Mississippi River. Control of the Mississippi would effectively cut off Texas, Arkansas, and Louisiana from the rest of the Confederacy. It would also open the door for Union advances anywhere along the Mississippi River. Finally, the plan called for continuous pressure against the Confederate armies by Union land forces. The theory was that this combination of naval and land pressure would force the Confederacy to stretch its forces too thin, leaving weak spots in the defenses that Union forces could exploit. The blockade would isolate the South from international aid and cause its economy to collapse on itself. The plan did work; however, the South proved much more resilient than Northern planners had expected. As a result it took four years for the South to finally collapse, rather than the one to two years envisioned by Union planners when the Anaconda Plan was adopted.

39. **C**

The correct answer is (C) France and the Ottoman Empire. Austria was attacked twice during the period from 1660 to 1685 by the Ottoman Turks and was confronted during the same time by wars with France. (A) is incorrect because Italy did not exist as a nation-state, and Austria and Prussia were allies. (B) is incorrect because England was allied with Austria and Russia was undergoing political crises that were not stabilized until Peter the Great seized power and reformed the government. (D) is incorrect because of Austria's alliance with Prussia.

40. **B**

Democracy is the correct response because it is the antithesis of the authoritarianism of fascism. Indeed, the totalitarian, romantic, militaristic, and nationalistic characteristics were, in large part, a reaction against the perceived inadequacies of democracy.

41. **B**

The industrial economy of the nineteenth century was not based upon an equitable distribution of profits among all those who were involved in production. Marxists and other critics of capitalism condemned the creed of capitalists and the abhorrent conditions of the industrial proletariat. Raw materials, a constant labor supply, capital, and an expanding marketplace were critical elements in the development of the industrial economy.

42. **B**

Oscar Wilde's The Picture of Dorian Gray *and Thomas Mann's* Death in Venice *embodied a new symbolists' direction in literature that addressed themes that were ignored previously; these themes include fantasies relating to the perpetual "youth" in exchange for the soul, and homosexuality. These works and others of this vintage could not be (A) construed as examples of romantic literature in the literary tradition of romanticism nor can they be categorized as examples of the (C) new sense of realism in literature or examples (D) of any expressionist literary movement. Both of these works were applauded by intellectuals at the time of their publication.*

43. **A**

The response of the Catholic Church to the Reformation was delayed because the papacy feared the remnants of the Conciliar Movement within the church itself. The Conciliar Movement, which was clearly evident at the Council of Constance (1414) and later at the Councils of Basel and Florence, was a tradition in the Roman Catholic Church which asserted that authority within the church resided in the assembly of bishops; it was a challenge to the concept of Petrine Supremacy and the authority of the papacy. Rome (B) had little interest in coordinating its policy with secular leaders, although the early support of Charles V and Henry VIII was well received. By the 1530s most intelligent church leaders did not (C) think that Protestantism would self-destruct or that (D) the situation was not a serious crisis.

44. **B**

The whole "taxation without representation" issue revolved around Parliament's belief that its laws were sovereign (unchallengeable) in all parts of the empire, including the colonies. This sovereignty of parliamentary rule meant that Parliament could pass any taxes or laws in regard to the colonies and the colonies could not legally resist the enactment of these taxes or laws. The colonists, however, believed that without direct representation in Parliament, their rights as English citizens were being violated. In their view, the Parliament had no right to tax them or regulate them unless they were given direct parliamentary representation. Neither side was willing to compromise on the issue and without compromise, no solution to the problems related to this conflict could be developed.

45. **D**

Leopold von Ranke, a nineteenth-century German historian, was not a contributor to the Enlightenment. Edward Gibbon (The Decline and Fall of the Roman Empire), David Hume (History of England and many works in philosophy), and Adam Smith (Wealth of Nations) were English contributors. Benjamin Franklin, an American, was a multifaceted genius of the Enlightenment.

46. **D**

In the 1880s and 1890s, the U.S. Supreme Court struck down desegregation laws and upheld the doctrine of segregated "separate but equal" facilities for blacks and whites. These laws became known as "Jim Crow" laws. Their impact was to allow racist governments in the South to set up "separate but unequal" facilities in which blacks were forced to sit in the rear of streetcars and buses, in the back rooms of restaurants, or were excluded completely from white businesses, and had to use separate and usually inferior public restroom facilities. These laws allowed white supremacists to "put blacks in their place" and effectively kept blacks from achieving anything near equal status. It wasn't until the 1950s and 1960s that new Supreme Court decisions finally forced the repeal of these laws.

47. **A**

The Carolinas were granted to supporters of the Stuarts as a reward for their loyalty during the Stuarts' exile during the English civil war. With the Stuarts' restoration to the throne, eight courtiers loyal to the Stuarts were granted proprietorship of the land extending from Virginia to Florida.

48. **B**

A writ of habeas corpus is a court order that directs an official who is detaining someone to produce the person before the court so that the legality of the detention may be determined. The primary function of the writ is to effect the release of someone who has been imprisoned without due process of law. For example, if the police detained a suspect for an unreasonable time without officially charging the person with a crime, the person could seek relief from a court in the form of a writ of habeas corpus. (A) is incorrect because a writ of mandamus is a court order commanding an official to perform a legal duty of his or her office. It is not used to prevent persons from being improperly imprisoned. The Fourth Amendment requirement that police have probable cause in order to obtain a search warrant regulates police procedure. It is not itself a mechanism for affecting release of a person for improper imprisonment, so (C) is incorrect. Answer (D) is incorrect since the decision in Roe v. Wade *dealt with a woman's right to have an abortion. It had nothing to do with improper imprisonment.*

49. Ⓐ

(A) is the best answer since the term "casework" is used by political scientists to describe the activities of congressmen on behalf of individual constituents. These activities might include helping an elderly person secure social security benefits, or helping a veteran obtain medical services. Most casework is actually done by congressional staff and may take as much as a third of the staff's time. Congressmen supply this type of assistance for the good public relations it provides. Answer (B) fails because pork barrel legislation is rarely if ever intended to help individual citizens. Pork barrel legislation authorizes federal spending for special projects, such as airports, roads, or dams, in the home state or district of a congressman. It is meant to help the entire district or state. Also, there is no legal entitlement on the part of a citizen to a pork barrel project, such as there is with social security benefits. (C) is not the answer because lobbying is an activity directed toward congressmen, not one done by congressmen. A lobbyist attempts to get congressmen to support legislation that will benefit the group that the lobbyist represents. Logrolling, (D), is incorrect, because it does not refer to congressional service for constituents. It refers instead to the congressional practice of trading votes on different bills. Congressman A will vote for Congressman B's pork barrel project and in return B will vote for A's pork barrel project.

50. Ⓒ

The three largest countries of western Europe—the United Kingdom, France, and the Federal Republic of Germany—have either a multi-party system or a two-plus party system. A multi-party system is one in which three or more major parties compete for seats in the national legislature, while a two-plus party system has two large parties and one or more small parties. The United Kingdom has a two-plus party system. There are two large parties, the Conservatives and Labour. The Liberals are a smaller third party and there are even smaller regional parties in Scotland, Northern Ireland, and Wales. France has a multi-party system. The Socialists, Neo-Gaullists, and Republicans are major parties, while the Communists and the National Front are small parties with few seats in parliament. The Federal Republic of Germany has a two-plus party system. The major parties are the Christian Democratic Union and the Social Democratic Party. The Greens, the Free Democratic Party, and the Party of Democratic Socialism are smaller national parties with varying regional success. The United States, by contrast, has only two parties which successfully compete on a national basis from one election to the next. These are, of course, the Democrats and the Republicans. Answer (A) is incorrect. In western European countries, party leaders determine which persons will run for office under the party banner. In the United States, on the other hand, candidates for office are selected by the voters in primary elections. Sometimes in the United States a candidate whom the party leadership detests wins the primary, and thus the right to run for office under the party banner. In most western European countries, political parties are much more centralized than in the United States; therefore, (B) is false. Answer (D) is false. Because parties are centralized in western Europe, and because party leaders select candidates for national office, a party member in the national legislature seldom votes against the party. If one did, party leaders would remove his or her name from the ballot in future elections.

51. B

The correct answer is (B). Michelangelo is famous for his (A) sculpture of David and his (D) painting of the Sistine Chapel in the Vatican at Rome, Italy. He also produced masterful architecture (C) and his work led to the Renaissance style known as Mannerism.

52. B

(B) is the correct answer. The Seneca Indians were a member of the Iroquois Confederacy, which included the Mohawk, Onondaga, Oneida, Cayuga, and Tuscarora Indians. The (A) Seminole, (C) Cherokee, (D) Chickasaw, Creek, and Choctaw Indians made up the "Five Civilized Tribes."

Constructed-Response Questions Scoring Guide

3 • The examinee demonstrates a comprehensive understanding of the material presented.

- The examinee has responded effectively to every part of the question.

- The examinee has provided well-supported explanations.

- The examinee has demonstrated a strong knowledge of the subject matter, including relevant theories, concepts, and procedures.

2 • The examinee demonstrates a basic understanding of the material presented.

- The examinee has responded effectively to most parts of the question.

- The examinee has provided explanations.

- The examinee has demonstrated an adequate knowledge of the subject matter, including relevant theories, concepts, and procedures.

1 • The examinee demonstrates some misunderstanding of the material presented.

- The examinee fails to respond effectively to every part of the question.

- The examinee has provided only weak explanations.

- The examinee has demonstrated insufficient knowledge of the subject matter, including relevant theories, concepts, and procedures.

0 • The examinee has either not responded, responded off-topic, responded completely incorrectly, or simply rephrased the question.

Constructed-Response Questions: Sample Responses

53. **Response that received a score of 3:**

  A non-native speaker faces the challenge of competing syntaxes, for instance when an adult speaker of Spanish must learn to express in English a familiar thought, but in a syntax that would be incorrect in Spanish. There is also the challenge of learning the cultural, ethnic, and geographical differences in the way English is spoken and written. Also, the non-native speaker must also be aware of the ways in which various forms of English have proliferated among different groups and regions in the United States. Finally, the nature of standard written English continues to be reconceptualized as the language changes and evolves through the written and spoken word.

Response that received a score of 1:

  Because it is constantly changing, the English language is challenging to learn. Adults lose their ability to learn with age, and that includes learning new words. Examples of this can be found in how hard it is for adults to do simple tasks that children find so easy, like programming a VCR or opening a child-proof bottle. Because of this, adult learners have different and more complex obstacles to overcome than native speakers.

54. **Response that received a score of 3:**

  The poem is written in iambic pentameter, and its rhyme scheme is ababcdcdefefgg. It is a Shakespearean sonnet. The central metaphor is love, defined negatively (not all, not meat, not drink, not slumber, not a roof, and so on). Death is personified ("making friends with death," line 7). The poem contains many images of food (sustenance) in line 1; of shelter in line 2; of drowning in lines 3 and 4; and of healing in lines 5 and 6. Its use of paradox is related to the central argument of the poem: the opening lines state that "love is not all" but in fact the poem argues that love is central to the human condition. The tone changes in the last lines of the poem, from certitude to incertitude to certitude; the "do not think" implies tentativeness and hesitancy on the speaker's part.

Response that received a score of 1:

  The poem is a sonnet because it has fourteen lines. The main theme is love and the speaker is arguing that "love is not all." There seems to be some disagreement in the poem about what love is or is not. The speaker is not sure about what love is. There are many different images that seem to indicate conflict or doubt.

55. Response that received a score of 3:

The central government in the North expanded its power in many ways. It imposed excise taxes on manufacturers and the practice of nearly every profession. On top of the excises came an income tax. Additionally, Congress created a Bureau of Internal Revenue. The Union also created the National Banking system, which lasted without serious modification until 1913. The national banks issued bank notes backed by federal government bonds. In addition, the government borrowed from major institutions and private individuals to finance the war. Power over communication was increased with the federal government controlling the telegraph system. Transportation was affected as the government subsidized a transcontinental railroad route, controlled and coordinated all existing rail lines, and constructed 650 miles of new track.

Response that received a score of 1:

The central government in the North increased its power in many ways. Among those ways were taxation, borrowing, banking, transportation, and communication. Each factor helped contribute to the North prevailing in the Civil War.

56. Response that received a score of 3:

The Supreme Court case *Plessy vs. Ferguson* (1896) established that "separate but equal" status for blacks was constitutional. After Reconstruction failed, white Southerners kept blacks separate from whites by establishing Jim Crow laws, which were legal because the *Plessy* case made them so. Jim Crow laws were passed by individual cities and created separate public facilities for blacks and whites, including restrooms, drinking fountains, hospitals, schools, and other facilities. The facilities for blacks were separate, but not equal; in fact, they were notably inferior to the whites' facilities.

Response that received a score of 1:

Jim Crow laws were passed in the South. These laws made black people use separate drinking fountains and bathrooms, and made them sit in separate areas in theaters and restaurants.

Practice Test 1: Subtest II
Detailed Explanations of Answers

Multiple-Choice Section

1. **A**

   By definition, acids and bases combine to produce a salt and water. An example would be HCl (hydrochloric acid) and NaOH (sodium hydroxide) reacting to form NaCl (salt) and water.

2. **D**

   The atomic number is the number of protons in the atom. In neutral (un-ionized) atoms, the number of electrons equals the number of protons; therefore, the atomic number in neutral atoms is equal to the number of protons and to the number of electrons in the atom.

3. **D**

   (A), (B), and (C) all involve chemical changes, where iron, wood, and rocket fuel are reacted with other substances to produce a reactant product with different chemical properties. Melted ice in the form of water still has the same chemical formula.

4. **C**

Isotopes for a given element have the same atomic number (that is, the number of protons) but differ in the number of neutrons they contain.

5. **C**

Newton's second law states that an unbalanced force acting on a mass will cause the mass to accelerate. In equation form, F = ma, where F is force, m is mass, and a is acceleration. Only (C) involves a mass that is being accelerated by an unbalanced force.

6. **A**

Thermal energy is the total amount of internal energy of a given body, while temperature is a measure of the vibrational activity of atoms or molecules comprising the material. So, thermal energy involves both the mass and temperature of a given body. Thus, (A) is the most likely answer, as its mass far exceeds I g, a bucket of water, and Lake Michigan. (B) is ruled out because even though its temperature is very high, its mass is extremely small.

7. **A**

At the high point the velocity of the projectile must be zero. (B), (C), and (D) all have non-zero values at the high point. Thus, (A) is the answer.

8. **A**

(C) is ruled out because neutrons are uncharged and cannot influence charging. (D) is not observed and (due to neutrality) could not affect charging. Electrons relative to protons are much more mobile and can be easily transferred from body to body (B). Thus, (A) is the answer.

9. **D**

Since repulsion requires like charges, we rule out (A) and (B). (C) is ruled out, because "like" means same in polarity (+ or –) not necessarily equal.

10. **D**

The cell membrane (D) is a selectively permeable barrier that permits some substances to pass through while forming a barrier for others. None of the other choices have this property.

11. **D**

mRNA (D) is the messenger that carries genetic information. None of the others function in this way.

12. **B**

(B) A nucleotide is the connection of a base to a sugar molecule and a phosphate group. The nucleotide is named after the base it contains, e.g., adenine nucleotide contains the base adenine. All of the other answers have three components but none have all three of the essential groups.

13. **D**

(D) is correct, since the zygote of a human is a cell derived from a sperm containing 23 chromosomes and an egg containing 23 chromosomes. (A) cannot be the correct answer since it represents too few chromosome for either a haploid sex cell or a diploid body cell. (B) cannot be the correct answer since it also represents too few chromosome for either a haploid sex cell or a diploid body cell. (C) cannot be the correct answer since it represents the number of chromosomes in a sperm or an egg.

14. **A**

The epidermis is made of two layers: the layer of Malpighi and the stratum corneum. The stratum corneum is the outer layer, and the layer of Malpighi is directly under it. Under these two layers of the epidermis is the dermis. The order is incorrect on the other three answers.

15. **C**

The body regulates water and heat through perspiration. Transpiration describes a process not involving humans. Thus, (B) is not correct. Respiration (A) is breathing in humans and will cause some water loss. However, the question asks how the body regulates substances through the skin. (D), sensation, is the ability to process or perceive. The skin does have nerve endings that can sense, but this does not involve temperature or water regulation.

16. **A**

B, C, and D are ruled out because Darwin was unaware of the genetic work that was later done by Mendel. Darwin and most other nineteenth-century biologists never knew of Mendel and his research. It was not until the beginning of the twentieth century that Mendel's pioneer research into genetic inheritance was rediscovered.

17. Ⓑ

(A) is ruled out as plants in general do not emit light energy. (C) and (D) are ruled out because light is not directly consumed as food nor do plants warm the atmosphere. (B) is the answer because light is utilized as an energy input that aids in internal processes that produce glucose as food energy.

18. Ⓒ

The answer is (C) because by definition the chemical reaction cited in problem 17 is a reduction process.

19. Ⓑ

The lunar period is about 30 days, or one month, which is the time it takes for the moon to orbit the earth one time.

20. Ⓒ

(C) A star going nova is presumed to be at the end of its life. As hydrogen (or sometimes helium) is depleted, the fusion reaction becomes incapable of sustaining pressures required to push the star's mass outward against the pull of gravity. The star then collapses, resulting in a gigantic explosion known as a super nova. (A) is not observed nor possible. (B) is not observed. (D), while occasionally observed, does not trigger nova-sized explosions.

21. Ⓒ

(B) is ruled out because the rotation period is the same from season to season. (A) is ruled out because earth is actually somewhat closer to the sun in Dec–Jan than it is in June–July, which is winter for the Northern Hemisphere. (D) is ruled out, as this is a daily not seasonal phenomena. (C) is the answer, because the tilting of the earth's axis causes the Northern Hemisphere to point more sunward in the summer months and more antisunward in the winter months (with the reverse being true for the Southern Hemisphere).

22. Ⓐ

(A) is the answer, because igneous rocks are transformed or "metamorphed" into metamorphic. Thus, they are related to igneous, not sedimentary, and are found on this planet.

23. Ⓓ

(D) The east coast of South America and the west coast of Africa fit together like pieces of a jig-saw puzzle. Fossil remains in locations where "fit" is observed to be too well matched to be

coincidental. Earthquakes and volcanism are more prevalent in mountainous regions, where plates collided, than in other regions. Thus, all support the theory of plate tectonics.

24. **A**

According to the theory of plate tectonics, plate spreading is associated with magma upwelling to fill the vacated space, which forms ridges at these locations.

25. **D**

Raw material for igneous rock formation is magma, which when cooled either above or below ground becomes igneous rock.

26. **B**

Multiple investigators have confirmed the order given in (B).

27. **C**

When simplifying algebraic expressions, always work from left to right. First perform all multiplication and division. Once this is done, start again from the left and do all addition and subtraction.

SUGGESTION: *It can be helpful to translate the algebraic statement to English. For example, 6 + 2(x − 4) is "six plus two times the quantity x minus 4." The word times indicates multiplication, so we must first perform 2(x − 4) by using the distributive property a(b − c) = ab − ac:*

$6 + 2(x − 4) = 6 + 2 \times x − 2 \times 4 = 6 + 2x − 8.$

Then we perform the subtraction to combine the terms 6 and 8:

$6 + 2x − 8 = 2x + (6 − 8) = 2x − 2.$

Note that we did not combine the 2x term with the other terms. This is because they are not like terms. Like terms are terms that have the same variables (with the same exponents). Since the terms 6 and 8 have no variable x, they are not like terms with 2x.

28. **D**

Let x be the cost of one can of beans. Then 6x is the cost of six cans of beans. So 6x = \$1.50. Dividing both sides of the equation by 6, we get x = \$.25 and, hence, since 8x is the cost of eight cans of beans, we have 8x = 8 × \$.25 = \$2.00.

29. **A**

Let t_1, t_2, t_3 represent Bonnie's scores on tests one, two, and three, respectively. Then the equation representing Bonnie's average score is

$$\frac{t_1 + t_2 + t_3}{3} = 71.$$

We know that $t_1 = 64$ and $t_2 = 87$. Substitute this information into the equation above:

$$\frac{64 + 87 + t_3}{3} = 71.$$

Combining 64 and 87 and then multiplying both sides of the equation by 3 gives us

$$3 \times \frac{151 + t_3}{3} = 3 \times 71 + t_3 \text{ or } 151 + t_3 = 213.$$

Now subtract 151 from both sides of the equation so that

$t_3 = 213 - 151 = 62.$

30. **D**

Let s be the length of each side of square ABCD. Since triangle ADC is a right triangle, we can use the Pythagorean Theorem to solve for s. We have $AD^2 + DC^2 = AC^2$ or $s^2 + s^2 = 8^2$. Simplifying the equation, we get: $2s^2 = 64$. Now divide both sides of the equation by two:

$s^2 = 32$, so $s = \sqrt{32} = \sqrt{16} \times \sqrt{2} = 4\sqrt{2}$.

Therefore, the perimeter of square ABCD is

$P = 4s = 4 \times 4\sqrt{2} = 16\sqrt{2}$.

31. **B**

To solve the equation $2x^2 + 5x - 3 = 0$, we can factor the left side of the equation to get $(2x - 1)(x + 3) = 0$. Then use the following rule (this rule is sometimes called the Zero Product Property): If $a \times b = 0$, then either $a = 0$ or $b = 0$. Applying this to our problem gives us

$2x - 1 = 0$ or $x + 3 = 0$.

Solve these two equations:

$2x - 1 = 0 \rightarrow 2x = 1 \rightarrow x = \dfrac{1}{2}$ or $x + 3 = 0 \rightarrow x = -3$.

But $x > 0$, so $x = \dfrac{1}{2}$.

32. C

Note that the numbers 4, 8, 12, 16, and 20 are the only numbers from 1 through 20 that are divisible by 4. The probability that a ball chosen from the jar has a number on it that is divisible by 4 is given by total number of possible outcomes =

$$\frac{5}{20} = \frac{1}{4}.$$

33. D

First find the total sales for each year by reading the graph for the sales of (i) black and white televisions and (ii) color televisions. Then combine these numbers:

1950	$20,000,000 + $5,000,000	=	$25,000,000
1960	$10,000,000 + $20,000,000	=	$30,000,000
1970	$15,000,000 + $25,000,000	=	$40,000,000
1980	$10,000,000 + $45,000,000	=	$55,000,000
1990	$5,000,000 + $45,000,000	=	$50,000,000

The greatest total sales occurred in 1980.

34. A

A prime number is an integer that is greater than one and that has no integer divisors other than 1 and itself. So, the prime numbers between 1 and 20 (not including 1 and 20) are: 2, 3, 5, 7, 11, 13, 17, 19. But 2 is not an odd number, so the odd primes between 1 and 20 are: 3, 5, 7, 11, 13, 17, 19. Hence, there are seven odd primes between 1 and 20.

35. C

The area of the shaded region is equal to the area of the large circle (which has $\overline{OB}$ as a radius) minus the area of the smaller circle (which has $\overline{OA}$ as a radius). Since the area of a circle with radius r is $A = \pi r^2$, the area of the shaded region is:

$$\pi (OB)^2 - \pi (OA)^2 = 36\pi - 16\pi = 20\pi.$$

36. D

To solve this inequality, we shall use the following rules:

(i) If $a \le b$ and c is any number, then $a + c \le b + c$.
(ii) If $a \le b$ and $c < 0$, then $ca \ge cb$.

The goal in solving inequalities, as in solving equalities, is to change the inequality so that the variable is isolated (i.e., by itself on one side). So, in the equation 8 − 2x ≤ 10, we want the term −2x by itself. To achieve this, use rule (i) above and add −8 to both sides obtaining 8 − 2x + (−8) ≤ 10 + (−8) or −2x ≤ 2. Now we use rule (ii) and multiply both sides of the inequality by −¹/₂ as follows:

$$-\frac{1}{2} \times 2x \geq -\frac{1}{2} \times 2 \text{ or } x \geq -1.$$

37. **C**

Since ∠OPQ is a straight angle, m∠OPQ = 180°. But

> *m∠OPQ = m∠OPR + ∠RPQ, so*
> *m∠OPR + m∠RPQ = 180° or m∠OPR = 180° − m∠RPQ.*

Thus, we need to find m∠RPQ. Now, l₁ ∥ l₂, therefore, m∠RPQ = m∠TRS since ∠RPQ and ∠TRS are corresponding angles. Recall that corresponding angles are two angles that lie on the same side of the transversal (i.e., a line intersecting other lines, in this case line TP is a transversal since it intersects both line l₁ and l₂), are not adjacent, and one is interior (∠ RPQ in this problem) while the other is exterior (∠TRS). Also, we know that the sum of the measures of the interior angles of a triangle is 180° and

> *m∠T = 80°, so m∠TRS + m∠RST = 180° − m∠T = 100°.*

But m∠TRS = m∠RST since ΔRST is isosceles. Thus, m∠TRS = 50°. Thus,

> *m∠RPQ = 50° and m∠OPR = 180° − m∠RPQ = 180° − 50° = 130°.*

38. **D**

The midpoint of a segment with endpoints (x₁, y₁) and (x₂, y₂) is

$$\left(\frac{x_1 + x_2}{2}, \frac{y_1 + y_2}{2} \right).$$

The endpoints are M = (4,1) and N = (−2, −1), so the midpoint of $\overline{MN}$ is

$$\left(\frac{4 + (-2)}{2}, \frac{1 + (-1)}{2} \right) = (1, 0)$$

39. **A**

Let p be the original price of the jacket. Linda received a 25% discount so she paid 75% of the original price. Thus, 75% of p equals 54. Writing this in an equation, we get:

$$0.75p = 54 \text{ or } \frac{3}{4}p = 54.$$

To solve this equation, multiply both sides of the equation by the reciprocal of $^3/_4$ which is $^4/_3$. This will isolate the variable p.

$$\frac{4}{3}\left(\frac{3}{4}p\right) = \left(\frac{4}{3}\right)54 \; or \; p = \frac{216}{3} = 72$$

40. **A**

72104.58 is read "seventy-**two thousand**, one hundred four and fifty-eight hundredths."

41. **C**

Another way to phrase the second sentence is: She wants to divide her money equally among her six children. Therefore, each child is to receive 300,000 ÷ 6.

42. **B**

Bob wants to bake 12 cupcakes. The recipe is for 36 cupcakes. Therefore, Bob wants to make $^{12}/_{36}$ or $^1/_3$ of the usual amount of cupcakes. Thus, Bob should use $^1/_3$ of the recipe's flour or

$$\left(\frac{1}{3}\right)\left(\frac{8}{3}\right) = \frac{8}{9}.$$

Note, we used $^8/_3$ since

$$2\frac{2}{3} = \frac{8}{3}.$$

43. **C**

Let s_1 and s_2 be Ricky's speed (rate) on the trip from A to B and the return trip from B to A, respectively. Then, since he drove 15 miles per hour slower on the return trip, $s_2 = s_1 - 15$. Recall that rate times time equals distance. So the distance from A to B is $(s_1)\, 3 = 3s_1$ and the distance from B to A is $(s_2)5 = 5s_2 = 5(s_1 - 15) = 5s_1 - 75$. But the distance from Town A to Town B is the same as the distance from Town B to Town A, so we have the following equation:

$$3s_1 = 5s_1 - 75.$$

To solve this equation, first add 75 to both sides of the equation:

$$3s_1 + 75 = 5s_1 - 75 + 75 \; or \; 3s_1 + 75 = 5s_1.$$

Now isolate the variable; subtract $3s_1$ from both sides:

$$3s_1 + 75 - 3s_1 = 5s_1 - 3s_1 \; or \; 75 = 2s_1.$$

To finish the problem, divide both sides of the equation by 2:

$$s_1 = \frac{75}{2} = 37.5$$

Thus, Ricky drove 37.5 miles per hour on his trip from Town A to Town B.

44. D

The shaded region consists of all the points on the horizontal line passing through the point (0, 2) and those below the line. All of these points have y = coordinate less than or equal to 2: Thus, our answer is y ≤ 2.

45. C

The 1 is in the hundredths place. If the number to the immediate right of the 1 (i.e., the number in the thousandths place) is greater than or equal to 5, we increase 1 to 2; otherwise, do not change the 1. Then we leave off all the numbers to the right of the 1. In our problem, a 6 is in the thousandths place, so we change the 1 to a 2 to get 287.42 as our answer.

46. D

If a = b³ and a = ¹/₈, then substituting into the first equation we have:

$$\frac{1}{8} = b^3 \ or \ \left(\frac{1}{2}\right)^3 = b^3 \ so \ b = \frac{1}{2}.$$

47. D

Let x be the number of people in the barn. Then, since each person and lamb has only one head, the number of lambs must be 30 – x. Since people have two legs, the number of human legs totals 2x. Similarly, since the number of legs each lamb has is 4, the total number of lamb legs in the barn is 4(30 – x). Thus, we have this equation:

2x + 4(30 – x) = 104.

To solve this equation, use the distributive property:

a(b – c) = ab – ac.

We get:

4(30 – x) = (4 × 30) – (4 × x) = 120 – 4x.

Our equation reduces to:

2x + 120 − 4x = 104 or 120 − 2x = 104.

Now subtract 120 from both sides of the equation to get −2x = 104 − 120 = −16. Dividing both sides of the equation by −2: x = 8. Therefore, there were 8 people and 30 − 8 = 22 lambs in the barn.

---

48. B

If two lines l_1 and l_2, which lie in the same plane, are both perpendicular to a third line, l_3, then l_1 and l_2 are parallel.

---

49. D

First, the least common multiple (LCM) of 2 and 3 is 2 × 3 = 6, so let's rewrite the expression so that both fractions have 6 as a common denominator:

$$\frac{1}{2} + \frac{1}{3} = \left(\frac{3}{3} \times \frac{1}{2}\right) + \left(\frac{2}{2} \times \frac{1}{3}\right) = \frac{3}{6} + \frac{2}{6} = \frac{5}{6}$$

---

50. A

Note that there is a solid dot on −1. This means to include −1 in the set. The numbers to the right of −1 are shaded; this means to include these numbers also. Hence, this is the graph of all numbers greater than or equal to

−1 ($\{x \mid x \geq -1\}$).

---

51. C

According to the graph, the supply was greater than the demand in March and May only.

---

52. D

The greatest common divisor (GCD) is the greatest integer that divides both 120 and 252. To find the GCD, factor both numbers and look for common factors.

$120 = 2^3 \times 3 \times 5$ and $252 = 2^2 \times 3^2 \times 7$,

so the GCD = $2^2 \times 3 = 12$.

Constructed-Response Questions Scoring Guide

---

3 • The examinee demonstrates a comprehensive understanding of the material presented.

 • The examinee has responded effectively to every part of the question.

 • The examinee has provided well-supported explanations.

 • The examinee has demonstrated a strong knowledge of the subject matter, including relevant theories, concepts, and procedures.

---

2 • The examinee demonstrates a basic understanding of the material presented.

 • The examinee has responded effectively to most parts of the question.

 • The examinee has provided explanations.

 • The examinee has demonstrated an adequate knowledge of the subject matter, including relevant theories, concepts, and procedures.

---

1 • The examinee demonstrates some misunderstanding of the material presented.

 • The examinee fails to respond effectively to every part of the question.

 • The examinee has provided only weak explanations.

 • The examinee has demonstrated insufficient knowledge of the subject matter, including relevant theories, concepts, and procedures.

---

0 • The examinee has either not responded, responded off-topic, responded completely incorrectly, or simply rephrased the question.

Constructed-Response Questions: Sample Responses

Constructed-Response Question 53

1. **Response that received a score of 3:**

   Region 1 = ionosphere or thermosphere, Region 2 = stratosphere and Region 3 = troposphere.

   Response that received a score of 1:

   Candidate would know names but would mix them up.

2. **Response that received a score of 3:**

   Troposphere: This is the lower 10–15 km of the atmosphere and its densest part, containing about 90% of the atmosphere's mass. It is where weather takes place thanks to the presence of abundant water vapor and vertical mixing caused by convection. Its composition is mainly molecular nitrogen, oxygen, and carbon dioxide. Very little ionization occurs due to the absorption of most of the sun's ultraviolet rays in the upper atmosphere. Temperature steadily decreases with altitude in the troposphere.

   Stratosphere: Extending for about 15–40 km above the troposphere, its density ranges from about 1/10 to 1/100 of the troposphere. There is little to no vertical mixing in the stratosphere with a nearly uniform temperature of about –60°C. Due to the low temperatures, there is virtually no water vapor in the stratosphere. Composition is the same as the troposphere, except for the lack of water vapor and the presence of ozone. Ozone is formed at the upper limits of the stratosphere by the absorption of solar ultraviolet light, forming a protective layer that screens lower reaches from the harmful rays.

   Thermosphere or Ionosphere: Thermosphere extends from about 40–50 km on up with the ionosphere beginning at about 80 km. Densities range from about 1/1,000 to 1/1,000,000 of that of the troposphere. Temperature steadily increases with altitude due to direct interaction with solar radiation. Composition in this area changes from primarily molecular gas to mainly atomic with ions and electrons in abundance above 80 km or so. The change in composition is due to the strength of the sun's UV radiation when first entering the atmosphere. The ionization is especially important, because it influences certain forms of long-distance radio communication. It also comes into play in formation of the aurora at the poles, where ions and electrons interact with the Earth's magnetosphere.

Response that received a score of 1:

Omitting mention that weather takes place in the troposphere. Not knowing where/why ionization occurs. Failing to mention or recognize the importance of vertical mixing. Not mentioning that density of the atmosphere decreases with altitude. Not explaining the relationship between the composition of the atmosphere and solar radiation at each level.

3. **Response that received a score of 3:**

Carbon dioxide is the most important gas because it is transparent to visible light, but highly absorbent to infrared. When visible light from the sun shines down on the Earth, it passes through the atmosphere with very little loss. However, absorption by land masses causes surface warming of these masses. Heated masses then reradiate infrared radiation, but the carbon dioxide in the atmosphere is not transparent to IR so the heat is trapped. Much the same thing happens in cars parked in a parking lot on a sunny day. Visible light passes through the windshield glass and is absorbed by the car's interior, which causes it to heat up. Radiated IR then is emitted by the interior, but cannot escape because the glass is not transparent to IR.

It is feared that global warming is occurring due to the presence of excess carbon dioxide produced by both auto exhausts and industrial emissions.

Response that received a score of 1:

Not knowing that carbon dioxide is the most important gas. Also, failing to explain how/why that particular gas traps heat (IR radiation) and acts as a blanket. Also, failing to support the explanation of the phenomena with an example.

Constructed-Response Question 54

1. **Response that received a score of 3:**

Potential energy is energy that is stored and kinetic energy is energy of motion. In this instance, the block is associated with energy of motion and the spring is associated with stored energy. Respective formulas for each are: $KE = (1/2)mv^2$ and $PE = (1/2)kx^2$. Here m = mass of the block, v = block velocity, k = spring constant, and x = deflection of the spring.

Response that received a score of 1:

Not explaining the difference between potential and kinetic energy or failing to point out that KE is associated with the moving block and PE is associated with the spring. Must state one or the other to get credit.

2. Response that received a score of 3:
At the high point, the block momentarily slows to zero, so its kinetic energy is zero.

Response that received a score of 1:
Stating that the block has zero energy at the high point without associating it with zero velocity.

3. Response that received a score of 3:
When the block is halfway between the high and low points, there is no potential energy stored in the spring. Therefore, all of the system energy is kinetic and the speed is maximum.

Response that received a score of 1:
Stating that the block has maximum kinetic energy without associating it with speed or conservation of energy, e.g., explaining how one knows that it is a maximum.

4. Response that received a score of 3:
Block speed is maximum at the mid point and minimum at the extremes of high and low. This is because total energy for the system is conserved. When the block is at the high and low point, the kinetic energy is zero and the potential energy stored in the spring is maximum; therefore, the speed is zero. When at the midpoint, the speed is maximum, because no energy is stored in the spring and all the system energy is kinetic.

Response that received a score of 1:
Stating the correct max/min position associations without explaining why as above.

5. Response that received a score of 3:
The sum will remain a constant for high, low, and all points in between. This is because of the Law of Conservation of Energy, which states that energy is neither destroyed nor created. For this system, therefore, the total energy is continuously being repartitioned between the block and the spring as it oscillates up and down, the repartitioning occurring in such a way that the sum of KE and PE is a constant. In an ideal system, there would be no friction and the oscillation would continue indefinitely. However, in real systems, friction is always present, so

eventually all of the system energy is converted into heat by means of friction and the block comes to a stop.

Response that received a score of 1: ──────────────────────────

Stating that the total will remain constant without an explanation as above. The role of conservation of energy, the continuous repartitioning of PE and KE, and the role of friction all play a role in a thorough answer to this question.

55. **Response that received a score of 3:** ──────────────────────────

The median salary is a more appropriate method of determining the measure of central tendency in this example because of the small sample size and the fact that a few large values ($90,000 and $95,000) skew the average. The mean value is influenced too much by the two high salary figures and is not a good representation of the average salary within this company.

Response that received a score of 1: ──────────────────────────

Because of the small sample size, the mean would not be a good method of calculating this company's average salary. By taking the mean value, this company's average salary appears higher than it is. Therefore, the median salary is a more appropriate indication of this company's average salary.

56. **Response that received a score of 3:** ──────────────────────────

Given the information above, it can be assumed that the ladder, tree, and ground form a right triangle. Therefore, the angle between the tree and the ground is 90°. Since the ladder forms a 45° angle with the ground, the angle between the ladder and the tree has to be 45° as well. (The sum of the measures of the angles of a triangle is 180°.) If a triangle has two equal angles, then the sides opposite those angles are equal. Therefore, since the distance between the tree and the ladder is 4 feet, the height of the tree also equals 4 feet.

Response that received a score of 1: ──────────────────────────

Since the ladder forms a 45° angle with the ground, the tree's height has to equal the distance from the tree to the ladder.

Practice Test 1: Subtest III
Detailed Explanations of Answers

Multiple-Choice Section

1. **D**

   Public Law 94-142 provides a legal definition for the term "handicapped children." It includes children who have been evaluated as being mentally retarded, hearing impaired, deaf, speech impaired, visually handicapped, seriously emotionally disturbed, orthopedically impaired, having other health impairments (e.g., anemia, arthritis, etc.), deaf-blind, multi-handicapped, or with specific learning disabilities. P.L. 94-142 states that these children need special education and services.

2. **A**

   Epilepsy refers to different kinds of seizures. Most epileptic children can participate in regular physical education classes, regardless of the type of seizure previously experienced (B). Seizures are caused by an electrochemical imbalance in the brain. A minor motor seizure (C) causes localized contractions of muscles on one side or in one part of the body. Sweating and rapid heart rate (D) are characteristic of an autonomic seizure.

3. **A**

Gross visual-motor skills involve movement of the body's large muscles as visual information is processed. A ball is always used to perfect these skills. In some cases a bat or racquet will also aid in developing these skills.

4 **C**

A volleyball game ends with 25 points, as long as the score differs by two points. One point is scored every time a team is unable to propel the ball across the net within the boundaries of the rules.

5. **B**

Interval training (A), (C), is associated with the development of cardiovascular endurance and performance of aerobic activities (e.g., swimming, running, and cycling). Weight training involves a progressive increase in workload to develop muscular strength. With isometric exercise, the muscle does not change its length as a person exerts force against a resistance. In this case the force is static. However, with isokinetic exercise, the resistance pushes back with force equal to the one that the person exerts.

6. **C**

Fluid is always reestablished by drinking water. A common practice is to drink before, during, and after an event. It is not necessary to take salt tablets (A) since normal salting of food is adequate to replenish the salt lost with sweat. Vitamin (B) and mineral supplements (D) will not replenish water.

7. **C**

Roughly 60% of the calories consumed should be derived from carbohydrates. These should mostly include complex carbohydrates that come from foods such as bread and pasta.

8. **D**

The grip strength test (C), pull-ups (for boys) (A), and flexed arm hang (for girls) (B), are all tests to measure muscular strength and endurance. The sit and reach test measures flexibility.

9. **A**

The skills required to master a certain dance will determine the suggested grade level for that dance. The simplest steps used are "walk and/or skip" and are therefore appropriate for grades 1–2. The steps "run and/or skip" (B) and "skip and slide" (C) are more difficult, and therefore are suggested for grades 2–3. Even more difficult is the "step-hop" (D), and it is incorporated in dances appropriate for grades 3–6.

10. **D**

Sodium is important to normal water balance inside and outside cells. It also regulates blood pressure and helps balance electrolytes and chemicals. Calcium (A), magnesium (B), and potassium (C) all help prevent muscle weakness and cramping.

11. **B**

Elevation is a key component to the R.I.C.E. treatment process for sprains. The other components are Rest, Ice, and Compression. One should not return to exercise (A) until significant healing has been acheived, though bearing a tolerable amount of weight on the sprain has been shown to help quicken the healing process. The sprain should be bandaged properly to prevent exposure (D) to potential reinjury.

12. **B**

Exercising cardiovascularly for a minimum of twenty minutes per session, as part of an exercise program, will lead to effective physical results with a proper nutritional diet. Forty-five minutes (D) is an effective time period when performing a weight-lifting exercise session.

13. **D**

Complex carbohydrates should comprise at least half of the calories consumed for the healthy diet of an active person. Carbohydrates are the primary and most efficient source of energy for the body. Proteins should make up about 20% (A) of the caloric intake of an active person.

14. **C**

The correct response is (C). This response recognizes that children learn at different rates and suggests a structured method to limit the number of children per center. It is impossible for all students to work at the same rate (A). Children who finish early should not be given extra work merely to keep them busy (B). Speed is not the primary goal of this activity (D).

15. **D**

The correct response is (D). A concluding activity should encourage students to summarize what they have learned and share this information with other students. A class party celebrating scientists is a valuable experience but does not allow students to share what they have learned (A). A topic for cumulative reviews should not be limited to only medical discoveries when the unit's topic was much broader (B). A test is considered an evaluation technique and should not be confused with a concluding activity (C).

16. **B**

The correct response is (B). Materials should represent a wide range of topics and people, thereby fostering an appreciation for diversity in the students. An appropriate reading level (A), related information (C), and a majority of interest (D) are all important, but cannot be called the main reason for selecting a book.

17. **D**

According to Piaget, concrete operations is the level of cognitive development in which children understand conservation. At this level, they can reason abstractly enough to realize that changing the shape of an object (rolling a ball of clay into a cigar shape, for example) doesn't change the amount of material they have to work with.

18. **C**

The correct response is (C). The use of instructional strategies that make learning relevant to individual student interests is a powerful motivating force that facilitates learning and independent thinking. (A) and (B) are both important factors to consider during a brainstorming session of this type, but both of these factors should influence the teacher only after the student interests have been included. (D) indicates a misunderstanding of the situation described. The students are setting the objectives for the unit as they brainstorm questions.

19. **B**

The correct response is (B). Choice is an important element in motivating students to learn. (A) is contradictory with the stated purpose of the activity. The students proposed the questions, so covering all the questions should not be a problem. (C) is incorrect because the students have chosen what they consider to be key questions; the teacher should select different or additional key questions. (D) is a possibility, but only if there is a specific reason why all the students should not research all the questions.

20. **C**

In Piaget's concrete operational period, which lasts from age 7 to 11 years, the child consistently conserves such qualities as length, quantity, weight, and volume. The child also classifies concrete objects by category and begins to understand the relations among categories.

21. **B**

The correct response is (B). The best way to teach children to read, regardless of grade level, is to use a program of emergent literacy that includes pattern books and journal writing with invented spelling. (A) is incorrect because although an intensive phonics program that includes drill and practice seat work on basic sight words may be effective with some students, it is not the most effective way to teach all students to read. (D) is incorrect because an ESL program is intended to provide assistance to only those students who are learning English as a second language. Additionally, the learning resource teacher should provide assistance to only those students who have been identified as having a learning disability that qualifies them to receive services.

22. **A**

The correct response is (A). By selecting books for the classroom library that match students' independent reading abilities, the teacher is recognizing that students must improve their reading ability by beginning at their own level and progressing to more difficult materials. (B) is incorrect because books that are so difficult that they are challenging will most likely be frustrating to many students. (C) is incorrect because the presence or absence of separate word lists should not be a determining factor in selecting books for a classroom library. (D) is incorrect because all children need access to a classroom library regardless of their reading abilities.

23. **C**

The correct response is (C). A post office center, restaurant center, and weather center all encourage a variety of reading and writing activities, which is what these students need most. (A) and (B) are incorrect because they are incomplete. (D) is incorrect because the science center is included and combining the chemicals in that center poses an obvious danger to young children.

24. **A**

The correct response is (A). One of the most reliable ways to identify individual learning styles is to observe the students over a period of time and make informal notes about their work habits and the choices they make within the classroom. (B) is incorrect because although a school psychologist could provide information about each student's learning style, the teacher can identify this information on his or her own. (C) is incorrect because although administering a group screening test will identify learning styles, such a test may be difficult to obtain, and the teacher could gain the same knowledge through simple observation. (D) is incorrect because each student's permanent file may or may not contain this information, and an individual student's learning style may have changed over the years and there is no guarantee that this change will be noted in the permanent record.

25. **C**

According to Freud, fixation is the result of abnormal personality development. In his scheme of personality development, consisting of progressive stages, Freud stated that there is a certain amount of frustration and anxiety as the person passes from one stage to the next. If the amount of frustration and anxiety over the next stage is too great, development will halt and the person becomes fixated at one stage. A very dependent child is an example of an early fixation preventing him or her from becoming independent.

26. **B**

Maslow's heirarchy of needs consists of the following: air, food, water, and shelter; safety and security; love and belonging; esteem and self-esteem; and self-actualization. Theoretically, a person must satisfy basic needs before moving up the heirarchy to satisfy higher order needs.

27. **B**

The ziggurat at Ur is the finest extant example of Sumerian architecture; actually, it is the best preserved ancient temple tower in all of Mesopotamia (present-day Iraq). To be specific, the ziggurat at Ur was built about 2100 B.C.E. by a group known as the Neo-Sumerians, the last civilization to embrace the customs and language of the earlier Sumerians (active from about 3000 to 2350 B.C.E.). The Egyptians neither lived in Mesopotamia nor built ziggurats, although their pyramids (which served as royal tombs not temple platforms) are sometimes confused with ziggurats. The Assyrians and Babylonians lived in Mesopotamia, but these civilizations had nothing to do with the great ziggurat at Ur, built centuries before the Assyrians and Babylonians came along. The Minoans lived on the Island of Crete and did not build ziggurats.

28. **D**

Flying buttresses, pointed arches and stained glass windows appear together only on Gothic-style buildings, most of which were built between 1150 and 1500. Buildings of the Romanesque period (c.1050–1150) usually employ wall buttresses and rounded arches; only a few employ pointed arches. The flying buttress was a device invented specifically to support the high vaults of Gothic churches. Byzantine buildings, like the famous Hagia Sophia in Istanbul, are characterized by domes and rounded arches, among other things. The same is true for Renaissance and Baroque architecture.

29. **D**

Pollock's Lucifer is a monument of Abstract Expressionism, one of the most influential artistic movements of the twentieth century. Pollock's work is characterized by drips and splotches of paint arranged in rhythmic patterns on large canvases. Pablo Picasso is the best known practitioner of Cubism, an early twentieth-century style characterized by fractured, though straight, lines and, at least at times, recognizable subject matter. Henri Matisse was the leader of the Fauvists, a group of French artists active in the early twentieth century and known for their use of intensely bright colors.

30. **C**

St. Paul (or Saul, as he was known at this point) has just been knocked from his horse and blinded by the light of God. Caravaggio renders the scene with a dark background strongly broken by a beam of light coming from above. It is a dramatic scene, a climactic moment in the life of the apostle. The figure of Paul has been foreshortened such that his head is closer to the viewer than the rest of his body. The artist has filled the composition almost completely; there is very little unoccupied, or "negative," space. He has also used clear, precise contour lines and detailed brushwork.

31. **A**

In conventional lithography a limestone block, obtained preferably from quarries in Bavaria, is used as the support for the crayon marks, acids, and inks needed for a lithograph. The support for woodcuts is wood. Metal plates, usually of zinc or copper, serve for engravings and etchings.

32. **B**

This question asks you to look at a set of costumes for a play and to match the costumes with the appropriate play. The costumes are definitely from the Elizabethan era, and even if you do not know the other authors and titles listed, you should be able to match a Shakespearean play with these Elizabethan costumes. The correct answer is (B).

33. **C**

Red, yellow, and blue are the primary colors. Their respective complements are green, purple, and orange.

34. **A**

Produced in 1915, Archipenko's Woman Combing Her Hair—*with its facet-like planes and displaced body parts—was a pioneering effort in Cubist sculpture.*

35. **C**

One of the best-known artifacts of the Paleolithic or Old Stone Age era, the so-called Venus of Willendorf, *was made around 20,000 B.C.E. The statue's emphasis on genitalia and breasts suggests its purpose had something to do with human reproduction.*

36. **B**

"Stupas" is the correct response. Pagodas are towers, usually with curved-up roofs, that are built as temples or memorials in the Far East (A). Mastabas are tombs built by Egyptians during the Old Kingdom (C). A mandorla is an almond-shaped halo surrounding medieval images of Christ.

37. **B**

Louis Sullivan, an architect best known for his late nineteenth-century skyscrapers, promoted the idea that a building's form should follow its function. His slogan "form follows function" became one of the Great Truths for modern architects of the twentieth century, among them Gropius and Mies van der Rohe.

38.

Exhibited in 1913 at the famous Armory Show in New York City, Duchamp's Nude Descending a Staircase *became one of the most vilified (and celebrated) paintings of the twentieth century. For many Americans, this painting represented everything that was perverse about modern European painting. Stylistically, Duchamp's work relies on the slightly earlier Cubist compositions of Picasso and Braque. However, unlike the static figures of Picasso and Braque, Duchamp's nude is captured in the process of moving.*

39.

Developed in Italy in the fifteenth century, one-point linear perspective uses a mathematical system based on orthogonals, where all lines appear to recede perpendicular to the picture plane, converging at a single vanishing point on the horizon. Imagines are wax ancestor portraits favored by the ancient Romans (D). Hatching is a drawing and printmaking technique in which fine lines are placed close together to achieve an effect of shading (C). Epigones are members of any generation that is less distinguished than the one before, e.g., the artists who followed Giotto (A).

Constructed-Response Questions Scoring Guide

---

3 • The examinee demonstrates a comprehensive understanding of the material presented.

• The examinee has responded effectively to every part of the question.

• The examinee has provided well-supported explanations.

• The examinee has demonstrated a strong knowledge of the subject matter, including relevant theories, concepts, and procedures.

---

2 • The examinee demonstrates a basic understanding of the material presented.

• The examinee has responded effectively to most parts of the question.

• The examinee has provided explanations.

• The examinee has demonstrated an adequate knowledge of the subject matter, including relevant theories, concepts, and procedures.

---

1 • The examinee demonstrates some misunderstanding of the material presented.

• The examinee fails to respond effectively to every part of the question.

• The examinee has provided only weak explanations.

• The examinee has demonstrated insufficient knowledge of the subject matter, including relevant theories, concepts, and procedures.

---

0 • The examinee has either not responded, responded off-topic, responded completely incorrectly, or simply rephrased the question.

Constructed-Response Questions: Sample Responses

40. Response that received a score of 3:

One of the best ways physical education teachers can enhance their students' self-esteem is to ask individual students to demonstrate skills to be learned. Many students who are not successful in the academic arena find that they can achieve in their physical education classes. Most students enjoy this type of demonstration and are made to feel successful by modeling the proper execution of an activity.

Another way to enhance students' self-esteem is to be absolutely sure that gender equity is practiced in their physical education classes. Too often, girls are ignored in phys ed. Girls should be chosen as "captains" as often as their male counterparts and should be encouraged to live up to their full physical potential.

Response that received a score of 1:

One way to enhance self-esteem in physical education classes is to accentuate the achievements of the best athletes. Often these students don't do well in their other classes, so they should be chosen as captains every time, and should always be used to demonstrate whatever they are good at, like hitting or running.

Another way is to make the captains pick teams, because this will enhance the self-esteem of the first students picked, and for the last students picked, physical education is probably not a priority for them anyway.

41. Response that received a score of 3:

Educators now realize that individual students often learn best in ways that are very different from one another. For example, some students are visually oriented, and some others are more geared toward auditory education. Visual learners are those students that learn best by reading. Teachers can encourage these students to pursue supplemental reading, or they can teach them how to read more effectively. Teachers can encourage these students to underline in their texts when they read, or to write margin notes. Auditory learners learn best by listening. They can use audiocassettes as supplementary learning materials, and should be encouraged to participate in class discussions, and should be taught to take effective notes based on what they hear in class.

Response that received a score of 1:

Two styles of learning are motivated and unmotivated. Motivated students don't require as much attention from teachers and can basically be left on their own to pursue their studies. Unmotivated students will not work on their own, and teachers must constantly keep after them to make sure that they are working. Motivated students should be rewarded by allowing them to study on their own and read materials that they chose themselves. Teachers should make sure that unmotivated students do not waste their time on things like comic books, but rather read only school-oriented material.

42. Response that received a score of 3:

Theater can be said to encompass all the artistic disciplines because in many cases, music, dance, and visual art work in concert to create the overall mood. For example, song and dance have long been a staple of many theatrical productions, from opera to Broadway musicals, and set dressing and costume design are carried out by visual artists. When all these things function together in harmony, they create a comprehensive artistic experience.

Response that received a score of 1:

When I saw *Cats*, by Andrew Lloyd Weber, it was clear that a true artist created this show. Many people don't think of him as an artist because he's modern, but I disagree. I think that it doesn't matter what time period you're from, if you can make people happy like that, you're an artist. He wrote the music and the dialogue, and it was such an original idea!

CSET

California Subject Examinations for Teachers: Multiple Subjects

Practice Test 2

Answer Sheet

53–56 are Constructed-Response questions. See sample essays in Detailed Explanation of Answers section.

Subtest I:
Reading, Language & Literature; History & Social Science

1. Ⓐ Ⓑ Ⓒ Ⓓ
2. Ⓐ Ⓑ Ⓒ Ⓓ
3. Ⓐ Ⓑ Ⓒ Ⓓ
4. Ⓐ Ⓑ Ⓒ Ⓓ
5. Ⓐ Ⓑ Ⓒ Ⓓ
6. Ⓐ Ⓑ Ⓒ Ⓓ
7. Ⓐ Ⓑ Ⓒ Ⓓ
8. Ⓐ Ⓑ Ⓒ Ⓓ
9. Ⓐ Ⓑ Ⓒ Ⓓ
10. Ⓐ Ⓑ Ⓒ Ⓓ
11. Ⓐ Ⓑ Ⓒ Ⓓ
12. Ⓐ Ⓑ Ⓒ Ⓓ
13. Ⓐ Ⓑ Ⓒ Ⓓ

14. Ⓐ Ⓑ Ⓒ Ⓓ
15. Ⓐ Ⓑ Ⓒ Ⓓ
16. Ⓐ Ⓑ Ⓒ Ⓓ
17. Ⓐ Ⓑ Ⓒ Ⓓ
18. Ⓐ Ⓑ Ⓒ Ⓓ
19. Ⓐ Ⓑ Ⓒ Ⓓ
20. Ⓐ Ⓑ Ⓒ Ⓓ
21. Ⓐ Ⓑ Ⓒ Ⓓ
22. Ⓐ Ⓑ Ⓒ Ⓓ
23. Ⓐ Ⓑ Ⓒ Ⓓ
24. Ⓐ Ⓑ Ⓒ Ⓓ
25. Ⓐ Ⓑ Ⓒ Ⓓ
26. Ⓐ Ⓑ Ⓒ Ⓓ

27. Ⓐ Ⓑ Ⓒ Ⓓ
28. Ⓐ Ⓑ Ⓒ Ⓓ
29. Ⓐ Ⓑ Ⓒ Ⓓ
30. Ⓐ Ⓑ Ⓒ Ⓓ
31. Ⓐ Ⓑ Ⓒ Ⓓ
32. Ⓐ Ⓑ Ⓒ Ⓓ
33. Ⓐ Ⓑ Ⓒ Ⓓ
34. Ⓐ Ⓑ Ⓒ Ⓓ
35. Ⓐ Ⓑ Ⓒ Ⓓ
36. Ⓐ Ⓑ Ⓒ Ⓓ
37. Ⓐ Ⓑ Ⓒ Ⓓ
38. Ⓐ Ⓑ Ⓒ Ⓓ
39. Ⓐ Ⓑ Ⓒ Ⓓ

40. Ⓐ Ⓑ Ⓒ Ⓓ
41. Ⓐ Ⓑ Ⓒ Ⓓ
42. Ⓐ Ⓑ Ⓒ Ⓓ
43. Ⓐ Ⓑ Ⓒ Ⓓ
44. Ⓐ Ⓑ Ⓒ Ⓓ
45. Ⓐ Ⓑ Ⓒ Ⓓ
46. Ⓐ Ⓑ Ⓒ Ⓓ
47. Ⓐ Ⓑ Ⓒ Ⓓ
48. Ⓐ Ⓑ Ⓒ Ⓓ
49. Ⓐ Ⓑ Ⓒ Ⓓ
50. Ⓐ Ⓑ Ⓒ Ⓓ
51. Ⓐ Ⓑ Ⓒ Ⓓ
52. Ⓐ Ⓑ Ⓒ Ⓓ

53–56 are Constructed-Response questions. See sample essays in Detailed Explanation of Answers section.

Subtest II:
Science; Mathematics

1. Ⓐ Ⓑ Ⓒ Ⓓ
2. Ⓐ Ⓑ Ⓒ Ⓓ
3. Ⓐ Ⓑ Ⓒ Ⓓ
4. Ⓐ Ⓑ Ⓒ Ⓓ
5. Ⓐ Ⓑ Ⓒ Ⓓ
6. Ⓐ Ⓑ Ⓒ Ⓓ
7. Ⓐ Ⓑ Ⓒ Ⓓ
8. Ⓐ Ⓑ Ⓒ Ⓓ
9. Ⓐ Ⓑ Ⓒ Ⓓ
10. Ⓐ Ⓑ Ⓒ Ⓓ
11. Ⓐ Ⓑ Ⓒ Ⓓ
12. Ⓐ Ⓑ Ⓒ Ⓓ
13. Ⓐ Ⓑ Ⓒ Ⓓ

14. Ⓐ Ⓑ Ⓒ Ⓓ
15. Ⓐ Ⓑ Ⓒ Ⓓ
16. Ⓐ Ⓑ Ⓒ Ⓓ
17. Ⓐ Ⓑ Ⓒ Ⓓ
18. Ⓐ Ⓑ Ⓒ Ⓓ
19. Ⓐ Ⓑ Ⓒ Ⓓ
20. Ⓐ Ⓑ Ⓒ Ⓓ
21. Ⓐ Ⓑ Ⓒ Ⓓ
22. Ⓐ Ⓑ Ⓒ Ⓓ
23. Ⓐ Ⓑ Ⓒ Ⓓ
24. Ⓐ Ⓑ Ⓒ Ⓓ
25. Ⓐ Ⓑ Ⓒ Ⓓ
26. Ⓐ Ⓑ Ⓒ Ⓓ

27. Ⓐ Ⓑ Ⓒ Ⓓ
28. Ⓐ Ⓑ Ⓒ Ⓓ
29. Ⓐ Ⓑ Ⓒ Ⓓ
30. Ⓐ Ⓑ Ⓒ Ⓓ
31. Ⓐ Ⓑ Ⓒ Ⓓ
32. Ⓐ Ⓑ Ⓒ Ⓓ
33. Ⓐ Ⓑ Ⓒ Ⓓ
34. Ⓐ Ⓑ Ⓒ Ⓓ
35. Ⓐ Ⓑ Ⓒ Ⓓ
36. Ⓐ Ⓑ Ⓒ Ⓓ
37. Ⓐ Ⓑ Ⓒ Ⓓ
38. Ⓐ Ⓑ Ⓒ Ⓓ
39. Ⓐ Ⓑ Ⓒ Ⓓ

40. Ⓐ Ⓑ Ⓒ Ⓓ
41. Ⓐ Ⓑ Ⓒ Ⓓ
42. Ⓐ Ⓑ Ⓒ Ⓓ
43. Ⓐ Ⓑ Ⓒ Ⓓ
44. Ⓐ Ⓑ Ⓒ Ⓓ
45. Ⓐ Ⓑ Ⓒ Ⓓ
46. Ⓐ Ⓑ Ⓒ Ⓓ
47. Ⓐ Ⓑ Ⓒ Ⓓ
48. Ⓐ Ⓑ Ⓒ Ⓓ
49. Ⓐ Ⓑ Ⓒ Ⓓ
50. Ⓐ Ⓑ Ⓒ Ⓓ
51. Ⓐ Ⓑ Ⓒ Ⓓ
52. Ⓐ Ⓑ Ⓒ Ⓓ

Answer Sheet (cont.)

40–42 are Constructed-Response questions. See sample essays in Detailed Explanation of Answers section.

Subtest III:

Physical Education; Human Development; Visual and Performing Arts

1. Ⓐ Ⓑ Ⓒ Ⓓ
2. Ⓐ Ⓑ Ⓒ Ⓓ
3. Ⓐ Ⓑ Ⓒ Ⓓ
4. Ⓐ Ⓑ Ⓒ Ⓓ
5. Ⓐ Ⓑ Ⓒ Ⓓ
6. Ⓐ Ⓑ Ⓒ Ⓓ
7. Ⓐ Ⓑ Ⓒ Ⓓ
8. Ⓐ Ⓑ Ⓒ Ⓓ
9. Ⓐ Ⓑ Ⓒ Ⓓ
10. Ⓐ Ⓑ Ⓒ Ⓓ
11. Ⓐ Ⓑ Ⓒ Ⓓ
12. Ⓐ Ⓑ Ⓒ Ⓓ
13. Ⓐ Ⓑ Ⓒ Ⓓ

14. Ⓐ Ⓑ Ⓒ Ⓓ
15. Ⓐ Ⓑ Ⓒ Ⓓ
16. Ⓐ Ⓑ Ⓒ Ⓓ
17. Ⓐ Ⓑ Ⓒ Ⓓ
18. Ⓐ Ⓑ Ⓒ Ⓓ
19. Ⓐ Ⓑ Ⓒ Ⓓ
20. Ⓐ Ⓑ Ⓒ Ⓓ
21. Ⓐ Ⓑ Ⓒ Ⓓ
22. Ⓐ Ⓑ Ⓒ Ⓓ
23. Ⓐ Ⓑ Ⓒ Ⓓ
24. Ⓐ Ⓑ Ⓒ Ⓓ
25. Ⓐ Ⓑ Ⓒ Ⓓ
26. Ⓐ Ⓑ Ⓒ Ⓓ

27. Ⓐ Ⓑ Ⓒ Ⓓ
28. Ⓐ Ⓑ Ⓒ Ⓓ
29. Ⓐ Ⓑ Ⓒ Ⓓ
30. Ⓐ Ⓑ Ⓒ Ⓓ
31. Ⓐ Ⓑ Ⓒ Ⓓ
32. Ⓐ Ⓑ Ⓒ Ⓓ
33. Ⓐ Ⓑ Ⓒ Ⓓ
34. Ⓐ Ⓑ Ⓒ Ⓓ
35. Ⓐ Ⓑ Ⓒ Ⓓ
36. Ⓐ Ⓑ Ⓒ Ⓓ
37. Ⓐ Ⓑ Ⓒ Ⓓ
38. Ⓐ Ⓑ Ⓒ Ⓓ
39. Ⓐ Ⓑ Ⓒ Ⓓ

CSET

Practice Test 2

Subtest I

Reading, Language & Literature;
History & Social Science

Practice Test 2: Subtest I
Reading, Language & Literature; History & Social Science

DIRECTIONS: This test consists of two sections: multiple-choice and constructed-response questions. The former is composed of 52 multiple-choice questions and the latter is composed of four questions that involve written responses. You may work on the questions in any order, keeping in mind that when taking the actual test you will have one five-hour test session in which to complete the subtest(s) for which you are assigned.

Multiple-Choice Questions

Reading, Language & Literature

QUESTIONS 1–2 are based on the following poem. Read the poem carefully before choosing your answers.

> Now thou art dead, no eye shall ever see,
> For shape and service, spaniel like to thee.
> This shall my love do, give thy sad death one
> Tear, that deserves of me a million.

1.   The above poem is an example of a(n)

   (A) allegory.   (C) ballad.

   (B) elegy.   (D) kenning.

2.   Lines 3–4 contain an example of

(A) enjambment.   (C) onomatopoeia.

(B) personification.   (D) Homeric simile.

QUESTIONS 3–4 are based on the following poem.

> Study is like the heaven's glorious sun,
> That will not be deep-searched with saucy looks.
> Small have continual plodders won
> Save base authority from others' books.
> These earthly godfathers of heaven's lights,
> That give a name to every fixed star
> Have no more profit of their shining nights
> Than those who walk and wot* not what they are.
> *know

3.   The speaker of these lines is most likely a

(A) student.   (C) clergyman.

(B) professor.   (D) thief.

4.   The lines "Small have continual plodders won / Save base authority from others' books" mean

(A) only one's opinions are important—not facts found in books.

(B) study is long and tedious, but ultimately rewarding.

(C) knowledge and authority are eventually given to those who pursue them.

(D) all that is gained by study are the simple and worthless opinions of others.

QUESTION 5 is based on the following passage.

There was a time when I went every day into a church, since a girl I was in love with knelt there in prayer for half an hour in the evening and I was able to look at her in peace.

Once when she had not come and I was reluctantly eyeing the other supplicants I noticed a young fellow who had thrown his whole lean length along the floor. Every now and then he clutched his head as hard as he could and sighing loudly beat it in his upturned palms on the stone flags.

5.   By using the term "supplicants," the author implies that

(A) everyone in the church is there to celebrate a mass.

(B) everyone in the church is devout.

(C) everyone in the church is guilty of something.

(D) everyone in the church is a hypocrite.

QUESTION 6 is based on the following poem.

WHEN BRITAIN REALLY RULED THE WAVES

When Britain really ruled the waves
    (In good Queen Bess's time)—
The House of Peers made no pretense
To intellectual eminence,
    Or scholarship sublime;
Yet Britain won her proudest bays*
In good Queen Bess's glorious days!
When Wellington thrashed Bonaparte,
    As every child can tell,
The House of Peers, throughout the war,
Did nothing in particular,
    And did it very well:
Yet Britain set the world ablaze
In good King George's glorious days!
And while the House of Peers withholds
    Its legislative hand,
And noble statesman do not itch
To interfere with matters which
    They do not understand,
As bright will shine Great Britain's rays
As in good King George's glorious days!
*honors

6. In this poem, the ruling body of Britain is described as

(A) a very successful legislative institution.

(B) a body that makes wise decisions.

(C) a body that is supported by the British.

(D) a group of disinterested and unintelligent noblemen.

QUESTIONS 7–8 are based on the following passage.

It was the best of times, it was the worst of times, it was the age of wisdom, it was the age of foolishness, it was the epoch of belief, it was the epoch of incredulity, it was the season of Light, it was the season of Darkness, it was the spring of hope, it was the winter of despair, we had everything before us, we had nothing before us, we were all going direct to Heaven, we were all going direct the other way—in short, the period was so far like the present period, that some of its noisiest authorities insisted on its being received, for good or for evil, in the superlative degree of comparison only.

There were a king with a large jaw, and a queen with a plain face, on the throne of England; there were a king with a large jaw, and a queen with a fair face, on the throne of France. In both countries it was clearer than crystal to the lords of the State preserves of loaves and fishes, that things in general were settled for ever.

7. The vast comparisons in the above passage indicate that the speaker is describing

   (A) a placid historical time period.

   (B) a time of extreme political upheaval.

   (C) a public event.

   (D) a time when anything was possible.

8. The last sentence of the passage

   (A) mocks the self-assuredness of the governments of England and France.

   (B) comments on the horrible poverty of the two nations.

   (C) most likely foreshadows an upcoming famine or drought.

   (D) attacks the two governments for neglecting the poor, hungry masses.

QUESTION 9 is based on the following passage.

And thus have these naked Nantucketers, these sea hermits, issuing from their ant-hill in the sea, overrun and conquered the watery world like so many Alexanders...

9. In this passage the author is illustrating

   (A) a symbolic connection to the sea.

   (B) the strength and power of whalers.

   (C) the vulnerability of the Nantucketers

   (D) the fragility of community

QUESTION 10 is based on the following passage.

Once upon a time and a very good time it was there was a moocow coming down along the road and this moocow that was coming down along the met a nicens little boy named baby tuckoo…

10. This passage is written in baby talk to convey to the reader

(A) the age, speech, and mental set of the narrator.

(B) the irony of the situation.

(C) the nature of existence.

(D) the a parody of a child's life.

QUESTION 11 is based on the following passage.

Emma was not required, by any subsequent discovery to retract her ill opinion of Mrs. Elton. Her observation had been pretty correct. Such as Mrs. Elton appeared to her on the second interview, such she appeared whenever they met again—self-important, presuming, familiar, ignorant, and ill-bred. She had a little beauty and a little accomplishment, but so little judgement that she thought herself coming with superior knowledge of the world, to enliven and improve a country neighborhood…

11. This passage is taken from a nineteenth-century novel of manners, and it employs all of the following themes EXCEPT:

(A) the importance (or unimportance) of "good breeding."

(B) the elation (and suffocation) caused by society.

(C) the interation of individuals within the confines of a closed country community.

(D) the tragic nature of self-importance.

QUESTION 12 is based on the following passage.

Gather ye rosebuds while ye may,
Old Time is still a-flying;
And this same flower that smiles today
Tomorrow will be dying.

12. This passage aspouses the philosophy of carpe diem, which means

(A) the day is long

(C) tomorrow will come.

(B) life is long.

(D) seize the day.

QUESTION 13 is based on the following passage.

> Hark, hark!
> Bow-wow,
> The watch-dogs bark!
> Bow-wow.
> Hark, hark! I hear
> The strain of strutting chanticleer
> Cry, "Cock-a-doodle-doo!"

13. The above passage illustrates the use of

   (A) personfication.   (C) allusion.

   (B) onomatopoeia.   (D) symbolism.

QUESTION 14 is based on the following passage.

> A narrow fellow in the grass
> Occasionally rides;
> You may have met him. Did you not,
> His notice sudden is:
> The grass divides as with a comb,
> A spotted shaft is seen,
> And then it closes at your feet
> And open further on.

14. Line 6 in the above passage employs the technique of

   (A) anaphora.   (C) alliteration.

   (B) enjambment.   (D) assonance.

QUESTION 15 is based on the following passage.

It pleased God that I was still spared, and very hearty and sound in health, but very impatient of being pent up within doors without air, as I had been for fourteen days or thereabouts, and I could not restrain myself, but I would go to carry a letter for my brother to the post-house.

15. This utterenace is expressed in the literary form known as the journal. The journal possesses the following qualities of expression EXCEPT:

(A) written in first person.

(B) includes everyday events.

(C) usually contains mythic overtones.

(D) includes everyday emotions.

QUESTION 16 is based on the following passage.

> Apparently with no surprise
> To any happy Flower
> The Frost begeads it at its play –
> In accidental power —
> The blonde Assassin passes on –
> The Sun proceeds unmoved
> To measure off another Day
> For an Approving God.

16. The "blonde Assassin" in the lines cited above is the

(A) Sun.   (C) Frost.

(B) Day.   (D) Flower.

17. Which of the following lines is an example of iambic pentameter?

(A) The an/gry spot / doth glow /on Cae/sar's brow.

(B) Here goes / the try / I've al/ways known/

(C) She loves the / way I hold / her hand/

(D) Although I / knew the road / led home/

QUESTIONS 18–19 refer to the following passage.

> Oh God, do you hear it, this persecution,
> These my sufferings from this hateful
> Woman, this monster, murderess of children?
> Still what I can do that I will do:
> I will lament and cry upon heaven,
> Calling the gods to bear me witness
> How you have killed my boys to prevent me from
> Touching their bodies or giving them burial.

I wish I never begot them to see them
Afterward slaughtered by you.

18. These lines are spoken by

    (A) the murderer.   (C) one of the gods.

    (B) the father of dead children   (D) a bystander.

19. It can be inferred from this passage that

    (A) the woman had a right to kill her children.

    (B) the man deserved to lose his children.

    (C) the rites and ceremonies of burial are extremely important.

    (D) the gods decreed the death of the children.

QUESTIONS 20–22 are based on the following passage.

It is very seldom that mere ordinary people like John and myself secure ancestral halls for the summer.

A colonial mansion, a hereditary estate, I would say a haunted house and reach the height of romantic felicity—but that would be asking too much of fate!

Still I will proudly declare that there is something queer about it.

Else, why should it be let so cheaply? And why have stood so long untenanted?

John laughs at me, of course, but one expects that.

John is practical in the extreme. He has no patience with faith, an intense horror of superstition, and he scoffs openly at any talk of things not to be felt and seen and put down in figures.

John is a physician, and *perhaps* (I would not say it to a living soul, of course, but this is dead paper and a great relief to my mind)—*perhaps* that is one reason I do not get well faster.

You see, he does not believe I am sick! And what can one do?

If a physician of high standing, and one's own husband, assures friends and relatives that there is really nothing the matter with one but temporary nervous depression—a slight hysterical tendency—what is one to do?

My brother is also a physician, and also of high standing, and he says the same thing.

So I take phosphates or phosphites—whichever it is—and tonics, and air and exercise, and journeys, and am absolutely forbidden to "work" until I am well again.

Personally, I disagree with their ideas.

20. John is characterized by the speaker as

    (A) arrogant.   (C) cunning.

    (B) trustworthy.   (D) realistic.

21. The speaker views writing as

    (A) annoying.   (C) laborious.

    (B) therapeutic.   (D) painful.

22. We can infer from the passage that the speaker

    (A) is insane.

    (B) is of no solid mental health.

    (C) has no real occupation.

    (D) strongly dislikes her husband.

QUESTION 23 refers to the following passage.

It was Phaethon who drove them to Fiesole that memorable day, a youth all irresponsibility and fire, recklessly urging his master's horses up the stony hill. Mr. Beebe recognized him at once. Neither the Ages of Faith nor the Age of Doubt had touched him; he was on the way, saying that she was his sister—Persephone, tall and slender and pale, returning with the Spring to her mother's cottage, and still shading her eyes from the unaccustomed light. To her Mr. Eager objected, saying that here was the thin edge of the wedge, and one must guard against imposition. But the ladies interceded, and when it had been made clear that it was a very great favour, the goddess was allowed to mount beside the god.

23. Which of the following helps characterize Phaethon and Persephone as a "god" and "goddess?"

    I.   Their names   III. Her eyes

    II. His occupation   IV.   Her build

    (A) I only.   (C) I, II, and III.

    (B) I and II.   (D) II, III, and IV.

24. The stages of language acquisition in infants and young children are

    (A) fluid.   (C) set in rigid parameters.

    (B) easily traced.   (D) mirrored in adults.

25. All of the following statements about grammar are correct EXCEPT:

    (A) grammar represents a constructed code.

    (B) grammar rules are at times arbitrary.

    (C) grammar has a direct relationship to the way people speak.

    (D) Standard English provides a general understanding and competence in the language.

26. Read the paragraph below; then answer the question that follows.

    [1]Just 12 miles north of San Francisco but with an unmistakenly small-town feel, Corte Madera, California, is a kind of metropolitan paradise. [2]Situated near the base of scenic Mt. Tamalpais, the town reflects the mellow, outdoor lifestyle that characterizes the Golden State as a whole, with open space and parks aplenty.[3]Corte Madera is ensconsed in the verdant Marin County countryside. [4]Many of its 8,300 residents enjoy running, hiking, and biking, and relish some of the most spectacular vistas in the West.

    Which of the following is the topic sentence of this paragraph?

    (A) Sentence 1

    (B) Sentence 2

    (C) Sentence 3

    (D) Sentence 4

History and Social Science

27. The nomadic warriors who would later become the lords of feudal Japan arrived in the

    (A) Kofun Era.   (C) Sengoku Era.

    (B) Heian Era.   (D) Warring States Era.

28. *Bakfu*, literally translated, means

    (A) shogunate.   (C) landed estate.

    (B) tent Government.   (D) feudal lord.

29. All of the following were unifiers of feudal Japan EXCEPT:

    (A) Oda Nobunaga.   (C) Tokugawa Ieyasu.

    (B) Toyotomi Hideyoshi. (D) Minamoto no Yorimoto.

30. Which of the following religions facilitated the conversion of Asoka into Indian society?

    (A) Taoism   (C) Buddhism

    (B) Hinduism   (D) Jainism

31. Which of the following Meso-American civilizations first established the concept of zero?

    (A) Toltec   (C) Aztec

    (B) Maya   (D) Inca

32. Which of the following is NOT one of the five pillars of the Islamic faith?

    (A) Confession of faith

    (B) Payment of alms

    (C) Fasting from sunrise to sunset during Ramadhan

    (D) The jihad

33. Which of the following Sub-Saharan peoples created life-sized figures of humans and animals in terra cotta?

    (A) The Nok   (C) The Ghana

    (B) The Songhai   (D) The Bantu

34. Which of the following Pre-Columbian American cultures were sun worshippers?

    (A) Aztec   (C) Inca

    (B) Andean   (D) Hohokam

35. Which Revolutionary War battle is considered the turning point in the war because it led to direct French assistance for the Americans?

    (A) Trenton   (C) Yorktown

    (B) Bunker Hill   (D) Saratoga

36. During the campaign to ratify the Constitution, the Federalists argued

    (A) for a return to the Articles of Confederation as the framework of federal government.

    (B) that a bill of rights, to correct flaws in the Constitution, must be in place before the Constitution could be ratified.

(C) for ratification of the Constitution, with a possible bill of rights to be discussed after ratification.

(D) against a strong national government of any kind and an increase in the powers of the states to govern themselves.

37. Which battle is considered to be the "turning point" of the Civil War and the last chance at a military victory by the Confederacy?

(A) Antietam   (C) Gettysburg

(B) Shiloh   (D) Chattanooga

38. All of the following helped shape the development of colonial American agriculture EXCEPT:

(A) availability of land.

(B) abundance of capital.

(C) limitations of climate and land.

(D) shortage of labor.

39. The Credit Mobilier Scandal involved

(A) a dummy construction company used by railroad magnates to defraud the government.

(B) a tax-collection contract sold in exchange for a kickback to Republican campaign coffers.

(C) a conspiracy to defraud the government of large amounts of money from the excise tax on whiskey.

(D) an attempt by Congress to raise its own pay retroactively.

40. The LEAST important issue during the era of "Jacksonian Democracy" was

(A) the removal of Indians from southeastern states.

(B) federal financing of internal improvements.

(C) the right of states to nullify federal laws.

(D) the growing trend toward industrialization.

41. Spanish explorers Hernando de Soto and Francisco Vasquez de Coronado sought

(A) an all-water route to the Orient.

(B) rich Indian civilizations to plunder.

(C) a route to East Asia.

(D) sources of raw materials for Spain.

42. Which of the following was NOT one of the purposes of the Lewis and Clark expedition?

(A) Establishing friendly relations with the western Indians

(B) Gaining geographic knowledge about the western part of North America

(C) Discovering sources of gold

(D) Gaining scientific knowledge about the flora and fauna of western North America

43. The Black Death of the fourteenth century resulted in the

(A) decline of the movement toward nation-states in western Europe.

(B) rise of modern medicine.

(C) enhancement of the value of labor.

(D) flight of millions of Europeans overseas.

44. The major responsibility of the Federal Reserve Board is to

(A) implement monetary policy.

(B) control government spending.

(C) regulate commodity prices.

(D) help the president run the executive branch.

45. Which of the following best describes the relationship between educational background and participation in politics?

(A) The more schooling one has, the more likely one is to vote.

(B) The less schooling one has, the more likely one is to run for public office.

(C) There is no relationship between educational background and participation in politics.

(D) People with a high school education are more likely to vote than either those who did not finish high school or those with a college degree.

46. The Great Awakening of the mid-eighteenth century refers to

   (A) a series of religious revivals that swept through the English colonies spreading evangelistic fervor and challenging the control of traditional clerics over their congregations.

   (B) the intellectual revolution that served as a precursor to the Enlightenment and challenged Orthodox religion's claim to knowledge of humankind and the universe.

   (C) the beginnings of the Industrial Revolution in England and its New World colonies.

   (D) the growing realization among English colonists that independence from England was only a matter of time and was the key to their future success.

47. Which of the following best defines the term "judicial restraint"?

   (A) A decision by judges to limit the number of cases they decide per year

   (B) Refusal by judges to lobby Congress for funds

   (C) A practice by which judges remove themselves from cases in which they have a personal interest

   (D) The tendency of judges to interpret the Constitution in light of the original intent of its framers

48. The Missouri Compromise provided that Missouri be admitted as a slave state, Maine be admitted as a free state, and

   (A) all of the Louisiana Territory north of the northern boundary of Missouri be closed to slavery.

   (B) all of the Louisiana Territory north of 36° 30´ be closed to slavery.

   (C) the entire Louisiana Territory be open to slavery.

   (D) the lands south of 36° 30´ be guaranteed to slavery and the lands north of it negotiable.

49. The most common form of resistance on the part of black American slaves prior to the Civil War was

   (A) attempts to escape and reach Canada by means of the "Underground Railroad."

   (B) passive resistance, including breaking tools and slightly slowing the pace of work.

   (C) arson of plantation buildings and cotton gins.

   (D) poisoning of the food consumed by their white masters.

50. The Constitution places legislative power in Congress and Executive power in the President. This is an example of

    (A) separation of power.   (C) constitutional interpretation.

    (B) checks and balances.   (D) fundamental rights.

51. Which of the following constitutional amendments officially ended slavery in the United States?

    (A) Thirteenth Amendment

    (B) Fourteenth Amendment

    (C) Fifteenth Amendment

    (D) Sixteenth Amendment

52. The *Marbury v. Madison* case was important because it

    (A) firmly established the principle of one man, one vote.

    (B) affirmed the Supreme Court's power to judge the constitutionality of law passed by Congress.

    (C) limited the power of the individual states to interfere with legal business contracts or commercial activity.

    (D) found that Congress had the constitutional power to issue bank characters, thus opening the door for a strong national bank.

Constructed-Response Questions

Constructed-Response Directions

Prepare a written response for each constructed-response assignment. Read each assignment carefully before you begin to write. Think about how you will organize what you plan to write.

Scoring of responses to CSET: Multiple Subjects constructed response assignments is based on the following criteria:

PURPOSE: the extent to which the response addresses the constructed-response assignment's charge in relation to relevant CSET content specifications.

SUBJECT MATTER KNOWLEDGE: the application of accurate subject matter knowledge as described in the relevant CSET content specifications.

SUPPORT: the appropriateness and quality of the supporting evidence in relation to relevant CSET content specifications.

The assignments are intended to assess subject matter knowledge and skills, not writing ability. Your responses, however, must be communicated clearly enough to permit a valid judgment of your knowledge and skills. Your responses should be written for an audience of educators in the field.

You may wish to write each of your responses to the CSET: Multiple Subjects Subtest I practice test constructed-response assignments and ask a mentor, advisor, or teacher to help evaluate them. Sample responses are provided for these assignments following the detailed answers section of the Subtest I practice test.

53. Read carefully the selection below, the opening paragraph from Herman Melville's short story "Bartleby the Scrivener: A Story of Wall Street," and discuss the significance of point of view. How does the narrator describe the character of Bartleby? What does the narrator reveal about his own character? What themes will the story explore, based on this opening?

"I am an elderly man. The nature of my avocations, for the last thirty years, has brought me into more than ordinary contact with what would seem an interesting and somewhat singular set of men, of whom, as yet, nothing, that I know of, has ever been written – I mean, the law copyists, or scriveners. I have known very many of them, professionally and privately, and, if I pleased, could realte divers histories, at which good-natured gentlemen might smile, and sentimental souls might weep. but I waive the biographies of all other scriveners, for a few passages in the life of Bartleby, who was a scrivener, the strangest I ever saw, or heard of. While, of other law-copyists, I might write the complete life, of Bartleby nothing of that sort can be done. I believe that no materials exist for a full and satisfactory biography of this man. It is an irreperable loss to literature. Bartleby was one of those beings of whom nothing is ascertainable, except from the original sources, and, in his case, those are very small. What my own astonished eyes saw of Bartleby, *that* is all I know of him, except, indeed, one vague report, which will appear in the sequel.

54. How does the short story as a genre or mode of writing differ significantly from the novel? Explain. In your essay, point to at least two short stories and one novel, and comment on the historical development of these two genres.

55. What was the Great Awakening? What impact did it have on the colonies?

56. Discuss the United States as it existed under the Articles of Confederation. What were the strengths and weaknesses of the Confederation government and how did the Constitution attempt to correct those flaws?

CSET

Practice Test 2
Subtest II:
Science
Mathematics

Practice Test 2: Subtest II

Science
Mathematics

DIRECTIONS: This test consists of two sections: multiple-choice and constructed-response questions. The former is composed of 52 multiple-choice questions and the latter is composed of four questions that involve written responses. You may work on the questions in any order, keeping in mind that when taking the actual test you will have one five-hour test session in which to complete the subtest(s) for which you are registered.

Multiple-Choice Questions

Science

1. DNA nucleotides are found in which part of the cell?

    (A) The lysosomes

    (B) The endoplasmic reticulum

    (C) The cytoplasmic matrix

    (D) The nucleus

2. DNA strands that are coiled around and interwoven with protein molecules form

    (A) RNA.   (C) nucleotides.

    (B) chromosomes.   (D) genes.

3. Which of the following is NOT a correct statement about water?

   (A) Ice cubes float because solid water is less dense than liquid water.

   (B) Water exists as both a liquid and a solid in the range of normal Earth temperatures.

   (C) Hydrogen bonding is especially weak in water.

   (D) Bonds between the oxygen and hydrogen of water are covalent.

4. The speed of light in a vacuum is

   (A) independent of the wavelength of light.

   (B) independent of the frequency of the light.

   (C) dependent on the distance traveled by the light.

   (D) Both (A) and (B).

5. Which sequence of life is correct?

   (A) Invertebrates, fish, reptiles, mammals

   (B) Fish, invertebrates, mammals, birds

   (C) Plants, invertebrates, forests, fish

   (D) Invertebrates, mammals, birds, plants

6. If the distance between the Moon and Earth were doubled, then the gravitational pull on the Earth by the moon would be

   (A) unchanged.   (C) halved.

   (B) doubled.   (D) quartered.

7. There are 46 chromosomes found in the cheek cell of a human male. If this cell were to undergo mitosis, how many chromosomes would be found in each resulting daughter cell?

   (A) 2   (C) 24

   (B) 10   (D) 46

8. If mitosis were not to occur in both a male and a female human and their sperm and egg were to unite to form a zygote, how many chromosomes would the zygote have?

(A) 2   (C) 46

(B) 23   (D) 92

9. An atom absorbs a photon of visible light. The most likely result is

(A) the atom nucleus splits.

(B) a valence electron assumes a lower energy state.

(C) a valence electron assumes a higher energy state.

(D) the photon is stored in the nucleus.

10. Earthquakes produce *P* and *S* waves that travel through the Earth from earthquake epicenters. The waves are

(A) both transverse and traveling at the same speed.

(B) both longitudinal and traveling at the same speed.

(C) one transverse and the other longitudinal and traveling at the same speed.

(D) one transverse and the other longitudinal and traveling at different speeds.

11. The reason metals are good electrical conductors is because

(A) atomic nuclei in metals are mobile.

(B) valence electrons in metals are mobile.

(C) protons in metals are mobile.

(D) neutrons in metals are mobile.

12. In the equation $F = ma$, F = unbalanced force, m = mass, and a = acceleration. A valid interpretation of the equation is

(A) increasing mass for a given force will increase accleration.

(B) decreasing mass for a given force will increase acceleration.

(C) increasing F for a given mass will decrease acceleration.

(D) decreasing F for a given mass will increase acceleration.

13. The density of a given substance has units of

   (A) mass per unit mass.

   (B) mass per unit mole.

   (C) mass per unit volume.

   (D) volume per unit mass.

14. The high tides are most likely to occur when the

   (A) Earth, sun, and moon are in alignment and the moon is in between the sun and the earth.

   (B) Earth, sun, and moon are in alignment and the earth is in between the sun and the moon.

   (C) Earth, sun, and moon are not in alignment and a line drawn through the earth–moon center is at right angles to the line drawn through the earth-sun centers.

   (D) None of the above.

15. The chemical properties of any element are most strongly determined by

   (A) the element's number of neutrons.

   (B) the element's nuclear structure.

   (C) the number of electrons in the element's outer or valence shell.

   (D) the element's density.

16. Avogadro's number of 6.023×1023 is a chemical constant and refers to the

   (A) number of atoms per mole.

   (B) number of atoms per cubic centimeter.

   (C) number of moles per atom.

   (D) number of electrons per atom.

17. A mercury thermometer is heated and the column of mercury is seen to rise to a higher temperature. If the thermometer is shaded from the sun, what is the most likely mechanism of heat transfer that caused the mercury to expand?

   (A) Radiation from the sun

   (B) Conduction from the surrounding air

   (C) Convection within the thermometer

   (D) None of the above

18. Consider a location on the equator at a certain longitude and another location at the same longitude in the Northern Hemisphere 3,000 miles to the north. Both locations will be

(A) in same time zone, but only in the summer months.

(B) in the same time zone.

(C) Cannot tell from information given

(D) in the same time zone, but only in the winter months.

19. A certain mass of salt is completely dissolved in distilled water, forming

(A) a chemical bond between the water and salt.

(B) a water-salt solution.

(C) a water-salt mixture.

(D) a water-salt compound.

20. A calculator is used to multiply 3.4 and 6.21. The answer displayed should be rounded to

(A) three places.

(B) two places.

(C) one place.

(D) as many places as are displayed.

21. Use the picture below to answer the question that follows.

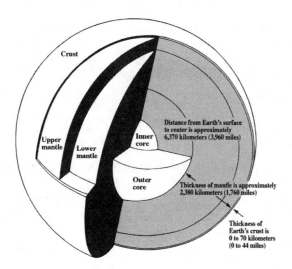

Which area of this illustration represents the *focus* of most earthquakes?

(A)   the inner core and outer core

(B)   the outer core and lower mantle

(C)   the lower mantle and the upper mantle

(D)   the upper mantle and the crust

22.   An experiment requires measurement of an electrical current passing through a resistor. The means of measurement of the current requires

(A)   a voltmeter connected in series with the resistor.

(B)   an ammeter connected in series with the resistor.

(C)   an ammeter connected in parallel with the resistor.

(D)   a voltmeter connected in parallel with the resistor.

23.   An experiment is conducted in which a graph is generated, showing a straight line relationship between two measured quantities. It is required to measure the slope of the line. This can be accomplished by

(A)   reading off the maximum of the graph.

(B)   reading off the miminum of the graph.

(C)   calculating the slope of the line as rise divided by run.

(D)   calculating the slope of the line as run divided by rise.

24.   An irregularly shaped object is dropped into a graduated cylinder partly filled with water and sinks. The object is now completely submerged. The fluid level in the cylinder will

(A)   remain unchanged.

(B)   increase by an amount proportional the object's mass.

(C)   increase by an amount proportional to the object's volume.

(D)   decrease by an amount proportional to the object's volume.

25.   Two sets of data are plotted in a parabolic-shaped graph, one set representing a controlled variable V and the other a dependent variable D. The controlled variable set ranges from 2 to 60. However, the experimenter wants to estimate what the value of D will be when $V = 80$, but for technical reasons cannot actually adjust $V = 80$. The experimenter could obtain the required value by

(A)   extrapolation of the existing data.

(B)   reduction of the existing data.

(C)   averaging the existing data.

(D)   finding the mean of the existing data.

26.   A charged particle initially traveling in a straight line at a constant speed enters a region of magnetic field. Its path within the region of the magnetic field will be

(A)   always altered by the magnetic field.

(B)   never altered by the magnetic field.

(C)   always circular.

(D)   sometimes circular, depending on particle direction relative to field direction.

Mathematics

27.   If 406.725 is rounded off to the nearest tenth, the result is

(A)   406.3.   (C)   406.7.

(B)   406.5.   (D)   406.8.

28.   The mean IQ score for 1,500 students is 100, with a standard deviation of 15. Assuming normal curve distribution, how many students have an IQ between 85 and 115? Refer to the figure shown below.

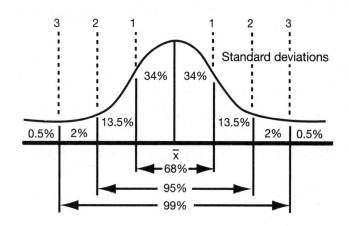

(A)   510   (C)   1,020

(B)   750   (D)   1,275

29. Twice the sum of 10 and a number is 28. Find the number.

    (A) 4   (C) 12

    (B) 8   (D) 14

30. You can buy a telephone for $24. If you are charged $3 per month for renting a telephone from the telephone company, how long will it take you to recover the cost of the phone if you buy one.

    (A) 6 months   (C) 8 months

    (B) 7 months   (D) 9 months

31. Two college roommates spent $2,000 for their total monthly expenses. The circle graph below indicates a record of their expenses.

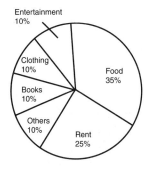

    Based on the above information, which of the following statements is accurate?

    (A) The roommates spent $700 on food alone.

    (B) The roommates spent $550 on rent alone.

    (C) The roommates spent $300 on entertainment alone.

    (D) The roommates spent $300 on clothing alone.

32. What would be the measure of the third angle in the following triangle?

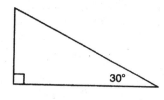

    (A) 45°   (C) 60°

    (B) 50°   (D) 70°

33. Assuming that the quadrilateral in the following figure is a parallelogram, what would be its area?

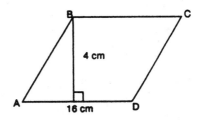

(A) 32 cm

(C) 40 cm²

(B) 40 cm

(D) 64 cm²

34. Which of the following statements includes a cardinal number?

(A) There are 15 volumes in the set of periodicals.

(B) I received my 14th volume recently.

(C) The students meet at Room 304.

(D) My phone number is 213-617-8442.

35. Find the next three terms in this sequence: 1, 4, 9, 16,…

(A) 19, 24, 31

(C) 21, 28, 36

(B) 20, 25, 31

(D) 25, 36, 49

36. Assume that one pig eats 4 pounds of food each week. There are 52 weeks in a year. How much food do 10 pigs eat in a week?

(A) 40 lb.

(C) 208 lb.

(B) 520 lb.

(D) 20 lb.

37. Suppose that a pair of pants and a shirt cost $65 and the pants cost $25 more than the shirt. What did they each cost?

(A) The pants cost $35 and the shirt costs $30.

(B) The pants cost $40 and the shirt costs $25.

(C) The pants cost $43 and the shirt costs $22.

(D) The pants cost $45 and the shirt costs $20.

38. There are five members in a basketball team. Supposing each member shakes hands with every other member of the team before the game starts, how many handshakes will there be in all?

    (A) 6   (C) 9

    (B) 8   (D) 10

39. Six dice are thrown. What is the probability of getting six ones?

    (A) 0.0000214   (C) 0.1667

    (B) 0.0278   (D) 0.1

40. Tom bought a piece of land selling for $20,000. If he had to pay 20% of the price as a down payment, how much was the down payment?

    (A) $2,500   (C) $4,000

    (B) $3,000   (D) $4,500

41. A certain company produces two types of lawnmowers. Type A is self-propelled while type B is not. The company can produce a maximum of 18 mowers per week. It can make a profit of $15 on mower A and a profit of $20 on mower B. The company wants to make at least 2 mowers of type A but not more than 5. They also plan to make at least 2 mowers of type B. Let x be the number of type A produced, and let y be the number of type B produced.

    Which of the following is not one of the listed constraints?

    (A) $x \le 2$ (C) $x + y \le 18$

    (B) $x \le 5$ (D) $y < 5$

42. Mr. Smith died and left an estate to be divided among his wife, two children, and a foundation of his choosing in the ratio of 8:6:6:1. How much did his wife receive if the estate was valued at $300,000?

    (A) $114,285.71   (C) $85,714.29

    (B) $120,421.91   (D) $14,285.71

43. There were 19 hamburgers for 9 people on a picnic. How many whole hamburgers were there for each person if they were divided equally?

    (A) 1   (C) 3

    (B) 2   (D) 4

44. George has four ways to get from his house to the park. He has seven ways to get from the park to the school. How many ways can George get from his house to school by way of the park?

    (A) 4   (C) 28

    (B) 7   (D) 3

45. If it takes 1 minute per cut, how long will it take to cut a 15-foot-long timber into 15 equal pieces?

    (A) 5   (C) 14

    (B) 10   (D) 20

46. Ed has 6 new shirts and 4 new pairs of pants. How many combinations of new shirts and pants does he have?

    (A) 10   (C) 18

    (B) 14   (D) 24

47. Ralph kept track of his gardening time. Refer to the broken-line graph below:

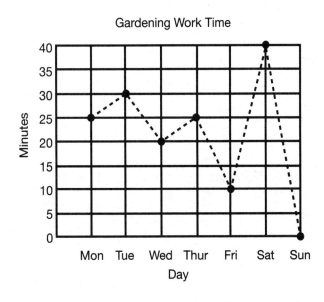

How many minutes did he average per day?

    (A) 10 minutes   (C) 21.43 minutes

    (B) 20 minutes   (D) 23.05 minutes

48. Mary had been selling printed shirts in her neighborhood. She made this pictograph to show how much money she made each week.

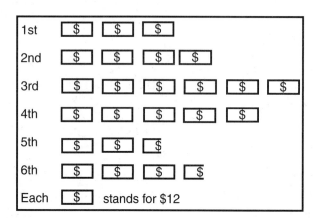

How many weeks were sales more than $55?

(A) 1 week

(C) 3 weeks

(B) 2 weeks

(D) 4 weeks

49. In a biology class at International University, the grades on the final examination were as follows:

91	81	65	81
50	70	81	93
36	90	43	87
96	81	75	81

Find the mode.

(A) 36

(C) 81

(B) 70

(D) 87

50. Which of the following figures below represent simple closed curves?

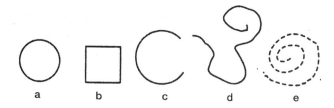

(A) a and b

(C) c and d

(B) a, b, and c

(D) d and e

51. How many lines of symmetry, if any, does the following figure have?

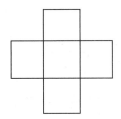

(A) 1

(C) 3

(B) 2

(D) 4

52. A car rental agency charges $139 per week plus $0.08 per mile for an average size car. How far can you travel to the nearest mile on a maximum budget of $350?

(A) 2,637 miles

(C) 2,110 miles

(B) 2,640 miles

(D) 1,737 miles

Constructed-Response Questions

Constructed-Response Directions

Prepare a written response for each constructed-response assignment. Read each assignment carefully before you begin to write. Think about how you will organize what you plan to write.

Scoring of responses to CSET: Multiple Subjects constructed response assignments is based on the following criteria:

PURPOSE: the extent to which the response addresses the constructed-response assignment's charge in relation to relevant CSET content specifications.

SUBJECT MATTER KNOWLEDGE: the application of accurate subject matter knowledge as described in the relevant CSET content specifications.

SUPPORT: the appropriateness and quality of the supporting evidence in relation to relevant CSET content specifications.

The assignments are intended to assess subject matter knowledge and skills, not writing ability. Your responses, however, must be communicated clearly enough to permit a valid judgment of your knowledge and skills. Your responses should be written for an audience of educators in the field.

You may wish to write each of your responses to the CSET: Multiple Subjects Subtest II practice test constructed-response assignments and ask a mentor, advisor, or teacher to help evaluate them. Sample responses are provided for these assignments following the detailed answers section of the Subtest II practice test.

53. Using your knowledge of Life Sciences answer the following questions

    1.   Discuss the relationship of amino acids to proteins.

    2.   Define a protein and give an example

    3.   Define an amino acid and give an example.

54. Using your knowledge of properties of waves answer the following questions.

    1.   Make a sketch of a single wave, labeling amplitude and wavelength

    2.   Define wave frequency and relate it to wavelength.

    3.   Describe the difference between transverse and longitudinal waves. Give an example of each

    4.   Describe the essential differences between light waves and sound waves.

55. If you square an integer and subtract 1, the result equals the product of that integer plus 1 and that integer minus 1. Why?

56. Why does the product of two irrational numbers not have to be another irrational number?

CSET

Practice Test 2

Subtest III:
Physical Education
Human Development
Visual and Performing Arts

Practice Test 2: Subtest III
Physical Education
Human Development
Visual and Performing Arts

DIRECTIONS: This test consists of two sections: multiple-choice and constructed-response questions. The former is composed of 39 multiple-choicequestions and the latter is composed of 3 questions that involve written responses. You may work on the questions in any order, keeping in mind that when taking the actual test you will have one five-hour test session in which to complete the subtest(s) for which you are registered.

Multiple-Choice Questions

Physical Education

1. Which of the following conditions would cause a child to be classified as handicapped according to P.L. 94–142?

    (A) Pregnancy   (C) Obesity

    (B) Deafness   (D) Acne

2. Which of the following vitamins is NOT fat soluble?

    (A) Vitamin D   (C) Vitamin E

    (B) Vitamin C   (D) Vitamin K

3. The primary and most efficient energy source of the body comes from

   (A) proteins.   (C) complex carbohydrates.

   (B) fats.   (D) simple sugars.

4. The body produces cholesterol in the

   (A) liver.   (C) stomach.

   (B) pancreas.   (D) pituitary gland.

5. A break in the bone with a corresponding break in the skin is called a

   (A) comminuted fracture.   (C) compound fracture.

   (B) simple fracture.   (D) complex fracture.

6. In order to achieve lasting weight loss, people should

   (A) enter a commercial diet program.

   (B) combine permanent dietary changes with exercise.

   (C) cut calories to below 100 per day.

   (D) exercise for two hours a day.

7. Which of the following is a locomotive skill?

   (A) Bouncing a ball   (C) Throwing

   (B) Catching   (D) Leaping

8. Exercises that cause actual contraction of the muscle fibers are called

   (A) isotonic.   (C) static.

   (B) isometric.   (D) aerobic.

9. Which is NOT a principle of aerobic conditioning?

   (A) Requires oxygen

   (B) Continuous and rhythmic

   (C) Burns protein for energy

   (D) Uses major muscle groups

10. The knee is an example of which of the following types of joints?

   (A) Hinge   (B) Angular

   (C) Ball and socket   (D) Gliding

11. Which of the following is not a characteristic of cholesterol?

    (A) Cholesterol plays a role in the function of the brain.

    (B) Cholesterol is a component in the creation of certain hormones.

    (C) Cholesterol is produced in the liver.

    (D) Excess cholesterol found in the blood of many people usually comes from internal production.

12. A table tennis game is scored to

    (A) 15 points.

    (B) 15 points, with a margin of two.

    (C) 21 points, with a margin of two.

    (D) 21 points.

13. What percentage of a diet should be comprised of protein?

    (A) 20%   (C) 40%

    (B) 25%   (D) 50%

Human Development

QUESTIONS 14-16 refer to the following statement.

Mr. Drake is a first-grade teacher who is using the whole language method while teaching about animals.

14. Before reading a story to the students, Mr. Drake tells the students what he is expecting them to learn from reading the story. What is his reason for doing this?

    (A) The students should know why the instructor chose this text over any other.

    (B) It is important for teachers to share personal ideas with their students in order to foster an environment of confidence and understanding.

    (C) Mr. Drake wants to verify that all students are on-task before he begins the story.

    (D) Mr. Drake is modeling a vital pre-reading skill in order to teach it to the young readers.

15. Mr. Drake has a heterogeneously grouped reading class. He has the students in groups of two—one skilled reader and one remedial reader—reading selected stories to one another. The students read the story and question each other until they feel that they both understand the story. By planning the lesson this way, Mr. Drake has

    (A) set a goal for his students.

    (B) condensed the number of observations necessary, thereby creating more time for class instruction.

    (C) made it possible for another teacher to utilize the limited materials.

    (D) utilized the students' strengths and weaknesses to maximize time, materials, and the learning environment.

16. Before reading a story about a veterinary hospital, Mr. Drake constructs a semantic map of related words and terms using the students' input. What is his main intention for doing this?

    (A) To demonstrate a meaningful relationship between the concepts of the story and the prior knowledge of the students

    (B) To serve as a visual means of learning

    (C) To determine the level of understanding the students will have at the conclusion of the topic being covered

    (D) To model proper writing using whole words

17. According to Piaget, a person who cannot consistently use abstract logic has not reached the stage of

    (A) concrete operations.

    (B) preoperational development.

    (C) formal operations.

    (D) initiative vs. guilt.

QUESTIONS 18-21 refer to the following passage

Mr. Dobson teaches fifth-grade mathematics at Valverde Elementary. He encourages students to work in groups of two or three as they begin homework assignments so they can answer questions for each other. Mr. Dobson notices immediately that some of his students chose to work alone even though they had been asked to work in groups. He also notices that some students are easily distracted even though the other members of their group are working on the assignment as directed.

18. Which of the following is the most likely explanation for the students' behavior?

    (A) Fifth-grade students are not physically or mentally capable of working in small groups; small groups are more suitable for older students.

    (B) Fifth-grade students vary greatly in their physical development and maturity; this variance influences students' interests and attitudes.

    (C) Fifth-grade students lack the ability for internal control, and therefore learn best in structured settings. It is usually best to seat fifth graders in single rows.

    (D) Mr. Dobson needs to be more specific in his expectations for student behavior.

19. Mr. Dobson wants to encourage all of his students to participate in discussions related to the use of math in the real world. Five students in one class are very shy and introverted. Which of the following would most likely be the best way to encourage these students to participate in the discussion?

    (A) Mr. Dobson should call on these students by name at least once each day and give participation grades.

    (B) Mr. Dobson should not be concerned about these students because they will become less shy and introverted as they mature during the year.

    (C) Mr. Dobson should divide the class into small groups for discussion so these students will not be overwhelmed by speaking in front of the whole class.

    (D) Mr. Dobson should speak with these students individually and encourage them to participate more in class discussions.

20. In the same class, Mr. Dobson has two students who are overly talkative. These two students volunteer to answer every question. Which of the following is the best way to deal with these students?

    (A) Mr. Dobson should call on the overly talkative students only once during each class.

    (B) Mr. Dobson should ask these students to be the observers in small group discussions, and take notes about participation and topics discussed.

    (C) Mr. Dobson should place these students in a group by themselves so they can discuss all they want and not disturb the other students.

    (D) Mr. Dobson should recognize that overly talkative students need lots of attention and should be called on to participate throughout the class period.

21. Mr. Dobson wants to use a variety of grouping strategies during the year. Sometimes he groups students with others of similar ability; sometimes he groups students with varying ability. Sometimes he permits students to choose their own groupings. Sometimes he suggests that students work with a particular partner; sometimes he assigns a partner. Sometimes he allows students to elect to work individually. This flexibility in grouping strategies indicates that Mr. Dobson recognizes that

    (A) fifth graders like surprises and unpredictable teacher behavior.

    (B) grouping patterns affect students perceptions of self-esteem and competence.

    (C) frequent changes in the classroom keep students alert and interested.

    (D) it is not fair to place the worst students in the same group consistently.

22. The theory that we all experience a series of psychosocial crises throughout our lives was proposed by

    (A) Piaget   (C) Freud

    (B) Maslow   (D) Erikson

QUESTION 23 refers to the following passage.

Genevieve Thompson is a first-year teacher who has accepted a position as a first-grade teacher. In college, Genevieve's elementary teaching field was science. She is eager to begin working with her first graders so that in addition to teaching them literacy skills, she can teach them to enjoy science and mathematics.

23. Of all of her students who do not have documented handicaps, which of her students are likely to be poor readers?

    (A) Those whose parents seldom read aloud to them.

    (B) Those whose parents place them in daycare for more than three hours per day.

    (C) Those whose parents allow them to watch more than two hours of television daily.

    (D) Those who are being raised by a grandparent.

24. One advantage of using interactive videodisk technology is that students have the opportunity to actually observe demonstrations of how such phenomena as sound waves work. Teaching students by allowing them to see the natural phenomenon of sound waves taking place instead of merely offering complex theoretical descriptions of sound waves is most important for students at what stage of development?

    (A) Piaget's sensorimotor stage

    (B) Piaget's concrete operational stage

(C) Piaget's formal operational stage

(D) Piaget's interpersonal concordance stage

QUESTIONS 25-26 refer to the following passage

Suppose you are playing "Monopoly" with a group of children. These children understand the basic instructions and will play by the rules. They are not capable of hypothetical transactions dealing with mortgages, loans, and special pacts with other players.

25. According to Piaget, these children are in which stage of cognitive development?

(A) Sensorimotor stage

(B) Formal operations stage

(C) Preconceptual stage

(D) Concrete operational stage

26. What are the probable ages of these children?

(A) 8–13   (C) 2–4

(B) 4–7   (D) 7–11

Visual and Performing Arts

27. Which of the statements that follow best describes the building pictured below?

Georges Pompidou National Center of Art and Culture, Paris

(A)   It relies on broad areas of unbroken surfaces.

(B)   It uses industrial forms and materials to suggest a living organism.

(C)   It is conceived and designed on a human scale.

(D)   It owes a debt to the Classical past.

28.   Use the picture of the Chartres Cathedral, France, below to answer the question that follows.

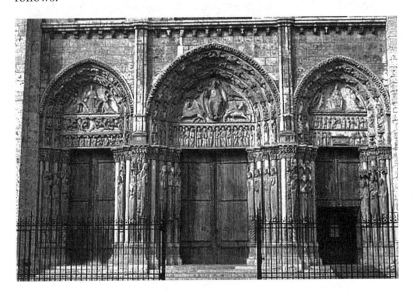

Which of the following best describes the sculpture on the building pictured above?

(A)   It tells a detailed story with a definite sequence.

(B)   It dominates the facade of the building.

(C)   It draws heavily on Classical mythology.

(D)   It is contained by the architectural forms of the doorways.

29. In the example pictured below, the folds of the garment serve to

Kiyotada, *Dancing Kabuki Actor*
c. 1725 Metropolitan Museum of Art, New York

(A) create a dynamic surface pattern that dominates the composition.

(B) counteract the vigorous motion of the figure.

(C) establish a sense of three-dimensional space.

(D) help tell the story behind the figure's movements.

Antonio Pollaiuolo, *Hercules and
Antaeus,* c. 1475. Museo Nazionale, Florence

30. The sculpture pictured above suggests which of the following?

(A) The rolling motion of a wheel

(B) The balanced action of a lever

(C) The twisting spiral of a screw

(D) The flowing motion of liquid

31. Use the picture below to answer the question that follows.

In the example shown above, which of the following contributes most to the effect of a photographic snapshot?

(A) The inclusion of the horse and dog

(B) The middle-class character of the subjects

(C) The perspective grid behind the figures

(D) The off-center composition and the random cropping of figures

32. Use the picture below of the Abbey Church of St. Michael, Hildesheim, Germany, to answer the question that follows.

The building pictured depends on which effect?

    (A)   The interplay of diagonal and vertical lines

    (B)   The broad expanse of window glass

    (C)   A subtle arrangement of curving, rhythmic forms

    (D)   The bold massing of simple cubic forms

33.   Use the picture below of the Temple of Hera at Paestum, Italy, to answer the question that follows.

Which of the following is fundamental to the design of the building?

    (A)   A combination of intersecting diagonal lines

    (B)   A simple repetition of vertical and horizontal forms

    (C)   A continuous expanse of unbroken wall surface

    (D)   A combination of columns and arches

QUESTIONS 34–36 refer to the following pictures.

(A)

National Gallery, Washington D.C.

New York

(B)

Metropolitan Museum of Art,

New York

(C)

Albright-Knox Art Gallery, Buffalo

Lugano, Italy.

(D)

Sammlung Thyssen-Bornemisza

34. Which of the examples pictured above makes the most direct contact with the viewer?

35. In which example does the pose and expression of the sitter convey artistic disdain?

36. Which example breaks down the forms of the subject and merges them with the background?

37. Use the picture below to answer the question that follows.

Wu Chen, *Bamboo*, National Palace Museum, Taipei, Taiwan.

Which of the following seems most true of the example pictured above?

(A) The artist attempted a realistic depiction of three-dimensional space.

(B) The picture probably illustrates an episode in a narrative.

(C) The execution was slow, painstaking, and deliberate.

(D) Both the script and the leaves share a quality of quick, fluid calligraphy.

QUESTIONS 38-39 refer to the following pictures.

(A)

Winslow Homer, *Snap the Whip*, 1872. Butler Institute of Art, Ohio.

(B)

Jean Baptiste Camille Corot, *The Harbor of La Rochelle*, 1851.

(C)

John Sloan, *The Lafayette*, 1927.

(D)

Andrew Wyeth, *Christina's World*, 1948. Museum of Modern Art, New York.

38. In which example does the landscape act as a backdrop for a carefully composed figure group?

39. In which example does the location of the horizon line emphasize the figure's isolation?

Constructed-Response Questions

Constructed-Response Directions

Prepare a written response for each constructed-response assignment. Read each assignment carefully before you begin to write. Think about how you will organize what you plan to write.

Scoring of responses to CSET: Multiple Subjects constructed-response assignments is based on the following criteria:

PURPOSE: the extent to which the response addresses the constructed-response assignment's charge in relation to relevant CSET content specifications.

SUBJECT MATTER KNOWLEDGE: the application of accurate subject matter knowledge as described in the relevant CSET content specifications.

SUPPORT: the appropriateness and quality of the supporting evidence in relation to relevant CSET content specifications.

The assignments are intended to assess subject matter knowledge and skills, not writing ability. Your responses, however, must be communicated clearly enough to permit a valid judgment of your knowledge and skills. Your responses should be written for an audience of educators in the field.

You may wish to write each of your responses to the CSET: Multiple Subjects Subtest III practice test constructed-response assignments and ask a mentor, advisor, or teacher to help evaluate them. Sample responses are provided for these assignments following the detailed answers section of the Subtest III practice test.

40. Elimination of everyday risk factors is an important part of physical education. Briefly describe two of these risk factors, and how physical education can be used to help reduce them.

41. Choose any one of Maslow's hierarchy of human needs, and briefly describe how it is relevant to elementary educators.

42. Most art historians agree that people began to create art in the Paleolithic period, about 30,000 years ago, carving small female fertility symbols, now called Venuses. What about this prehistoric art connects it with the art of today?

Answer Key

Subtest I:
Reading, Language & Literature; History & Social Science

1.	(B)	14.	(C)	27.	(A)	40.	(D)
2.	(A)	15.	(C)	28.	(B)	41.	(B)
3.	(A)	16.	(C)	29.	(D)	42.	(C)
4.	(D)	17.	(A)	30.	(C)	43.	(C)
5.	(C)	18.	(B)	31.	(B)	44.	(A)
6.	(D)	19.	(C)	32.	(D)	45.	(A)
7.	(D)	20.	(D)	33.	(A)	46.	(A)
8.	(A)	21.	(B)	34.	(C)	47.	(D)
9.	(B)	22.	(C)	35.	(D)	48.	(B)
10.	(A)	23.	(B)	36.	(C)	49.	(B)
11.	(D)	24.	(A)	37.	(C)	50.	(A)
12.	(D)	25.	(C)	38.	(B)	51.	(A)
13.	(B)	26.	(A)	39.	(A)	52.	(B)

Subtest II:
Science; Mathematics

1.	(D)	14.	(A)	27.	(C)	40.	(C)
2.	(B)	15.	(C)	28.	(C)	41.	(D)
3.	(C)	16.	(A)	29.	(A)	42.	(A)
4.	(D)	17.	(B)	30.	(C)	43.	(B)
5.	(A)	18.	(B)	31.	(A)	44.	(C)
6.	(D)	19.	(B)	32.	(C)	45.	(C)
7.	(D)	20.	(B)	33.	(D)	46.	(D)
8.	(D)	21.	(D)	34.	(A)	47.	(C)
9.	(C)	22.	(B)	35.	(D)	48.	(B)
10.	(D)	23.	(C)	36.	(A)	49.	(C)
11.	(B)	24.	(C)	37.	(D)	50.	(A)
12.	(B)	25.	(A)	38.	(D)	51.	(D)
13.	(C)	26.	(D)	39.	(A)	52.	(A)

Answer Key (cont.)

Subtest III:
Physical Education; Human Development; Visual and Performing Arts

1.	(B)	14.	(D)	27.	(B)
2.	(B)	15.	(D)	28.	(D)
3.	(C)	16.	(A)	29.	(A)
4.	(A)	17.	(C)	30.	(B)
5.	(C)	18.	(B)	31.	(D)
6.	(B)	19.	(C)	32.	(D)
7.	(D)	20.	(B)	33.	(B)
8.	(A)	21.	(B)	34.	(C)
9.	(C)	22.	(D)	35.	(B)
10.	(A)	23.	(A)	36.	(A)
11.	(D)	24.	(B)	37.	(D)
12.	(C)	25.	(D)	38.	(A)
13.	(A)	26.	(D)	39.	(D)

Practice Test 2: Subtest I
Detailed Explanations of Answers

Multiple-Choice Section

1. **B**

An elegy is a serious poem lamenting the death of an individual or group of individuals. Passage (B) is Robert Herrick's "Upon His Spaniel Tracy," an elegy that mourns the death of his favorite dog. Thus, passage (B) is the correct answer.

2. **A**

Enjambment occurs when a line of poetry "runs on" to the next line, causing a slight pause in mid-sentence or thought. Line three reads, "This shall my love do, give thy sad death one." The reader is left wondering, "One what"? It is not until line four that the poet explains that he will give one "Tear." Thus, choice (A) is the correct answer.

3. **A**

The speaker of these lines is Berowne, a reluctant student in Shakespeare's Love's Labor's Lost. You can discern that the lines are spoken by a student because they are a reaction against study and those who pursue it ("Small have continual plodders won..."). It would be highly unusual for a professor to say such things, and the other three choices are, of course, possible, but not within the limited context of the passage.

4. **D**

Restated, the lines mean, "Little (small) have those who constantly (continually) plod through their studies gained (won), except (save) for some common, throwaway knowledge (base authority) from others' books." Choice (D) comes closest to this, and is thus the correct answer.

5. **C**

A supplicant is one who seeks forgiveness in a religious sense. Therefore, by labeling the parishioners as such, the author is implying that they are all guilty of various crimes against their religion, and have come to the church seeking forgiveness.

6. **D**

This poem, written by William S. Gilbert in 1882, is a satiric look at the ineffectuality of the British Parliament and its inability (in the poet's opinion) to do anything worthwhile. Phrases such as "The House of Peers made no pretense / To intellectual eminence" and "The House of Peers, throughout the war, / Did nothing in particular, / And did it very well" show the author's disdain for the noble men who inherited their Parliament seats and had no real interest in the political goings-on of England. The fact that, as the poet mentions, Britain becomes an empire in spite of the House of Peers adds to the satiric yet humorous tone of the poem.

7. **D**

The passage, which opens Charles Dickens's A Tale of Two Cities, contains numerous and vast comparisons. By making these comparisons and descriptions of the time period ("we had everything before us, we had nothing before us, we were all going direct to Heaven, we were all going direct the other way," etc.), Dickens is illustrating how during this period (just before the French Revolution) anything was possible: "wisdom," "foolishness," "Light," or "Darkness." This anything-is-possible tone also foreshadows the French Revolution, which the aristocracy never expected. Dickens will, later in the novel, describe extreme political upheaval, but does not here, so (B) is wrong. (A) is wrong because "placid" implies settled and calm; if "anything is possible," then the times are exact opposite. There is no mention of a public event or the attitudes of people at war, so (C) is incorrect.

8. **A**

The Bible tells of how Christ was able to feed hundreds of hungry people with only seven loaves of bread and fish until all were satiated. By jokingly suggesting that the two governments contain the positions "lords of the state preserves of loaves and fishes," Dickens mocks their self-assuredness and unflinching certainty that the "preserves" will never be depleted and that "things in general [are] settled for ever." The phrase "clearer than crystal" helps, through its sarcasm, to give this attack more sting. All of the other choices are not alluded to or discussed in the passage, and are thus incorrect.

9. **B**

This passage from Melville's Moby-Dick *contains an allusion in the phrase, "like so many Alexanders." Melville is illustrating the strength and power of whalers ("naked Nantucketers") by comparing them to Alexander the Great, the famous conqueror who died in 323 B.C.E.*

10. **A**

This passage, which opens James Joyce's A Portrait of the Artist as a Young Man *is written in "baby talk" ("moocow," "nicens," "baby tuckoo") to convey to readers the age, speech, and mental set of the narrator.*

11. **D**

Nineteenth-century novels of manners employed such themes as the importance (or unimportance) of "good breeding," the elation (and suffocation) caused by society, and the interaction of individuals within the confines of a closed country community (to name just a few). This passage, taken from Jane Austen's Emma, *mentions "opinions" of other characters, the importance of "beauty" and "accomplishment" (note how Emma sees them as almost saving graces for Mrs. Elton), and the "improvement" of a "country neighborhood."*

12. **D**

The theme of carpe diem, Latin for "seize the day," urges people to enjoy their present pleasures and lives, because the future is so uncertain. Passage (D), taken from Robert Herrick's, "To the Virgins to Make Much of Time," urges its readers to act now ("Gather ye...while ye may") because time will never stop and all things must come to an end ("...Tomorrow will be dying").

13. **B**

Onomatopoeia refers to the formation of words imitating the sound of the object or action expressed, such as "Buzz," "clang," "boom," and "meow." Passage (B) contains two examples of onomatopoeia: "Bow-wow" to imitate the barking of a dog, and "Cock-a-doodle-doo" to imitate the sound of the rooster.

14. **C**

Alliteration refers to the repetition of consonant sounds at the beginning of successive (or nearly successive) words in a line (or lines) of poetry. Passage (C) contains the line, "A spotted shaft is seen," which alliterates the "s" sound for poetic effect. Thus, choice (C) is correct.

15. **C**

A journal, or diary, is written in first person, as the excerpt is. Also, it puts forth everyday events and feelings, the purpose we normally associate with a journal. A myth (D) is a traditional story, usually connected with the religion of people, and attempts to account for something in nature. This quote gives no indication of mythological allusions. The correct answer is (C).

16. **C**

The correct answer is (C) Frost. The frost here is personified and "beheads" the unwitting flower, exerting its power in an "acccidental" and apparently random manner.

17. **A**

Choice (A) is the only correct scanned line. It contains five iambic feet and is an example of iambic pentameter. The other examples have incorrectly marked accents and feet.

18. **B**

This passage comes from the Greek play Medea, *by Euripides. Medea, a woman who is being cast aside so her husband, Jason, can marry a princess, kills their two sons in retaliation. This passage shows Jason lamenting over the boys' deaths and invoking the gods to punish his ex-wife.*

19. **C**

In the passage Jason mourns that Medea killed the boys "to prevent me from/Touching their bodies or giving them burial." In Greek society, the dead were honored by elaborate burial rites and ceremonies. To be buried without ceremony was considered to be dishonorable to the dead, especially when they were related to great warriors, such as Jason.

20. **D**

John is portrayed by the speaker as condescending. The speaker tells us that she thinks that there is something queer about the house and that "John laughs at me, of course, but one expects that." The speaker expects her husband to laugh at her, which indicates that that is his usual reaction to her ideas. Also, the speaker reports that John does not believe that she is sick, and dismisses her illness as "temporary nervous tension" and "a slight hysterical tendency;" he believes he knows more about her than she does herself. Choice (D) is the correct answer.

21. **B**

The speaker says of her story that she "would not say it to living soul, of course, but this is dead paper and a great relief to my mind." Writing is, for her, an outlet, a way for her to address her problems. Choice (B) is the correct answer.

22. **C**

The speaker feels limited by her husband. She tells us that she thinks the reason she does not get well faster is because John does not believe that she is sick. To cure her depression and "hysteria" he prescribes, in addition to tonics and exercize, a prohibition on her writing. She disagrees with him, as her writing serves as an outlet and is "a great relief to (her) mind."

23. **B**

Phaethon was (in classical myth) the son of Helios, the Sun, who at one time undertook to drive his father's chariot. Persephone was (in classical myth) queen of the underworld and the reviving crops. Thus, their names (I) as well as Phaethon's occupation (II) characterize them as "gods"; choice (B) is correct.

24. **A**

The correct answer is (A) fluid. Infants and young children move in and out of various stages of language acquisition at different times. There is no strict or inherent logic by which children acquire language.

25. **C**

The correct response is (C). Grammar often has very little relationship to the way people in the world actually speak; nevertheless, learning standard English provides a good starting point for students to then learn English in all its complexity and nuance.

26. **A**

The correct response is (A). Sentence 1, in characterizing Corte Madera as a "metropolitan paradise," creates a theme that the subsequent sentences build on. Sentences 2, 3, and 4 relate to this idea by offering supporting details.

27. **A**

The nomadic warriors who would later become the lords of feudal Japan arrived in the Kofun Era. The Heian Era (B) marked their rise to power, and the Sengoku Era (C), also called the Warring States Era (D), marked the beginning of the decline of their power due to political fragmentation.

28. **B**

Literally translated, "bakfu" means tent government. Shogunate (A) refers to the customary translation of the term. A landed estate (C) was known as a shoen, and a local feudal lord (D) was called a daimyo.

29. **D**

(A), (B), and (C) were all unifiers of Japan, while Minamoto no Yorimoto was the founder of the first feudal government, called Kamakura Shogunate.

30. **C**

Asoka converted to Buddhism in the third century B.C.E., facilitating its acceptance by Indian society. Taoism (A), and Jainism (D) flourished in China rather than the Indian subcontinent. Hinduism (B) was the prominent religion in India before, as well as after, the conversion of Asoka.

31. **B**

The Maya were the first of these civilizations to develop the concept of zero. While each of the other civilizations achieved a great deal artistically, mathematically, and culturally, the Maya were the first to develop this esoteric concept.

32. **D**

The jihad, or holy war, is a concept central to the Islamic faith; however, it is not one of the five pillars. In addition to (A), (B), and (C), a Muslim is expected to make a pilgrimage to Mecca once in their lifetime, completing the five pillars of faith.

33. **(A)**

The Nok created life-sized terra cotta figures. The Songhai (B) were originally part of the Mali Empire, and were known for gaining their independence in the early 1400s. The Ghana (C) were noted for their building of impressive stone structures, but their society mysteriously disappeared after an invasion by the Mali in the thirteenth century. The Bantu (D) society was loosely organized throughout Sub-Saharan Africa, and their walled city, Great Zimbabwe, was a prominent trading center.

34. **(C)**

The Inca were a sun worshipping people and believed themselves to be the viceregent of the sun god on Earth. The Aztec (A) were a polytheistic culture and practiced routine human sacrifice for the appeasement of their chief diety. The term Andean (B) refers to the Andes Mountains of South America, where several cultures flourished. The Hohokam (D) were mound builders that lived in what is now the southwestern United States.

35. **(D)**

Saratoga marked the doomed ending to a British three-pronged campaign to split New England from the other colonies. With the surrender of Burgoyne's army, the Americans had won a major victory and captured an entire British army. This victory gave the French the evidence they needed that the Americans could actually win the war, and gave them a chance to avenge their loss to the British in the Seven Years' War. The French now recognized the American government and declared war on England. The entrance of France into the war steadily turned the tide in favor of the Americans. England now found itself fighting not only its American colonists, but a global struggle against its chief European rival. Of the remaining battles, only Yorktown rivals Saratoga in significance because it marked the end of active large-scale hostilities in the war and led the British Parliament to request peace negotiations.

36. **(C)**

The Federalists' name implied that they did not support a strong national government. However, the leaders of the Federalist movement believed strongly in the necessity of a relatively strong central government. They strongly supported ratification of the Constitution and believed that discussion of a bill of rights should be delayed until after the Constitution was ratified. Alexander Hamilton, James Madison, and John Jay wrote a series of essays contained within The Federalist, *which brilliantly argued the Federalist position and captured support of all the nation's major newspapers. This campaign made the difference in the battles for ratification in several key states.*

The chief opponents of ratification, the Antifederalists, argued against ratification primarily on the basis of choice (B), that a bill of rights needed to be in place before ratification of the Constitution. Many Antifederalists opposed the Constitution entirely based on the belief in choice (D), that no strong national government could or should ever exist. They believed that a strong national government would become corrupt and lose touch with the needs of the local people. They believed that the best path was for the states to govern themselves within the framework of an extremely limited national government. Few people wanted (A) a return to the Articles of Confederation, which had clearly not worked.

37.

Gettysburg marked the "high tide" of Robert E. Lee's army of northern Virginia. In June of 1863, the Confederacy was still hoping for recognition by France and England. Confederate leaders believed a major military victory on Northern territory would give the Europeans the proof they needed that the Union could never defeat the South militarily. On that basis, Lee who had just defeated Union forces at Chancellorsville, pushed his army into Maryland and Pennsylvania. He hoped to force a battle on his terms in Northern territory that would demoralize the numerically superior army of the Potomac and perhaps even allow Confederate forces to isolate or capture Washington, D.C. Such a success would have relieved Union pressure on the South and almost assuredly obtained formal European recognition for the Confederacy. Unfortunately for Lee, the two forces met unexpectedly at the little Pennsylvania town of Gettysburg. Outnumbered Union forces held on throughout the first day and were reinforced that night by the remainder of the army of the Potomac. From that point on, the battle was basically fought on Union terms, despite Lee pressing the initiative. After futile efforts to break the superior Union lines for two days, and inflicting only 28,000 casualties (out of 67,000 soldiers at the start of the battle), Lee was forced to retreat. Followed by news of Union victory at Vicksburg at the same time Lee was being defeated at Gettysburg, the South never regained the initiative. There were no further major incursions into Northern territory, and while Lee fought doggedly on the defensive, no European recognition was ever announced. Now it was only a matter of time until the superior manpower and industrial capacity of the North wore down and finished the South. While all of the remaining Civil War battles influenced the course of the war, none of them had the decisive impact of Gettysburg.

38.

Though the land was abundant (A), capital (B) and labor (D) were scarce in early America. Limitations of climate and land (C) prevented New England from developing the staple-crop agriculture in demand in Europe.

39.

Credit Mobilier was the name of the dummy construction company set up by officials of Union Pacific in order to embezzle millions of dollars the government was paying to subsidize the construction of a transcontinental railroad. The contract for the collection of $427,000 in unpaid taxes, for a 50% commission that later found its way into Republican campaign coffers (B), was the centerpiece of a scandal known as the Sanborn Contract Fraud. The Whiskey Ring Fraud was the name given to the conspiracy of distillers and treasury officials to defraud the government of large amounts of money from the excise tax on whiskey (C), and Congress's attempt to raise its own pay retroactively (D) was christened the Salary Grab Act. The exposure of all of *these sordid affairs during the presidency of U. S. Grant helped give his administration a reputation for corruption.*

40. **D**

While farms were disappearing and industry was growing during the era of Jacksonian Democracy, industrialization would not become an issue until after the Civil War. Federal financing of internal improvements (B), states' rights (C), and the removal of southeastern Indians to reservations (A) all were, with other issues such as the Second Bank of the United States, important issues during this era.

41. **B**

De Soto and Coronado hoped to repeat the success of Hernando Cortes, who had sacked the rich Aztec Empire of Mexico. For Coronado, the hope first focused on the mythical "Seven Cities of Cibola" and then on the equally fictional "Gran Quivira." Both Spaniards were disappointed but did play important roles in exploring the hitherto unknown interior of North America and in establishing Spain's claims to the southern portions of the continent.

42. **C**

In sending out the Lewis and Clark expedition, President Thomas Jefferson was not concerned with the possibility that they might discover gold (they did not). He did desire that they establish friendly relations with the western Indians (A), and gain both geographic (B) and scientific (D) knowledge about western North America.

43. **C**

The devastation of the Black Death enhanced the value of labor during the fourteenth century because of the enormous depletion of the labor pool. The plague did not have any meaningful impact on the development of nation-states (A), nor was a flight of millions of Europeans overseas (D) associated with this event. (B) is incorrect because modern medicine did not develop for centuries.

44. **A**

The Federal Reserve Board is a government agency consisting of seven members appointed for 14-year terms by the president, with the consent of the Senate. This board is at the head of the Federal Reserve System, which is comprised of member banks across the country. The primary function of the Federal Reserve Board is to implement monetary policy. The Federal Reserve Board has three methods of implementing monetary policy. First, it can change the reserve requirement, which is the amount of cash that member banks must keep on deposit in a regional Federal Reserve Bank. An increase in the requirement reduces the amount of cash a bank has on hand to loan. Second, the board can change the discount rate, which is the interest rate that member banks must pay to borrow money from a Federal Reserve Bank. A higher rate discourages a member bank from borrowing and lending more money. Third, the board can buy and sell government securities. To increase the money supply, the board sells securities. To decrease the money supply, the board buys securities. Answer (B) is the most plausible alternative to (A), but fails because controlling government spending is a function of Congress and the president. Answer (C) is incorrect because the Federal Reserve Board has nothing to do with regulating commodity prices. Answer (D) is incorrect because the Board does not help the president run the executive branch.

45.

There is a direct correlation between voter turnout and educational level. Those with four years or more of college are more likely to vote than those with one to three years of college. Those with one to three years of college are more likely to vote than are high school graduates. High school graduates are, in turn, more likely to vote than are those with less than a high school education. The answer is (A), the more schooling one has, the more likely one is to vote. Voting is only one form of political participation. Other forms are running for office, working in political campaigns, and contributing to campaigns. While it is difficult to find statistics that show the correlation between educational status and running for office, we do know that most people who are completely inactive (that is, do not participate in politics in any way) typically have little education and low incomes and are relatively young. Therefore, it is safe to conclude that the less education one has, (B), the less likely one is to run for office; so (B) is not the answer. Answer (C) is clearly wrong, since many studies have shown a direct correlation between advanced educational status and political participation by voting. Answer (D) is wrong, as is clear from the graph. Those with a high school education are not more likely to vote than are those with a college degree.

46.

The Great Awakening was a series of religious awakenings, or rebirths, centered primarily in New England but spread throughout the colonies, which changed the lives of English colonists. It challenged the old hierarchical religious order in which ordained clergy were deferred to and were believed to have knowledge based on extensive formal learning that the average member of a congregation lacked. It brought a much broader sense of community to colonists making them aware of others with similar questions and beliefs who lived outside their village or town. In many ways, it was the first of a series of events that helped to forge distinctively American regional identities, separate from their European heritage, among the North American colonists.

47.

There are two schools of thought on the proper method of constitutional interpretation by the judiciary. One is called "judicial activism." Advocates of this school believe that the intentions of those who wrote the Constitution should not be authoritative for the decision of controversial matters in the present. They say that judges should be free to adapt the Constitution to changing political and social circumstances. The other school is called "judicial restraint." Advocates of this school stress that the Constitution was a great contract by which the American people created a government. This contract laid the ground rules for the operation of the government, and it provided a formal process of amendment for changing those ground rules. In order to understand the ground rules, say advocates of restraint, one must determine the original intentions of those who wrote and ratified the Constitution. For unelected judges to assume to themselves the power to change the Constitution, according to this school, is for the judges to usurp a power that was not given them by the Constitution or the people. Therefore, the correct answer is (D). Answer (A) is incorrect because there is no general process by which judges limit the number of cases they hear in a year. Justices on the Supreme Court do have a lot of control over which cases they hear, through a process called certiorari. When litigants appeal to the court to have their cases heard, the justices vote on the merits of the cases. If four justices vote to hear a particular case, they issue a "writ of certiorari" to the lower court, ordering all documents relevant to the case to be sent up to the Supreme Court. Answer (B) is incorrect because judges do not lobby funds from Congress. Answer (C) is incorrect because when judges remove themselves from a case they are said to recuse themselves.

48 **B**

As part of the 1820 Missouri Compromise, all of the Louisiana Territory north of 36°30′—that is, the southern (A) boundary of most of Missouri—was closed (C) to slavery. According to the compromise, this was to be permanent, though subsequent behavior on the part of some politicians—the 1854 Kansas-Nebraska Act—might lead one to believe the free areas had been left negotiable (D)—but such was not the case.

49. **B**

Blacks most commonly resisted slavery passively, if at all. The Underground Railroad (A), though celebrated in popular history, involved a relatively minute number of slaves. Arson (C) and poisoning (D), though they did sometimes occur and were the subject of much fear on the part of white Southerners, were also relatively rare.

50. **A**

The distribution of governmental powers between the branches is known as "separation of powers." A related concept, "checks and balances" (B) most frequently refers to situations where power is "shared," and is therefore "checked" by the power of another branch. Federalism (A) refers to the distribution of power between levels of government (state, national), while constitutional interpretation (C) could refer to any aspect of the constitution, not just the distribution of power. The notion of fundamental rights would refer to such basic liberties as freedom of the press.

51. **A**

The correct answer is (A). The Thirteenth Amendment, adopted in 1865, banned slavery and involuntary servitude except as punishment for a crime for which one has been convicted. The (B) Fourteenth Amendment granted citizenship to "all persons born or naturalized in the United States, and subject to the jurisdiction thereof." The (C) Fifteenth Amendment provided U.S. citizens the right to vote, regardless of "race, color, or previous condition of servitude." The (D) Sixteenth Amendment allows Congress to pass legislation to collect income tax.

52. **B**

Marbury v. Madison *was a landmark case in which Justice John Marshall steered the court through a minefield of potentially disastrous constitutional confrontations to a stronger and more respected position than ever before. The case was used by Marshall to affirm the court's right to judge the constitutionality of congressional legislation by declaring part of the Judiciary Act (previously passed by Congress) to be unconstitutional. In the case the court restricted some of its own rights to issue legal writs, making it difficult for opponents of the decision to launch any broad-based attacks upon the court itself. The case served to elevate the court to equal standing with the other two branches of government.*

Constructed-Response Questions Scoring Guide

3 • The examinee demonstrates a comprehensive understanding of the material presented.

• The examinee has responded effectively to every part of the question.

• The examinee has provided well-supported explanations.

• The examinee has demonstrated a strong knowledge of the subject matter, including relevant theories, concepts, and procedures.

2 • The examinee demonstrates a basic understanding of the material presented.

• The examinee has responded effectively to most parts of the question.

• The examinee has provided explanations.

• The examinee has demonstrated an adequate knowledge of the subject matter, including relevant theories, concepts, and procedures.

1 • The examinee demonstrates some misunderstanding of the material presented.

• The examinee fails to respond effectively to every part of the question.

• The examinee has provided only weak explanations.

• The examinee has demonstrated insufficient knowledge of the subject matter, including relevant theories, concepts, and procedures.

0 • The examinee has either not responded, responded off-topic, responded completely incorrectly, or simply rephrased the question.

Constructed-Response Questions: Sample Responses

53. **Response that received a score of 3:**

  The narrator, a lawyer who has employed a law-copyist named Bartleby, is the speaker. The point of view used here is first person. The narrator is an older man who has had a good amount of worldly experience, especially in his profession. He has seen many types of humanity, yet Bartleby has eluded the narrator's understanding, and still intrigues the narrator. Bartleby, according to the lawyer, is beyond being accounted for in writing; his biography is unknown. He is an "astonishing" person, mysterious and unsettling. Thus, the themes that this story will explore, as indicated in these opening lines, have to do with identity and selfhood, the mystery of the self, and the responsibility of one human being toward another in unraveling identity.

Response that received a score of 1:

  The person who is telling the story is confused and unable to express himself very well. He is older and has worked a long time, in some kind of professional way. One person named Bartleby seems to have caught his interest but he does not really know who Bartleby is. He seems like a very sad and lonely old man who has a story to tell but no one who will listen to him.

54. **Response that received a score of 3:**

  Because the short story has less opportunity than the novel to develop characters, this mode of fiction must rely on epiphanic moments to convey significance. Point of view is also much more important as a technique in the short story. Historically, the short story developed as a genre in the nineteenth century and was generally realistic, relying on the details of the lives of middle-class characters. Writers such as Edgar Allan Poe and Nathaniel Hawthorne helped to popularize the short story as a mode of writing. The novel has a much longer history and may be traced back some 600 years to Boccaccio and Chaucer. It has developed into many different forms and may be classified by subject matter such as the historical novel (Sir Walter Scott) and the stream-of-consciousness novel (James Joyce).

Response that receive a score of 1:

  The difference between the short story and the novel is primarily length. The novel is much longer than the short story. Because of this, the short story must be much more condensed and must get to the point more quickly. The novel can be more developed and include more characters and more description. Charles Dickens wrote novels. Mark Twain and Ernest Hemingway wrote short stories.

55. Response that received a score of 3:

     The American Great Awakening was a series of religious revivals that swept over the American colonies during the second quarter of the eighteenth century, almost simultaneously in New England, the Middle colonies, and the South. It began in different ways in different places, but much of its activity began among the Presbyterians and the Dutch reformed churches in the Middle colonies. During the 1730s, emotional and passionate revivalists called people back to God by threatening them with eternal damnation for sin. Noted revivalist preachers, like Jonathan Edwards and George Whitfield, magnified the revival into a religious event spreading throughout the colonies.

     The preachers of the Great Awakening were often poorly educated; their exhortations were emotional, popular, and anti-intellectual, frequently touching off extravagant reactions by their audiences.

     In terms of pure religion, it is impossible to estimate the effects of the Great Awakening but its social significance was immense. It brought more people into the Protestant churches, which it also helped splinter. By the end of the eighteenth century, America had so many different religions that religious conformity could not be imposed.

Response that received a score of 1:

     The Great Awakening was a series of religious revivals that swept over the American colonies, threatening eternal damnation to those who did not return to God. The movement brought more people to the Protestant churches it assisted in dispersing. A religious conformity in the colonies could not be established as a result of the movement.

56. Response that received a score of 3:

     The Articles of Confederation established a federal government consisting of one branch of government: Congress. There was no federal judiciary, nor was there an executive branch. Under the Articles of Confederation, the power of the individual states reigned supreme. The federal government's only role was to coordinate the activities of the various states, and then only if they agreed with federal desires. The states retained sovereignty, as independent nations, and were granted all legal control over commerce and legislation within their boundaries, except those not "expressly delegated to the United States" government. The Articles granted very few powers expressly to that government. In addition, ratification of the Articles or amendments of those Articles required unanimous consent of the states, which proved quite difficult to achieve. It took nearly three years to get the Articles themselves adapted because Maryland refused to ratify them until concerns over land acquisition were resolved.

     Most considered the strength of the Confederation to be its focus on local self-government. By limiting the federal government, people could rule themselves as they felt best at the state and local level. While the Articles guaranteed there could be no autocracy in America, this very strength was the weakness that undid the Articles. Under the rules of the Articles, there could be no effective central government at all. States could virtually do whatever they wanted, resulting in no cohesive national policies.

Under the Constitution, the sovereignty of the federal government replaced the sovereignty of the individual states. While states retained certain rights, state laws were subservient to federal laws. Congress was given the power to raise taxes, and states could not refuse to pay for them. An executive branch was created with an elected president who controlled foreign policy. A federal judiciary was set up to resolve legal disputes regarding the Constitution and the actions of Congress, the executive branch, and the various states. This "checks and balances" structure prevented any one branch of government from totally dominating the system. While it protected many of the rights of states, it placed enough power in the hands of the federal government to ensure that the government could carry out effective foreign policy, could regulate interstate commerce, and collect taxes.

Response that received a score of 1:

The Articles of Confederation established a central government made up of one branch: Congress. States were given ultimate authority over the federal government. They retained sovereignty as independent nations and controlled commerce and legislation within their boundaries. Amendments could only be made to the Articles upon unanimous ratification of the states. Many considered the focus on local government to be the strength of the Articles, which also served as its weakness. As a result of states holding the power, no cohesive national policies could be made. The Constitution replaced state sovereignty with the sovereignty of the federal government. An executive branch and judicial branch were developed.

Practice Test 2: Subtest II
Detailed Explanations of Answers

Multiple-Choice Section

1. **D**

   (D) is correct, as the nucleus contains the chromosomes, which are composed of DNA nucleotides and some protein. (A) is ruled out because lysosomes contain digestive enzymes. (B) is incorrect, since this is a series of membranes found in the cytoplasm, serving as a site of protein synthesis. (C) is incorrect, since DNA nucleotides are not found outside the nucleus.

2. **B**

   (B) is correct, as the DNA and its associated proteins form these rodlike or threadlike structures. (A) is incorrect, since RNA does not interweave itself with proteins to form chromosomes. (C) is incorrect, as DNA strands are composed of nucleotides. (D) is incorrect, since genes are composed of DNA and are found on chromosomes.

3. **C**

   Hydrogen bonding is especially strong in water, not weak. (A), (B), and (D) are all correct.

4. **D**

   In a vacuum like outer space, the speed of light is c and independent of both wavelength (color) and frequency. All electromagnetic radiation travels at c in a vacuum. Answer (C) is incorrect because light speed c is independent of distance.

5. **A**

   Fossil records show that the evolutionary sequence of life is as stated in (A).

6. **D**

   Gravitational attraction between masses varies inversely as the square of the distance between them. So, if the distance is doubled, the attractive force is decreased by a factor of 4 or quartered.

7. **D**

   (D) is correct, since a cell undergoing mitosis will first double its chromosome number and then divide its chromosome number and then divide. During that division, the chromosomes will be evenly and correctly divided between the two daughter cells. (A) is incorrect, as the information in the question states that a cell starts out with 46 chromosomes. (B) is wrong, since this number is still too small to make up even one set of chromosomes, much less two. (C) is incorrect, since humans are sexually reproducing organism and in a body cell there are two sets of chromosomes; therefore, 24 would be more than a single set but less than two sets.

8. **D**

   (D) is the correct answer since the egg and sperm, in this case, would have the diploid number of chromosomes (46), and if they were to unite, then the number of chromosomes would be doubled. (A) is incorrect since this number represents too few chromosomes for even a human sex cell. (B) is incorrect, since this is the haploid chromosome number of a normal human sex cell. (C) is incorrect since this is the diploid chromosome number of a normal zygote.

9. **C**

   The absorbed photon must result in an energy increase. Visible light is not energetic enough to split a nucleus, thus ruling out (A). (B) is ruled out because a lowered energy state would violate conservation of energy. (D) is ruled out, because photon energy is not stored by atoms in this way.

10. D

It has been observed with seismographs that both waves travel at different speeds and are of different types. The transverse waves shake structures in an up/down direction and the longtitudinal waves shake structures in the horizontal direction.

11. B

Electrical conductivity in metals is due to mobile or "free" electrons. (A), (C), and (D) are ruled out because nuclei and their constituent parts are fixed in place and do not enter into the flow of current.

12. B

Solving the equation for a, we obtain a = F/m. A decreased m in the denominator for a given F in the numerator will produce an increased acceleration. Solving the equation for each of the parameters listed in (A), (C), and (D) and applying the conditions stated will lead to a result that contradicts the stated outcome.

13. C

By definition, density is mass per unit volume (C) or (in units) kg/cubic meter. All other answers do not correspond to the definition.

14. A

Maximum tidal force is experienced by the earth when the moon and Sun's gravitational force, are pulling together, e.g., when the moon is between the Earth and the Sun. Under this condition, the tidal bulge of earth's oceans is maximized. All of the other answers will not produce a maximum force.

15. C

Valences for chemical activity are determined by an element's tendency to either gain (become more negative) or lose (become more positive) outer shell or valence electrons. (D) is incorrect because density does not in any direct manner involve valence electrons. (A) and (B) are ruled out because nuclei do not enter into ordinary chemical reactions.

16. A

By definition the number of molecules in I mole = mass of an element in grams equal to atomic weight. All of the other answers are either confusions of the definition or misunderstandings of it.

17. B

(B) is correct, since shading shields the thermometer from direct radiation (light) from the sun. (C) is ruled out, as the heat source is not within the mercury but outside of it, e.g., the heated air transfers heat to the thermometer from the air. Convection is a method of heat transfer that is internal (D) and relies on changes in density of the convective substance.

18. B

Time zones are determined by latitude (east-west position), not longitude locations (north-south position). (A) and (D) are ruled out because longitude and, therefore, location do not change from season to season.

19. B

(B) is correct, since complete dissolution means that the composition is the same at every point. (A) and (D) are ruled out because the water and salt do not enter into chemical combination. (C) is ruled out because a mixture would have varying composition from point to point.

20. B

The number of significant digits in a product of two numbers cannot exceed the number of significant digits in the number with the least significant digits.

21. D

The correct answer is the upper mantle and the crust. The focus of an earthquake is the region where a quake's energy originates. Earthquakes with a focal depth of about 43 miles are classified as shallow. Earthquakes with focal depths from about 43 miles to about 186 miles are classified as intermediate. Deep earthquakes may reach as far as 450 miles beneath the Earth's surface, within the region known as the upper mantle.

22. B

Ammeters are used to measure current and must be connected properly. In this case, the current must be made to flow through the ammeter by connecting it in series with the resistor. (A) and (D) are ruled out because voltmeters cannot measure current. (C) is ruled out because the connection method is improper.

23. C

By definition slope = rise/run, where rise = vertical change in dependent quantity variable and run = horizontal change in independent quantity variable. All of the others do not fit the definition.

24. **C**

By Archimedes' Principle, the object will displace an amount of fluid equal to its volume. The fluid level in the cylinder will, accordingly, increase by an amount proportional to the object's volume. (A) and (B) are incorrect because they violate the principle. (D) is incorrect, because it is a misunderstanding of the principle.

25. **A**

Extrapolation is to extend a curve into regions where the controlled variable was not adjusted. This amounts to continuing the curve in a way suggested by the known data. If a straight line had resulted, for example, then the natural extrapolation would be to continue the straight line. In this case a parabola-shaped curve is involved, so any extrapolated extention would have to be consistent with a parabolic curve. (B), (C), and (D) are all ruled out as being vague and/or meaningless.

26. **D**

In general, a magnetic field will cause a charged particle to move in a circular path at a constant speed. However, if the direction of the particle's movement is parallel to the magnetic field upon entering, then the particle's motion will be unaffected.

27. **C**

7 is in the tenths place. Since the next digit (2) is below 5, drop this digit and retain the 7. The answer, therefore, is 406.7.

28. **C**

The mean IQ score of 100 is given. One standard deviation above the mean is 34% of the cases, with an IQ score up to 115. One standard deviation below the mean is another 34% of the cases, with an IQ score ranging to 85. So, a total of 68% of the students have an IQ between 85 and 115. Therefore, $1,500 \times .68 = 1,020$.

29. **A**

$$
\begin{aligned}
(10 + x)2 &= 28 \\
20 + 2x &= 28 \\
2x &= 28 - 20 \\
2x &= 8
\end{aligned}
$$

$$x = \frac{8}{2}$$
$$x = 4$$

30. **C**

Let x = length of time (# of mos) to recover cost.
$$3x = 24$$
$$x = \frac{24}{3}$$
$$x = 8 \text{ mos.}$$

31. **A**

$2,000 \times .35 = \$700$. The rest have wrong computations.

32. **C**

With one right angle (90°) and a given 30° angle, the missing angle, therefore, is a 60° angle. (90° + 30° = 120°; 180° − 120° = 60°.)

33. **D**

The area of a parallelogram is base × height. Therefore, $A = bh = 16cm \times 4\,cm = 64\ cm^2$.

34. **A**

Fifteen is used as a cardinal number. The rest are either ordinal (B) or nominal (C,D) numbers.

35. **D**

The sequence 1, 4, 9, 16 is the sum of serialized odd numbers.

1. 1
2. 1 + 3 = 4
3. 1 + 3 + 5 = 9
4. 1 + 3 + 5 + 7 = 16
5. 1 + 3 + 5 + 7 + 9 = 25
6. 1 + 3 + 5 + 7 + 9 + 11 = 36
7. 1 + 3 + 5 + 7 + 9 + 11 + 13 = 49

36. **A**

Here one must use only needed information. Do not be distracted by superfluous data. Simple multiplication will do. If one pig eats four pounds of food per week, how much will 10 pigs eat in one week? 10 × 4 = 40 pounds. The problem intentionally contains superfluous data (52 weeks), which should not distract the reader from its easy solution. Ratio and proportion will also work here:

$$\frac{1}{10} = \frac{4}{x},$$

x = 40 pounds/week.

37. **D**

Let the variable S stand for the cost of the shirt. Then the cost of the pair of pants is S + 25 and

$$
\begin{aligned}
S + (S + 25) &= 65 \\
2S &= 65 - 25 \\
2S &= 40 \\
S &= 20
\end{aligned}
$$

$20 (cost of shirt)
$20 + $25 = $45 (cost of pants)

38. **D**

The possible handshakes are illustrated by listing all the possible pairs of letters, thus

AB	AC	AD	AE
BC	BD	BE	
CD	CE		
DE			

(a total of 10 handshakes)

39. **A**

The six throws are independent events. Thus,

$$= P(1) \times P(1) \times P(1) \times P(1) \times P(1) \times P(1)$$

$$= \frac{1}{6} \times \frac{1}{6} \times \frac{1}{6} \times \frac{1}{6} \times \frac{1}{6} \times \frac{1}{6}$$

$$= \frac{1}{6^6}$$

$$= \frac{1}{46,656}$$

$$= 0.0000214$$

40. **C**

Let

D = down payment
D = $20,000 × .20
D = $4,000

41. **D**

All but (D) are constraints. The constraint for y is to at least make 2 mowers.

42. **A**

The ratio 8:6:6:1 implies that for each $8 the wife received, each child received $6 and the foundation $1. The estate is divided into 8 + 6 + 6 + 1, or 21 equal shares. The wife received $8/_{21}$ of $300,000 or $114,285.71, each child received $6/_{21}$ of $300,000, or $85,714.29, and the foundation received $1/_{21}$ of $300,000 or $14,285.71. As a check, $114,285.71 + $85,714.29 + $85,714.29 + $14,285.71 = $300,000.

43. **B**

Simple division. $19/_9$ = 2 whole hamburgers with one left over.

44. **C**

Simple multiplication. 7 × 4 = 28.

45. **C**

For a 15-ft. log, it will take 14 cuts to make 15 equal pieces. Therefore, 14 minutes for 14 cuts.

46. **D**

Simple multiplication. 6 × 4 = 24.

47. **C**

Find the sum of the seven days. Thus:

$$M = 25;$$
$$T = 30;$$
$$W = 20;$$
$$Th = 25;$$
$$F = 10;$$
$$Sat = 40;$$
$$Sun = 0,$$

or a total of 150 minutes. Find the average by dividing 150 by 7 = 21.43 minutes.

48. **B**

If each $ stands for $12, only weeks 3 and 4 had a sale of $72 and $60, respectively. The rest are below $55.

49. **C**

Mode is the most frequent score. The score of 81 appeared five times and is therefore the mode.

50. **A**

By definition, a simple curve is a curve that can be traced in such a way that no point is traced more than once with the exception that the tracing may stop where it started. A closed curve is a curve that can be traced so that the starting and stopping points are the same. Therefore, A and B are simple closed curves. The rest are not.

51. **D**

A line of symmetry for a figure is a line in which you can stand a mirror, so that the image you see in the mirror is just like the part of the figure that the mirror is hiding. In this case, there are four lines.

52.

m = number of miles you can travel
$0.08 *m* = amount spent for *m* miles travelled at 8 cents per mile,
rental fee + mileage charge = total amount spent

$139 + $0.08 *m* = $350
Solution: 139 – 139 + 0.08 *m* = 350 – 139

0.08 *m* = 211

$$\frac{0.08m}{0.08} = \frac{211}{0.08}$$

m = 2,637.5
m = 2,637

Therefore, you can travel 2,637 miles (if you go 2,638 miles, you have travelled too far).

Constructed-Response Questions Scoring Guide

---

3 • The examinee demonstrates a comprehensive understanding of the material presented.

• The examinee has responded effectively to every part of the question.

• The examinee has provided well-supported explanations.

• The examinee has demonstrated a strong knowledge of the subject matter, including relevant theories, concepts, and procedures.

---

2 • The examinee demonstrates a basic understanding of the material presented.

• The examinee has responded effectively to most parts of the question.

• The examinee has provided explanations.

• The examinee has demonstrated an adequate knowledge of the subject matter, including relevant theories, concepts, and procedures.

---

1 • The examinee demonstrates some misunderstanding of the material presented.

• The examinee fails to respond effectively to every part of the question.

• The examinee has provided only weak explanations.

• The examinee has demonstrated insufficient knowledge of the subject matter, including relevant theories, concepts, and procedures.

---

0 • The examinee has either not responded, responded off-topic, responded completely incorrectly, or simply rephrased the question.

Constructed-Response Questions: Sample Responses

Constructed-Response Answer 53

1. **Response that received a score of 3:**

A protein molecule is itself composed of amino acid molecules. The amino acids are chemcally bonded together to form chains or protein molecules. In short, the amino acids are building blocks for proteins.

They are incorporated into proteins by transfer RNA according to the genetic code while messenger RNA is being decoded by ribosomes. During and after the final assembly of a protein, the amino acid content dictates the spatial and biochemical properties of the protein.

Response that received a score of 1:

Stating only that proteins are made up of amino acid molecules without supporting evidence and examples as above.

2. **Response that received a score of 3:**

Proteins make up our skin, hair, muscles, cartilage, and many other components of our body. The human body for the most part is made of protein. As mentioned above, proteins are molecular combinations of amino acids of which there are some 20 different types.

Response that received a score of 1:

Stating only that proteins are amino acid combinations without supporting examples as above.

3. **Response that received a score of 3:**

Amino acids are generally composed of carbon, hydrogen, oxygen, and nitrogen. Every amino acid is basically alike except for one molecular component, called the "R" factor. The "R" factor makes each amino acid unique. The 20 different amino acids make up hundreds of thousands of different kinds of proteins. An example of an amino acid would be glycine, which is classified as hydrophobic and aliphatic.

Response that received a score of 1:

Stating only its elemental composition without mention of the "R" factor or the 20 different types that make possible a multiplicity of proteins.

Constructed-Response Answer 54

1. **Response that received a score of 3:**

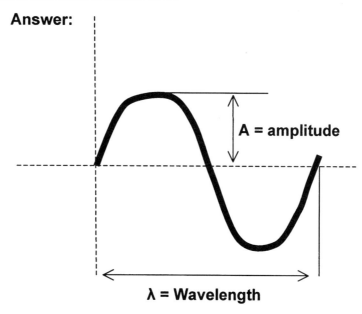

Answer:

A = amplitude

λ = Wavelength

Response that received a score of 1:

Drawing a wave but incorrectly labeling amplitude and wavelength.

2. **Response that received a score of 3:**

Frequency is the time it takes for a wave to repeat itself. Alternatively, it is the reciprocal of its period. Tides are a good example. If the period between high and low tide is about 12 hours, then the frequency is 1/12 tides per hour. To measure frequency, one chooses a fixed position in space to observe the wave and then measures the time it takes for the wave amplitude to repeat itself at that position. The frequency will be the reciprocal of that time.

The product of frequency and wavelength is the speed of wave propagation in a medium.

Response that received a score of 1:

Being able to define frequency either by a method used or with a formula or even with an example. Not relating it or incorrectly relating it to wavelength would also decrease the score.

3. **Response that received a score of 3:** ————————————————

Transverse: the wave disturbance (amplitude) is perpendicular to the direction of propagation. Light is a transverse wave. Transverse waves can be polarized.

Longitudinal: the wave disturbance (amplitude) is parallel to the direction of propagation. Sound is a longitudinal wave. Longitudinal waves cannot be polarized.

Response that received a score of 1: ————————————————

Must know that "transverse" and "longitudinal" are associated with disturbance and direction of propagation. Errors in specifying how they are related along with failure to provide a specific example of each will decrease the score.

4. **Response that received a score of 3:** ————————————————

Light waves are transverse waves and sound waves are longitudinal. Light waves are electromagnetic waves that are caused by oscillations of electrical charges. Sound waves are mechanical waves that are caused by mechanical oscillations in a medium. Light waves will have various speeds in various mediums, but can also propagate in a vacuum. Sound waves will also have various speeds in various mediums, but cannot propagate in a vacuum. Finally, the speed of light is much greater than the speed of sound, typically differing by a factor of about 1,000,000.

Response that received a score of 1: ————————————————

There are numerous differences as specified above. At least two of these essential differences (transverse vs. longitudinal and mechanical vs. electromagnetic, for example) should be cited to receive credit.

55. **Response that received a score of 3:** ————————————————

This is true because of polynomial factors. It can be shown in the equation:

$$n^2 - 1 = (n + 1)(n - 1)$$

$n + 1$ and $n - 1$ are factors of the polynomial $n^2 - 1$. The factors of every polynomial equal that polynomial if multiplied together.

Response that received a score of 1: ————————————————

When multiplied together, the product of $(n + 1)$ and $(n - 1)$ equals $n^2 - 1$. This is due to polynomials and factoring.

56. Response that received a score of 3: ─────────────────────────

The product of two irrational numbers is not limited to the set of irrational numbers. An irrational number is a nonterminating, nonrepeating decimal number. The product of two irrational numbers can be a rational number. The best way to illustrate this is by an example,

$$\sqrt{2} \times \sqrt{2} = 2$$

Therefore, the product of two irrational numbers can be a rational number.

Response that received a score of 1: ─────────────────────────

The product of two irrational numbers can be a rational number. This is because products of any real number are not limited to the set of irrational numbers.

Practice Test 2: Subtest III
Detailed Explanations of Answers

Multiple-Choice Section

1. **B**

   Deafness is the only one that would cause a child to be classified as handicapped. Pregnancy (A) is not a permanent condition, and obesity (C) and acne (D) are not debilitating enough to be considered handicaps.

2. **B**

   Vitamin C is water soluble—the remaining choices are fat soluble.

3. **C**

   Complex carbohydrates are the most efficient energy source for the body. While other choices provide some energy, they are not nearly as efficient as complex carbohydrates.

4. **A**

Cholesterol is produced naturally in the liver. The pancreas (B) produces insulin and digestive enzymes; the stomach (C) is the organ of digestion; and the pituitary gland (D) produces a variety of hormones.

5. **C**

A broken bone with a corresponding break in the skin is called a compound fracture. In a comminuted fracture (A), a bone has been shattered. A simple fracture (B) does not break the skin. A complex fracture (D) concerns a bone with more than one break.

6. **B**

Permanent dietary changes and exercise are the only way to produce lasting weight loss. Commercial diets (A) do not always include a program of exercise, but rather concentrate on diet. Radically reducing calorie intake (C) will cause the body to go into starvation mode and slow down digestion to conserve energy. Two hours of daily exercise (D) is not very practical and without controlling calorie intake, it would be ineffective.

7. **D**

Leaping is the only locomotive skill listed. Bouncing (A), catching (B), and throwing (C) are manipulative movements.

8. **A**

Isotonic exercises cause the muscles to contract. Isometric (B) exercises do not effect a change in muscle length. Static (C) is not a type of exercise, and an exercise does not have to change muscle length to be considered aerobic (D).

9. **C**

(A), (B), and (D) are principles of aerobic conditioning. (C) is not.

10. **A**

The knee is an example of a hinge joint. An example of a ball-and-socket joint (B) is the shoulder. The wrist is an angular joint (C) and the carpal and tarsal bones are gliding joints (D).

11. **D**

Excess cholesterol found in the blood typically comes from cholesterol in a diet rather than internal production. Cholesterol, which is produced in the liver (C), plays a vital role in brain function (A) and is important for creating certain hormones (B).

12. **C**

Table tennis is scored to 21 and must be won by a margin of two points. In doubles play for badminton, the winner must score 15 points (A). Singles badminton is also scored to 21 points with a margin of two points needed for victory.

13. **A**

One-fifth of the caloric intake of a diet should consist of protein. Complex carbohydrates should comprise nearly half of a person's diet (D).

14. **D**

The correct response is (D). Comprehension is shown when the reader questions his or her intent for reading. For example, one may be reading a story to find out what terrible things may befall the main character. The rationale for choosing a book may be an interesting bit of information (A), but it is not a major topic of discussion with the students. Sharing personal information (B) creates a certain bond, but this is not directly relevant to the question. It is also important that all students are on-task before the beginning of a lesson (C), but this is a smaller part of the skill modeled in response (D).

15. **D**

The correct response is (D). By having a mixed level pair read together, the remedial student receives instruction and the skilled student receives reinforcement. It uses alternative teaching resources, the students themselves, to enhance the learning environment. A certain goal, comprehension, has been set (A), but this is not the most likely outcome. The teacher will need to observe fewer groups (B), but it is unlikely that this will change the time needed to work with all groups as long as quality is to be maintained. Although reading in pairs, each student should have a book, and it would be impractical to permit another teacher to utilize the books while one teacher is using them (C).

16. **A**

The correct response is (A). By mapping out previous knowledge, information already known can be transferred to support new information. Although words on the board are visual (B), this is not the underlying motive. Semantic mapping done at the beginning of a story tests how much prior knowledge the students have about the topic at the outset (C). This does model proper use of words (D), but this is not the main intent of the exercise.

17. **C**

The stage of formal operations is noted for the ability of the individual to deal with abstract problems and concepts. It usually begins around puberty but research shows that some people never develop these skills and continue to function at the level of concrete operations for life.

18. **B**

The correct response is (B). The variance in fifth graders' physical size and development has a direct influence on their interests and attitudes, including their willingness to work with others and a possible preference for working alone. Working in small groups enhances student achievement. It is a learned skill that must be practiced. (A) is incorrect because fifth graders do have the physical and mental maturity to work in small groups. (C) is incorrect because not all fifth-grade students lack the ability for internal control. (D) is incorrect because although Mr. Dobson might need to be more specific in his directions to the students, this is not the main reason for the behavior.

19. **C**

The correct response is (C). Students who are naturally shy are usually more willing to participate in small groups than in discussions involving the entire class. Answer (A) is incorrect because calling on each student once per day will not necessarily assist shy students to participate in class discussions even if participation grades are assigned. (B) is incorrect because although students may become less shy as the year progresses, the teacher still has a responsibility to encourage students to participate. Choice (D) is incorrect because although speaking to each student individually may help some students participate, it is likely more students will participate if the procedure outlined in choice (A) is implemented.

20. **B**

The correct response is (B). Students who are overly talkative are usually flattered to be asked to take a leadership role. Asking these students to take notes also assigns them a task that allows other students to voice their opinions uninterrupted. Choice (A) is incorrect because calling on these students only once during the class period will most likely frustrate them and create problems. Answer (C) is incorrect because placing overly talkative students in a group by themselves does not teach them to listen to other students' opinions. (D) is incorrect because although overly talkative students usually need attention, they must be helped to recognize that other students also have opinions, even though they may not be assertive in voicing them.

21. **B**

The correct response is (B). Grouping patterns affect a student's perceptions of self-esteem and competence. Maintaining the same groups throughout the year encourages students in the average group to view themselves as average, students in the above-average group to view themselves as above average. Choice (A) is incorrect because most students do not like unpredictable teacher behavior. Response (C) is incorrect because changes in the classroom often create an atmosphere of mistrust and uneasiness, and do not cause students to be more alert. Answer (D) is incorrect because although the explanation is correct, it is incomplete when compared to (B).

22. **D**

Erikson determined that there were eight developmental crises in our lives corresponding to the eight developmental periods. These crises in their developmental order are (1) trust vs. mistrust; (2) autonomy vs. doubt and shame; (3) initiative vs. guilt; (4) industry vs. inferiority; (5) identity crisis; (6) intimacy vs. isolation; (7) crisis of child rearing; and (8) integrity vs. despair in old age.

23. **A**

The correct response is (A). The most important predictor variable of reading success is whether or not a child's parents immerse her in print (read to her) before she starts school. An enriched day care environment can be beneficial to a child's development (B), especially if shared reading and story activities are stressed. While research suggests that excessive television watching by young students may have deleterious effects, the amount of time spent watching television is not the important predictor of reading success that being read to by a parent is (C). Being raised by a grandparent is not a predictor of poor reading ability (D).

24. **B**

The correct response is (B). Children operating at the concrete operating stage greatly benefit from direct observation. Infants operate at the sensorimotor stage; observing a demonstration of how sound waves work would be of no use to infants (A). While students operating at the formal operational level would greatly benefit from direct observation of sound waves in addition to complex theoretical descriptions, the direct observation is absolutely essential to the understanding of the concrete thinker (C). There is no Piagetian interpersonal concordance stage. Interpersonal concordance is a stage of moral development described by Lawrence Kohlberg (D).

25. **D**

Based on the description of the way these children understood the game rules, one could determine that they are in the concrete operational stage of development. This stage empha-

sizes concrete understanding of rules and logical thinking as it relates to real concrete objects. Abstract and hypothetical thinking are largely undeveloped.

26. D ———

The concrete operational stage lasts from ages seven to eleven years. This is the usual age span, but it may be shorter or longer in an individual child.

27. B ———

The building pictured in the example—the contemporary "Beaubourg" art museum and cultural center in Paris—dispenses entirely with the ideas and philosophies of the classical past and with the styles and forms of traditional architecture. It is conceived instead on a huge industrial scale and, rather than projecting an atmosphere of quiet balance and poetic calm, it seeks to involve itself and its visitors in the dynamic life and culture of the modern city. Therefore, rather than concealing its structural and mechanical components behind a finished, exterior wall, the Beaubourg intentionally exposes its "anatomy," using pipes, ducts, tubes, and funnels of a modern industrial plant to reveal both its structure and its functions to the people in attendance. The visitor's ability to perceive the building's processes at work creates the sense that both building and people are part of a huge living organism.

28. D ———

The jamb statues on the Early Gothic cathedral at Chartres, France (c. 1145–1170 C.E.), draw their subject matter and thematic content not from classical mythology but from Christian ideology and belief. The figure groupings in the three main portals illustrate scenes from the Life and Passion of Christ, such as His birth, the Presentation in the Temple, and, in the center, the Second Coming. However, these scenes are not specifically arranged in a continuous narrative sequence and do not "tell a story." The sculpture itself, though it covers much of the building's facade, cannot be said to dominate, since it is strictly controlled and contained within the space allotted to it. The static, motionless figures conform closely to their architectural framework and are therefore subordinate to the structural forms of the doorways.

29. A ———

In the eighteenth century Japanese woodblock print pictured in the example, the artist used the folds of the garment and its bold design to create an animated surface pattern of diagonal lines and shapes. These diagonals, far from minimizing the motion of the dancer, emphasize his athletic leaps and turns, although they give no specific information about the story behind his dance. Further, the drapery folds do not cling to the dancer's body and define the three-dimensional forms of his anatomy, as they would in a Western tradition, but, rather, obscure his body almost completely, reassert the picture surface, and deny any sense of actual, three-dimensional space.

30. B

The Renaissance sculptor who created the small figure group shown in the example was intent on conveying the physical stresses and strains of two wrestlers in violent conflict. To express the ferocity of the fight, he has exaggerated the tautness of the muscles and the rigid tension of the bodies; to illustrate the climactic moment at which one fighter lifts the other from the ground to break his back, he has shown the brief instant during which the raised figure is balanced against his opponent's stomach. In the viewpoint shown, there is no suggestion of either the rolling motion of a wheel or the flowing of liquid, and there is apparently none of the spiral torsion of a screw. The figures do seem to interlock somewhat like a set of gears, but the simple machine they most resemble is the lever, with the fulcrum located at the balance point between the two men's abdomens.

31. D

Edgar Degas (1834–1917), the French Impressionist artist who painted the picture shown in the example, was strongly influenced by the ability of the camera to capture a subject in a fleeting moment and in a spontaneous, seemingly unposed manner. In Viscount Lepic and His Daughters, 1873, *the artist has constructed an off-center composition in which the main subject moves to the right and seems about to exit the picture. Both the viscount and his two young daughters are abruptly cut off at or near the waist, the dog is half-hidden behind one of the children, and the man standing to the left barely enters the picture. This random cropping of objects is reminiscent of a photographic snapshot. Further, the focal center of the picture is located in the empty plaza behind the figures. The painting therefore owes little either to Greek sculpture, which usually represented the full human figure in idealized form, or to Renaissance perspective, which carefully balanced its figures within an illusionistic space. It also shows no apparent debt to the numerous styles of children's book illustrations or to the severe abstractions of much primitive art.*

32. D

The example shows the church of St. Michael's at Hildesheim, Germany (c. 1001–1003 c.e.). It is typical of Early Romanesque architecture in its dependence on thick blank walls with little or no ornamental decoration, and in its massing of simple cubic and cylindrical forms. The effect of this building is less that of a structural framework supporting walls, roofs, and windows, than of a combination of building blocks that have been sectioned and then glued together. Except for the arched shape of the windows, with their tiny glassed areas, the building completely avoids curving forms, while the only diagonals are those of the roof lines, which are functionally necessary but not fundamental to the building's cubic character. Finally, a spectator's ground-level point of view might make this building seem larger and more dramatic, but it, too, is not essential to the architects' conception.

33. **B**

The Greek Doric temple pictured in the example illustrates a type of architecture known as post-and-lintel (or trabeated) construction, in which long horizontal beams rest atop a series of vertical supports. In the Greek temple, the cylindrical columns act as supports for the large marble "beam" (or the architrave), which, in turn, supports the roof. The Doric temple thus achieves an appearance of Classical balance and perfection through the calculated repetition of a minimum variety of forms. The temple avoids unbroken wall surfaces, instead playing off the solids and voids of the columns and the spaces between, while the only diagonals are those of the triangular front gable (the pediment). The building is completely devoid of arches, which were known to the Greeks but were rarely used and gained prominence only in Roman architecture.

34. **C**

One of the examples shown, choice (D), is a profile portrait, in which the sitter does not turn her gaze out of the picture space, thus eliminating any possibility of eye contact with the viewer. Two other examples, choices (A) and (B), show the subjects in nearly full face, but the sitter in choice (A) glances introspectively down to his left, while the subject in choice (B) looks toward us but, with aristocratic remove, keeps his own gaze just out of the line of our view. Only choice (C) presents a subject in full face who looks directly at the viewer with his large, warm eyes. This sarcophagus portrait from Roman Egypt, c. 160 C.E., intent on expressing the warmth and humanity of the deceased subject, not only effected full eye contact with the viewer, but also portrayed the subject's eyes as abnormally large and deep.

35. **B**

Neither the clothing, the sitters, the expressions, nor the styles of choices (A) and (C) convey in any specific way that the subjects are aristocrats. Only choices (B) and (D) show subjects who are clearly wealthy, well-born, and well-bred. Choice (D), however, is a profile portrait that is so formalized as to be neutral and devoid of expression. Choice (B), by contrast, presents a subject whose rich clothing, haughty posture, elegantly cocked wrists, and, especially, distant expression mark him as a wealthy young man whose circumstances make him superior to most.

36. **A**

The two Renaissance portraits, choices (B) and (D), show the forms and features of their subjects as clearly defined, well-modelled, and set within a basically naturalistic space. The portrait in choice (C), too, though painted in a sketchier style, models the forms of the face in a lucid, convincing, realistic manner in order to project the sitter's personality. Only choice (A) begins to abstract the figure and undermine the conventional sense of form in the search for new pictorial styles. Only in choice (A), the Boy in a Red Vest by the French painter Paul Cézanne, is the specific subject less important than the way the artist treats it. Here, the painter breaks the outlines of the figure and disintegrates its forms, linking them with the background space in a new kind of picture and construction.

37. **D**

In the Chinese ink painting shown in the example, the artist exploited the fluid, calligraphic character of the ink-and-brush technique. In rendering the graceful bamboo leaves, he did not attempt to suggest illusionistic three-dimensional space, as a Western artist might, but let his forms lie firmly on the two-dimensional picture plane. Further, he restricted his range of tones to a dense black and one grey, and, even though written script is included in the picture, this isolated image of the bamboo plant does not relate an episode in a story. Instead, the artist has drawn upon years of technical training and practice to create a picture in which both the script and the plant forms act as kind of spontaneous, rhythmic "writing."

38. **A**

Of the four answer choices, only (A) and (B) can be said to show groups of figures in a landscape; choice (D) shows one or two isolated figures in a landscape setting, and choice (C) contains no landscape elements at all. Choice (B), however, though it presents a number of figures within a topographic view, carefully avoids formally composed and arranged groups and seeks instead to achieve an effect of direct, unposed observation. Only choice (A) uses a composed group as its focal point: the line of schoolboys, seemingly engaged in a moment of spontaneous play, has been painstakingly arranged to lead the viewer's eye from the darker forms at the right to the white-shirted boy at the center. The entire group is set in a broad meadow against a distant, level horizon line that lends balance and stability to the whole composition.

39. **D**

Only choices (A), (B), and (D) include visible horizon lines: in choice (A) the horizon is integrated with the figure group, and in choice (B) the figures, though small and insignificant within the broad landscape space, are busy in normal workday activities and do not seem especially isolated. Choice (D), however, Andrew Wyeth's Christina's World, *1948, places a solitary figure in a broad, empty landscape space bounded by a high, distant horizon. The helpless isolation of the stricken woman in the field is emphasized by the distance that separates her from her home high on the horizon.*

Constructed-Response Questions Scoring Guide

3 • The examinee demonstrates a comprehensive understanding of the material presented.

• The examinee has responded effectively to every part of the question.

• The examinee has provided well-supported explanations.

• The examinee has demonstrated a strong knowledge of the subject matter, including relevant theories, concepts, and procedures.

2 • The examinee demonstrates a basic understanding of the material presented.

• The examinee has responded effectively to most parts of the question.

• The examinee has provided explanations.

• The examinee has demonstrated an adequate knowledge of the subject matter, including relevant theories, concepts, and procedures.

1 • The examinee demonstrates some misunderstanding of the material presented.

• The examinee fails to respond effectively to every part of the question.

• The examinee has provided only weak explanations.

• The examinee has demonstrated insufficient knowledge of the subject matter, including relevant theories, concepts, and procedures.

0 • The examinee has either not responded, responded off-topic, responded completely incorrectly, or simply rephrased the question.

Constructed-Response Questions: Sample Responses

40. **Responses that received a score of 3:**

Students face threats to their health and well being every day, and one of the best ways that physical education can combat their effects is to instill the value of a healthy life. For example, students that are encouraged to gain self-esteem through their physical fitness will be less likely to compromise that fitness by smoking or using drugs.

Another method is to make use of the more relaxed environment present in many physical education classes for a frank discussion about safer sex practices—what they are and why they are important.

Response that received a score of 1:

Physical education can be used to reduce risks by educating students about what the risks are and how to avoid them. For example, a student who smokes can be asked to perform several aerobic exercises and when they can't do any more, a student who doesn't smoke can be asked to do the same thing. When the non smoking student performs better, the other student can see the risk of smoking first hand. Another way physical education can be used is to teach stress relieving activities like yoga.

41. **Response that received a score of 3:**

The second level of need in Maslow's hierarchy concerns an individual's need to feel safe. With violence in our schools becoming an increasing problem, a student's need to feel safe is more important than ever. Maslow's hierarchy states that until these basic needs are met, it is impossible for a student to engage in real, productive learning. Many schools have taken steps to make students feel safer such as the installation of metal detectors. There is an argument to be made, however, that metal detectors make students feel less safe, both as a reminder of the presence of weapons in the school, and also the feeling that the school's administration is an oppressive omnipresent authority figure.

Response that received a score of 1:

The first level of Maslow's hierarchy has to do with the very basic needs of life. The need not to be hungry or thirsty, and to be warm enough in winter and cool enough in summer. I know that my elementary school did not satisfy any of these needs. It was always either too hot or too cold, and the food was so bad that students often went hungry rather than eat it. Then they were surprised when we didn't do well on tests. If teachers hope that their students will perform well in school, they should press the administration to get better food, as well as better heaters and air conditioners.

42. **Response that received a score of 3:**

   Paleolithic art reflects the same impulses that are alive in the art world today. The conscious manipulation of materials based upon some aesthetic criteria is the one constant in the art world. The motivations for this creativity might be different, but the art is the same. Perhaps they were trying to manipulate and influence the world around them. Perhaps these Venuses had some religious significance, or maybe they were just pretty to look at, but in any case, the result is the same. Art is created when people take one thing, like a rock, or some paint, and transform it into something completely different based upon their own unique creativity.

Response that received a score of 1:

   This art is the same as the art of today because it has no practical use. Paleolithic people were the first to create objects that they didn't really need, just liked to have around. Just like today, art might be nice to look at, but it doesn't do anything. Until the Paleolithic times, people only made things that they actually needed, like weapons or axes. In Paleolithic times, people actually started being creative instead of just making things that they needed to stay alive.

CSET

California Subject Examinations
for Teachers: Multiple Subjects

Appendix

CSET: Writing Skills Test
Review and Sample Essays

Appendix
CSET: Writing Skills Test Review and Sample Essays

One of California's options for meeting the state's basic skills requirement is the CSET: Writing Skills Test. The test is made up of two constructed-response questions that assess the individual's ability to write effectively. One question asks the candidate to analyze a given situation or statement—the answer will be a sample of expository writing. The other question asks the candidate to write about a specified personal experience—the answer will be a sample of expressive writing. The questions are designed so the candidates can demonstrate their ability to write; they don't call for any specialized knowledge. These are not trick questions—you don't need to worry about reading a lot into these questions; just read them carefully and answer them to the best of your ability.

Qualified California educators using "focused holistic scoring" will score the responses to the questions. Holistic means that the essay's overall effect is more important than any one piece of it; a run-on sentence would not be a fatal flaw in an otherwise excellent essay (but it wouldn't be overlooked, either). The performance characteristics the CSET: Writing Skills assessment emphasizes are:

- **RHETORICAL FORCE**—The way the main idea is stated and how well it is focused on; with how the entire essay holds together, including the quality of reasoning the writer demonstrates.

- **ORGANIZATION**—How well and how clearly the ideas are put together and how well they flow and hold together.

- **SUPPORT AND DEVELOPMENT**—The information within the essay—how pertinent and specific the supporting details are and how the argument is built using those details.

- **USAGE**—Basically, the writer's choice of words and how she/he handles them.

- **STRUCTURE AND CONVENTIONS**—Whether the writing is free of mistakes in both simple mechanics like spelling and punctuation and grammatical areas like sentence structure and paragraph structure.

- **APPROPRIATENESS**—How well the writer addresses the topic and uses language and style that are appropriate to the given audience and purpose.

The highest score an essay can receive is a 4. Below, we'll go through the elements a paper needs to have to get the highest score. A paper would receive a "U" if it were off topic, illegible, not in English, or very, very short. Taking the points in turn, the most important is, of course, to answer the question. (You don't want to receive a U!)

The first point in the CSET "4" list is "The writer clearly presents a central idea and/or point of view and maintains focus on that topic; the response is well reasoned."

- Be sure that your response is appropriate and focused. If the topic is animal rights, don't somehow migrate to an essay about solar energy, even though that may be a topic that burns intensely in your heart and mind. The way the questions are designed, you can take almost any approach you wish with the topic; just be sure you stay with your approach.

- Take the time to plan out the approach—you might start out talking about animal rights as the topic relates to animal testing and cosmetics, then wander over to how people treat their pets, then spend time describing spay and neuter clinics. Unless you are a consummate writer, this broad approach isn't going to earn you a 4; it's best to take a single point, such as animal testing, and talk about it in terms of cosmetics, medicine, rats in mazes (testing behavior), and so forth.

- Think about how you state your response—"well reasoned" means you don't make wild assertions that you can't support.

Secondly, "Ideas or points of discussion are logically arranged, and their meaning is clearly communicated."

- This is all about organization, and planning is essential here. You have a series of ideas about how to present your response.
  - ✓ Start with a clear introduction
  - ✓ Build your support paragraphs carefully and bring it all to a clear conclusion that briefly summarizes your main points.

"Generalizations and assertions are well supported with relevant, specific, and detailed development."

- This is another point where planning is essential. You may have a brilliant concept of how to solve the looming energy crisis but basically it boils down to saying we need to use renewable energy. Although this is a laudable sentiment, if you don't have concrete examples of how to get there from here—at least three or four concrete, compelling examples of renewable energy programs—choose another topic.

- Choose to focus on something closer to home—a series of classes in your academic specialty, the two summers that you spent as a camp counselor—something that will enable you to bring relevant, specific, detailed examples to your essays. That way, you will have made a significant impact on not only the "development" area of your essay but the focus and organization areas as well.

The following points are more about the nitty gritty of the mechanics of writing:

"Choice of words is precise; usage is careful and accurate."

Note that the emphasis here is on precise, careful, and accurate. If you are a poet and you've done a lot of writing—maybe journaling, maybe songwriting or verse—use that gift to craft an essay that has a lot of pizzazz. If you're not used to using words in a creative writing sense, stick with being precise, careful, and accurate.

- Use verbs that are active but make sure they fit the situation.

- Use modifiers sparingly.

- Use the nouns that best fit the situations, people, and events you are trying to describe or discuss—avoid generic terms like "stuff" and "things."

- Think about your subject and, if it helps, make a list of words on your scratch paper, then use them as the context dictates.

"The writer composes sentences of syntactic complexity and variety and constructs coherent paragraphs, although the response may contain minor flaws in mechanical conventions."

- In other words, don't put one declarative sentence right after another. Instead, use a blend of sentences that have main and subordinate clauses and coordinate subjects, punctuated with the occasional simple sentence—just the subject, verb, and object or, if appropriate, a simple question. That adds variety.

- Pay attention to your paragraph structure; shorter paragraphs help a lot with organization. Think of paragraphs as the roadmap that leads your reader smoothly from one point to the next.

- Note that "minor flaws in mechanical conventions" are not a major point. If you misspell a word or two or miss a comma, those errors will be overlooked (noted, but not counted heavily). Although you must take time to proof your work, a small error is not, in a holistic evaluation, a major sin. Still, the closer you come to a mechanically correct paper, the better. If you tend to rely on spell check, remember that you're doing this "in person" and there isn't a computer standing by that will catch your spelling errors; you need to do that as you write and as you proofread.

The following are some general points that will help you as you craft your essays.

Pre-Writing/Planning

Before you begin to actually write, here are some preliminary steps. A few minutes spent planning really pays off—your final essay will be more focused, organized, and well developed.

Keep a close eye on your time. You should spend from 10 to 20 percent of the time allotted collecting your thoughts; use your favorite outlining technique to jot them down and organize them.

Understand the Question

Sometimes a writer fails to understand the question the essay is meant to address. The resulting answer may be very well written, but if it is totally off topic it will receive a U; if it is partially off topic, or takes a strange turn and winds up addressing a different issue, it will receive a low score because the focus will not be strong. Read the essay question very carefully and ask yourself the following questions:

- What is the meaning of the topic statement?

- Is the question asking me to write an expressive essay or an expository essay?

- Do I agree or disagree with the statement? (Remember to take one position and stay with it.)

- What kinds of examples can I use to support my thesis? (Pull from everything you have—personal experience, reading, current events, your academic experience.)

Consider Your Audience

The CSET tells you who your audience will be in the body of the question: "In an essay to be read by an audience of educated adults. . . ." Consider this as you frame your essay.

- You want to "speak" as you would to a well-regarded teacher or senior colleague rather than as you might to a casual friend.

- Don't use slang and consider that your audience won't be swayed by blanket statements—they will want details put forth in a clear, organized fashion using language that is clear and easy to follow and also keeps the reader motivated.

Writing Your Essay

Once you have decided on a topic and created a plan for organizing it, including jotting down a number of appropriate examples, you are ready to begin writing.

Organizing Your Essay

Decide how many paragraphs you will write. You will probably have time for four or five paragraphs. In that type of format, the first paragraph will be the introduction, the next two or three will develop your thesis with specific examples, and the final paragraph should be a strong conclusion.

The Introduction

The focus of your introduction should be the thesis statement. The thesis is the heart of the essay. If you do not state your thesis clearly, your essay won't have the focus and clarity it needs. This statement allows your reader to understand the point and direction of your essay. The statement identifies the central idea of your essay and should clearly state your attitude about the topic. It will also dictate the basic content and organization of your essay.

Take your cue about your thesis from the question you need to answer. If the prompt reads, "Explain why you would or would not want to live in a large city," any of the following responses could be a strong thesis: "I have lived the bulk of my life in the suburbs and look forward to spending some significant time in a large city." Or "Big-city living has never appealed to me because I like knowing the people around me and feeling a part of a small community." Either of these thesis statements (and countless others) would be good leads into essays that support the position you are taking as you defend your position (expository writing) or share your experiences (expressive writing).

When writing under time constraints, your essay may take a turn you hadn't expected when you began. While doing proofreading, if you discover that your thesis statement is no longer accurate, or if the emphasis has shifted, go back and revise your statement to reflect the essay that you have, in fact, written.

Supporting Paragraphs

The next two or three paragraphs of your essay should elaborate on the supporting examples you have in your introductory paragraph. Each paragraph should discuss only one idea. Like the introduction, each paragraph should be coherently organized with a topic sentence and supporting details and examples.

Don't overload your essay with too many ideas, and be sure to explore each concept thoroughly—bring in those examples that will help you develop a strong essay.

The topic sentence is to each paragraph what the thesis statement is to the essay as a whole. It tells the reader what you plan to discuss in the paragraph. It has a specific subject and is neither too broad nor too narrow. It establishes your attitude and gives your reader guidance about where this paragraph is going, what this example is all about.

The topic sentence, like the thesis statement, is usually placed at the beginning of the sentence, although skilled writers may plant it in the middle or end of the paragraph. In a timed writing exercise, it's best to stick with beginning the paragraph with the topic sentence.

The remainder of the paragraph should support the topic sentence by bringing in detailed examples. Don't suddenly add material that doesn't belong to the topic sentence, even if it's a great idea you suddenly thought of. Material that is off topic or that interrupts the logical flow of the essay will lower your score.

Conclusion

In your conclusion, briefly restate your thesis. For the expository essay, explain how you have proved your point; for the expressive essay, give a good summary of the points you have made. Because you want to end your essay on a strong note, your conclusion should be concise and effective.

Do not introduce any new topics in your conclusion and don't make a statement that shifts the reader's attention away from the main focus of the essay. If you were watching a movie that suddenly shifted plot and characters at the end, you would be disappointed or even angry. Similarly, your readers would feel confused and disappointed if the conclusion didn't reflect the points and strengths of your essay.

The conclusion is your last chance to grab and impress your reader. A strong close will remind the reader that you are serious, even passionate, about your subject.

Effective Use of Language

Clear organization, while vitally important, is not the only factor your adult, educated readers will consider. You must also show that you can express your ideas clearly, using correct grammar, diction, usage, spelling, and punctuation. For rules on grammar, usage, and mechanics, consult your college notes or your favorite book or Web site. It can be enjoyable and enlightening to Google something like "misplaced modifiers." If you were consistently told in your classes that you made mistakes with sentence construction, spend a little time delving into different types of sentences, common faults in sentence formation, and the like.

Point of View

Depending on the audience, essays may be written from one of three points of view:

1.   First Person point of view (I)

      "I think if I lived in a large city . . ."

      "I feel that living in a large city. . . ."

2. Second Person point of view (You)

    "If you live in a big city, you might find. . . ."

3. Third Person point of view (focuses on the idea, not on what "you" or "I" think about it in a personal way)

    "Living in a big city is. . . ."

What's important about point of view is sticking with it throughout your essay. Don't start by saying "I think I would feel great if I lived in a big city. You might find yourself meeting fascinating people from a great range of backgrounds. It would be a fulfilling and educational experience to live in a big city." Instead, say something like:

- "I believe living in a big city would be fulfilling and educational. Fascinating people from a wide range of backgrounds tend to live in large metropolitan areas; the experience of rubbing shoulders with such a diverse bunch of people would be exciting and exhilarating."

- Or, "I think I'd feel great if I lived in a big city. I know I would find a number of fascinating people with diverse backgrounds there, and rubbing shoulders with them would give me a lot of educational and fulfilling experiences."

Tone and Voice

A writer's tone expresses his or her attitude toward the subject and the reader. If the essay question requires you to take a strong stand, the tone of your essay should reflect this.

Your tone should also be appropriate for the subject matter. A serious topic demands a serious tone. For a more light-hearted topic, using humor or a lighter touch would be perfectly appropriate (just stay away from slang, unless you are clearly using it for humor's sake).

Whatever tone you take, be consistent. Do not make any abrupt shifts in tone in the middle of your essay.

Your voice is the way you project your personality. Voice is used sparingly in expository writing, where the emphasis is on the topic. In expressive writing, you have a chance to reveal aspects of who you are. If you are enthusiastic, have fun with sprightly adjectives and adverbs (as long as they are words you know well). If you feel strongly about your subject, choose some dynamic verbs. Don't be afraid to use language to let your reader get to know you a bit, but don't let your enthusiasm take over—focus, organization, and development are the most important aspects of these essays.

Verb Tense

Choose one verb tense for your essay and stick with it. If you start in the past, stay there—unless you have a compelling reason to switch tense to make an already well-supported point. Staying in the same verb tense improves your continuity and flow of ideas. Avoid phrases such as "now was," a confusing blend of present and past. Remember, your goal is to craft an essay that is easy for your educated adult reader to follow.

Transitions

Transitions are like the links of a bracelet, holding the "beads," or major points, of your essay together. They help the reader follow the smooth flow of your ideas and see the connections you're making between major and minor ideas. Transitions come either at the beginning of a paragraph to show how it relates to the paragraph above it, or in a paragraph to show the connection of ideas within that paragraph.

Use strong and appropriate transitions when you introduce your ideas and examples. Make sure you give each idea its own paragraph and introduce new or supporting ideas with an appropriate phrase like "on the other hand," "additionally," "therefore," "however," "also," "furthermore," "consequently," "and then," "moreover," and on and on. You can consult a book of grammar or the World Wide Web for helpful lists of transitions.

Common Writing Errors

Remember your penmanship! You will be writing on lined paper with pencil. If you've been using keyboards pretty exclusively, take some time to practice good handwriting so your readers can easily decipher your words. If you're used to writing in longhand you should also have fewer problems with completing your essay and having time for proofreading.

Five major writing errors are run-ons (also known as fused sentences), fragments, lack of subject-verb agreement, incorrect use of objects, and misplaced modifiers.

- Run-ons. "She swept the floor it was dirty" is a run-on because "it" starts a new sentence. The should be a period or semicolon after "floor." If a period is used, "it" should start with a capital *I*.

- Fragments: "Because Jimmy knew how to play baseball" is a fragment even though it has a subject (Jimmy) and an object (knew), the word "because" turns the phrase into a clause that needs an object—what happened because Jimmy knew how to play baseball? This sentence could be made complete by saying something like "Because Jimmy knew how to play baseball, he was asked to coach his little brother's Little League team."

- Problems with subject-verb agreement: "Either Maria or Roberta are going to the game" is incorrect because Maria is going or Robert is going, but not both. The sentence should say, "Either Maria or Robert is going to the game."

- Incorrect objects: Probably the most common offense in this area is saying "between you and I," which sounds correct but isn't. "Between" is a preposition that takes the objective case "me." You wouldn't say, "It's a problem between he and she," you'd say, "It's a problem between him and her." Similarly, the correct usage is "between you and me."

- Misplaced modifiers: Sometimes, a modifying word or phrase is placed too far away from the noun or verb it is modifying, which confuses the reader. For instance, "By accident, he poked the little girl with his finger **in the eye**" is incorrect; this is the way to say it: "By accident, he poked the little girl **in the eye** with his finger."

Five Words Weak Writers Overuse

Weak and beginning writers sometimes use the pronouns "you," "we," "they," "this," and "it" without explaining who or what the pronoun stands for. Vagueness can sap the life out of your writing, driving your reader to distraction, or at least to a good bit of head-scratching. Here are some telltale signs that your prose may need a tune-up:

1. Shifting to second-person "you" when you really mean "a person." This shift confuses readers and weakens the flow of the essay. Of course, "you" is commonly accepted in creative writing, journal and other areas, and may be fine in your expressive essay, but not in your expository essay. We use "you" in this book because we (the author and publishers) know exactly who's reading it and the very point of much of what we're writing is to address you personally!) In a brief, formal essay it is best to avoid using "you."

2. Don't slip into the use of "we" without explaining who "we" are. If you mean "Americans" or "society," let the reader know by using some phrase like "We Americans love the small towns like Mayberry that exist on TV, but we might be disappointed by life in a real small town" rather than "We all know that a town like Mayberry is only a figment of the TV writers' imagination."

3. "They" is often misused in essay writing, probably because it is so often used in casual conversation. How often have you heard something like this? "I went to the doctor and they told me to take an antibiotic." Tell the reader who "they" are, and if it turns out that you are only talking about one person, use the correct pronoun—"he," "she," or "it." (The same is true for "them," "him," and "her.")

4. "This" is often used incorrectly. If you say, 'She told me she received a present. This sounded good to me," the reader doesn't know what "this" refers to—the present? The idea? The news? Be clear; don't make your readers guess what you mean. The word "this" should be followed by a noun or other referent.

5. Weak writers often use "it" as shorthand, but readers don't appreciate having to struggle to figure out what "its" referent is. Take the time to be clear, logical, and complete when you express yourself.

Use Your Own Vocabulary

Should you use big words that look good in the dictionary or thesaurus but that you don't use or fully understand? No. You should use your own words.

This doesn't mean that you should slide into slang; use your best vocabulary, the one you used when writing a serious paper for an upper division class. You can take a bit more liberty in the expressive essay if you can make it fit, but even here, be careful.

Use the Active Voice

When you write, choose the active voice as often as possible; it adds punch to your prose. A weak, passive verb leaves the actor unknown or seemingly unimportant (compare "It seems to me that small-town living is boring" with "I find small-town living boring."). However, sometimes the passive voice is appropriate—if you want to emphasize the action rather than the actor, you don't know who the actor is, or the person acted on is more important than the actor. For instance, "He suffered a concussion," is usually, in the moment, the most important message; the person or activity that caused the concussion is information to be passed along a little later: "Joe hit him with a rock" or "He fell while mountain-climbing."

Proofreading

Set aside five minutes at the end to copyedit and proofread your work—remember, you need to do this by hand and spell check isn't going to help you.

This is the time to catch any errors such as misspellings, omitted words, or incorrect punctuation. You won't have enough time to make large-scale revisions, but use this chance to make any small changes that will strengthen your essays. Consider the following points when proofreading your work:

- Are all your sentences really sentences? Have you written any fragments or run-ons?

- Are you using vocabulary correctly?

- Did you leave out or garble any punctuation? Did you capitalize correctly?

- Are there any misspellings? Check both difficult words and the simple ones; mistakes in words like "than" versus "then" are annoying to the educated adult reader.

- If you have time, go back and proof once more. This time, read your essay backwards, from the last paragraph to the first. By doing so, you may catch errors that you missed reading it from start to finish.

Sample Essays

For the CSET: Writing Skills you will write two essays:

1. Write about a specified personal experience.

2. Analyze a given situation or statement.

Below are examples of two analysis (expository) essays and two personal experience (expressive) essays. These samples would most probably receive the highest score on the test, a "4."

Prompt 1 (Personal Experience Essay):

In an essay to be read by an audience of educated adults, explain how your experiences in college affect your position on the following statement: Today's college student should declare a major and begin specializing right away because the world gets more competitive all the time and it's important to start on a career immediately.

Sample Response:

Although it is true that the world out there is a very challenging one, I disagree that college students should start specializing immediately. In fact, many of the most highly regarded liberal arts colleges emphasize giving students a well-rounded experience in their first four years. These are some of the best schools in the country and a large percentage of their graduates go on to medical school, law school, and so on and wind up with very successful careers.

In my college experience, I saw many instances when not specializing right away was the preferred course of action. A person who is 18 years old, even if she thinks she knows exactly what she wants to do, really hasn't experienced that much of the world yet. College is a time to explore and learn new things, to get outside your comfort zone, stretch your wings, and all those other cliches that really have a lot of truth in them. If you decide at 18 years old that you're going to be a marine biologist, you might find out that you really get excited by studying physics. In my case, I had early thoughts about pursuing fashion design and am now excited at the prospect of teaching design and art at the high school level.

In general, I believe that the student who begins specializing when she is 18 years old is cheating herself of a world of knowledge. She can just as easily declare a major in her junior year and spend the first two years sampling the riches that her school has to offer. I would never give up the anthropology and psychology courses I took as I was exploring different fields.

College students may have a chance to study abroad in their junior year. By staying flexible, more choices of destination are open to students. I had the good fortune to spend a semester in Italy studying art history in Florence, an experience that was extremely enriching and that I would not have chosen when I first entered school (I had a strong interest in Japan at that time).

Finally, I have read many times that the average person will change careers six or seven times during her lifetime. By staying flexible in college, I have, I believe, prepared myself for changes in the future.

Although it is true that the world is a competitive place, college is a time for learning, sampling, and reflecting. The graduate will be on a career path soon enough. The person who has learned a variety of things and had a variety of experiences will be better richer for them, and the exposure she has had to a large number of different fields will serve her well in the future, no matter how competitive it is.

Discussion:

This writer takes a question that could be answered either as the analysis of a statement or as a personal experience and explains, drawing on her own experiences, to explain why not declaring a major early on in college can be valuable to the individual's growth and development. The essay does not precisely build from Point A to Point B; instead, the writer presents a number of points of equal weight (pointing out that students are often too young, at 18, to know what they want to do; that they might miss learning about areas they had not even considered before; and that flexibility in the college years may improve their ability to be flexible later in their careers). All the examples are nicely supported with personal examples and the writer finishes with a strong conclusion that ties the elements of the essay together.

Prompt 2 (Personal Experience Essay):

In an essay to be read by an audience of educated adults, describe a volunteer or internship experience you've had during the past three or four years, both the work you did and what you got out of it.

Sample Response:

In the summer between my sophomore and junior years in college, I was an intern at my home town's public radio station. At the time, I was majoring in communications and journalism and this position seemed to be tailor-made for me.

When I started work at the station, I thought I'd be helping with the music. The station has a lot of volunteer DJs who play an incredible range of types of music, everything from classical to hip-hop, bluegrass, jazz . . . you name it. I learned a vast amount about kinds of music I had never been exposed to and gained a great appreciation for almost all genres.

At first, I filled in wherever the station needed me, and that meant I did everything from stuffing envelopes to taking out the recycling to filing CDs and entering play lists into the computer. I never resented this low-level work because the volunteers, many of them highly educated community members who had interesting jobs and lives, were cheerfully doing the same work right alongside me.

I had no idea how many different aspects there were to audio broadcasting, but the station people trained me on how to work the on-air equipment (this is training that's required by the government for anyone who does programming), work all sorts of interesting computer programs for recording and editing audio files, and generally get familiar with how a radio station works.

After sampling many different aspects of the station, I found myself gravitating to the news and public affairs side of things. The station runs a half-hour news show every morning and afternoon. It's amazing to learn about all the work that goes into creating that half hour. When people do an interview, they often will condense an hour interview into a couple of minutes of broadcast time. Incidentally, I learned some basics of interviewing—it can be quite a challenge to get your interviewee to stay on topic and to say things that are both interesting and demonstrate the person's range and knowledge of the topic you're trying to zoom in on. I have a lot more respect for people who do this kind of work in the broadcast world.

The job that became mine, and that I did for the last two months of my internship (along with stuffing envelopes and take out the recycling) was the station's community calendar. The volunteer who had been doing this work trained me on how to check the stations computer for the events that community organizations sent in. Sometimes, I had to contact those organizations, like a summer school program, a church that was running a fair, groups staging a 5-K benefit run, and check details. Then—and this was the fun part—I got to go into the recording studio and make an announcement that went on air every day, letting community people know about what was going on for the upcoming days.

This work was exciting and I received almost the equivalent of a year's worth of work in classes about broadcasting. In addition, my experience with community radio and its volunteers showed me that there are people who love what they do and manage to make their work and their life one and the same. I know my entire life will be richer for this experience.

Discussion:

This essay about a specified personal situation is rich in detail and in reflection. The writer does a nice job of describing the various aspects of the experience. In addition, the organization is well done. The second paragraph, about music, seems a little off topic but it helps paint a picture of a summer filled with interesting experiences. Although many aspects of the internship are discussed, the author ties the essay together in the last sentence by emphasizing the effect the spirit of the volunteers has had on him or her; a nice way of wrapping up what had been a somewhat scattered collection of thoughts. (Note that the theme of the volunteers recurs in several spots throughout the essay.)

Prompt 3 (Analysis Essay):

In an essay to be read by an audience of educated adults, discuss the topic of poverty—what it means to you or to the world, or both.

Sample Response:

I believe there are basically two kinds of poverty. Of course, the most important kind is the terrible poverty that many people in the world suffer with. Who hasn't seen pictures of mothers in Africa holding poor little babies who aren't even strong enough to sit up? When a person lives in that kind of poverty, it is hard to imagine that they can think about anything but just getting their next meal. When people are extremely emaciated, they can't possibly be healthy, either. And if they have no money, they would have very little access to healthcare. This type of poverty supercedes any other kind that exists, but there is another type of poverty.

The other type of poverty is the poverty of spirit. There are people who are wealthy but very unhappy. They have plenty to eat, dress well, and drive fancy cars, but they have a gnawing hunger and feel that what they have is not enough. I think this is because they don't have any purpose in life beyond buying the next car or the next house.

The sales of antidepressants in the United States are off the charts—some people may need this medicine, but I believe that a large number of them are actually suffering from a poverty of spirit. Without a goal, without a thought for ideas and people outside yourself, you aren't going to be truly happy and you will feel empty and poor. Those people who are truly empty and poor because they don't have enough to eat and can't feed their hungry children would be so happy just to have enough to eat. Somehow, people in wealthier countries need to learn how to be happy and satisfied. We have to know when enough is enough.

The answer to the question, what does poverty mean to me and to the world, is a complicated one. I believe that human beings are meant to be able to rise above poverty of both the spirit and of lack of material things like food. In a perfect world, the people with plenty to eat and wear would make sure that the people without enough to eat have plenty of food and other things, an activity that would enrich them in spirit. If everyone were rich in sprit, I believe there would be no poverty of want.

Discussion:

This analysis of a given situation shows the writer doing a good job with a topic he or she isn't deeply familiar with. The author apparently does not have a specialized knowledge of poverty (or isn't sharing such knowledge with the readers) and perhaps for that reason, he/she chooses to tackle the topic of poverty from a rather philosophical perspective, making a distinction between actual and spiritual poverty. The writer is able to put together some strong examples from a general knowledge of current events (poverty in Africa, the rampant use of antidepressants). The paper is well organized and the author does a nice job of relating the two types of poverty in the final paragraph, concluding that richness of spirit could lead to a lessening of material poverty.

Prompt (Analysis Essay):

In an essay to be read by an audience of educated adults, discuss the statement, "Monsters and demons are a part of the human experience."

Sample Response:

A study of folk tales from around the world would show that all folklore contains stories of monsters and demons. From the trolls under the bridge in the Three Billy Goats Gruff to the witch in Snow White to the monsters represented by the terrifying masks from cultures in the South Pacific, Africa, North and South America, and elsewhere that we see in museums, it is clear that all human societies have had their own types of these supernatural creatures.

Even in today's modern American society, plenty of people believe in ghosts, evil spirits, and entities such as Bigfoot and the Loch Ness Monster. In addition, we seem to love to be frightened by monsters and demons like Count Dracula (how many iterations of the original Mary Shelley story have we had now?), Frankenstein's monster, and modern-day incarnations like Freddy Kruger?

When so many cultures and societies seem to have demons and monsters, it raises the question, do these creatures play a role in society? I believe that they do. In a time when there were many dangers lurking in the woods, monsters must have served a useful function—parents and village elders could frighten their children by telling them that the bogeyman lurked outside the village boundaries, thus keeping the youngsters from roaming too far into unknown areas. Monsters played a useful role in social control.

In fact, I believe we are still at work making monsters today for other than entertainment purposes. People are often accused "demonizing" someone—demonizing an enemy, demonizing a group—and what is that but a way of making someone or something into a monster?

One example of demonizing is the way various political groups paint the opposition as everything that is evil. This kind of demonizing is clearly done for control—if you are terrified of or repelled by the Republican or Democratic candidate, you are not going to listen to what he or she has to say.

Another type of demonizing happens when something like global warming becomes a terrifying subject. This issue is, of course, extremely important, but the way in which it is presented often seems to be done to create fear and thus action. But in our current society, it sometimes just causes the "other side" to demonize the people who are promoting awareness of the situation.

From the troll under the bridge to global warming, it seems that all societies have their demons and monsters; maybe they will always be with us. Monsters and demons seem to speak to something deep inside us. We must enjoy being frightened, and these entities may always be used as a form of social control.

Discussion:

This writer explores the topic of monsters and demons in an interesting way, bringing in appropriate examples from preliterate societies and weaving them nicely with similarly appropriate examples from the present day. The writer shows some knowledge of the role monsters and demons play in various cultures vis-à-vis social control. The "demonizing" theme is handled well and raises interesting questions about the role of demons in human behavior. The conclusion nicely summarizes the essay and restates the author's points that human societies seem to need and enjoy their monsters and demons.

Index

A

Abelard, Peter, 98
abolitionist movements, 199
Abraham, 84
absolute value, 257–258
abstract art, 366
Abstract Expressionism, 367
Abu Bakr, 89
abuse, of children, 352–353
acceleration, 225
accentual meter, 38–39
accommodation stage, of
        cognitive development, 327
acids, 224
acute angles, 294
Adams, John, 160, 177–178
Adams, John Quincy, 184, 186,
        187, 188
Adams, Samuel, 158
adaptive physical education,
        311–312
addends, 262
addition
        decimal fractions, 268
        fractions, 266
        integers, 262–263
adjacent angles, 294
The Admirable Crichton (Barrie),
        53
adolescents, 325–326, 351
Adrianople, Battle of, 80
*The Adventures of Huckleberry
        Finn* (Twain), 53–54
The Adventures of Tom Sawyer
        (Twain), 20
Aeneid (Vergil), 80
aerobic exercise, 307–308, 316
Aeschylus, 76
affiliation, need for, 331
affirmations, 351
Africa, 91–92, 112, 131, 133
African Americans
        in California, 218
        citizenship of, 206
        Jim Crow Laws, 208

during Reconstruction
        period, 205–208
religious movements, 181
voting rights, 188, 207
See also slavery, in U.S.
Agincourt, Battle of, 100
agriculture
        ancient India, 73
        eighteenth century, 113
        Europe in Middle Ages, 95
        Native Americans, 127–
                128, 129, 130
        prehistoric period, 68, 127
        in Southern U.S., 191
air movement, 250
Akhenaton, 71–72
Akkadians, 70
Alabama, 201
Alais, Peace of, 111
Alaric, 80
Alexander the Great, 73, 76, 77
Alexandrine, 48
Alfred the Great (England), 94, 96
algebra, 271–289
        algebraic expressions,
                271–273
        formulas, 279
        functions, 281–283
        inequalities, 277–278
        linear equations, 273–276
        quadratic equations,
                283–288
        relations, 279–281
        slope, 274–275
        word problems, 288–289
Algonquians, 130
Alien Act (U.S.), 177, 178
allegorical characters, 20
alliteration, 44
allusion, 41, 44
alternative interior/exterior
        angles, 296
amendments, to the Constitution,
        170–174, 180
American English, 59–60
American Fur Company, 185

Americas, discovery of, 112
        See also North America;
                South America
AmonRe, 72
Amorites, 70
Anabaptists, 105
anapest, 38
Anasazi civilization, 93, 128–129
anatomy, 234–236, 308–309
Andean civilization, 92–93
anger, 332–333
angles, 294, 295, 296
animals
        domestication of, 68
        within ecosystem, 237
        interaction with
                environment, 238–
                239
        vs. plants, 236
        propagation of, 240
antagonists, 19
antebellum period, 195
antibody molecules, 235
Antietam, Battle of, 203
Anti-Federalists, 165–166
Antony, Mark, 79
apostrophe, poetry, 44
applied art, 356
applied instructional style, 344
"A&P" (Updike), 25–26
Aquinas, Thomas, 99
Arabs, 131
"Araby" (Joyce), 26
architecture
        Bauhaus School, 366
        cultural differences, 360
        definition of, 358
        of Middle Ages, 99
        Renaissance period, 362
        Romanesque style, 361
arcs, of circles, 292
area, 290, 291, 293
Argentina, 136
argumentative essays, 27
aristocracy
        England, 110

Europe, 94–95, 101
France, 111, 114–115, 124–125
Japan, 89
Aristophanes, 76
Aristotle, 76
Arkansas, 201, 205
Arkwright, Richard, 114
Armada, 108, 138
Arminius, 109
Arnold, Benedict, 163
Arouet, Francois Marie, 123
art, 355–376
    of ancient Greece, 76
    critical judgment of, 374–376
    cultural differences, 359–360
    dance, 311, 358, 371–373
    of early civilizations, 356
    fine vs. applied art, 356
    music, 99, 358, 360, 368–371
    pre-historic cave paintings, 67, 360
    of Renaissance, 102–103
    theater, 53, 76, 80, 359, 373–374
    types of, 357–359
    visual art, 360–367
Articles of Confederation, 164–165, 170
Aryans, 73
Ashikaga Shogunate, 90
Ashley, Andrew and William, 186
Asprin, Robert, 54
assessment, information processing theory, 342
assimilation stage, of cognitive development, 327
associative property, 256
assonance, 45
Assyrians, 71, 72, 85
asteroids, 243
Astor, John Jacob, 185
astrolabe, 132
astronomy, 120–121, 242–245
Athens, 75–76
atmosphere, 247
atoms, 222

ATP (adenosine triphosphate), 234
Attila the Hun, 80, 93
aubade, 50
auditory learners, 338, 339–340
Augsburg, Peace of, 108–109
Augustus, 79
Austen, Jane, 22
autobiography, 16
autonomic system, 234
average, 301
Axum, 72
Aztec civilization, 92, 112, 135

B

Babel, Isaac, 40
Babylonians, 70
Bacon, Nathaniel, 142–143
badminton, 310
Balanchine, George, 373
ballads, 49
ballad stanza, 49
ballet, 373
banking, 185, 186
Bantu peoples, 91–92
Baroque period, 363, 369
Barrie, James Matthew, 53
bases (mathematics), 260, 261, 271
base solutions (science), 224
basketball, 309
bathos, 45
Baton Rouge, 182
Bauhaus School of Design, 366
Baxter-Magolda, Marcia, 347, 348
Beauregard, Pierre Gustave Toutant, 201, 202
Becket, Thomas, 96
Bede, Venerable, 95
Beethoven, Ludwig van, 369
Belisarius, 81
Bell, Alexander Graham, 209
Beowulf, 95
Beringia, 126–127
Berkeley, William, 142
Bharata Natyam, 372
bias, of teachers, 335–336
Bill of Rights, 170–172, 175
binomials, 271

birth rates, 238
Black Death/Plague, 83–84, 99
Black Hawk War, 190
Blake, William, 31, 42–44
blank verse, 37, 50–51
"Bliss" (Mansfield), 24
Bloom, Benjamin, 323
Boccaccio, 100, 102
body fat, 315
Boleyn, Anne, 105
"Boom!" (Nemerov), 52
Boston Massacre, 158
Boston Tea Party, 158–159
Bourbon dynasty, 114–115, 125
bowling, 310
Bradford, William, 143
Brazil, 135
Britain. *See* Great Britain
Bronze Age, 69
Brown, R., 328–329
Browning, Robert, 47
Bruni, Leonardo, 103
Brutus, 79
Bucer, Martin, 105
Buchanan, James, 201
Buddhism, 86–87
Bull Run, Battle of, 202
Bunker Hill, Battle of, 161
Burgoyne, 162
Burgundians, 100
Burkhardt, Jacob, 101
B-Vitamins, 313–314
Byron, Lord, 31, 36
Byzantine Empire, 81–82

C

Cabot, John, 112, 137
Cabot, Sebastian, 112
Caesar, Julius, 78–79
caesura, 45
"The Caged Skylark" (Hopkins), 39
Cahokia, 129
calcium, 314
calendar, Roman, 79
Calhoun, John C., 189
California, 209–219
    environmental issues, 219
    Gold Rush, 196, 213–214, 215

during Great Depression, 216–217
Los Angeles, 216
Mexican War effects, 212–213
Native Indians, 209–211
pioneer settlement, 195
social and political issues, 218
statehood, 197, 198
transcontinental railroad, 214–215
water sources, 216, 219
during World War II, 217–218
californios, 212, 213
Calvert, Cecilius, George, and Leonard, 141
Calvinism, 105, 106, 107, 108, 109
Canada, 155, 183, 184
canals, 113
Candide (Voltaire), 53
Cannae, Battle of, 78
Canterbury Tales (Chaucer), 17, 49, 101
Capetian dynasty, 96–97
carbohydrates, 312
cardiovascular fitness, 306–307
Carnegie, Andrew, 209
Carolina, Colony of, 146
Carolingian dynasty, 94, 95
Carthage, 78
Cartier, Jacques, 112
Cartwright, Edward, 114
Cassius, 79
Cataline, 78
Catch-22 (Heller), 53
Carteret, George, 147
Catherine of Aragon, 105
Catherine the Great (Russia), 124
Cato the younger, 79
Catullus, 79
Cavaliers, 111, 117
cell rate theory, of life span, 239–240
cells, 232–234
center, of circle, 291
Central Pacific Railroad, 215
Chaldeans, 85

Champlain, Samuel de, 112
Chandragupta Maurya, 73
chansons de geste, 99
chapters, in novels, 18–19
characters, in literature, 19–20, 22, 23
Charlemagne (Charles the Great), 94
Charles I (England), 110–111, 116, 143, 145, 146
Charles II (England), 117, 146, 149
Charles IV (France), 97
Charles the Bald (Holy Roman Empire), 94
Charles V (Holy Roman Empire), 107
Charles VII (France), 100
Chaucer, Geoffrey, 17, 49, 99, 100–101
chemical energy, 227
chemical properties, of matter, 223–224
Cherokees, 190
child abuse and neglect, 352, 353
Chile, 136
"The Chimney Sweeper" (Blake), 43–44
China, 73–74, 83, 87–88
Chinese railroad workers, in California, 215
Chippewas, 130
chloroplasts, 234
cholesterol, 313, 315
chord, 292
Christianity
in America (early), 152–153, 181
Calvinism, 105, 106, 107, 108, 109
Church of England, 115–116, 117, 152
Crusades, 82, 97–98
first Christians, 81
Lutherans, 107, 108–109
Protestant Reformation, 103–105
Puritans, 105, 106, 108, 110, 137, 143–144

wars between Protestants and Catholics, 107, 108–109
See also Roman Catholic Church
"A Christmas Memory" (Capote), 24–25
chromaticism, 369
Cicero, 79
Cid, El, 97
"Cinderella," 20–21
circles, 291–293
circulatory system, 235
circumference, 292
city-states, of Greece, 75, 76
The Civilization of the Renaissance in Italy (Burkhardt), 101–102
civilizations, first, 68–74
civil wars
England, 111, 115–118, 145–146
U.S., 201–204
Clark, William, 180
Classical period, 369
classroom environment, 336–337
Clay, Henry, 184, 187–188, 189, 195, 198
Cleisthenes, 75
Clement VII (Pope), 105
Cleopatra, 79
climate, 248–249
climax stage, of novels, 18
closed form, of poems, 48–50
Clovis I, 94
Code of Hammurabi, 70
coefficients, 271
Coeur, Jacques, 101
coevolution, 239
cognition, definition of, 326
cognitive development and skills, 326–331, 341, 342, 343
Coleridge, Samuel Taylor, 41–42, 49
Coles, Robert, 349
colonialism, of Europeans, 137–138
colonies, American
Carolina, 146
Declaration of Independence, 159, 160

Delaware, 148
differentiation of, 153–154
Enlightenment influence, 153
Georgia, 148
Hartford, Connecticut, 144
Jamestown settlement, 139–140
Maine, 145
Maryland, 141–142, 145
Massachusetts Bay, 143–144
New Hampshire, 145
New Jersey, 146–147
New York, 146–147
Pennsylvania, 147–148
Plymouth, 143
religion of, 152–153
Revolutionary War, 113, 160–163
Revolutionary War causes, 156–159
Rhode Island, 143–144
Roanoke, 138
slave trade, 150
trade, 149–150, 151
Virginia, 140–141
witchcraft trials, 151
color, of matter, 223
Columbus, Christopher, 112, 133–134
comets, 243
Commodius, 80
common denominators, 266
common fractions, 265–268, 270
"Common Sense" (Paine), 160
commutative property, 256
compass, 132
competition, 238
complementary angles, 294
complication stage, of novels, 18
composite numbers, 259
compounds, 222
Compromise of 1850, 198
Compromise of 1877, 207
conceits, 45
concentric circles, 292
conceptual instructional style, 344

conclusion stage, of novels, 18
Concordat of Worms, 96
concrete operations stage, of cognitive development, 327–328
conduction, of heat, 229
conductivity, 223
Confederate States of America, 200–204
Confucius and Confucianism, 74, 87–88
Congress, U.S., 166–167, 206–207
congruent angles, 294
congruent arcs, 292
congruent circles, 292
congruent spheres, 293
Connecticut, 144
Conquistadors, 135–136
consecutive interior/exterior angles, 296
consonance, 45
Constable, John, 364
Constantine, 80, 81
Constantinople, 80, 81, 82, 98
Constitution, U.S., 165–175, 180, 206
Continental Congress, 159–160, 164
continental drift, 247, 248
convection, 229–230
conversions (mathematics)
arithmetic, 270
measurement, 300–301
coordinate geometry, 297–298
Copernicus, Nikolai, 120, 153
Cordoba, 97
core, of Earth, 247
Cornwallis, Charles, 163
corresponding angles, 296
Cortes, Hernando, 112, 135
cotton, 191
cotton gin, 191
Counter-Enlightenment, 123
Counter-Reformation, 106–107
couplets, 48
Courbet, Gustave, 364
CPR (Cardiopulmonary Resuscitation), 317
crafts, prehistoric, 68

Cranmer, Thomas, 105
Crassus, 78–79
Crawford, William H., 187
Crecy, Battle of, 100
Crees, 130
Crick, Francis, 242
critical judgment, of art, 374–376
Crocker, Charles, 215
Crockett, Davy, 196
Croesus, 70
Cromwell, Oliver, 111, 117, 118, 145–146
Crusades, 82, 97–98
cube root, 261
cubes, 294
Currency Act (American Colonies), 156
cytoplasm, 233

D

dactyl, 38
daimyo, 90
dance, 311, 358, 371–373
Dante, 99, 102
Daoism, 88
Darius I, 75
Darwin, Charles, 241
Daumier, Honoré, 364
David, Jacques-Louis, 364, 365
David, King of Israel, 70, 84
Davis, Jefferson, 201, 202
The Dead (Joyce), 18
death rates, 238
Debussy, Claude, 370
The Decameron (Boccaccio), 102
decimal fractions, 268–269, 270
Declaration of Independence, 159, 160, 164
Declaration of Indulgence, 119
degrees, of angles, 294
Deism, 124, 181
Delacroix, Eugene, 364
Delaware, 147, 201
Delian League, 76
De Mille, Agnes, 373
democracy, 75, 124, 188
Democrats, 188, 190, 199, 207
denominator, 265

denotation, 40
denouement stage, of novels, 18
density, 223
Depression, Great, 216–217
Descartes, Rene, 122
deserts, 245–246
development.
    See human development
Diaghilev, Sergei, 373
diameter, of circle, 291–292
Dias, Bartholomew, 112
Diaz de Bivar, Rodrigo, 97
Dickinson, Emily, 30–31, 33, 51
diction, 45
Diderot, Denis, 123
diet, 312–316
Diet of Worms, 104
difference, 263
digestive system, 235–236
dimeter, 38
Diocletian, 80
discriminant, of quadratic
    equation, 286–288
diseases and illness
    along trade routes, 83–84
    Black Death/Plague,
        83–84, 99
    of colonists, 139
    of Native Americans, 137,
        211
dislocations, first aid for,
    316–317
displacement (science), 225
distance formula, 297
distributive property, 256
diversity, 335–336
dividend, 264
Divine Comedy (Dante), 102
division
    decimal fractions, 269
    fractions, 267–268
    integers, 264
divisors, 258, 264
DNA (deoxyribonucleic acid),
    233, 242
doggerel, 50
domain, of relation, 279
Domesday Book, 96
Donatello, 362
Donne, John, 45, 46

"Do not go gentle into that good
    night" (Thomas), 50
Dorr, Thomas, 188
Douglas, Stephen, 198, 199,
    200
Draco, 75
Drake, Francis, 112, 138
drama, 53, 76, 80, 359, 373–374
dramatic monologues, 47
drawing, 358
Dred Scott Decision, 200
Dunn, Kenneth, 336–338
Dunn, Rita, 336–338
dynamic characters, 19

E

Earth
    age of, 67
    geology, 245–249
    rotation of, 243
East India Company, 158
eating, in classroom, 337
*Ecclesiastical History of the
    English People* (Bede), 95
ecology, 236–239
economic theory, 124
ecosystems, 236–237
Edgar the Peaceable, 96
edge, of cubes, 294
Edict of Milan, 81
Edison, Thomas, 209
education, 98, 180
Edward I (England), 96
Edward III (England), 97, 100
Edwards, Jonathan, 153
Edward VI (England), 106
Egypt, 71–72
electrical energy, 227
electrical properties, of matter,
    223
electricity, 153, 209
electrons, 222
elegy, 49
Eliot, T.S., 30, 37, 39
Elizabeth I (England), 106, 108
Elkind, David, 325
Emancipation Proclamation, 203
Embargo Act (1807) (U.S.), 182
emotions, 31, 332–334, 337

empathy, 334
empiricism, 122
empowerment, of students,
    349–351
encomienda system, 136
The Encyclopedia (Diderot), 123
end rhymes, 36
energy, 226–228
England. *See* Great Britain
England, Church of, 115–116,
    117, 152
English language, standard
    American, 59–60
enjambment, 45
The Enlightenment, 121–124,
    153
environmental factors, of
    learning, 336–337
The Epic of Gilgamesh, 69
epic poems, 48–49
Epictetus, 80
epigrams, 50
equal protection, 189
equal rights, 169
equilateral triangles, 295
equilibrium, 327
equivalent fractions, 265
Era of Good Feelings, 186
Erikson, Erik, 328–329
Eriksson, Leif, 131
error theory, of life span, 239
essays, 16, 26–29
Estates General, 97, 114, 115,
    125
estuary, 250
ethnocentrism, 335–336
Etruscans, 77
Euphrates River, 69
Euripides, 76
Europe
    colonialism of, 137–138
    explorers from, 132–134
    in Middle Ages, 93–101
    Reformation, 103–105
    Renaissance Period,
        101–103
    See also specific country
even numbers, 259
evidence (science), 253
evolution, 239, 241–242

Executive Branch, 168–169
exercise, 305–308, 309,315–316
experiments, scientific, 251–254
exploration, 112, 131–134
exponents, 260–261
exposition stage, of novels, 18
expository essays, 27
Expressionism, 17, 366
exterior angles, 296
exteroceptors, 234

F

fabliaux, 99
factors and factoring, 258, 264, 273
falling action stage, of novels, 18
fall season, 244
fat, in diet, 312–313
Faulkner, William, 22, 24
Federalists, 165–166, 175–176, 177, 178, 184, 186
feminine rhymes, 37
Ferdinand (Holy Roman Empire), 107
Ferdinand of Aragon (Spain), 101, 133–134
Fertile Crescent, 69
feudalism, 89, 90, 95, 96, 101
fiction, 16, 17
field hockey, 309
Fifteenth Amendment, 207
figurative images and language, 39–44
fine art, 356
    See also art
fire, 67
first aid, 316–317
first person, 23–26
First Triumvirate, 78
fitness, 305–308
Fitzhugh, George, 192
fixed form, of poems, 48
flag football, 309
Flavell, J. H., 343, 346
Florida, 113, 136, 148, 182–183, 201
fluorescent light, 230
flying shuttle, 114

FOIL method (First, Outside, Inside, Last), 273
foils, characters as, 20
folk music and dancing, 370–371, 372
foot, 38
force, 226–227
form, of poems, 47–48
formal operations development stage, 328
formulas, evaluation of, 279
Fort Sumter, Battle of, 201
Fourteenth Amendment, 206
Fox, George, 147
Fox Indians, 190
fractions, 257, 265–271
fractures, first aid for, 316
France
    American Revolutionary War support, 162
    ballet of, 373
    Bourbon dynasty, 114–115, 125
    Capetian dynasty, 96–97
    colonies of, 138
    conflict with U.S. (late 18th century), 177
    The Enlightenment, 123
    Estates General, 97, 114, 115, 125
    exploration, 112
    French and Indian War, 148, 154–155
    under Holy Roman Empire, 94
    Hundred Years' War, 99–100
    in North America, 112–113
    Revolution of, 115, 124–125
    in seventeenth century, 111
    war with Great Britain, 181
Franciscans, 211, 212
Franconian dynasty, 95–96
Franklin, Benjamin, 153, 160, 163, 165
Franks, Kingdom of, 94
Frederick II (Holy Roman Empire), 98

Frederick III (Saxony), 104
Frederick the Great (Prussia), 124
free verse, 37
French and Indian War, 148, 154–155, 156
Freytag's Pyramid, 18
Fronde, 111
Frost, Robert, 37
Fugitive Slave Act (U.S.), 198
functions, 281–283
fur trade, 185–186

G

Gage, Thomas, 159
Gaius Gracchus, 78
galaxies, 244
Galen, 80
Galileo Galilei, 121
Gama, Vasco da, 112, 134
gas, 222
Gates, Thomas, 140
Gaul, 94
gender bias, in teaching, 335
gender equity, in physical education, 320–321
genetics, 241–242
genre, 16
gente de razon, 212, 213
geology, 245–249
geometry, 290–298
George I (England), 120
George II (England), 120
George III (England), 120, 156
George IV (England), 120
Georgia, 148, 160, 190, 201
Gericault, Theodore, 364
Germanic tribes, 80, 93
Germany, 94, 109
Gettysburg, Battle of, 204
Ghana, 91
Ghent, Treaty of, 184–185
Gilbert, Humphrey, 138
Gilligan, Carol, 330
Ginsberg, Allen, 47
Glorious Revolution, 150
gods and goddesses, 72, 74
gold, 133, 135
Gold Rush, 196, 213–214, 215

golf, 311
"Good Country People"
 (O'Connor), 24
Gothic art and architecture, 99,
 361
Goths, 80, 93
Goya, Francisco de, 364
gram (g), 299
grammar, 58, 59
Grand Testament (Villon), 101
Grant, Ulysses, 203, 204, 207
Granville, George, 156
The Grapes of Wrath (Steinbeck),
 18–19, 20
graphs and graphing
 coordinate geometry,
  297–298
 inequalities, 277–278
 linear equations, 275–276
 plotting points on, 298
Gray, Thomas, 41
Great Awakening, 152–153, 181
Great Britain
 American War of
  Independence, 113,
  160–163
 Church of England, 115–
  116, 117, 152
 Civil War, 111, 115–118,
  145–146
 Declaration of Rights, 119
 Elizabethan Period, 106
 exploration of, 112
 French and Indian War,
  148, 154–155
 Glorious Revolution, 150
 Hanover dynasty, 119–120
 Hundred Years' War, 97,
  99–100
 under Mary I, 106, 108
 Middle Ages, 96
 Parliament, 110, 116,
  117, 118, 150
 Reformation, 105–106
 Rush-Bagot Agreement, 184
 seventeenth century,
  109–111
 Toleration Act, 119
 treaties with U.S., 163,
  177

Treaty of Paris, 113
Trials for Treason Act, 119
U.S. Civil War side, 203
War of 1812, 183–184
War of the Roses, 100
war with France, 181
under William and Mary,
 119
See also colonies,
 American
great circle, of sphere, 293
Great Ice Age, 126–127
Great Rebellion, 111
Greece, ancient, 74–77, 82,
 360–361, 368
Gregorian chants, 368
Gregory I (Pope), 95
Gregory VII (Pope), 96
Griswold, Roger, 178
Guadeloupe Hidalgo, Treaty of,
 213
guilt, 328
Gulliver's Travels (Swift), 53
gymnastics, 310

H

habitat, 237
Hamilton, Alexander, 165,
 175–176
Hammurabi, 70
handicapped children, definition
 of, 311
Hannibal, 78
Hanover dynasty, 120
"Happy Families" (Jenning), 32
Hapsburgs, 96, 107
Harappan civilization, 72
hardness, of matter, 223
Hargreaves, James, 114
Harrison, William Henry, 182,
 191
Hartford, Connecticut, 144
Hasidism, 123
Hastings, Battle of, 94
Hawthorne effect, 335
Hayes, Rutherford B., 207
HDL (high-density lipoproteins),
 313
heart, 235

heart attacks, first aid for, 317
heart rate, target, 307
heat, 227, 228
heat stroke/exhaustion, first aid
 for, 317
heat transfer, 229–230
Hebrews, 70–71, 84–85
Heian Era (Japan), 89
Hellenistic Age, 77
Heller, Joseph, 53
Hemingway, Ernest, 22, 23
Henry I (England), 96
Henry II (England), 96
Henry III (England), 96
Henry IV (France), 111
Henry IV (Holy Roman Empire),
 96
Henry the Navigator, 112,
 131–132
Henry VIII (England), 105–106,
 137
heptameter, 38
Hermandad, 101
Herodotus, 77
heroic couplet, 48
Hesiod, 75
hexameter, 38
hieroglyphics, 71
Hinduism, 85–86
history, study of, 77, 80
Hittites, 70
Hohokam civilization, 93
Holy Roman Empire, 94, 95,
 104, 107
Homer, 49, 75
hominids, 67
Homo sapiens sapiens, 67
Hooker, Thomas, 144
Hopkins, Gerard Manley, 30,
 38–39, 44, 45
Hopkins, Mark, 215
Horace, 80
House of Commons, 117, 118
House of Representatives, U.S.,
 166–167
Houston, Sam, 196, 197
Howe, William, 161, 162
Hudson, Henry, 138
Huguenots, 111, 115
human anatomy, 234–236

human development, 323–353
    cognitive development and
        skills, 326–331
    importance of learning
        about, 323–324
    learning process, 345–351
    metacognition, 343–345
    nature vs. nurture debate,
        331–332
    physiological changes,
        325–326
    and students' perceptions,
        332–334
    See also learning style
humanism, 102, 103
humans, first, 67
Hume, David, 122
Hundred Years' War, 97, 99–100
Huns, 80, 93
hunting, 127
Huntington, Collis P., 215
Hutchinson, Anne, 145
Hydrologic Cycle, 250
hydrosphere, 247
hyperbole, 45–46
hypotenuse, 295
hypothesis, 251, 253
Hyskos, 71

I

iambic foot, 38
iambic meter, 37
iambic pentameter, 37–38, 48, 51
iambic rhythm, 37
Ice Age, 126–127
identity achievement, 329–330
Ignatius of Loyola, 106–107
igneous rocks, 246
Iliad (Homer), 49, 75
illness. *See* diseases and illness
imagery, 42–43
imaginary audience, 325–326
imagism, 42
immune system, 235
immune theory, of life span, 240
The Importance of Being Earnest
    (Wilde), 53
Impressionism, 17, 365
improper fractions, 266

Inca civilization, 93, 112, 135
independent instructional style,
    344
India, 72–73, 372
Indians, American.
    See also Native Americans
indulgences, 104
industrialization, 191, 209
Industrial Revolution, 191
industry, developmental stage,
    328
inequalities, 277–278
inference, 253
inferiority, 328
information processing theory,
    341–342
initiation story, 24–26
initiative, 328
instructional objectives and
    outcomes, 342
instructional style, 344–345
integers, 256, 262–264
intelligence, Sternberg's theory
    of, 341–342
intention, and meaning of words,
    57
interindividual knowledge, 343,
    344
interior angles, 296
internal rhymes, 36–37
interoceptors, 235
intersecting lines, 295
interval training, 308
intimacy, 329
Intolerable Acts, 159
introduction stage, of novels, 18
inventions
    compass, 132
    electricity, 209
    fire, 67
    shipbuilding, 132
    steam engine, 113
    telephone, 209
    textiles machines, 114
Ireland, 117
iron, 314
irony, 36, 46, 52
Iroquois, 130, 154
irrational numbers, 257
Irving, Washington, 180

Isabella I of Castile (Spain), 101,
    133–134
Islam, 88–89, 91, 94, 97, 98,
    101
isolation, 329
isosceles triangles, 295
Israel, 85
Israelites, 70–71, 84–85

J

Jackson, Andrew, 183–184, 187,
    188–191, 197
Jackson, Stonewall, 204
Jainism, 87
James I (England), 110, 120,
    139, 143
James II (England), 119, 146–
    147, 149–150
Jamestown settlement, 139–140
Jansenism, 123
Japan, 89–90, 372
Japanese Americans, internment
    of, 217
Jay, John, 177
Jefferson, Thomas, 160, 178–
    180, 182, 189–190
Jenning, Elizabeth, 32
Jerusalem, 84, 85, 97–98
Jesuits, 107
Jesus, 81
Jews, 70–71, 84–85, 123, 152
Jim Crow Laws, 208
Joan of Arc, 100
John I (England), 96
Johns, Jasper, 368
Johnson, Andrew, 206–207
Johnston, Joseph, 202, 204
jointly constructed meaning,
    348–351
Joseph II (Austria), 124
Joyce, James, 18, 26, 39, 50
Judah, Kingdom of, 85
Judah, T.D., 215
Judicial Branch, U.S., 169, 179
Judiciary Act (1789) (U.S.), 175,
    179
Julius Caesar, 78–79
Justinian I, 81
Juvenal, 80

K

Kamakura Shogunate, 90
Kansas-Nebraska Act, 198–199
Kathakali, 372
Kathek, 372
Kay, John, 114
Keats, John, 31–32, 42, 44, 46, 50
Kentucky, 201
Kepler, Johannes, 120
Key, Francis Scott, 183
kinesthetic learners, 338–339, 340
"Kitchen Cabinet," 189
knowledge, metacognition types, 343
knowledge, of self, 351
Knox, John, 105
Koch, Kenneth, 52
Kofun Era (Japan), 89
Kohlberg, L., 330
Koran, 89
Kush, Kingdom of, 72
Kyoto, 89

L

laissez-faire economic approach, 124
lakes, 250
language and linguistics, 54–61
   across educational disciplines, 60–61
   American English, teaching of, 59–60
   development stages, 58, 328–329
   grammar standardization, 59
   language, defined, 57
   meaning of words, 54–57
   system of, 57–58
   See also writing
lasers, 230
Latin, 99
latitude, 243
Laud, William, 110, 117
lava, 246, 247
law, scientific, 253

laws, development and codification of, 70, 75, 80, 81–82
LDL (low-density lipoproteins), 313
learning process, 348–351
learning style, 336–344
Lee, Robert E., 202, 204
legs, of triangles, 295
Leibniz, Gottfried Wilhelm, 122
L'Enfant, Pierre, 181
Leo III (Pope), 94
Leonardo da Vinci, 103, 363
Leo X (Pope), 104
Lepidus, 79
Lewis, Meriwether, 180
Lexington and Concord, Battles of, 159–160
life cycle, 239–240
life science, 232–236
life spans, 239–240
light, 227, 230
like terms, 272
limericks, 50
Lincoln, Abraham, 200, 201, 202, 205, 206
linear equations, 273–276
lines, 295–297
line segment, 291
lipids, 233
liquid, 222
literal images, 42
literal meaning, of words, 40
literary ballads, 49
literature
   early American, 180
   essays, 16, 26–29
   of late Middle Ages, 100–101
   monasteries' preservation of in Middle Ages, 95
   novels, 16, 17–22, 52–53
   of Renaissance, 102
   short stories, 23–26
liter (l), 299
lithosphere, 247
Livy, 80
Locke, John, 122, 124
locomotor skills, 318
Lombards, 93, 94

"London" (Blake), 42–43
London Company, 139, 140
longitude, 243
longitudinal waves, 231
Lord of the Flies (Golding), 22
Los Angeles, 216, 217, 218
Lothair I, 94
Louisiana, 154, 201, 205
Louisiana Purchase, 179–180, 187
Louis II the German (Holy Roman Empire), 94, 95
Louis IX (France), 98
Louis the Fat (France), 96
Louis the Pious (Holy Roman Empire), 94
Louis VIII (France), 97
Louis XI (France), 101
Louis XIII (France), 111
Louis XIV (France), 111, 114
Louis XV (France), 114–115
Louis XVI (France), 115, 125
lowest common denominator, 266
Lucretius, 79
lungs, 235
Luther, Martin, 103–104
Lutherans, 107, 108–109
Lycurgus, 75
lymphocytes, 235
Lyon, Mathew, 178
lyric poems, 49
Lysimachus, 77

M

Macbeth (Shakespeare), 39
Macedonians, 77, 78
Machiavelli, 103
machines, 227
Macon's Bill No. 2, 182
Madame Bovary (Flaubert), 22
Madison, James, 165, 179, 181–182, 183
Madison, Marbury v., 179
Magellan, Ferdinand, 112, 134
Magna Carta, 96
magnesium, 315
magnetic energy, 227
Magyars, 94

Mahavira, 87
Maine, 139, 145, 186
Mali Kingdom, 91
Manet, Edouard, 364–365
Manifest Destiny, 185, 195, 213
manipulative skills, 318–319
Manipuri, 372
Mannerism, 103
manorialism, 94, 118
mantle, 247
Marathon, 75
Marbury v. Madison, 179
March to the Sea, 204
Marcus Aurelius, 80
Marie Antoinette, 115
Marius, 78
Marshall, John, 190
Mary I (England), 106, 108
Mary II (England), 119, 150
Maryland, 141–142, 145, 152, 201
Maryland, McCulloch v., 167
masculine rhymes, 37
Maslow, Abraham, 330–331
Massachusetts, 143–144, 149, 150
Massachusetts Bay Company, 143–144
mathematics, 255–304
    algebra, 271–289
    arithmetic, 255–271
    geometry, 290–298
    measurement, 298–301
    statistics and probability, 301–304
Mather, Cotton, 153
matter, 222–224
Mauryan Empire, 73
Mayan civilization, 92
Mayflower, 143
Mayflower Compact, 143
Mazarin, Cardinal, 111
McClellan, George, 202, 204
McCulloch v. Maryland, 167
mean, 301
meaning, of words, 54–57
"meaning is use," 54–55, 58, 59
mean length of utterance (MLU), 328–329
measurement, 298–301

median, 301
Meiji Restoration, 90
membrane, of cells, 233
Menander, 76
Mencius, 74, 88
Mendel, Gregor, 241
Mennonites, 105
mercantilism, 113, 137–138
Merovingian dynasty, 94
Merriam, Frank, 217
Mesolithic Age, 68
Mesopotamia, 69–71
Messenia, 75
Mesta, 101
metacognition, 343–345, 346
metamorphic rocks, 246
Metamorphoses (Ovid), 80
metaphors, 40
meteorology, 249–250
meter (m), 37–39, 299
metonymy, 46
metric system, 298–301
Mexicans, in California, 213, 217
Mexican War, 212–213
Mexico, 92–93, 137, 196, 211–212
Michelangelo, 103, 363
Middle Ages
    in America, 92–93
    dance in, 371
    Europe, 93–101
    Japan, 89–90
    music of, 368
    sub-Saharan kingdoms, 91
    visual art/architecture, 361
Middle Stone Age, 68
midpoint, of arcs, 292
Millet, Jean-Francois, 364
Milton, John, 37, 49
minerals, 245, 314–315
minimalism, in music, 371
Minoans, 74
minuend, 263
missionary activities, 133, 211
Mississippi, 201
Missouri, 186, 201
Missouri Compromise, 186–187, 199

mitochondria, 234
mixed numerals, 265–266
mixtures, 222
mobility needs, of students, 338
mock-heroic poems, 48
mode, 16, 17, 302
Mohenjo-Daro, 72
moieties, 210
molecules, 222
Molière, 374
monarchy
    China, 73–74
    England, 96, 110, 115, 118
    European Middle Ages, 101
    France, 96
    Voltaire on, 124
monasteries, 95
monochromatic light, 230
monometer, 38
monomials, 271
Monroe, James, 186, 187
Monroe Doctrine, 187
Montesquieu, Baron de, 123
Montezuma, 135
moral development, 330
More, Thomas, 105–106
morphemes, 58
Moses, 84
motifs, of novels, 21–22
motion, 224–225
motivation, of students, 337, 346–347, 349–351
mountains, 246
movement education, 317–319
Mozart, Wolfgang Amadeus, 369
Muhammad, 88–89
Multiple Subject Teaching Credential, 3
multiplication
    decimal fractions, 269
    fractions, 267
    integers, 264
    whole numbers, 258
muscular system, 234, 308–309
music, 99, 358, 360, 368–371
musical theater, 373–374
Muslims, 88–89, 91, 94, 97, 98, 101

Mutiny Act (American Colonies), 156
Mycenaeans, 74
Myth Adventures (Asprin), 54

N

Napoleon Bonaparte, 177, 179
narrative essays, 27
narrative poems, 49
narrators, short stories, 23–26
Natchez peoples, 129–130
nationalism, 100, 370
Native Americans
    agriculture, 127–128, 129, 130
    Algonquians, 130
    Anasazi, 93, 128–129
    Battle of Tippecanoe, 182
    Cahokia civilization, 129
    in California, 209–211, 212
    dance of, 372
    forced migration and resettlement of, 190
    Hohokam, 93
    Iroquois, 130, 154
    and Jamestown colonists, 139–140
    Natchez, 129–130
    and Pilgrims, 143
    practices, 128
    Second Great Awakening, 181
    Virginia Colony conflict, 142
naturalism, 17, 51
nature vs. nurture debate, 331–332
Navigation Acts (American Colonies), 149, 156, 158
Navy, U.S., 177
Nebraska, 199
needs, Maslow's hierarchy, 330–331
negative numbers, 256, 262
Nemerov, Howard, 52
neo-classicism, 17, 364
Neolithic Age, 68
Neolithic Revolution, 68
nervous system, 234–235
Netherlands, 138, 143, 146–147
Newcomen, Thomas, 113

New Hampshire, 145
New Haven, Connecticut, 144
New Jersey, 146–147
New Mexico, 136–137
New Orleans, 155
New Orleans, Battle of, 183–184
New Stone Age, 68
Newton, Isaac, 121, 153
New World, discovery of, 112
    See also North America; South America
New York, 146–147, 161, 166
niches, of animal species, 237
Nigeria, 91
Nika revolt, 81
Nirvana, Buddhist belief of, 86
Nok culture, 91
nomadic tribes, 93
non-fiction, 16, 17
Non-Intercourse Act (1809) (U.S.), 182
nonlocomotor skills, 318
Normans, 94
Norsemen, 93
North America
    European colonies, 137–138
    exploration of, 131–134
    first humans in, 126–127
    Mexico, 92–93, 137, 196, 211–212
    native cultures, 127–130
    Spanish settlements, 135–136
    See also United States of America
North Carolina, 146, 201
Northwest Passage, 211
novella, 17
novels, 16, 17–22, 52–53
Nubia, 72
nucleic acids, 233
nullification theory, 189
numerator, 265
nutrition, 312–315

O

obesity, 315
observation, 252

obtuse angles, 294
oceanography, 250–251
oceans, 249–250, 251
octameter, 38
octave sonnet, 48
Octavian, 79
odd numbers, 259
ode, 49–50
"Ode on a Distant Prospect of Eton College" (Gray), 41
Odes (Horace), 80
"Ode to a Nightingale" (Keats), 42
Odoacer, 81
Odyssey (Homer), 75
Oglethorpe, James, 148
Oklahoma, 190
Old Stone Age, 67
Onate, Don Juan de, 136
onomatopoeia, 46
open form, of poems, 48
opera, 370, 373, 376
opinion, 253
optical methods, of temperature measurement, 229
Orations (Cicero), 79
ordered pairs, 297
Order of Things (Lucretius), 79
Oregon, 195
organization, 252
Osiris, 72
Otto I, 94
Ottoman Turks, 82
Ovid, 80
oxymoron, 46

P

Paine, Thomas, 160
painting, 358, 360–367, 375
Paleolithic Age, 67, 356
Palestine, 84
Panic of 1819, 186
Paradise Lost (Milton), 37, 49
paradox, 46
parallel lines, 296
Paris, Treaty of (1763), 112, 113, 155
Parliament (Great Britain), 110, 116, 117, 118, 150

Paul III (Pope), 107
Paul of Tarsus, 81
Pax Romana, 80, 81
peasants, in France, 114
Peisistratus, 75
Peloponnesian War, 76
Penn, William, 147
Pennsylvania, 147–148, 176
percents, 270–271
perceptions, of students,
    332–334
performing arts, 356, 358–359,
    368–374
Pericles, 76
perimeter, 290
periodic table, 224
perpendicular lines, 296–297
Persians, 85, 87
Persian War, 75
persistence, of students, 337
personal fable, 326
personification, 41–42
person knowledge, 343
Peru, 136
Petrarch, 48, 102
pharaohs, 71–72
Philadelphia, 147, 162
Philip Augustus (France), 96
Philip II (Holy Roman Empire),
    107, 108
Philip II (Macedonia), 77
Philip IV, "The Fair" (France), 97
Philistines, 70, 84
philosophy
    of ancient Greece, 76
    of ancient Rome, 79, 80
    Confucianism, 87–88
    Daoism, 88
    The Enlightenment,
        121–124
phonic quality, of language, 16
phonology, 57
phosphorous, 315
photoemission, 231
photosynthesis, 231, 234
physical education, 305–322
    adaptive programs,
        311–312
    anatomy and physiology,
        308–309

dance, 311
diet, 312–315
exercise, 305–308
first aid, 316–317
gender equity, 320–321
importance of, 320
movement education,
    317–319
social skill development,
    321
sports, 309–311
weight control, 315–316
physiological factors, of learning,
    337–338
physiological needs, 331
physiology, 308–309
Piaget, Jean, 326–327, 330,
    341
Pilgrims, 143–144
Pinckney Treaty, 177
Pindar, 76
Pitt, William, 155, 157
Pizarro, Francisco, 112, 135
place value, 259
The Plague, 83–84
planetary system, 242
plants
    vs. animals, 236
    cellular makeup, 233
    domestication of, 68
    within ecosystem, 237
    photosynthesis, 234
    propagation, 241
plasma, 222
plate tectonics, 247, 248–249
Plato, 76
Plautus, 79
play activities, 329
Pliny the Elder, 80
plot (literature), 18–19, 20, 21,
    22, 23
plotting, of points on graphs, 298
Plutarch, 80
Plymouth Colony, 143, 150
Plymouth Company, 139
Plymouth Rock, 143
Pocahontas, 140
poetry, 29–51
    of ancient Greece, 76
    of ancient Rome, 79, 80

examination tips, 33–35
figurative language, 39–44
form of, 47–48
meter, 37–39
of Middle Ages, 99
poetic devices, 44–47
vs. prose, 16
purpose of, 29–33
rhythm of, 32
types of, 47–51
verse, 36–37
point of tangency, 292
point of view, author's, 23–26
Poitiers, Battle of, 100
Poland, 97
polis, 75
political parties, in U.S., 176
Polk, James K., 212–213
Polya method, for solving word
    problems, 288
polychromatic light, 230
polynomials, 271, 273
polysaccharides, 233
polytheism, 84
Pompey, 78–79
Pope, Alexander, 45, 48, 50
popular sovereignty, 198
population growth, 238
*A Portrait of the Artist as a
    Young Man* (Joyce), 50
Portugal
    Brazil, 135
    explorations of, 112, 131,
        132, 133
    under Spanish rule, 107
position (science), 225
positive numbers, 256, 262
potassium, 314
Pound, Ezra, 42
powers (mathematics), 260–261
Powhatan, 139–140
predation, 238
prediction, 253
pre-history, 67–68
preoperational stage, of cognitive
    development, 327
Presbyterians, 115–116
President of the United States,
    168–169
prime number, 259

The Prince (Machiavelli), 103
Princeton, Battle of, 162
Principia (Newton), 121
printmaking, 358
probability, 303–304
product (mathematics), 258, 264
proprioceptors, 235
prose, 16–29
    essays, 26–29
    novels, 17–22
    short stories, 23–26
Proser, Gabriel, 181
protagonists, 19
proteins, 233, 312
Providence, Rhode Island, 143–144
Ptolemy, 80, 120
Ptolemy I, 77
public schools, 180
Publius Cornelius Scipio, 78
Pueblo peoples, 129, 136–137
pun, 46
Punic Wars, 78
Puritan Revolution, 111
Puritans
    American settlement, 138, 143–144
    Calvinistic beliefs, 105
    in England, 106, 108, 110, 137
    in Netherlands, 143
Pythagorean Theorem, 295

Q

quadrant, 292
quadratic equations, 283–288
Quakers, 147
quatrains, 48, 50
Quebec, fall of, 155
quotient, 264
Quran, 89

R

radiation, 229
radius, of circle, 291
railroad, transcontinental, 199, 214–215

Raleigh, Walter, 138
Ramses II, 72
rancherias, 210
ranchos, 212
range, of relation, 279
range (statistics), 302
"The Rape of the Lock" (Pope), 45, 48
Raphael, 103
rate, 271
rationalism, 121–122
rational numbers, 257
Ravel, Maurice, 370
reading, 60–61
realism, 17, 23, 51, 364
real numbers or reals, 255–256
receptors, 234–235
reciprocal, 267
Reconquista, 97
Reconstruction Period, 205–208
rectangles
    area of, 291
    perimeter of, 290
rectangle solids, 294
reference, 55–56
reflection, 232
Reformation, 103–105
refraction, 232
relations, 279–281
religion
    in America (early), 152–153, 181
    Buddhism, 86–87
    Hinduism, 85–86
    Islam, 88–89, 91, 94, 97, 98, 101
    Judaism, 70–71, 84–85, 152
    Vedic religions, 85
    Zoroastrianism, 87
    See also Christianity
Religion, Wars of, 107
remainder, 263
Rembrandt, 363
Renaissance period, 101–103, 361–363, 368–369, 372
Republican Party, 199, 207
Republicans, 175, 176, 178, 184, 188
The Republic (Plato), 76

respiratory system, 235
responsibility, of students, 337
Revere, Paul, 159
Revolutionary War, 113, 160–163
"Revolution of 1800," 178
Rhode Island, 144–145, 188
rhyme schemes, 36–37
rhythmics, 311
Richard II (England), 100
Richard the Lionhearted, 96, 98
Richelieu, Cardinal, 111
right angles, 294
"The Rime of the Ancient Mariner" (Coleridge), 41–42
"The Ring of Time" (White), 27
rising action stage, of novels, 18
rivers, 246, 250
RNA (ribonucleic acid), 233
Roanoke Colony, 138
Robbins, Jerome, 373
Rockefeller, John D., 209
rocks, 245, 246
Rocky Mountain Fur Company, 186
rococo style, 363
Rodriguez, Juan, 211
Rolfe, John, 140
Roman Catholic Church
    in American colonies, 141, 148, 150, 152
    Counter-Reformation, 106–107
    of Middle Ages, 95
    missionary activities, 133
    music of, 368
    origins of, 81
    Protestant Reformation, 103–105
    Spanish Crusades, 107–108
    Thirty Years' War, 108–109
    and Thomas Aquinas, 99
    Wars of Religion, 107
romances or romans (novels), 17
Romanesque style of art, 361
Romans, ancient, 77–81, 93, 94, 361, 371
romanticism, 17, 51, 364, 368, 371

Rome, city of, 77, 81, 93, 107
Romulus Augustulus, 81, 93
roots, 261
"A Rose for Emily" (Faulkner), 24
Roundheads, 111, 117
Rousseau, Jean-Jacques, 123, 124
Rush-Bagot Agreement, 184
Russia, 97, 124, 373

S

safety, 331
Saladin, 98
Salamis, Battle of, 75
Salem Witch Trials, 151
Samaria, 85
San Antonio, 196
Sandy, Edwin, 140
San Francisco, 196, 213, 214, 216, 217
San Jacinto, Battle of, 197
Santa Anna, 197
Santa Fe, New Mexico, 136
Sappho, 76
Saratoga, Battle of, 162
sarcasm, 46–47
Sargon I, 70
Sassanids, 80
satire, 16, 17, 51–54
Saul, King of Israel, 70, 84
Saul of Tarsus, 81
Saussure, Ferdinand de, 55
Saxons, 93, 94, 96
scalene triangles, 295
Schoenberg, Arnold, 370, 371
Scholasticism, 98
science, 221–254
      ancient Rome, 80
      astronomy, 242–245
      definition of, 221
      ecology, 236–239
      energy, 226–228
      evolution, 241–242
      experiments, 251–254
      geology, 245–249
      heat transfer, 229–230
      life cycles, 239–240
      life science, 232–236
      light/matter interaction,

230–231
      light sources, 230
      matter, 222–224
      meteorology, 249–250
      motion, 224–225
      oceanography, 250–251
      Renaissance
            achievements, 120–121
      reproduction, 240–241
      temperature, 228–229
      waves, 231–232
scientific notation, 262
scientific revolution, 120–121
scoring, of CSET exam, 6–7
Scots, 116, 118
Scott, Winfield, 190, 202
sculpture, 357, 361–362, 366
sea-floor spreading, 247
seasons, 244
secant, 292
secession crisis, U.S., 200–201
Second Great Awakening, 181
sedimentary rocks, 246
Sedition Act (U.S.), 178
seizures, first aid for
Seleucus I, 77
self-efficacy, 349–350
self-esteem, 320–321, 349
self-knowledge, 351
self-respect, 350
semicircles, 292
Senate, U.S., 166–167
Seneca, 80
Seneca Falls Convention, 207
sensorimotor stage, of cognitive development, 327
Serra, Junipero, 211
sestet sonnet, 48
sestina, 50
setting, 22, 23
Settlement Act (1701) (England), 119
Seven Years' War, 148, 155
Shakespeare, William, 37, 39, 48, 374
Shang Dynasty, 73–74
Shelley, Percy Bysshe, 46
Sherman, William T., 204
Shi'ites, 89

shipbuilding, 132
shock, first aid for, 316
shoguns, 90
"Shooting an Elephant" (Orwell), 28–29
short stories, 23–26, 99
shuffleboard, 310
sibilance, 30
Sic et Non (Abelard), 98
Siddhartha Gautama, 86
signed numbers, 262
Silk Road, 74, 83, 84
similes, 40
Simons, Menno, 105
Sinclair, Upton, 217
Single Subject Teaching Credential, 3
situational meaning, 56
skeletal system, 234
slant rhymes, 37
slavery, in U.S.
      anti-slavery movements, 199–200
      Compromise of 1850, 198
      Constitutional issues, 165
      Dred Scott decision, 200
      early, 150
      Emancipation Proclamation, 203
      end of, 205, 206
      Fugitive Slave Act, 198
      Missouri Compromise, 186–187
      popular sovereignty, 198
      system of, 192–194
      See also African Americans
slave trade, 133, 137, 150, 165
Slavs, 93
"slice of life," 23
slope, 274–275
smallpox vaccine, 153
Smith, Adam, 124
Smith, John, 139–140
soccer, 309
Social Contract (Rousseau), 123
social dancing, 373
social instructional style, 344
sociological factors, of learning, 337
Socrates, 76

sodium, 314
softball, 309
soil processes, 246–247
solar radiation, 227
solar system, 242
solids, 222
Solomon, King of Israel, 53–54, 70, 85
Solon, 75
somatic system, 234
Songhai peoples, 91
sonnets, 48
Sophists, 76
Sophocles, 76
sound, 227
The South, 191–195, 200–206
South America
    diseases spread by contact with Europeans, 137
    early civilizations, 92–93
    first humans in, 126–127
    Spanish control of, 135, 136
South Carolina, 146, 189, 201
Southern Pacific Railroad, 215
Spain
    California missions, 211
    Catholic Crusades, 107–108
    decline from world power, 109
    explorations of, 112, 134, 135
    under Isabella I and Ferdinand, 101
    Muslims in, 94, 97, 101
    New World settlements, 112, 113, 136, 148, 182–183
    Seven Years' War, 148
    treaties with U.S., 177
    war with England, 108
Sparta, 75, 76
Spartacus, 78
specialized movement skills, 319
speculative essays, 26–27
speech, parts of, 58
speed, 225
Spenser, Edmund, 45

spheres, 293
spinning jenny, 114
Spinoza, Benedict de, 122
Spirit of the Laws (Montesquieu), 123
sports, 309–311
sprains, first aid for, 316
spring season, 244
square, completing the, 285
square root, 261
squares
    area of, 291
    perimeter of, 290
St. Augustine, Florida, 136
stage theories, of human development, 327, 330
Stamp Act (American Colonies), 156
standard deviation, 302–303
Stanford, Leland, 215
Stanton, Edwin M., 206
Stanton, Elizabeth Cady, 207
stanzas, 36
"Stanzas" (Byron), 36–37
stars, 244–245
"The Star-Spangled Banner," 183
static characters, 19
statistics and probability, 301–304
steam engine, invention of, 113
stereotyped characters, 19
Sternberg, 341–342
Stevens, Thaddeus, 205
stock characters, 19
Stoicism, 79, 80
stone ages, 67–68
Stowe, Harriet Beecher, 199
strains, first aid for, 316
strategy knowledge, 343, 345
Stravinsky, Igor, 370
stress, 333–334
structure, of classroom, 337
structure, of essays, 28
Stuart dynasty, 119
stucture (science), 222
study strategies
    for CSET exam, 7–8, 10–11
    for learners, 345–348

style, of literature, 22, 27–28
subtraction
    decimal fractions, 269
    fractions, 267
    integers, 263
subtrahend, 263
Sugar Act (American Colonies), 156
Sulla, 78
sum, 262
Sumerians, 69, 70
Summa Theologica (Aquinas), 99
summer season, 244
Sun, 242, 243–244, 249, 250
Sunni Ali, 91
Sunnis, 89
supplementary angles, 294
Supreme Court, U.S., 175, 178, 179, 200
Swift, Jonathan, 52, 53
swimming, 310
symbolism, 43–44, 366
synecdoche, 47
syntax, 47
syphilis, 137

T

table tennis, 310
tabula rasa, learner as, 324
Tacitus, 80
tactile or kinesthetic learners, 338–339, 340
Taira-Minamoto War, 90
Tallmadge, James, 186
tangent circles, 292
task knowledge, 343, 345
Tavris, Carol, 332, 347
taxation without representation, 157
teachers
    classroom environment, 334
    ethnocentrism, 335
    expectations of student, 335
    instructional strategies, 341–343
    instructional style, 344–345

principles for effective teaching, 347–348
role of, 323–324
Tecumseh, 182, 183
teenagers, 325–326, 351
telephone, 209
temperature, 228–229
Tennessee, 201, 205
tennis, 310
Tenure of Office Act, 206
tercets, 50
terms, 271
test-taking tips
    administration of, 3–4
    exam day, 8–10
    format, 4–5
tetrameter, 38
Tetzel, John, 104
Texas, 196–197, 201, 212
textiles machines, 114
theater, 53, 76, 80, 359, 373–374
Thebes, 76
theme, of novels, 20–21, 22
Theodosius I, 81
Theodosius II, 81
Theogony (Hesiod), 75
theory, scientific, 253
Theory of Ideas or Forms (Plato), 76
thermal properties, of matter, 223
thermocouples, 228
thermometers, 228
thinking skills, 346
third person, 23
Thirteenth Amendment, 206
Thirty Years' War, 108–109
Thomas, Dylan, 50
thought element, of essays, 28
Thucydides, 77
Thutmose II, 71
Tiberius Gracchus, 78
tides, 251
Tigris River, 69
Timbuktu, 91
time zones, 243
Tippecanoe, Battle of, 182
tobacco, 191
To Kill a Mockingbird (Lee), 20
Tokugawa Shogunate, 90
Toleration Act (England), 119

tone, of literature and poetry, 27, 36, 47
tool-making, 67, 127
topic, of novels, 20
Torah, 71
Townshend, Charles, 157–158
track and field, 310
trade
    American colonies, 149–150, 151
    of ancient world, 82–84
    exploration prompted by, 131
"Trail of Tears," 190
transcontinental railroad, 199, 214–215
transversals, 296
transverse waves, 231
treaties
    Guadeloupe Hidalgo, 213
    Jay Treaty, 177
    Pinckney Treaty, 177
    Treaty of Aix-la-Chapelle, 94
    Treaty of Ghent, 184–185
    Treaty of Paris, 112, 113, 155
    Treaty of Verdun, 94, 95
Trenton, Battle of, 162
Trials for Treason Act (England), 119
triangles
    area of, 291
    perimeter of, 290
    Pythagorean Theorem, 295
    types of, 295
Triennial Act (England), 117
trimeter, 38
trinomials, 271
trochee, 38
Turner, Joseph, 364
Tutankhamen, 72
Twain, Mark, 20, 22, 53–54
Twelfth Amendment, 180
Tyler, John, 191, 197

U

"The Ugly Duckling," 20
ultraviolet light, 230
Uncle Tom's Cabin (Stowe), 199
Underground Railroad, 199

United States of America
    Adams administration, 177–178
    Articles of Confederation, 164–165
    California gold rush, 196, 213–214
    Civil War, 201–204
    Congress, 166–167
    Constitution, 165–175
    discovery of, 112
    early settlements, 112
    Era of Good Feelings, 186
    Executive Branch, 168–169
    exploration of, 131–134
    federal vs. state powers, 174–175
    first city in, 136
    first humans in, 126–127
    industrialization, 191, 209
    Jackson administration, 188–190
    Jefferson administration, 178–180
    Judicial Branch, 169
    Louisiana Purchase, 179–180
    Madison administration, 181–184
    Mexican War, 212–213
    Panic of 1819, 186
    presidential election of 1824, 187
    Reconstruction period, 205–208
    Revolutionary War, 113, 160–163
    secession crisis, 200–201
    the South (pre-Civil War), 191–195
    Texas, 196–197
    War of 1812, 183–184
    Washington administration, 175–177
    westward expansion, 185, 195, 212
    See also colonies, American; Native Americans; slavery, in U.S.

universal knowledge, 343, 344
universities, first, 98
Uthman, 89

V

Valens, 80
Valerian, 80
Van Buren, Martin, 189
Vandals, 81, 93
variables, 271
"Variations on a Theme by
    William Carlos Williams"
    (Koch), 52
Vedic religions, 85
velocity, 225
Verdun, Treaty of, 94, 95
Vergil, 80
verse, 36–37
vertex, 294
vertical angles, 294
Vespucci, Amerigo, 134
Vicksburg, Battle of, 204
Victoria (England), 120
Vikings, 93, 94
villanelle, 50
Villon, Francois, 101
Vinci, Leonardo da, 103, 363
Virginia, 138, 140–141, 142,
    166, 201
Visigoths, 80, 93, 97
vision, 230
visual art, 356–358, 360–367,
    375
visualizations, 351
visual learners, 338, 339
vitamins and minerals, 313–315
voice, in non-fiction, 27
volcanoes, 247–248
volleyball, 309
Voltaire, 53, 123, 124
volume, 293–294
voting rights, 188, 207
Vygostsky, L., 329

W

Wade-Davis Bill, 205–206
Wagner, Richard, 370
War of 1812, 183–184
War of the Roses, 100

Washington, George, 155, 160,
    161, 175–177
Washington, D.C., 181, 183, 198
water, 222, 233
Watson, James, 242
Watt, James, 113
wavelength, 230
waves, 231–232
weapons, used in Hundred
    Years' War, 100
weather, 249–250
weight training, 310
Wentworth, Thomas, 116–117
West Indies, 113
Whigs, 190–191, 199
Whiskey Rebellion, 176
white light, 230
Wilde, Oscar, 50, 53
William II (England), 96
William III (England), 119, 150
William IV (England), 120
William of Orange, 150
Williams, Roger, 144–145
William the Conqueror, 94
winter season, 244
Winthrop, John, 144
Witch Trials, in Salem, 151
Wittgenstein, Ludwig, 54, 61
Wolsey, Thomas, 105
women
    bias toward when teaching,
        335
    equity in physical
        education, 320–321
    human development
        research, 330
    role of, 192
    voting rights, 207
word problems, 288–289
words, 54–57, 58
Wordsworth, William, 30, 49
Works and Days (Hesiod), 75
work (science), 227
Worms, Concordat of, 96
Wright, Frank Lloyd, 366
writing
    of ancient Greeks, 75
    connection with reading,
        60–61
    early river valley
        civilizations, 69

hieroglyphics, 71
Minoan civilization, 74
origins of, 58
prehistoric period, 68
Wyatt, Thomas, 37

X

Xavier, Francis, 107
x-axis, 297
Xerxes, 75
Xia Dynasty, 73

Y

y-axis, 297
Yorktown, Battle of, 163

Z

Zama, Battle of, 78
zero, 258
Zhou Dynasty, 74
zinc, 314
Zoot Suit riots, 217
Zoroastrianism, 87

REA's Test Prep Books Are The Best!

(a sample of the <u>hundreds of letters</u> REA receives each year)

" I am writing to congratulate you on preparing an exceptional study guide. In five years of teaching this course I have never encountered a more thorough, comprehensive, concise and realistic preparation for this examination. "
Teacher, Davie, FL

" I have found your publications, The Best Test Preparation..., to be exactly that. "
Teacher, Aptos, CA

" I am writing to thank you for your test preparation... your books helped me immeasurably and I have nothing but praise for your GRE preparation. "
Student, Benton Harbor, MI

" Your GMAT book greatly helped me on the test. Thank you. "
Student, Oxford, OH

" I recently got the French SAT II Exam book from REA. I congratulate you on first-rate French practice tests. "
Instructor, Los Angeles, CA

" The REA LSAT Test Preparation guide is a winner! "
Instructor, Spartanburg, SC

" This book is great. Most of my friends who used the REA AP book and took the exam received 4's or 5's (mostly 5's. which is the highest score!)! "
Student, San Jose, CA